A History of Western Society

A History of Western Society

Volume B
From the Renaissance to 1815

Seventh Edition

John P. McKay

University of Illinois at Urbana-Champaign

Bennett D. Hill

Georgetown University

John Buckler

University of Illinois at Urbana-Champaign

HOUGHTON MIFFLIN COMPANY
Boston New York

Editor-in-Chief: Jean L. Woy
Senior Sponsoring Editor: Nancy Blaine
Development Editor: Julie Dunn
Senior Project Editor: Christina M. Horn
Editorial Assistant: Talia M. Kingsbury
Manufacturing Manager: Florence Cadran
Senior Marketing Manager: Sandra McGuire

Text credits:
Page 556: Poem by Joost van den Vondel quoted from *Europe in the Seventeenth Century,* by David Ogg. Copyright © 1967 by A & C Black, Ltd.

Volume B cover image: *Portrait of Madame Aymon La Belle Zelie,* by Jean-August-Dominque Ingres (1780–1867), French. Musée des Beaux-Arts/Superstock.

Printed in the U.S.A.

Library of Congress Control Number: 2001133312

ISBN: 0-618-17052-9

2 3 4 5 6 7 8 9-VH-06 05 04 03

About the Authors

John P. McKay Born in St. Louis, Missouri, John P. McKay received his B.A. from Wesleyan University (1961), his M.A. from the Fletcher School of Law and Diplomacy (1962), and his Ph.D. from the University of California, Berkeley (1968). He began teaching history at the University of Illinois in 1966 and became a professor there in 1976. John won the Herbert Baxter Adams Prize for his book *Pioneers for Profit: Foreign Entrepreneurship and Russian Industrialization, 1885–1913* (1970). He has also written *Tramways and Trolleys: The Rise of Urban Mass Transport in Europe* (1976) and has translated Jules Michelet's *The People* (1973). His research has been supported by fellowships from the Ford Foundation, the Guggenheim Foundation, the National Endowment for the Humanities, and IREX. He has written well over a hundred articles, book chapters, and reviews, which have appeared in numerous publications, including *The American Historical Review, Business History Review, The Journal of Economic History,* and *Slavic Review.* He contributed extensively to C. Stewart and P. Fritzsche, eds., *Imagining the Twentieth Century* (1997).

Bennett D. Hill A native of Philadelphia, Bennett D. Hill earned an A.B. from Princeton (1956) and advanced degrees from Harvard (A.M., 1958) and Princeton (Ph.D., 1963). He taught history at the University of Illinois at Urbana, where he was department chairman from 1978 to 1981. He has published *English Cistercian Monasteries and Their Patrons in the Twelfth Century* (1968), *Church and State in the Middle Ages* (1970), and articles in *Analecta Cisterciensia, The New Catholic Encyclopaedia, The American Benedictine Review,* and *The Dictionary of the Middle Ages.* His reviews have appeared in *The American Historical Review, Speculum, The Historian,* the *Journal of World History,* and *Library Journal.* He is one of the contributing editors to *The Encyclopedia of World History* (2001). He has been a Fellow of the American Council of Learned Societies and served on the editorial board of *The American Benedictine Review,* on committees of the National Endowment for the Humanities, and as Vice President of the American Catholic Historical Association (1995–1996). A Benedictine monk of St. Anselm's Abbey in Washington, D.C., he is also a Visiting Professor at Georgetown University.

John Buckler Born in Louisville, Kentucky, John Buckler received his B.A. (summa cum laude) from the University of Louisville in 1967. Harvard University awarded him the Ph.D. in 1973. From 1984 to 1986 he was an Alexander von Humboldt Fellow at the Institut für Alte Geschichte, University of Munich. He has lectured at the Fondation Hardt at the University of Geneva and at the University of Freiburg. He has also participated in numerous international conferences. He is currently a professor of Greek history at the University of Illinois. In 1980 Harvard University Press published his *Theban Hegemony, 371–362* B.C. He has also published *Philip II and the Sacred War* (Leiden 1989) and co-edited *BOIOTIKA: Vorträge vom 5. Internationalen Böotien-Kolloquium* (Munich 1989). He has contributed articles to *The American Historical Association's Guide to Historical Literature* (Oxford 1995), *The Oxford Classical Dictionary* (Oxford 1996), and *Encyclopedia of Greece and the Hellenic Tradition* (London 1999). His other articles have appeared in journals both in the United States and abroad, including the *American Journal of Ancient History, Classical Philology, Rheinisches Museum für Philologie, Klio, Classical Quarterly, Wiener Studien,* and many others.

Brief Contents

Contents

Chapter 20

Chapter 21

Maps

Listening to the Past

Preface

A History of Western Society grew out of the authors' desire to infuse new life into the study of Western civilization. We knew that historians were using imaginative questions and innovative research to open up vast new areas of historical interest and knowledge. We also recognized that these advances had dramatically affected the subject of European economic, intellectual, and, especially, social history, while new research and fresh interpretations were also revitalizing the study of the traditional mainstream of political, diplomatic, and religious development. Despite history's vitality as a discipline, however, it seemed to us that both the broad public and the intelligentsia were generally losing interest in the past.

It was our conviction, based on considerable experience introducing large numbers of students to the broad sweep of Western civilization, that a book reflecting current trends could excite readers and inspire a renewed interest in history and our Western heritage. Our strategy was twofold. First, we made social history a core element of our work. We not only incorporated recent research by social historians but also sought to recreate the life of ordinary people in appealing human terms. At the same time we were determined to give great economic, political, cultural, and intellectual developments the attention they unquestionably deserve. We wanted to give individual readers and instructors a balanced, integrated perspective so that they could pursue—on their own or in the classroom—those themes and questions that they found particularly exciting and significant. In an effort to realize fully the potential of our fresh yet balanced approach, we made many changes, large and small, in the editions that followed.

Changes in the Seventh Edition

In preparing the Seventh Edition we have worked hard to keep our book up-to-date and to strengthen our distinctive yet balanced approach. Six main lines of revision guided our many changes.

New "Images in Society" Feature

A photo essay, "Images in Society," represents a new and distinctive feature of this Seventh Edition. The complete text contains four essays, each consisting of a short narrative with questions, accompanied by several images. The goal of the feature is to encourage students to think critically: to view and compare visual images and draw conclusions about the societies and cultures that produced those images. Thus, "The Roman Villa at Chedworth" in Britain mirrors Roman provincial cuture (Chapter 6). The essay "From Romanesque to Gothic" treats the architectural shift in medieval church building and aims to show how the Gothic cathedral reflected the ideals and values of medieval society (Chapter 11). Moving to modern times, the essay "Class and Gender Boundaries in Women's Fashion, 1850–1914" studies women's clothing in relationship to women's evolving position in society and gender relations (Chapter 24), while "Pablo Picasso and Modern Art" looks at Picasso's greatest paintings to gain insight into his principles and practices and the modernist revolution in art (Chapter 28).

"Individuals in Society" Feature

In the Sixth Edition of the text, we introduced the feature "Individuals in Society," including in each chapter a brief study of a woman, man, or group that informed us about the societies in which they lived; each study or biographical sketch was carefully integrated into the body of the text. Readers' positive response to this feature encouraged us to continue it in the Seventh Edition. The "Individuals in Society" feature grew out of our longstanding focus on people's lives and the varieties of historical experience, and we believe that readers will empathize with these human beings as they themselves seek to define their own identities. The spotlighting of individuals, both famous and obscure, perpetuates the greater attention to cultural and intellectual developments that we used to invigorate our social history in earlier editions, and it reflects changing interests within the historical profession as well as the development of "micro history."

The range of men and women we consider is broad. For this edition, and sometimes at readers' suggestion, we have dropped eight individuals and replaced them with others who we believe will prove more exciting or significant. Several are famous historical actors, such as Queen Nefertiti, the fourteenth-century B.C. queen of Egypt (Chapter 1); the mystical Saint Teresa of Ávila (Chapter 14); the charismatic Russian rebel Stenka Razin (Chapter 17); the ruthless British imperialist Cecil Rhodes (Chapter 26); the great Renaissance artist and polymath Leonardo da Vinci (Chapter 13); and the creator of communist Yugoslavia, Marshal Tito (Chapter 30). Other individuals illuminate aspects of their times but are not well known: a Roman soldier stationed in the provinces (Chapter 6); a serf who gained freedom and success in thirteenth-century France (Chapter 10); a Jewish businesswoman and mother of thirteen in seventeenth-century Germany (Chapter 16); Madame du Coudray, who traveled through eighteenth-century France instructing, in the king's name, midwives on the safest delivery practices (Chapter 20); and the Zionist leader Theodor Herzl, who made the creation of a Jewish state in Palestine his life's work (Chapter 25). Creative artists and intellectuals include the Muslim-Spanish mulatto artist Juan de Pareja (Chapter 15) and the controversial German statesman Gustav Stresemann (Chapter 28).

Expanded Ethnic and Geographic Scope

In this edition we have added significantly more discussion of groups and regions that are frequently shortchanged in the general histories of Europe and Western civilization. This expanded scope is, we feel, an important improvement. It reflects the renewed awareness within the profession of Europe's enormous historical diversity, as well as the efforts of contemporary Europeans to understand the ambivalent and contested meanings of their national, regional, ethnic, and pan-European identities. Examples of this enlarged scope include early Greek influence in the western Mediterranean (Chapter 3) and subsequent developments there (Chapter 4); greatly expanded treatment of Europe's borderlands—Iberia, Ireland, Scotland, eastern Europe, and the Baltic area—in the Middle Ages and coverage of racism in these regions (Chapters 9, 11, 12); developments in absolutist Sweden and southern Russia (Chapter 17); Spanish urban life (Chapter 24); and completely new and detailed discussion of twentieth-century eastern Europe (Chapters 27, 30, and 31). A broader treatment of Jewish history has been integrated into the text throughout this edition, just as the history of women and gender was integrated in the Fifth Edition. Examples include anti-Semitism and Europeans' hostility toward Muslims (Chapter 9); anti-Semitism in the period of the Black Death (Chapter 12), in the Spanish inquisition (Chapter 13), and in tsarist Russia (Chapter 27); Jewish Enlightenment thought in Germany (Chapter 18); a new section on Jewish emancipation in nineteenth-century Europe, which is tied to the "Individuals in Society" feature on Theodor Herzl (Chapter 25); and the unfolding of the Holocaust before and during the Second World War (Chapter 29).

Organizational Changes

Our expanded ethnic and geographic scope is one of several organizational improvements. Chapter 23 has undergone extensive revision, including a reconceptualized section on nationalism and an entirely new section on Ireland and the Great Famine. In Chapter 28, material on the United States has been tightened. Perhaps most important, the book's final chapter dealing with the period from 1985 to the present has been greatly reorganized. Material on the cold war has been reduced, there are new sections on the 1990s, and Western relations with the Islamic world are treated, leading up to the fall of the Taliban. The book concludes with a discussion of European population decline, the surge of immigration, and the European Union's search for identity in the global age.

Incorporation of Recent Scholarship

As in all previous revisions we have made a conscientious effort to keep our book up-to-date with new and significant scholarship. Because the authors are committed to a balanced approach that reflects the true value of history, we have continued to incorporate important new findings on political, economic, cultural, and intellectual developments in this edition. Revisions of this nature include extensive work on early Judaism based on archaeological evidence, and on the Phoenicians (Chapter 2); on the origins and development of the polis, revised in cooperation with the Copenhagen Polis Center (Chapter 3); on the catacombs as pilgrimage sites (Chapter 6); on Muslim-Christian relations (Chapters 7 and 9); on the work of ordinary and elite women in the Renaissance (Chapter 13); on recent interpretations of the sixteenth-century Reformations (Chapter 14); on the Atlantic economy, including a new subsection on the slave trade (Chapter 19); on nationalism in the French Revolution (Chapter 21); and on women and the women's movement in the post–World War II era (Chapter 30). In short, recent research keeps the broad sweep of our history fresh.

Revised Full-Color Art and Map Programs

Finally, the illustrative component of our work has been carefully revised. We have added many new illustrations to our extensive art program, which includes nearly two hundred color reproductions, letting great art and important events come alive. As in earlier editions, all illustrations have been carefully selected to complement the text, and all carry informative captions, based on thorough research, that enhance their value. Artwork remains an integral part of our book; the past can speak in pictures as well as in words. The use of full color serves to clarify the maps and graphs and to enrich the textual material. The maps and map captions have been updated to correlate directly to the text, and new maps have been added in Chapters 7, 14, and 15.

Distinctive Features

In addition to the new "Images in Society" studies and the revised "Individuals in Society" essays, distinctive features from earlier editions guide the reader in the process of historical understanding. Many of these features also show how historians sift through and evaluate evidence. Our goal is to suggest how historians actually work and think. We want the reader to think critically and to realize that history is neither a list of cut-and-dried facts nor a senseless jumble of conflicting opinions. To help students and instructors realize this goal, we have significantly expanded the discussion of "what is history" in Chapter 1 of this edition.

Revised Primary-Source Feature

In the Fifth Edition we added a two-page excerpt from a primary source at the end of each chapter. This important feature, entitled "Listening to the Past," extends and illuminates a major historical issue considered in the chapter, and it has been well received by instructors and students. In the new edition we have reviewed our selections and made judicious substitutions. For example, in Chapter 4 Antiochus III meets the Jews, and in Chapter 5, students may explore Titus Flamininus on the liberty of the Greeks. In Chapter 13 Desiderius Erasmus explains why his era was an "Age of Gold," while in Chapter 14 students may reflect on Martin Luther's concept of liberty. Chapter 20 provides a new selection from Rousseau's influential treatise *Emile,* which deals with the gendered needs of education for girls; in Chapter 26 the French political leader Jules Ferry gives a spirited defense of French imperialism before the French Assembly, and in Chapter 28 the novelist and critic George Orwell analyzes the multiple consequences of prolonged unemployment in Britain during the Great Depression.

Each primary source opens with a problem-setting introduction and closes with "Questions for Analysis" that invite students to evaluate the evidence as historians would. Drawn from a range of writings addressing a variety of social, cultural, political, and intellectual issues, these sources promote active involvement and critical interpretation. Selected for their interest and importance and carefully fitted into their historical context, these sources do indeed allow the student to "listen to the past" and to observe how history has been shaped by individual men and women, some of them great aristocrats, others ordinary folk.

Problems of Historical Interpretation

The addition of more problems of historical interpretation in the Fifth Edition was well received, and so we have increased their number again in this edition. We believe that the problematic element helps our readers develop the critical-thinking skills that are among the most precious benefits of studying history. New examples of this more open-ended, interpretive approach include the debate over the transition from Antiquity to the early Middle Ages (Chapter 6), the question of European racism in the Middle Ages (Chapter 12), the issue of gender in the Italian cities of the Renaissance (Chapter 13), the renewed debate on personal and collective responsibilities for the Holocaust (Chapter 29), the dynamics of the great purges in the Soviet Union (Chapter 29), the process of reconstruction in eastern Europe, and the debate over globalization (Chapter 31).

Improved Chapter Features

Other distinctive features from earlier editions have been reviewed and improved in this Seventh Edition. To help guide the reader toward historical understanding, we pose specific historical questions at the beginning of each chapter. These questions are then answered in the course of each chapter, and each chapter concludes with a concise summary of its findings. All of the questions and summaries have been re-examined and frequently revised in order to maximize the usefulness of this popular feature.

A list of Key Terms concludes each chapter, another new feature of this edition. These terms are highlighted in boldface in the text. The student may use these terms to test his or her understanding of the chapter's material.

In addition to posing chapter-opening questions and presenting more problems in historical interpretation, we have quoted extensively from a wide variety of primary sources in the narrative, demonstrating in our use of these quotations how historians evaluate evidence. Thus primary sources are examined as an integral part of the narrative as well as presented in extended form in the "Listening to the Past" chapter feature. We believe that such an extensive program of both integrated and separate primary source excerpts will help readers learn to interpret and think critically.

Each chapter concludes with carefully selected suggestions for further reading. These suggestions are briefly described to help readers know where to turn to continue thinking and learning about the Western world. Also, chapter bibliographies have been thoroughly revised and updated to keep them current with the vast amount of new work being done in many fields.

Revised Timelines

New comparative timelines now begin each chapter. These timelines organize historical events into three categories: political/military, social/economic, and intellectual/religious. In addition, the topic-specific timelines appearing in earlier editions have been revised for this edition. Once again we provide a unified timeline in an appendix at the end of the book. Comprehensive and easy to locate, this useful timeline allows students to compare simultaneous political, economic, social, cultural, intellectual, and scientific developments over the centuries.

Flexible Format

Western civilization courses differ widely in chronological structure from one campus to another. To accommodate the various divisions of historical time into intervals that fit a two-quarter, three-quarter, or two-semester period, *A History of Western Society* is being published in four versions, three of which embrace the complete work:

- One-volume hardcover edition: A HISTORY OF WESTERN SOCIETY
- Two-volume paperback: A HISTORY OF WESTERN SOCIETY, *Volume I: From Antiquity to the Enlightenment* (Chapters 1–17); *Volume II: From Absolutism to the Present* (Chapters 16–31)
- Three-volume paperback: A HISTORY OF WESTERN SOCIETY, *Volume A: From Antiquity to 1500* (Chapters 1–13); *Volume B: From the Renaissance to 1815* (Chapters 12–21); *Volume C: From the Revolutionary Era to the Present* (Chapters 21–31)
- A HISTORY OF WESTERN SOCIETY, *Since 1300* (Chapters 12–31), for courses on Europe since the Renaissance

Note that overlapping chapters in both the two- and the three-volume sets permit still wider flexibility in matching the appropriate volume with the opening and closing dates of a course term.

Ancillaries

Learning and teaching ancillaries, listed below, also contribute to the usefulness of the text.

- *Study Guide*
- *Online Study Guide*
- *Instructor's Resource Manual*
- *Test Items*
- *Computerized Test Items*
- *ClassPrep: an instructor's resource CD-ROM*
- *Web site for instructors and students*
- *Blackboard™ and WebCT™ course cartridges*
- *Mosaic: Perspectives on Western Civilization web site*
- *GeoQuest™: an interactive map CD-ROM*
- *Bibliobase™: custom coursepacks in Western civilization*
- *Map Transparencies*

The excellent *Study Guide* has been thoroughly revised by Professor James Schmiechen of Central Michigan University. Professor Schmiechen has been a tower of strength ever since he critiqued our initial prospectus, and he has continued to give us many valuable suggestions as well as his warmly appreciated support. His *Study Guide* contains learning objectives, chapter summaries, chapter outlines, review questions, extensive multiple-choice exercises, self-check lists of important concepts and events, and a variety of study aids and suggestions. The Seventh Edition also retains the study-review exercises on the interpretation of visual sources and major political ideas, as well as suggested issues for discussion and essay, chronology reviews, and sections on studying effectively. These sections take the student through reading and studying activities such as underlining, summarizing, identifying main points, classifying information according to sequence, and making historical comparisons. For the Seventh Edition, new essay activities have been added for each of the four "Images in Society" features. The multiple-choice questions now offer five potential responses to coincide more directly with the Advanced Placement examination.

To enable both students and instructors to use the *Study Guide* with the greatest possible flexibility, the guide is available in two volumes, with considerable overlapping of chapters. Instructors and students who use only Volumes A and B of the text have all the pertinent study materials in a single volume, *Study Guide, Volume I* (Chapters 1–21); likewise, those who use only Volumes B and C of the text also have all the necessary materials in one volume, *Study Guide, Volume II* (Chapters 12–31). An *Online Study Guide* is also available for students. Accessible through Houghton Mifflin's @history web site (college.hmco.com), it functions as a tutorial, providing rejoinders to all multiple-choice questions that explain why the student's response is or is not correct.

The *Instructor's Resource Manual* and *Test Items* have been thoroughly revised for this edition by Professor Matthew Lenoe of Assumption College. The *Instructor's Resource Manual* contains instructional objectives, annotated chapter outlines, suggestions for lectures and discussion, term paper and class activity topics, primary-source exercises, map activities, and lists of audiovisual resources. For the Seventh Edition, a new section has been added on the "Images in Society" photo essays. The accompanying *Test Items* offer identification, multiple-choice, map, and essay questions for a total of approximately two thousand test items. In order to make the multiple-choice questions more useful to the Advanced Placement market, a fifth answer option has been added. These test items are available to adopters in a Windows™ version that includes editing capability.

New to this edition is the *ClassPrep CD-ROM* for instructors. This resource includes an electronic version of the *Instructor's Manual* and *Test Items,* PowerPoint™ maps from the text, a testbank of questions from GeoQuest™, a transition guide, and other teaching aids.

The text-specific web site has been thoroughly revised and expanded for this edition. It now includes a glossary of Key Terms, a searchable bibliography, web activities, links to web resources, interactive exercises on the "Individuals in Society" and "Images in Society" features, chronological ordering activities, and the ACE self-testing quiz program. Visitors to the site can also access some of the older "Individuals in Society" features that did not make it into the Seventh Edition.

For institutions using either the Blackboard™ or WebCT™ platforms, we have designed a premium version of the course cartridge. Students can access a wealth of information, including learning objectives, chapter summaries, study outlines, review questions and self-quizzes, web research projects, and geography activities.

Houghton Mifflin is pleased to announce *Mosaic: Perspectives on Western Civilization.* This web site is a comprehensive, interactive resource that includes primary and secondary documents, interactive maps, fine art, and audio files, providing students with a direct connection to the raw material of Western civilization. Please contact your Houghton Mifflin Company representative for more information about this innovative multimedia program.

An exciting addition to our map program is a CD-ROM of thirty interactive maps—GeoQuest™, available for both instructors and students.

We are also proud to call attention to our on-line primary-source collection, Bibliobase™. This resource allows instructors to select from over six hundred documents to create their own customized readers for courses in Western civilization. Visit our web site at **www.bibliobase.com** for more information.

Finally, a set of full-color Map Transparencies of all the maps in the text is available on adoption.

Acknowledgments

It is a pleasure to thank the many instructors who read and critiqued the manuscript through its development:

Mary Elizabeth Ailes
University of Nebraska at Kearney

Ann Taylor Allen
University of Louisville

Robert J. Antony
Western Kentucky University

James Rushton Bishop
Holmes Community College

Gary B. Blumenshine
Indiana University, Fort Wayne

Donna L. Boutelle
California State University, Long Beach

Denvy A. Bowman
Coastal Carolina University

Jerry H. Brookshire
Middle Tennessee State University

James Burns
Clemson University

David Cherry
Montana State University, Bozeman

Stephanie Christelow
Idaho State University

Marc Cooper
Southwest Missouri State University

Jeffrey Cox
University of Iowa

Robert L. Dise, Jr.
University of Northern Iowa

Peter Dykema
University of Arizona

Carla C. Falkner
Northeast Mississippi Community College

James Felak
University of Washington

Malia B. Formes
Western Kentucky University

J. Drew Harrington
Troy State University, Montgomery

Jeffrey Hyson
Saint Joseph's University

Allen E. Jones
Troy State University

Sarah A. Kent
University of Wisconsin, Stevens Point

Danton Kostandarithes
Bolles School

Lisa M. Lane
MiraCosta College

Oliver L. Larkin
Hawkeye Community College

Michael V. Leggiere
Louisiana State University, Shreveport

Paul Douglas Lockhart
Wright State University

Martin C. J. Miller
Metropolitan State College of Denver

Michael Mini
Montgomery County Community College

R. Scott Moore
University of Dayton

Kathleen Paul
University of South Florida

Penne L. Prigge
Rockingham Community College

John B. Reid
Truckee Meadows Community College

Thomas S. Reid
Valencia Community College

Anna Marie Roos
University of Minnesota, Duluth

Thomas Schaeper
St. Bonaventure University

Richard Schellhammer
University of West Alabama

Linda Bregstein Scherr
Mercer County Community College

Jeffrey Smith
Northwestern State University

Philip M. Soergel
Arizona State University

Janet Thompson
Tallahassee Community College

Victoria E. Thompson
Arizona State University

Rosemary Fox Thurston
New Jersey City University

Laura Trauth
The Community College of Baltimore County, Essex Campus

George S. Vascik
Miami University

Sydney E. Watts
University of Richmond

Henry Weisser
Colorado State University

Terri York
Kilgore College

Mary E. Zamon
Marymount University

It is also a pleasure to thank our many editors at Houghton Mifflin for their efforts over many years. To Christina Horn, who guided production in the ever-more intensive email age, and to Julie Dunn, our development editor, we express our special appreciation. And we thank Carole Frohlich for her contributions in photo research and selection.

Many of our colleagues at the University of Illinois and at Georgetown University continued to provide information and stimulation, often without even knowing it. We thank them for it. Bennett Hill wishes to express his appreciation to Donald Franklin for his support and encouragement in the preparation of this Seventh Edition. John Buckler thanks Professor Jack Cargill for his advice on topics in Chapter 2. And he wishes to thank Professor Nicholas Yalouris, former General Inspector of Antiquities, for his kind permission to publish the newly discovered mosaic from Elis, Greece, in Chapter 3. He also wishes to thank Dr. Amy C. Smith, Curator of the Ure Museum of Archaeology of the University of Reading for her kind permission to publish the vase on page 61. John McKay happily acknowledges the excellent research assistance provided by Bryan Ganaway and Irina Gigova and he thanks them for it. He also expresses his deep appreciation to Jo Ann McKay for her sharp-eyed editorial support and unfailing encouragement.

Each of us has benefited from the criticism of his co-authors, although each of us assumes responsibility for what he has written. John Buckler has written the first six chapters; Bennett Hill has continued the narrative through Chapter 16; and John McKay has written Chapters 17 through 31. Finally, we continue to welcome the many comments and suggestions that have come from our readers, for they have helped us greatly in this ongoing endeavor.

J. P. M. B. D. H. J. B.

Dante's Inferno: frontispiece from an early manuscript of the *Divine Comedy*. Dante, wearing a red robe, is guided by Virgil, in blue, through the agonies of Hell. *(Bibliothèque Nationale, Paris)*

chapter

12 The Crisis of the Later Middle Ages

chapter outline

- Prelude to Disaster
- The Black Death
- The Hundred Years' War (ca 1337–1453)
- The Decline of the Church's Prestige
- The Life of the People
- Vernacular Literature

During the later Middle Ages, the last book of the New Testament, the Book of Revelation, inspired thousands of sermons and hundreds of religious tracts. The Book of Revelation deals with visions of the end of the world, with disease, war, famine, and death. It is no wonder this part of the Bible was so popular. Between 1300 and 1450, Europeans experienced a frightful series of shocks: economic dislocation, plague, war, social upheaval, and increased crime and violence. Death and preoccupation with death make the fourteenth century one of the most wrenching periods of Western civilization. Yet, in spite of the pessimism and crises, important institutions and ideas, such as representative assemblies and national literatures, emerged.

The miseries and disasters of the later Middle Ages bring to mind a number of questions.

- What economic difficulties did Europe experience?
- What were the social and psychological effects of repeated attacks of plague and disease?
- Some scholars maintain that war is often the catalyst for political, economic, and social change. Does this theory have validity for the fourteenth century?
- What provoked schism in the church, and what impact did it have on the lives of ordinary people?
- How did new national literatures reflect political and social developments?
- How and why did the laws of settlers in frontier regions reveal a strong racial or ethnic discrimination?

This chapter will focus on these questions.

Prelude to Disaster

In the first decade of the fourteenth century, the countries of northern Europe experienced a considerable price inflation. The cost of grain, livestock, and dairy products rose sharply. Severe weather, which historical geographers label the "Little Ice Age," made a serious situation frightful. An unusual number of storms brought torrential rains, ruining the wheat, oat, and hay crops on which people and animals almost everywhere depended. Since long-distance transportation of food was expensive and difficult, most urban areas depended for bread and meat on areas no more than a day's journey away. Poor harvests—and one in four was likely to be poor—led to scarcity and starvation. Almost all of northern Europe suffered a **"Great Famine"** in the years 1315–1322, which contemporaries interpreted as a recurrence of the biblical "seven lean years" (Genesis 42).

Reduced caloric intake meant increased susceptibility to disease, especially for infants, children, and the elderly. Workingmen and workingwomen on a reduced diet had less energy, which in turn meant lower productivity, lower output, and higher grain prices. The great famine proved a demographic disaster in France; in Burgundy perhaps one-third of the population died. The many religious houses of Flanders experienced a high loss of monks, nuns, and priests.

Hardly had western Europe begun to recover from this disaster when another struck. An epidemic of typhoid fever carried away thousands. In 1316, 10 percent of the population of the city of Ypres may have died between May and October alone. Then in 1318 disease hit cattle and sheep, drastically reducing the herds and flocks. Another bad harvest in 1321 brought famine and death.

The province of Languedoc in France presents a classic example of agrarian crisis. For over 150 years, Languedoc had enjoyed continual land reclamation, steady agricultural expansion, and enormous population growth. Then the fourteenth century opened with four years of bad harvests. Torrential rains in 1310 ruined the harvest and brought on terrible famine. Harvests failed again in 1322 and 1329. In 1332 desperate peasants survived the winter on raw herbs. In the half century from 1302 to 1348, poor harvests occurred twenty times. The undernourished population was ripe for the Grim Reaper, who appeared in 1348 in the form of the Black Death.

These catastrophes had grave social consequences. Poor harvests and famine led to the abandonment of homesteads. In parts of the Low Countries and in the Scottish-English borderlands, entire villages were abandoned. This meant a great increase in the number of vagabonds, what we call "homeless people." In Flanders and East Anglia (eastern England), where aspects of the famine have been carefully analyzed, some rustics were forced to mortgage, sublease, or sell their holdings to get money to buy food. Rich farmers bought out their poorer neighbors. When conditions improved, debtors tried to get their lands back, leading to a very volatile land market. To reduce the labor supply and the mouths to feed in the countryside, young males sought work in the towns.[1] Poor harvests probably meant that marriage had to be postponed. Later marriages and the deaths caused by famine and disease meant a reduction in population. Meanwhile, the international character of trade and commerce meant that a disaster in one country had serious implications elsewhere. For example, the infection that attacked English sheep in 1318 caused a sharp decline in wool exports in the following years. Without wool, Flemish weavers could not work, and thousands were laid off. Without woolen cloth, the businesses of Flemish, Hanseatic, and Italian merchants suffered. Unemployment encouraged people to turn to crime.

To none of these problems did governments have effective solutions. The three sons of Philip the Fair who sat on the French throne between 1314 and 1328 condemned speculators, who held stocks of grain back until conditions were desperate and prices high, forbade the sale of grain abroad, and published legislation prohibiting fishing with traps that took large catches. These measures had few positive results. As the subsistence crisis deepened, popular discontent and paranoia increased. Starving people focused their anger on the rich, speculators, and the Jews, who were targeted as creditors fleecing the poor through pawnbroking. (Expelled from France in 1306, Jews were readmitted in 1315 and granted the privilege of lending at high interest rates.) Rumors spread of a plot by Jews and their agents, the lepers, to kill Christians by poisoning the wells. With "evidence" collected by torture, many lepers and Jews were killed, beaten, or hit with heavy fines.

In England Edward I's incompetent son, Edward II (r. 1307–1327), used Parliament to set price controls, first on the sale of livestock after disease and poor lambing had driven prices up, and then on ale, which was made from barley (the severe rains of 1315 had contributed to molds and mildews, sharply reducing the crop). Baronial conflicts and wars with the Scots dominated Edward II's reign. Fearing food riots and violence, Edward condemned speculators, which proved easier than enforcing price controls. He did try to buy grain abroad, but yields in the Baltic were low; the French crown, as we have seen, forbade exports; and the grain shipped from Castile in northern Spain was grabbed by Scottish, English, and rogue Hanseatic pirates on the high seas. Such grain as reached southern English ports was stolen by looters and sold on the black market. The Crown's efforts at famine relief failed.

In Scandinavia and the Baltic countries, low cereal harvests, declines in meat and dairy production, economic

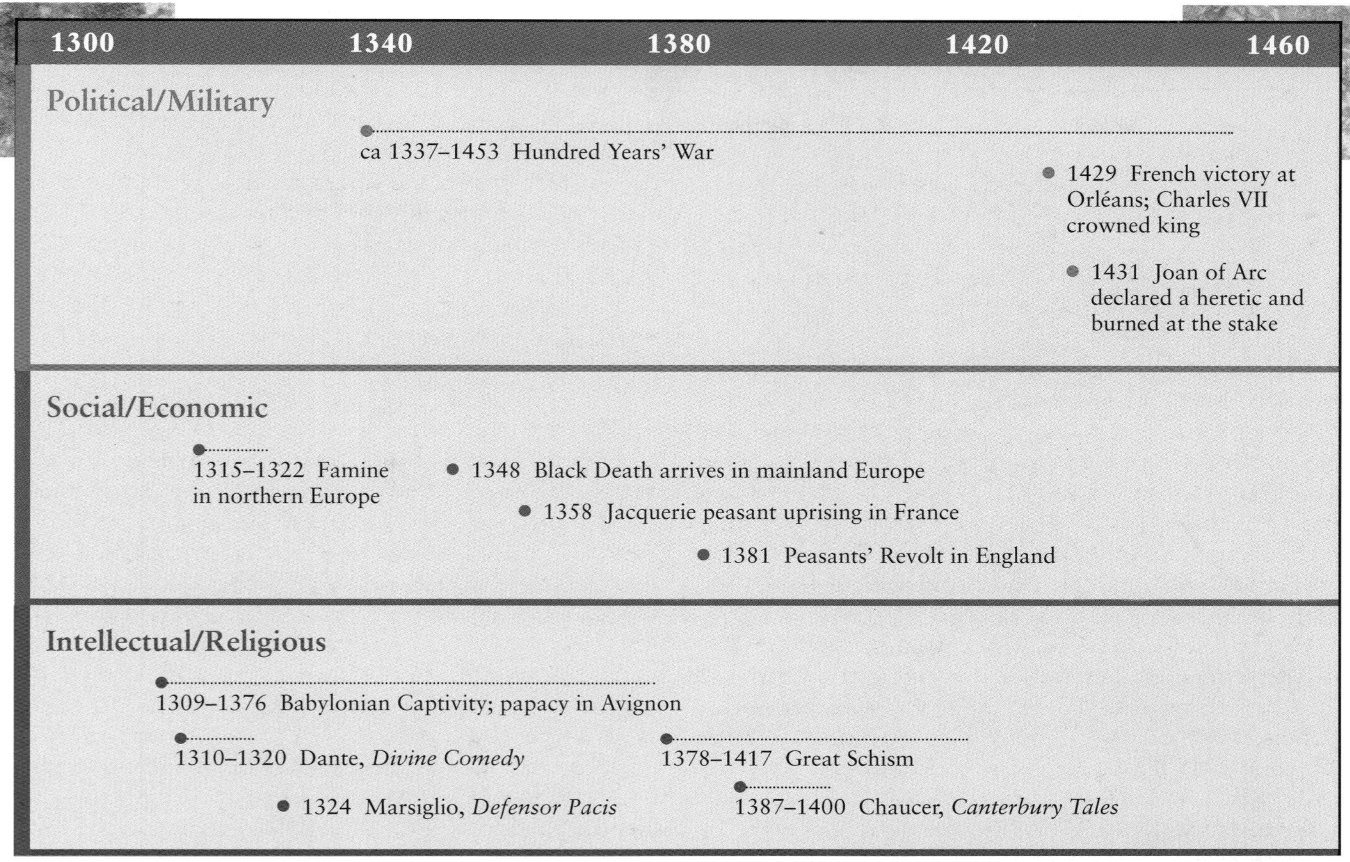

recessions, and the lack of salt, used for preserving herring, resulted in terrible food shortages. One scholar describes conditions there as "catastrophic."[2] Economic and social problems were aggravated by the appearance of a frightful disease.

The Black Death

In 1291 Genoese sailors had opened the Strait of Gibraltar to Italian shipping by defeating the Moroccans. Then, shortly after 1300, important advances were made in the design of Italian merchant ships. A square rig was added to the mainmast, and ships began to carry three masts instead of just one. Additional sails better utilized wind power to propel the ship. The improved design permitted year-round shipping for the first time, and Venetian and Genoese merchant ships could sail the dangerous Atlantic coast even in the winter months. With ships continually at sea, their rats too were constantly on the move, and thus any rat-transmitted disease could spread rapidly.

Scholars dispute the origins of the bubonic plague, often known as the **Black Death**. One legend holds that the plague broke out in the Tartar (or Tatar) army under Khan Djani-Beg that was besieging the city of Caffa (modern Feodosiya) in the Crimea, in southern Russia. The Khan ordered the heads of Tartar victims hurled into Caffa to infect the defenders.[3] Some scholars hold that the plague broke out in China or Central Asia around 1331, and during the next fifteen years merchants and soldiers carried it over the caravan routes until in 1346 it reached the Crimea. Other scholars believe the plague was endemic in southern Russia. In either case, from the Crimea the plague had easy access to Mediterranean lands and western Europe.

In October 1347, Genoese ships brought the plague to Messina, from which it spread across Sicily. Venice and Genoa were hit in January 1348, and from the port of Pisa the disease spread south to Rome and east to Florence and all of Tuscany. By late spring, southern Germany was attacked. Frightened French authorities chased a galley bearing the disease from the port of Marseilles,

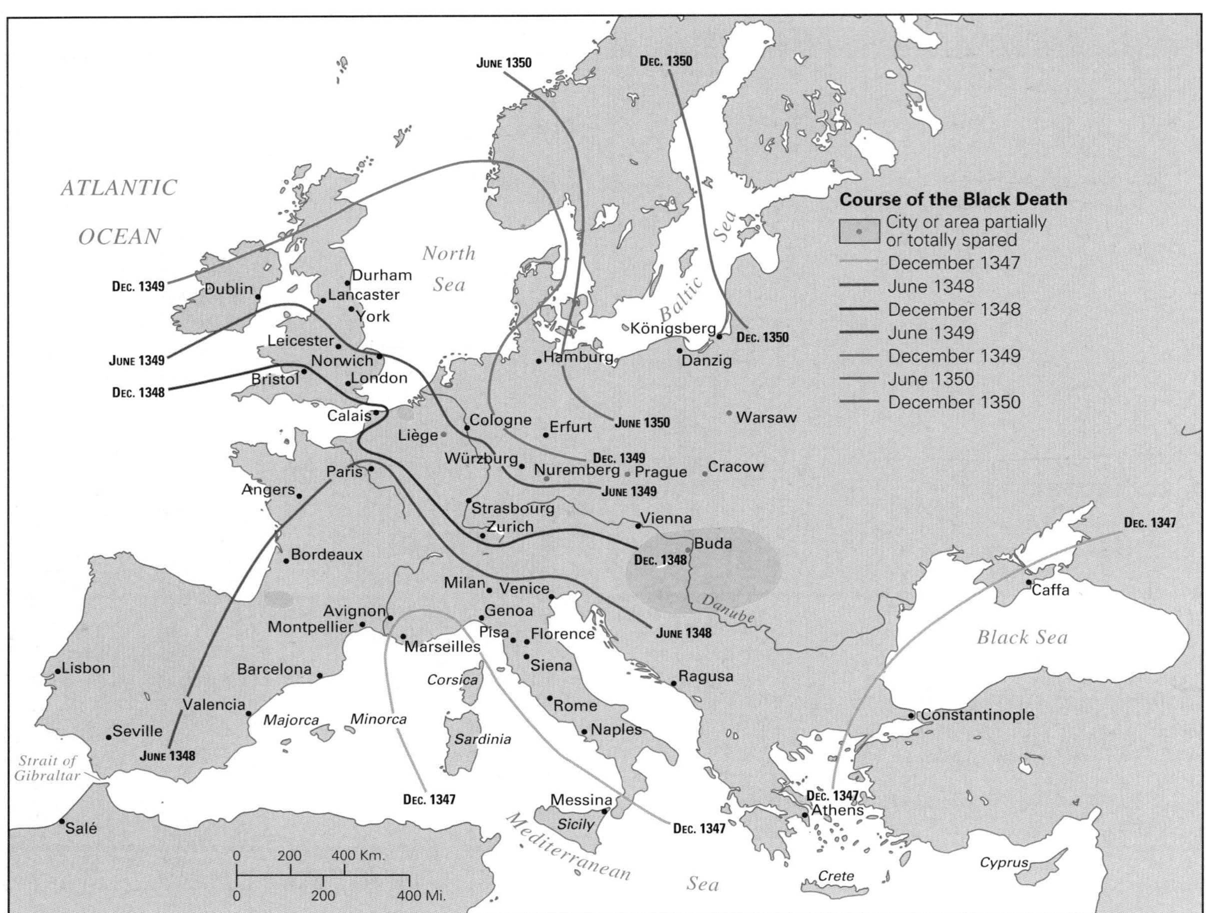

MAP 12.1 The Course of the Black Death in Fourteenth-Century Europe Note the routes that the bubonic plague took across Europe. How do you account for the fact that several regions were spared the "dreadful death"?

but not before plague had infected the city, from which it spread to Languedoc and Spain. In June 1348, two ships entered the Bristol Channel and introduced it into England. All Europe felt the scourge of this horrible disease (see Map 12.1).

Pathology and Care

Modern understanding of the bubonic plague rests on the research of two bacteriologists, one French and one Japanese, who in 1894 independently identified the bacillus that causes the plague, *Pasteurella pestis* (so labeled after the French scientist's teacher, Louis Pasteur). The bacillus liked to live in the bloodstream of an animal or, ideally, in the stomach of a flea. The flea in turn resided in the hair of a rodent, sometimes a squirrel but preferably the hardy, nimble, and vagabond black rat. Why the host black rat moved so much, scientists still do not know, but it often traveled by ship. There the black rat could feast for months on a cargo of grain or live snugly among bales of cloth. Fleas bearing the bacillus also had no trouble nesting in saddlebags.[4] Comfortable, well-fed, and having greatly multiplied, the black rats ended their ocean voyage and descended on the great cities of Europe.

The plague took two forms—bubonic and pneumonic. In the bubonic form, the flea was the vector, or transmitter, of the disease. In the pneumonic form, the plague was communicated directly from one person to another.

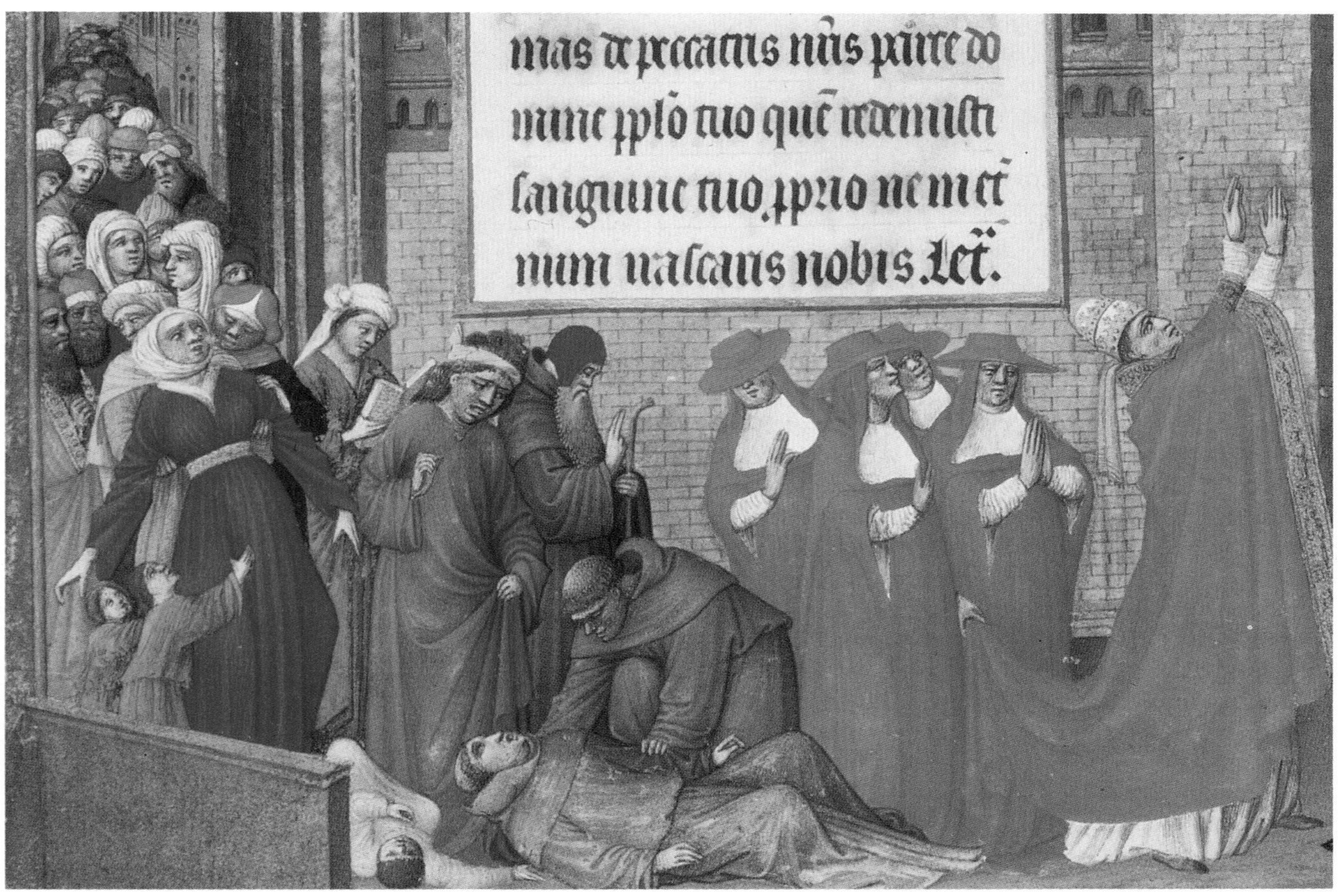

Procession of Saint Gregory According to the *Golden Legend,* a thirteenth-century collection of saints' lives, the bubonic plague ravaged Rome when Gregory I was elected pope (590–604). He immediately ordered special prayers and processions around the city. Here, as people circle the walls, new victims fall (*center*). The architecture, the cardinals, and the friars all indicate that this painting dates from the fourteenth, not the sixth, century. *(Musée Condé, Chantilly/Art Resource, NY)*

Although by the fourteenth century urban authorities from London to Paris to Rome had begun to try to achieve a primitive level of sanitation, urban conditions remained ideal for the spread of disease. Narrow streets filled with refuse and human excrement were as much cesspools as thoroughfares. Dead animals and sore-covered beggars greeted the traveler. Houses whose upper stories projected over the lower ones eliminated light and air. And extreme overcrowding was commonplace. When all members of an aristocratic family lived and slept in one room, it should not be surprising that six or eight persons in a middle-class or poor household slept in one bed—if they had one. Closeness, after all, provided warmth. Houses were beginning to be constructed of brick, but many remained of wood, clay, and mud. A determined rat had little trouble entering such a house.

Standards of personal hygiene remained frightfully low. True, most large cities had public bathhouses, but we have no way of knowing how frequently ordinary people used them. Lack of personal cleanliness, combined with any number of temporary ailments such as diarrhea and the common cold, weakened the body's resistance to serious disease. Fleas and body lice were universal afflictions: everyone from peasants to archbishops had them. One more bite did not cause much alarm. But if that nibble came from a bacillus-bearing flea, an entire household or area was doomed.

The symptoms of the bubonic plague started with a growth the size of a nut or an apple in the armpit, in the groin, or on the neck. This was the boil, or **buba,** that gave the disease its name and caused agonizing pain. If the buba was lanced and the pus thoroughly drained, the victim had a chance of recovery. The secondary stage was the appearance of black spots or blotches caused by bleeding under the skin. (This syndrome did not give the disease its common name; contemporaries did not call the plague the Black Death. Sometime in the fifteenth century, the Latin phrase *atra mors,* meaning "dreadful death," was translated "black death," and the phrase stuck.) Finally, the victim began to cough violently and spit blood. This stage, indicating the presence of millions of bacilli in the bloodstream, signaled the end, and death followed in two or three days. Rather than evoking compassion for the victim, a French scientist has written, everything about the bubonic plague provoked horror and disgust: "All the matter which exuded from their bodies let off an unbearable stench; sweat, excrement, spittle, breath, so fetid as to be overpowering; urine turbid, thick, black or red."[5]

Fourteenth-century medical literature indicates that physicians could sometimes ease the pain, but they had no cure. Most people—lay, scholarly, and medical—believed that the Black Death was caused by some "vicious property in the air" that carried the disease from place to place. When ignorance was joined to fear and ancient bigotry, savage cruelty sometimes resulted. Many people believed that the Jews had poisoned the wells of Christian communities and thereby infected the drinking water. This charge led to the murder of thousands of Jews across Europe. According to one chronicler, sixteen thousand were killed at the imperial city of Strasbourg alone in 1349. Though sixteen thousand is probably a typical medieval numerical exaggeration, the horror of the massacre is not lessened. Scholars have yet to explain the economic impact that the loss of such a productive people had on Strasbourg and other cities.

The Italian writer Giovanni Boccaccio (1313–1375), describing the course of the disease in Florence in the preface to his book of tales *The Decameron,* pinpointed the cause of the spread:

Moreover, the virulence of the pest was the greater by reason that intercourse was apt to convey it from the sick to the whole, just as fire devours things dry or greasy when they are brought close to it. Nay, the evil went yet further, for not merely by speech or association with the sick was the malady communicated to the healthy with consequent peril of common death, but any that touched the clothes of the sick or aught else that had been touched or used by them, seemed thereby to contract the disease.[6]

The highly infectious nature of the plague, especially in areas of high population density, was recognized by a few sophisticated Muslims. When the disease struck the town of Salé in Morocco, Ibu Abu Madyan shut in his household with sufficient food and water and allowed no one to enter or leave until the plague had passed. Abu Madyan was entirely successful. The rat that carried the disease-bearing flea avoided travel outside the cities. Thus the countryside was relatively safe. City dwellers who could afford to move fled to the country.

If medical science had no effective treatment, could victims' suffering be eased? Perhaps in hospitals. What was the geographical distribution of hospitals, and, although our estimates of medieval populations remain rough, what was the hospital-to-population ratio? How many patients could a hospital serve? Whereas earlier the feudal lord had made philanthropic foundations, beginning in the thirteenth century individual merchants—out of compassion, generosity, and the custom of giving to parish collections, and in the belief that the sick would be prayerful intercessors with God for the donors' sins—endowed hospitals. Business people established hospitals in the towns of northern France and Flanders; Milan, Genoa, and Venice were well served, and the 30 hospitals in Florence provided 1,000 beds in 1339. Sixty hospitals served Paris in 1328—but probably not enough for its population of 200,000. The many hospitals in the Iberian Peninsula continued the Muslim tradition of care for the poor and ill. Merchants in the larger towns of the German Empire, in Poland, and in Hungary also founded hospitals in the fourteenth century, generally later than those in western Europe. Sailors, long viewed as potential carriers of disease, benefited from hospitals reserved for them; in 1300 the Venetian government paid a surgeon to care for sick sailors. At the time the plague erupted, therefore, most towns and cities had hospital facilities.

When trying to determine the number of people a hospital could accommodate, the modern researcher considers the number of beds, the size of the staff, and the building's physical layout. Since each hospital bed might serve two or more patients, we cannot calculate the number of patients on the basis of the beds alone. We do know that rural hospices usually had twelve to fifteen beds, and city hospitals, as at Lisbon, Narbonne, and Genoa, had on average twenty-five to thirty beds, but these figures do not tell us how many patients were accommodated. Only the very rare document listing the number of wrapping sheets and coffins for the dead pur-

Patients in a Hospital Ward, Fifteenth Century In many cities hospitals could not cope with the large numbers of plague victims. The practice of putting two or more adults in the same bed, as shown here, contributed to the spread of the disease. At the Hôtel-Dieu in Paris, nurses complained of being forced to put eight to ten children in a single bed in which a patient had recently died. *(Musée de l'Assistance Publique, Paris/Giraudon/Art Resource, NY)*

chased in a given period provides the modern scholar with information on the number of patients a hospital had. Hospitals could offer only shelter, compassion, and care for the dying.[7]

Mortality rates cannot be specified, because population figures for the period before the arrival of the plague do not exist for most countries and cities. The largest amount of material survives for England, but it is difficult to use; after enormous scholarly controversy, only educated guesses can be made. Of a total English population of perhaps 4.2 million, probably 1.4 million died of the Black Death in its several visits.[8] Densely populated Italian cities endured incredible losses. Florence lost between one-half and two-thirds of its 1347 population of 85,000 when the plague visited in 1348.

Nor did central and eastern Europe escape the ravages of the disease. Moving northward from the Balkans, eastward from France, and southward from the Baltic, the plague swept through the German Empire. In the Rhineland in 1349, Cologne and Mainz endured heavy losses. In 1348 it swept through Bavaria, entered the Moselle Valley, and pushed into northern Germany. One chronicler records that in the summer and autumn of 1349, between five hundred and six hundred died every day in Vienna. Styria, in what today is central Austria, was very hard hit, with cattle straying unattended in the fields.

As the Black Death took its toll on the German Empire, waves of emigrants fled to Poland, Bohemia, and Hungary. The situation there was better, though not completely absent of disease. The plague seems to have entered Poland through the Baltic seaports and spread from there. Still, population losses were lower than elsewhere in Europe. In Hungary, at least, that may have been due to blood type. Historians of medicine have postulated that people with type O blood, which predominated in that area, are immune to the bubonic plague. The plague spread from Poland to Russia, reaching Pskov, Novgorod, and Moscow, where it felled Grand Duke Simeon.[9] No estimates have been made of population losses there or in the Balkans. In Serbia, though, the plague left vast tracts of land unattended, which prompted an increase in Albanian immigration to meet the labor shortage.

Across Europe the Black Death recurred intermittently in the 1360s and 1370s. It reappeared many times with reduced virulence, making its last appearance in the French port city of Marseilles in 1721. Survivors became more prudent. Because periods of famine had caused malnutrition, making people vulnerable to disease, Europeans controlled population growth so that population did not outstrip food supply. Western Europeans improved navigation techniques and increased long-distance trade, which permitted the importation of grain from sparsely populated Baltic regions (see page 380). They strictly enforced quarantine measures.[10] They worked on the development of vaccines. But it was only in 1947, six hundred years after the arrival of the plague in the West, that the American microbiologist Selman Waksman discovered an effective vaccine, streptomycin.

Social, Economic, and Cultural Consequences

It is noteworthy that, in an age of mounting criticism of clerical wealth (see page 395), the behavior of the clergy during the plague was often exemplary. Priests, monks, and nuns cared for the sick and buried the dead. In places like Venice, from which even physicians fled, priests remained to give what ministrations they could. Consequently, their mortality rate was phenomenally high. The German clergy especially suffered a severe decline in personnel in the years after 1350. With the ablest killed off, the wealth of the German church fell into the hands of the incompetent and weak. The situation was ripe for reform (see Chapter 14).

In taking their pastoral responsibilities seriously, some clergy did things that the church in a later age would vigorously condemn. The institutional church has traditionally opposed laymen, and especially laywomen, administering the sacraments. But the shortage of priests was so great that in 1349 Ralph, bishop of Bath and Wells in England (1329–1363), advised his people that "if they are on the point of death and cannot secure the services of a priest, then they should make confession to each other, as is permitted in the teaching of the Apostles, whether to a layman or, if no man is present, even to a woman."[11]

Economic historians and demographers sharply dispute the impact of the plague on the economy in the late fourteenth century. The traditional view that the plague had a disastrous effect has been greatly modified. The clearest evidence comes from England, where the agrarian economy showed remarkable resilience. While the severity of the disease varied from region to region, it appears that by about 1375 most landlords enjoyed revenues near those of the pre-plague years. By the early fifteenth century, seigneurial prosperity reached a medieval peak. Why? The answer appears to lie in the fact that England and many parts of Europe suffered from overpopulation in the early fourteenth century. Population losses caused by the Black Death "led to increased productivity by restoring a more efficient balance between labour, land, and capital."[12]

What impact did visits of the plague have on urban populations? The rich evidence from a census of the city of Florence and its surrounding territory taken between 1427 and 1430 is fascinating. The region had suffered repeated epidemics since 1347. In a total population of 260,000 persons, 15 percent were age sixty or over (a very high proportion), suggesting that the plague took the young rather than the mature. Children and youths up to age nineteen constituted 44 percent of the people. Adults between the ages of twenty and fifty-nine, the most economically productive group, represented 41 percent of Florentine society.

The high mortality rate of craftsmen led Florentine guilds to recruit many new members. For example, between 1328 and 1347 the silk merchants guild accepted 730 members, and between 1408 and 1427 it admitted 784. It appears that economic organizations tried to keep their numbers constant, even though the size of the population and its pool of potential guild members was shrinking. Moreover, in contrast to the pre-1348 period, many new members of the guilds were not related to existing members. Thus the post-plague years represent an age of "new men."[13]

The Black Death brought on a general European inflation. High mortality produced a fall in production, shortages of goods, and a general rise in prices. The shortage of labor and workers' demands for higher wages put guild masters on the defensive. They retaliated with measures such as the English Statute of Laborers (1351), which attempted to freeze salaries and wages at pre-1347 levels. The statute could not be enforced and thus was unsuccessful. The price of wheat in most of Europe increased, as did the costs of meat, sausage, and cheese. This inflation continued to the end of the fourteenth century. But wages in the towns rose faster, and the broad mass of people enjoyed a higher standard of living. "A more efficient balance between labour, land, and capital" brought increased productivity.[14] Population decline meant a sharp increase in per capita wealth. The greater demand for labor meant greater mobility for peasants in rural areas and for industrial workers in the towns and cities.

Labor shortages caused by the Black Death throughout the Mediterranean region, from Constantinople to Spain, presented aggressive businessmen with a golden opportunity. The price of slaves rose sharply. Venetian slavers from their colony at Tana on the Sea of Azov in the Crimea took advantage of the boom in demand as prices soared between 1350 and 1410. "By about 1408, no less than 78 per cent of Tana's export earnings came from slaves. Out of their misery, and out of the profits born of the Black Death, one palace after another was raised along the (Venetian) Rialto."[15]

Even more significant than the social effects were the psychological consequences. The knowledge that the disease meant almost certain death provoked the most profound pessimism. Imagine an entire society in the grip of the belief that it was at the mercy of a frightful affliction about which nothing could be done, a disgusting disease from which family and friends would flee, leaving one to die alone and in agony. It is not surprising that some sought release in orgies and gross sensuality, while others turned to the severest forms of asceticism and frenzied religious fervor. Some extremists joined groups of **flagellants**, who whipped and scourged themselves as penance for their and society's sins, in the belief that the Black Death was God's punishment for humanity's wickedness.

Plague ripped apart the social fabric. In the thirteenth century, funerals, traditionally occasions for the mutual consolation of the living as much as memorial services for the dead, grew increasingly elaborate, with large corteges and many mourners. In the fourteenth century, public horror at the suffering of the afflicted and at the dead reduced the size of mourning processions and eventually resulted in failure even to perform the customary death rites. Fear of infection led to the dead being buried hastily, sometimes in mass graves.

People often used pilgrimages to holy places as justification for their flight from cities. Suspected of being carriers of plague, travelers, pilgrims, and the homeless aroused deep hostility. All European port cities followed the example of Ragusa (modern Dubrovnik in southwestern Croatia on the Dalmatian coast) and quarantined arriving ships, crews, passengers, and cargoes to determine whether they brought the plague. Deriving from a Venetian word, the English term *quarantine* originally meant forty days' isolation.

Popular endowments of educational institutions multiplied. The years of the Black Death witnessed the foundation of new colleges at old universities, such as Corpus Christi and Clare Colleges at Cambridge and New College at Oxford, and of entirely new universities. The beginnings of Charles University in Prague (1348) and the Universities of Florence (1350), Vienna (1364), Cracow (1364), and Heidelberg (1385) were all associated with the plague: their foundation charters specifically mention the shortage of priests and the decay of learning. Whereas universities such as those at Bologna and Paris had an international student body, new institutions established in the wake of the Black Death had more national or local constituencies. Thus the international character of medieval culture weakened. The decline of cultural cohesion paved the way for schism in the Catholic church even before the Reformation.[16]

The literature and art of the fourteenth century reveal a terribly morbid concern with death. One highly popular artistic motif, the Dance of Death, depicted a dancing skeleton leading away a living person. No wonder survivors experienced a sort of shell shock and a crisis of faith. Lack of confidence in the leaders of society, lack of hope for the future, defeatism, and malaise wreaked enormous anguish and contributed to the decline of the Middle Ages. A long international war added further misery to the frightful disasters of the plague.

The Hundred Years' War (ca 1337–1453)

In January 1327, Queen Isabella of England, her lover Mortimer, and a group of barons, having deposed and murdered Isabella's incompetent husband, King Edward II, proclaimed his fifteen-year-old son king as Edward III. Isabella and Mortimer, however, held real power until 1330, when Edward seized the reins of government. In 1328 Charles IV of France, the last surviving son of Philip the Fair, died childless. With him ended the Capetian dynasty. An assembly of French barons, meaning to exclude Isabella—who was Charles's sister and the daughter of Philip the Fair—and her son Edward III from the French throne, proclaimed that "no woman nor her son could succeed to the [French] monarchy."  The French barons rested their position on the Salic Law, a Germanic law code that forbade females or those descended in the female line to succeed to offices. The barons passed the crown to Philip VI of Valois (r. 1328–1350), a nephew of Philip the Fair. In these actions lie the origins of another phase of the centuries-old struggle between the English and French monarchies, one that was fought intermittently from 1337 to 1453.

Causes

The Hundred Years' War had both distant and immediate causes. In 1259 France and England signed the Treaty of Paris, in which the English king agreed to become—for himself and his successors—vassal of the French crown for the duchy of Aquitaine. The English claimed Aquitaine as an ancient inheritance. French policy, however, was strongly expansionist, and the French kings resolved to absorb the duchy into the kingdom of France. In 1329 Edward III paid homage to Philip VI for Aquitaine. In 1337 Philip, eager to exercise full French jurisdiction in Aquitaine, confiscated the duchy. Edward III interpreted this action as a gross violation of the treaty of 1259 and as a cause for war. Moreover, Edward argued, as the eldest directly surviving male descendant of Philip the Fair, he must assume the title of king of France in order to wield his rightful authority in Aquitaine.[17] In short, Edward rejected the decision of the French barons excluding him from the throne. Edward III's dynastic argument upset the feudal order in France: to increase their independent power, French vassals of Philip VI used the excuse that they had to transfer their loyalty to a more legitimate overlord, Edward III. One reason the war lasted so long was that it became a French civil war, with some French barons supporting English monarchs in order to thwart the centralizing goals of the French crown.

Economic factors involving the wool trade and the control of Flemish towns had served as justifications for war between France and England for centuries. The wool trade between England and Flanders served as the cornerstone of both countries' economies; they were closely interdependent. Flanders was a fief of the French crown, and the Flemish aristocracy was highly sympathetic to the monarchy in Paris. But the wealth of Flemish merchants and cloth manufacturers depended on English wool, and Flemish burghers strongly supported the claims of Edward III. The disruption of commerce with England threatened their prosperity.

The Popular Response

The governments of both England and France manipulated public opinion to support the war. Whatever significance modern scholars ascribe to the economic factor,

Flanders and the English Merchant Staplers Flanders was officially on the French side during the Hundred Years' War, but Flemish cities depended heavily on English wool for their textile manufacturing. Hence the Merchant Staplers, the English trading company with a monopoly on trade in wool, sought concessions. In this 1387 illustration, the master of the staple and his fellow merchants plead their case to the count of Flanders. *(Courtesy of the Trustees of the British Museum)*

public opinion in fourteenth-century England held that the war was waged for one reason: to secure for King Edward the French crown he had been unjustly denied.[18] Edward III issued letters to the sheriffs describing in graphic terms the evil deeds of the French and listing royal needs. Kings in both countries instructed the clergy to deliver sermons filled with patriotic sentiment. The royal courts sensationalized the wickedness of the other side and stressed the great fortunes to be made from the war. Philip VI sent agents to warn communities about the dangers of invasion and to stress the French crown's revenue needs to meet the attack.

The royal campaign to rally public opinion was highly successful, at least in the early stage of the war. Edward III gained widespread support in the 1340s and 1350s. The English developed a deep hatred of the French and feared that King Philip intended "to have seized and slaughtered the entire realm of England." When England was successful in the field, pride in the country's military proficiency increased.

Most important of all, the Hundred Years' War was popular because it presented unusual opportunities for wealth and advancement. Poor knights and knights who were unemployed were promised regular wages. Criminals who enlisted were granted pardons. The great nobles expected to be rewarded with estates. Royal exhortations to the troops before battles repeatedly stressed that, if victorious, the men might keep whatever they seized. The French chronicler Jean Froissart wrote that, at the time of Edward III's expedition of 1359, men of all ranks flocked to the English king's banner. Some came to acquire honor, but many came "to loot and pillage the fair and plenteous land of France."[19]

The Decline of Medieval Chivalry

The period of the Hundred Years' War witnessed the final flowering of the aristocratic code of medieval chivalry. Indeed, the enthusiastic participation of the nobility in both France and England was in response primarily to the opportunity the war provided to display chivalric behavior. What better place to display chivalric qualities than on the field of battle?

War was considered an ennobling experience; there was something elevating, manly, fine, and beautiful about it. When Shakespeare in the sixteenth century wrote of "the pomp and circumstance of glorious war," he was echoing the fourteenth- and fifteenth-century chroniclers who had glorified the trappings of war. Describing the French army before the Battle of Poitiers (1356), a contemporary said: "Then you might see banners and pennons unfurled to the wind, whereon fine gold and azure shone, purple, gules and ermine. Trumpets, horns and clarions—you might hear sounding through the camp; the Dauphin's [title borne by the eldest son of the king of France] great battle made the earth ring."[20]

This romantic view of war holds little appeal for modern men and women, who are more conscious of the slaughter, brutality, dirt, and blood that war inevitably involves. Also, modern thinkers are usually conscious of the broad mass of people, while the chivalric code applied only to the aristocratic military elite. Chivalry had no reference to those outside the knightly class.

The knight was supposed to show courtesy, graciousness, and generosity to his social equals, but certainly not to his social inferiors. When English knights fought French ones, they were social equals fighting according to a mutually accepted code of behavior. The infantry troops were looked on as inferior beings. When a French peasant force at Longueil destroyed a contingent of English knights, their comrades mourned them because "it was too much that so many good fighters had been killed by mere peasants."[21]

The Course of the War to 1419

The war was fought almost entirely in France and the Low Countries (see Map 12.2). It consisted mainly of a series of random sieges and cavalry raids. In 1335 the French began supporting Scottish incursions into northern England, ravaging the countryside in Aquitaine, and sacking and burning English coastal towns, such as Southampton. Such tactics lent weight to Edward III's propaganda campaign. In fact, royal propaganda on both sides fostered a kind of early nationalism.

During the war's early stages, England was highly successful. At **Crécy** in northern France in 1346, English longbowmen scored a great victory over French knights and crossbowmen. Although the aim of the longbow was not very accurate, it allowed for rapid reloading, and English archers could send off three arrows to the French crossbowmen's one. The result was a blinding shower of arrows that unhorsed the French knights and caused mass confusion. The firing of cannon—probably the first use of artillery in the West—created further panic. Thereupon the English horsemen charged and butchered the French.

This was not war according to the chivalric rules that Edward III would have preferred. Nevertheless, his son Edward the Black Prince used the same tactics ten years later to smash the French at Poitiers, where he captured the French king and held him for ransom. Again, at **Agincourt** near Arras in 1415, the chivalric English

The Battle of Crécy, 1346 Pitched battles were unusual in the Hundred Years' War. At Crécy, the English (on the right with lions on their royal standard) scored a spectacular victory. The longbow proved a more effective weapon over the French crossbow, but characteristically the artist concentrated on the aristocratic knights. *(Bibliothèque Nationale, Paris)*

soldier-king Henry V (r. 1413–1422) gained the field over vastly superior numbers. Henry followed up his triumph at Agincourt with the reconquest of Normandy. By 1419 the English had advanced to the walls of Paris (see Map 12.2). But the French cause was not lost. Though England had scored the initial victories, France won the war.

Joan of Arc and France's Victory

The ultimate French success rests heavily on the actions of an obscure French peasant girl, **Joan of Arc**, whose vision and work revived French fortunes and led to victory. A great deal of pious and popular legend surrounds Joan the Maid, because of her peculiar appearance on the scene, her astonishing success, her martyrdom, and her canonization by the Catholic church. The historical fact is that she saved the French monarchy, which was the embodiment of France.

Born in 1412 to well-to-do peasants in the village of Domrémy in Champagne, Joan of Arc grew up in a religious household. During adolescence she began to hear voices, which she later said belonged to Saint Michael, Saint Catherine, and Saint Margaret. In 1428 these voices spoke to her with great urgency, telling her that the dauphin (the uncrowned King Charles VII) had to be crowned and the English expelled from France. Joan went to the French court, persuaded the king to reject the rumor that he was illegitimate, and secured his support for her relief of the besieged city of Orléans.

The astonishing thing is not that Joan the Maid overcame serious obstacles to see the dauphin, not even that Charles and his advisers listened to her. What is amazing is the swiftness with which they were convinced. French fortunes had been so low for so long that the court believed only a miracle could save the country. Because Joan cut her hair short and dressed like a man, she scandalized the court. But hoping she would provide the miracle, Charles allowed her to accompany the army that was preparing to raise the English siege of Orléans.

In the meantime Joan, herself illiterate, dictated this letter calling on the English to withdraw:

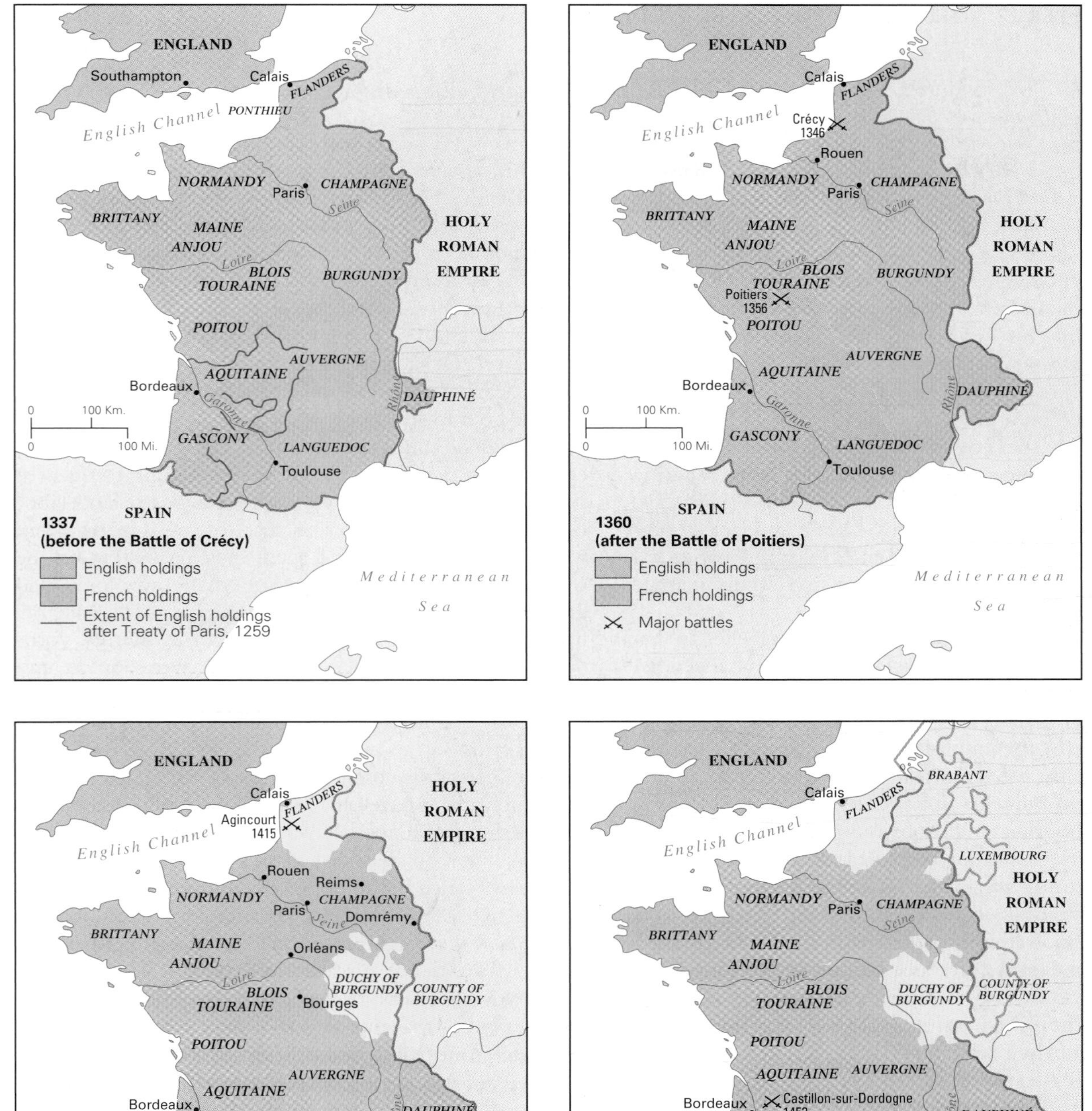

MAP 12.2 English Holdings in France During the Hundred Years' War The year 1429 marked the greatest extent of English holdings in France. Why is it unlikely that England could have held these territories permanently?

Jhesus Maria
King of England, and you Duke of Bedford, calling yourself regent of France, you William Pole, Count of Suffolk . . . , do right in the King of Heaven's sight. Surrender to The Maid *sent hither by God the King of Heaven, the keys of all the good towns you have taken and laid waste in France. She comes in God's name to establish the Blood Royal, ready to make peace if you agree to abandon France and repay what you have taken. And you, archers, comrades in arms, gentles and others, who are before the town of Orléans, retire in God's name to your own country.*[22]

Joan arrived before Orléans on April 28, 1429. Seventeen years old, she knew little of warfare and believed that if she could keep the French troops from swearing and frequenting brothels, victory would be theirs. On May 8 the English, weakened by disease and lack of supplies, withdrew from Orléans. Ten days later, Charles VII was crowned king at Reims. These two events marked the turning point in the war.

Joan's presence at Orléans, her strong belief in her mission, and the fact that she was wounded enhanced her reputation and strengthened the morale of the army. In 1430 England's allies, the Burgundians, captured Joan and sold her to the English. When the English handed her over to the ecclesiastical authorities for trial, the French court did not intervene. While the English wanted Joan eliminated for obvious political reasons, sorcery (witchcraft) was the ostensible charge at her trial. Witch persecution was increasing in the fifteenth century, and Joan's wearing of men's clothes appeared not only aberrant but indicative of contact with the Devil. In 1431 the court condemned her as a heretic—her claim of direct inspiration from God, thereby denying the authority of church officials, constituted heresy—and burned her at the stake in the marketplace at Rouen. A new trial in 1456 rehabilitated her name. In 1920 she was canonized and declared a holy maiden, and today she is revered as the second patron saint of France. The nineteenth-century French historian Jules Michelet extolled Joan of Arc as a symbol of the vitality and strength of the French peasant classes.

The relief of Orléans stimulated French pride and rallied French resources. As the war dragged on, loss of life mounted, and money appeared to be flowing into a bottomless pit, demands for an end increased in England. The clergy and intellectuals pressed for peace. Parliamentary opposition to additional war grants stiffened. Slowly the French reconquered Normandy and, finally, ejected the English from Aquitaine. At the war's end in 1453, only the town of Calais remained in English hands.

Costs and Consequences

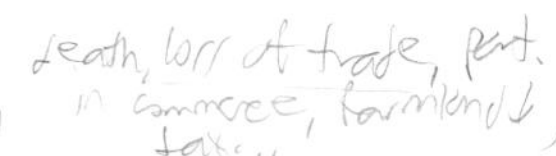

In France the English had slaughtered thousands of soldiers and civilians. In the years after the sweep of the Black Death, this additional killing meant a grave loss of population. The English had laid waste to hundreds of thousands of acres of rich farmland, leaving the rural economy of many parts of France a shambles. The war had disrupted trade and the great fairs, resulting in the drastic reduction of French participation in international commerce. Defeat in battle and heavy taxation contributed to widespread dissatisfaction and aggravated peasant grievances.

In England only the southern coastal ports experienced much destruction, and the demographic effects of the Black Death actually worked to restore the land-labor balance (see page 386). The costs of the war, however, were tremendous. England spent over £5 million on the war effort, a huge sum at the time. Manpower losses had greater social consequences. The knights who ordinarily handled the work of local government as sheriffs, coroners, jurymen, and justices of the peace were abroad, and their absence contributed to the breakdown of order at the local level. The English government attempted to finance the war effort by raising taxes on the wool crop. Because of steadily increasing costs, the Flemish and Italian buyers could not afford English wool. Consequently, raw wool exports slumped drastically between 1350 and 1450.

Many men of all social classes had volunteered for service in France in the hope of acquiring booty and becoming rich. The chronicler Walsingham, describing the period of Crécy, wrote: "For the woman was of no account who did not possess something from the spoils of . . . cities overseas in clothing, furs, quilts, and utensils . . . tablecloths and jewels, bowls of murra [semiprecious stone] and silver, linen and linen cloths."[23] Walsingham is referring to 1348, in the first generation of war. As time went on, most fortunes seem to have been squandered as fast as they were made.

If English troops returned with cash, they did not invest it in land. In the fifteenth century, returning soldiers were commonly described as beggars and vagabonds, roaming about making mischief. Even the large sums of money received from the ransom of the great—such as the £250,000 paid to Edward III for the freedom of King John of France—and the money paid as indemnities by captured towns and castles did not begin to equal the more than £5 million spent. England suffered a serious net loss.[24]

The long war also had a profound impact on the political and cultural lives of the two countries. Most notably, it stimulated the development of the English Parliament.

Between 1250 and 1450, representative assemblies flourished in many European countries. In the English Parliament, German diets, and Spanish cortes, deliberative practices developed that laid the foundations for the representative institutions of modern liberal-democratic nations. While representative assemblies declined in most countries after the fifteenth century, the English Parliament endured. Edward III's constant need for money to pay for the war compelled him to summon not only the great barons and bishops, but knights of the shires and burgesses from the towns as well. Between the outbreak of the war in 1337 and the king's death in 1377, parliamentary assemblies met twenty-seven times. Parliament met in thirty-seven of the fifty years of Edward's reign.[25]

The frequency of the meetings is significant. Representative assemblies were becoming a habit. Knights and burgesses—or the "Commons," as they came to be called—recognized their mutual interests and began to meet apart from the great lords. The Commons gradually realized that they held the country's purse strings, and a parliamentary statute of 1341 required that all nonfeudal levies have parliamentary approval. When Edward III signed the law, he acknowledged that the king of England could not tax without Parliament's consent. Increasingly, during the course of the war, money grants were tied to royal redress of grievances: if the government was to raise money, it had to correct the wrongs its subjects protested.

In England theoretical consent to taxation and legislation was given in one assembly for the entire country. France had no such single assembly; instead, there were many regional or provincial assemblies. Why did a national representative assembly fail to develop in France? The initiative for convening assemblies rested with the king, who needed revenue almost as much as the English ruler. But the French monarchy found the idea of representative assemblies thoroughly distasteful. Large gatherings of the nobility potentially or actually threatened the king's power. The advice of a counselor to King Charles VI (r. 1380–1422), "above all things be sure that no great assemblies of nobles or of *communes* take place in your kingdom," was accepted.[26] Charles VII (r. 1422–1461) even threatened to punish those proposing a national assembly.

No one in France wanted a national assembly. Linguistic, geographical, economic, legal, and political differences were very strong. People tended to think of themselves as Breton, Norman, Burgundian, or whatever, rather than French. Through much of the fourteenth and early fifteenth centuries, weak monarchs lacked the power to call a national assembly. Provincial assemblies, highly jealous of their independence, did not want a national assembly. The costs of sending delegates to it would be high, and the result was likely to be increased taxation. Finally, the Hundred Years' War itself hindered the growth of a representative body. Possible violence on dangerous roads discouraged people from travel.

In both countries, however, the war did promote the growth of **nationalism**—the feeling of unity and identity that binds together a people. After victories, each country experienced a surge of pride in its military strength. Just as English patriotism ran strong after Crécy and Poitiers, so French national confidence rose after Orléans. French national feeling demanded the expulsion of the enemy not merely from Normandy and Aquitaine but from French soil. Perhaps no one expressed this national consciousness better than Joan of Arc, when she exulted that the enemy had been "driven out of *France*."

The Decline of the Church's Prestige

In times of crisis or disaster, people of all faiths have sought the consolation of religion. In the fourteenth century, however, the official Christian church offered little solace. In fact, the leaders of the church added to the sorrow and misery of the times.

The Babylonian Captivity

From 1309 to 1376, the popes lived in Avignon in southeastern France. In order to control the church and its policies, Philip the Fair of France pressured Pope Clement V to settle in Avignon (see Map 11.5 on page 357). Clement, critically ill with cancer, lacked the will to resist Philip. This period in church history is often called the **Babylonian Captivity** (referring to the seventy years the ancient Hebrews were held captive in Mesopotamian Babylon).

The Babylonian Captivity badly damaged papal prestige. The Avignon papacy reformed its financial administration and centralized its government. But the seven popes at Avignon concentrated on bureaucratic matters to the exclusion of spiritual objectives. Though some of the popes led austere lives, the general atmosphere was one of luxury and extravagance. The leadership of the church was cut off from its historic roots and the source of its ancient authority, the city of Rome. In the absence of the papacy, the Papal States in Italy lacked stability and good government. The economy of Rome had been based on the presence of the papal court and the rich tourist trade the papacy attracted. The Babylonian Captivity left Rome poverty-stricken.

In 1377 Pope Gregory XI brought the papal court back to Rome. Unfortunately, he died shortly after the return. At Gregory's death, Roman citizens demanded an Italian pope who would remain in Rome. Between the time of Gregory's death and the opening of the conclave, great pressure was put on the cardinals to elect an Italian. At the time, none of them protested this pressure.

Sixteen cardinals—eleven Frenchmen, four Italians, and one Spaniard—entered the conclave on April 7, 1378. After two ballots, they unanimously chose a distinguished administrator, the archbishop of Bari, Bartolomeo Prignano, who took the name Urban VI. Each of the cardinals swore that Urban had been elected "sincerely, freely, genuinely, and canonically."

Urban VI (1378–1389) had excellent intentions for church reform. He wanted to abolish simony, *pluralism* (holding several church offices at the same time), absenteeism, and clerical extravagance. These were the very abuses being increasingly criticized by Christian people across Europe. Unfortunately, Pope Urban went about the work of reform in a tactless and bullheaded manner. The day after his coronation, he delivered a blistering attack on cardinals who lived in Rome while drawing their income from benefices elsewhere. His criticism was well-founded but ill-timed and provoked opposition before Urban had consolidated his authority.

In the weeks that followed, Urban stepped up attacks on clerical luxury, denouncing individual cardinals by name. He threatened to strike the cardinal archbishop of Amiens. Urban even threatened to excommunicate certain cardinals, and when he was advised that such excommunications would not be lawful unless the guilty had been warned three times, he shouted, "I can do anything, if it be my will and judgment."[27] Urban's quick temper and irrational behavior have led scholars to question his sanity. Whether he was medically insane or just drunk with power is a moot point. In any case, Urban's actions brought on disaster.

In groups of two and three, the cardinals slipped away from Rome and met at Anagni. They declared Urban's election invalid because it had come about under threats from the Roman mob, and they asserted that Urban himself was excommunicated. The cardinals then proceeded to the city of Fondi between Rome and Naples and elected Cardinal Robert of Geneva, the cousin of King Charles V of France, as pope. Cardinal Robert took the name Clement VII. There were thus two popes—Urban at Rome and the antipope Clement VII (1378–1394), who set himself up at Avignon in opposition to the legally elected Urban. So began the Great Schism, which divided Western Christendom until 1417.

The Great Schism

The powers of Europe aligned themselves with Urban or Clement along strictly political lines. France naturally recognized the French antipope, Clement. England, France's historic enemy, recognized Pope Urban. Scotland, whose attacks on England were subsidized by France, followed the French and supported Clement. Aragon, Castile, and Portugal hesitated before deciding for Clement at Avignon. The emperor, who bore ancient hostility to France, recognized Urban VI. At first the Italian city-states recognized Urban; when he alienated them, they opted for Clement.

John of Spoleto, a professor at the law school at Bologna, eloquently summed up intellectual opinion of the **schism,** or division: "The longer this schism lasts, the more it appears to be costing, and the more harm it does; scandal, massacres, ruination, agitations, troubles and disturbances."[28] The common people, wracked by inflation, wars, and plague, were thoroughly confused about which pope was legitimate. The schism weakened the religious faith of many Christians and gave rise to instability and religious excesses. It brought the church leadership into serious disrepute. At a time when ordinary Christians needed the consolation of religion and confidence in religious leaders, church officials were fighting among themselves for power. The schism also brought to the fore conciliar ideas about church government.

The Conciliar Movement

Theories about the nature of the Christian church and its government originated in the very early church, but the years of the Great Schism witnessed their maturity. **Conciliarists** believed that reform of the church could best be achieved through periodic assemblies, or general councils, representing all the Christian people. While acknowledging that the pope was head of the church, conciliarists, such as the French theologian Pierre d'Ailly and the German Conrad of Gelnhausen, held that the pope derived his authority from the entire Christian community, whose well-being he existed to promote. Thus the pope was not an absolute authority incapable of doctrinal error. Conciliarists favored a balanced or constitutional form of church government, with papal authority shared with a general council, in contrast to the monarchical one that prevailed.

A half century before the Great Schism, in 1324, Marsiglio of Padua, then rector of the University of Paris, had published *Defensor Pacis* (The Defender of the Peace). Dealing as it did with the authority of state and church, *Defensor Pacis* proved to be one of the most controversial works written in the Middle Ages.

Marsiglio argued that the state was the great unifying power in society and that the church was subordinate to the state. He put forth the revolutionary ideas that the church had no inherent jurisdiction and should own no property. Authority in the Christian church, according to Marsiglio, should rest in a general council, made up of laymen as well as priests and superior to the pope. These ideas directly contradicted the medieval notion of a society governed by the church and the state, with the church supreme. *Defensor Pacis* was condemned by the pope, and Marsiglio was excommunicated.

Even more earthshaking than the theories of Marsiglio of Padua were the ideas of the English scholar and theologian John Wyclif (ca 1330–1384). Wyclif wrote that papal claims of temporal power had no foundation in the Scriptures and that the Scriptures alone should be the standard of Christian belief and practice. He urged the abolition of such practices as the veneration of saints, pilgrimages, pluralism, and absenteeism. Sincere Christians, according to Wyclif, should read the Bible for themselves. In response to that idea, the first English translation of the Bible was produced and circulated. Wyclif's views had broad social and economic significance. He urged that the church be stripped of its property. His idea that every Christian free of mortal sin possessed lordship was seized on by peasants in England during a revolt in 1381 and used to justify their goals.

In advancing these views, Wyclif struck at the roots of medieval church structure. Consequently, he has been hailed as the precursor of the Reformation of the sixteenth century. Although Wyclif's ideas were vigorously condemned by ecclesiastical authorities, they were widely disseminated by humble clerics and enjoyed great popularity in the early fifteenth century. Wyclif's followers were called "Lollards." The term, which means "mumblers of prayers and psalms," refers to what they criticized. Lollard teaching allowed women to preach and to consecrate the Eucharist. Women, some well educated, played a significant role in the movement. After Anne, sister of Wenceslaus, king of Germany and Bohemia, married Richard II of England, members of her household carried Lollard principles back to Bohemia.

In response to continued calls throughout Europe for a council, the two colleges of cardinals—one at Rome, the other at Avignon—summoned a council at Pisa in 1409.

Spoon with Fox Preaching to Geese (southern Netherlands, ca 1430) Taking as his text a contemporary proverb, "When the fox preaches, beware your geese," the artist shows, in the bowl of a spoon, a fox dressed as a monk or friar, preaching with three dead geese in his hood, while another fox grabs one of the congregation. The preaching fox reads from a scroll bearing the word *pax* (peace), implying the perceived hypocrisy of the clergy. The object suggests the widespread criticism of churchmen in the later Middle Ages. *(Painted enamel and gilding on silver; 17.6 cm [6⅞ in]. Museum of Fine Arts, Boston, Helen and Alice Coburn Fund, 51.2472)*

That gathering of prelates and theologians deposed both popes and selected another. Neither the Avignon pope nor the Roman pope would resign, however, and the appalling result was the creation of a threefold schism.

Finally, because of the pressure of the German emperor Sigismund, a great council met at the imperial city of Constance (1414–1418). It had three objectives: to end the schism, to reform the church "in head and members" (from top to bottom), and to wipe out heresy. The council condemned the Czech reformer Jan Hus (see the feature "Individuals in Society: Jan Hus"), and he was burned at the stake. The council eventually deposed both the Roman pope and the successor of the pope chosen at Pisa, and it isolated the Avignon antipope. A conclave elected a new leader, the Roman cardinal Colonna, who took the name Martin V (1417–1431).

Martin proceeded to dissolve the council. Nothing was done about reform. The schism was over, and though councils subsequently met at Basel and at Ferrara-Florence, in 1450 the papacy held a jubilee, celebrating its triumph over the conciliar movement. In the later fifteenth century, the papacy concentrated on Italian problems to the exclusion of universal Christian interests. But the schism and the conciliar movement had exposed the crying need for ecclesiastical reform, thus laying the foundations for the great reform efforts of the sixteenth century.

The Life of the People

In the fourteenth century, economic and political difficulties, disease, and war profoundly affected the lives of European peoples. Decades of slaughter and destruction, punctuated by the decimating visits of the Black Death, made a grave economic situation virtually disastrous. In many parts of France and the Low Countries, fields lay in ruin or untilled for lack of labor power. In England, as taxes increased, criticisms of government policy and mismanagement multiplied. Crime, aggravated economic troubles, and throughout Europe the frustrations of the common people erupted into widespread revolts. But for most people, marriage and the local parish church continued to be the center of their lives.

Marriage

Marriage and the family provided such peace and satisfaction as most people attained. What do we know about peasant marriages in the later Middle Ages? Scholars long believed that because peasants were illiterate and left very few statements about their marriages, generalizations could not be made about them. Recent research in English manorial, ecclesiastical, and coroners' records, however, has uncovered fascinating material. Evidence abounds of teenage flirtations, and many young people had sexual contacts—some leading to conception. Premarital pregnancy may have been deliberate: because children were economically important, the couple wanted to be sure of fertility before entering marriage.

"Whether rich or poor, male or female, the most important rite de passage for peasant youth was marriage."[29] Did they select their own spouses or accept parents' choices? Church law stressed that for a marriage to be valid, both partners must freely consent to it. The evidence overwhelmingly shows, above all where land or property accompanied the union, that parents took the lead in arranging their children's marriages; if the parents were dead, the responsibility fell to the inheriting son. Marriage determined not only the life partner and the economic circumstances in which the couple would live, but also the son-in-law who might take over the family land or the daughter-in-law who might care for her elderly in-laws. These kinds of interests required careful planning.

Most marriages were between men and women of the same village; where the name and residence of a husband is known, perhaps 41 percent were outsiders. Once the prospective bride or groom had been decided on, parents paid the **merchet** (fine to the lord for a woman's marriage—since he stood to lose a worker). Parents saw that the parish priest published on three successive Sundays the **banns**, public announcements that the couple planned to marry, to allow for objections to the union. And parents made the financial settlement. The couple then proceeded to the church door, where they made the vows, rings were blessed and exchanged, and the ceremony concluded with some kind of festivity.[30]

Although most peasants were illiterate, the gentry could write. The letters exchanged between Margaret and John Paston, who lived in Norfolk, England, in the fifteenth century, provide evidence for the experience of one couple. John and Margaret Paston were married about 1439, after an arrangement concluded entirely by their parents. John spent most of his time in London fighting through the law courts to increase his family properties and business interests; Margaret remained in Norfolk to supervise the family lands. Her enormous responsibilities involved managing the Paston estates, hiring workers, collecting rents, ordering supplies for the large household, hearing complaints and settling disputes among tenants, and marketing her crops. In these duties, she proved herself a remarkably shrewd businessperson. Moreover, when an army of over a thousand men led by the aristocratic thug Lord Moleyns attacked her house, she successfully withstood the siege. When the Black Death entered her area, Margaret moved her family to safety.

Margaret Paston did all this on top of raising eight children (there were probably other children who did not survive childhood). Her husband died before she was

Individuals in Society

Jan Hus

In May 1990, the Czech Republic's parliament declared July 6, the date of Jan Hus's execution in 1415, a Czech national holiday. The son of free farmers, Hus (ca 1369–1415) was born in Husinec in southern Bohemia, an area of heavy German settlement, and grew up conscious of the ethnic differences between Czechs and Germans. Most of his professors at Charles University in Prague were Germans. In 1396 he received a master's degree, and just before his ordination as a priest in 1400, he wrote that he would not be a "clerical careerist," implying that ambition for church offices motivated many of his peers.

The young priest lectured at the university and preached at the private Bethlehem Chapel. During his twelve years there, Hus preached only in Czech. He denounced superstition, the sale of indulgences, and other abuses, but his remarks were thoroughly orthodox. He attracted attention among artisans, the small Czech middle class, but not Germans. His austere life and lack of ambition enhanced his reputation.

Around 1400, Czech students returning from study at Oxford introduced into Bohemia the reforming ideas of the English theologian John Wyclif. When German professors condemned Wyclif's ideas as heretical, Hus and the Czechs argued "academic freedom," the right to read and teach Wyclif's works regardless of their particular merits. When popular demonstrations against ecclesiastical abuses and German influence at the university erupted, King Vaclav IV (1378–1419) placed control of the university in Czech hands. Hus was elected rector, the top administrative official.

The people of Prague, with perhaps the largest urban population in central Europe, 40 percent of it living below the poverty line and entirely dependent on casual labor, found Hus's denunciations of an overendowed church appealing. Hus considered the issues theological; his listeners saw them as socioeconomic.

Hus went into exile, where he wrote *On the Church*. He disputed papal authority, denounced abuses, and approved *utraquism,* the reception of the Eucharist under both species, bread and wine. Hus also defended transubstantiation (see page 463); insisted that church authority rested on Scripture, conscience, and tradition (in contrast to sixteenth-century Protestant reformers, who placed authority in Scripture alone); and made it clear that he had no intention of leaving the church or inciting a popular movement.

The execution of Jan Hus. (University Library, Prague)

In 1413 the emperor Sigismund urged the calling of a general council to end the schism. Hus was invited, and, given the emperor's safe conduct (protection from attack or arrest), agreed to go. What he found was an atmosphere of inquisition. The safe conduct was disregarded, and Hus was arrested. Under questioning about his acceptance of Wyclif's ideas, Hus repeatedly replied, "I have not held; I do not hold." Council members were more interested in proving Hus a Wyclifite than in his responses. They took away his priesthood, banned his teachings, burned his books, and burned Hus himself at the stake. He then belonged to the ages.

The ages have made good use of him. His death aggravated the divisions between the bishops at Constance and the Czech clerics and people. In September 1415, 452 nobles from all parts of Bohemia signed a letter saying that Hus had been unjustly executed and rejecting council rulings. This event marks the first time that an ecclesiastical decision was publicly defied. Revolution swept through Bohemia, with Hussites—Czech nobles and people—insisting on clerical poverty and Communion under both species, and German citizens remaining loyal to the Roman church. In the sixteenth century, reformers hailed Hus as the forerunner of Protestantism. In the eighteenth century, Enlightenment philosophes evoked Hus as a defender of freedom of expression. In the nineteenth century, central European nationalists used Hus's name to defend national sentiment against Habsburg rule. And in the twentieth century, Hus's name was used against German fascist and Russian communist tyranny.

Questions for Analysis

1. Since Jan Hus lived and died insisting that his religious teaching was thoroughly orthodox, why has he been hailed as a reformer?
2. What political and cultural interests did the martyred Hus serve?

forty-three, and she later conducted the negotiations for the children's marriages. Her children's futures, like her estate management, were planned with an eye toward economic and social advancement. When one daughter secretly married the estate bailiff, an alliance considered beneath her, the girl was cut off from the family as if she were dead.[31]

The many letters surviving between Margaret and John reveal slight tenderness toward their children. They seem to have reserved their love for each other, and during many of his frequent absences they wrote to express mutual affection and devotion. How typical the Paston relationship was modern historians cannot say, but the marriage of John and Margaret, although completely arranged by their parents, was based on respect, responsibility, and love.[32]

At what age did people usually marry? The largest amount of evidence on age at first marriage survives from Italy, and a comparable pattern probably existed in northern Europe. For girls population surveys at Prato place the age at 16.3 years in 1372 and 21.1 in 1470. Chaucer's Wife of Bath says that she married first in her twelfth year. Among the German nobility, recent research has indicated that in the Hohenzollern family in the late Middle Ages, "five brides were between 12 and 13; five about 14, and five about 15."

Men were older. An Italian chronicler writing about 1354 says that men did not marry before the age of 30. At Prato in 1371, the average age of men at first marriage was 24 years, very young for Italian men, but these data may represent an attempt to regain population losses due to the recent attack of the plague. In England Chaucer's Wife of Bath describes her first three husbands as "goode men, and rich, and old." Among seventeen males in the noble Hohenzollern family, eleven were over 20 years when married, five between 18 and 19, one 16. The general pattern in late medieval Europe was marriage between men in their middle or late 20s and women under 20.[33] Poor peasants and wage laborers did not marry until their mid- or late 20s.

With marriage for men postponed, was there any socially accepted sexual outlet? Research on the southern French province of Languedoc in the fourteenth and fifteenth centuries has revealed the establishment of legal houses of prostitution. Prostitution involves "a socially definable group of women [who] earn their living primarily or exclusively from the [sexual] commerce of their bodies."[34] Municipal authorities in Toulouse, Montpellier, Albi, and other towns set up houses or red-light districts either outside the city walls or away from respectable neighborhoods. For example, authorities in Montpellier set aside Hot Street for prostitution, required public women to live there, and forbade anyone to molest them. Prostitution thus passed from being a private concern to a social matter requiring public supervision.[35] Publicly owned brothels were more easily policed

Prostitute Invites a Traveling Merchant Poverty and male violence drove women into prostitution, which, though denounced by moralists, was accepted as a normal part of the medieval social fabric. In the cities and larger towns where prostitution flourished, public officials passed laws requiring prostitutes to wear a special mark on their clothing, regulated hours of business, forbade women to drag men into their houses, and denied business to women with the "burning sickness," gonorrhea. *(Bodleian Library, MS. Bodl. 264, fol. 245V)*

and supervised than privately run ones. Prostitution was an urban phenomenon, because only populous towns had large numbers of unmarried young men, communities of transient merchants, and a culture accustomed to a cash exchange. Although the risk of disease limited the number of years a woman could practice this profession, many women prospered. Some acquired sizable incomes. In 1361 Françoise of Florence, a prostitute working in a brothel in Marseilles, made a will in which she made legacies to various charities and left a large sum as a dowry for a poor girl to marry. Archives in several cities show expensive properties bought by women who named their occupation as prostitution.

The towns of Languedoc were not unique. Public authorities in Amiens, Dijon, Paris, Venice, Genoa, London, Florence, Rome, most of the larger German towns, and the English port of Sandwich set up brothels. Legalized prostitution suggests that public officials believed the prostitute could make a positive contribution to society; it does not mean the prostitute was respected. Rather, she was scorned and distrusted. Legalized brothels also reflect a greater tolerance for male than for female sexuality.[36]

In the later Middle Ages, as earlier—indeed, until the late nineteenth century—economic factors, rather than romantic love or physical attraction, determined whom and when a person married. The young agricultural laborer on the manor had to wait until he had sufficient land. Thus most men had to wait until their fathers died or yielded the holding. Late marriage affected the number of children a couple had. The journeyman craftsman in the urban guild faced the same material difficulties. Once a couple married, the union ended only with the death of one partner.

Deep emotional bonds knit members of medieval families. Most parents delighted in their children, and the church encouraged a cult of paternal care. The church stressed its right to govern and sanctify marriage, and it emphasized monogamy. Tighter moral and emotional unity within marriages resulted.

Divorce did not exist in the Middle Ages. The church held that a marriage validly entered into could not be dissolved. A valid marriage consisted of the mutual oral consent or promise of two parties. Church theologians of the day urged that the couple's union be celebrated and witnessed in a church ceremony and blessed by a priest.

Many couples did not observe the church's regulations. Some treated marriage as a private act—they made the promise and spoke the words of marriage to each other without witnesses and then proceeded to enjoy the sexual pleasures of marriage. This practice led to a great number of disputes, because one of the two parties could later deny having made a marriage agreement. The records of the ecclesiastical courts reveal many cases arising from privately made contracts. Evidence survives of marriages contracted in a garden, in a blacksmith's shop, at a tavern, and, predictably, in a bed. The records of church courts that relate to marriage reveal that, rather than suing for divorce, the great majority of petitions asked the court to enforce the marriage contract that one of the parties believed she or he had validly made. Annulments were granted in extraordinary circumstances, such as male impotence, on the grounds that a lawful marriage had never existed.[37]

Life in the Parish

In the later Middle Ages, the land and the parish remained the focus of life for the European peasantry. Work on the land continued to be performed collectively. Both men and women cooperated in the annual tasks of planting and harvesting. The close association of the cycle of agriculture and the liturgy of the Christian calendar endured. The parish priest blessed the fields before the annual planting, offering prayers on behalf of the people for a good crop. If the harvest was rich, the priest led the processions and celebrations of thanksgiving.

How did the common people feel about their work? Since the vast majority were illiterate, it is difficult to say. Certainly the peasants hated the ancient services and obligations on the lords' lands and tried to get them commuted for money rents. When lords attempted to reimpose service duties, the peasants revolted.

In the thirteenth century, the craft guilds provided the small minority of men and women living in towns and cities with the psychological satisfaction of involvement in the manufacture of a superior product. The guild member also had economic security. The craft guilds set high standards for their merchandise. The guilds looked after the sick, the poor, the widowed, and the orphaned. Masters and employees worked side by side.

In the fourteenth century, those conditions began to change. The fundamental objective of the craft guild was to maintain a monopoly on its product, and to do so recruitment and promotion were carefully restricted. Some guilds required a high entrance fee for apprentices; others admitted only relatives of members. Apprenticeship increasingly lasted a long time, seven years. Even after a young man had satisfied all the tests for full membership in the guild and had attained the rank of master, other hurdles had to be passed, such as finding the funds to open his own business or special connections just to get into a guild. Restrictions limited the

Spanish Bullfight Muslims introduced bullfighting to Spain in the eleventh century. The sport takes place in a large outdoor arena, the object being for the bullfighter or matador (*torero*) to kill a wild bull (*toro*) with a sword. Here unsporting spectators goad the bull with whips. *(From the* Cantigas *of Alfonso X, ca 1283. El Escorial/Laurie Platt Winfrey, Inc.)*

number of apprentices and journeymen to match the anticipated openings for masters.

Women experienced the same exclusion. A careful study of the records of forty-two craft guilds in Cologne shows that in the fifteenth century all but six had become male preserves, either greatly restricting women's participation or allowing so few female members that they cannot be considered mixed guilds.[38] Popular and educated culture, supporting a patriarchal system that held women to be biologically and intellectually inferior, consigned them to low-status and low-paying jobs.

The larger a particular business was, the greater was the likelihood that the master did not know his employees. The separation of master and journeyman and the decreasing number of openings for master craftsmen created serious frustrations. Strikes and riots occurred in the Flemish towns, in France, and in England.

The recreation of all classes reflected the fact that late medieval society was organized for war and that violence was common. The aristocracy engaged in tournaments or jousts; archery and wrestling had great popularity among ordinary people. Everyone enjoyed the cruel sports of bullbaiting and bearbaiting. The hangings and mutilations of criminals were exciting and well-attended events, with all the festivity of a university town before a Saturday football game. Chroniclers exulted in describing executions, murders, and massacres. Here a monk gleefully describes the gory execution of William Wallace (ca 1270–1305), the Scottish hero who led a revolt against Edward I of England and retains importance as a symbol of resistance to English rule and of Scottish nationalism:

> *Wilielmus Waleis, a robber given to sacrilege, arson and homicide . . . was condemned to most cruel but justly deserved death. He was drawn through the streets of London at the tails of horses, until he reached a gallows of unusual height, there he was suspended by a halter; but taken down while yet alive, he was mutilated, his bowels torn out and burned in a fire, his head then cut off, his body divided into four, and his quarters transmitted to four principal parts of Scotland.*[39]

Violence was as English as roast beef and plum pudding, as French as bread, cheese, and *potage*.

If violent entertainment was not enough to dispel life's cares, alcohol was also available. Beer or ale commonly provided solace to the poor, and the frequency of drunkenness reflects their terrible frustrations.

During the fourteenth and fifteenth centuries, the laity began to exercise increasing control over parish affairs. The constant quarrels of the mendicant orders (the Franciscans and Dominicans), the mercenary and grasping attitude of the parish clergy, the scandal of the Great Schism and a divided Christendom—all these did much to weaken the spiritual mystique of the clergy in the popular mind. The laity steadily took responsibility for the management of parish lands. Laypeople organized associations to vote on and purchase furnishings for the church. And ordinary laypeople secured jurisdiction over the structure of the church building and its vestments, books, and furnishings. These new responsibilities of the laity reflect the increased dignity of parishioners in the late Middle Ages.[40]

Fur-Collar Crime

The Hundred Years' War had provided employment and opportunity for thousands of idle and fortune-seeking knights. But during periods of truce and after the war finally ended, many nobles once again had little to do. Inflation hurt them. Although many were living on fixed incomes, their chivalric code demanded lavish generosity and an aristocratic lifestyle. Many nobles turned to crime as a way of raising money. The fourteenth and fifteenth centuries witnessed a great deal of "fur-collar crime," so called for the miniver fur the nobility alone were allowed to wear on their collars.

Fur-collar crime rarely involved such felonies as homicide, robbery, rape, and arson. Instead, nobles used their superior social status to rob and extort from the weak and then to corrupt the judicial process. Groups of noble brigands roamed the English countryside stealing from both rich and poor. Sir John de Colseby and Sir William Bussy led a gang of thirty-eight knights who stole goods worth £3,000 in various robberies. Operating like modern urban racketeers, knightly gangs demanded that peasants pay "protection money" or else have their hovels burned and their fields destroyed.

Attacks on the rich often took the form of kidnapping and extortion. Individuals were grabbed in their homes, and wealthy travelers were seized on the highways and held for ransom. In northern England a gang of gentry led by Sir Gilbert de Middleton abducted Sir Henry Beaumont; his brother, the bishop-elect of Durham; and two Roman cardinals in England on a peacemaking visit. Only after a ransom was paid were the victims released.[41]

Fur-collar criminals were terrorists, but like some modern-day white-collar criminals who commit nonviolent crimes, medieval aristocratic criminals got away with their outrages. When accused of wrongdoing, fur-collar criminals intimidated witnesses. They threatened jurors. They used "pull" or cash to bribe judges. As a fourteenth-century English judge wrote to a young nobleman, "For the love of your father I have hindered charges being brought against you and have prevented execution of indictment actually made."[42]

The ballads of Robin Hood, a collection of folk legends from late medieval England, describe the adventures of the outlaw hero and his band of followers, who lived in Sherwood Forest and attacked and punished those who violated the social system and the law. Most of the villains in these simple tales are fur-collar criminals—grasping landlords, wicked sheriffs such as the famous sheriff of Nottingham, and mercenary churchmen. Robin and his merry men performed a sort of retributive justice. Robin Hood was a popular figure because he symbolized the deep resentment of aristocratic corruption and abuse; he represented the struggle against tyranny and oppression.

Criminal activity by nobles continued decade after decade because governments were too weak to stop it. Then, too, much of the crime was directed against a lord's own serfs, and the line between a noble's legal jurisdiction over his peasants and criminal behavior was a fine one indeed. Persecution by lords, on top of war, disease, and natural disaster, eventually drove long-suffering and oppressed peasants all across Europe to revolt.

Peasant Revolts

Early in the thirteenth century, the French preacher Jacques de Vitry asked rhetorically, "How many serfs have killed their lords or burnt their castles?"[43] And in the fourteenth and fifteenth centuries, social and economic conditions caused a great increase in peasant uprisings (see Map 12.3).

In 1358, when French taxation for the Hundred Years' War fell heavily on the poor, the frustrations of the French peasantry exploded in a massive uprising called the **Jacquerie,** after a mythical agricultural laborer, Jacques Bonhomme (Good Fellow). Two years earlier, the English had captured the French king John and many nobles and held them for ransom. The peasants resented paying for their lords' release. Recently hit by plague, experiencing famine in some areas, and harassed by fur-collar criminals, the peasants in Picardy, Champagne, and the Île-de-France erupted in anger and frustration. Crowds swept through the countryside slashing the throats of nobles, burning their castles, raping their wives and daughters, killing or maiming their horses and cattle.

MAP 12.3 Fourteenth-Century Peasant Revolts In the later Middle Ages and early modern times, peasant and urban uprisings were endemic, as common as factory strikes in the industrial world. The threat of insurrection served to check unlimited exploitation.

Peasants blamed the nobility for oppressive taxes, for the criminal brigandage of the countryside, for defeat in war, and for the general misery. Artisans, small merchants, and parish priests joined the peasants. Urban and rural groups committed terrible destruction, and for several weeks the nobles were on the defensive. Then the upper class united to repress the revolt with merciless ferocity. Thousands of the "Jacques," innocent as well as guilty, were cut down.

This forcible suppression of social rebellion, without some effort to alleviate its underlying causes, served to drive protest underground. Between 1363 and 1484, serious peasant revolts swept the Auvergne; in 1380 uprisings occurred in the Midi; and in 1420 they erupted in the Lyonnais region of France.

The Peasants' Revolt in England in 1381, involving perhaps a hundred thousand people, was probably the largest single uprising of the entire Middle Ages (see Map 12.3). The causes of the rebellion were complex and varied from place to place. In general, though, the thirteenth century had witnessed the steady commutation of labor services for cash rents, and the Black Death had drastically cut the labor supply. As a result, peasants demanded higher wages and fewer manorial obligations. Thirty years earlier, the parliamentary Statute of Laborers of 1351 (see page 386) had declared:

Whereas to curb the malice of servants who after the pestilence were idle and unwilling to serve without securing excessive wages, it was recently ordained . . . that such servants, both men and women, shall be bound to serve in return for salaries and wages that were customary . . . five or six years earlier.[44]

This attempt by landlords to freeze wages and social mobility could not be enforced. As a matter of fact, the condition of the English peasantry steadily improved in the course of the fourteenth century. Some scholars believe that the peasantry in most places was better off in the period 1350 to 1450 than it had been for centuries before or was to be for four centuries after.

Why then was the outburst in 1381 so serious? It was provoked by a crisis of rising expectations. The relative

John Ball A priest of Kent, Ball often preached his radical egalitarianism out-of-doors after Mass: "Matters goeth not well . . . in England nor shall (they) till everything be common and . . . there be no villains (serfs) nor gentlemen. . . . What have we deserved, or why should we be kept thus in servage (servitude)?" All contemporary writers blamed Ball for fomenting the rebellion of 1381. But the evidence of peasant demands shows that they were limited and local: hunting rights in the woods, freedom from miscellaneous payments, exemption from special work on the lord's bridges or parks. *(Private Collection)*

prosperity of the laboring classes led to demands that the upper classes were unwilling to grant. Unable to climb higher, the peasants found release for their economic frustrations in revolt. But economic grievances combined with other factors. The south of England, where the revolt broke out, had been subjected to destructive French raids. The English government did little to protect the south, and villages grew increasingly scared and insecure. This fear erupted into revolt. Moreover, decades of aristocratic violence, much of it perpetrated against the weak peasantry, had bred hostility and bitterness. The social and religious agitation of the popular preacher John Ball fanned the embers of discontent. Such sayings as Ball's famous couplet "When Adam delved and Eve span; Who was then the gentleman?" reflect real revolutionary sentiment.

The straw that broke the camel's back in England was the reimposition of a head tax on all adult males. Although the tax met widespread opposition in 1380, the royal council ordered the sheriffs to collect it again in 1381 on penalty of a huge fine. Beginning with assaults on the tax collectors, the uprising in England followed much the same course as had the Jacquerie in France. Castles and manors were sacked; manorial records were destroyed. Many nobles, including the archbishop of Canterbury, who had ordered the collection of the tax, were murdered.

Although the center of the revolt lay in the highly populated and economically advanced south and east, sections of the north and the Midlands also witnessed rebellions. Violence took different forms in different places. The townspeople of Cambridge expressed their hostility toward the university by sacking one of the colleges and building a bonfire of academic property. In towns containing skilled Flemish craftsmen, fear of competition led to their being attacked and murdered. Urban discontent merged with rural violence. Apprentices and journeymen, frustrated because the highest positions in the guilds were closed to them, rioted.

The boy-king Richard II (r. 1377–1399) met the leaders of the revolt, agreed to charters ensuring peasants' freedom, tricked them with false promises, and then proceeded to crush the uprising with terrible ferocity. Although the nobility tried to restore ancient duties of serfdom, virtually a century of freedom had elapsed, and the commutation of manorial services continued. Rural serfdom had disappeared in England by 1550.

Conditions in England and France were not unique. In Florence in 1378, the *ciompi,* the poor propertyless workers, revolted. Serious social trouble occurred in Lübeck, Brunswick, and other German cities. In Spain in 1391, aristocratic attempts to impose new forms of serfdom, combined with demands for tax relief, led to massive working-class and peasant uprisings in Seville and Barcelona. These took the form of vicious attacks on Jewish communities. Rebellions and uprisings everywhere reveal deep peasant and working-class frustration and the general socioeconomic crisis of the time.

Race and Ethnicity on the Frontiers

Large numbers of people in the twelfth and thirteenth centuries migrated from one part of Europe to another: the English into Scotland and Ireland; Germans, French, and Flemings into Poland, Bohemia, and Hungary; the French into Spain. In the fourteenth century, many Germans moved into eastern Europe, fleeing the Black Death. The colonization of frontier regions meant that peoples of different ethnic or racial backgrounds lived side by side. Race relations became a basic factor in the lives of peoples living in those frontier areas.

Racial categories rest on socially constructed beliefs and customs, not on any biological or anthropological classification. When late medieval chroniclers used the language of race—words such as *gens* (race or clan) and *natio* (species, stock, or kind)—they meant cultural differences. Medieval scholars held that peoples differed according to descent, language, customs, and laws. Descent or blood, basic to the color racism of the United States, played an insignificant part in eleventh- and twelfth-century ideas about race and ethnicity. Rather, the chief marks of an ethnic group were language (which could be learned), customs (for example, dietary practices, dance, marriage and death rituals, clothing, and hairstyles, all of which could be adopted), and laws (which could be changed or modified). How did the law reflect attitudes and race relations in the Middle Ages? Did greater harmony exist in regions such as Ireland, where native peoples and settlers were of the same religious faith, than in countries such as Spain, where colonists and natives held different faiths? What role did race and ethnicity play in relations between the two groups in the later Middle Ages?

In the early periods of conquest and colonization, and in all frontier regions, a legal dualism existed: native peoples remained subject to their traditional laws; newcomers brought and were subject to the laws of the countries from which they came. On the Prussian and Polish frontier, for example, the law was that "men who come there . . . should be judged on account of any crime or contract engaged in there according to Polish custom if they are Poles and according to German custom if they are Germans."[45] Likewise, in Spain Mudéjars, Muslim subjects of Christian kings, received guarantees of separate but equal judicial rights. King Alfonso I of Aragon's charter to the Muslims of Toledo states, "They shall be in lawsuits and pleas under their (Muslim) qadi (judges) . . . as it was in the times of the Moors."[46] Thus conquered peoples, whether Muslims in Spain, or minority immigrant groups, such as Germans in eastern Europe, had legal protection and lived in their own juridical enclaves. Subject peoples experienced some disabilities, but the broad trend was toward a legal pluralism.

The great exception to this broad pattern was Ireland. From the start, the English practiced an extreme form of racial discrimination toward the native Irish. The English distinguished between the free and the unfree, and the entire Irish population, simply by the fact of Irish birth, was unfree. In 1210 King John declared that "English law and custom be established there (in Ireland)." Accordingly, a legal structure modeled on that of England, with county courts, itinerant justices, and the common law (see pages 341–342), was set up. But the Irish had no access to the common-law courts. In civil (property) disputes, an English defendant need not respond to his Irish plaintiff; no Irish person could make a will; and an Irish widow could not claim her dower rights (enjoyment of part of the estate during her lifetime). In criminal procedures, the murder of an Irishman was not considered a felony. In 1317–1318, Irish princes sent a Remonstrance to the pope complaining that "any non-Irishman is allowed to bring legal action against an Irishman, but an Irishman . . . except any prelate (bishop or abbot) is barred from every action by that fact alone." An English defen-

English View of the Irish Depicting a subject or colonial people as barbaric and uncivilized has long been a way of denigrating and dehumanizing the enemy. In this thirteenth-century miniature, a king (in a bath) and his courtiers devour horseflesh with their hands, without plates or eating utensils. The viewer is supposed to think that this is how Irish kingship was conferred. *(Bodleian Library, MS. Laud. Misc. 720f. 226R)*

dant in the criminal matter would claim "that he is not held to answer . . . since he [the plaintiff] is Irish and not of free blood."[47] This emphasis on blood descent naturally provoked bitterness, but only in the Tudor period (see Chapter 14) was the English common law opened to the subject Irish population.

The later Middle Ages witnessed a movement away from legal pluralism or dualism and toward a legal homogeneity and an emphasis on blood descent. Competition for ecclesiastical offices and the cultural divisions between town and country people became arenas for ethnic tension and racial conflict. Since bishoprics and abbacies carried religious authority, spiritual charisma, and often rights of appointment to subordinate positions, they were natural objects of ambition. When prelates of a language or "nationality" different from those of the local people gained church positions, the latter felt a loss of influence. Bishops were supposed to be pastors. Their pastoral work involved preaching, teaching, and comforting, duties that could be performed effectively only when the bishop (or priest) could communicate with the people. Ideally in a pluralistic society, he should be bilingual; often he was not.

In the late thirteenth century, as waves of Germans migrated into Danzig on the Baltic, into Silesia, and into the Polish countryside and towns, they encountered Jakub Swinka, archbishop of Gniezno (1283–1314), whose jurisdiction included these areas of settlement. The bishop hated Germans and referred to them as "dog heads." His German contemporary, Bishop John of Cracow, detested the Poles, wanted to expel all Polish people, and refused to appoint Poles to any church office. In Ireland, English colonists and the native Irish competed for ecclesiastical offices until 1217, when the English government in London decreed:

> *Since the election of Irishmen in our land of Ireland has often disturbed the peace of that land, we command you . . . that henceforth you allow no Irishman to be elected . . . or preferred in any cathedral . . . (and) you should seek by all means to procure election and promotion to vacant bishoprics of . . . honest Englishmen.*[48]

Although criticized by the pope and not totally enforceable, this law remained in effect in many dioceses for centuries.

Likewise, the arrival of Cistercians and mendicants (Franciscans and Dominicans) from France and Germany in Baltic and Slavic lands provoked racial and "national" hostilities. In the fourteenth and fifteenth centuries, in contrast to earlier centuries, racial or ethnic prejudices became conspicuous. Slavic prelates and princes saw the German mendicants as "instruments of cultural colonization," and Slavs were strongly discouraged from becoming friars. In 1333, when John of Drazic, bishop of Prague, founded a friary at Roudnice (Raudnitz), he specified that "we shall admit no one to this convent or monastery of any nation except a Bohemian [Czech], born of two Czech-speaking parents."[49]

Everywhere in Europe, towns recruited people from the countryside (see pages 346–347). In frontier regions, townspeople were usually long-distance immigrants and, in eastern Europe, Ireland, and Scotland, ethnically different from the surrounding rural population. In eastern Europe, German was the language of the towns; in Ireland, French, the tongue of Norman or English settlers, predominated. In fourteenth-century Prague, between 63 percent and 80 percent of new burgesses bore identifiable German names, as did almost all city council members. Towns in eastern Europe "had the character of German islands in Slav, Baltic, Estonian, or Magyar seas."[50] Although native peoples commonly held humbler positions, both immigrant and native townspeople prospered during the expanding economy of the thirteenth century. When economic recession hit during the fourteenth century, ethnic tensions multiplied.

On the frontiers of Latin Europe discrimination, ghettoization, and **racism**—now based on blood descent—characterized the attitudes of colonists toward native peoples. But the latter also could express racial savagery. In the ***Dalimil Chronicle,*** a survey of Bohemian history pervaded with Czech hostility toward Germans, one anti-German prince offered 100 marks of silver "to anyone who brought him one hundred noses cut off from the Germans."[51] Regulations drawn up by various guilds were explicitly racist, with protectionist bars for some groups and exclusionist laws for others. The Deutschtum paragraph of the *Chronicle,* applicable to parts of eastern Europe, required that applicants for guild membership be of German descent. Cobblers in fourteenth-century Beeskow, a town close to the large Slavic population of Lausitz in Silesia, required that "an apprentice who comes to learn his craft should be brought before the master and guild members. . . . We forbid the sons of barbers, linen workers, shepherds, Slavs." The bakers of the same town decreed:

Whoever wishes to be a member must bring proof to the councillors and guildsmen that he is born of legitimate, upright, German folk. . . . No one of Wendish (Slavic) race may be in the guild. In Limerick and Dublin in Ireland, guild masters agreed to accept "noo apprentice but that he be of English berthe."[52]

Intermarriage was forbidden in many places, such as Riga on the Baltic (now the capital of Latvia), where legislation for the bakers guild stipulated that "whoever wishes to have the privilege of membership in our company shall not take as a wife any woman who is ill-famed . . . or non-German; if he does marry such a woman, he must leave the company and office." Not only the guilds but eligibility for public office depended on racial purity, as at the German burgher settlement of Pest in Hungary, where a town judge had to have four German grandparents. The most extensive attempt to prevent intermarriage and protect racial purity is embodied in Ireland's **Statute of Kilkenny** (1366), which states that "there were to be no marriages between those of immigrant and native stock; that the English inhabitants of Ireland must employ the English language and bear English names; that they must ride in the English way (i.e., with saddles) and have English apparel; that no Irishmen were to be granted ecclesiastical benefices or admitted to monasteries in the English parts of Ireland. . . ."[53] Rulers of the Christian kingdoms of Spain drew up comparable legislation discriminating against the Mudéjars.

All these laws had an economic basis: to protect the financial interests of the privileged German, English, or Spanish colonial minorities. The laws also reflect a racism that not only pervaded the lives of frontier peoples at the end of the Middle Ages but also sowed the seeds of difficulties still unresolved today.

Vernacular Literature

Across Europe people spoke the language and dialect of their particular locality and class. In England, for example, the common people spoke regional English dialects, while the upper classes conversed in French. Official documents and works of literature were written in Latin or French. Beginning in the fourteenth century, however, national languages—the vernacular—came into widespread use not only in verbal communication but in literature as well. Three masterpieces of European culture, Dante's *Divine Comedy* (1310–1320), Chaucer's *Canterbury Tales* (1387–1400), and Villon's *Grand Testament* (1461), brilliantly manifest this new national pride.

Dante Alighieri (1265–1321) descended from an aristocratic family in Florence, where he held several positions in the city government. Dante called his work a "comedy" because he wrote it in Italian and in a different style from the "tragic" Latin; a later generation added the adjective *divine,* referring both to its sacred subject and to Dante's artistry. The *Divine Comedy* is an allegorical trilogy of one hundred cantos (verses) whose three equal parts (1 + 33 + 33 + 33) each describe one of the realms of the next world: Hell, Purgatory, and Paradise. The Roman poet Virgil, representing reason, leads Dante through Hell, where he observes the torments of the damned and denounces the disorders of his own time, especially ecclesiastical ambition and corruption. Passing up into Purgatory, Virgil shows the poet how souls are purified of their disordered inclinations. From Purgatory, Beatrice, a woman Dante once loved and the symbol of divine revelation in the poem, leads him to Paradise. In Paradise, home of the angels and saints, Saint Bernard—representing mystic contemplation—leads Dante to the Virgin Mary. Through her intercession, he at last attains a vision of God.

The *Divine Comedy* portrays contemporary and historical figures, comments on secular and ecclesiastical affairs, and draws on Scholastic philosophy. Within the framework of a symbolic pilgrimage to the City of God, the *Divine Comedy* embodies the psychological tensions of the age. A profoundly Christian poem, it also contains bitter criticism of some church authorities. In its symmetrical structure and use of figures from the ancient world, such as Virgil, the poem perpetuates the classical tradition, but as the first major work of literature in the Italian vernacular, it is distinctly modern.

Geoffrey Chaucer (1340–1400), the son of a London wine merchant, was an official in the administrations of the English kings Edward III and Richard II and wrote poetry as an avocation. Chaucer's *Canterbury Tales* is a collection of stories in lengthy, rhymed narrative. On a pilgrimage to the shrine of Saint Thomas Becket at Canterbury (see page 342), thirty people of various social backgrounds each tell a tale. The Prologue sets the scene and describes the pilgrims, whose characters are further revealed in the story each one tells. For example, the gentle Christian Knight relates a chivalric romance; the gross Miller tells a vulgar story about a deceived husband; the earthy Wife of Bath, who has buried five husbands, sketches a fable about the selection of a spouse; and the elegant Prioress, who violates her vows by wearing jewelry, delivers a homily on the Virgin. In depicting the interests and behavior of all types of people, Chaucer presents a rich panorama of English social life in the fourteenth century. Like the *Divine Comedy, Canterbury Tales* reflects the cultural tensions of the times. Ostensibly Christian, many of the pilgrims are also materialistic, sensual, and worldly, suggesting the ambivalence of the broader society's concern for the next world and frank enjoyment of this one.

Our knowledge of François Villon (1431–1463), probably the greatest poet of late medieval France, derives from Paris police records and his own poetry. Born to poor parents in the year of Joan of Arc's execution, Villon was sent by his guardian to the University of Paris, where he earned the master of arts degree. A rowdy and free-spirited student, he disliked the stuffiness of academic life. In 1455 Villon killed a man in a street brawl; banished from Paris, he joined one of the bands of wandering thieves that harassed the countryside after the Hundred Years' War. For his fellow bandits, he composed ballads in thieves' jargon.

Villon's *Lais* (1456), a pun on the word *legs* ("legacy"), is a series of farcical bequests to friends and enemies. "Ballade des Pendus" (Ballad of the Hanged) was written while contemplating that fate in prison. (His execution was commuted.) Villon's greatest and most self-revealing work, the *Grand Testament,* contains another string of bequests, including a legacy to a prostitute, and describes his unshakable faith in the beauty of life on earth. The *Grand Testament* possesses elements of social rebellion, bawdy humor, and rare emotional depth. While the themes of Dante's and Chaucer's poetry are distinctly medieval, Villon's celebration of the human condition brands him as definitely modern. Although he used medieval forms of versification, Villon's language was the despised vernacular of the poor and the criminal.

Perhaps the most versatile and prolific French writer of the later Middle Ages was Christine de Pisan (1363?–1434?). The daughter of a professor of astrology at Bologna, Christine had a broad knowledge of Greek, Latin, French, and Italian literature. The deaths of her father and husband left her with three small children and her mother to support; she had to earn her living with her pen. In addition to poems and books on love, religion, and morality, Christine produced the *Livre de la mutacion de fortune,* a major historical work; a biography of King Charles V; the *Ditié,* celebrating Joan of Arc's victory; and many letters. *The City of Ladies* lists the great women of history and their contributions to society, and *The Book of Three Virtues* provides practical advice on household management for women of all social classes. Christine de Pisan's wisdom and wit are illustrated in her autobiographical *Avison-Christine*. She records that a man told her an educated woman is unattractive, since there are so few, to which she responded that an ignorant man was even less attractive, since there are so many. (See

Schoolmaster and His Wife Teaching Ambrosius Holbein, elder brother of the more famous Hans Holbein, produced this signboard for the Swiss educator Myconius; it is an excellent example of what we would call commercial art—art used to advertise, in this case Myconius's profession. The German script above promised that all who enrolled would learn to read and write. By modern standards the classroom seems bleak: the windows have glass panes but they don't admit much light, and the schoolmaster is prepared to use the sticks if the boy makes a mistake. *(Öffentliche Kunstsammlung Basel/Martin Bühler, photographer)*

the feature "Listening to the Past: Christine de Pisan" on pages 412–413.)

In Bohemia the immigration of large numbers of Germans elicited increasing Czech self-consciousness, leading to an interest among the Czechs in their own language. Fourteenth-century translations of knightly sagas from German into Czech multiplied. So did translations of religious writings—Psalters, prayers, a life of Christ—from Latin into Czech. Vernacular literature in eastern Europe especially represents an ethnic and patriotic response to foreigners.

Beginning in the fourteenth century, a variety of evidence attests to the increasing literacy of laypeople. Wills and inventories reveal that many people, not just nobles, possessed books, mainly devotional, but also romances, manuals on manners and etiquette, histories, and sometimes legal and philosophical texts. In England the number of schools in the diocese of York quadrupled between 1350 and 1500. Information from Flemish and German towns is similar: children were sent to schools and received the fundamentals of reading, writing, and arithmetic. Laymen increasingly served as managers or stewards of estates and as clerks to guilds and town governments; such positions obviously required that they be able to keep administrative and financial records.

The penetration of laymen into the higher positions of governmental administration, long the preserve of clerics, also illustrates rising lay literacy. For example, in 1400 beneficed clerics held most of the posts in the English Exchequer; by 1430 clerics were the exception. With growing frequency, the upper classes sent their daughters to convent schools, where, in addition to instruction in singing, religion, needlework, deportment, and household management, girls gained the rudiments of reading and sometimes writing. Reading and writing represent two kinds of literacy. Scholars estimate that many more people, especially women, possessed the first literacy, but not the second. The spread of literacy represents a response to the needs of an increasingly complex society. Trade, commerce, and expanding governmental bureaucracies required more and more literate people. Late medieval culture remained an oral culture in which most people received information by word of mouth. But by the mid-fifteenth century, even before the printing press was turning out large quantities of reading materials, the evolution toward a literary culture was already perceptible.[54]

Summary

The crises of the fourteenth and fifteenth centuries were acids that burned deeply into the fabric of traditional medieval society. Bad weather brought poor harvests, which contributed to the international economic depression. Disease, over which people also had little control, fostered widespread depression. Population losses caused by the Black Death and the Hundred Years' War encouraged the working classes to try to profit from the labor shortage by selling their services higher: they wanted to move up the economic ladder. The theological ideas of thinkers like John Wyclif, John Hus, and John Ball fanned the flames of social discontent. When peasant frustrations exploded in uprisings, the frightened nobility and upper middle class joined to crush the revolts and condemn heretical preachers as agitators of social rebellion.

The Hundred Years' War served as a catalyst for the development of representative government in England. In France, on the other hand, the war stiffened opposition to national assemblies.

The war also stimulated technological experimentation, especially with artillery. Cannon revolutionized warfare, because the stone castle was no longer impregnable. Because only central governments, and not private nobles, could afford cannon, they strengthened the military power of national states.

The migration of peoples from the European heartland to the frontier regions of Ireland, the Baltic, eastern Europe, and Spain led to ethnic frictions between native peoples and new settlers. Economic difficulties heightened ethnic consciousness and spawned a vicious racism.

Religion held society together. European culture was a Christian culture. But the Great Schism weakened the prestige of the church and people's faith in papal authority. The conciliar movement, by denying the church's universal sovereignty, strengthened the claims of secular government to jurisdiction over all their peoples. The later Middle Ages witnessed a steady shift of basic loyalty from the church to the emerging national states.

The increasing number of schools leading to the growth of lay literacy represents another positive achievement of the later Middle Ages. So also does the development of national literatures. The first signs of a literary culture appeared.

Key Terms

Great Famine
Black Death
buba
flagellants
Crécy
Agincourt
Joan of Arc
representation
nationalism
Babylonian Captivity
schism
conciliarists
merchet
banns
Jacquerie
racism
Dalimil Chronicle
Statute of Kilkenny

Notes

1. W. C. Jordan, *The Great Famine: Northern Europe in the Early Fourteenth Century* (Princeton, N.J.: Princeton University Press, 1996), pp. 97–102.
2. Ibid., pp. 167–179.
3. N. Ascherson, *Black Sea* (New York: Hill & Wang, 1996), pp. 95–96.
4. W. H. McNeill, *Plagues and Peoples* (New York: Doubleday, 1976), pp. 151–168.
5. Quoted in P. Ziegler, *The Black Death* (Harmondsworth, England: Pelican Books, 1969), p. 20.
6. J. M. Rigg, trans., *The Decameron of Giovanni Boccaccio* (London: J. M. Dent & Sons, 1903), p. 6.
7. M. Mollatt, *The Poor in the Middle Ages: An Essay in Social History,* trans. A. Goldhammer (New Haven, Conn.: Yale University Press, 1986), pp. 146–153, 193–197.
8. Ziegler, *The Black Death,* pp. 232–239.
9. Ibid., p. 84.
10. G. Huppert, *After the Black Death: A Social History of Early Modern Europe* (Bloomington, Ind.: Indiana University Press, 1986), p. ix.
11. Quoted in D. Herlihy, *The Black Death and the Transformation of the West* (Cambridge, Mass.: Harvard University Press, 1997), p. 42.
12. J. Hatcher, *Plague, Population, and the English Economy, 1348–1530* (London: Macmillan Education, 1986), p. 33.
13. See Herlihy, *The Black Death,* pp. 43–45.
14. Ibid., pp. 46–47; Hatcher, *Plague,* p. 33. The quotation is from Hatcher.
15. Ascherson, *Black Sea,* p. 96.
16. See Herlihy, *The Black Death,* pp. 59–81.
17. See P. Cuttino, "Historical Revision: The Causes of the Hundred Years' War," *Speculum* 31 (July 1956): 463–472.
18. J. Barnie, *War in Medieval English Society: Social Values and the Hundred Years' War* (Ithaca, N.Y.: Cornell University Press, 1974), p. 6.

19. Quoted ibid., p. 34.
20. Quoted ibid., p. 73.
21. Quoted ibid., pp. 72–73.
22. W. P. Barrett, trans., *The Trial of Jeanne d'Arc* (London: George Routledge, 1931), pp. 165–166.
23. Quoted in Barnie, *War in Medieval English Society,* pp. 36–37.
24. M. M. Postan, "The Costs of the Hundred Years' War," *Past and Present* 27 (April 1964): 34–53.
25. See G. O. Sayles, *The King's Parliament of England* (New York: W. W. Norton, 1974), app., pp. 137–141.
26. Quoted in P. S. Lewis, "The Failure of the Medieval French Estates," *Past and Present* 23 (November 1962): 6.
27. Quoted in J. H. Smith, *The Great Schism, 1378: The Disintegration of the Medieval Papacy* (New York: Weybright & Talley, 1970), p. 141.
28. Ibid., p. 15.
29. B. A. Hanawalt, *The Ties That Bound: Peasant Families in Medieval England* (New York: Oxford University Press, 1986), p. 197. This section leans heavily on Hanawalt's work.
30. Ibid., pp. 194–204.
31. A. S. Haskell, "The Paston Women on Marriage in Fifteenth Century England," *Viator* 4 (1973): 459–469.
32. Ibid., p. 471.
33. See D. Herlihy, *Medieval Households* (Cambridge, Mass.: Harvard University Press, 1985), pp. 103–111.
34. L. L. Otis, *Prostitution in Medieval Society: The History of an Urban Institution in Languedoc* (Chicago: University of Chicago Press, 1987), p. 2.
35. Ibid., pp. 25–27, 64–66, 100–106.
36. Ibid., pp. 118–130.
37. See R. H. Helmholz, *Marriage Litigation in Medieval England* (Cambridge: Cambridge University Press, 1974), pp. 28–29, et passim.
38. See M. C. Howell, *Women, Production, and Patriarchy in Late Medieval Cities* (Chicago: University of Chicago Press, 1986), pp. 134–135.
39. A. F. Scott, ed., *Everyone a Witness: The Plantagenet Age* (New York: Thomas Y. Crowell, 1976), p. 263.
40. See E. Mason, "The Role of the English Parishioner, 1000–1500," *Journal of Ecclesiastical History* 27 (January 1976): 17–29.
41. B. A. Hanawalt, "Fur Collar Crime: The Pattern of Crime Among the Fourteenth-Century English Nobility," *Journal of Social History* 8 (Spring 1975): 1–14.
42. Quoted ibid., p. 7.
43. Quoted in M. Bloch, *French Rural History,* trans. J. Sondeimer (Berkeley: University of California Press, 1966), p. 169.
44. C. Stephenson and G. Marcham, eds., *Sources of English Constitutional History,* rev. ed. (New York: Harper & Row, 1972), p. 225.
45. Quoted in R. Bartlett, *The Making of Europe: Conquest, Colonization and Cultural Change, 950–1350* (Princeton, N.J.: Princeton University Press, 1993), p. 205. For an alternative, if abstract, discussion of medieval racism, see I. Hannaford, *Race: The History of an Idea in the West* (Baltimore: Johns Hopkins University Press, 1995), pp. 87–146.
46. Quoted in Bartlett, *The Making of Europe,* p. 208.
47. Quoted ibid., p. 215.
48. Quoted ibid., p. 224.
49. Quoted ibid., p. 228.
50. Quoted ibid., p. 233.
51. Quoted ibid., p. 236.
52. Quoted ibid., p. 238.
53. Quoted ibid., p. 239.
54. See M. Keen, *English Society in the Later Middle Ages, 1348–1500* (New York: Penguin Books, 1990), pp. 219–239.

Suggested Reading

The best starting point for study of the great epidemic that swept the European continent is D. Herlihy, *The Black Death and the Transformation of the West* (1997), a fine treatment of the causes and cultural consequences of the disease. P. Binski, *Medieval Death: Ritual and Representation* (1995), discusses the impact of the Black Death on medieval art and literature. For the social implications of the Black Death, see L. Poos, *A Rural Society After the Black Death: Essex, 1350–1525* (1991), and G. Huppert, *After the Black Death: A Social History of Early Modern Europe* (1986). For the economic effects of the plague, see J. Hatcher, *Plague, Population, and the English Economy, ca. 1300–1450* (1977). The older study of P. Ziegler, *The Black Death* (1969), remains important.

For the background and early part of the long military conflicts of the fourteenth and fifteenth centuries, see the provocative M. M. Vale, *The Origins of the Hundred Years War: The Angevin Legacy, 1250–1340* (1996). The standard study of this subject is still E. Perroy, *The Hundred Years War* (1959), but see also C. Allmand, *The Hundred Years War: England and France at War, ca 1300–1450* (1988). The broad survey of J. Keegan, *A History of Warfare* (1993), contains a useful summary of significant changes in military technology during the war. The main ruler of the age has found his biographer in W. M. Ormrod, *The Reign of Edward III: Crown and Political Society in England, 1327–1377* (1990). J. Henneman, *Royal Taxation in Fourteenth Century France: The Development of War Financing, 1322–1356* (1971), is an important technical work. J. Keegan, *The Face of Battle* (1977), chap. 2, "Agincourt," describes what war meant to the ordinary soldier. B. Tuchman, *A Distant Mirror: The Calamitous Fourteenth Century* (1980), gives a vivid picture of many facets of fourteenth-century life, while concentrating on war. For strategy, tactics, armaments, and costumes of war, see H. W. Koch, *Medieval Warfare* (1978), a beautifully illustrated book. R. Barber, *The Knight and Chivalry* (1982), and M. Keen, *Chivalry* (1984), give interpretations of the cultural importance of chivalry.

For political and social conditions in the fourteenth and fifteenth centuries, see the works by Lewis, Sayles, Bloch, and especially Hanawalt and Helmholz cited in the Notes. C. Dyer, *Standards of Living in the Later Middle Ages* (1989), contains much valuable social history. The papers in R. H. Hilton and T. H. Aston, eds., *The English Rising of 1381* (1984), stress the importance of urban, as well as rural, participation in the movement, but see also R. Hilton, *Bond Men Made Free: Medieval Peasant Movements and the English Rising of 1381* (1973), a comparative study; and

M. Keen, *The Outlaws of Medieval Legend* (1961). T. F. Glick, *From Muslim Fortress to Christian Castle: Social and Cultural Change in Medieval Spain* (1995), which is based in part on rare archaeological information, explores the reorganization of Spanish society after the reconquest, bringing considerable cultural change. J. S. Gerber, *The Jews of Spain: A History of the Sephardic Experience* (1992), treats growing anti-Jewish sentiment in the wake of the Black Death. P. C. Maddern, *Violence and Social Order: East Anglia, 1422–1442* (1991), deals with social disorder in eastern England. I. M. W. Harvey, *Jack Cade's Rebellion of 1450* (1991), is an important work in local history. J. C. Holt, *Robin Hood* (1982), is a soundly researched and highly readable study of the famous outlaw. For the Pastons, see R. Barber, ed., *The Pastons: Letters of a Family in the Wars of the Roses* (1984). The starting point for study of the widespread starvation of the early fourteenth century is the prizewinning work by Jordan cited in the Notes. For social attacks on various ethnic and religious minorities, see D. Nirenberg, *Communities of Violence: Persecution of Minorities in the Middle Ages* (1996).

D. Herlihy, *Women, Family and Society in Medieval Europe: Historical Essays, 1978–1991* (1995), contains valuable articles dealing with the later Middle Ages, while the exciting study by B. Gottlieb, *The Family in the Western World from the Black Death to the Industrial Age* (1993), explores the family's political, emotional, and cultural roles. For prostitution, see, in addition to the title by Otis cited in the Notes, J. Rossiaud, *Medieval Prostitution* (1995), a very good treatment of prostitution's social and cultural significance.

For women's economic status in the late medieval period, see the titles by Howell and Hanawalt cited in the Notes. J. S. Bennett, *Ale, Beer, and Brewsters in England: Women's Work in a Changing World, 1300–1600* (1996), uses the experience of women in the brewing industry to stress the persistence of patriarchal attitudes. P. J. P. Goldberg, *Women, Work, and Life Cycle in a Medieval Economy: Women in York and Yorkshire, c 1300–1520* (1992), explores the relationship between economic opportunity and marriage.

The poetry of Dante, Chaucer, and Villon may be read in the following editions: D. Sayers, trans., *Dante: The Divine Comedy,* 3 vols. (1963); N. Coghill, trans., *Chaucer's Canterbury Tales* (1977); P. Dale, trans., *The Poems of Villon* (1973). The social setting of *Canterbury Tales* is brilliantly evoked in D. W. Robertson, Jr., *Chaucer's London* (1968). Students interested in further study of Christine de Pisan should consult A. J. Kennedy, *Christine de Pisan: A Bibliographical Guide* (1984), and C. C. Willard, *Christine de Pisan: Her Life and Works* (1984).

For religion and lay piety, A. D. Brown, *Popular Piety in Late Medieval England: The Diocese of Salisbury, 1250–1550* (1995), is a good case study showing the importance of guilds, charity, and heresy and how they affected parish life. F. Oakley, *The Western Church in the Later Middle Ages* (1979), is an excellent broad survey, while R. N. Swanson, *Church and Society in Late Medieval England* (1989), provides a good synthesis of English conditions. For great detail, consult H. Beck et al., *From the High Middle Ages to the Eve of the Reformation,* trans. A. Biggs, vol. 14 in the History of the Church series edited by H. Jedin and J. Dolan (1980). J. Bossy, "The Mass as a Social Institution, 1200–1700," *Past and Present* 100 (August 1983): 29–61, provides a technical study of the central public ritual of the Latin church. The important achievement of A. Vauchez, *The Laity in the Middle Ages: Religious Beliefs and Devotional Practices,* ed. D. E. Bornstein and trans. M. J. Schneider (1993), explores many aspects of popular piety and contains considerable material on women.

Listening to the Past

Christine de Pisan

The passage below is taken from The Book of the City of Ladies, *one of the many writings of Christine de Pisan (1363?–1434?). Christine was a highly educated woman who wrote prolifically in French, her native tongue. Her patron was the queen of France. Christine wrote amid the chaos of the Hundred Years' War about a wide range of topics. The excerpt below is not reflective of all French women. Rather, it focuses on the behavior of courtly women only. And it expresses Christine's and her patron's views about women's role in the creation and stabilization of an elite court culture during a time of political and social upheaval.*

Just as the good shepherd takes care that his lambs are maintained in health, and if any of them becomes mangy, separates it from the flock for fear that it may infect the others, so the princess will take upon herself the responsibility for the care of her women servants and companions, who she will ensure are all good and chaste, for she will not want to have any other sort of person around her. Since it is the established custom that knights and squires and all men (especially certain men) who associate with women have a habit of pleading for love tokens from them and trying to seduce them, the wise princess will so enforce her regulations that there will be no visitor to her court so foolhardy as to dare to whisper privately with any of her women or give the appearance of seduction. If he does it or if he is noticed giving any sign of it, immediately she should take such an attitude towards him that he will not dare to importune them any more. The lady who is chaste will want all her women to be so too, on pain of being banished from her company.

She will want them to amuse themselves with decent games, such that men cannot mock, as they do the games of some women, though at the time the men laugh and join in. The women should restrain themselves with seemly conduct among knights and squires and all men. They should speak demurely and sweetly and, whether in dances or other amusements, divert and enjoy themselves decorously and without wantonness. They must not be frolicsome, forward, or boisterous in speech, expression, bearing or laughter. They must not go about with their heads raised like wild deer. This kind of behaviour would be very unseemly and greatly derisory in a woman of the court, in whom there should be more modesty, good manners and courteous behaviour than in any others, for where there is most honour there ought to be the most perfect manners and behaviour. Women of the court in any country would be deceiving themselves very much if they imagined that it was more appropriate for them to be frolicsome and saucy than for other women. For this reason we hope that in time to come our doctrine in this book may be carried into many kingdoms, so that it may be valuable in all places where there might be any shortcoming.

We say generally to all women of all countries that it is the duty of every lady and maiden of the court, whether she be young or old, to be more prudent, more decorous, and better schooled in all things than other women. The ladies of the court ought to be models of all good things and all honour to other women, and if they do otherwise they will do no honour to their mistress nor to themselves. In addition, so that everything may be consistent in modesty, the wise princess will wish that the clothing and the ornaments of her women, though they be appropriately

Christine de Pisan, shown here producing her *Collected Works,* was devoted to scholarship. *(British Library)*

beautiful and rich, be of a modest fashion, well fitting and seemly, neat and properly cared for. There should be no deviation from this modesty nor any immodesty in the matter of plunging necklines or other excesses.

In all things the wise princess will keep her women in order just as the good and prudent abbess does her convent, so that bad reports about it may not circulate in the town, in distant regions or anywhere else. This princess will be so feared and respected because of the wise management that she will be seen to practise that no man or woman will be so foolhardy as to disobey her commands in any respect or to question her will, for there is no doubt that a lady is more feared and respected and held in greater reverence when she is seen to be wise and chaste and of firm behaviour. But there is nothing wrong or inconsistent in her being kind and gentle, for the mere look of the wise lady and her subdued reception is enough of a sign to correct those men and women who err and to inspire them with fear.

Questions for Analysis

1. How did Christine think courtly women should behave around men?
2. How did women fit into the larger picture of court culture? What was their role at court?

Source: Christine de Pisan, "The Book of the City of Ladies," in *Treasures of the City of Ladies,* trans. Sarah Lawson (Penguin, 1985), pp. 74–76. Reprinted by permission of Penguin Books Ltd.

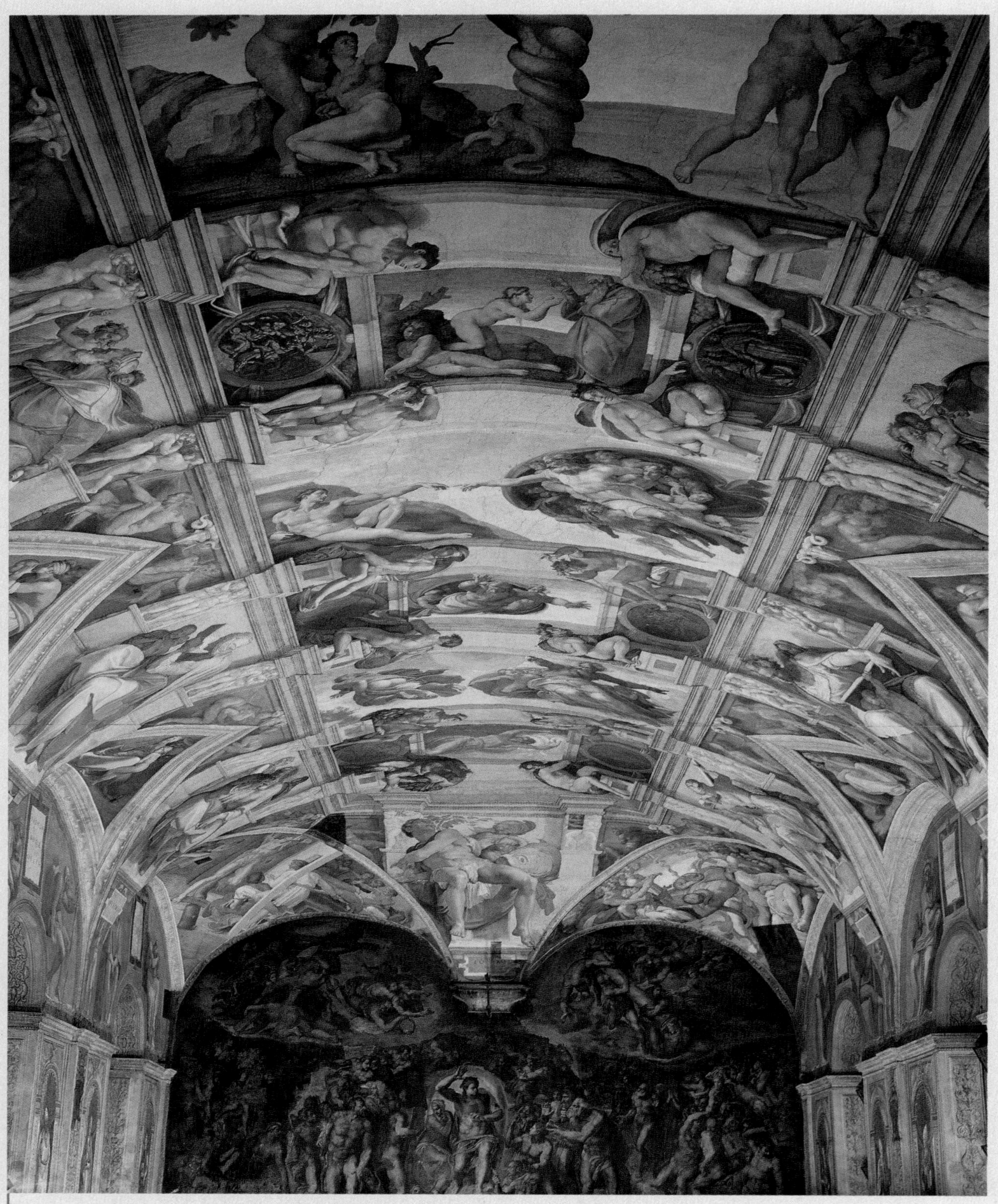

Michelangelo painted the entire Sistine Chapel ceiling by himself, in 1508–1512. *(Vatican Museum)*

chapter

13 European Society in the Age of the Renaissance

chapter outline

- The Evolution of the Italian Renaissance
- Intellectual Hallmarks of the Renaissance
- Art and the Artist
- Social Change
- The Renaissance in the North
- Politics and the State in the Renaissance (ca 1450–1521)

While the Four Horsemen of the Apocalypse seemed to be carrying war, plague, famine, and death across northern Europe, a new culture was emerging in southern Europe. The fourteenth century witnessed the beginnings of remarkable changes in many aspects of Italian society. In the fifteenth century, these phenomena spread beyond Italy and gradually influenced society in northern Europe. These cultural changes have been collectively labeled the "Renaissance."

- What does the term *Renaissance* mean?
- How was the Renaissance manifested in politics, government, and social organization?
- What were the intellectual and artistic hallmarks of the Renaissance?
- Did the Renaissance involve shifts in religious attitudes?
- What developments occurred in the evolution of the nation-state?

This chapter will concentrate on these questions.

The Evolution of the Italian Renaissance

Economic growth laid the material basis for the Italian Renaissance. The period extending roughly from 1050 to 1300 witnessed phenomenal commercial and financial development, the growing political power of self-governing cities, and great population expansion. Then the period from the late thirteenth to the late sixteenth century was characterized by an incredible efflorescence of artistic energies.[1] Scholars commonly use the term **Renaissance** to describe the cultural achievements of the fourteenth through sixteenth centuries; those achievements rest on the economic and political developments of earlier centuries.

In the great commercial revival of the eleventh century, northern Italian cities led the way. By the middle of the twelfth century, Venice, supported by a huge merchant marine, had grown enormously rich through overseas trade. It profited tremendously from the diversion of the Fourth Crusade to Constantinople (see page 355). Genoa and Milan also enjoyed the benefits of a

A Bank Scene, Florence Originally a "bank" was just a counter; if covered with a carpet like this Ottoman geometric rug with a kufic border, it became a bank of distinction. Moneychangers who sat behind the counter became "bankers," exchanging different currencies and holding deposits for merchants and business people. *(Prato, San Francesco/Scala/Art Resource, NY)*

large volume of trade with the Middle East and northern Europe. These cities fully exploited their geographical positions as natural crossroads for mercantile exchange between the East and West. Furthermore, in the early fourteenth century, Genoa and Venice made important strides in shipbuilding that allowed their ships for the first time to sail all year long. Advances in ship construction greatly increased the volume of goods that could be transported; improvements in the mechanics of sailing accelerated speed. Most goods were purchased directly from the producers and sold a good distance away. For example, Italian merchants bought fine English wool directly from the Cistercian abbeys of Yorkshire in northern England. The wool was transported to the bazaars of North Africa either overland or by ship through the Strait of Gibraltar. The risks in such an operation were great, but the profits were enormous. These profits were continually reinvested to earn more. The Florentine wool industry was the major factor in that city's financial expansion and population increase.

Scholars tend to agree that the first artistic and literary manifestations of the Italian Renaissance appeared in Florence, which possessed enormous wealth despite geographical constraints: it was an inland city without easy access to sea transportation. But toward the end of the thirteenth century, Florentine merchants and bankers acquired control of papal banking. From their position as tax collectors for the papacy, Florentine mercantile families began to dominate European banking on both sides of the Alps. These families had offices in Paris, London, Bruges, Barcelona, Marseilles, Tunis and other North African ports, and, of course, Naples and Rome. The profits from loans, investments, and money exchanges that poured back to Florence were pumped into urban industries. Such profits contributed to the city's economic vitality. Banking families, such as the Medici in Florence, controlled the politics and culture of their cities.

By the first quarter of the fourteenth century, the economic foundations of Florence were so strong that even severe crises could not destroy the city. In 1344 King Edward III of England repudiated his huge debts to Florentine bankers and forced some of them into bankruptcy. Florence suffered frightfully from the Black Death, losing at least half of its population. Serious labor unrest, such as the *ciompi* revolts of 1378 (see page 404), shook the political establishment. Nevertheless, the basic Florentine economic structure remained stable. Driving enterprise, technical know-how, and competitive spirit saw Florence through the difficult economic period of the late fourteenth century.

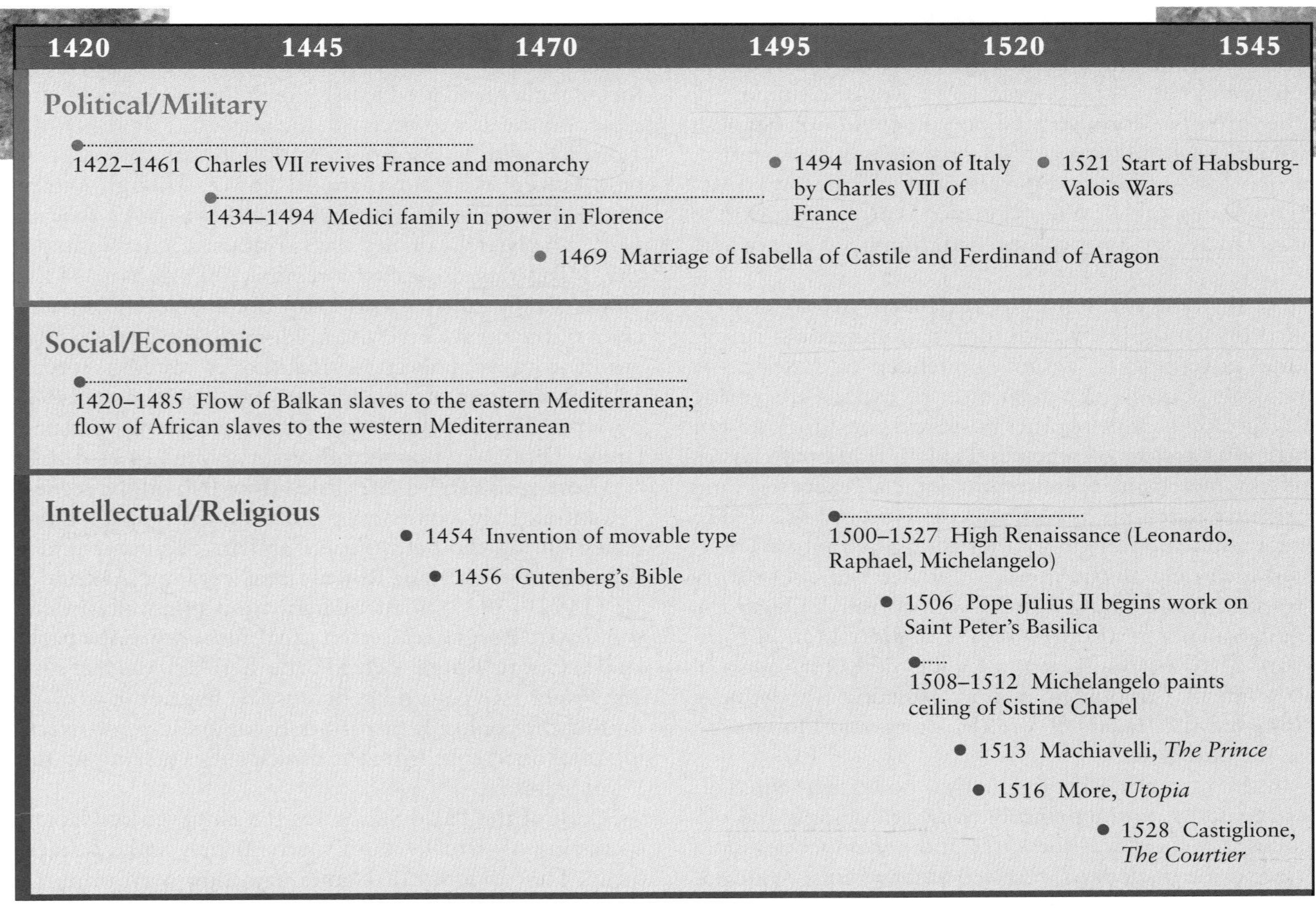

Communes and Republics

The northern Italian cities were **communes**, sworn associations of free men seeking complete political and economic independence from local nobles. The merchant guilds that formed the communes built and maintained the city walls, regulated trade, raised taxes, and kept civil order. In the course of the twelfth century, communes at Milan, Florence, Genoa, Siena, and Pisa fought for and won their independence from surrounding feudal nobles. The nobles, attracted by the opportunities of long-distance and maritime trade, the rising value of urban real estate, the new public offices available in the expanding communes, and the chances for advantageous marriages into rich commercial families, frequently settled within the cities. Marriage vows often sealed business contracts between the rural nobility and the mercantile aristocracy. This merger of the northern Italian feudal nobility and the commercial aristocracy constituted the formation of a new social class, an urban nobility. Within this nobility, groups tied by blood, economic interests, and social connections formed tightly knit alliances to defend and expand their rights.

This new class made citizenship in the communes dependent on a property qualification, years of residence within the city, and social connections. Only a tiny percentage of the male population possessed these qualifications and thus could hold office in the commune's political councils. A new force, called the **popolo**, disenfranchised and heavily taxed, bitterly resented their exclusion from power. The popolo wanted places in the communal government and equality of taxation. Throughout most of the thirteenth century, in city after city, the popolo used armed force and violence to take over the city governments. Republican governments—in which political power theoretically resides in the people and is exercised by its chosen representatives—were established in Bologna, Siena, Parma, Florence, Genoa, and other cities. The victory of the popolo, however, proved temporary. Because they practiced the same sort of political exclusivity as had the noble communes—denying influence to the classes below them, whether the poor, the unskilled, or new immigrants—the popolo never won the support of other groups. Moreover, the popolo could not establish civil order within their cities. Consequently, these movements for republican government failed. By 1300 **signori** (despots, or one-man rulers) or **oligarchies** (the rule of merchant aristocracies) had triumphed everywhere in Italy.[2]

For the next two centuries, the Italian city-states were ruled by signori or by constitutional oligarchies. In signorial governments, despots pretended to observe the law while actually manipulating it to conceal their basic illegality. Oligarchic regimes possessed constitutions, but through a variety of schemes a small, restricted class of wealthy merchants exercised the judicial, executive, and legislative functions of government. Thus in 1422 Venice had a population of eighty-four thousand, but two hundred men held all the power; Florence had about forty thousand people, but six hundred men ruled. Oligarchic regimes maintained only a façade of republican government. The Renaissance nostalgia for the Roman form of government, combined with calculating shrewdness, prompted the leaders of Venice, Milan, and Florence to use the old forms.

In the fifteenth century, political power and elite culture centered on the **princely courts** of despots and oligarchs. "A court was the space and personnel around a prince as he made laws, received ambassadors, made appointments, took his meals, and proceeded through the streets."[3] The princely court afforded the despot or oligarch the opportunity to display and assert his wealth and power. He flaunted his patronage of learning and the arts by munificent gifts to writers, philosophers, and artists. He used ceremonies connected with family births, baptisms, marriages, funerals, or triumphant entrances into the city as occasions for magnificent pageantry and elaborate ritual.

The Balance of Power Among the Italian City-States

Renaissance Italians had a passionate attachment to their individual city-states: political loyalty and feeling centered on the local city. This intensity of local feeling perpetuated the dozens of small states and hindered the development of one unified state.

In the fifteenth century, five powers dominated the Italian peninsula: Venice, Milan, Florence, the Papal States, and the kingdom of Naples (see Map 13.1). The rulers of the city-states—whether despots in Milan, patrician elitists in Florence, or oligarchs in Venice—governed as monarchs. They crushed urban revolts, levied taxes, killed their enemies, and used massive building programs to employ, and the arts to overawe, the masses.

Venice, with its enormous trade and vast colonial empire, ranked as an international power. Though Venice had a sophisticated constitution and was a republic in name, an oligarchy of merchant aristocrats actually ran the city. Milan was also called a republic, but despots of the Sforza family ruled harshly and dominated the smaller cities of the north. Likewise in Florence the form of government was republican, with authority vested in several councils of state. In reality, between 1434 and 1494, power in Florence was held by the great Medici banking family. Though not public officers, Cosimo (1434–1464) and Lorenzo (1469–1492) ruled from behind the scenes.

Central Italy consisted mainly of the Papal States, which during the Babylonian Captivity had come under the sway of important Roman families. Pope Alexander VI (1492–1503), aided militarily and politically by his son Cesare Borgia, reasserted papal authority in the papal lands. Cesare Borgia became the hero of Machiavelli's *The Prince* (see page 431) because he began the work of uniting the peninsula by ruthlessly conquering and exacting total obedience from the principalities making up the Papal States.

South of the Papal States was the kingdom of Naples, consisting of virtually all of southern Italy and, at times, Sicily. The kingdom of Naples had long been disputed by the Aragonese and by the French. In 1435 it passed to Aragon.

The major Italian city-states controlled the smaller ones, such as Siena, Mantua, Ferrara, and Modena, and competed furiously among themselves for territory. The large cities used diplomacy, spies, paid informers, and any other available means to get information that could be used to advance their ambitions. While the states of northern Europe were moving toward centralization and consolidation, the world of Italian politics resembled a jungle where the powerful dominated the weak.

In one significant respect, however, the Italian city-states anticipated future relations among competing European states after 1500. Whenever one Italian state appeared to gain a predominant position within the peninsula, other states combined to establish a *balance of power* against the major threat. In 1450, for example, Venice went to war against Milan in protest against Francesco Sforza's acquisition of the title of duke of Milan. Cosimo de' Medici of Florence, a long-time supporter of a Florentine-Venetian alliance, switched his position and aided Milan. Florence and Naples combined

MAP 13.1 The Italian City-States, ca 1494 In the fifteenth century, the Italian city-states represented great wealth and cultural sophistication. The political divisions of the peninsula invited foreign intervention.

with Milan against powerful Venice and the papacy. In the peace treaty signed at Lodi in 1454, Venice received territories in return for recognizing Sforza's right to the duchy. This pattern of shifting alliances continued until 1494. In the formation of these alliances, Renaissance Italians invented the machinery of modern diplomacy: permanent embassies with resident ambassadors in capitals where political relations and commercial ties needed continual monitoring. The resident ambassador was one of the great achievements of the Italian Renaissance.

At the end of the fifteenth century, Venice, Florence, Milan, and the papacy possessed great wealth and represented high cultural achievement. However, their imperialistic ambitions at one another's expense and their

Uccello: Battle of San Romano Fascinated by perspective—the representation of spatial depth or distance on a flat surface—the Florentine artist Paolo Uccello (1397–1475) celebrated the Florentine victory over Siena (1432) in a painting with three scenes. Though a minor battle, it started Florence on the road to domination over smaller nearby states. The painting hung in Lorenzo de' Medici's bedroom. *(National Gallery, London/Erich Lessing/Art Resource, NY)*

resulting inability to form a common alliance against potential foreign enemies made Italy an inviting target for invasion. When Florence and Naples entered into an agreement to acquire Milanese territories, Milan called on France for support.

At Florence the French invasion had been predicted by Dominican friar Girolamo Savonarola (1452–1498). In a number of fiery sermons between 1491 and 1494, Savonarola attacked what he called the paganism and moral vice of the city, the undemocratic government of Lorenzo de' Medici, and the corruption of Pope Alexander VI. For a time, Savonarola enjoyed popular support among the ordinary people; he became the religious leader of Florence and as such contributed to the fall of the Medici dynasty. Eventually, however, people tired of his moral denunciations, and he was excommunicated by the pope and executed. Savonarola stands as proof that the common people did not share the worldly outlook of the commercial and intellectual elite. His career also illustrates the internal instability of Italian cities such as Florence, an instability that invited foreign invasion.

The invasion of Italy in 1494 by the French king Charles VIII (r. 1483–1498) inaugurated a new period in Italian and European power politics. Italy became the focus of international ambitions and the battleground of foreign armies. Charles swept down the peninsula with little opposition, and Florence, Rome, and Naples soon bowed before him. When Piero de' Medici, Lorenzo's son, went to the French camp seeking peace, the Florentines exiled the Medici and restored republican government.

Charles's success simply whetted French appetites. In 1508 his cousin and heir, Louis XII, formed the League of Cambrai with the pope and the German emperor Maximilian for the purpose of stripping rich Venice of its mainland possessions. Pope Leo X (1513–1521) soon found France a dangerous friend and in a new alliance called on the Spanish and Germans to expel the French from Italy. This anti-French combination was temporarily successful. In 1519 Charles V succeeded his grandfather Maximilian (1493–1519) as Holy Roman emperor. When the French returned to Italy in 1522, a series of conflicts called the Habsburg-Valois Wars (named for the German and French dynasties) began. The battlefield was often Italy.

In the sixteenth century, the political and social life of Italy was upset by the relentless competition for dominance between France and the empire. The Italian cities suffered severely from continual warfare, especially in the frightful sack of Rome in 1527 by imperial forces under Charles V. Thus the failure of the city-states to form some federal system, consolidate, or at least establish a common foreign policy led to the continuation of the centuries-old subjection of the peninsula by outside invaders. Italy was not to achieve unification until 1870.

Intellectual Hallmarks of the Renaissance

The Renaissance was characterized by self-conscious awareness among fourteenth- and fifteenth-century Italians that they were living in a new era. The realization that something new and unique was happening first came to men of letters in the fourteenth century, especially to the poet and humanist Francesco Petrarch (1304–1374). Petrarch thought that he was living at the start of a new age, a period of light following a long night of Gothic gloom. He considered the first two centuries of the Roman Empire to represent the peak in the development of human civilization. Medieval people had believed that they were continuing the glories that had been ancient Rome and had recognized no cultural division between the world of the emperors and their own times. But for Petrarch, the Germanic invasions had caused a sharp cultural break with the glories of Rome and inaugurated what he called the "Dark Ages." He believed, with many of his contemporaries, that the thousand-year period between the fourth and the fourteenth centuries constituted a barbarian, Gothic, or "middle" age. The sculptors, painters, and writers of the Renaissance spoke contemptuously of their medieval predecessors and identified themselves with the thinkers and artists of Greco-Roman civilization. Petrarch believed that he was witnessing a new golden age of intellectual achievement—a rebirth or, to use the French word that came into English, a renaissance. The division of historical time into periods is often arbitrary and done for the convenience of historians. In terms of the way most people lived and thought, no sharp division exists between the Middle Ages and the Renaissance. Some important poets, writers, and artists, however, believed they were living in a new golden age.

The Renaissance also manifested itself in a new attitude toward men, women, and the world—an attitude that may be described as individualism. A humanism characterized by a deep interest in the Latin classics and a deliberate attempt to revive antique lifestyles emerged, as did a bold new secular spirit.

Individualism

Though the Middle Ages had seen the appearance of remarkable individuals, recognition of such persons was limited. The examples of Saint Augustine in the fifth century and Peter Abelard and Guibert of Nogent in the twelfth—men who perceived themselves as unique and produced autobiographical statements—stand out for that very reason: Christian humility discouraged self-absorption. In the fourteenth and fifteenth centuries, moreover, such characteristically medieval and corporate attachments as the guild and the parish continued to provide strong support for the individual and to exercise great social influence. Yet in the Renaissance, intellectuals, unlike their counterparts in the Middle Ages, developed a new sense of historical distance from earlier periods. A large literature specifically concerned with the nature of individuality emerged. This literature represented the flowering of a distinctly Renaissance individualism.

The Renaissance witnessed the emergence of many distinctive personalities who gloried in their uniqueness. Italians of unusual abilities were self-consciously aware of their singularity and unafraid to be unlike their neighbors; they had enormous confidence in their ability to achieve great things. Leon Battista Alberti (1404–1474), a writer, architect, and mathematician, remarked, "Men can do all things if they will."[4] Florentine goldsmith and sculptor Benvenuto Cellini (1500–1574) prefaced his *Autobiography* with a declaration:

My cruel fate hath warr'd with me in vain:
Life, glory, worth, and all unmeasur'd skill,
Beauty and grace, themselves in me fulfill
That many I surpass, and to the best attain.[5]

Cellini, certain of his genius, wrote so that the whole world might appreciate it.

Individualism stressed personality, uniqueness, genius, and full development of one's capabilities and talents.

Benvenuto Cellini: Saltcellar of Francis I (ca 1539–1543) In gold and enamel, Cellini depicts the Roman sea god, Neptune (with trident, or three-pronged spear), sitting beside a small boat-shaped container holding salt from the sea. Opposite him, a female figure personifying Earth guards pepper, which derives from a plant. Portrayed on the base are the four seasons and the times of day, symbolizing seasonal festivities and daily meal schedules. The grace, poise, and elegance of the figures reflect Mannerism, an artistic style popular during the Italian High Renaissance (1520–1600). *(Kunsthistorisches Museum, Vienna/The Bridgeman Art Library International Ltd)*

Artist, athlete, painter, scholar, sculptor, whatever—a person's abilities should be stretched until fully realized. Thirst for fame, a driving ambition, and a burning desire for success drove such people to the complete achievement of their potential. The quest for glory was a central component of Renaissance individualism.

Humanism

In the cities of Italy, especially Rome, civic leaders and the wealthy populace showed phenomenal archaeological zeal for the recovery of manuscripts, statues, and monuments. Pope Nicholas V (1447–1455), a distinguished scholar, planned the Vatican Library for the nine thousand manuscripts he had collected. Pope Sixtus IV (1471–1484) built that library, which remains one of the richest repositories of ancient and medieval documents.

The revival of antiquity also took the form of profound interest in and study of the Latin classics. This feature of the Renaissance became known as the "new learning," or simply **humanism,** the term of Florentine rhetorician and historian Leonardo Bruni (1370–1444). The words *humanism* and *humanist* derive ultimately from the Latin *humanitas,* which Cicero used to mean the literary culture needed by anyone who would be considered educated and civilized. Humanists studied the Latin classics to learn what they reveal about human nature. Humanism emphasized human beings, their achievements, interests, and capabilities. Although churchmen supported the new learning, by the later fifteenth century Italian humanism was increasingly a lay phenomenon.

Appreciation for the literary culture of the Romans had never died in the West. Bede and John of Salisbury, for example, had studied and imitated the writings of the ancients. Medieval writers, however, had studied the ancients in order to come to know God. Medieval scholars had interpreted the classics in a Christian sense and had invested the ancients' poems and histories with Christian meaning.

Renaissance humanists, although deeply Christian, approached the classics differently. Whereas medieval writers accepted pagan and classical authors uncritically, Renaissance humanists were skeptical of their authority, conscious of the historical distance separating themselves from the ancients, and fully aware that classical writers often disagreed among themselves. Whereas medieval writers looked to the classics to reveal God, Renaissance humanists studied the classics to understand human nature, and while they fully grasped the moral thought of pagan antiquity, Renaissance humanists viewed humanity from a strongly Christian perspective: men and women were made in the image and likeness of God. For example, in a remarkable essay, *On the Dignity of Man,* the Florentine writer Pico della Mirandola stressed that man possesses great dignity because he was made as Adam in the image of God before the Fall and as Christ after the Resurrection. According to Pico, man's place in the universe is somewhere between the beasts and the angels, but because of the divine image planted in him, there are no limits to what he can accomplish. Humanists rejected classical ideas that were opposed to Christianity. Or they sought through reinterpretation an underlying harmony between the pagan and secular and the Christian faith. The fundamental difference between Renaissance humanists and medieval ones is that the former were more self-conscious about what they were doing, and they stressed the realization of human potential.[6]

The fourteenth- and fifteenth-century humanists loved the language of the classics and considered it superior to the corrupt Latin of the medieval schoolmen. They eventually became concerned more about form than about content, more about the way an idea was expressed than about the significance and validity of the idea. Literary humanists of the fourteenth century wrote each other highly stylized letters imitating ancient authors, and they held witty philosophical dialogues in conscious imitation of the Platonic Academy of the fourth century B.C. Renaissance humanists heaped scorn on the "barbaric" Latin style of the medievalists. The leading humanists of the early Renaissance were rhetoricians, seeking effective and eloquent communication, both oral and written.

Secular Spirit

Secularism involves a basic concern with the material world instead of with the eternal world of spirit. A secular way of thinking tends to find the ultimate explanation of everything and the final end of human beings within the limits of what the senses can discover. Even though medieval business people ruthlessly pursued profits and medieval monks fought fiercely over property, the dominant ideals focused on the otherworldly, on life after death. Renaissance people often held strong and deep spiritual interests, but in their increasingly secular society, attention was concentrated on the here and now, often on the acquisition of material things. Church doctrine, relying on Scripture (Leviticus 25:36–37, Psalms 37:26, Luke 11:15), frowned on usury (lending money at interest), but the law had always been difficult to enforce. In the twelfth century, Cistercian monks had been severely criticized for practicing usury. During the Renaissance, the practice became widespread, even acceptable. Considerable wealth derived from interest on loans. The fourteenth and fifteenth centuries witnessed the slow but steady growth of such secularism in Italy.

The economic changes and rising prosperity of the Italian cities in the thirteenth century worked a fundamental change in social and intellectual attitudes and values. Worries about shifting rates of interest, shipping routes, personnel costs, and employee relations did not leave much time for thoughts about penance and purgatory. The busy bankers and merchants of the Italian cities calculated ways of making and increasing their money. Such wealth allowed greater material pleasures, a more comfortable life, the leisure time to appreciate and patronize the arts. Money could buy many sensual gratifications, and the rich, social-climbing patricians of Venice, Florence, Genoa, and Rome came to see life more as an opportunity to be enjoyed than as a painful pilgrimage to the City of God.

In *On Pleasure,* humanist Lorenzo Valla (1406–1457) defends the pleasures of the senses as the highest good. Scholars praise Valla as a father of modern historical criticism. His study *On the False Donation of Constantine* (1444) demonstrates by careful textual examination that an anonymous eighth-century document supposedly giving the papacy jurisdiction over vast territories in western Europe was a forgery. Medieval people had accepted the Donation of Constantine as a reality, and the proof that it was an invention weakened the foundations of papal claims to temporal authority. Lorenzo Valla's work exemplifies the application of critical scholarship to old and almost-sacred writings as well as the new secular spirit of the Renaissance.

The tales in *The Decameron* by the Florentine Giovanni Boccaccio (1313–1375), which describe ambitious merchants, lecherous friars, and cuckolded husbands, portray a frankly acquisitive, sensual, and worldly society. Although Boccaccio's figures were stock literary characters, *The Decameron* contains none of the "contempt of the world" theme so pervasive in medieval literature. Renaissance writers justified the accumulation and enjoyment of wealth with references to ancient authors.

Nor did church leaders do much to combat the new secular spirit. In the fifteenth and early sixteenth centuries, the papal court and the households of the cardinals were just as worldly as those of great urban patricians. Of course, most of the popes and higher church officials had come from the bourgeois aristocracy. Renaissance popes beautified the city of Rome, patronized artists and men of letters, and expended enormous enthusiasm and huge sums of money. A new papal chancellery, begun in 1483 and finished in 1511, stands as one of the architectural masterpieces of the High Renaissance. Pope Julius II (1503–1513) tore down the old Saint Peter's Basilica and began work on the present structure in 1506. Michelangelo's dome for Saint Peter's is still considered his greatest work. Papal interests, which were far removed from spiritual concerns, fostered, rather than discouraged, the new worldly attitude.

The broad mass of the people and the intellectuals and leaders of society remained faithful to the Christian church. Few people questioned the basic tenets of the Christian religion. Italian humanists and their aristocratic patrons were anti-ascetic, anti-Scholastic, and ambivalent, but they were not agnostics or skeptics. The thousands of pious paintings, sculptures, processions, and pilgrimages of the Renaissance period prove that strong religious feeling persisted.

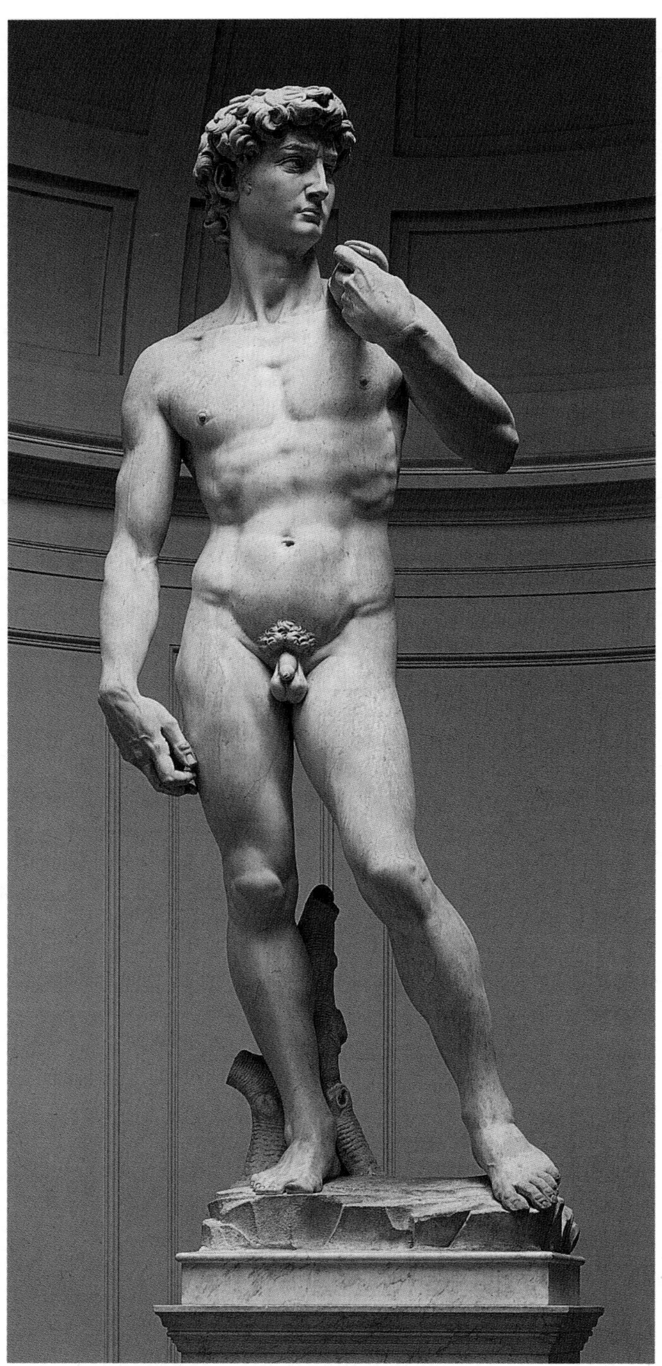

Michelangelo: David In 1501 the new republican government of Florence commissioned the twenty-six-year-old Michelangelo to carve David as a symbol of civic independence and resistance to oligarchial tyranny. Tensed in anticipation of action but certain of victory over his unseen enemy Goliath (1 Samuel 17), this male nude represents the ideal of youthful physical perfection. *(Scala/Art Resource, NY)*

Art and the Artist

No feature of the Renaissance evokes greater admiration than its artistic masterpieces. The 1400s (*quattrocento*) and 1500s (*cinquecento*) bore witness to a dazzling creativity in painting, architecture, and sculpture. In all the arts, the city of Florence led the way. According to Renaissance art historian Giorgio Vasari (1511–1574), the painter Perugino once asked why it was in Florence and not elsewhere that men achieved perfection in the arts. The first answer he received was, "There were so many good critics there, for the air of the city makes men quick and perceptive and impatient of mediocrity."[7] But Florence was not the only artistic center. In the period art historians describe as the "High Renaissance" (1500–1527), Rome took the lead. The main characteristics of High Renaissance art—classical balance, harmony, and restraint—are revealed in the masterpieces of Leonardo da Vinci (1452–1519), Raphael (1483–1520), and Michelangelo (1475–1564), all of whom worked in Rome.

Art and Power

In early Renaissance Italy, art manifested corporate power. Powerful urban groups such as guilds or religious confraternities commissioned works of art. The Florentine cloth merchants, for example, delegated Filippo Brunelleschi to build the magnificent dome on the cathedral of Florence and selected Lorenzo Ghiberti to design the bronze doors of the Baptistry. These works represented the merchants' dominant influence in the community. Corporate patronage was also reflected in the Florentine government's decision to hire Michelangelo to create the sculpture of David, the great Hebrew hero and king. The subject matter of art through the early fifteenth century, as in the Middle Ages, remained overwhelmingly religious. Religious themes appeared in all media—woodcarvings, painted frescoes, stone sculptures, paintings. As in the Middle Ages, art served an educational purpose. A religious picture or statue was intended to spread a particular doctrine, act as a profession of faith, or recall sinners to a moral way of living.

Increasingly in the later fifteenth century, individuals and oligarchs, rather than corporate groups, sponsored works of art. Patrician merchants and bankers, popes and princes, supported the arts as a means of glorifying themselves and their families. Vast sums were spent on family chapels, frescoes, religious panels, and tombs. Writing about 1470, Florentine oligarch Lorenzo de' Medici declared that over the previous thirty-five years his family

Andrea Mantegna: Adoration of the Magi (ca 1495–1505) Applying his study of ancient Roman relief sculpture, and elaborating on a famous scriptural text (Matthew 2:1), Mantegna painted for the private devotion of the Gonzaga family of Mantua this scene of the Three Kings coming to recognize the divinity of Christ. The Three Kings represent the entire world—that is, the three continents known to medieval Europeans: Europe, Asia, and Africa. They also symbolize the three stages of life: youth, maturity, and old age. Here Melchior, the oldest, his large cranium symbolizing wisdom, personifies Europe. He offers gold in a Chinese porcelain cup from the Ming Dynasty. Balthazar, with an olive complexion and dark beard, stands for Asia and maturity. He presents frankincense in a stunning vessel of Turkish tombac ware. Caspar, representing Africa and youth, gives myrrh in an urn of striped marble. The child responds with a blessing. The black background brings out the rich colors. *(The J. Paul Getty Museum, Los Angeles. Mantegna, Andrea,* Adoration of the Magi, *ca 1495–1505, distemper on linen, 54.6 × 70.7 cm [85.PA.417])*

had spent the astronomical sum of 663,755 gold florins for artistic and architectural commissions. Yet "I think it casts a brilliant light on our estate [public reputation] and it seems to me that the monies were well spent and I am very pleased with this." Powerful men wanted to exalt themselves, their families, and their offices. A magnificent style of living, enriched by works of art, served to prove the greatness and the power of the despot or oligarch.[8]

In addition to power, art reveals changing patterns of consumption in Renaissance Italy. "Consumer habits introduced into economic life a creative and dynamic process for growth and change that was fundamental to the development of the West."[9] If modern consumerism has its roots in the eighteenth century, the latter period's consumer practices can be traced to the Italian Renaissance.

In the rural world of the Middle Ages, society had been organized for war. Men of wealth spent their money on military gear—swords, armor, horses, crenelated castles, towers, family compounds—all of which represent offensive or defensive warfare. As Italian nobles settled in towns (see page 417), they adjusted to an urban culture. Rather than employing knights for warfare, cities hired mercenaries. Expenditure on military hardware declined. For the rich merchant or the noble recently arrived from the countryside, the urban palace represented the greatest outlay of cash. It was his chief luxury, and although a private dwelling, the palace implied grandeur.[10] Within the palace, the merchant-prince's chamber, or bedroom, where he slept and received his intimate guests, was the most important room. In the fourteenth and fifteenth centuries, a large, intricately carved wooden bed, a chest, and perhaps a bench served as its sole decorations. The chest held the master's most precious goods—silver, tapestries, jewelry, clothing. Other rooms, even in palaces of fifteen to twenty rooms, were very sparsely furnished. As the fifteenth century advanced and wealth increased, other rooms were gradually furnished with carved chests, tables, benches, chairs, tapestries for the walls, paintings (an innovation), and sculptural decorations, and a private chapel was added. By the late sixteenth century, the Strozzi banking family of Florence spent more on household goods than on anything else except food; the value of those furnishings was three times that of their silver and jewelry.[11]

After the palace itself, the private chapel within the palace symbolized the largest expenditure. Equipped with the ecclesiastical furniture—tabernacles, chalices, thuribles, and other liturgical utensils—and decorated with religious scenes, the chapel served as the center of the household's religious life and its cult of remembrance of the dead. In fifteenth-century Florence, only the Medici had a private chapel, but by the late sixteenth century, most wealthy Florentine families had private chapels. Since the merchant banker or prince appointed the chaplain, usually a younger son of the family, religious power passed into private hands.[12]

As the fifteenth century advanced, the subject matter of art became steadily more secular. The study of classical texts brought deeper understanding of ancient ideas. Classical themes and motifs, such as the lives and loves of pagan gods and goddesses, figured increasingly in painting and sculpture. Religious topics, such as the Annunciation of the Virgin and the Nativity, remained popular among both patrons and artists, but frequently the patron had himself and his family portrayed. People were conscious of their physical uniqueness and wanted their individuality immortalized. Paintings were also means of displaying wealth.

The content and style of Renaissance art were decidedly different from those of the Middle Ages. The individual portrait emerged as a distinct artistic genre. In the fifteenth century, members of the newly rich middle class often had themselves painted in a scene of romantic chivalry or courtly society. Rather than reflecting a spiri-

Renaissance Wedding Chest (Tuscany, late fifteenth century) A wedding chest was a gift from the groom's family to the bride. Appreciated more for their decorative value than for practical storage purposes, these chests were prominently displayed in people's homes. This 37" × 47" × 28" chest is carved with scenes from classical mythology. *(Philadelphia Museum of Art. Purchased with the Joseph E. Temple Fund)*

tual ideal, as medieval painting and sculpture tended to do, Renaissance portraits mirrored reality. The Florentine painter Giotto (1276–1337) led the way in the use of realism; his treatment of the human body and face replaced the formal stiffness and artificiality that had for so long characterized representation of the human body. The sculptor Donatello (1386–1466) probably exerted the greatest influence of any Florentine artist before Michelangelo. His many statues express an appreciation of the incredible variety of human nature. Whereas medieval artists had depicted the nude human body only in a spiritualized and moralizing context, Donatello revived the classical figure, with its balance and self-awareness. The short-lived Florentine Masaccio (1401–1428), sometimes called the father of modern painting, inspired a new style characterized by great realism, narrative power, and remarkably effective use of light and dark. As important as realism was the new "international style," so called because of the wandering careers of influential artists, the close communications and rivalry of princely courts, and the increased trade in works of art. Rich color, decorative detail, curvilinear rhythms, and swaying forms characterized the international style. As the term *international* implies, this style was European, not merely Italian.

Narrative artists depicted the body in a more scientific and natural manner. The female figure is voluptuous and sensual. The male body, as in Michelangelo's *David* and *The Last Judgment,* is strong and heroic. Renaissance glorification of the human body revealed the secular spirit of the age. Filippo Brunelleschi (1377–1446) and Piero della Francesca (1420–1492) seem to have pioneered *perspective* in painting, the linear representation of distance and space on a flat surface. *The Last Supper* by Leonardo da Vinci, with its stress on the tension between Christ and the disciples, is an incredibly subtle psychological interpretation.

The Status of the Artist

In the Renaissance, the social status of the artist improved. Whereas the lower-middle-class medieval master mason had been viewed in the same light as a mechanic, the Renaissance artist was considered a free intellectual worker. Artists did not produce unsolicited pictures or statues for the general public; that could mean loss of status. They usually worked on commission from a powerful prince. The artist's reputation depended on the support of powerful patrons, and through them some artists and architects achieved not only economic security but also very great wealth.

Lorenzo Ghiberti's salary of 200 florins a year compared very favorably with that of the head of the city government, who earned 500 florins. Moreover, at a time when a person could live in a princely fashion on 300 ducats a year, Leonardo da Vinci was making 2,000 annually.[13]

Renaissance society respected and rewarded the distinguished artist. In 1537 the prolific letter writer, humanist, and satirizer of princes Pietro Aretino (1492–1556) wrote to Michelangelo while he was painting the Sistine Chapel:

> *To the Divine Michelangelo:*
> *Sir, just as it is disgraceful and sinful to be unmindful of God so it is reprehensible and dishonourable for any man of discerning judgment not to honour you as a brilliant and venerable artist whom the very stars use as a target at which to shoot the rival arrows of their favour. . . . It is surely my duty to honour you with this salutation, since the world has many kings but only one Michelangelo.*[14]

When Holy Roman Emperor Charles V (r. 1519–1556) visited the workshop of the great Titian (1477–1576) and stooped to pick up the artist's dropped paintbrush, the emperor was demonstrating that the patron himself was honored in the act of honoring the artist.

Renaissance artists were not only aware of their creative power; they also boasted about it. Describing his victory over five others, including Brunelleschi, in the competition to design the bronze doors of Florence's Baptistry, Ghiberti exulted, "The palm of victory was conceded to me by all the experts and by all my fellow-competitors. By universal consent and without a single exception the glory was conceded to me."[15] Some medieval painters and sculptors had signed their works; Renaissance artists almost universally did so, and many of them incorporated self-portraits, usually as bystanders, in their paintings.

The Renaissance, in fact, witnessed the birth of the concept of the artist as genius. In the Middle Ages, people believed that only God created, albeit through individuals; the medieval conception recognized no particular value in artistic originality. Renaissance artists and humanists came to think that a work of art was the deliberate creation of a unique personality who transcended traditions, rules, and theories. A genius had a peculiar gift, which ordinary laws should not inhibit. Cosimo de' Medici described a painter, because of his genius, as "divine," implying that the artist shared in the powers of God. The word *divine* was widely applied to Michelangelo. (See the feature "Individuals in Society: Leonardo da Vinci.")

But students must guard against interpreting Italian Renaissance culture in twenty-first-century democratic

Benozzo Gozzoli: Journey of the Magi Few Renaissance paintings better illustrate art in the service of the princely court, in this case the Medici, than this one, commissioned by Piero de' Medici to adorn his palace chapel. Everything in this fresco—the large crowd, the feathers and diamonds adorning many of the personages, the black servant in front—serves to flaunt the power and wealth of the House of Medici. There is nothing especially religious about it; the painting could more appropriately be called "Journey of the Medici." The artist has discreetly placed himself in the crowd; the name Benozzo is embroidered on his cap. *(Scala/Art Resource, NY)*

terms. The culture of the Renaissance was that of a small mercantile elite, a business patriciate with aristocratic pretensions. Renaissance culture did not directly affect the broad middle classes, let alone the vast urban proletariat. A small, highly educated minority of literary humanists and artists created the culture of and for an exclusive elite. The Renaissance maintained a gulf between the learned minority and the uneducated multitude that has survived for many centuries.

Social Change

Renaissance ideals permeated educational theory and practice and political thought. The era's most stunning technological invention, printing, affected many forms of social life. Renaissance culture witnessed a shift in the status and experience of women. Numbers of slaves also played a role in Renaissance society.

Individuals in Society

Leonardo da Vinci

What makes a genius? An infinite capacity for taking pains? A deep curiosity about an extensive variety of subjects? A divine spark as manifested by talents that far exceed the norm? Or is it just "one percent inspiration and ninety-nine percent perspiration," as Thomas Edison said? By whatever criteria, Leonardo da Vinci was one of the greatest geniuses in the history of the Western world.

He was born in Vinci, near Florence, the illegitimate son of Caterina, a local peasant girl, and Ser Piero da Vinci, a notary public. Caterina later married another native of Vinci. When Ser Piero's marriage to Donna Albrussia produced no children, they took in Leonardo, who remained with them until Ser Piero secured Leonardo's apprenticeship with the painter and sculptor Andrea del Verrocchio. In 1472, when Leonardo was just twenty years old, he was listed as a master in Florence's "Company of Artists."

Leonardo contributed to the modern concept of the artist as an original thinker and as a special kind of human being: an isolated figure with exceptional creative powers. Leonardo's portrait *Ginevra de' Benci* anticipates his most famous portrait, *Mona Lisa,* with the enigmatic smile that Giorgio Vasari described as "so pleasing that it seemed divine rather than human." Leonardo's experimental method of fresco painting of *The Last Supper* caused the picture to deteriorate rapidly, but it has been called "the most revered painting in the world." To the annoyance of his patrons, none of these paintings was ever completed to Leonardo's satisfaction. For example, *The Last Supper* was left unfinished because he could not find a model for the face of Christ that would evoke the spiritual depth he felt it deserved.

Leonardo once said that "a painter is not admirable unless he is universal." He left notes and plans on drawing, painting, sculpture, music, architecture, town planning, optics, astronomy, biology, zoology, mathematics, and various branches of engineering, such as a model for a submarine, designs for tank warfare, and cranes for dredging. These drafts suggest the astonishing versatility of his mind. One authority has said that Leonardo "saw art from the scientific point of view and science from the artist's point of view."

Vasari described Leonardo as a handsome man with a large body and physical grace, a "sparkling conversationalist" talented at singing while accompanying himself on the lyre. According to Vasari, "his genius was so wonderfully inspired by God, his powers of expression so powerfully fed by a willing memory and intellect . . . that his arguments confounded the most formidable critics."

Leonardo da Vinci, Lady with an Ermine. *The whiteness of the ermine's fur symbolizes purity.* (Czartoryski Museum, Krakow/ The Bridgeman Art Library International Ltd)

In a famous essay, the Viennese psychiatrist Sigmund Freud argued that Leonardo was a homosexual who sublimated, pouring his sexual energy into his art. Freud wrote that it is doubtful that Leonardo ever touched a woman or even had an intimate spiritual relationship with one. Although as a master artist he surrounded himself with handsome young men and even had a long emotional relationship with one, Francesco Melzi, the evidence suggests that his male relationships never resulted in sexual activity. On a page of his *Codex Atlanticus,* which includes his sketch of the Florentine navigator Amerigo Vespucci, Leonardo wrote, "Intellectual passion drives out sensuality." For Freud, Leonardo transferred his psychic energy into artistic and scientific study. This thesis has attracted much attention, but no one has refuted it.

Leonardo worked in Milan for the despot Ludovico Sforza, planning a gigantic equestrian statue in honor of Ludovico's father, Duke Francesco Sforza. The clay model collapsed, and only notes survived. Leonardo also worked as a military engineer for Cesare Borgia (see page 418). In 1516 he accepted King Francis I's invitation to France. At the French court and in the presence of his faithful companion Francesco Melzi, Leonardo died in the arms of the king.

Questions for Analysis

1. How would you explain Leonardo's genius?
2. Consider sublimation as a source of artistic and scientific creativity.

Sources: Giorgio Vasari, *Lives of the Artists,* vol. 1, trans. G. Bull (London: Penguin Books, 1965); S. B. Nuland, *Leonardo da Vinci* (New York: Lipper/Viking, 2000); Sigmund Freud, *Leonardo da Vinci: A Study in Psychosexuality* (New York: Random House, 1947).

Education and Political Thought

One of the central preoccupations of the humanists was education and moral behavior. Humanists poured out treatises, often in the form of letters, on the structure and goals of education and the training of rulers. In one of the earliest systematic programs for the young, Peter Paul Vergerio (1370–1444) wrote Ubertinus, the ruler of Carrara:

> *For the education of children is a matter of more than private interest; it concerns the State, which indeed regards the right training of the young as, in certain aspects, within its proper sphere. . . . Tutors and comrades alike should be chosen from amongst those likely to bring out the best qualities, to attract by good example, and to repress the first signs of evil. . . . Above all, respect for Divine ordinances is of the deepest importance; it should be inculcated from the earliest years. Reverence towards elders and parents is an obligation closely akin.*
>
> *We call those studies liberal which are worthy of a free man; those studies by which we attain and practice virtue and wisdom.*[16]

Part of Vergerio's treatise specifies subjects for the instruction of young men in public life: history teaches virtue by examples from the past, ethics focuses on virtue itself, and rhetoric or public speaking trains for eloquence.

No book on education had broader influence than Baldassare Castiglione's *The Courtier* (1528). This treatise sought to train, discipline, and fashion the young man into the courtly ideal, the gentleman. According to Castiglione, the educated man of the upper class should have a broad background in many academic subjects, and his spiritual and physical as well as intellectual capabilities should be trained. The courtier should have easy familiarity with dance, music, and the arts. Castiglione envisioned a man who could compose a sonnet, wrestle, sing a song and accompany himself on an instrument, ride expertly, solve difficult mathematical problems, and, above all, speak and write eloquently.

In the sixteenth and seventeenth centuries, *The Courtier* was widely read. It influenced the social mores and patterns of conduct of elite groups in Renaissance and early modern Europe. The courtier became the model of the European gentleman.

In the cities of Renaissance Italy, well-to-do girls received an education similar to boys'. Young ladies learned their letters and studied the classics. Many read Greek as well as Latin, knew the poetry of Ovid and Virgil, and could speak one or two "modern" languages, such as French or Spanish. In this respect, Renaissance humanism represented a real educational advance for women. Some women, though a small minority among humanists, acquired great learning and fame. (See the feature "Listening to the Past: Christine de Pisan" on pages 412–413.) In the later sixteenth century, at least twenty-five women published books in Italy, Sofonisba Anguissola (1530–1625) and Artemisia Gentileschi (1593–1653) achieved international renown for their paintings, and Isabella Andreini (1562–1604) enjoyed a reputation as the greatest actress of her day.

Laura Cereta (1469–1499) illustrates the successes and failures of educated Renaissance women. Educated by her father, who was a member of the governing elite of Brescia in Lombardy, she learned languages, philosophy, theology, and mathematics. She also gained self-confidence and a healthy respect for her own potential. By the age of fifteen, when she married, her literary career was already launched, as her letters to several cardinals attest. For Laura Cereta, however, as for all educated women of the period, the question of marriage forced the issue: she could choose a husband, family, and full participation in social life or study and withdrawal from the world. Marriage brought domestic responsibilities and usually prevented women from fulfilling their scholarly potential. Although Cereta chose marriage, she was widowed at eighteen, and she spent the remaining twelve years of her life in study. But she had to bear the envy of other women and the hostility of men who felt threatened. In response, Cereta condemned "empty women, who strive for no good but exist to adorn themselves. . . . These women of majestic pride, fantastic coiffures, outlandish ornament, and necks bound with gold or pearls bear the glittering symbols of their captivity to men." For Laura Cereta, women's inferiority was derived not from the divine order of things but from women themselves: "For knowledge is not given as a gift, but through study. . . . The free mind, not afraid of labor, presses on to attain the good."[17] Despite Cereta's faith in women's potential, men frequently believed that in becoming learned, a woman violated nature and thus ceased to be a woman.

Laura Cereta was a prodigy. Ordinary girls of the urban upper middle class, in addition to a classical education, received some training in painting, music, and dance. What were they to do with this training? They were to be gracious, affable, charming—in short, decorative. So although Renaissance women were better educated than their medieval counterparts, their education prepared them for the social functions of the home. An educated woman was supposed to know how to attract artists and literati to her husband's court and how to grace her husband's household, whereas an educated man was supposed to know how to rule and participate in public affairs.

No Renaissance book on any topic, however, has been more widely read and studied in all the centuries since its publication (1513) than the short political treatise ***The Prince,*** by Niccolò Machiavelli (1469–1527). The subject of *The Prince* is political power: how the ruler should gain, maintain, and increase it. Machiavelli implicitly addresses the question of the citizen's relationship to the state. As a good humanist, he explores the problems of human nature and concludes that human beings are selfish and out to advance their own interests. This pessimistic view of humanity led him to maintain that the prince may have to manipulate the people in any way he finds necessary:

> *For a man who, in all respects, will carry out only his professions of good, will be apt to be ruined amongst so many who are evil. A prince therefore who desires to maintain himself must learn to be not always good, but to be so or not as necessity may require.*[18]

The prince should combine the cunning of a fox with the ferocity of a lion to achieve his goals. Asking rhetorically whether it is better for a ruler to be loved or feared, Machiavelli writes: "It will naturally be answered that it would be desirable to be both the one and the other; but as it is difficult to be both at the same time, it is much more safe to be feared than to be loved, when you have to choose between the two."[19]

Medieval political theory had derived ultimately from Saint Augustine's view that the state arose as a consequence of Adam's fall and people's propensity to sin. The test of good government was whether it provided justice, law, and order. Political theorists and theologians from Alcuin to Marsiglio of Padua had stressed the way government *ought* to be; they had set high moral and Christian standards for the ruler's conduct.

Machiavelli maintained that the ruler should be concerned not with the way things ought to be but with the way things actually are. The sole test of a "good" government is whether it is effective, whether the ruler increases his power. Machiavelli did not advocate amoral behavior, but he believed that political action cannot be restricted by moral considerations. While amoral action might be the most effective approach in a given situation, he did not argue for generally amoral, rather than moral, behavior. Nevertheless, on the basis of a crude interpretation of *The Prince,* the word *Machiavellian* entered the language as a synonym for the politically devious, corrupt, and crafty, indicating actions in which the end justifies the means. The ultimate significance of Machiavelli rests on two ideas: first, that one permanent social order reflecting God's will cannot be established, and second, that politics has its own laws and ought to be a science.[20]

The Printed Word

Sometime in the thirteenth century, paper money and playing cards from China reached the West. They were *block-printed*—that is, Chinese characters or pictures were carved into a wooden block, the block was inked, and the words or illustrations were transferred to paper. Since each word, phrase, or picture was on a separate block, this method of reproduction was extraordinarily expensive and time-consuming.

Around 1454, probably through the combined efforts of three men—Johann Gutenberg, Johann Fust, and Peter Schöffer, all experimenting at Mainz—movable type came into being. The mirror image of each letter (rather than entire words or phrases) was carved in relief on a small block. Individual letters, easily movable, were put together to form words; words separated by blank spaces formed lines of type; and lines of type were brought together to make up a page. Since letters could be arranged into any format, an infinite variety of texts could be printed by reusing and rearranging pieces of type.

By the middle of the fifteenth century, acquiring paper was no problem. The knowledge of paper manufacture had originated in China, and the Arabs introduced it to the West in the twelfth century. Europeans quickly learned that durable paper was far less expensive than the vellum (calfskin) and parchment (sheepskin) on which medieval scribes had relied for centuries.

The effects of the invention of movable-type printing were not felt overnight. Nevertheless, within a half century of the publication of Gutenberg's Bible of 1456, movable type had brought about radical changes. Printing transformed both the private and the public lives of Europeans (see Map 13.2). Governments that "had employed the cumbersome methods of manuscripts to communicate with their subjects switched quickly to print to announce declarations of war, publish battle accounts, promulgate treaties or argue disputed points in pamphlet form. Theirs was an effort 'to win the psychological war.'" Printing made propaganda possible, emphasizing differences between opposing groups, such as Crown and nobility, church and state. These differences laid the

The Print Shop Sixteenth-century printing involved a division of labor. Two persons (*left*) at separate benches set the pieces of type. Another (*center, rear*) inks the chase (or locked plate containing the set type). Yet another (*right*) operates the press, which prints the sheets. The boy removes the printed pages and sets them to dry. Meanwhile, a man carries in fresh paper on his head. *(Giraudon/Art Resource, NY)*

basis for the formation of distinct political parties. Printed materials reached an invisible public, allowing silent individuals to join causes and groups of individuals widely separated by geography to form a common identity; this new group consciousness could compete with older, localized loyalties.[21]

Printing also stimulated the literacy of laypeople and eventually came to have a deep effect on their private lives. Although most of the earliest books and pamphlets dealt with religious subjects, students, housewives, businessmen, and upper- and middle-class people sought books on all subjects. Printers responded with moralizing, medical, practical, and travel manuals. Pornography as well as piety assumed new forms. For example, satirist Pietro Aretino (1492–1556) used the shock of sex in pornography as a vehicle to criticize: his *Sonnetti Lussuriosi* (1527) and *Ragionamenti* (1534–1536), sonnets accompanying sixteen engravings of as many sexual positions, attacked princely court life, humanist education, and false clerical piety.[22] Broadsides and flysheets allowed great public festivals, religious ceremonies, and political events to be experienced vicariously by the stay-at-home. Since books and other printed materials were read aloud to illiterate listeners, print bridged the gap between written and oral cultures.

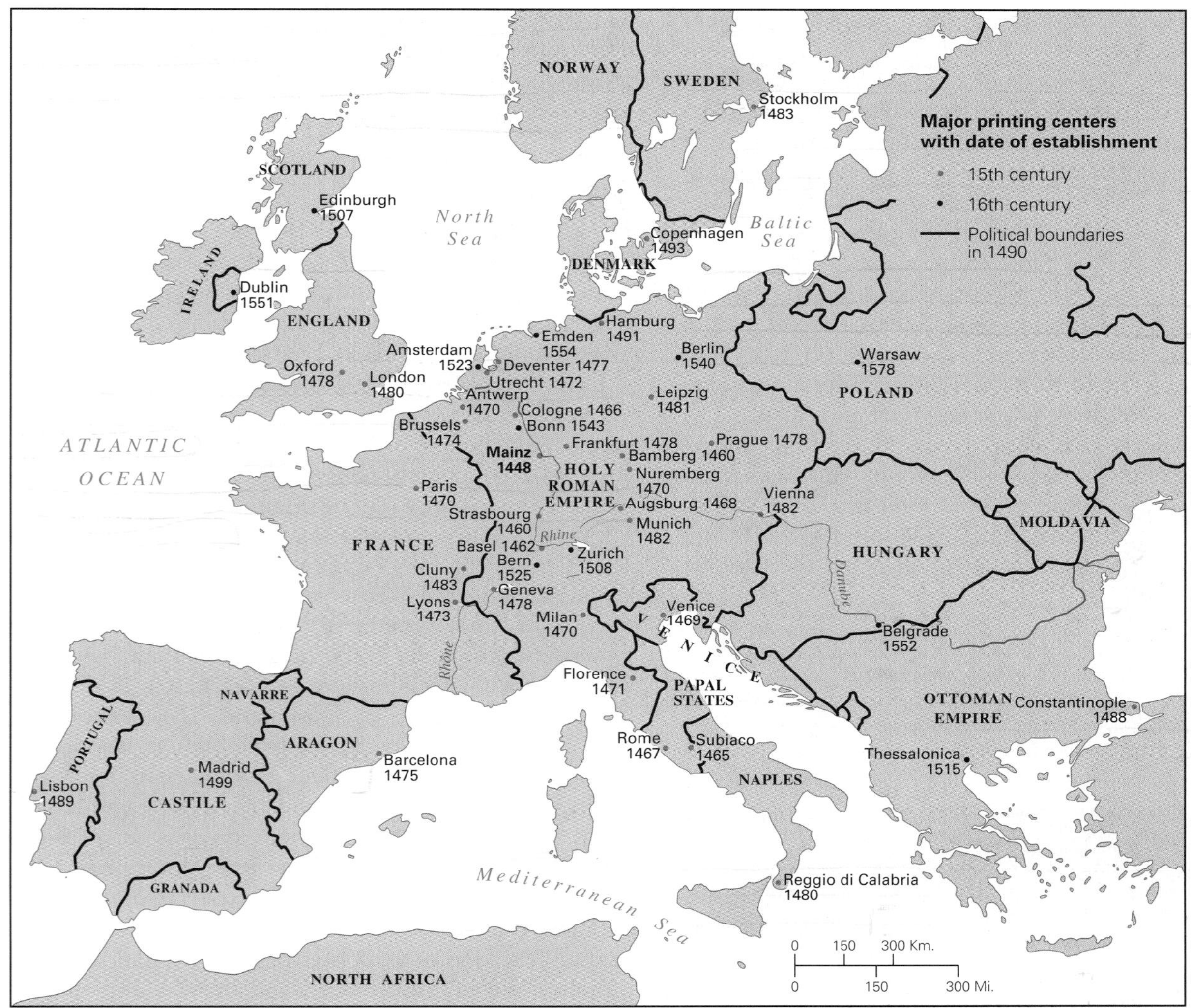

MAP 13.2 The Growth of Printing in Europe Although many commercial and academic centers developed printing technology, the press at Venice, employing between four hundred and five hundred people and producing one-eighth of all printed books, was by far the largest in Europe.

Clocks

The English word *quantification* was first used in 1840, but five centuries earlier, before the invention of movable type, Europeans learned how to quantify, or measure, time with the mechanical clock. Who invented the clock remains a subject of scientific debate. Between A.D. 700 and 1000, Arabs relied on the sundial, using their knowledge of astronomy to correct for the varying motion of the sun during the course of the year. The Arabs knew that the length of daylight, caused by the changing distance between the earth and the sun as the earth moves in elliptical orbit, varies with the seasons. Chinese knowledge of mechanical clocks may have allowed Gerbert, later Pope Sylvester II (999–1003), to build the first mechanical clock in the West.

The English word *clock* resembles the French *cloche* and the German *Glocke,* all meaning "bells." In monastic houses, bells determined the times for the recitation of the Hours, the Work of God. Bells also paced the life of the rural world nearby, but country people needed only approximate times—dawn, noon, sunset—for their work.

The measurement of time played a much more urgent role for city people.

Buying and selling goods had initiated city people into the practice of quantification: they needed precise measurement of the day's hours. City people's time was what the American polymath Benjamin Franklin later called it: money. In the Italian cities, clocks must have been widespread, since the poet Dante, writing about 1320, took them for granted. Mechanical clocks, usually installed on the cathedral or town church, were in general use in Germany by the 1330s, in England by the 1370s, and in France by the 1380s.[23]

Clocks contributed to the development of a mentality that conceived of the universe in visual and quantitative terms. Measuring the world brought not only understanding of it but the urge to control it. The mechanical clock enabled Europeans to divide time into equal hours, allowing the working day to be fixed in both winter and summer. The Maya in Central America and the Chinese had theoretical knowledge of time, but Europeans put that knowledge to practical use. Along with cannon and printing, clocks gave Europeans technological advantages over other peoples.[24]

Mechanical Clock Slowly falling weights provide the force that pushes the figures' arms to strike the bells on the quarter-hour in this sixteenth-century German clock. The sound of a machine now marked time. *(Biblíothèque royale Albert 1er, Brussels)*

Women and Work

We know relatively little about the lives of individual women of the middle and working classes in the period from about 1300 to 1600. Most women married and thus carried all the domestic responsibilities of the home. They also frequently worked outside the home.

In the Venetian Arsenal, the state-controlled dock and shipbuilding area (the largest single industrial plant in Europe and the builder of the biggest fleet) women made the ships' sails. Women were heavily involved in the Florentine textile industry, weaving cloth and reeling and winding silk. In the 1560s, a woman named Suzanne Erkur managed the imperial silver mint at Kutná Hora in Bohemia. Women conducted the ferry service across the Rhône River at Lyons. Throughout Europe rural women assisted fathers and husbands in the many agricultural tasks, and urban women helped in shops and businesses. Widows often ran their husbands' establishments. Tens of thousands of women worked as midwives, maids, cooks, laundresses, and household servants. From the port city of Dubrovnik (formerly Ragusa) on the Dalmatian coast came tens of thousands of female slaves to enter domestic service in upper-class households throughout Italy[25] (see page 438).

What of women of the upper classes? During the Renaissance, the status of upper-class women declined. In terms of the kind of work they performed, their access to property and political power, and their role in shaping the outlook of their society, women in the Renaissance ruling classes generally had less power than comparable women in the feudal age. As mentioned earlier (see page 430), well-to-do girls generally received an education, but even so, men everywhere held the conviction that a woman's attention should be focused on the domestic affairs of family life. The Italian humanist and polymath Leon Battista Alberti (1404–1472), discussing morality in his *On the Family,* stressed that a wife's role should be restricted to the orderliness of the household, food and the serving of meals, the education of children, and the supervision of servants. The Spanish humanist Juan Luis Vives (1492–1540), in his *Instruction of the Christian Woman,* held that a woman's sphere should be the home, not the public arena, where she might compete with men. The English statesman Sir Thomas Smith (1513–1577) wrote in *The English Commonwealth* that women were "those whom nature hath made to keepe home and

Working Women Women did virtually every kind of work in Renaissance Europe. They often sold food, cloth, handmade jewelry, trinkets, and other merchandise in the town marketplace, just as many women in developing countries do today. *(Scala/Art Resource, NY)*

to nourish the familie and children, and not to meddle with affairs abroad."[26] Wealthy women might support charitable organizations, but men denied them any sort of political or legal activity.

Excluded from the public arena, the noblewoman or spouse of a rich merchant managed the household or court (see page 418), where the husband displayed his wealth and power (the larger the number of servants and retainers, the greater his prestige). Households depended on domestic servants, and the lady of the house had to have the shrewdness and managerial prudence to employ capable cooks, maids, tailors and seamstresses, laundresses, gardeners, coachmen, stable hands, nurses, and handymen. If a prosperous Florentine or Venetian merchant's household had fifteen to twenty servants, a great lord or a Medici banker could easily employ four times that number. The lady of the house had to make sure that all these people were adequately fed and clothed; to maintain harmony among them; to tend anyone who fell ill, meaning that she must have at least a rudimentary knowledge of medications; and to look after the girl who "accidentally" became pregnant and then her child. Custom also laid on the lady the responsibility for providing the servants with religious instruction. Then there was the education of her own children and possibly the care of aged or infirm in-laws. Her husband expected her to entertain (which, depending on his position, could be an elaborate and complicated undertaking) and preside over each occasion with grace and, if possible, charm. All of these burdens, in addition to her own pregnancies, added up to an enormous responsibility.

Culture and Sexuality

With respect to love and sex, the Renaissance witnessed a downward shift in women's status. In contrast to the medieval tradition of relative sexual equality, Renaissance humanists laid the foundations for the bourgeois double standard. Castiglione, the foremost spokesman of Renaissance love and manners, completely separated love from sexuality. For women, sex was restricted entirely to marriage. Women were bound to chastity and then to the roles of wife and mother in a politically arranged marriage. Men, however, could pursue sensual indulgence outside marriage.[27]

Artemesia Gentileschi: Judith Slaying Holofernes The Old Testament Book of Judith tells the tale of the beautiful widow Judith, who first charms and then decapitates the Assyrian general Holofernes, thus saving Israel. The message is that trust in God will bring deliverance. The talented Roman artist Artemesia Gentileschi (1593–1652/3), elected to the Florentine Academy of Design at age twenty-three, rendered the story in this dramatic and gruesome painting, whose light and gushing blood give it great power. Some scholars hold that the painting is Gentileschi's pictorial revenge for her alleged rape by the decorative artist Agostino Tassi. *(Uffizi, Florence/Alinari/Art Resource, NY)*

Official attitudes toward rape provide an index of the status of women in the Renaissance. According to a study of the legal evidence from Venice in the years 1338 to 1358, rape was not considered a particularly serious crime against either the victim or society. Noble youths committed a higher percentage of rapes than their small numbers in Venetian society would imply. The rape of a young girl of marriageable age or a child under twelve was considered a graver crime than the rape of a married woman. Nevertheless, the punishment for rape of a noble, marriageable girl was only a fine or about six months' imprisonment. In an age when theft and robbery were punished by mutilation, and forgery and sodomy by burning, this penalty was very mild indeed. When a youth of the upper class was convicted of the rape of a non-noble girl, his punishment was even lighter. By contrast, the sexual assault of a noblewoman by a working-class man, which was extraordinarily rare, resulted in severe penalization because the crime had social and political overtones.

In the eleventh century, William the Conqueror had decreed that rapists be castrated, implicitly according women protection and a modicum of respect. But in the early Renaissance, Venetian laws and their enforcement show that the governing oligarchy believed that rape damaged, but only slightly, men's property—women.[28]

A new study of country women based on fifteenth-century Florentine court records raises interesting questions but provides inconclusive evidence about women's condition. These records read like twenty-first-century tabloids, with virtually every sensational criminal activity: incest, wife beatings, sexual assaults on children and nuns, murders provoked by adulterous relationships. For instance, one priest had a long love affair with a married woman and hired a "hit man" to kill the husband. Indicted for homicide and adultery, the priest was decapitated. In another case, while his wife was out shopping, middle-aged Muccino raped his eleven-year-old niece. The court ordered Muccino whipped with branches to the place of justice, where his penis was mutilated. The courts saw sexual crimes as "originating in bodily parts that had to be punished or removed."[29] But sexual crimes, however broadly defined, never constituted more than 5 percent of the courts' annual caseload. Fewer women appear in these fifteenth-century records than had appeared in similar records a century earlier. Why? We do not know.[30]

The term *homosexuality* was coined only in 1892, but erotic activity with a person of the same sex goes back very far in human history (see pages 202, 345–346). Medieval and Renaissance people used two terms concerning such activity: *sodomy,* meaning all sexual acts between persons of the same sex, whether male with male or female with female, and *sexual acts against nature,* meaning any act that did not lead to conception.[31] When early modern Italians used the term *sodomite,* they usually had males in mind, partly because those acts were most conspicuous, partly because theological and "scientific" teaching held that women could not have erotic pleasure without a man. While we tend to classify people according to the gender of their sexual partners, Renaissance people did not frame their understanding and representation of sexuality on this basis.

In the cities of Renaissance Italy, the sermons of the Franciscan Bernardino of Siena (1380–1444) and the Dominican Savonarola (1452–1498) severely condemned sodomitical activities, and civil authorities seem to have been preoccupied with it: Siena passed legislation against it in 1425, Venice in 1496, Florence in 1415, 1418, 1432, 1494, and 1542.[32] When a law is repeatedly put on the statute books, it is not observed or cannot be enforced. How prevalent was homosexuality? Florence provides a provocative case study.

On April 17, 1432, the Florentine government set up a special magistracy, the Office of the Night, to "root out . . . the abominable vice of sodomy." This board of professional men at least forty-five years of age and married was elected annually and charged with pursuing and punishing sodomitical activity between males.[33] The name of the magistracy derived from the nocturnal activities of most male encounters, especially in the spring and summer months, and on feast days and Sundays. Between 1432 and the abolition of the magistracy in 1502, about seventeen thousand men came to its attention, which, even over a seventy-year period, represents a great number in a population of about forty thousand. Sodomy was not a marginal practice.

Moreover, careful and statistical analysis of judicial records shows that all classes of society engaged in it—those in the textile trade, in commerce, in education, and in the food industry, especially butchers, as well as construction workers, tavern keepers, and innkeepers. Evidence also reveals that adult males rarely had sex together, or if they did, it did not come to the Office of the Night's attention. Rather, boys were the objects of desire. These roles carried cultural values. Florentines believed in a generational model in which different roles were appropriate to different stages in life. In a socially and sexually hierarchical world, the boy in the passive role was identified as subordinate, dependent, and mercenary, words usually applied to women. Florentines, however, never described the dominant partner in feminine terms, for he had not compromised his masculine

Thirteenth-Century Moral Code This illustration, from a French book of morals, interprets female and male homosexuality as the work of devils; modern science offers other explanations. *(Österreichische Nationalbibliothek)*

identity or violated a gender ideal. Only if an adult male assumed the passive role was his masculinity jeopardized. Such cases were extremely rare.[34]

Why was this kind of sexual activity so common? The evidence offers a variety of explanations. First among these is the general seclusion of "respectable" women and the late marriages of men. Perhaps 30 percent of the adult male population never married, and three-fourths of those who did postponed it, largely for economic reasons, until about age thirty-two. An occasional sexual experience with a boy did not preclude sex with women. Other explanations include the construction of male identity and of forms of male sociability.

In 1476 an informer denounced the carpenter Piero di Bartolomeo for sexual relations with Bartolomeo di Jacopo, son of a grocer. When interrogated, fifteen-year-old Bartolomeo di Jacopo confessed that Piero "did [this] out of great love and good brotherhood, because they are in a confraternity together, and he did as good neighbors do." Bartolomeo di Jacopo understood their relationship as being based on the traditional emotional bonds between members of their confraternity and neighborhood associations. Their sexual relationship, though forbidden, was woven into the entire fabric of their community life.[35]

Other explanations for youthful homoerotic activity include the desire for gifts, money, or some material reward from the adult partner; parental complicity in urging attractive teenage sons to accept the attentions of wealthy suitors; the need for companionship and same-age cohorts—that is, peer pressure; gang rapes; and soldiers' demands that youthful servants satisfy their sexual needs. Sex among males—kinsmen, neighbors, coworkers, and groups of friends—fashioned the collective male experience. Homoerotic relationships played important roles in defining stages of life, expressing distinctions of status, and shaping masculine gender identity.[36]

Slavery and Ethnicity

In a famous essay, the French historian Marc Bloch observed that "Western and Central Europe, taken as a whole, were never free of slaves during the High Middle Ages."[37] In central and eastern Europe, where political conditions were very unstable and permitted the enslavement of pagans, slavery allowed strong lords to satisfy cheaply the needs of their estates; slaves also offered merchants a commodity for profitable exchange with foreigners. Thus, in the period of eastward expansion (see Chapter 12), German lords seized Polish and Bohemian peoples; used them as agricultural laborers, domestics, and concubines; and sold the rest. In the thirteenth century, Prague was a large slave market. The word *slave* always carried a definite ethnic connotation: it meant an unfree person of Slavic background.[38]

In the fourteenth century, Genoa and Venice dominated the Mediterranean slave trade. The labor shortage caused by the Black Death led to the flow of Russians, Tartars, and Circassian slaves from Azov in the Crimea and of Serbs, Albanians, Greeks, and Hungarians from the Balkans. Venetian control of the northern regions of the Dalmatian coast enabled Venetian slavers to import large numbers of female slaves from the port city of Dubrovnik.[39] All of these people, Slavic but of different ethnic backgrounds, gradually intermingled with the native Italian population.

Ever since the time of the Roman republic, a few black people had lived in western Europe. They had come, along with white slaves, as the spoils of war. Even after the collapse of the Roman Empire, Muslim and Christian merchants continued to import them. The evidence of medieval art attests to the presence of Africans in Europe and to Europeans' awareness of them.

As in Slavic regions, unstable political conditions in many parts of Africa enabled enterprising merchants to seize people and sell them into slavery. Local authorities afforded them no protection. Long tradition, moreover, sanctioned the practice of slavery. Beginning in the fifteenth century, sizable numbers of black slaves entered Europe. Portuguese explorers imported perhaps a thousand a year and sold them at the markets of Seville, Barcelona, Marseilles, and Genoa. By the mid-sixteenth century, blacks, slave and free, constituted about 10 percent of the populations of the Portuguese cities of Lisbon and Évora; other cities had smaller percentages. In all, blacks made up roughly 3 percent of the Portuguese population. The Venetians specialized in the importation of white slaves, but blacks were so greatly in demand at the Renaissance courts of northern Italy that the Venetians defied papal threats of excommunication to secure them. Although blacks were concentrated in the Iberian Peninsula, there must have been some Africans in northern Europe as well. In the 1580s, for example, Queen Elizabeth I of England complained that there were too many "blackamoores" competing with needy English people for places as domestic servants.[40]

What roles did blacks play in Renaissance society? Although few written records survive, obviously black slaves in Europe hated the loss of their freedom, separation from their societal roots, and forced labor without

Carpaccio: Black Laborers on the Venetian Docks (detail) Enslaved and free blacks, besides working as gondoliers on the Venetian canals, served on the docks: here seven black men careen—clean, caulk, and repair—a ship. Carpaccio's reputation as one of Venice's outstanding painters rests on his eye for details of everyday life. *(Gallerie dell'Accademia, Venice/Scala/Art Resource, NY)*

compensation. No doubt, too, they disliked the alien culture, the cold climate, and the strange foods. But so far as we know, few who managed to secure their freedom through manumission or escape chose to return to Africa. The lack of black slave revolts in Europe, so common in South and North America and in Africa under colonial rule, attests to the small numbers and wide dispersion of blacks and to a relatively benign pattern of slavery. Moreover, the legal definition of *slave* never took on the rigid character in Europe that it did in the United States.

Within Africa, the economic goals of rulers and merchants took priority over any cultural, ethnic, or racial hostilities they may have felt toward Europeans. For example, in 1492 the king of the Congo learned of the arrival of Portuguese ships off the Congo estuary. He needed support in a local war and new resources; his biggest asset was a large concentration of slaves near his capital. So he accepted Christian baptism and began to exchange slaves for weapons and other Portuguese goods. His son Alfonso Mbemba Nzinga adopted a European lifestyle: he renamed his capital São Salvador; took on Portuguese dress, etiquette, and literacy; and assigned Portuguese titles to his officials and courtiers. Meanwhile, the flow of slaves from the region accelerated. Between 1500 and 1525, about seventeen hundred slaves a year were traded to the Portuguese. By 1530 between four thousand and five thousand were being sold to the Portuguese each year.[41] What does this tell us about Africans' attitudes toward white Europeans? First, obviously, the interests of African rulers and those of their peoples diverged considerably. Second, African rulers' and merchants' desire for revenue and goods was the driving force in the sale of black people to white Europeans.

Westerners tend to lump all sub-Saharan Africans into one category: black. However, Africans, like Europeans and Asians, belonged to and identified themselves by ethnic groups. In Africa, the world's second-largest continent, there were (and are) more than six hundred distinct ethnic groups. In addition, African slaves in the Iberian Peninsula (and elsewhere in Europe), like Slavic ones in Italy, intermingled with the people they lived among, and their offspring were, in fact, biracial.

However Africans may have been defined in Europe, black servants were much sought after, as the medieval interest in curiosities, the exotic, and the marvelous continued into the Renaissance. In the late fifteenth century, Isabella, the wife of Gian Galazzo Sforza, took pride in the fact that she owned ten blacks, seven of them females. A black lady's maid was both a curiosity and a symbol of wealth. In 1491 Isabella of Este, duchess of Mantua, instructed her agent to secure a black girl between four and eight years old, "shapely and as black as possible." The duchess saw the child as a source of entertainment: "We shall make her very happy and shall have great fun with her." She hoped the girl would become "the best buffoon in the world,"[42] as the cruel ancient practice of a noble household retaining a professional "fool" for the family's amusement persisted through the Renaissance—and even down to the twentieth century.

Adult black slaves served as maids, valets, and domestic servants. Italian aristocrats such as Marchesa Elena Grimaldi had their portraits painted with their black pageboys to indicate their wealth. The Venetians employed blacks—slave and free—as gondoliers and stevedores on the docks. In Portugal kings, nobles, laborers, monasteries and convents, and prostitutes owned slaves. They supplemented the labor force in virtually all occupations—as agricultural laborers, craftsmen, and seamen on ships going to Lisbon and Africa.[43] Tradition, stretching back at least as far as the thirteenth century, connected blacks with music and dance. In Renaissance Spain and Italy, blacks performed as dancers, as actors and actresses in courtly dramas, and as musicians, sometimes making up full orchestras.[44] Slavery during the Renaissance foreshadowed the American, especially the later Brazilian, pattern.

Before the sixteenth-century "discoveries" of the non-European world, Europeans had little concrete knowledge of Africans and their cultures. What Europeans did know was based on biblical accounts. The European attitude toward Africans was ambivalent. On the one hand, Europeans perceived Africa as a remote place, the home of strange people isolated by heresy and Islam from superior European civilization. Africans' contact, even as slaves, with Christian Europeans could only "improve" the blacks. Most Europeans' knowledge of the black as a racial type was based entirely on theological speculation. Theologians taught that God was light. Blackness, the opposite of light, therefore represented the hostile forces of the underworld: evil, sin, and the Devil. Thus the Devil was commonly represented as a black man in medieval and early Renaissance art (see the illustration on page 437). On the other hand, blackness possessed certain positive qualities. It symbolized the emptiness of worldly goods, the humility of the monastic way of life. Black clothes permitted a conservative and discreet display of wealth. Black vestments and funeral trappings indicated grief, and Christ had said that those who mourn are blessed. Until the exploration and observation of the sixteenth, seventeenth, and nineteenth centuries allowed, ever so slowly, for the development of more scientific knowledge, the Western conception of black people remained bound up with religious notions.[45] As for the sterile and meaningless concept of race, recent scholarship stresses that it emerged only in the late seventeenth century.[46] In Renaissance society, blacks, like women, were signs of wealth; both were used for display.

The Renaissance in the North

In the last quarter of the fifteenth century, students from the Low Countries, France, Germany, and England flocked to Italy, imbibed the "new learning," and carried it back to their countries. Northern humanists interpreted Italian ideas about and attitudes toward classical antiquity, individualism, and humanism in terms of their own traditions. The cultural traditions of northern Europe tended to remain more distinctly Christian, or at least pietistic, than those of Italy. But in Italy, secular and pagan themes and Greco-Roman motifs received more humanistic attention. North of the Alps, the Renaissance had a distinctly religious character, and humanists stressed biblical and early Christian themes. What fundamentally distinguished Italian humanists from northern ones is that the latter had a program for broad social reform based on Christian ideals.

Christian humanists were interested in the development of an ethical way of life. To achieve it, they believed that the best elements of classical and Christian cultures should be combined. For example, the classical ideals of calmness, stoical patience, and broad-mindedness should be joined in human conduct with the Christian virtues of love, faith, and hope. Northern humanists also stressed the use of reason, rather than acceptance of dogma, as the foundation for an ethical way of life. Like the Italians, they were impatient with Scholastic philosophy. Christian humanists had a profound faith in the power of human intellect to bring about moral and institutional reform. They believed that, although human nature had been corrupted by sin, it was fundamentally good and capable of improvement through education.

The Englishman Thomas More (1478–1535) towered above other figures in sixteenth-century English social and intellectual history. Trained as a lawyer, More lived as a student in the London Charterhouse, a Carthusian monastery. He subsequently married and practiced law but became deeply interested in the classics; his household served as a model of warm Christian family life and as a mecca for foreign and English humanists. In the career pattern of such Italian humanists as Petrarch, More entered government service under Henry VIII and was sent as ambassador to Flanders. There More found the time to write *Utopia* (1516), which presents a revolutionary view of society.

Utopia, which means "nowhere," describes an ideal socialistic community on an island somewhere off the mainland of the New World. All its children receive a good education, primarily in the Greco-Roman classics, and learning does not cease with maturity, for the goal of all education is to develop rational faculties. Adults divide their days between manual labor or business pursuits and various intellectual activities.

Because profits from business and property are held in common, there is absolute social equality. The Utopians use gold and silver to make chamber pots and to prevent wars by buying off their enemies. By this casual use of precious metals, More meant to suggest that the basic problems in society are caused by greed. Citizens of Utopia lead an ideal, nearly perfect existence because they live by reason; their institutions are perfect. More punned on the word *utopia,* which he termed "a good place. A good place which is no place."

More's ideas were profoundly original in the sixteenth century. Contrary to the long-prevailing view that vice and violence existed because women and men were basically corrupt, More maintained that acquisitiveness and private property promoted all sorts of vices and civil disorders. Since society protected private property, society's flawed institutions were responsible for corruption and war. According to More, the key to improvement and reform of the individual was reform of the social institutions that molded the individual. Today this view is so much taken for granted that it is difficult to appreciate how radical More's approach was in the sixteenth century.

Better known by contemporaries than Thomas More was the Dutch humanist Desiderius Erasmus (1466?–1536) of Rotterdam. Orphaned as a small boy, Erasmus was forced to enter a monastery. Although he intensely disliked the monastic life, he developed there an excellent knowledge of the Latin language and a deep appreciation for the Latin classics. During a visit to England in 1499, Erasmus met the scholar John Colet, who decisively influenced his life's work: the application of the best humanistic learning to the study and explanation of the Bible. As a mature scholar with an international reputation stretching from Cracow to London, a fame that rested largely on his exceptional knowledge of Greek, Erasmus could boast with truth, "I brought it about that humanism, which among the Italians . . . savored of nothing but pure paganism, began nobly to celebrate Christ."[47]

Erasmus's long list of publications includes *The Education of a Christian Prince* (1504), a book combining idealistic and practical suggestions for the formation of a ruler's character through the careful study of Plutarch, Aristotle, Cicero, and Plato; *The Praise of Folly* (1509), a satire of worldly wisdom and a plea for the simple and spontaneous Christian faith of children; and, most important, a critical edition of the Greek New Testament (1516). In the preface to the New Testament, Erasmus explained the purpose of his great work:

> *For I utterly dissent from those who are unwilling that the sacred Scriptures should be read by the unlearned translated into their vulgar tongue, as though Christ had taught such subtleties that they can scarcely be understood even by a few theologians. . . . Christ wished his mysteries to be published as openly as possible. I wish that even the weakest woman should read the Gospel—should read the epistles of Paul. And I wish these were translated into all languages, so that they might be read and understood, not only by Scots and Irishmen, but also by Turks and Saracens.*[48]

Two fundamental themes run through all of Erasmus's work. First, education is the means to reform, the key to moral and intellectual improvement. The core of education ought to be study of the Bible and the classics. (See the feature "Listening to the Past: An Age of Gold" on pages 452–453.) Second, the essence of Erasmus's thought is, in his own phrase, "the philosophy of Christ." By this Erasmus meant that Christianity is an inner attitude of the heart or spirit. Christianity is not formalism, special ceremonies, or law; Christianity is Christ—his life and what he said and did, not what theologians have written. The Sermon on the Mount, for Erasmus, expresses the heart of the Christian message.

Whereas the writings of Erasmus and More have strong Christian themes and have drawn the attention primarily of scholars, the stories of French humanist François Rabelais (1490?–1553) possess a distinctly secular flavor and have attracted broad readership among the literate public. Rabelais's *Gargantua* and *Pantagruel*

Rogier van der Weyden: Deposition Taking as his subject the suffering and death of Jesus, a popular theme of Netherlandish piety, van der Weyden describes (in an inverted **T**) Christ's descent from the cross, surrounded by nine sorrowing figures. An appreciation of the human anatomy, the rich fabrics of the clothes, and the pierced and bloody hands of Jesus were all intended to touch the viewers' emotions. *(Museo del Prado/Scala/Art Resource, NY)*

(serialized between 1532 and 1552) belong among the great comic masterpieces of world literature. These stories' gross and robust humor introduced the adjective *Rabelaisian* into the language.

Gargantua and *Pantagruel* can be read on several levels: as a comic romance about the adventures of the giant Gargantua and his son, Pantagruel; as a spoof on contemporary French society; as a program for educational reform; or as an illustration of Rabelais's prodigious learning. The reader enters a world of Renaissance vitality, ribald joviality, and intellectual curiosity. In his travels, Gargantua meets various absurd characters, and within their hilarious exchanges occur serious discussions of religion, politics, philosophy, and education. Like More and Erasmus, Rabelais did not denounce institutions directly. Like Erasmus, Rabelais satirized hypocritical monks, pedantic academics, and pompous lawyers. But whereas Erasmus employed intellectual cleverness and sophisticated wit, Rabelais applied wild and gross humor. Like Thomas More, Rabelais believed that institutions molded individuals and that education was the key to a moral and healthy life. Whereas the middle-class inhabitants of More's Utopia lived lives of restrained moderation, the aristocratic residents of Rabelais's Thélème lived for the gratification of their physical instincts and rational curiosity.

The distinctly religious orientation of the literary works of the Renaissance in the north also characterized northern art and architecture. Some Flemish painters, notably Rogier van der Weyden (1399/1400–1464) and Jan van Eyck (1366–1441), were considered the artistic equals of Italian painters, were much admired in Italy, and worked a generation before Leonardo and Michelangelo. Van Eyck, one of the earliest artists to use oil-based paints successfully, shows the Flemish love for detail in paintings such as *Ghent Altarpiece* and the portrait *Giovanni Arnolfini and His Bride;* the effect is great realism and remarkable attention to human personality.

Another Flemish painter, Jerome Bosch (1450?–1516), frequently used religious themes, but in combination with grotesque fantasies, colorful imagery, and peasant folk legends (see page 461). Many of Bosch's paintings reflect the confusion and anguish often associated with the end of the Middle Ages.

A quasi-spiritual aura infuses architectural monuments in the north. The city halls of wealthy Flemish towns such as Bruges, Brussels, Louvain, and Ghent strike the viewer more as shrines to house the bones of saints than as settings for the mundane decisions of politicians and business people. Northern architecture was little influenced by the classical revival so obvious in Renaissance Rome and Florence.

Politics and the State in the Renaissance (ca 1450–1521)

The High Middle Ages had witnessed the origins of many of the basic institutions of the modern state. Sheriffs, inquests, juries, circuit judges, professional bureaucracies, and representative assemblies all trace their origins to the twelfth and thirteenth centuries (see pages 340–344). The linchpin for the development of states, however, was strong monarchy, and during the period of the Hundred Years' War, no ruler in western Europe was able to provide effective leadership. The resurgent power of feudal nobilities weakened the centralizing work begun earlier.

Beginning in the fifteenth century, rulers utilized the aggressive methods implied by Renaissance political ideas to rebuild their governments. First in Italy, then in France, England, and Spain, rulers began the work of reducing violence, curbing unruly nobles, and establishing domestic order. Divided into scores of independent principalities, Germany could not deal with the Roman church as an equal.

The dictators and oligarchs of the Italian city-states, together with Louis XI of France, Henry VII of England, and Ferdinand of Aragon, were tough, cynical, calculating rulers. In their ruthless push for power and strong governments, they subordinated morality to hard results. They preferred to be secure, if feared, rather than loved. They could not have read Machiavelli's *The Prince,* but they acted as though they understood its ideas.

Some historians have called Louis XI, Henry VII, and Ferdinand and Isabella in Spain "new monarchs." The term is only partly appropriate. These monarchs were new in that they invested kingship with a strong sense of royal authority and national purpose. They stressed that monarchy was the one institution that linked all classes and peoples within definite territorial boundaries. These rulers emphasized royal majesty and royal sovereignty and insisted on the respect and loyalty of all subjects. These monarchs ruthlessly suppressed opposition and rebellion, especially from the nobility. They loved the business of kingship and worked hard at it.

In other respects, however, the methods of these rulers, which varied from country to country, were not so new. They reasserted long-standing ideas and practices of strong monarchs in the Middle Ages. They seized on the maxim of the Justinian *Code,* "What pleases the prince has the force of law," to advance their authority. Some medieval rulers, such as Henry I of England, had depended heavily on middle-class officials. Renaissance rulers, too, tended to rely on middle-class civil servants. With tax revenues, medieval rulers had built armies to crush feudal anarchy. Renaissance townspeople with commercial and business interests naturally wanted a reduction of violence, and usually they were willing to pay taxes in order to achieve it.

France

The Hundred Years' War left France drastically depopulated, commercially ruined, and agriculturally weak. Nonetheless, the ruler whom Joan of Arc had seen crowned at Reims, Charles VII (r. 1422–1461), revived the monarchy and France. He seemed an unlikely person to do so. Frail, indecisive, and burdened with questions about his paternity (his father had been deranged; his mother, notoriously promiscuous), Charles VII nevertheless began France's long recovery.

Charles reconciled the Burgundians and Armagnacs, who had been waging civil war for thirty years. By 1453 French armies had expelled the English from French soil except in Calais. Charles reorganized the royal council, giving increased influence to middle-class men, and strengthened royal finances through such taxes as the **gabelle** (on salt) and the *taille* (land tax). These taxes remained the Crown's chief sources of income until the Revolution of 1789.

By establishing regular companies of cavalry and archers—recruited, paid, and inspected by the state—Charles created the first permanent royal army. In 1438 Charles published the **Pragmatic Sanction of Bourges**, asserting the superiority of a general council over the papacy, giving the French crown major control over the appointment of bishops, and depriving the pope of French ecclesiastical revenues. The Pragmatic Sanction established Gallican (or French) liberties because it affirmed the special rights of the French crown over the French church. Greater control over the church and the army helped to consolidate the authority of the French crown.

Charles's son Louis XI (r. 1461–1483), called the "Spider King" because of his treacherous character, was very much a Renaissance prince. Facing the perpetual French problem of reduction of feudal disorder, he saw money as the answer. Louis promoted new industries, such as silk weaving at Lyons and Tours. He welcomed foreign craftsmen and entered into commercial treaties with England, Portugal, and the towns of the Hanseatic League (see page 354). He used the revenues raised through these economic activities and severe taxation to improve the army. With the army, Louis stopped aristocratic brigandage and slowly cut into urban independence.

Luck favored his goal of expanding royal authority and unifying the kingdom. On the timely death of Charles the Bold, duke of Burgundy, in 1477, Louis invaded Burgundy and gained some territories. Three years later, the extinction of the house of Anjou brought Louis the counties of Anjou, Bar, Maine, and Provence.

Two further developments strengthened the French monarchy. The marriage of Louis XII (r. 1498–1515) and Anne of Brittany added the large western duchy of Brittany to the state. Then the French king Francis I and Pope Leo X reached a mutually satisfactory agreement in 1516. The new treaty, the Concordat of Bologna, rescinded the Pragmatic Sanction's assertion of the superiority of a general council over the papacy and approved the pope's right to receive the first year's income of new bishops and abbots. In return, Leo X recognized the French ruler's right to select French bishops and abbots. French kings thereafter effectively controlled the appointment and thus the policies of church officials within the kingdom.

England

English society suffered severely from the disorders of the fifteenth century. The aristocracy dominated the government of Henry IV (r. 1399–1413) and indulged in mischievous violence at the local level. Population, decimated by the Black Death, continued to decline. Between 1455 and 1471, adherents of the ducal houses of York and Lancaster waged civil war, commonly called the Wars of the Roses because the symbol of the Yorkists was a white rose and that of the Lancastrians a red one. The chronic disorder hurt trade, agriculture, and domestic industry. Under the pious but mentally disturbed Henry VI, the authority of the monarchy sank lower than it had been in centuries.

The Yorkist Edward IV (r. 1461–1483) began establishing domestic tranquillity. He succeeded in defeating the Lancastrian forces and after 1471 began to reconstruct the monarchy. Edward, his brother Richard III (r. 1483–1485), and Henry VII (r. 1485–1509) of the Welsh house of Tudor worked to restore royal prestige, to crush the power of the nobility, and to establish order and law at the local level. All three rulers used methods that Machiavelli himself would have praised—ruthlessness, efficiency, and secrecy.

The Hundred Years' War had been financed by Parliament. Dominated by baronial factions, Parliament had been the arena where the nobility exerted its power. As long as the monarchy was dependent on the Lords and the Commons for revenue, the king had to call Parliament. Edward IV and subsequently the Tudors, excepting Henry VIII, conducted foreign policy on the basis of diplomacy, avoiding expensive wars. Thus the English monarchy did not depend on Parliament for money, and the Crown undercut that source of aristocratic influence.

Henry VII did summon several meetings of Parliament in the early years of his reign primarily to confirm laws, but the center of royal authority was the **royal council**, which governed at the national level. There Henry VII revealed his distrust of the nobility: though not completely excluded, very few great lords were among the king's closest advisers. Regular representatives on the council numbered between twelve and fifteen men, and while many gained high ecclesiastical rank (the means, as it happened, by which the Crown paid them), their origins were in the lesser landowning class, and their education was in law. They were, in a sense, middle-class.

The royal council handled any business the king put before it—executive, legislative, and judicial. For example, the council conducted negotiations with foreign governments and secured international recognition of the Tudor dynasty through the marriage in 1501 of Henry VII's eldest son, Arthur, to Catherine of Aragon, the daughter of Ferdinand and Isabella of Spain. The council dealt with real or potential aristocratic threats through a judicial offshoot, the **court of Star Chamber,** so called because of the stars painted on the ceiling of the room. The court applied principles of Roman law, and its methods were sometimes terrifying: accused persons were not entitled to see evidence against them, sessions were secret, torture could be applied to extract confessions, and juries were not called. These procedures ran directly counter to English common-law precedents, but they effectively reduced aristocratic troublemaking.

Unlike the continental countries of Spain and France, England had no standing army or professional civil service bureaucracy. The Tudors relied on the support of unpaid local officials, the **justices of the peace.** These influential landowners in the shires handled all the work of local government. They apprehended and punished criminals, enforced parliamentary statutes, fixed wages and prices, maintained proper standards of weights and measures, and even checked up on moral behavior.

The Tudors won the support of the influential upper middle class because the Crown linked government policy with the interests of that class. A commercial or agricultural upper class fears and dislikes few things more than disorder and violence. The Tudors promoted peace and social order, and the gentry did not object to arbitrary methods, like those of the court of Star Chamber, because the government had halted the long period of anarchy.

Secretive, cautious, and thrifty, Henry VII rebuilt the monarchy. He encouraged the cloth industry and built up the English merchant marine. English exports of wool and the royal export tax on that wool steadily increased. Henry crushed an invasion from Ireland and secured peace with Scotland through the marriage of his daughter Margaret to the Scottish king. When Henry VII died in 1509, he left a country at peace both domestically and internationally, a substantially augmented treasury, and the dignity and role of the royal majesty much enhanced.

Spain

While England and France laid the foundations of unified nation-states during the Renaissance, Spain remained a conglomerate of independent kingdoms. Castile and León formed a single political organization, but Aragon consisted of the principalities of Aragon, Valencia, Majorca, Sicily, Cardeña, and Naples, each tied to the crown of Aragon in a different way. On the one hand, the legacy of Hispanic, Roman, Visigothic, Jewish, and Muslim peoples made for rich cultural diversity; on the other hand, the Iberian Peninsula lacked a common cultural tradition.

The centuries-long reconquista—the wars of the northern Christian kingdoms to control the entire peninsula (see pages 285–286)—had military and religious objectives: conversion or expulsion of the Muslims and Jews and political control of the south. By the middle of the fifteenth century, the kingdoms of Castile and Aragon dominated the weaker Navarre, Portugal, and Granada, and the Iberian Peninsula, with the exception of Granada, had been won for Christianity. But even the wedding in 1469 of the dynamic and aggressive Isabella of Castile and the crafty and persistent Ferdinand of Aragon did not bring about administrative unity. Rather, their marriage constituted a dynastic union of two royal houses, not the political union of two peoples. Although Ferdinand and Isabella (r. 1474–1516) pursued a common foreign policy, Spain existed until about 1700 as a loose confederation of separate kingdoms (see Map 13.3), each maintaining its own *cortes* (parliament), laws, courts, and systems of coinage and taxation.

To curb the rebellious and warring aristocracy, Ferdinand and Isabella revived an old medieval institution: the **hermandades,** or "brotherhoods," which were popular groups in the towns given authority to act as local police forces and as judicial tribunals. The hermandades repressed violence with such savage punishments that by 1498 they could be disbanded.

The decisive step Ferdinand and Isabella took to curb aristocratic power was the restructuring of the royal council. Aristocrats and great territorial magnates were rigorously excluded; thus the influence of the nobility on state policy was greatly reduced. Ferdinand and Isabella intended the council to be the cornerstone of their government system, with full executive, judicial, and legislative powers under the monarchy. The council was also to be responsible for the supervision of local authorities. The king and queen therefore appointed to the council only people of middle-class background. The council and various government boards recruited men trained in Roman law, which exalted the power of the Crown as the embodiment of the state.

In the extension of royal authority and the consolidation of the territories of Spain, the church was the linchpin. If the Spanish crown could select the higher clergy, then the monarchy could influence ecclesiastical policy, wealth, and military resources. Through a diplomatic alliance with the Spanish pope Alexander VI, the Spanish

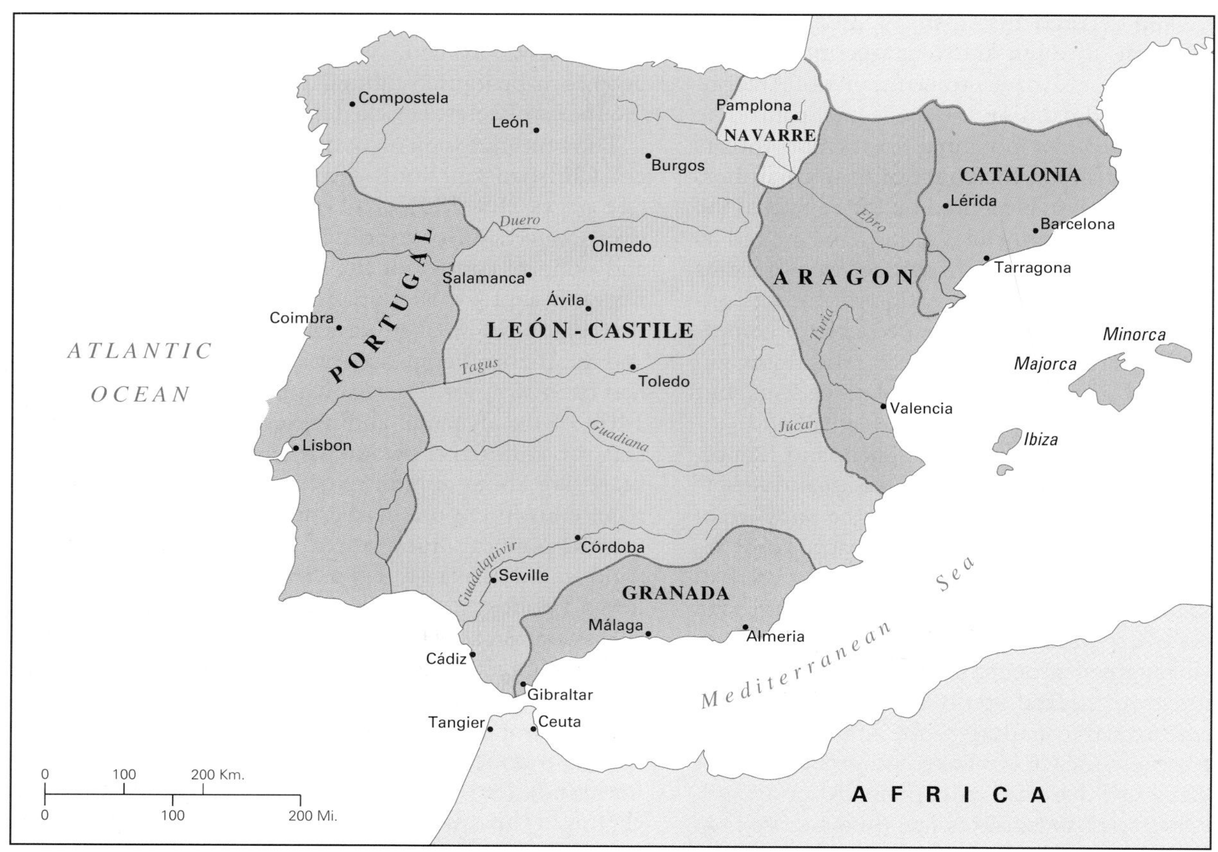

MAP 13.3 Spain in 1492 The marriage of Ferdinand of Aragon and Isabella of Castile in 1469 represented a dynastic union of two houses, not a political union of two peoples. Some principalities, such as León (part of Castile) and Catalonia (part of Aragon), had their own cultures, languages, and legal systems. Barcelona, the port city of Catalonia, controlled a commercial empire throughout the Mediterranean. The culture of Granada was heavily Muslim.

monarchs secured the right to appoint bishops in Spain and in the Hispanic territories in America. This power enabled the "Catholic Kings of Spain," a title granted Ferdinand and Isabella by the papacy, to establish, in effect, a national church.[49]

Revenues from ecclesiastical estates provided the means to raise an army to continue the reconquista. The victorious entry of Ferdinand and Isabella into Granada on January 6, 1492, signaled the culmination of eight centuries of Spanish struggle against the Arabs in southern Spain and the conclusion of the reconquista (see Map 9.3 on page 286). Granada in the south was incorporated into the Spanish kingdom, and in 1512 Ferdinand conquered Navarre in the north.

There still remained a sizable and, in the view of the majority of the Spanish people, potentially dangerous minority, the Jews. During the long centuries of the reconquista, Christian kings had renewed Jewish rights and privileges; in fact, Jewish industry, intelligence, and money had supported royal power. While Christians of all classes borrowed from Jewish moneylenders, and while all who could afford them sought Jewish physicians, a strong undercurrent of resentment of Jewish influence and wealth festered. When the kings of France and England had expelled the Jews from their kingdoms (see pages 344–345), many had sought refuge in Spain. In the fourteenth century, Jews formed an integral and indispensable part of Spanish life. With vast numbers of

Muslims, Jews, and Moorish Christians, medieval Spain represented the most diverse and cosmopolitan country in Europe. Diversity and cosmopolitanism, however, were not medieval social ideals.

Since ancient times, governments had seldom tolerated religious pluralism; religious faiths that differed from the official state religion were considered politically dangerous. But in the fourteenth century, anti-Semitism in Spain rose more from popular sentiment than from royal policies. Aggravated by fiery anti-Jewish preaching, by economic dislocation, and by the search for a scapegoat during the Black Death, the fourteenth century witnessed rising anti-Semitic feeling. In 1331 a mob attacked the Jewish community of Gerona in Catalonia. In 1355 royal troops massacred Jews in Toledo. On June 4, 1391, inflamed by "religious" preaching, mobs sacked and burned the Jewish community in Seville and compelled such Jews as survived to accept baptism. From Seville anti-Semitic pogroms swept the towns of Valencia, Barcelona, Burgos, Madrid, and Segovia. One scholar estimates that 40 percent of the Jewish population of Spain was killed or forced to convert.[50] Those converted were called *conversos, Marranos,* or **New Christians,** the three terms here used interchangeably.

King Ferdinand was not a religious fanatic. He was a Renaissance prince who wanted to *appear* as a moral and devout Christian, respectful of public opinion. He feared urban rioting and disorder, but he knew that the vast majority of the Spanish people hated the conversos. If the Crown protected them, it would lose popular support. Ferdinand resolved the dilemma by seeking papal permission to set up the Inquisition in Spain; if the actions of the Inquisition provoked public criticism, the papacy could be blamed. Pope Sixtus IV's bull authorizing the Inquisition reached Spain in November 1478, and on September 28, 1480, Ferdinand and Isabella ordered the establishment of tribunals to "search out and punish converts from Judaism who had transgressed against Christianity by secretly adhering to Jewish beliefs and performing rites of the Jews."[51]

What do we know of these New Christians? Why did they inspire such hostility? How did they view their religious position? In the administration of Castile, New Christians held the royal secretaryship, controlled the royal treasury, and composed a third of the royal council. In the church, they held high positions as archbishops, bishops, and abbots. In the administration of the towns, conversos often held the highest public offices; in Toledo they controlled the collection of royal revenues. They included some of the leading merchants and business people. They also served great magnates, and by intermarrying with the nobility, they gained political leverage. In the professions of medicine and law, New Christians held the most prominent positions. Numbering perhaps 200,000 in a total Spanish population of about 7.5 million, New Christians and Jews exercised influence disproportionate to their numbers. Aristocratic grandees resented their financial dependence, the poor hated the converso tax collectors, and churchmen doubted the sincerity of their conversions.

Recent scholarship has carefully analyzed documents written by New Christians for their reactions to the rising anti-Semitism. They identified themselves as Christians. In the 1480s, they unanimously insisted that they were happy to be Christians and failed to see why they should be labeled New Christians: many came from families that had received baptism generations before. They argued that just as Christ had never abandoned the ancient (Hebrew) Law, so they had not abandoned it; in fact, they had a better and clearer understanding of the Christian faith. For the New Christians, the issue was not that they had relinquished the faith of the Jews (and secretly reconverted); rather, in accepting Christianity, they had become real Jews and, in following Jesus, real Christians.[52]

This argument satisfied neither the Jews nor the conversos' enemies. The Jewish reaction to persecution of the conversos was, bluntly put, "Well, we told you so; it's just what you get."[53] Searching for a viable principle to use against both New Christians and Jews, their detractors hit not on what conversos believed, not on what they did, but on what they *were* as human beings. Hence arose the following racial theory: "Since race, they maintained, formed man's qualities and indeed his entire mental constitution, the Marranos, who were all offspring of Jews, retained the racial makeup of their forebears. . . . [E]thnically they were what they (or their ancestors) had been before their conversion to Christianity; in other words, they were Jews."[54] This absurd racist theory, which violated scriptural teaching, maintained that all conversos were malicious, immoral, and criminally inclined by their nature, and thus they could not be truly converted to Christianity.

Fifteenth-century Spanish anti-Semitism emerged at the very time a Spanish national feeling was emerging, a national sentiment that looked to the building of a single nation. Whereas earlier anti-Semitism, such as that during the time of the Black Death, alleged Jewish schemes to kill off entire Christian populations—by poisoning the wells, for example, from which Jews derived no profit—fifteenth-century theories held that Jews or

Felipe Bigarny: Ferdinand the Catholic and Isabella the Catholic All governments try to cultivate a popular image. For Ferdinand and Isabella, it was the appearance of piety. Contemporaries, such as the Burgundian sculptor Bigarny, portrayed them as paragons of Christian piety, as shown in these polychrome wooden statues. If Isabella's piety was perhaps more genuine, she used it—together with rich ceremony, elaborate dress, and a fierce determination—to assert royal authority. *(Capilla Real, Granada/Laurie Platt Winfrey, Inc.)*

New Christians planned to take over all public offices in Spain. Jews, therefore, represented a grave threat to national unity.[55]

Although the Inquisition was a religious institution established to ensure the Catholic faith, it was controlled by the Crown and served primarily as a politically unifying tool. Because the Spanish Inquisition commonly applied torture to extract confessions, first from lapsed conversos, then from Muslims, and later from Protestants, it gained a notorious reputation. Thus the word *inquisition,* meaning "any judicial inquiry conducted with ruthless severity," came into the English language. The methods of the Spanish Inquisition were cruel, though not as cruel as the investigative methods of some twentieth-century governments. Shortly after the reduction of the Moorish stronghold at Granada in 1492, Isabella and Ferdinand issued an edict expelling all practicing Jews from Spain. Of the community of perhaps 200,000 Jews, 150,000 fled. (Efforts were made, through last-minute conversions, to retain good Jewish physicians.) Absolute religious orthodoxy and purity of blood (untainted by Jews or Muslims) served as the theoretical foundation of the Spanish national state.

The diplomacy of the Catholic rulers of Spain achieved a success they never anticipated. Partly out of hatred for the French and partly out of a desire to gain international recognition for their new dynasty, Ferdinand and Isabella in 1496 married their second daughter, Joanna, heiress to Castile, to the archduke Philip, heir through his mother to the Burgundian Netherlands and through his father to the Holy Roman Empire. Philip and Joanna's son, Charles V (r. 1519–1556), thus succeeded to a vast patrimony. When Charles's son Philip II joined Portugal to the Spanish crown in 1580, the Iberian Peninsula was at last politically united. The various kingdoms, however, were administered separately.

Summary

The Italian Renaissance rested on the phenomenal economic growth of the High Middle Ages. In the period from about 1050 to 1300, a new economy emerged based on Venetian and Genoese shipping and long-distance trade and on Florentine banking and cloth manufacture. These commercial activities, combined with the struggle of urban communes for political independence from surrounding feudal lords, led to the appearance of a new aristocratic class. The centuries extending roughly from 1300 to 1600 witnessed a remarkable intellectual flowering. Based on a strong interest in the ancient world, the Renaissance had a classicizing influence on many facets of culture: law, literature, government, education, religion, and art. In the city-states of fifteenth- and sixteenth-century Italy, oligarchic or despotic powers governed; Renaissance culture was manipulated to enhance the power of those rulers.

Expanding outside Italy, the intellectual features of this movement affected the culture of all Europe. The intellectual characteristics of the Renaissance were a secular attitude toward life, a belief in individual potential, and a serious interest in the Latin classics. The printing press revolutionized communication. Meanwhile, the status of women in society declined, and black people entered Europe in sizable numbers for the first time since the collapse of the Roman Empire. Male culture in Italian cities had a strongly homoerotic character, reflecting a significant contrast between Renaissance attitudes toward male sexuality and attitudes today. In northern Europe, city merchants and rural gentry allied with rising monarchies. With taxes provided by business people, kings established greater peace and order, both essential for trade. Northern humanism had a more pietistic strain than did the Italian. In Spain, France, and England, rulers also emphasized royal dignity and authority, and they utilized Machiavellian ideas to ensure the preservation and continuation of their governments. Feudal monarchies gradually evolved in the direction of nation-states.

Key Terms

Renaissance
communes
popolo
signori
oligarchies
republic
princely courts
individualism
humanism
secularism
The Prince
gabelle
Pragmatic Sanction of Bourges
royal council
court of Star Chamber
justices of the peace
hermandades
New Christians

Notes

1. See L. Martines, *Power and Imagination: City-States in Renaissance Italy* (New York: Vintage Books, 1980), esp. pp. 332–333.
2. Ibid., pp. 22–61.
3. Ibid., p. 221.
4. Quoted in J. Burckhardt, *The Civilization of the Renaissance in Italy* (London: Phaidon Books, 1951), p. 89.
5. *Memoirs of Benvenuto Cellini; A Florentine Artist; Written by Himself* (London: J. M. Dent & Sons, 1927), p. 2.
6. See C. Trinkaus, *In Our Image and Likeness: Humanity and Divinity in Italian Humanist Thought,* vol. 2 (London: Constable, 1970), pp. 505–529.
7. B. Burroughs, ed., *Vasari's Lives of the Artists* (New York: Simon & Schuster, 1946), pp. 164–165.
8. See Martines, *Power and Imagination,* chap. 13, esp. pp. 241, 243.
9. R. A. Goldthwaite, *Wealth and the Demand for Art in Italy, 1300–1600* (Baltimore: Johns Hopkins University Press, 1993), p. 5.
10. Ibid., p. 213.
11. Ibid., pp. 224–229.
12. Ibid., pp. 121–129.
13. See A. Hauser, *The Social History of Art,* vol. 2 (New York: Vintage Books, 1959), chap. 3, esp. pp. 60, 68.
14. G. Bull, trans., *Aretino: Selected Letters* (Baltimore: Penguin Books, 1976), p. 109.
15. Quoted in P. and L. Murray, *A Dictionary of Art and Artists* (Baltimore: Penguin Books, 1963), p. 125.
16. Quoted in W. H. Woodward, *Vittorino da Feltre and Other Humanist Educators* (Cambridge: Cambridge University Press, 1897), pp. 96–97.
17. M. L. King, "Book-Lined Cells: Women and Humanism in the Early Italian Renaissance," in *Beyond Their Sex: Learned Women of the European Past,* ed. P. H. Labalme (New York: New York University Press, 1980), pp. 66–81, esp. p. 73.
18. C. E. Detmold, trans., *The Historical, Political and Diplomatic Writings of Niccolò Machiavelli* (Boston: J. R. Osgood, 1882), pp. 51–52.
19. Ibid., pp. 54–55.
20. See F. Gilbert, *Machiavelli and Guicciardini: Politics and History in Sixteenth Century Florence* (New York: W. W. Norton, 1984), pp. 197–200.
21. E. L. Eisenstein, *The Printing Press as an Agent of Change: Communications and Cultural Transformations in Early Modern Europe,* vol. 1 (New York: Cambridge University Press, 1979), p. 135. For an overall discussion, see pp. 126–159.

22. See L. Hunt, *The Invention of Pornography: Obscenity and the Origins of Modernity, 1500–1800* (New York: Zone Books, 1993), pp. 10, 93–95.
23. See A. W. Crosby, *The Measure of Reality: Quantification and Western Society* (New York: Cambridge University Press, 1997), pp. 76–78.
24. Ibid., pp. 49–74.
25. See Susan Mosher Stuard, "Ancillary Evidence for the Decline of Medieval Slavery," *Past and Present* 149 (November 1995): 3–28.
26. Quoted in J. Hale, *The Civilization of Europe in the Renaissance* (New York: Atheneum, 1994), p. 270.
27. This account rests on J. Kelly-Gadol, "Did Women Have a Renaissance?" in *Becoming Visible: Women in European History*, ed. R. Bridenthal and C. Koonz (Boston: Houghton Mifflin, 1977), pp. 137–161, esp. p. 161.
28. G. Ruggerio, "Sexual Criminality in Early Renaissance Venice, 1338–1358," *Journal of Social History* 8 (Spring 1975): 18–31.
29. For these and a variety of other remarkable court cases, see S. K. Cohn, Jr., *Women in the Streets: Essays on Sex and Power in Renaissance Italy* (Baltimore: Johns Hopkins University Press, 1996), pp. 103–121.
30. Ibid., pp. 30–35, 105–115.
31. M. Rocke, *Forbidden Friendships: Homosexuality and Male Culture in Renaissance Florence* (New York: Oxford University Press, 1996), pp. 10–11.
32. Ibid.
33. Ibid., p. 45.
34. See ibid., chap. 3, "Age and Gender in the Social Organization of Sodomy," and chap. 4, "Social Profiles."
35. Ibid., p. 148.
36. Ibid., pp. 190–191.
37. Marc Bloch, *Slavery and Serfdom in the Middle Ages*, trans. William R. Beer (Berkeley: University of California Press, 1975), p. 30.
38. Ibid., p. 28.
39. See S. M. Stuard, *op. cit.*
40. Hale, *The Civilization of Europe*, p. 44.
41. J. Iliffe, *Africans: The History of a Continent* (Cambridge: Cambridge University Press, 1995), p. 130; H. Thomas, *The Slave Trade: The Story of the Atlantic Slave Trade, 1440–1870* (New York: Simon & Schuster, 1997), pp. 109–110.
42. Quoted in J. Devisse and M. Mollat, *The Image of the Black in Western Art*, vol. 2, trans. W. G. Ryan (New York: William Morrow, 1979), pt. 2, pp. 187–188.
43. See A. C. DE. C. M. Saunders, *A Social History of Black Slaves and Freedmen in Portugal, 1441–1555* (New York: Cambridge University Press, 1982), pp. 59, 62–88, 176–179.
44. Ibid., pp. 190–194.
45. Ibid., pp. 255–258.
46. See I. Hannaford, *Race: The History of an Idea in the West* (Washington, D.C.: Woodrow Wilson Center Press, 1996), pp. 3–182 passim, 182–187.
47. Quoted in E. H. Harbison, *The Christian Scholar and His Calling in the Age of the Reformation* (New York: Charles Scribner's Sons, 1956), p. 109.
48. Quoted in F. Seebohm, *The Oxford Reformers* (London: J. M. Dent & Sons, 1867), p. 256.
49. See J. H. Elliott, *Imperial Spain, 1469–1716* (New York: Mentor Books, 1963), esp. pp. 75, 97–108.
50. See B. F. Reilly, *The Medieval Spains* (New York: Cambridge University Press, 1993), pp. 198–203.
51. B. Netanyahu, *The Origins of the Inquisition in Fifteenth Century Spain* (New York: Random House, 1995), p. 921.
52. Ibid., pp. 934–935.
53. Ibid., p. 930.
54. Ibid., p. 982.
55. Ibid., pp. 996–1005.

Suggested Reading

The best comprehensive treatment of the period is J. Hale, *The Civilization of Europe in the Renaissance* (1994), a magisterial achievement, while G. Holmes, ed., *The Oxford History of Italy* (1997), contains valuable articles on politics, society, and culture. P. Burke, *The Historical Anthropology of Early Modern Italy* (1987), contains useful essays on Italian cultural history in a European framework. G. Holmes, ed., *Art and Politics in Renaissance Italy* (1993), treats the art of Florence and Rome against a political background. For an explanation of why Italy lagged in developing a national state, see G. Chittolini, "Cities, 'City-States,' and Regional States in North-Central Italy," in *Cities and the Rise of States in Europe, A.D. 1000 to 1800,* ed. C. Tilly and W. P. Blockmans (1994). For the Renaissance court, see the splendid achievement of G. Lubkin, *A Renaissance Court: Milan Under Galeazzo Maria Sforza* (1994), as well as the title by Martines cited in the Notes.

For Renaissance humanism and education, see D. R. Kelley, *Renaissance Humanism* (1991), a good survey of humanism as a cultural movement; A. Grafton and L. Jardine, *From Humanism to the Humanities: Education and the Liberal Arts in Fifteenth and Sixteenth Century Europe* (1986), a sophisticated study; P. F. Grendler, *Schooling in Renaissance Italy: Literacy and Learning, 1300–1600* (1989); and J. F. D'Amico, *Renaissance Humanism in Papal Rome: Humanists and Churchmen on the Eve of the Reformation* (1983), another work of outstanding scholarship.

J. R. Hale, *Machiavelli and Renaissance Italy* (1966), is a sound short biography, but advanced students may want to consult the sophisticated intellectual biography S. de Grazia, *Machiavelli in Hell* (1989), which is based on Machiavelli's literary as well as political writing. C. Singleton, trans., *The Courtier* (1959), presents an excellent picture of Renaissance court life.

The best introduction to the Renaissance in northern Europe and a book that has greatly influenced modern scholarship is J. Huizinga, *The Waning of the Middle Ages: A Study of the Forms of Life, Thought, and Art in France and the Netherlands in the Dawn of the Renaissance* (1954): it challenges the whole idea of the Renaissance. R. J. Knecht, *Renaissance Warrior and Patron: The Reign of Francis I* (1994), is the standard study of that important French ruler. The leading northern humanist is sensitively treated in J. McConica, *Erasmus* (1991). Advanced students interested in his program for the reform of Christian society should see J. D. Tracy, *Erasmus of the Low Countries* (1996). R. Marius, *Thomas More: A Biography* (1984), is a useful study of the English humanist and statesman, while the works of Rabelais, the French humanist and wit, are available in J. Leclercq, trans., *The Complete Works of Rabelais* (1963).

For the experiences of women as wives, mothers, slaves, servants, and workers in the crafts, see B. Hanawalt, ed., *Women and Work in Pre-industrial Europe* (1986), and M. L. King, *Women of the Renaissance* (1991). For the status of women, see C. Klapisch-Zuper, ed., *A History of Women,* vol. 3 (1994); R. Chartier, ed., *A History of Private Life,* vol. 3: *Passions of the Renaissance* (1990); and I. Maclean, *The Renaissance Notion of Women* (1980). J. C. Brown, *The Life of a Lesbian Nun in Renaissance Italy* (1985), and J. M. Saslow, *Ganymede in the Renaissance* (1986), both treat sexual issues, as do the titles by Rocke and Cohn cited in the Notes.

Renaissance art has understandably inspired vast research. In addition to Burroughs's edited version of Vasari's volume of biographical sketches on the masters referred to in the Notes, see, for Vasari's aims and methods of interpretation, P. L. Rubin, *Giorgio Vasari: Art and History* (1995). For Venice, see the highly readable and beautifully illustrated G. Wills, *Venice, Lion City: The Religion of Empire* (2001), which tells the story of the republic through an appreciation of its art and architecture; P. F. Brown, *Venice and Antiquity: The Venetian Sense of the Past* (1997), which treats the ways Venice invented its past to celebrate the city and its people; P. F. Brown, *Venetian Narrative Painting in the Age of Carpaccio* (1989); P. Humfrey, *Painting in Renaissance Venice* (1995), a useful survey for the beginning student; and P. Humfrey, *Lorenzo Lotto* (1997), a fine study of a distinctive Venetian painter. For artist families, see P. Burke, *The Italian Renaissance: Culture and Society in Italy* (1986). For the city of Milan, see E. S. Welch, *Art and Authority in Milan* (1996); and for Rome, see C. Hibbert, *Rome: The Biography of a City* (1985), an elegantly illustrated work, and P. Partner, *Renaissance Rome, 1500–1559: A Portrait of a Society* (1979). For Florence, see R. W. B. Lewis, *The City of Florence: Historical Vistas and Personal Sightings* (1995), an evocative appreciation of the city with a good study of the Medici achievement; and D. C. Ahl, *Benozzo Gozzoli* (1996), which places Gozzoli's art in its social context. M. Baxandall, *Painting and Experience in Fifteenth Century Italy* (1988), has important material on Florentine art. The magisterial achievement of J. Pope-Hennessy, *Cellini* (1985), is a superb evocation of that artist's life and work, while R. Jones and N. Penny, *Raphael* (1983), celebrates the work of that master. Leonardo's scientific and naturalistic ideas and drawings are available in I. A. Richter, ed., *The Notebooks of Leonardo da Vinci* (1985). The best introduction to the art of northern Europe is C. Harbison, *The Mirror of the Artist: Northern Renaissance Art in Its Historical Context* (1995).

The following studies should be helpful to students interested in issues relating to the political and religious history of Spain: N. Rubin, *Isabella of Castile: The First Renaissance Queen* (1991); P. Lis, *Isabel the Queen: Life and Times* (1992); J. S. Gerber, *The Jews of Spain: A History of the Sephardic Experience* (1992); H. Kamen, *Inquisition and Society in Spain in the Sixteenth and Seventeenth Centuries* (1985); P. F. Albaladejo, "Cities and the State in Spain," in *Cities and the Rise of States in Europe, A.D. 1000 to 1800,* eds. C. Tilly and W. M. Blockmans (1994); and B. Netanyahu, *The Origins of the Inquisition in Fifteenth Century Spain* (1995).

Listening to the Past

An Age of Gold

As the foremost scholar of the early sixteenth century and a writer with international contacts, Desiderius Erasmus (1466?–1536) maintained a vast correspondence. In the letters here, he explains his belief that Europe was entering a golden age. The letters also reflect the spiritual ideals of northern European humanists. Wolfgang Capito (1478?–1541), a German scholar, was professor of theology at the University of Basel. Pope Leo X (1513–1521), second son of Lorenzo de' Medici, extended the hospitality of the papal court to men of letters, sought to rebuild Rome as a Renaissance capital, and pushed the building of the new Saint Peter's Basilica by licensing the sale of indulgences *(see pages 459–460)**.*

To Capito

It is no part of my nature, most learned Wolfgang, to be excessively fond of life; whether it is that I have, to my own mind, lived nearly long enough, having entered my fifty-first year, or that I see nothing in this life so splendid or delightful that it should be desired by one who is convinced by the Christian faith that a happier life awaits those who in this world earnestly attach themselves to piety. But at the present moment I could almost wish to be young again, for no other reason but this, that I anticipate the near approach of a golden age, so clearly do we see the minds of princes, as if changed by inspiration, devoting all their energies to the pursuit of peace. The chief movers in this matter are Pope Leo and Francis, King of France.

There is nothing this king does not do or does not suffer in his desire to avert war and consolidate peace . . . and exhibiting in this, as in everything else, a magnanimous and truly royal character. Therefore, when I see that the highest sovereigns of Europe—Francis of France, Charles the King Catholic, Henry of England, and the Emperor Maximilian—have set all their warlike preparations aside and established peace upon solid and, as I trust, adamantine foundations, I am led to a confident hope that not only morality and Christian piety, but also a genuine and purer literature, may come to renewed life or greater splendour; especially as this object is pursued with equal zeal in various regions of the world—at Rome by Pope Leo, in Spain by the Cardinal of Toledo,* in England by Henry, eighth of the name, himself not unskilled in letters, and among ourselves by our young King Charles.† In France, King Francis, who seems as it were born for this object, invites and entices from all countries men that excel in merit or in learning. Among the Germans the same object is pursued by many of their excellent princes and bishops, and especially by Maximilian Caesar,‡ whose old age, weary of so many wars, has determined to seek rest in the employments of peace, a resolution more becoming to his own years, while it is fortunate for the Christian world. To the piety of these princes it is due, that we see everywhere, as if upon a given signal, men of genius are arising and conspiring together to restore the best literature.

Polite letters, which were almost extinct, are now cultivated and embraced by Scots, by Danes, and by Irishmen. Medicine has a host of champions. . . . The Imperial Law is restored at Paris by William Budé, in Germany by Udalric Zasy; and mathematics at Basel by Henry of Glaris. In the theological sphere there was no little to be done, because this science has been hitherto mainly professed by those who are most

*Francisco Jiménez de Cisneros (1436–1517), Spanish statesman and adviser to Queen Isabella who gained renown for his reform of the monasteries and the Spanish church.

†After 1516 king of Spain and much of the Netherlands; after 1519 Holy Roman emperor.

‡Holy Roman emperor (1493–1519), he was succeeded by his grandson Charles (above).

pertinacious in their abhorrence of the better literature,[§] and are the more successful in defending their own ignorance as they do it under pretext of piety, the unlearned vulgar being induced to believe that violence is offered to religion if anyone begins an assault upon their barbarism. . . . But even here I am confident of success if the knowledge of the three languages continues to be received in schools, as it has now begun. . . .

The humblest part of the work has naturally fallen to my lot. Whether my contribution has been worth anything I cannot say; . . . although the work was not undertaken by me with any confidence that I could myself teach anything magnificent, but I wanted to construct a road for other persons of higher aims, so that they might be less impeded by pools and stumbling blocks in carrying home those fair and glorious treasures.

Why should I say more? Everything promises me the happiest success. But one doubt still possesses my mind. I am afraid that, under cover of a revival of ancient literature, paganism may attempt to rear its head—as there are some among Christians that acknowledge Christ in name but breathe inwardly a heathen spirit—or, on the other hand, that the restoration of Hebrew learning may give occasion to a revival of Judaism. This would be a plague as much opposed to the doctrine of Christ as anything that could happen. . . . Some books have lately come out with a strong flavour of Judaism. I see how Paul exerted himself to defend Christ against Judaism, and I am aware that some persons are secretly sliding in that direction. . . . So much the more do I wish you to undertake this province; I know that your sincere piety will have regard to nothing but Christ, to whom all your studies are devoted. . . .

To Pope Leo X

While on the one hand, as a private matter, I acknowledge my own felicity in obtaining the approbation not only of the Supreme Pontiff but of Leo, by his own endowments supreme among the supreme, so on the other hand, as a matter of public concern, I congratulate this our age—which bids fair to be an age of gold, if ever such there was—wherein I see, under your happy auspices and by your holy counsels, three of the chief blessings of humanity are about to be restored to her. I mean, first, that truly Christian piety, which has in many ways fallen into decay; secondly, learning of the best sort, hitherto partly neglected and partly corrupted; and thirdly, the public and lasting concord of Christendom, the source and parent of piety and erudition. These will be the undying trophies of the tenth Leo, which, consecrated to eternal memory by the writings of learned men, will forever render your pontificate and your family[||] illustrious. I pray God that he may be pleased to confirm this purpose in you, and so protract your life, that after the affairs of mankind have been ordered according to your designs, Leo may make a long-delayed return to the skies.

[§]Latin, Greek, and Hebrew.

Hans Holbein the Younger, *Erasmus* (ca 1521). Holbein persuaded his close friend Erasmus to sit for this portrait and portrayed him at his characteristic work, writing. *(Louvre/Scala/Art Resource, NY)*

Questions for Analysis

1. What does Erasmus mean by a "golden age"? What are its characteristics?
2. Does education and learning ensure improvement in the human condition?
3. What would you say are the essential differences between Erasmus's educational goals and those of modern society?

[||]The Florentine House of Medici, whose interests Leo X, himself a Medici, was known always to support.

Source: The Portable Renaissance Reader, ed. James Bruce Ross and Mary Martin McLaughlin (New York: Penguin Books, 1981), pp. 80–84.

Josse Lieferinxe, *Pilgrims in a Sanctuary*. Christians, especially those who were ill or handicapped, flocked to the shrines of saints in hopes of a cure. *(Scala/Art Resource, NY)*

chapter

14 Reform and Renewal in the Christian Church

chapter outline

- The Condition of the Church (ca 1400–1517)
- Martin Luther and the Birth of Protestantism
- Germany and the Protestant Reformation
- The Growth of the Protestant Reformation
- The Catholic Reformation and the Counter-Reformation

The idea of reform is as old as Christianity itself. In his letter to the Christians at Rome, Saint Paul exhorted, "Do not model yourselves on the behavior of the world around you, but let your behavior change, reformed by your new mind. That is the only way to discover the will of God." In the early fifth century, Saint Augustine of Hippo, describing the final stage of world history, wrote, "In the sixth age of the world our reformation becomes manifest, in newness of mind, according to the image of Him who created us." In the middle of the twelfth century, Saint Bernard of Clairvaux complained about the church of his day: "There is as much difference between us and the men of the primitive Church as there is between muck and gold." The Christian humanists of the late fifteenth and early sixteenth centuries—More, Erasmus, and Colet—urged reform of the church on the pattern of the early church, primarily through educational and social change.

Men and women of every period believed the early Christian church represented a golden age, and critics in every period called for reform. Thus sixteenth-century cries for reformation were hardly new. What was new, however, were the criticisms of educated laypeople whose religious needs were not being met. Many scholars interpret the sixteenth-century Reformation against the background of reforming trends begun in the fourteenth century. Unlike any other period, the sixteenth century experienced religious changes that had profound social, political, and cultural consequences.

- What late medieval religious developments paved the way for the adoption and spread of Protestant thought?
- Why did the strictly theological ideas of Martin Luther trigger political, social, and economic reactions?
- What were the consequences of religious schism?
- Do the various reform movements represent revolution or continuity? How?

These are some of the questions that this chapter will explore.

The Condition of the Church (ca 1400–1517)

The papal conflict with the German emperor Frederick II in the thirteenth century, followed by the Babylonian Captivity and then the Great Schism, badly damaged the prestige of church leaders. In the fourteenth and fifteenth centuries, leaders of the conciliar movement reflected educated public opinion when they called for the reform of the church "in head and members." Humanists denounced corruption in the church. As Machiavelli put it, "We Italians are irreligious and corrupt above others, because the Church and her representatives set us the worst example."[1] In *The Praise of Folly,* Erasmus condemned the superstitions of the parish clergy and the excessive rituals of the monks. The records of episcopal visitations of parishes, civil court records, and even such literary masterpieces as Chaucer's *Canterbury Tales* and Boccaccio's *Decameron* tended to confirm the sarcasm of the humanists.

Signs of Disorder

The religious life of most people in early-sixteenth-century Europe took place at the village or local level. At this parish level, priests were peasants, and they were poor. All too frequently, the spiritual quality of their lives was not much better than that of the people to whom they ministered. The clergy identified religion with life; that is, they injected religious symbols and practices into everyday living. Some historians have therefore accused the clergy of cheapening, or vulgarizing, religion. But even if the level of belief and practice was vulgarized, the lives of rural, isolated, and semipagan people were still spiritualized.

In the early sixteenth century, critics of the church concentrated their attacks on three disorders: clerical immorality, clerical ignorance, and clerical pluralism, with the related problem of absenteeism. There was little pressure for doctrinal change; the emphasis was on moral and administrative reform.

Since the fourth century, church law had required that candidates for the priesthood accept absolute celibacy. That requirement had always been difficult to enforce. Many priests, especially those ministering to country people, had concubines, and reports of neglect of the rule of celibacy were common. Immorality, of course, included more than sexual transgressions. Clerical drunkenness, gambling, and indulgence in fancy dress were frequent charges. Because such conduct was so much at odds with the church's rules and moral standards, it scandalized the educated faithful.

The bishops only casually enforced regulations regarding the education of priests. As a result, standards for ordination were shockingly low. When Saint Antonio, archbishop of Florence, conducted a visitation of his metropolitan see in the late fifteenth century, he found churches and service books in a deplorable state and many priests barely able to read and write. The evidence points consistently to the low quality of the Italian clergy, although in northern Europe—in England, for example—recent research shows an improvement in clerical educational standards in the early sixteenth century. Nevertheless, parish priests throughout Europe were not as educated as the educated laity. Predictably, Christian humanists, with their concern for learning, condemned the ignorance or low educational level of the clergy. Many priests could barely read and write, and critics laughed at the illiterate priest mumbling Latin words of the Mass that he could not understand.

In regard to absenteeism and **pluralism**, many clerics, especially higher ecclesiastics, held several *benefices* (or offices) simultaneously but seldom visited their benefices, let alone performed the spiritual responsibilities those offices entailed. Instead, they collected revenues from all of them and hired a poor priest, paying him just a fraction of the income to fulfill the spiritual duties of a particular local church. King Henry VIII's chancellor Thomas Wolsey was archbishop of York for fifteen years before he set foot in his diocese. The French king Louis XII's famous diplomat Antoine du Prat was perhaps the most notorious example of absenteeism: as archbishop of Sens, he entered his cathedral for the first time in his own funeral procession.

Many Italian officials in the papal curia held benefices in England, Spain, and Germany. Revenues from those countries paid the Italian priests' salaries, provoking not only charges of absenteeism but also nationalistic resentment. Critics condemned pluralism, absenteeism, and the way money seemed to change hands when a bishop entered into his office.

Although royal governments strengthened their positions and consolidated their territories in the fifteenth and sixteenth centuries, rulers lacked sufficient revenues to pay and reward able civil servants. The Christian church, with its dioceses and abbeys, possessed a large proportion of the wealth of the countries of Europe. What better way to reward government officials, who were usually clerics, than with high church offices? After all, the practice was sanctioned by centuries of tradition. Thus all over Europe—because church officials served

1470	1500	1530	1560	1590

Political/Military

- 1477 Union of Burgundy and Habsburg dynasties
- 1521–1555 Charles V's wars against Valois kings
- 1553–1558 Reign of Mary Tudor and restoration of Roman Catholicism in England
- 1555 Peace of Augsburg
- 1558–1603 Reign of Elizabeth and the "Elizabethan Settlement" in England

Social/Economic

- 1525 Peasants' Revolt in Germany

Intellectual/Religious

- 1517 Martin Luther, "Ninety-five Theses on the Power of Indulgences"
- 1521 Diet of Worms
- 1527 Henry VIII asks Pope Clement VII to annul his marriage to Catherine of Aragon
- 1541 John Calvin, *Genevan Catechism*
- 1542 Sacred Congregation of the Holy Office and Roman Inquisition
- 1545–1563 Council of Trent
- 1555 Peace of Augsburg officially recognizes Lutheranism

their monarchs, those officials were allowed to govern the church. Churchmen served as royal councilors, diplomats, treasury officials, chancellors, viceroys, and judges. These positions had nothing whatsoever to do with spiritual matters. Bishops worked for their respective states as well as for the church, and they were paid by the church for their services to the state. It is astonishing that so many conscientiously tried to carry out their religious duties on top of their public burdens.

In most countries except England, members of the nobility occupied the highest church positions. The spectacle of proud, aristocratic prelates living in magnificent splendor contrasted very unfavorably with the simple fishermen who had been Christ's disciples.

Nor did the popes of the period 1450 to 1550 set much of an example. They lived like secular Renaissance princes. Pius II (1458–1464), although deeply learned and a tireless worker, enjoyed a reputation as a clever writer of love stories and Latin poetry. Sixtus IV (1471–1484) beautified the city of Rome, built the famous Sistine Chapel, and generously supported several artists. Innocent VIII (1484–1492) made the papal court a model of luxury and scandal. All three popes used papal power and wealth to advance the material interests of their own families. The court of the Spanish pope Alexander VI (Rodrigo Borgia) (1492–1503), who publicly acknowledged his mistress and children, reached new heights of impropriety. Because of the prevalence of

Arm Reliquary of Saint Babylas Silver, glass paste, stones, rock crystals, and an amethyst were attached to an oak base to create this arm reliquary for a third-century martyred bishop of Antioch. Containers for relics were designed in forms related to the objects they held; here the bishop's hand is raised in blessing. Shrines possessing saints' relics drew pilgrims, who represented a demand for food, shelter, and souvenirs. *(Germany, Brunswick, 1467. Philadelphia Museum of Art, purchased with Museum funds. 1951-12-1)*

intrigue, sexual promiscuity, and supposed poisonings, the name *Borgia* became a synonym for moral corruption. Julius II (1503–1513), the nephew of Sixtus IV, donned military armor and personally led papal troops against the French invaders of Italy in 1506. After him, Giovanni de' Medici, the son of Lorenzo de' Medici, carried on as Pope Leo X (1513–1521) the Medicean tradition of being a great patron of the arts.

Signs of Vitality

Calls for reform testify to the spiritual vitality of the church as well as to its numerous problems. In the late fifteenth and early sixteenth centuries, both individuals and groups within the church were working actively for reform. In Spain, for example, Cardinal Francisco Jiménez de Cisneros (1436–1517) visited religious houses, encouraged the monks and friars to uphold their rules and constitutions, and set high standards for the training of the diocesan clergy.

In Holland beginning in the late fourteenth century, a group of pious laypeople called the "Brethren of the Common Life" lived in stark simplicity while daily carrying out the Gospel teaching of feeding the hungry, clothing the naked, and visiting the sick. The Brethren also taught in local schools with the goal of preparing devout candidates for the priesthood. The Brethren sought to make religion a personal, inner experience. The spirituality of the Brethren of the Common Life found its finest expression in the classic ***The Imitation of Christ*** by Thomas à Kempis, which gained wide appeal among laypeople. It urges Christians to take Christ as their model and seek perfection in a simple way of life. Like the later Protestants, the Brethren stressed the centrality of the Scriptures in spiritual life.[2] In the mid-fifteenth century, the movement had founded houses in the Netherlands, in central Germany, and in the Rhineland; it was a true religious revival.

If external religious observances are a measure of depth of heartfelt conviction, Europeans in the early sixteenth century remained deeply pious and loyal to the Roman Catholic church. Villagers participated in processions honoring the local saints. Middle-class people made pilgrimages to the great shrines, such as Saint Peter's in Rome. The upper classes continued to remember the church in their wills. In England, for example, between 1480 and 1490 almost 30,000 pounds, a prodigious sum in those days, was bequeathed to religious foundations. People of all social classes devoted an enormous amount of their time and income to religious causes and foundations.

The papacy also expressed concern for reform. Pope Julius II summoned an **ecumenical council,** which met in Rome from 1512 to 1517. Since most of the bishops were Italian and did not represent a broad cross section of international opinion, the term *ecumenical* (universal) is not really appropriate to describe their meetings. Nevertheless, the bishops and theologians present strove earnestly to reform the church. The council recommended higher standards for education of the clergy and instruction of the common people. The bishops placed the responsibility for eliminating bureaucratic corruption squarely on the papacy and suggested significant doctrinal reforms. But many obstacles stood in the way of ecclesiastical change. Meantime, difficulties were brewing in Germany.

Martin Luther and the Birth of Protestantism

As the result of a personal religious struggle, a German Augustinian friar, Martin Luther (1483–1546), launched the Protestant Reformation of the sixteenth century. Luther was not a typical person of his time; miners' sons who become professors of theology are never typical. But Luther was representative of his time in the sense that he articulated the widespread desire for reform of the Christian church and a deep yearning for salvation. In the sense that concern for salvation was an important motivating force for Luther and other reformers, the sixteenth-century Reformation was in part a continuation of the medieval religious search.

Luther's Early Years

Martin Luther was born at Eisleben in Saxony, the second son of a copper miner and, later, mine owner. At considerable sacrifice, his father sent him to school and then to the University of Erfurt, where he earned a master's degree with distinction at the young age of twenty-one. Hans Luther intended his son to proceed to the study of law and a legal career, which for centuries had been the steppingstone to public office and material success. Badly frightened during a thunderstorm, however, Martin Luther vowed to become a friar. Without consulting his father, he entered the monastery of the Augustinian friars at Erfurt in 1505. Luther was ordained a priest in 1507 and after additional study earned a doctorate of theology. From 1512 until his death in 1546, he served as professor of the Scriptures at the new University of Wittenberg. Luther was deadly serious when he said, years later, "I would not take all the world's goods for my doctorate." His doctorate led to his professorship, and his professorship conferred on him the *authority* to teach: throughout his life, he frequently cited his professorship as justification for his reforming work.

Martin Luther was a very conscientious friar. His scrupulous observance of the religious routine, frequent confessions, and fasting, however, gave him only temporary relief from anxieties about sin and his ability to meet God's demands. These apprehensions in turn led him to doubt the value of the monastic life itself. Since the medieval church had long held that the monastic life was a sure and certain road to salvation, Luther's confusion and anxieties increased.

Luther's wise and kindly confessor, John Staupitz, directed him to the study of Saint Paul's letters. Gradually, Luther arrived at a new understanding of the Pauline letters and of all Christian doctrine. He came to believe that salvation comes not through external observances and penance but through a simple faith in Christ. Faith is the means by which God sends humanity his grace, and faith is a free gift that cannot be earned. Thus Martin Luther discovered himself, God's work for him, and the centrality of faith in the Christian life.

The Ninety-five Theses

An incident illustrative of the condition of the church in the early sixteenth century propelled Martin Luther onto the stage of history and brought about the Reformation. The University of Wittenberg lay within the ecclesiastical jurisdiction of the archdiocese of Magdeburg. The twenty-seven-year-old archbishop of Magdeburg, Albert, was also administrator of the see of Halberstadt and had been appointed archbishop of Mainz. To hold all three offices simultaneously—blatant pluralism—required papal dispensation. At that moment, Pope Leo X was eager to continue the construction of Saint Peter's Basilica but was hard-pressed for funds. Archbishop Albert borrowed money from the Fuggers, a wealthy banking family of Augsburg, to pay for the papal dispensation allowing him to hold the several episcopal benefices. Only a few powerful financiers and churchmen knew the details of the arrangement, but Leo X authorized Archbishop Albert to sell indulgences in Germany to repay the Fuggers.

Wittenberg was in the political jurisdiction of Frederick of Saxony, one of the seven electors of the Holy Roman Empire. When Frederick forbade the preaching and sale of indulgences within his duchy, the people of Wittenberg, including some of Professor Luther's students, streamed across the border from Saxony into Jütenborg in Thuringia to buy indulgences.

What exactly was an **indulgence**? According to Catholic theology, individuals who sin alienate themselves from God and his love. In order to be reconciled to God, the sinner must confess his or her sins to a priest and do the penance assigned. For example, a person who steals must first return the stolen goods and then perform the penance given by the priest, usually certain prayers or good works. This is known as the temporal (or earthly) penance since no one knows what penance God will ultimately require.

The doctrine of indulgence rested on three principles. First, God is merciful, but he is also just. Second, Christ and the saints, through their infinite virtue, established a "treasury of merits" on which the church, through its special relationship with Christ and the saints, can draw. Third, the church has the authority to grant sinners the spiritual benefits of those merits. Originally an indulgence was a remission of the temporal (priest-imposed) penalties for sin. Beginning in the twelfth century, the papacy and bishops had given Crusaders such indulgences. By the later Middle Ages, people widely believed that an indulgence secured total remission of penalties for sin—on earth or in purgatory—and ensured swift entry into Heaven.

The Folly of Indulgences In this woodcut the church's sale of indulgences is viciously satirized. With one claw in the holy water symbolizing the rite of purification (Psalm 50), and the other claw resting on the coins paid for indulgences, the church, in the form of a rapacious eagle with its right hand stretched out for offerings, writes out an indulgence with excrement—which represents its worth. Fools, in a false security, sit in the animal's gaping mouth, representing Hell, to which a devil delivers the pope in a three-tiered crown and holding the keys to Heaven originally given to Saint Peter. *(Kunstsammlungen der Veste Coburg)*

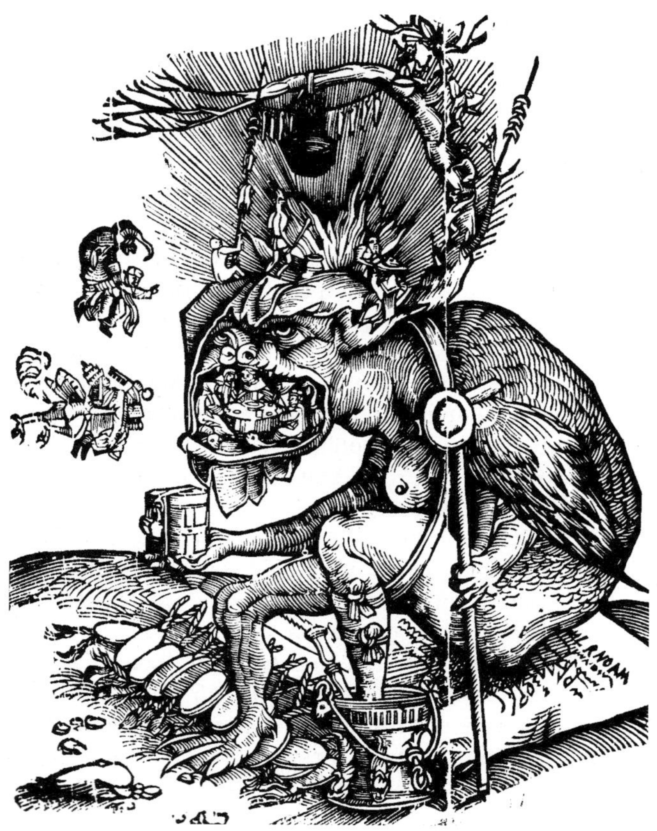

Archbishop Albert hired Dominican friar John Tetzel to sell the indulgences. Tetzel mounted an advertising blitz. One of his slogans—"As soon as coin in coffer rings, the soul from purgatory springs"—brought phenomenal success. Men and women could buy indulgences not only for themselves but also for deceased parents, relatives, or friends. Tetzel even drew up a chart with specific prices for the forgiveness of particular sins.

Luther was severely troubled that ignorant people believed they had no further need for repentance once they had purchased an indulgence. He wrote a letter to Archbishop Albert on the subject and enclosed in Latin "Ninety-five Theses on the Power of Indulgences." His argument was that indulgences undermined the seriousness of the sacrament of penance, competed with the preaching of the Gospel, and downplayed the importance of charity in Christian life. After Luther's death, his disciple Philipp Melanchthon reported that the theses were also posted on the door of the church at Wittenberg Castle on October 31, 1517. Some modern scholars believe that event never happened, meaning all the subsequent dramatic and artistic renderings of it rest on myth.

In any case, Luther intended the theses for academic debate. By December 1517, they had been translated into German and were read throughout the empire.

Luther firmly rejected the notion that salvation could be achieved by good works, such as indulgences. Some of his theses challenged the pope's power to grant indulgences, and others criticized papal wealth. When questioned, Luther rested his fundamental argument on the principle that there was no biblical basis for indulgences. But, replied Luther's opponents, to deny the legality of indulgences was to deny the authority of the pope who had authorized them. The issue was drawn: where did authority lie in the Christian church?

Through 1518 and 1519, Luther studied the history of the papacy. In 1519 in a large public disputation with Catholic debater John Eck at Leipzig, Luther denied both the authority of the pope and the infallibility of a general council. The Council of Constance, he said, had erred when it had condemned Jan Hus (see page 396).

The papacy responded with a letter condemning some of Luther's propositions, ordering that his books be

Jerome Bosch: Christ Before Pilate Pilate (*right*) grasps the pitcher of water as he prepares to wash his hands. The peasant faces around Christ are vicious, grotesque, even bestial, perhaps signifying humanity's stupidity and blindness. Notice the dunce cap on one man, Christ's embroidered undergarment, and the nose and lip rings on some faces. *(The Art Museum, Princeton University. Gift of Allan Marquand)*

burned, and giving him two months to recant or be excommunicated. Luther retaliated by publicly burning the letter. By January 3, 1521, when the excommunication was supposed to become final, the controversy involved more than theological issues. The papal legate wrote, "All Germany is in revolution. Nine-tenths shout 'Luther' as their war cry; and the other tenth cares nothing about Luther, and cries 'Death to the court of Rome.'"[3]

In this highly charged atmosphere, the twenty-one-year-old emperor Charles V held his first diet (assembly of the Estates of the empire). Charles summoned Luther to appear before the **Diet of Worms.** When ordered to recant, Luther replied in language that rang all over Europe:

Unless I am convinced by the evidence of Scripture or by plain reason—for I do not accept the authority of the Pope or the councils alone, since it is established that they have often erred and contradicted themselves—I am bound by the Scriptures I have cited and my conscience is captive to the Word of God. I cannot and will not recant anything, for it is neither safe nor right to go against conscience. God help me. Amen.[4]

When Charles V declared Luther an outlaw, meaning he was denied legal protection, Duke Frederick of Saxony protected him.

Meanwhile, the Swiss humanist and admirer of Erasmus, Ulrich Zwingli (1484–1531), introduced the reformation in Switzerland. Elected People's Priest at the New Minster in Zurich, Zwingli first mounted the pulpit on January 1, 1519, and announced that he would preach not from the church's prescribed readings but, relying on Erasmus's New Testament, go right through the New Testament "from A to Z," that is, from Matthew to Revelations. Zwingli was convinced that Christian life rested on the Scriptures, which were the pure words of God and the sole basis of religious truth. He went on to attack indulgences, the Mass, the institution of monasticism, and clerical celibacy. In his gradual reform of the church in Zurich, where he remained the rest of his life, he had the strong support of the town's civil authorities. He disagreed, however, with Luther on various theological issues, notably the nature of the Eucharist. The Colloquy of Marburg, summoned in 1529 to unite Protestant opinion, failed to resolve those differences.

Protestant Thought

Between 1520 and 1530, Luther worked out the basic theological tenets that became the articles of faith for his new church and subsequently for all Protestant groups. The word **Protestant** derives from the protest drawn up by a small group of reforming German princes at the Diet of Speyer in 1529. The princes "protested" the decisions of the Catholic majority. At first Protestant meant "Lutheran," but with the appearance of many protesting sects, it became a general term applied to all non-Catholic Christians. Lutheran Protestant thought was officially formulated in the Confession of Augsburg in 1530.

Ernst Troeltsch, a German student of the sociology of religion, has defined Protestantism as a "modification of Catholicism, in which the Catholic formulation of questions was retained, while a different answer was given to them." Luther provided new answers to four old, basic theological issues.

First, how is a person to be saved? Traditional Catholic teaching held that salvation is achieved by both faith and good works. Luther held that salvation comes by faith alone. Women and men are saved, said Luther, by the arbitrary decision of God, irrespective of good works or the sacraments. God, not people, initiates salvation.

Second, where does religious authority reside? Christian doctrine had long maintained that authority rests both in the Bible and in the traditional teaching of the church. Luther maintained that authority rests in the Word of God as revealed in the Bible alone and as interpreted by an individual's conscience. (Luther, of course, did not have the advantage of modern biblical research, which has demonstrated that tradition *preceded* the writing of the New Testament—that is, the New Testament is not exactly contemporaneous with Jesus but is based on the traditional understanding of his life and teachings current in first-century Christian communities.) He urged that each person read and reflect on the Scriptures.

Third, what is the church? Luther re-emphasized the Catholic teaching that the church consists of the entire community of Christian believers. Medieval churchmen, however, had tended to identify the church with the clergy.

Fourth, what is the highest form of Christian life? The medieval church had stressed the superiority of the monastic and religious life over the secular. Luther argued that all vocations have equal merit, whether ecclesiastical

Lucas Cranach: The Ten Commandments (early sixteenth century) Protestants condemned images of all kinds but recognized their value for instructional purposes. Here Cranach, an early adherent of Luther's Reformation, illustrates the Ten Commandments. Can you name the commandments? Is it unfair to say that the painting has a misogynistic tinge, given the female devil in number 5 and the wife in number 9? The semicircular rainbow running through the ten scenes symbolizes the covenant between God and humankind. *(Lutherhalle, Wittenberg/The Bridgeman Art Library International Ltd)*

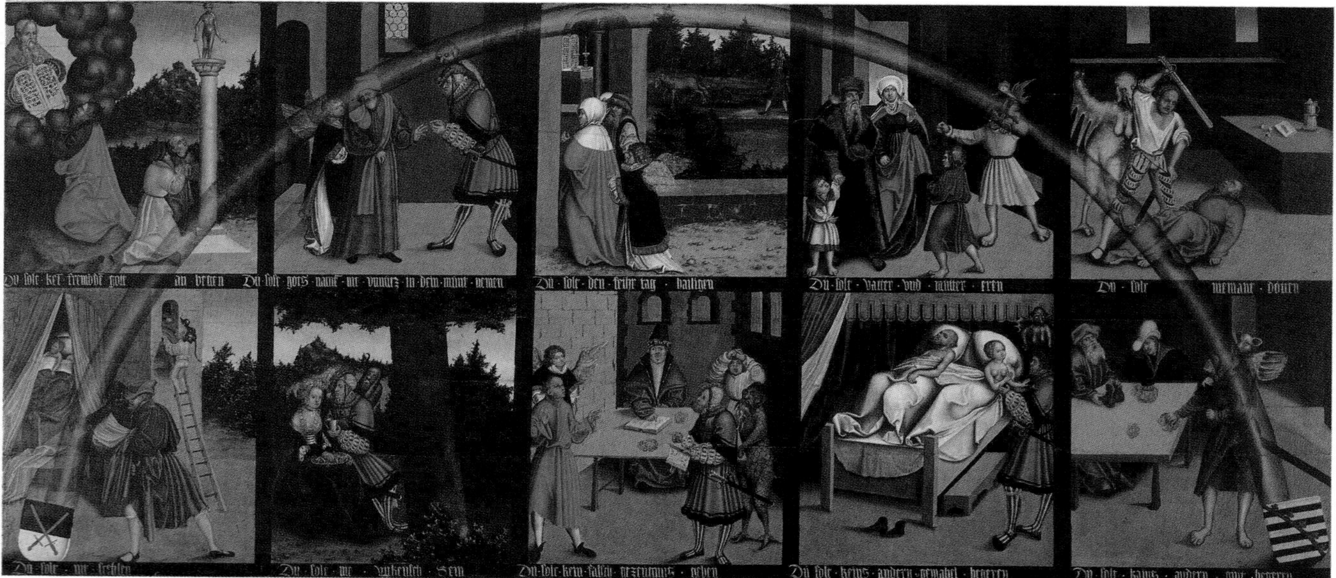

or secular, and that every person should serve God in his or her individual calling.[5]

As Protestant thought developed, it differed from Roman Catholic teaching on several other fundamental issues. Luther's idea of the church as a spiritual *priesthood of all believers,* an invisible fellowship not fixed in any place or person, differed markedly from the Roman Catholic practice of a clerical, hierarchical institution headed by the pope in Rome. Because faith required no institutional structure, Luther stressed the invisibility of the church. Whereas Catholic doctrine holds that there are seven sacraments, Luther believed that the Scriptures support only three sacraments—baptism, penance, and the Eucharist, or Lord's Supper. Protestant sects, as they emerged, developed a theology of the Eucharist. Catholics hold the dogma of **transubstantiation:** by the consecrating words of the priest during the Mass, the bread and wine become the actual body and blood of Christ, who is then fully present in the bread and wine. In opposition, Luther defined **consubstantiation,** the belief that after consecration the bread and wine undergo a spiritual change whereby Christ is really present (the Real Presence) but the bread and wine are not transformed. Swiss reformer Ulrich Zwingli affirmed that the **Lord's Supper** is a *memorial* of the Last Supper and that no change whatever occurs in the elements. John Calvin believed that the body and blood of Christ are spiritually but not physically present in the bread and wine, and they are consumed spiritually. Catholics and Protestants agreed that the sacrament must be received worthily and that it is a source of grace.

The Social Impact of Luther's Beliefs

Every encounter Luther had with ecclesiastical or political authorities attracted attention. Pulpits and printing presses spread his message all over Germany. By the time of his death, people of all social classes had become Lutheran. What was the immense appeal of Luther's religious ideas?

Historical research on the German towns has shown that two significant late medieval developments prepared the way for Luther's ideas. First, since the fifteenth century, city governments had expressed resentment of clerical privileges and immunities. Priests, monks, and nuns paid no taxes and were exempt from civic responsibilities, such as defending the city. Yet religious orders frequently held large amounts of urban property. At Zurich in 1467, for example, religious orders held one-third of the city's taxable property. City governments were determined to integrate the clergy into civic life by reducing their privileges and giving them public responsibilities. Accordingly, the Zurich magistracy subjected the religious to taxes, inspected wills so that legacies to the church and legacies left by churchmen could be controlled, and placed priests under the jurisdiction of the civil courts.

Second, critics of the late medieval church, especially educated townspeople, condemned the irregularity and poor quality of sermons. As a result, prosperous burghers in many towns established **preacherships.** Preachers were men of superior education who were required to deliver about a hundred sermons a year, each lasting about forty-five minutes. Endowed preacherships had important consequences after 1517. Luther's ideas attracted many preachers, and in such towns as Stuttgart, Reutlingen, Eisenach, and Jena, preachers became Protestant leaders. Preacherships also encouraged the Protestant form of worship, in which the sermon, not the Eucharist, was the central part of the service.[6]

In the countryside, the attraction of German peasants to Lutheran beliefs was predictable. Luther himself came from a peasant background, and he admired the peasants' ceaseless toil. They thrilled to the words of Luther used in his treatise *On Christian Liberty* (1520)—"A Christian man is the most free lord of all and subject to none"—choosing to ignore the second clause of Luther's statement: "A Christian man is the most dutiful servant of all, and subject to everyone." (See the feature "Listening to the Past: Martin Luther, *On Christian Liberty*" on pages 486–487.) Taken by itself, the first clause contributed to social unrest.

Fifteenth-century Germany had witnessed several **peasant revolts.** In the early sixteenth century, the economic condition of the peasantry varied from place to place but was generally worse than it had been in the fifteenth century and was deteriorating. Crop failures in 1523 and 1524 aggravated an explosive situation. In 1525 representatives of the Swabian peasants met at the city of Memmingen and drew up the Twelve Articles, which expressed their grievances. The Twelve Articles condemned lay and ecclesiastical lords and summarized the agrarian crisis of the early sixteenth century. The articles complained that nobles had seized village common lands, which traditionally had been used by all; that they had imposed new rents on manorial properties and new services on the peasants working those properties; and that they had forced the poor to pay unjust death duties in the form of the peasants' best horses or cows. Wealthy, socially mobile peasants especially resented these burdens, which they emphasized as new. The peasants believed their demands conformed to the Scriptures and cited Luther as a theologian who could prove that they did.

German Burgher Domestic Scene With what Jesus called the greatest commandment ("You shall love the Lord your God with all your heart and all your soul and your neighbor as yourself" [Deut. 6, Matt. 22]) inscribed on tablets over the room, a German family begins a meal. The father listens as his son says grace, the mother passes bread, the older daughters seem to have begun eating, and a small child biting a chicken drumstick seems dangerously close to the fire. The little dog begs for food; the cat laps milk. *(Mary Evans Picture Library)*

Luther wanted to prevent rebellion. Initially he sided with the peasants, and in his tract *An Admonition to Peace* (1525) he blasted the lords:

> *We have no one on earth to thank for this mischievous rebellion, except you lords and princes, especially you blind bishops and mad priests and monks. . . . In your government you do nothing but flay and rob your subjects in order that you may lead a life of splendor and pride, until the poor common folk can bear it no longer.*[8]

But, he warned, nothing justified the use of armed force: "The fact that rulers are unjust and wicked does not excuse tumult and rebellion; to punish wickedness does not belong to everybody, but to the worldly rulers who bear the sword." As for biblical support for the peasants' demands, he maintained that Scripture had nothing to do with earthly justice or material gain.[9]

Massive revolts first broke out near the Swiss frontier and then swept through Swabia, Thuringia, the Rhineland, and Saxony. The crowds' slogans came directly from Luther's writings. "God's righteousness" and the "Word of God" were invoked in an effort to secure social and economic justice. The peasants who expected Luther's support were soon disillusioned. Freedom for Luther meant independence from the authority of the Roman church; it did *not* mean opposition to legally established secular powers. Firmly convinced that rebellion hastened the end of civilized society, he wrote the tract *Against the Murderous, Thieving Hordes of the Peasants:* "Let everyone who can smite, slay, and stab [the peasants], secretly and openly, remembering that nothing can be more poisonous, hurtful or devilish than a rebel."[10] The nobility ferociously crushed the revolt. Historians estimate that over seventy-five thousand peasants were killed in 1525.

Luther took literally these words of Saint Paul's Letter to the Romans: "Let every soul be subject to the higher powers. For there is no power but of God: the powers that be are established by God. Whosoever resists the power, resists the ordinance of God: and they that resist shall receive to themselves damnation."[11] As Lutheran theology developed, it exalted the state, subordinated the church to the state, and everywhere championed "the powers that be." The revolt of 1525 greatly strengthened the authority of lay rulers. Peasant economic conditions, however, moderately improved. For example, in many parts of Germany, enclosed fields, meadows, and forests were returned to common use.

Scholars in many disciplines have attributed Luther's fame and success to the invention of the printing press, which rapidly reproduced and made known his ideas.

Equally important was Luther's incredible skill with language. Some thinkers have lavished praise on the Wittenberg reformer; others have bitterly condemned him. But in the words of psychologist Erik Erikson:

> *The one matter on which professor and priest, psychiatrist and sociologist, agree is Luther's immense gift for language: his receptivity for the written word; his memory for the significant phrase; and his range of verbal expression (lyrical, biblical, satirical, and vulgar) which in English is paralleled only by Shakespeare.*[12]

Language proved to be the weapon with which this peasant's son changed the European world.

Like the peasants, educated people and humanists were much attracted by Luther's words. He advocated a simpler, personal religion based on faith, a return to the spirit of the early church, the centrality of the Scriptures in the liturgy and in Christian life, and the abolition of elaborate ceremonies—precisely the reforms the northern humanists had been calling for.

Luther's linguistic skill, together with his translation of the New Testament into German in 1523, led to the acceptance of his dialect of German as the standard version of German. His insistence that everyone should read and reflect on the Scriptures attracted the literate and thoughtful middle classes partly because Luther appealed to their intelligence. Moreover, the business classes envied the church's wealth, disapproved of the luxurious lifestyle of some churchmen, and resented tithes and ecclesiastical taxation. Luther's doctrines of salvation by faith and the priesthood of all believers not only raised the religious status of the commercial classes but also protected their pocketbooks.

Hymns, psalms, and Luther's two catechisms (1529), compendiums of basic religious knowledge, also show the power of language in spreading the ideals of the Reformation. The reformers knew "that rhyme, meter, and melodies could forcefully impress minds and affect sensibilities." Such hymns as the famous "A Mighty Fortress Is Our God" expressed deep human feelings, were easily remembered, and imprinted on the mind central points of doctrine. Luther's *Larger Catechism* contained brief sermons on the main articles of faith, whereas the *Shorter Catechism* gave concise explanations of doctrine in question-and-answer form. Both catechisms stressed the importance of the Ten Commandments, the Lord's Prayer, the Apostle's Creed, and the sacraments for the believing Christian. Although originally intended for the instruction of pastors, these catechisms became powerful techniques for the indoctrination of men and women of all ages, especially the young.[13]

What appeal did Luther's message have for women? Luther's argument that all vocations have equal merit in the sight of God gave dignity to those who performed

Martin Luther and Katharina von Bora The couple married on June 13, 1525, when Katharina was twenty-six and Luther forty-two. His parents were present for the ceremony. She brewed beer; managed the house, garden, and accounts; and produced six children. She also gave her husband her complete devotion, but having a no-nonsense character, she scolded him for what she perceived as his excessive generosity. For Luther, it was an exceptionally happy union. *(Uffizi, Florence/Scala/Art Resource, NY)*

ordinary, routine, domestic tasks. The abolition of monasticism in Protestant territories led to the exaltation of the home, which Luther and other reformers stressed as the special domain of the wife. The Christian home, in contrast to the place of business, became the place for the exercise of the gentler virtues—love, tenderness, reconciliation, the carrying of one another's burdens. The Protestant abolition of private confession to a priest freed women from possibly embarrassing explorations of their sexual lives. Protestants established schools where girls as well as boys became literate in the catechism and the Bible. Finally, the reformers stressed marriage as the cure for clerical concupiscence. Protestantism thus proved attractive to the many women who had been priests' concubines and mistresses: now they became legal and honorable wives.[14]

For his time, Luther held enlightened views on matters of sexuality and marriage. He wrote a letter to a young man, "Dear lad, be not ashamed that you desire a girl, nor you my maid, the boy. Just let it lead you into matrimony and not into promiscuity, and it is no more cause for shame than eating and drinking."[15] Luther was confident that God took delight in the sexual act and denied that original sin affected the goodness of creation. He believed, however, that marriage was a woman's career. A student recorded Luther as saying early in his public ministry, "Let them bear children until they are dead of it; that is what they are for." A happy marriage to ex-nun Katharina von Bora mellowed him, and another student later quoted him as saying, "Next to God's Word there is no more precious treasure than holy matrimony. God's highest gift on earth is a pious, cheerful, God-fearing, home-keeping wife, with whom you may live peacefully, to whom you may entrust your goods, and body and life."[16] With many relatives and constant visitors, Luther's home was a large and happy household, a model for Protestants, if an abomination for Catholics. The wives of other reformers, though they exercised no leadership role in the reform, shared their husbands' work and concerns.

Germany and the Protestant Reformation

Unlike Spain, France, and England, the German Empire lacked a strong central power. The Golden Bull of 1356 legalized what had long existed—government by an aristocratic federation. Each of seven electors—the archbishops of Mainz, Trier, and Cologne, the margrave of Brandenburg, the duke of Saxony, the count palatine of the Rhine, and the king of Bohemia—gained virtual sovereignty in his own territory. The agreement ended disputed elections in the empire; it also reduced the central authority of the emperor. Germany was characterized by weak borders, localism, and chronic disorder. The nobility strengthened its hold on its territories, while imperial power declined.

Against this background of decentralization and strong local power, Martin Luther had launched a movement to reform the church. Two years after Luther published the Ninety-five Theses, the electors chose as emperor a nineteen-year-old Habsburg prince who ruled as Charles V. Luther's interests and motives were primarily religious, but many people responded to his teachings for political, social, or economic reasons.

The Rise of the Habsburg Dynasty

The marriage in 1477 of Maximilian I of the house of Habsburg and Mary of Burgundy was a decisive event in early modern European history. Burgundy consisted of two parts: the French duchy, with its capital at Dijon, and the Burgundian Netherlands, with its capital at Brussels. Through this union with the rich and powerful duchy of Burgundy, the Austrian house of Habsburg, already the strongest ruling family in the empire, became an international power.

In the fifteenth and sixteenth centuries, as in the Middle Ages, relations among states continued to be greatly affected by the connections of royal families. Marriage often determined the diplomatic status of states. The Habsburg-Burgundian marriage angered the French, who considered Burgundy French territory and had lusted after the Burgundian Netherlands (Flanders) for centuries. Louis XI of France repeatedly ravaged parts of the Burgundian Netherlands until he was able to force Maximilian to accept French terms: the Treaty of Arras (1482) declared French Burgundy a part of the kingdom of France. The Habsburgs, however, never really renounced their claim to Burgundy, and intermittent warfare over it continued between France and Maximilian. But Louis could not conquer it. It remained outside French control. Within the empire, German principalities that resented Austria's pre-eminence began to see that they shared interests with France. The marriage of Maximilian and Mary inaugurated centuries of conflict between the Austrian house of Habsburg and the kings of France. And Germany was to be the chief arena of the struggle.

"Other nations wage war; you, Austria, marry." Historians dispute the origins of this adage, but no one questions its accuracy. The heir of Mary and Maximilian, Philip of Burgundy, married Joanna of Castile, daughter

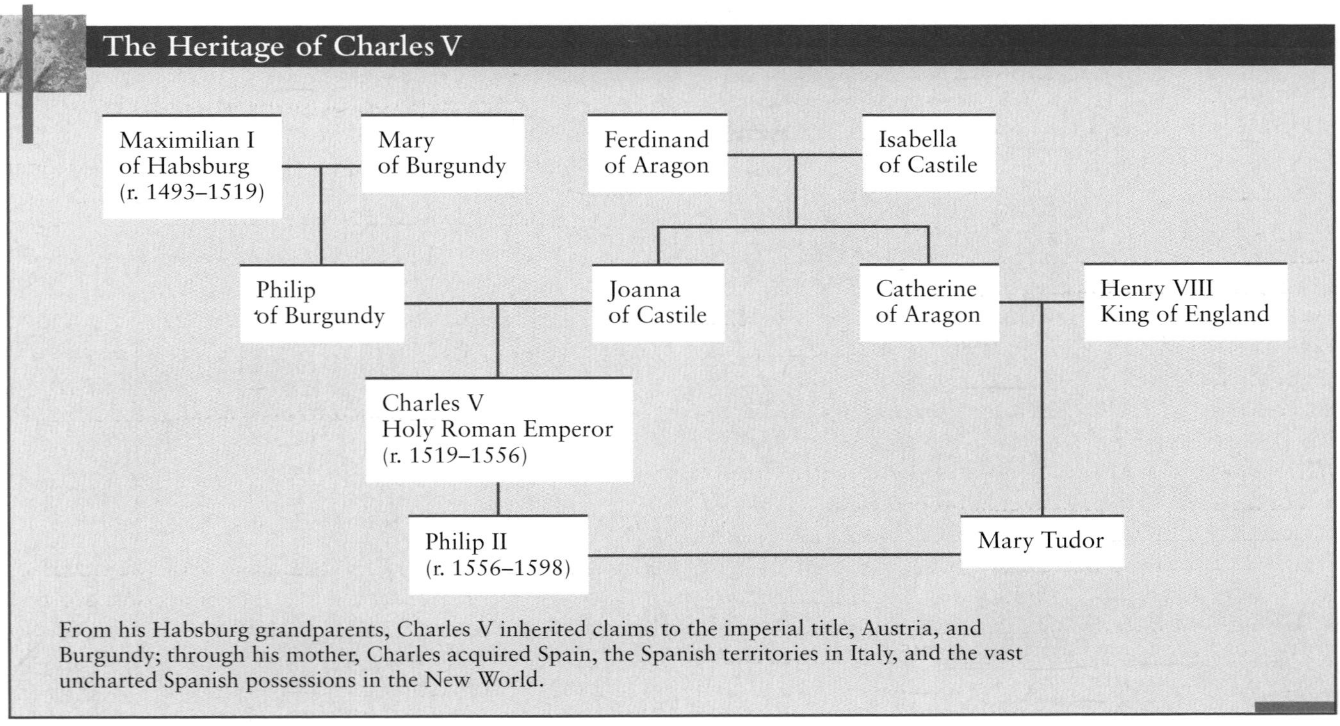

From his Habsburg grandparents, Charles V inherited claims to the imperial title, Austria, and Burgundy; through his mother, Charles acquired Spain, the Spanish territories in Italy, and the vast uncharted Spanish possessions in the New World.

of Ferdinand and Isabella of Spain. Philip and Joanna's son Charles V (1500–1558) fell heir to a vast conglomeration of territories. Through a series of accidents and unexpected deaths, Charles inherited Spain from his mother, her New World possessions, and the Spanish dominions in Italy, Sicily, and Sardinia. From his father he inherited the Habsburg lands in Austria, southern Germany, the Low Countries, and Franche-Comté in east-central France.

Charles's inheritance was an incredibly diverse collection of states and peoples, each governed in a different manner and held together only by the person of the emperor (see Map 14.1). Charles's Italian adviser, the grand chancellor Gattinara, told the young ruler, "God has set you on the path toward world monarchy." Charles not only believed this, but also was convinced that it was his duty to maintain the political and religious unity of Western Christendom. In this respect, Charles V was the last medieval emperor.

Charles needed and in 1519 secured the imperial title. Forward-thinking Germans proposed placing the administration in the hands of an imperial council whose president, the emperor's appointee, would have ultimate executive power. Reforms of the imperial finances, the army, and the judiciary were also recommended. Such ideas did not interest the young emperor at all. When he finally arrived in Germany from Spain and opened his first diet at Worms in January 1521, he naively announced that "the empire from of old has had not many masters, but one, and it is our intention to be that one." In view of the long history of aristocratic power, Charles's notions were pure fantasy. He continued the Burgundian policy of his grandfather Maximilian. That is, German revenues and German troops were subordinated to the needs of other parts of the empire, first Burgundy and then Spain. Habsburg international interests came before the need for reform in Germany.

The Political Impact of Luther's Beliefs

In the sixteenth century, the practice of religion remained a public matter. Everyone participated in the religious life of the community, just as almost everyone shared in the local agricultural work. Whatever spiritual convictions individuals held in the privacy of their consciences, the emperor, king, prince, magistrate, or other civil authority determined the official form of religious practice within his jurisdiction. Almost everyone believed that the presence of a faith different from that of the majority represented a political threat to the security of the

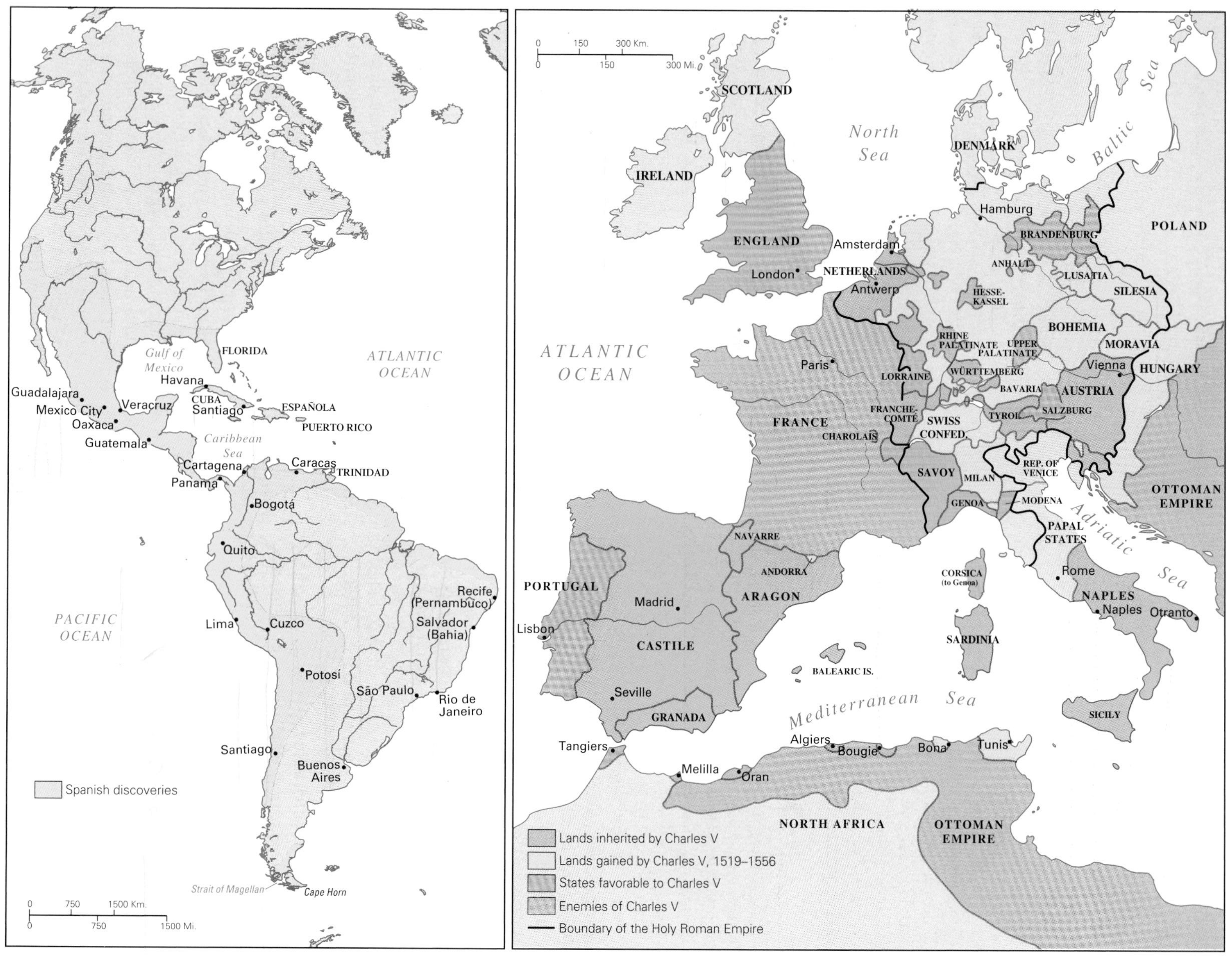

MAP 14.1 The Global Empire of Charles V Charles V exercised theoretical jurisdiction over more European territory than anyone since Charlemagne. He also claimed authority over large parts of North and South America.

state. Only a tiny minority, and certainly none of the princes, believed in religious liberty.

Against this background, the religious storm launched by Martin Luther swept across Germany. Elements in his religious reformation stirred patriotic feelings. Anti-Roman sentiment ran high. Humanists lent eloquent intellectual support. And Luther's translation of the New Testament evoked national pride.

For decades devout laypeople and churchmen had called on the German princes to reform the church. In 1520 Luther took up the cry in his *Appeal to the Christian Nobility of the German Nation*. Unless the princes destroyed papal power in Germany, Luther argued, reform was impossible. He urged the princes to confiscate ecclesiastical wealth and to abolish indulgences, dispensations, pardons, and clerical celibacy. He told them that it was their public duty to bring about the moral reform of the church. Luther based his argument in part on the papacy's financial exploitation of Germany:

> *How comes it that we Germans must put up with such robbery and such extortion of our property at the hands of the pope? If the Kingdom of France has prevented it, why do we Germans let them make such fools and apes of us? It would all be more bearable if in this way they only stole our property; but they lay waste the churches and rob Christ's sheep of their pious shepherds, and destroy the worship and the Word of God. As it is they do nothing for the good of Christendom; they only wrangle about the incomes of bishoprics and prelacies, and that any robber could do.*[17]

These words fell on welcome ears and itchy fingers. Luther's appeal to German patriotism gained him strong support, and national feeling influenced many princes otherwise confused by or indifferent to the complexities of the religious issues.

The rejection of Roman Catholicism and adoption of Protestantism would mean the legal confiscation of lush farmlands, rich monasteries, and wealthy shrines. Some German princes, such as the prince-archbishop of Cologne, Hermann von Wied, were sincerely attracted to Lutheranism, but material considerations swayed many others to embrace the new faith. A steady stream of duchies, margraviates, free cities, and bishoprics secularized church property, accepted Lutheran theological doctrines, and adopted simpler services conducted in German. The decision reached at Worms in 1521 to condemn Luther and his teaching was not enforced because the German princes did not want to enforce it.

Charles V was a vigorous defender of Catholicism, and contemporary social and political theory denied the possibility of two religions coexisting peacefully in one territory. Thus many princes used the religious issue to extend their financial and political independence. When doctrinal differences became linked to political ambitions and financial receipts, the results were unfortunate for the improvement of German government. The Protestant movement ultimately proved a political disaster for Germany.

Charles V must share blame with the German princes for the disintegration of imperial authority in the empire. He neither understood nor took an interest in the

Fresco of Pope Clement VII and the Emperor Charles V by Giorgio Vasari Since Vasari's *Lives of the Most Eminent Italian Painters, Sculptors, and Architects* (rev. ed. 1568), still the basic historical source for Renaissance art and culture, held that "art is the imitation of nature," we may assume that these are faithful likenesses of the Medici pope and the Holy Roman emperor. *(Alinari/Art Resource, NY)*

constitutional problems of Germany, and he lacked the material resources to oppose Protestantism effectively there. Throughout his reign, he was preoccupied with his Flemish, Spanish, Italian, and American territories. Moreover, the Turkish threat prevented him from acting effectively against the Protestants; Charles's brother, Ferdinand, needed Protestant support against the Turks who besieged Vienna in 1529.

Five times between 1521 and 1555, Charles V went to war with the Valois kings of France. The issue each time was the Habsburg lands acquired by the marriage of Maximilian and Mary of Burgundy. Much of the fighting occurred in Germany. The cornerstone of French foreign policy in the sixteenth and seventeenth centuries was the desire to keep the German states divided. Thus Europe witnessed the paradox of the Catholic king of France supporting the Lutheran princes in their challenge to his fellow Catholic, Charles V. French foreign policy contributed to the continuing division of Germany. The long dynastic struggle commonly called the Habsburg-Valois Wars advanced the cause of Protestantism and promoted the political fragmentation of the German Empire.

Finally, in 1555 Charles agreed to the Peace of Augsburg, which, in accepting the status quo, officially recognized Lutheranism. Each prince was permitted to determine his territory's religion. Most of northern and central Germany became Lutheran, while the south remained Roman Catholic. There was no freedom of religion, however. Princes or town councils established state churches to which all subjects of the area had to belong. Dissidents, whether Lutheran or Catholic, had to convert or leave. The political difficulties Germany inherited from the Middle Ages had been compounded by the religious crisis of the sixteenth century.

The Growth of the Protestant Reformation

By 1555 much of northern Europe had broken with the Roman Catholic church. All of Scandinavia, England (except under Mary Tudor), Scotland, and such self-governing cities as Geneva and Zurich in Switzerland and Strasbourg in Germany had rejected the religious authority of Rome and adopted new faiths. Because a common religious faith had been the one element uniting all of Europe for almost a thousand years, the fragmentation of belief led to profound changes in European life and society. The most significant new form of Protestantism was Calvinism, of which the Peace of Augsburg had made no mention at all.

Calvinism

In 1509 while Luther was studying for a doctorate at Wittenberg, John Calvin (1509–1564) was born in Noyon in northwestern France. Luther inadvertently launched the Protestant Reformation. Calvin, however, had the greater impact on future generations. His theological writings profoundly influenced the social thought and attitudes of Europeans and English-speaking peoples all over the world, especially in Canada and the United States. Although he had originally intended to have an ecclesiastical career, Calvin studied law, which had a decisive impact on his mind and later thought. In 1533 he experienced a religious crisis, as a result of which he converted to Protestantism.

Convinced that God selects certain people to do his work, Calvin believed that God had specifically called him to reform the church. Accordingly, he accepted an invitation to assist in the reformation of the city of Geneva. There, beginning in 1541, Calvin worked assiduously to establish a Christian society ruled by God through civil magistrates and reformed ministers. Geneva, "a city that was a Church," became the model of a Christian community for sixteenth-century Protestant reformers.

To understand Calvin's Geneva, it is necessary to understand Calvin's ideas. These he embodied in ***The Institutes of the Christian Religion,*** first published in 1536 and definitively issued in 1559. The cornerstone of Calvin's theology was his belief in the absolute sovereignty and omnipotence of God and the total weakness of humanity. Before the infinite power of God, he asserted, men and women are as insignificant as grains of sand.

Calvin did not ascribe free will to human beings because that would detract from the sovereignty of God. Men and women cannot actively work to achieve salvation; rather, God in his infinite wisdom decided at the beginning of time who would be saved and who damned. This viewpoint constitutes the theological principle called **predestination:**

Predestination we call the eternal decree of God, by which he has determined in himself, what he would have become of every individual. . . . For they are not all created with a similar destiny; but eternal life is foreordained for some, and eternal damnation for others. . . . In conformity, therefore, to the clear doctrine of the Scripture, we assert, that by an eternal and immutable counsel, God has once for all determined, both whom he would admit to salvation, and whom he would condemn to destruction. . . . To those whom he devotes to condemnation, the gate of life is closed by a just and irreprehensible, but incomprehensible, judgment. How exceedingly presumptuous it is only to inquire into the causes of the Divine will; which is in fact, and is justly entitled to be, the cause of everything that exists. . . . For the will of God is the highest justice; so that what he wills must be considered just, for this very reason, because he wills it.[18]

Many people have found the doctrine of predestination, which dates back to Saint Augustine and Saint Paul, a pessimistic view of the nature of God, who, they feel, revealed himself in the Old and New Testaments as merciful as well as just. But "this terrible decree," as even Calvin called it, did not lead to pessimism or fatalism. Rather, the Calvinist believed in the redemptive work of Christ and was confident that God had elected (saved) him or her. Predestination served as an energizing dynamic, forcing a person to undergo hardships in the constant struggle against evil.

Calvin aroused Genevans to a high standard of morality. He had two remarkable assets: complete mastery of the Scriptures and exceptional eloquence. Through his sermons and a program of religious education, God's laws and man's were enforced in Geneva. Calvin's powerful sermons delivered the Word of God and thereby monopolized the strongest contemporary means of communication: preaching. Through his *Genevan Catechism,* published in 1541, children and adults memorized set questions and answers and acquired a summary of their faith and a guide for daily living. Calvin's sermons and his *Catechism* gave a whole generation of Genevans thorough instruction in the reformed religion.[19]

In the reformation of the city, the Genevan Consistory also exercised a powerful role. This body consisted of twelve laymen plus the Company of Pastors, of which Calvin was the permanent moderator (presider). The duties of the Consistory were "to keep watch over every man's life [and] to admonish amiably those whom they see leading a disorderly life." Even though Calvin emphasized that the Consistory's activities should be thorough and "its eyes may be everywhere," corrections were considered only "medicine to turn sinners to the Lord."[20]

Although all municipal governments in early modern Europe regulated citizens' conduct, none did so with the severity of Geneva's Consistory under Calvin's leadership. Nor did it make any distinction between what we would consider crimes against society and simple un-Christian conduct. Absence from sermons, criticism of ministers, dancing, card playing, family quarrels, and heavy drinking were all investigated and punished by the Consistory. Serious crimes and heresy were handled by the civil authorities, which, with the Consistory's approval, sometimes used torture to extract confessions. Between 1542 and 1546 alone, seventy-six persons were banished from Geneva and fifty-eight executed for heresy, adultery, blasphemy, and witchcraft.

John Calvin The lean, ascetic face with the strong jaw reflects the iron will and determination of the organizer of Protestantism. The fur collar represents his training in law. *(Bibliothèque Nationale/Snark/Art Resource, NY)*

Calvin reserved his harshest condemnation for religious dissenters, declaring them "dogs and swine":

God makes plain that the false prophet is to be stoned without mercy. We are to crush beneath our heel all affections of nature when His honor is concerned. The father should not spare his child, . . . nor husband his own wife or the friend who is dearer to him than life. No human relationship is more than animal unless it be grounded in God.[21]

In the 1550s, Spanish humanist Michael Servetus had gained international notoriety for his publications denying the Christian dogma of the Trinity. Servetus had been arrested by the Inquisition but escaped to Geneva, where he was promptly rearrested. At his trial, he not only held to his belief that there is no scriptural basis for the Trinity but also rejected child baptism and insisted that a person under twenty cannot commit a mortal sin. The city fathers considered this last idea dangerous to public morality, "especially in these days when the young are so corrupted." Though Servetus begged that he be punished by banishment, Calvin and the town council maintained that the denial of child baptism and the Trinity amounted to a threat to all society. Servetus was burned at the stake.

To many sixteenth-century Europeans, Calvin's Geneva seemed "the most perfect school of Christ since the days of the Apostles." Religious refugees from France, England, Spain, Scotland, and Italy visited the city. Subsequently, the Reformed church of Calvin served as the model for the Presbyterian church in Scotland, the Huguenot church in France, and the Puritan churches in England and New England. For women, the Calvinist provision for congregational participation and vernacular liturgy helped satisfy their desire to belong to and participate in a meaningful church organization.

On women the views of reformers such as Calvin did not differ much from those of medieval Scholastic theologians. Protestants exalted marriage, stressing the husband's authority over his family and the wife's duty of obedience to her husband. Marriage provided the outlet for women's sexual urges, which reformers believed were stronger than men's. Calvin and other reformers did not distinguish between noblewomen and commoners, but they recognized that noblewomen had influence and power. Thus Calvin maintained a large correspondence with them and worked hard to persuade Marguerite d'Angoulême and her daughter Jeanne of Navarre to

Calvinist Worship A converted house in Lyons, France, serves as a church for the simple Calvinist service. Although Calvin's followers believed in equality and elected officials administered the church, here men and women are segregated, and some people sit on hard benches while others sit in upholstered pews. Beside the pulpit an hourglass hangs to time the preacher's sermon. (Could the dog sit still for that long?) *(Bibliothèque publique et universitaire, Geneva)*

support the Calvinist cause. Most women expressed their religious feelings in a domestic setting—praying, reciting the catechism, and reading the Bible with their children and servants. As public welfare, long the responsibility of local Catholic institutions, became secularized, well-to-do Protestant women aided the poor on a case-by-case basis; some wealthy women founded and endowed schools, orphanages, and dowries for girls and provided funds for poor widows. Women's charitable interests focused specifically on other women.[22]

Calvinism became the compelling force in international Protestantism. The Calvinist ethic of the "calling" dignified all work with a religious aspect. Hard work, well done, was pleasing to God. This doctrine encouraged an aggressive, vigorous activism. These factors, together with the social and economic applications of Calvin's theology, made Calvinism the most dynamic force in sixteenth- and seventeenth-century Protestantism.

The Anabaptists

The name *Anabaptist* derives from a Greek word meaning "to baptize again." The **Anabaptists** believed that only adults could make a free choice about religious faith, baptism, and entry into the Christian community. Thus they considered the practice of baptizing infants and children preposterous and claimed there was no scriptural basis for it. They wanted to rebaptize believers who had been baptized as children. Anabaptists took the Gospel and, at first, Luther's teachings absolutely literally and favored a return to the kind of church that they thought had existed among the earliest Christians—a voluntary association of believers who had experienced an inner light.

Anabaptists maintained that only a few people would receive the inner light. This position meant that the Christian community and the Christian state were not identical. In other words, Anabaptists believed in religious toleration. They almost never tried to force their values on others. In an age that believed in the necessity of state-established churches, Anabaptist views on religious liberty were thought to undermine that concept. Each Anabaptist community or church was entirely independent; it selected its own ministers and ran its own affairs.

Anabaptists admitted women to the ministry. They shared goods as the early Christians had done, refused all public offices, and would not serve in the armed forces. In fact, they laid great stress on pacifism. A favorite Anabaptist scriptural quotation was "By their fruits you shall know them," suggesting that if Christianity was a religion of peace, then the Christian should not fight. Good deeds were the sign of Christian faith, and to be a Christian meant to imitate the meekness and mercy of Christ. With such beliefs Anabaptists were inevitably a minority. Anabaptism later attracted the poor, the unemployed, and the uneducated. Geographically, Anabaptists drew their members from depressed urban areas—from among the followers of Zwingli in Zurich and from Basel, Augsburg, and Nuremberg.

Ideas such as absolute pacifism and the distinction between the Christian community and the state brought down on these unfortunate people fanatical hatred and bitter persecution. Zwingli, Luther, Calvin, and Catholics all saw—quite correctly—the separation of church and state as leading ultimately to the complete secularization of society. The powerful rulers of Swiss and German society immediately saw the connection between religious heresy and economic dislocation. Civil authorities feared that the combination of religious differences and economic grievances would lead to civil disturbances. In Saxony, in Strasbourg, and in the Swiss cities, Anabaptists were either banished or cruelly executed by burning, beating, or drowning. Their community spirit and the edifying example of their lives, however, contributed to the survival of Anabaptist ideas. Later, the Quakers, with their gentle pacifism; the Baptists, with their emphasis on an inner spiritual light; the Congregationalists, with their democratic church organization; and, in 1787, the authors of the U.S. Constitution, with their opposition to the "establishment of religion" (state churches), would all trace their origins, in part, to the Anabaptists of the sixteenth century.

The English Reformation

As on the continent, the Reformation in England had economic causes as well as religious ones. When the personal matter of the divorce of King Henry VIII (r. 1509–1547) became enmeshed with political issues, a complete break with Rome resulted.

Demands for ecclesiastical reform dated back at least to the fourteenth century. The Lollards (see page 395) had been driven underground in the fifteenth century but survived in parts of southern England and the Midlands. Working-class people, especially cloth workers, were attracted to their ideas. The Lollards stressed the individual's reading and interpretation of the Bible, which they considered the only standard of Christian faith and holiness. Consequently, they put no stock in the value of the sacraments and were vigorously anticlerical. Lollards opposed ecclesiastical wealth, the veneration of the saints, prayers for the dead, and all war. Although they had no notion of justification by faith, like Luther they insisted on the individual soul's direct responsibility to God.

The work of English humanist William Tyndale (1494?–1536) stimulated cries for reform. Tyndale visited Luther at Wittenberg in 1524 and a year later at Antwerp began printing an English translation of the New Testament. From Antwerp, merchants carried the New Testament into England, where it was distributed by Lollards. Fortified with copies of Tyndale's English Bible and some of Luther's ideas, the Lollards represented the ideal of "a personal, scriptural, non-sacramental, and lay-dominated religion."[23] In this manner, doctrines that would later be called Protestant flourished underground in England before any official or state-approved changes. The Lollards, however, represented a very small group.

Recent scholarship indicates that the English church was in a very healthy condition in the early sixteenth century. Traditional Catholicism exerted an enormously strong and vigorous hold over the imagination and loyalty of the people. The teachings of Christianity were graphically represented in the liturgy, reiterated in sermons, enacted in plays, carved and printed on walls, screens, and the windows of churches. A zealous clergy, increasingly better educated, engaged in a "massive catechetical enterprise." No substantial gulf existed between the religion of the clergy and educated elite and the broad mass of the English people.[24] The Reformation in England was an act of state initiated by the king's emotional life.

In 1527, having fallen in love with Anne Boleyn, Henry wanted his marriage to Catherine of Aragon annulled. When Henry had married Catherine, he had secured a dispensation from Pope Julius II eliminating all legal technicalities about Catherine's previous union with Henry's late brother, Arthur (see page 445). Henry claimed that a disputed succession and the anarchy of the Wars of the Roses would be repeated if a woman, the princess Mary, sole surviving child of his marriage to Catherine, inherited the throne. Accordingly, Henry petitioned Pope Clement VII for an annulment, stating that a valid marriage to Catherine had never existed. The pope was an indecisive man whose attention at the time was focused on the Lutheran revolt in Germany and the Habsburg-Valois struggle for control of Italy. But there is a stronger reason Clement could not grant Henry's petition. Henry argued that Pope Julius's dispensation had contradicted the law of God—that a man may not marry his brother's widow. The English king's request reached Rome at the very time that Luther was publishing tracts condemning the papacy as the core of wickedness. Had Clement granted Henry's annulment and thereby admitted that his recent predecessor, Julius II, had erred, Clement would have given support to the Lutheran assertion that popes substituted their own evil judgments for the law of God. This Clement could not do, so he delayed acting on Henry's request.[25] The capture and sack of Rome in 1527 by the emperor Charles V (see page 479), Queen Catherine's nephew, thoroughly tied the pope's hands.

Since Rome appeared to be thwarting Henry's matrimonial plans, he decided to remove the English church from papal jurisdiction. Henry used Parliament to legalize the Reformation in England. The Act in Restraint of Appeals (1533) declared the king to be the supreme sovereign in England and forbade judicial appeals to the papacy, thus establishing the Crown as the highest legal authority in the land. The Act for the Submission of the Clergy (1534) required churchmen to submit to the king and forbade the publication of ecclesiastical laws without royal permission. The Supremacy Act (1534) declared the king the supreme head of the Church of England. Both the Act in Restraint of Appeals and the Supremacy Act led to heated debate in the House of Commons. An authority on the Reformation Parliament has written that probably only a small number of those who voted for the Restraint of Appeals actually knew they were voting for a permanent break with Rome.[26] Some opposed the king. John Fisher, the bishop of Rochester, a distinguished scholar and a humanist, lashed the clergy with scorn for its cowardice in abjectly bending to the king's will. Another humanist, Thomas More, resigned the chancellorship: he could not take the oath required by the Supremacy Act because it rejected papal authority and made the king head of the English church. Fisher, More, and other dissenters were beheaded.

When Anne Boleyn failed twice to produce a male child, Henry VIII charged her with adulterous incest and in 1536 had her beheaded. Parliament promptly proclaimed Anne's daughter, the princess Elizabeth, illegitimate and, with the royal succession thoroughly confused, left the throne to whomever Henry chose. His third wife, Jane Seymour, gave Henry the desired son, Edward, but died in childbirth. Henry went on to three more wives. Before he passed to his reward in 1547, he got Parliament to reverse the decision of 1536, relegitimating Mary and Elizabeth and fixing the succession first in his son and then in his daughters.

Between 1535 and 1539, under the influence of his chief minister, Thomas Cromwell, Henry decided to dissolve the English monasteries because he wanted their wealth. The king ended nine hundred years of English monastic life, dispersed the monks and nuns, and confiscated their lands. Hundreds of properties were sold to the middle and upper classes and the proceeds spent on war. The dissolution of the monasteries did not achieve a more

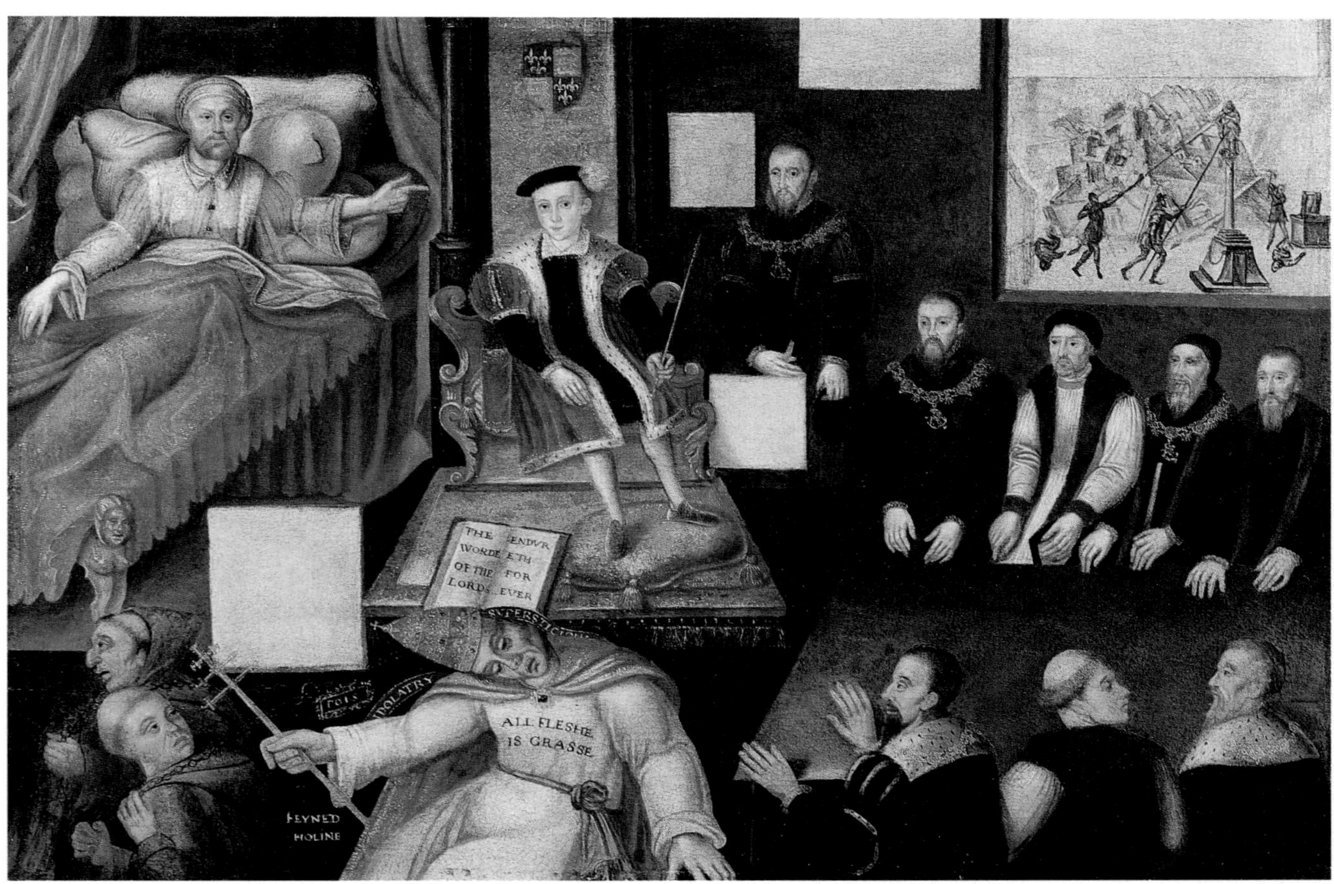

Allegorical Painting, ca 1548 Henry VIII on his deathbed points to his heir, Edward, surrounded by Protestant worthies, as the wave of the future. The pope collapses, monks flee, and through the window iconoclasts knock down statues, symbolizing error and superstition; stressing Protestantism's focus on Scripture, the Bible is open to 1 Peter 1:24: "The word of the Lord endures forever." Since the new order lacked broad popular support, propagandistic paintings like this and the printing press had to be mobilized to sway public opinion. *(Reproduced by courtesy of the Trustees, National Portrait Gallery, London)*

equitable distribution of land and wealth. Rather, the "bare ruined choirs where late the sweet birds sang"—as Shakespeare described in Sonnet 73 the desolate religious houses—testified to the loss of a valuable cultural force in English life. The redistribution of land strengthened the upper classes and tied them to the Tudor dynasty.

Did the religious changes accompanying this political upheaval have broad popular support? The surviving evidence does not allow us to gauge the degree of opposition to (or support for) Henry's break with Rome. Certainly, many laypeople wrote to the king begging him to spare the monasteries. "Most laypeople acquiesced in the Reformation because they hardly knew what was going on, were understandably reluctant to jeopardise life or limb, a career or the family's good name."[27] But all did not quietly acquiesce. In 1536 popular opposition in the north to the religious changes led to the Pilgrimage of Grace, a massive multiclass rebellion that proved the largest in English history. The "pilgrims" accepted a truce, and their leaders were arrested, tried, and executed. In 1546 serious rebellions in East Anglia and in the west, despite possessing economic and Protestant components, reflected considerable public opposition to the state-ordered religious changes.[28]

Henry's motives combined personal, political, social, and economic elements. Theologically he retained such traditional Catholic practices and doctrines as auricular confession, clerical celibacy, and transubstantiation. Meanwhile, Protestant literature circulated, and Henry approved the selection of men of Protestant sympathies as tutors for his son.

The nationalization of the church and the dissolution of the monasteries led to important changes in government administration. Vast tracts of formerly monastic land came temporarily under the Crown's jurisdiction, and new bureaucratic machinery had to be developed to manage those properties. Cromwell reformed and centralized the king's household, the council, the secretariats, and the Exchequer. New departments of state were set up. Surplus funds from all of the departments went into a liquid fund to be applied to areas where there were deficits. This balancing resulted in greater efficiency and economy. Henry VIII's reign saw the growth of the modern centralized bureaucratic state.

In the short reign of Henry's sickly son, Edward VI (r. 1547–1553), strongly Protestant ideas exerted a significant influence on the religious life of the country. Archbishop Thomas Cranmer simplified the liturgy, invited Protestant theologians to England, and prepared the first ***Book of Common Prayer*** (1549). In stately and dignified English, the *Book of Common Prayer* included, together with the Psalter, the order for all services of the Church of England.

The equally brief reign of Mary Tudor (r. 1553–1558) witnessed a sharp move back to Catholicism. The devoutly Catholic daughter of Catherine of Aragon, Mary rescinded the Reformation legislation of her father's reign and restored Roman Catholicism. Mary's marriage to her cousin Philip of Spain, son of the emperor Charles V, proved highly unpopular in England, and her execution of several hundred Protestants further alienated her subjects. During her reign, many Protestants fled to the continent. Mary's death raised to the throne her sister, Elizabeth (r. 1558–1603), and inaugurated the beginnings of religious stability.

Elizabeth had been raised a Protestant, but at the start of her reign sharp differences existed in England. On the one hand, Catholics wanted a Roman Catholic ruler. On the other hand, a vocal number of returning exiles wanted all Catholic elements in the Church of England eliminated. The latter, because they wanted to "purify" the church, were called "Puritans." Probably one of the shrewdest politicians in English history, Elizabeth chose a middle course between Catholic and Puritan extremes. She insisted on dignity in church services and political order in the land. She did not care what people believed as long as they kept quiet about it. Avoiding precise doctrinal definitions, Elizabeth had herself styled "Supreme Governor of the Church of England, Etc.," and left it to her subjects to decide what the "Etc." meant.

The parliamentary legislation of the early years of Elizabeth's reign—laws sometimes labeled the **Elizabethan Settlement**—required outward conformity to the Church of England and uniformity in all ceremonies. Everyone had to attend Church of England services; those who refused were fined. In 1563 a convocation of bishops approved the Thirty-nine Articles, a summary in thirty-nine short statements of the basic tenets of the Church of England. During Elizabeth's reign, the Anglican church (from the Latin *Ecclesia Anglicana*), as the Church of England was called, moved in a moderately Protestant direction. Services were conducted in English, monasteries were not re-established, and clergymen were allowed to marry. But the episcopate was not abolished and the bishops remained as church officials; apart from language, the services were quite traditional.

The Establishment of the Church of Scotland

In Scotland as elsewhere, political authority was the decisive influence in reform. The monarchy was weak, and factions of virtually independent nobles competed for power. King James V and his daughter, Mary, Queen of Scots (r. 1560–1567), staunch Catholics and close allies of Catholic France, opposed reform. The Scottish nobles supported it. One man, John Knox (1505?–1572), dominated the movement for reform in Scotland.

In 1559 Knox, a dour, single-minded, and fearless man with a reputation as a passionate preacher, set to work reforming the church. He had studied and worked with Calvin in Geneva and was determined to structure the Scottish church after the model of Calvin's Geneva. In 1560 Knox persuaded the Scottish parliament, which was dominated by reform-minded barons, to enact legislation ending papal authority. The Mass was abolished. Knox then established the Presbyterian Church of Scotland, so named because *presbyters,* or ministers, not bishops, governed it. The Church of Scotland was strictly Calvinist in doctrine, adopted a simple and dignified service of worship, and laid great emphasis on preaching. Knox's *Book of Common Order* (1564) became the liturgical directory for the church. The Presbyterian Church of Scotland was a national, or state, church, and many of its members maintained close relations with English Puritans.

Protestantism in Ireland

To the ancient Irish hatred of English political and commercial exploitation, the Reformation added the bitter antagonism of religion. Henry VIII wanted to "reduce that realm to the knowledge of God and obedience to us." English rulers in the sixteenth century regarded the Irish as barbarians, and a policy of complete extermination was rejected only because "to enterprise [attempt] the whole extirpation and total destruction of all the Irishmen in the land would be a marvelous sumptious charge and great difficulty."[29] In other words, it would have cost too much.

In 1536 on orders from London, the Irish parliament, which represented only the English landlords and the people of the Pale (the area around Dublin), approved the English laws severing the church from Rome and making the English king sovereign over ecclesiastical organization and practice. The Church of Ireland was established on the English pattern, and the (English) ruling class adopted the new reformed faith. Most of the Irish, probably for political reasons, defiantly remained Roman Catholic. Monasteries were secularized. Catholic property was confiscated and sold and the profits were shipped to England. With the Roman church driven underground, Catholic churchmen acted as national as well as religious leaders.

Lutheranism in Sweden, Norway, and Denmark

In Sweden, Norway, and Denmark, the monarchy took the initiative in the religious Reformation. The resulting institutions were Lutheran state churches. Since the late fourteenth century, the Danish kings had ruled Sweden and Norway as well as Denmark. In 1520 Swedish nobleman Gustavus Vasa (r. 1523–1560) led a successful revolt against Denmark, and Sweden became independent. As king, Gustavus Vasa seized church lands and required the bishops' loyalty to the Swedish crown. Wittenberg-educated Swedish reformer Olaus Petri (1493–1552) translated the New Testament into Swedish and, with the full support of Gustavus Vasa, organized the church along strict Lutheran lines. This consolidation of the Swedish monarchy in the sixteenth century was to profoundly affect the development of Germany in the seventeenth century.

Christian III, king of Denmark (r. 1503–1559) and of Norway (r. 1534–1559), secularized church property and set up a Lutheran church. Norway, which was governed by Denmark until 1814, adopted Lutheranism as its state religion under Danish influence.

The Catholic Reformation and the Counter-Reformation

Between 1517 and 1547, the reformed versions of Christianity known as Protestantism made remarkable advances. Nevertheless, the Roman Catholic church made a significant comeback. After about 1540, no new large areas of Europe, except for the Netherlands, accepted Protestant beliefs (see Map 14.2).

Historians distinguish between two types of reform within the Catholic church in the sixteenth and seventeenth centuries. The Catholic Reformation began before 1517 and sought renewal basically through the stimulation of a new spiritual fervor. The Counter-Reformation started in the 1540s as a reaction to the rise and spread of Protestantism. The Counter-Reformation involved Catholic efforts to convince or coerce dissidents or heretics to return to the church lest they corrupt the entire community of Catholic believers. Fear of the "infection" of all Christian society by the religious dissident was a standard sixteenth-century attitude. If the heretic could not be persuaded to reconvert, counter-reformers believed it necessary to call on temporal authorities to defend Christian society by expelling or eliminating the dissident. The Catholic Reformation and the Counter-Reformation were not mutually exclusive; in fact, after about 1540 they progressed simultaneously.

The Slowness of Institutional Reform

The Renaissance princes who sat on the throne of Saint Peter were not blind to the evils that existed. Modest reform efforts had begun with the Lateran Council called in 1512 by Pope Julius II. The Dutch pope Adrian VI (1522–1523) instructed his legate in Germany to "say that we frankly confess that God permits this [Lutheran] persecution of his church on account of the sins of men, especially those of the priests and prelates. . . . We know that in this Holy See now for some years there have been many abominations."[30] Adrian VI tried desperately to reform the church and to check the spread of Protestantism. His reign lasted only thirteen months, however, and the austerity of his life and his Dutch nationality provoked the hostility of pleasure-loving Italian curial bureaucrats.

Overall, why did the popes, spiritual leaders of the Western church, move so slowly? The answers lie in the personalities of the popes themselves, their preoccupation with political affairs in Italy, and the awesome difficulty of reforming so complicated a bureaucracy as the Roman curia.

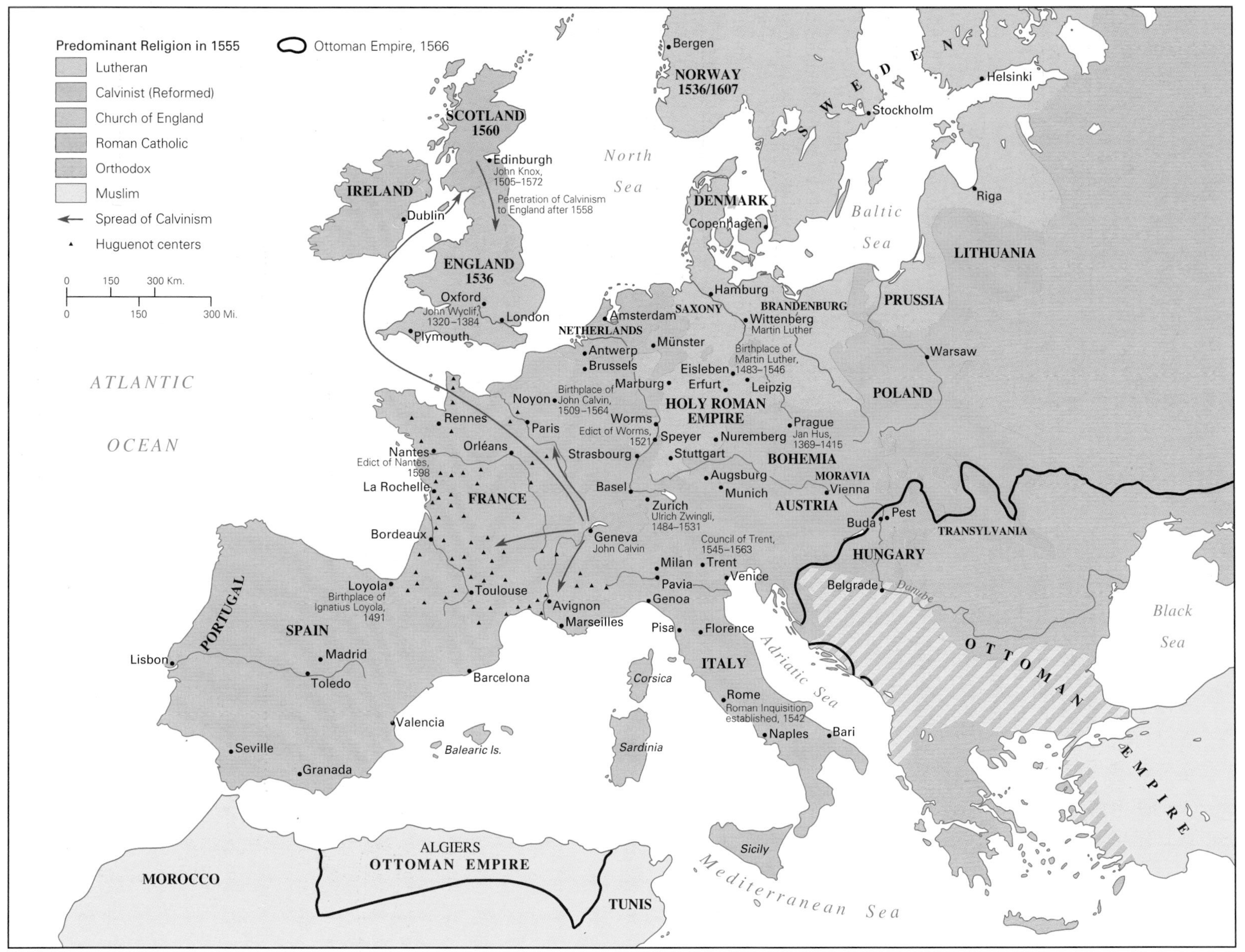

MAP 14.2 The Protestant and the Catholic Reformations The Reformations shattered the religious unity of Western Christendom. What common cultural traits predominated in regions where a particular branch of the Christian faith was maintained or took root?

Clement VII (r. 1523–1534), a true Medici, was far more interested in elegant tapestries and Michelangelo's painting of the Last Judgment than in theological disputes in barbaric Germany. Indecisive and vacillating, Pope Clement must bear much of the responsibility for the great spread of Protestantism. While Emperor Charles V and the French king Francis I competed for the domination of divided Italy, the papacy worried about the security of the Papal States. Clement tried to follow a middle course, backing first the emperor and then the French ruler. At the Battle of Pavia in 1525, Francis I suffered a severe defeat and was captured. In a reshuffling of diplomatic alliances, the pope switched from Charles and the Spanish to Francis I. In retaliation for Clement's diplomatic shift, and to pay his near mutinous soldiers, Charles allowed his German and Spanish troops to sack Rome (May 1527) and to capture the pope. With the city destroyed, its art treasures stolen, and its population decimated, a contemporary reported that "hell itself must have been a prettier sight." The event marked the end of the High Renaissance in Rome.

The idea of reform was closely linked to the idea of a general council representing the entire church. A strong contingent of countries beyond the Alps—Spain, Germany, and France—wanted to reform the vast bureaucracy of Latin officials, reducing offices, men, and revenues. Popes from Julius II to Clement VII, remembering fifteenth-century conciliar attempts to limit papal authority, resisted calls for a council. The papal bureaucrats who were the popes' intimates warned the popes against a council, fearing loss of power, revenue, and prestige.

The Council of Trent

In the papal conclave that followed the death of Clement VII, Cardinal Alexander Farnese promised two German cardinals that if he was elected pope, he would summon a council. He won the election and ruled as Pope Paul III (1534–1549). This Roman aristocrat, humanist, and astrologer, who immediately made his teenage grandsons cardinals, seemed an unlikely person to undertake serious reform. Yet Paul III appointed as cardinals several reform-minded men, such as Gian Pietro Caraffa (later Pope Paul IV); established the Inquisition in the Papal States; and—true to his word—called a council, which finally met at Trent, an imperial city close to Italy.

The Council of Trent met intermittently from 1545 to 1563. It was called not only to reform the church but also to secure reconciliation with the Protestants. Lutherans and Calvinists were invited to participate, but their insistence that the Scriptures be the sole basis for discussion made reconciliation impossible. International politics repeatedly cast a shadow over the theological debates. Charles V opposed discussions on any matter that might further alienate his Lutheran subjects, fearing the loss of additional imperial territory to Lutheran princes. Meanwhile, the French kings worked against the reconciliation of Roman Catholicism and Lutheranism. As long as religious issues divided the German states, the empire would be weakened, and a weak and divided empire meant a stronger France. Portugal, Poland, Hungary, and Ireland sent representatives, but very few German bishops attended.

Another problem was the persistence of the conciliar theory of church government (see page 394). Some bishops wanted a concrete statement asserting the supremacy of a church council over the papacy, but the centralizing tenet was established that all acts of the council required papal approval.

In spite of the obstacles, the achievements of the Council of Trent were impressive. It dealt with both doctrinal and disciplinary matters. The council gave equal validity to the Scriptures and to tradition as sources of religious truth and authority. It reaffirmed the seven sacraments and the traditional Catholic teaching on transubstantiation. Thus it rejected Lutheran and Calvinist positions.

The council tackled the problems arising from ancient abuses by strengthening ecclesiastical discipline. Tridentine (from *Tridentum,* the Latin word for Trent) decrees required bishops to reside in their own dioceses, suppressed pluralism and simony, and forbade the sale of indulgences. Clerics who kept concubines were to give them up. The jurisdiction of bishops over all the clergy of their dioceses was made almost absolute, and bishops were ordered to visit every religious house within the diocese at least once every two years. In a highly original canon, the council required every diocese to establish a seminary for the education and training of the clergy; the council even prescribed the curriculum and insisted that preference for admission be given to sons of the poor. Seminary professors were to determine if candidates for ordination had *vocations,* genuine callings as determined by purity of life, detachment from the broader secular culture, and a steady inclination toward the priesthood. This was a novel idea since from the time of the early church, parents had determined their sons' (and daughters') religious careers (see page 318). Finally, great emphasis was laid on preaching and instructing the laity, especially the uneducated.

One decision had especially important social consequences for laypeople. Since the time of the Roman Empire, many couples had treated marriage as a completely

School of Titian: The Council of Trent Since the early sessions were sparsely attended, this well-attended meeting seems to be a later session. Few bishops from northern Europe, however, ever attended. The Swiss guards (*forefront*) of the Vatican were founded by Pope Julius II in 1505 to defend the papacy. *(Louvre/Réunion des Musées Nationaux/Art Resource, NY)*

personal matter, exchanged vows privately without witnesses, and thus formed what were called clandestine (secret) unions. This widespread practice frequently led later to denials by one party, conflicts over property, and disputes in the ecclesiastical courts that had jurisdiction over marriage once it became a sacrament (which occurred in the twelfth century). The Tridentine decree Tametsi (November 1563) stipulated that for a marriage to be valid, consent (the essence of marriage) as given in the vows had to be made publicly before witnesses, one of whom had to be the parish priest. Trent thereby ended secret marriages in Catholic countries. (They remained a problem for civil and church courts in England until the Hardwicke Act of 1753 abolished them.)

The Council of Trent did not meet everyone's expectations. Reconciliation with Protestantism was not achieved, nor was reform brought about immediately. Nevertheless, the Tridentine decrees laid a solid basis for the spiritual renewal of the church and for the enforcement of correction. For four centuries, the doctrinal and disciplinary legislation of Trent served as the basis for Roman Catholic faith, organization, and practice.

New Religious Orders

The establishment of new religious orders within the church reveals a central feature of the Catholic Reformation. Most of these new orders developed in response to one crying need: to raise the moral and intellectual level of the clergy and people. (See the feature "Individuals in Society: Teresa of Ávila.") Education was a major goal of the two most famous orders.

The Ursuline order of nuns, founded by Angela Merici (1474–1540), attained enormous prestige for the education of women. The daughter of a country gentleman, Angela Merici worked for many years among the poor, sick, and uneducated around her native Brescia in northern Italy. In 1535 she established the Ursuline order to combat heresy through Christian education. The first women's religious order concentrating exclusively on

Individuals in Society

Teresa of Ávila

Seventeenth-century cloisonné enamelwork illustrating Teresa of Ávila's famous vision. (By gracious permission of Catherine Hamilton Kappauf)

Her family derived from Toledo, center of the Moorish, Jewish, and Christian cultures in medieval Spain. Her grandfather, Juan Sanchez, made a fortune in the cloth trade. A "New Christian" (see pages 447–448), he was accused of secretly practicing Judaism. Although he endured the humiliation of a public repentance, he moved his family south to Ávila. Beginning again, he recouped his wealth and, aspiring to the prestige of an "Old Christian," bought noble status. Juan's son Alzonzo Sanchez de Cepeda married a woman of thoroughly Christian background, giving his family an aura of impeccable orthodoxy. The third of their nine children, Teresa, became a saint and the first woman declared a Doctor of the Church—a theologian of outstanding merit and saintliness (1970).

At age twenty, inspired more by the fear of Hell than the love of God, Teresa (1515–1582) entered the Carmelite Convent of the Incarnation in Ávila. The 140 nuns there were supported by rents from their lands; they did not practice poverty. Nor did they observe enclosure, as guests were frequently entertained. The nuns, privileged daughters of Ávila's leading citizens, were obsessed with status and social prestige.

For twenty years Teresa remained in this worldly atmosphere that contradicted the convent's religious ideals. Francesco de Osuna's book *The Third Spiritual Alphabet* introduced Teresa to a more meaningful spiritual life, and she began to devour devotional literature. In her late thirties, she had profound mystical experiences—visions and voices in which Christ chastised her for her frivolous life and friends. She described one such experience in 1560:

> *It pleased the Lord that I should see an angel. . . . Short, and very beautiful, his face was so aflame that he appeared to be one of the highest types of angels. . . . In his hands I saw a long golden spear and at the end of an iron tip I seemed to see a point of fire. With this he seemed to pierce my heart several times so that it penetrated to my entrails. When he drew it out . . . he left me completely afire with the great love of God.**

Teresa responded with a new sense of purpose: although she encountered stiff opposition, she resolved to found a reformed house. Four basic principles were to guide the new convent. First, poverty was to be fully observed, symbolized by the nuns being barefoot, hence *discalced*. Ending a long-established monastic practice, Teresa rejected rents: charity and the nuns' own work must support the community. Second, the convent must keep strict enclosure; the visits of powerful benefactors with material demands were forbidden. Third, Teresa intended an egalitarian atmosphere where class distinctions were forbidden. She had always rejected the emphasis on "purity of blood," a distinctive and racist feature of Spanish society especially out of place in the cloister. All sisters, including those of aristocratic background, must share the manual chores. Finally, like Ignatius Loyola and the Jesuits, Teresa placed great emphasis on obedience, especially to one's confessor.

Between 1562 and Teresa's death in 1582, she founded or reformed fourteen other houses of nuns, no small feat for a woman in a very sexist society. She was the first spiritual author to provide a scientific description of the life of prayer from simple meditation to mystical union with God. Her books, along with her five hundred extant letters, show her as capable of great discernment of individual character. But for all her mystical experiences, Teresa was a motherly, practical, and down-to-earth woman with a strong sense of humor. From her brother who had obtained wealth in the Spanish colonies, Teresa learned about conditions in Peru and instructed her nuns "to pray unceasingly for the missionaries working among the heathens." In this way, they shared in evangelization.

Teresa of Ávila responded to change not with doubt, but with deeper belief.

Questions for Analysis

1. How did sixteenth-century convent life reflect the values of Spanish society?
2. How does Teresa of Ávila represent the spirit of the Catholic Reformation?

**The Autobiography of St. Teresa of Ávila,* trans. and ed. E. A. Peers (New York: Doubleday, 1960), pp. 273–274.

Juan de Valdes Leal: Pope Paul III Approves the Jesuit Constitutions Although Paul III devoted considerable energy to advancing the interests of his (Farnese) family, he also tried to meet the challenge of Protestantism—through the Council of Trent and new religious orders. When the Jesuit constitutions were read to him, Paul III supposedly murmured, "There is the finger of God." The portrait of Ignatius Loyola is a reasonable likeness, that of the pope an idealization: in 1540 he was a very old man. *(Institut Amatller d'Art Hispanic)*

teaching young girls, the Ursulines sought to re-Christianize society by training future wives and mothers. Because the Council of Trent placed great stress on the *claustration* (strict enclosure) of religious women and called for the end of all active ministries for women, Angela had great difficulty gaining papal approval. Official recognition finally came in 1565, and the Ursulines rapidly spread to France and the New World. Their schools in North America, stretching from Quebec to New Orleans, provided superior education for young women and inculcated the spiritual ideals of the Catholic Reformation.

The Society of Jesus, founded by Ignatius Loyola (1491–1556), a former Spanish soldier, played a powerful international role in resisting the spread of Protestantism, converting Asians and Latin American Indians to Catholicism, and spreading Christian education all over Europe. While recuperating from a severe battle wound in his legs, Loyola studied a life of Christ and other religious books and decided to give up his military career and become a soldier of Christ. During a year spent in seclusion, prayer, and personal mortification, he gained insights that went into his great classic, *Spiritual Exercises* (1548). This work, intended for study during a four-week period of retreat, directed the individual imagination and will to the reform of life and a new spiritual piety.

Loyola was a man of considerable personal magnetism. After study at universities in Salamanca and Paris, he gathered a group of six companions and in 1540 secured papal approval of the new Society of Jesus, whose members were called **Jesuits.** The first Jesuits, recruited primarily from the wealthy merchant and professional classes, saw the Reformation as a pastoral problem, its causes and cures related not to doctrinal issues but to people's spiritual condition. Reform of the church, as Luther and Calvin understood that term, played no role in the future the Jesuits planned for themselves. Their goal was "to help souls." Loyola also possessed a gift for leadership that consisted in spotting talent and in seeing "how at a given juncture change is more consistent with one's scope than staying the course."[31]

The Society of Jesus developed into a highly centralized, tightly knit organization. Candidates underwent a two-year novitiate, in contrast to the usual one-year probation. In addition to the traditional vows of poverty, chastity, and obedience, professed members vowed "special obedience to the sovereign pontiff regarding missions."[32] Thus as stability—the promise to live his life in the monastery—was what made a monk, so mobility—the commitment to go anywhere for the help of souls—was the defining characteristic of a Jesuit. Flexibility and the willingness to respond to the needs of time and circumstance formed the Jesuit tradition. In this respect, Jesuits were very modern, and they attracted many recruits.

They achieved phenomenal success for the papacy and the reformed Catholic church. Jesuit schools adopted the modern humanist curricula and methods, and though they first concentrated on the children of the poor, they were soon educating the sons of the nobility. As confessors and spiritual directors to kings, Jesuits exerted great political influence. Operating on the principle that the end sometimes justifies the means, they were not above spying. Indifferent to physical comfort and personal safety, they carried Christianity to India and Japan before 1550, to Brazil, North America, and the Congo in the seventeenth century. Within Europe the Jesuits brought southern Germany and much of eastern Europe back to Catholicism.

The Congregation of the Holy Office

In 1542 Pope Paul III established the Sacred Congregation of the **Holy Office**, with jurisdiction over the Roman Inquisition, a powerful instrument of the Counter-Reformation. The Inquisition was a committee of six cardinals with judicial authority over all Catholics and the power to arrest, imprison, and execute. Under the fanatical Cardinal Caraffa, it vigorously attacked heresy.

The Roman Inquisition operated under the principles of Roman law. It accepted hearsay evidence, was not obliged to inform the accused of charges against them, and sometimes applied torture. Echoing one of Calvin's remarks about heresy, Cardinal Caraffa wrote, "No man is to lower himself by showing toleration towards any sort of heretic, least of all a Calvinist."[33] The Holy Office published the *Index of Prohibited Books,* a catalogue of forbidden reading.

Within the Papal States, the Inquisition effectively destroyed heresy (and some heretics). Outside the papal territories, however, its influence was slight. In Venice, a major publishing center, the *Index* had no influence on scholarly research in nonreligious areas such as law, classical literature, and mathematics. As a result of the Inquisition, Venetians and Italians were *not* cut off from the main currents of European learning.

The Reformations: Revolution or Continuity?

The introduction to this chapter casts reformation in general in terms of the individual Christian's and the institutional church's continual need and search for reform. Indeed, the first critical moment came with one man, Martin Luther, whose inner questioning about his own salvation led to his criticism of the Roman papacy. Historians ask a central question: do the sixteenth-century religious movements represent continuity—a constant feature of the institutional faith—or do those movements demonstrate revolution and radical discontinuity? Recent scholarly research argues that the Reformations constituted both.

Revolution, by definition, rejects the status quo. Protestantism rejected the authority of the Roman papacy. The appearance and growth of new churches—such as Lutheran, Calvinist, Anabaptist, and Anglican in the sixteenth century and Baptist, Quaker, and Methodist, among others, in the seventeenth and eighteenth centuries—represent revolution and a radical discontinuity from the religious situation in Europe over the previous thousand years. Whereas previously there had been one Christian church to which all Christians at least nominally belonged, after 1555 there were many. Protestantism meant fragmentation.

Moreover, some historians, mainly Protestant ones, have identified Protestantism with "modernity," by which they mean not only rejection of the Middle Ages and that period's main symbol, the Roman church, but also the embrace of light and genius. By contrast, students of the Catholic church have seen the Reformations in terms of continuity. While acknowledging that there were grave abuses in the institutional church, these scholars stress that serious movements for reform began in the fifteenth century. The Brethren of the Common Life in the Low Countries, the reforming efforts of Francisco Jiménez de Cisneros in Spain, the preaching programs of the friars, and the Lateran Council of 1512 all antedate Martin Luther. Within the Roman church, there was a great deal of spiritual vitality and many serious attempts to spread the Gospel message (see pages 369–370). After about 1550, the focus shifted from an emphasis on the church as an institution—its powers and prerogatives—to what both the Council of Trent and the Jesuits called "what's good for souls." The Catholic church became a pastoral and a missionary church.[34]

Summary

Martin Luther's strictly religious call for reform, rapidly spread by preaching, hymns, and the printing press, soon became enmeshed in social, economic, and political issues. The German peasants interpreted Luther's ideas in an economic sense: Christian liberty for them meant the end of harsh manorial burdens. Princes used the cloak of the new religious ideas to acquire the material wealth of the church and to thwart the centralizing goals of the emperor. In England the political issue of the royal succession triggered that country's break with Rome, and in Switzerland and France the political and social ethos of Calvinism attracted many people. The Protestant doctrine that all callings have equal merit in God's sight and its stress on the home as the special domain of women drew women to Protestantism. The reformulation of Roman Catholic doctrine at the Council of Trent and the new religious orders such as the Jesuits and the Ursulines represented the Catholic response to the demands for reform.

Religious belief remained tremendously strong. In fact, the strength of religious convictions caused political fragmentation. In the later sixteenth century and through most of the seventeenth, religion and religious issues continued to play a major role in the lives of individuals and in the policies and actions of governments. Religion, whether Protestant or Catholic, decisively influenced the growth of national states.

Although most of the church reformers rejected the idea of religious toleration, they helped pave the way for it. They also paved the way for the eighteenth-century revolt against the Christian God, one of the strongest supports of life in Western culture. In this respect, the Reformation marked the beginning of the modern world, with its secularism and rootlessness. At the same time, it can equally be argued that the sixteenth century represented the culmination of the Middle Ages. Martin Luther's anxieties about salvation showed him to be very much a medieval man. His concerns had deeply troubled serious individuals since the time of Saint Augustine. In modern times, such concerns have tended to take different forms.

Key Terms

pluralism
The Imitation of Christ
ecumenical council
indulgence
Diet of Worms
Protestant
transubstantiation
consubstantiation
Lord's Supper
preacherships
German peasant revolts
The Institutes of the Christian Religion
predestination
Anabaptists
Book of Common Prayer
Elizabethan Settlement
Jesuits
Holy Office

Notes

1. Quoted in J. Burckhardt, *The Civilization of the Renaissance in Italy* (London: Phaidon Books, 1951), p. 262.
2. See R. R. Post, *The Modern Devotion: Confrontation with Reformation and Humanism* (Leiden: E. J. Brill, 1968), esp. pp. 237–238, 255, 323–348.
3. Quoted in O. Chadwick, *The Reformation* (Baltimore: Penguin Books, 1976), p. 55.
4. Quoted in E. H. Harbison, *The Age of Reformation* (Ithaca, N.Y.: Cornell University Press, 1963), p. 52.
5. This passage leans on ibid., pp. 52–55.
6. See S. E. Ozment, *The Reformation in the Cities: The Appeal of Protestantism to Sixteenth-Century Germany and Switzerland* (New Haven, Conn.: Yale University Press, 1975), pp. 32–45.
7. See S. E. Ozment, *The Age of Reform, 1250–1550: An Intellectual and Religious History of Late Medieval and Reformation Europe* (New Haven, Conn.: Yale University Press, 1980), pp. 273–279.
8. Quoted ibid., p. 280.
9. Ibid., p. 281.
10. Quoted ibid., p. 284.
11. Romans 13:1–2.
12. E. Erikson, *Young Man Luther: A Study in Psychoanalysis and History* (New York: W. W. Norton, 1962), p. 47.
13. G. Strauss, *Luther's House of Learning: Indoctrination of the Young in the German Reformation* (Baltimore: Johns Hopkins University Press, 1978), esp. pp. 159–162, 231–233.
14. See R. H. Bainton, *Women of the Reformation in Germany and Italy* (Minneapolis: Augsburg, 1971), pp. 9–10; and Ozment, *The Reformation in the Cities,* pp. 53–54, 171–172.
15. Quoted in H. G. Haile, *Luther: An Experiment in Biography* (Garden City, N.Y.: Doubleday, 1980), p. 272.
16. Quoted in J. Atkinson, *Martin Luther and the Birth of Protestantism* (Baltimore: Penguin Books, 1968), pp. 247–248.
17. *Martin Luther: Three Treatises* (Philadelphia: Muhlenberg Press, 1947), pp. 28–31.
18. J. Allen, trans., *John Calvin: The Institutes of the Christian Religion* (Philadelphia: Westminster Press, 1930), bk. 3, chap. 21, paras. 5, 7.
19. E. W. Monter, *Calvin's Geneva* (New York: John Wiley & Sons, 1967), pp. 98–108.
20. Ibid., p. 137.
21. Quoted in Bainton, *Women of the Reformation,* pp. 69–70.
22. See M. E. Wiesner-Hanks, "Women," in *The Oxford Encyclopedia of the Reformation,* ed. H. J. Hillerbrand, vol. 4 (New York: Oxford University Press, 1996), pp. 290–298.
23. A. G. Dickens, *The English Reformation* (New York: Schocken Books, 1964), p. 36.
24. E. Duffy, *The Stripping of the Altars: Traditional Religion in England, 1400–1580* (New Haven, Conn.: Yale University Press, 1992), pp. 2–6.
25. See R. Marius, *Thomas More: A Biography* (New York: Alfred A. Knopf, 1984), pp. 215–216.
26. See S. E. Lehmberg, *The Reformation Parliament, 1529–1536* (Cambridge: Cambridge University Press, 1970), pp. 174–176, 204–205.
27. J. J. Scarisbrick, *The Reformation and the English People* (Oxford: Basil Blackwell, 1984), p. 81.
28. Ibid.
29. Quoted in P. Smith, *The Age of the Reformation,* rev. ed. (New York: Henry Holt, 1951), p. 346.
30. Quoted ibid., p. 84.
31. See J. W. O'Malley, *The First Jesuits* (Cambridge, Mass.: Harvard University Press, 1993), p. 376.
32. Ibid., p. 298.
33. Quoted in Chadwick, *The Reformation,* p. 270.
34. See J. W. O'Malley, *Trent and All That: Renaming Catholicism in the Early Modern Era* (Cambridge, Mass.: Harvard University Press, 2000), chap. 2, et passim.

Suggested Reading

P. Chaunu, ed., *The Reformation* (1989), is a lavishly illustrated anthology of articles by an international team of scholars—a fine appreciation of both theological and historical developments. The best reference work is H. J. Hillerbrand, ed., *The Oxford Encyclopedia of the Reformation,* 4 vols. (New York: Oxford University Press, 1996). E. Cameron, *The European Reformation* (1991), provides a comprehensive survey based on recent research; A. Pettegree, ed., *The Early Reformation in Europe* (1992), compares developments in different parts of Europe; and the books by Chadwick and Harbison listed in the Notes are good general introductions. L. W. Spitz, *The Protestant Reformation, 1517–1559* (1985), provides a comprehensive survey that incorporates sound scholarly research. For the trend in scholarship interpreting the Reformation against the background of fifteenth-century reforming developments, see the excellent study of J. F. D'Amico, *Renaissance Humanism in Papal Rome: Humanists and Churchmen on the Eve of the Reformation* (1983); and J. H. Overfield, *Humanism and Scholasticism in Late Medieval Germany* (1984), which portrays the intellectual life of the German universities, the milieu from which the Protestant Reformation emerged.

For the central figure of the early Reformation, Martin Luther, students should see the works by Atkinson, Erikson, and Haile mentioned in the Notes; G. Brendler, *Martin Luther: Theology and Revolution* (1991), a response to the Marxist interpretation of Luther as a tool of the aristocracy who sold out the peasantry; and H. Boehmer, *Martin Luther: Road to Reformation* (1960), a well-balanced work treating Luther's formative years. Beginning as well as advanced students will find a vividly written interpretation of Luther's writings in the recent work by R. Marius, *Martin Luther: The Christian Between God and Death* (1999), which also contains a considerable amount of new information.

The best study of John Calvin is W. J. Bouwsma, *John Calvin: A Sixteenth-Century Portrait* (1988), an authoritative study that situates Calvin within Renaissance culture. D. C. Steinmetz, *Calvin in Context* (1995), treats Calvin as an interpreter of the Bible. See also F. Wendel, *Calvin: The Origins and Development of His Thought* (1963). W. E. Monter, *Calvin's Geneva* (1967), shows the effect of Calvin's reforms on the social life of that Swiss city. R. T. Kendall, *Calvinism and English Calvinism to 1649* (1981), presents English conditions. Students interested in the left wing of the Reformation should see the profound, though difficult, work of G. H. Williams, *The Radical Reformers* (1962). For reform in other parts of Switzerland, see T. Brady, *Turning Swiss* (1985), and L. P. Wendel, *Always Among Us: Images of the Poor in Zwingli's Zurich* (1990). W. P. Stephens, *Zwingli: An Introduction to His Thought* (1992), emphasizes the major themes in Zwingli's theology.

For various aspects of the social history of the period, see S. Ozment, *Magdalena and Balthasar* (1987), which reveals many features of social life through the letters of a Nuremberg couple; and K. von Greyerz, ed., *Religion and Society in Early Modern Europe, 1500–1800* (1984), which contains interesting essays on religion, society, and popular culture. For women, see M. E. Wiesner, *Women and Gender in Early Modern Europe* (1993); L. Roper, *The Holy Household: Women and Morals in Reformation Augsburg* (1991), an important study in local religious history as well as the history of gender; M. Wiesner, *Women in the Sixteenth Century: A Bibliography* (1983), a useful reference tool; and S. M. Wyntjes, "Women in the Reformation Era," in R. Bridenthal and C. Koonz, eds., *Becoming Visible: Women in European History* (1977), an interesting general survey. The best recent treatment of marriage and the family is S. Ozment, *When Fathers Ruled: Family Life in Reformation Europe* (1983). Ozment's edition of *Reformation Europe: A Guide to Research* (1982), contains helpful references.

For England, in addition to the fundamental works by Duffy and Dickens cited in the Notes, K. Thomas, *Religion and the Decline of Magic* (1971), provides a useful treatment of pre-Reformation popular religion, as does Scarisbrick, also mentioned in the Notes, and S. T. Bindoff, *Tudor England* (1959), a good short synthesis. S. J. Gunn and P. G. Lindley, eds., *Cardinal Wolsey: Church, State and Art* (1991), is a useful study of that important prelate. The marital trials of Henry VIII are treated in both the sympathetic study by G. Mattingly, *Catherine of Aragon* (1949), and A. Fraser, *The Wives of Henry VIII* (1992). The legal implications of Henry VIII's divorces have been thoroughly analyzed in J. J. Scarisbrick, *Henry VIII* (1968), an almost definitive biography. On the dissolution of the English monasteries, see D. Knowles, *The Religious Orders in England,* vol. 3 (1959), one of the finest examples of historical prose in English written in the twentieth century. G. R. Elton, *The Tudor Revolution in Government* (1959), discusses the modernization of English government under Thomas Cromwell, whereas the same author's *Reform and Reformation: England, 1509–1558* (1977), combines political and social history in a broad study.

P. Janelle, *The Catholic Reformation* (1951), is a comprehensive treatment of the Catholic Reformation from a Catholic point of view, and A. G. Dickens, *The Counter Reformation* (1969), gives the Protestant standpoint in a beautifully illustrated book. The definitive study of the Council of Trent was written by H. Jedin, *A History of the Council of Trent,* 3 vols. (1957–1961). For the Jesuits, see W. W. Meissner, *Ignatius of Loyola: The Psychology of a Saint* (1993), and J. W. O'Malley, *The First Jesuits* (1993). These books are basic not only for the beginnings of the Society of Jesus but also for the refutation of many myths. Perhaps the best recent work on the Spanish Inquisition is W. Monter, *Frontiers of Heresy: The Spanish Inquisition from the Basque Lands to Sicily* (1990). For the impact of the Counter-Reformation on ordinary Spanish people, see H. Kamen, *The Phoenix and the Flame: Catalonia and the Counter Reformation* (1993). In exceptionally lucid prose, J. W. O'Malley, *Trent and All That: Renaming Catholicism in the Early Modern Era* (2000), provides an excellent historiographical review of the literature and explains why early modern Catholicism influenced early modern European history.

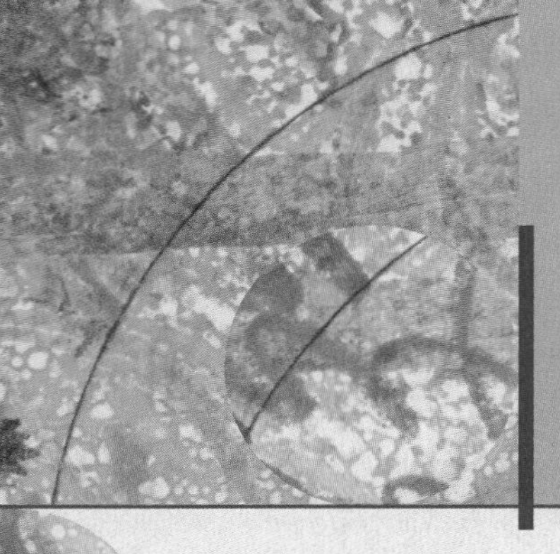

Listening to the Past

Martin Luther, *On Christian Liberty*

The idea of liberty has played a powerful role in the history of Western society and culture; that idea is unique to the European world. But the meaning and understanding of liberty has undergone continual change and interpretation. In the Roman world, where slavery was a basic institution, liberty meant the condition of being a free person, independent of obligations to a master. In the Middle Ages, possessing liberty meant having special privileges or rights that other persons or institutions did not have. A lord or a monastery, for example, might speak of his or its liberties. Likewise, the first chapter of Magna Carta (1215), often called the "Charter of Liberties," states: "Holy Church shall be free and have its rights entire and its liberties *inviolate," meaning that the English church was independent of the authority of the king.*

The idea of liberty also has a religious dimension, and the reformer Martin Luther formulated a classic interpretation of liberty in his treatise On Christian Liberty, *arguably his finest piece. It contains the main themes of Luther's theology: the importance of faith, the relationship of Christian faith and good works, the dual nature of human beings, and the fundamental importance of Scripture in Christian life.*

Christian faith has appeared to many an easy thing; nay, not a few even reckon it among the social virtues, as it were; and this they do because they have not made proof of it experimentally, and have never tasted of what efficacy it is. For it is not possible for any man to write well about it, or to understand well what is rightly written, who has not at some time tasted of its spirit, under the pressure of tribulation; while he who has tasted of it, even to a very small extent, can never write, speak, think, or hear about it sufficiently. . . .

I hope that . . . I have attained some little drop of faith, and that I can speak of this matter, if not with more elegance, certainly with more solidity. . . .

A Christian man is the most free lord of all, and subject to none; a Christian man is the most dutiful servant of all, and subject to everyone.

Although these statements appear contradictory, yet, when they are found to agree together, they will do excellently for my purpose. They are both the statements of Paul himself, who says, "Though I be free from all men, yet have I made myself a servant unto all" (I Cor. 9:19), and "Owe no man anything but to love one another" (Rom. 13:8). Now love is by its own nature dutiful and obedient to the beloved object. Thus even Christ, though Lord of all things, was yet made of a woman; made under the law; at once free and a servant; at once in the form of God and in the form of a servant.

Let us examine the subject on a deeper and less simple principle. Man is composed of a twofold nature, a spiritual and a bodily. As regards the spiritual nature, which they name the soul, he is called the spiritual, inward, new man; as regards the bodily nature, which they name the flesh, he is called the fleshly, outward, old man. The Apostle speaks of this: "Though our outward man perish, yet the inward man is renewed day by day" (II Cor. 4:16). The result of this diversity is that in the Scriptures opposing statements are made concerning the same man, the fact being that in the same man these two men are opposed to one another; the flesh lusting against the spirit, and the spirit against the flesh (Gal. 5:17).

We first approach the subject of the inward man, that we may see by what means a man becomes justified, free, and a true Christian; that is, a spiritual, new, and inward man. It is certain that absolutely none among outward things, under whatever name they may be reckoned, has any influence in producing Christian righteousness or liberty, nor, on the other hand, unrighteousness or slavery. This can be shown by an easy argument.

What can it profit to the soul that the body should be in good condition, free, and full of life, that it should eat, drink, and act according to its pleasure, when even the most impious slaves of every kind of vice are prosperous in these matters? Again, what harm can ill health, bondage, hunger, thirst, or any other outward evil, do to the soul, when even the most pious of men, and the freest in the purity of their conscience, are harassed by these things? Neither of these states of things has to do with the liberty or the slavery of the soul.

And so it will profit nothing that the body should be adorned with sacred vestment, or dwell in holy places, or be occupied in sacred offices, or pray, fast, and abstain from certain meats, or do whatever works can be done through the body and in the body. Something widely different will be necessary for the justification and liberty of the soul, since the things I have spoken of can be done by an impious person, and only hypocrites are produced by devotion to these things. On the other hand, it will not at all injure the soul that the body should be clothed in profane raiment, should dwell in profane places, should eat and drink in the ordinary fashion, should not pray aloud, and should leave undone all the things above mentioned, which may be done by hypocrites.

. . . One thing, and one alone, is necessary for life, justification, and Christian liberty; and that is the most Holy Word of God, the Gospel of Christ, as He says, "I am the resurrection and the life; he that believeth in me shall not die eternally" (John 9:25), and also, "If the Son shall make you free, ye shall be free indeed" (John 8:36), and "Man shall not live by bread alone, but by every word that proceedeth out of the mouth of God" (Matt. 4:4).

Let us therefore hold it for certain and firmly established that the soul can do without everything except the Word of God, without which none at all of its wants is provided for. But, having the Word, it is rich and wants for nothing, since that is the Word of life, of truth, of light, of peace, of justification, of salvation, of joy, of liberty, of wisdom, of virtue, of grace, of glory, and of every good thing. . . .

But you will ask, "What is this Word, and by what means is it to be used, since there are so many words of God?" I answer, "The Apostle Paul (Rom. 1) explains what it is, namely the Gospel of God, concerning His Son, incarnate, suffering, risen, and glorified through the Spirit, the Sanctifier." To preach Christ is to feed the soul, to justify it, to set it free, and to save it, if it believes the preaching. For faith alone, and the efficacious use of the Word of God, bring salvation. "If thou shalt confess with thy mouth the Lord Jesus, and shalt believe in thine heart that God hath raised Him from the dead, thou

On effective preaching, especially to the uneducated, Luther urged the minister "to keep it simple for the simple." *(Church of St. Marien, Wittenberg/The Bridgeman Art Library International Ltd)*

shalt be saved" (Rom. 9:9); . . . and "The just shall live by faith" (Rom. 1:17). . . .

But this faith cannot consist of all with works; that is, if you imagine that you can be justified by those works, whatever they are, along with it. . . . Therefore, when you begin to believe, you learn at the same time that all that is in you is utterly guilty, sinful, and damnable, according to that saying, "All have sinned, and come short of the glory of God" (Rom. 3:23). . . . When you have learned this, you will know that Christ is necessary for you, since He has suffered and risen again for you, that, believing on Him, you might by this faith become another man, all your sins being remitted, and you being justified by the merits of another, namely Christ alone.

. . . [A]nd since it [faith] alone justifies, it is evident that by no outward work or labour can the inward man be at all justified, made free, and saved; and that no works whatever have any relation to him. . . . Therefore the first care of every Christian ought to be to lay aside all reliance on works, and strengthen his faith alone more and more, and by it grow in knowledge, not of works, but of Christ Jesus, who has suffered and risen again for him, as Peter teaches (I Peter 5).

Questions for Analysis

1. What did Luther mean by liberty?
2. Why, for Luther, was Scripture basic to Christian life?

Source: Luther's Primary Works, ed. H. Wace and C. A. Buchheim (London: Holder and Stoughton, 1896). Reprinted in *The Portable Renaissance Reader,* ed. James Bruce Ross and Mary Martin McLaughlin (New York: Penguin Books, 1981), pp. 721–726.

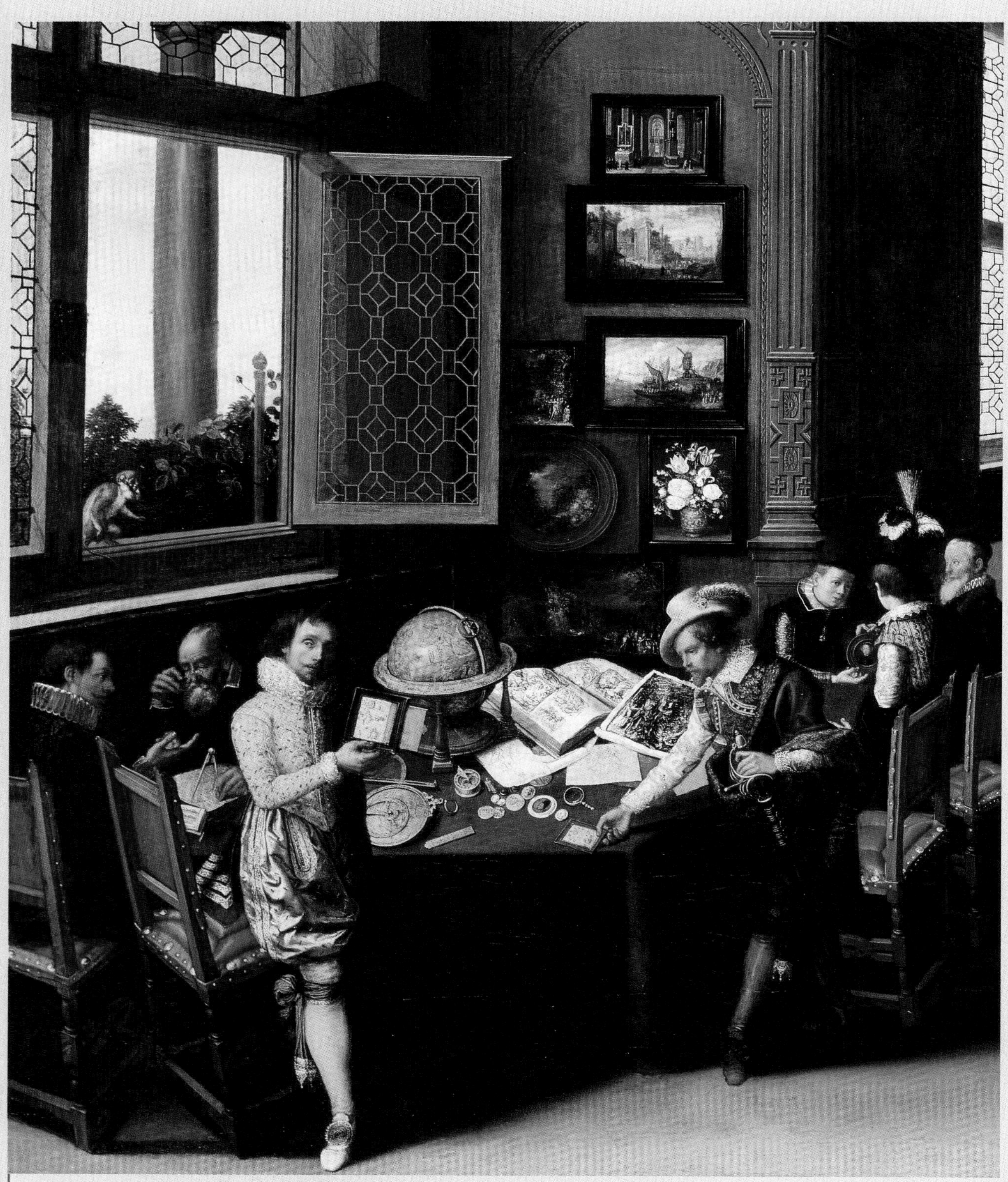

A detail from an early-seventeenth-century Flemish painting depicting maps, illustrated travel books, a globe, a compass, and an astrolabe. *(Reproduced by courtesy of the Trustees, The National Gallery, London)*

chapter

15 The Age of Religious Wars and European Expansion

chapter outline

Between 1560 and 1648, two developments dramatically altered the world in which Europeans lived: the Reformations of the Christian churches and overseas expansion. The Renaissance and the Reformations drastically changed cultural, political, religious, and social life in Europe and inspired magnificent literary, artistic, and musical achievements. Overseas expansion broadened the geographical horizons of Europeans and brought them into confrontation with ancient civilizations in Africa, Asia, and the Americas. These confrontations led first to conquest, then to exploitation, and finally to profound social changes in both Europe and the conquered territories. War and religious issues dominated politics and were intertwined: religion was commonly used to rationalize wars, which were often fought for power and territorial expansion. Meanwhile, Europeans carried their political, religious, and social attitudes to their newly acquired territories.

- What were the causes and consequences of the religious wars in France, the Netherlands, and Germany?
- How and why, in the sixteenth and seventeenth centuries, did a relatively small group living on the edge of the Eurasian landmass gain control of the major sea-lanes of the world and establish political and economic hegemony on distant continents?
- What immediate effect did overseas expansion have on Europe and on the conquered societies?
- How and why did slave labor become the dominant form of labor organization in the New World?
- How did the religious crises of this period affect religious faith, literary and artistic developments, and the status of women?

This chapter will address these questions.

François Clouet: Francis I Having succeeded his father as official painter at the French court, Clouet (1520?–1572) executed this royal portrait. The rich gold doublet has been embroidered with black velvet designs, satin, and more gold. His left hand rests on his golden sword hilt. *(Réunion des Musées Nationaux/Art Resource, NY)*

Politics, Religion, and War

In 1559 France and Spain signed the **Treaty of Cateau-Cambrésis,** which ended the long conflict known as the Habsburg-Valois Wars. Spain was the victor. France, exhausted by the struggle, had to acknowledge Spanish dominance in Italy, where much of the wars had been fought. Spanish governors ruled in Sicily, Naples, and Milan, and Spanish influence was strong in the Papal States and Tuscany. The Treaty of Cateau-Cambrésis ended an era of dynastic wars and initiated a period of conflicts in which politics and religion played the dominant roles. Governments used religious faiths to persuade people to acquiesce to heavier taxation. Religious differences served as the motivating force for ordinary people to participate in wars. Religious passions conditioned the mindsets of all elements of European society.

Wars of the late sixteenth century differed considerably from earlier wars. Sixteenth- and seventeenth-century armies were bigger than medieval ones; some forces numbered as many as fifty thousand men. Because large armies were expensive, governments had to reorganize their administrations to finance these armies. The use of gunpowder altered both the nature of war and popular attitudes toward it. Guns and cannon killed and wounded from a distance, indiscriminately. Writers scorned gunpowder as a coward's weapon that allowed a common soldier to kill a gentleman. Gunpowder weakened the notion, common during the Hundred Years' War, that warfare was an ennobling experience. At the same time, governments utilized propaganda, pulpits, and the printing press to arouse public opinion to support war.[1]

Late-sixteenth-century conflicts fundamentally tested the medieval ideal of a unified Christian society governed by one political ruler, the emperor, to whom all rulers were theoretically subordinate, and one church, to which all people belonged. The Protestant Reformation had killed this ideal, but few people recognized it as dead. Catholics continued to believe that Calvinists and Lutherans could be reconverted; Protestants persisted in thinking that the Roman church should be destroyed. Most people believed that a state could survive only if its members shared the same faith. Catholics and Protestants alike feared people of the other faith living in their midst. The settlement finally achieved in 1648, known as the Peace of Westphalia, signaled the end of the medieval ideal.

The Origins of Difficulties in France (1515–1559)

In the first half of the sixteenth century, France continued the recovery begun under Louis XI (see page 444). The population losses caused by the plague and the disorders accompanying the Hundred Years' War had created such a labor shortage that serfdom virtually disappeared. Cash rents replaced feudal rents and servile obligations. This development clearly benefited the peasantry. Meanwhile, the declining buying power of money hurt the nobility. The increase in France's population in the late fifteenth and sixteenth centuries brought new lands under cultivation, but the division of property among sons meant that most peasant holdings were very small. Domestic and foreign trade picked up, mercantile centers such as Rouen and Lyons expanded, and in 1517 a new port city was founded at Le Havre.

The charming and cultivated Francis I (r. 1515–1547) and his athletic, emotional son Henry II (r. 1547–1559)

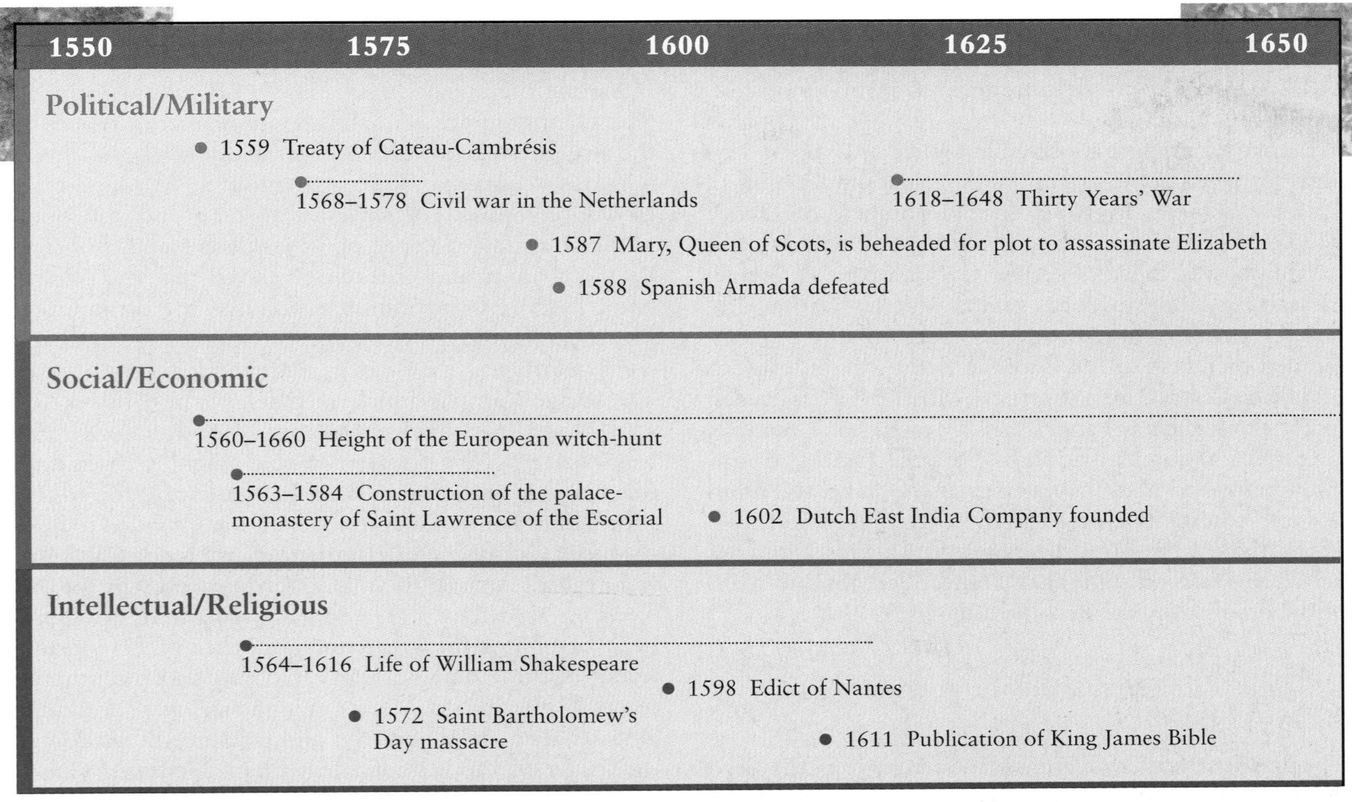

governed through a small, efficient council. Great nobles held titular authority in the provinces as governors, but Paris-appointed baillis and seneschals continued to exercise actual fiscal and judicial responsibility (see page 336). In 1539 Francis issued an ordinance that placed the whole of France under the jurisdiction of the royal law courts and made French the language of those courts. This act had a powerful centralizing impact. The taille, a tax on land, provided what strength the monarchy had and supported a strong standing army. Unfortunately, the tax base was too narrow for Francis's extravagant promotion of the arts and ambitious foreign policy.

The Habsburg-Valois Wars, waged intermittently through the first half of the sixteenth century, also cost more than the government could afford. Financing the wars posed problems. In addition to the time-honored practices of increasing taxes and engaging in heavy borrowing, Francis I tried two new devices to raise revenue: the sale of public offices and a treaty with the papacy. The former proved to be only a temporary source of money. The offices sold tended to become hereditary within a family, and once a man bought an office, he and his heirs were tax-exempt. The sale of public offices thus created a tax-exempt class called the "nobility of the robe," which held positions beyond the jurisdiction of the Crown.

The treaty with the papacy was the Concordat of Bologna (see page 444), in which Francis agreed to recognize the supremacy of the papacy over a universal council. In return, the French crown gained the right to appoint all French bishops and abbots. This understanding gave the monarchy a rich supplement of money and offices and a power over the church that lasted until the Revolution of 1789. The Concordat of Bologna helps explain why France did not later become Protestant: in effect, it established Catholicism as the state religion. Because French rulers possessed control over appointments and had a vested financial interest in Catholicism, they had no need to revolt against Rome.

However, the Concordat of Bologna perpetuated disorders within the French church. Ecclesiastical offices were used primarily to pay and reward civil servants. Churchmen in France, as elsewhere, were promoted to the hierarchy not because they possessed any special spiritual qualifications but because they had rendered services to the state. Such bishops were unlikely to work to elevate the intellectual and moral standards of the parish clergy. Few priests devoted scrupulous attention to the needs of their parishioners. Thus the teachings of Luther and Calvin, as the presses disseminated them, found a receptive audience.

Luther's tracts first appeared in France in 1518, and his ideas attracted some attention. After the publication of Calvin's *Institutes* in 1536, sizable numbers of French people were attracted to the "reformed religion," as Calvinism was called. Because Calvin wrote in French rather than Latin, his ideas gained wide circulation. Initially, Calvinism drew converts from among reform-minded members of the Catholic clergy, the industrious middle classes, and artisan groups. Most Calvinists lived in major cities, such as Paris, Lyons, Meaux, and Grenoble.

In spite of condemnation by the universities, government bans, and massive burnings at the stake, the numbers of Protestants grew steadily. When Henry II died in 1559, there were 40 well-organized Calvinist churches and 2,150 mission stations in France. Perhaps one-tenth of the population had become Calvinist.

Religious Riots and Civil War in France (1559–1598)

The feebleness of the French monarchy was the seed from which the weeds of civil violence sprang. The three weak sons of Henry II who occupied the throne could not provide the necessary leadership. Francis II (r. 1559–1560) died after seventeen months. Charles IX (r. 1560–1574) succeeded at the age of ten and was dominated by his mother, Catherine de' Medici. The intelligent, cultivated, and erratic Henry III (r. 1574–1589) followed his brother Charles on the French throne; Henry divided much of his attention between debaucheries with his male favorites and frantic acts of repentance. From 1560 to her death in 1589, Catherine genuinely wanted civil and religious peace—so long as her sons controlled the government. But she had no consistent religious policy, and her actions were guided by political motives.

The French nobility took advantage of this monarchical weakness. In the second half of the sixteenth century, between two-fifths and one-half of the nobility at one time or another became Calvinist. Just as German princes in the Holy Roman Empire had adopted Lutheranism as a means of opposition to Emperor Charles V, so French nobles frequently adopted the reformed religion as a religious cloak for their independence. No one believed that peoples of different faiths could coexist peacefully within the same territory. The Reformation thus led to a resurgence of feudal disorder. Armed clashes between Catholic royalist lords and Calvinist antimonarchical lords occurred in many parts of France.

Among the upper classes, the Catholic-Calvinist conflict was the surface issue, but the fundamental object of the struggle was power. At lower social levels, however, religious concerns were paramount. Working-class crowds composed of skilled craftsmen and the poor wreaked terrible violence on other people and property. Both Calvinists and Catholics believed that the others' books, services, and ministers polluted the community. Preachers incited violence, and ceremonies such as baptisms, marriages, and funerals triggered it.

A savage Catholic attack on Calvinists in Paris on August 24, 1572 (Saint Bartholomew's Day), followed the usual pattern. The occasion was a religious ceremony, the marriage of the king's sister Margaret of Valois to the Protestant Henry of Navarre, which was intended to help reconcile Catholics and **Huguenots,** as French Calvinists were called. Among the many Calvinists present for the wedding festivities was Admiral Gaspard de Coligny, head of one of the great noble families of France and leader of the Huguenot party. Coligny had recently replaced Catherine de' Medici in influence over the young king Charles IX. When, the night before the wedding, the leader of the Catholic aristocracy, Henry of Guise, had Coligny attacked, rioting and slaughter followed. The Huguenot gentry in Paris was massacred, and religious violence spread to the provinces. Between August 25 and October 3, perhaps twelve thousand Huguenots perished at Meaux, Lyons, Orléans, and Paris. The contradictory orders of Charles IX worsened the situation.

The **Saint Bartholomew's Day massacre** led to fighting called the War of the Three Henrys, a civil conflict among factions led by the Catholic Henry of Guise, the Protestant Henry of Navarre, and King Henry III, who succeeded the tubercular Charles IX. Though King Henry remained Catholic, he realized that the Catholic Guise group represented his greatest danger. The Guises wanted, through an alliance of Catholic nobles called the "Holy League," not only to destroy Calvinism but also to replace Henry III with a member of the Guise family. France suffered fifteen more years of religious rioting and domestic anarchy. Agriculture in many areas was destroyed, commercial life declined severely, and starvation and death haunted the land.

What ultimately saved France was a small group of moderates of both faiths called **politiques** who believed that only the restoration of strong monarchy could reverse the trend toward collapse. No religious creed was worth the incessant disorder and destruction. Therefore, the politiques favored accepting the Huguenots as an officially recognized and organized pressure group. (But religious toleration, the full acceptance of peoples of different religious persuasions within a pluralistic society, with minorities having the same civil liberties as the majority, developed only in the eighteenth century.) The death of Catherine de' Medici, followed by the assassinations of Henry of Guise and King Henry III, paved the way for the accession of Henry of Navarre, a politique who became Henry IV (r. 1589–1610).

This glamorous prince, "who knew how to fight, to make love, and to drink," as a contemporary remarked, wanted above all a strong and united France. He knew, too, that the majority of the French were Roman Catholics. Allegedly saying "Paris is worth a Mass," Henry knelt before the archbishop of Bourges and was received into the Roman Catholic church. Henry's willingness to sacrifice religious principles to political necessity saved France. The **Edict of Nantes,** which Henry published in 1598, granted to Huguenots liberty of conscience and liberty of public worship in 150 fortified towns, such as La Rochelle. The reign of Henry IV and the Edict of Nantes prepared the way for French absolutism in the seventeenth century by helping restore internal peace in France.

The Netherlands Under Charles V

In the last quarter of the sixteenth century, the political stability of England, the international prestige of Spain, and the moral influence of the Roman papacy all became mixed up with the religious crisis in the Low Countries. The Netherlands was the pivot around which European money, diplomacy, and war revolved. What began as a movement for the reformation of the church developed into a struggle for Dutch independence.

Emperor Charles V (r. 1519–1556) had inherited the seventeen provinces that compose present-day Belgium and Holland (see page 467). Since the time of the great medieval fairs, cities of the Low Countries (so called because much of the land lies below sea level) had been important sites for the exchange of products from the Baltic and Italy. Antwerp, ideally situated on the Scheldt River at the intersection of many trading routes, steadily expanded as the chief intermediary for international commerce and finance. English woolens; Baltic wheat, fur, and timber; Portuguese spices; German iron and copper; Spanish fruit; French wines and dyestuffs; Italian silks, marble, and mirrors; and vast amounts of cash—all were exchanged at Antwerp. The city's harbor could dock twenty-five hundred vessels at once, and five thousand merchants from many nations gathered daily in the **bourse** (or exchange). Other great towns—Bruges, Ghent, Brussels, Arras, and Amsterdam—made their living by trade and industry as well. The French-speaking southern towns produced fine linens and woolens, while the wealth of the Dutch-speaking northern cities rested on fishing, shipping, and international banking. In these cities, trade and commerce had produced a vibrant atmosphere, as personified in the urbane Erasmus of Rotterdam (see page 441).

Each of the seventeen provinces of the Netherlands possessed historical liberties: each was self-governing and enjoyed the right to make its own laws and collect its own taxes. In addition to important economic connections, only the recognition of a common ruler in the person of Emperor Charles V united the provinces. Delegates from the various provinces met together in the States General, but important decisions had to be referred back to each province for approval. In the middle of the sixteenth century, the provinces of the Netherlands had a limited sense of federation.

In the Low Countries as elsewhere, corruption in the Roman church and the critical spirit of the Renaissance provoked pressure for reform. Lutheran tracts and Dutch translations of the Bible flooded the seventeen provinces in the 1520s and 1530s, attracting many people to Protestantism. Charles V's government responded with condemnation and mild repression. This policy was not effective, however, because ideas circulated freely in the cosmopolitan atmosphere of the commercial centers. But Charles's loyalty to the Flemings checked the spread of Lutheranism. Charles had been born in Ghent and raised in the Netherlands; he was Flemish in language and culture. He identified with the Flemish and they with him.

In 1556, however, Charles V abdicated, dividing his territories between his brother Ferdinand, who received Austria and the Holy Roman Empire, and his son Philip, who inherited Spain, the Low Countries, Milan and the kingdom of Sicily, and the Spanish possessions in the Americas. Charles delivered his abdication speech before the States General at Brussels. The emperor was then fifty-five years old, white-haired, and so crippled in the legs that he had to lean for support on the young Prince William of Orange. According to one contemporary account of the emperor's appearance, "His under lip . . . was heavy and hanging, the lower jaw protruding so far beyond the upper that it was impossible for him to . . . speak a whole sentence in an intelligible voice."[2] Charles spoke in Flemish. Philip responded in Spanish; he could speak neither French nor Flemish. Netherlanders had always felt that Charles was one of their own. They were never to forget that Philip was Spanish.

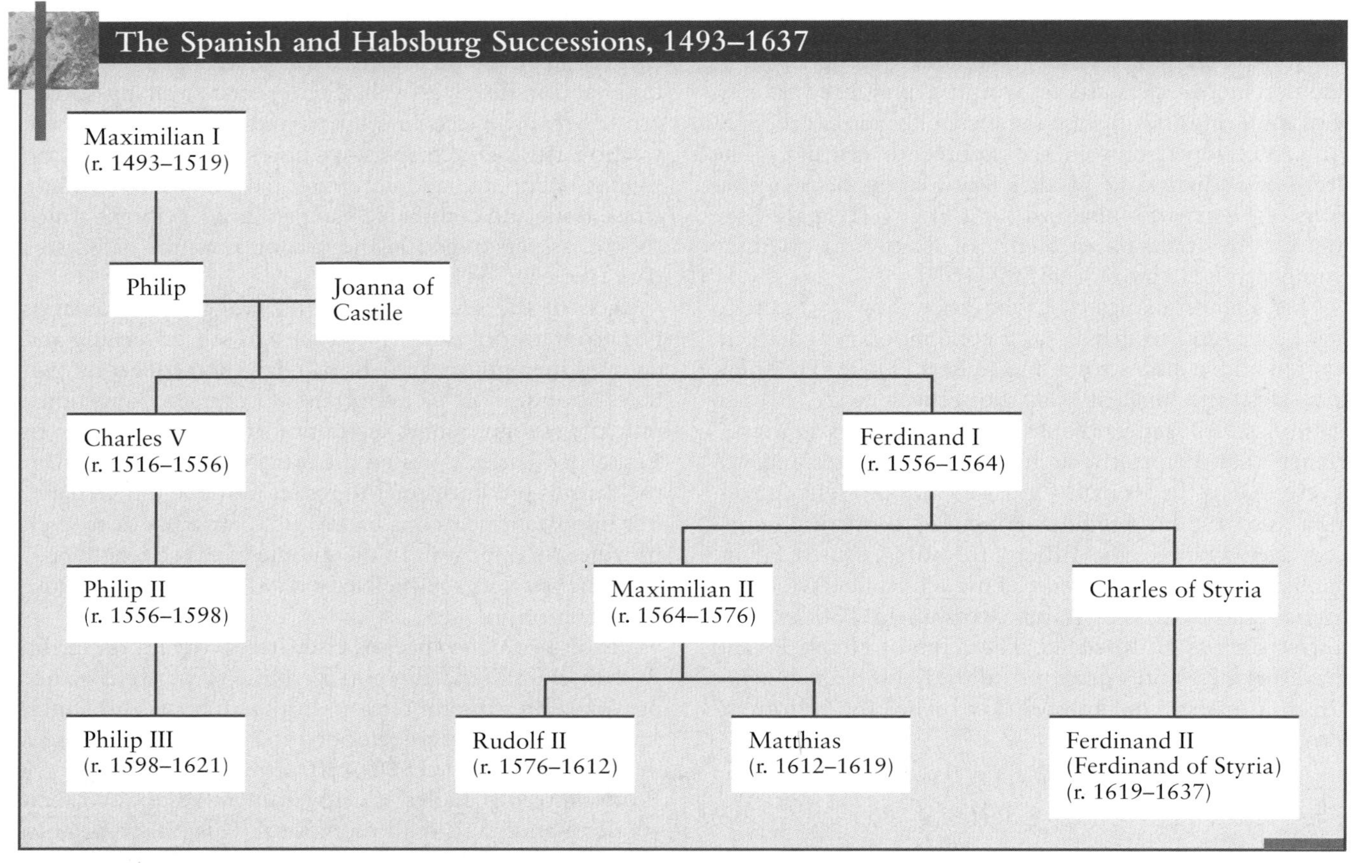

The Revolt of the Netherlands (1566–1587)

Lutheranism had posed no serious threat to Spanish rule; it was the spread of Calvinism that upset the apple cart. By the 1560s, there was a strong, militant minority of Calvinists in most of the cities of the Netherlands. The seventeen provinces possessed a large middle-class population, and the reformed religion, as a contemporary remarked, had a powerful appeal "to those who had grown rich by trade and were therefore ready for revolution."[3] Calvinism appealed to the middle classes because of its intellectual seriousness, moral gravity, and emphasis on any form of labor well done. It took deep root among the merchants and financiers in Amsterdam and the northern provinces. Working-class people were also converted, partly because their employers would hire only other Calvinists. Well organized and backed by rich merchants, Calvinists quickly gained a wide following. Whereas Lutherans taught respect for the powers that be, Calvinist reformed religion in the 1570s tended to encourage opposition to "illegal" civil authorities.

In 1559 Philip II appointed his half sister Margaret as regent of the Netherlands (r. 1559–1567). A proud, energetic, and strong-willed woman who once had Ignatius Loyola as her confessor, Margaret pushed Philip's orders to wipe out Protestantism. She introduced the Inquisition. Her more immediate problem, however, was revenue to finance the government of the provinces. Charles V had steadily increased taxes in the Low Countries. When Margaret appealed to the States General, it claimed that the Low Countries were more heavily taxed than Spain. Nevertheless, Margaret raised taxes and succeeded in uniting the opposition to the government's fiscal policy with the opposition to official repression of Calvinism.

In August 1566, a year of very high grain prices, fanatical Calvinists, primarily of the poorest classes, embarked on a rampage of frightful destruction. As in France, Calvinist destruction in the Low Countries was incited by popular preaching, and attacks were aimed at religious images as symbols of false doctrines, not at people. The cathedral of Notre Dame at Antwerp was the first target.

Begun in 1124 and finished only in 1518, this church stood as a monument to the commercial prosperity of Flanders, the piety of the business classes, and the artistic genius of centuries. On six successive summer evenings, crowds embarked on a rampage of destruction. Before the havoc was over, thirty more churches had been sacked and irreplaceable libraries burned. From Antwerp the destruction spread to Brussels and Ghent and north to the provinces of Holland and Zeeland.

From Madrid Philip II sent twenty thousand Spanish troops under the duke of Alva to pacify the Low Countries. Alva interpreted "pacification" to mean the ruthless extermination of religious and political dissidents. On top of the Inquisition, he opened his own tribunal, soon called the "Council of Blood." On March 3, 1568, fifteen hundred men were executed. Even Margaret was sickened and resigned her regency. Alva resolved the financial crisis by levying a 10 percent sales tax on every transaction, which in a commercial society caused widespread hardship and confusion.

For ten years, between 1568 and 1578, civil war raged in the Netherlands between Catholics and Protestants and between the seventeen provinces and Spain. Spanish generals could not halt the fighting. In 1576 the seventeen provinces united under the leadership of Prince William of Orange, called "the Silent" because of his remarkable discretion. In 1578 Philip II sent his nephew Alexander Farnese, duke of Parma, to crush the revolt once and for all. Farnese arrived with an army of German mercenaries. Avoiding pitched battles, he fought by patient sieges. One by one, the cities of the south fell—Maastricht, Tournai, Bruges, Ghent, and, finally, the financial capital

To Purify the Church The destruction of pictures and statues representing biblical events, Christian doctrine, or sacred figures was a central feature of the Protestant Reformation. Here Dutch Protestant soldiers destroy what they consider idols in the belief that they are purifying the church. *(Fotomas Index)*

of northern Europe, Antwerp (see Map 15.1). Calvinism was forbidden in these territories, and Protestants were compelled to convert or leave. The collapse of Antwerp marked the farthest extent of Spanish jurisdiction and ultimately the religious division of the Netherlands.

The ten southern provinces, the Spanish Netherlands (the future Belgium), remained under the control of the Spanish Habsburgs. The seven northern provinces, led by Holland, formed the **Union of Utrecht** and in 1581 declared their independence from Spain. The Dutch struggle for independence continued because it became inextricably tied up with English affairs.

Geography and sociopolitical structure differentiated the two countries. The northern provinces were ribboned with sluices and canals and therefore were highly defensible. Several times the Dutch had broken the dikes and flooded the countryside to halt the advancing Farnese. In the southern provinces, the Ardennes mountains interrupted the otherwise flat terrain. In the north, the commercial aristocracy possessed the predominant power; in the south, the landed nobility had the greater influence. The north was Protestant; the south remained Catholic.

MAP 15.1 The Netherlands, 1559–1609 Some provinces were overwhelmingly agricultural, some involved in manufacturing, others heavily commercial. Each of the seventeen was tied to the Spanish crown in a different way.

Philip II and Alexander Farnese did not accept this geographical division, and the struggle continued after 1581. The United Provinces repeatedly asked the Protestant queen of England, Elizabeth, for assistance. If Elizabeth responded favorably to Dutch pleas for military support against the Spanish, she would antagonize Philip II. But if she did not help the Protestant Netherlands and it was crushed by Farnese, the likelihood was that the Spanish would invade England.

Three developments forced Elizabeth's hand. First, the wars in the Low Countries—the chief market for English woolens—badly hurt the English economy. When wool was not exported, the Crown lost valuable customs revenues. Second, the murder of William the Silent in July 1584 eliminated not only a great Protestant leader but also the chief military check on the Farnese advance. Third, the collapse of Antwerp appeared to signal a Catholic sweep through the Netherlands. The next step, the English feared, would be a Spanish invasion of their island. For these reasons, Elizabeth pumped 250,000 pounds and two thousand troops into the Protestant cause in the Low Countries between 1585 and 1587.

Philip II and the Spanish Armada

Philip pondered the Dutch and English developments at the **Escorial**, northwest of Madrid. Begun in 1563 and completed under the king's personal supervision in 1584, the monastery of Saint Lawrence of the Escorial served as a residence for Jeromite monks, a tomb for the king's Habsburg ancestors, and a royal palace for Philip and his family. The vast buildings resemble a gridiron, the instrument on which Saint Lawrence (d. 258) had supposedly been roasted alive. The royal apartments were in the center of the Italian Renaissance building complex. King Philip's tiny bedchamber possessed a concealed sliding window that opened directly onto the high altar of the monastery church so that he could watch the services and pray along with the monks. In this somber atmosphere, surrounded by a community of monks and close to the bones of his ancestors, the Catholic ruler of Spain and much of the globe passed his days.

In 1587 Philip turned sixty, by the standards of his day an old man. Traditional scholarship, shaped largely by his Protestant enemies, has depicted Philip as morose and melancholic, a religious bigot determined to reimpose Roman Catholicism on northern Europe. Recent research

NOT LONGE TIME SINCE I SAWE A COWE.
DID FLAVNDERS REPRESENTE
VPON WHOSE BACKE KINGE PHILLIP RODE
AS BEING MALECONTNT.
THE QVEENE OF ENGLAND GIVING HAY
WHEARE ON THE COW DID FEEDE.
AS ONE THAT WAS HER GREATEST HELPE.
IN HER DISTRESSE AND NEEDE.
THE PRINCE OF ORANGE MILKT THE
AND MADE HIS PVRSE THE PAYLE.
THE COW DID SHYT IN MONSIEVRS
WHILE HE DID HOLD HER TAYLE.

The Milch Cow In this late-sixteenth-century allegorical cartoon, the cow is Flanders: Queen Elizabeth feeds it hay, King Philip rides and beats it, William of Orange milks it, and the duke of Anjou (of France) pulls its tail. The artist apparently thought all these rulers were exploiting the Low Countries. *(Rijksmuseum-Stichting Amsterdam)*

portrays him as a more complicated, even paradoxical, figure. In his youth, "he had visited northern Italy, the Alps, southern Germany, the Rhineland, the Netherlands, parts of France, and southern England." He had walked the streets of Antwerp, Augsburg, Brussels, Cologne, London, and Trent. With the exception of his father, Charles V, no other European ruler of the time had traveled or seen so much, or accumulated so much political experience in international relations. Philip impressed ambassadors as formal, tight-lipped, and forbidding, perhaps because he spoke only his native Castilian (and Latin) and thus was limited in his ability to communicate with others. He was deeply pious: attendance at daily Mass was always part of his routine, and every year he retired to a monastery during Holy Week. On the other hand, in his younger days, he was much given to pleasure, and a critical contemporary wrote, "He is dissipated with women, likes to go in disguise at night, and enjoys all types of gaming (gambling)." He also enjoyed jokes and had a good sense of humor.[4]

After Philip buried his fourth wife (enough to make any man "melancholic"), Anna of Austria, to whom he had been deeply devoted, contemporaries noticed a more marked devotion to religion. He relied more and more on God for political help. On the issues of the Inquisition and religious toleration, Philip was completely inflexible. He identified toleration with the growth of heresy, civil disorder, violence, and bloodshed: "Had there been no inquisition (in Spain) there would have been more heretics, and the country would be in a lamentable state like others (the Netherlands) where there is no inquisition as we have in Spain."[5] In this respect, Philip II differed little from the Protestant reformers Luther and Calvin, who initially called for individual liberty of conscience and then insisted on the right of church and civil powers to extirpate heresy within their jurisdictions.

Philip was a man of his times, and the times did not favor religious toleration. And just as the Protestant princes of northern Europe governed religious life within their states, so Philip II controlled ecclesiastical appointments and revenues in Spain.

With his determination to crush heresy in the Low Countries, and with the enormous wealth of American silver enabling him to hire the mercenary armies he needed, why did Philip II have such trouble achieving his goal? Philip ruled the first global empire in history. He was preoccupied with other parts of that empire, especially the advance of the Ottoman Turks into the western Mediterranean. This issue, combined with the death of his son and heir, Don Carlos; the death of his third wife, Elizabeth of Valois; and then a revolt of the Moriscos (Muslims) in Granada, made it impossible to concentrate on the Netherlands. At one point in 1566 he complained, "I have so much on my mind that I rarely know what I am doing or saying." Only after Philip learned that Suleiman the Magnificent had led a Turkish army into Hungary, ordered his fleet from the Mediterranean to the Adriatic, and died, did Philip feel able to focus on the Netherlands.[6]

But the Netherlands could not be separated in Philip's mind from what he perceived as the "British problem." In 1586, Mary, Queen of Scots, cousin and heir of Elizabeth of England, became implicated in a plot to assassinate Elizabeth. Philip, hoping to reunite England with Catholic Europe through Mary, gave the conspiracy his full backing. Mary was discovered and beheaded on February 18, 1587. News of her execution reached Philip in mid-April. When Pope Sixtus V (1585–1590) learned of Mary's death on March 24 (the dates suggest the slowness of communication in the late sixteenth century), the pope promised to pay Philip 1 million gold ducats the moment Spanish troops landed in England. Alexander Farnese had repeatedly warned that to subdue the Dutch, he would have to conquer England and cut off the source of Dutch support. Two plans for an expedition were considered. Philip's naval adviser recommended that a fleet of 150 ships sail from Lisbon, attack the English navy in the Channel, and invade England. Another proposal was to assemble a collection of barges and troops in Flanders to stage a cross-Channel assault. With the expected support of English Catholics, Spain would achieve a great victory. Farnese opposed this plan as militarily unsound.

As plans for an armada proceeded in 1587, two serious difficulties burdened the king. First, he was so badly crippled by gout that he could not sign documents and could walk, painfully, only with a cane. Second, official reports indicated that the Ottoman Turks might seize the moment of preoccupation with the Netherlands and England to attack Spain from the Mediterranean. With premonitions of disaster, Philip compromised between the two plans given him. He prepared a vast fleet to sail from Lisbon to Flanders, fight off Elizabeth's navy if it attacked, rendezvous with Farnese, and escort his barges across the English Channel. The expedition's purpose was to transport the Flemish army.

On May 9, 1588, *la felicissima armada*—"the most fortunate fleet," as it was ironically called in official documents—sailed from Lisbon harbor. The **Spanish Armada** of 130 vessels met an English fleet of about 150 ships in the Channel. The English fleet was composed of smaller, faster, more maneuverable ships, many of which had greater firing power than their Spanish counterparts. A combination of storms and squalls, spoiled food and rank water, inadequate Spanish ammunition, and, to a lesser extent, English fire ships that caused the Spanish to scatter gave England the victory. Many Spanish ships went down on the journey home around Ireland; perhaps 65 managed to reach home ports.

The battle in the Channel has frequently been described as one of the decisive battles in the history of the world. In fact, it had mixed consequences. Spain soon rebuilt its navy, and after 1588 the quality of the Spanish fleet improved. The destruction of the Spanish Armada did not halt the flow of silver from the New World. More silver reached Spain between 1588 and 1603 than in any other fifteen-year period. The war between England and Spain dragged on for years.

The defeat of the Spanish Armada was decisive, however, in the sense that it prevented Philip II from reimposing religious unity on western Europe by force. He did not conquer England, and Elizabeth continued her financial and military support of the Dutch. In the Netherlands, neither side gained significant territory. The borders of 1581 tended to become permanent. In 1609 Philip III of Spain (r. 1598–1621) agreed to a truce, in effect recognizing the independence of the United Provinces. In seventeenth-century Spain, memory of the loss of the Spanish Armada contributed to a spirit of defeatism. In England the victory contributed to a David and Goliath legend that enhanced English national sentiment.

The Thirty Years' War (1618–1648)

While Philip II dreamed of building a second armada and Henry IV began the reconstruction of France, the political-religious situation in central Europe deteriorated. An uneasy truce had prevailed in the Holy Roman Empire since the Peace of Augsburg of 1555 (see page 470). According to the Augsburg settlement, the faith of the prince determined the religion of his subjects. Later in the century, however, Catholics grew alarmed because Lutherans, in violation of the Peace of Augsburg, were steadily acquiring German bishoprics. The spread of Calvinism further confused the issue. The Augsburg settlement had pertained only to Lutheranism and Catholicism, so Calvinists ignored it and converted several princes. Lutherans feared that the Augsburg principles would be totally undermined by Catholic and Calvinist gains. Also, the militantly active Jesuits had reconverted several Lutheran princes to Catholicism. In an increasingly tense situation, Lutheran princes formed the **Protestant Union** (1608), and Catholics retaliated with the Catholic League (1609). Each alliance was determined that the other should make no religious (that is, territorial) advance. The empire was composed of two armed camps.

Dynastic interests were also involved in the German situation. The Spanish Habsburgs strongly supported the goals of their Austrian relatives: the unity of the empire and the preservation of Catholicism within it.

Violence erupted first in Bohemia (see Map 15.2), where in 1617 Ferdinand of Styria, the new Catholic king of Bohemia, closed some Protestant churches. On May 23, 1618, Protestants hurled two of Ferdinand's officials from a castle window in Prague. They fell seventy feet but survived: Catholics claimed that angels had caught them; Protestants said that the officials had fallen on a heap of soft horse manure. Called the "defenestration of Prague," this event marked the beginning of the Thirty Years' War (1618–1648).

Historians traditionally divide the war into four phases. The first, or Bohemian, phase (1618–1625) was characterized by civil war in Bohemia between the Catholic League, led by Ferdinand, and the Protestant Union,

Soldiers Pillage a Farmhouse Billeting troops among civilian populations caused untold hardships. In this late-seventeenth-century Dutch illustration, brawling soldiers take over a peasant's home, eat his food, steal his possessions, and insult his family. Peasant retaliation sometimes proved swift and bloody. *(Rijksmuseum-Stichting Amsterdam)*

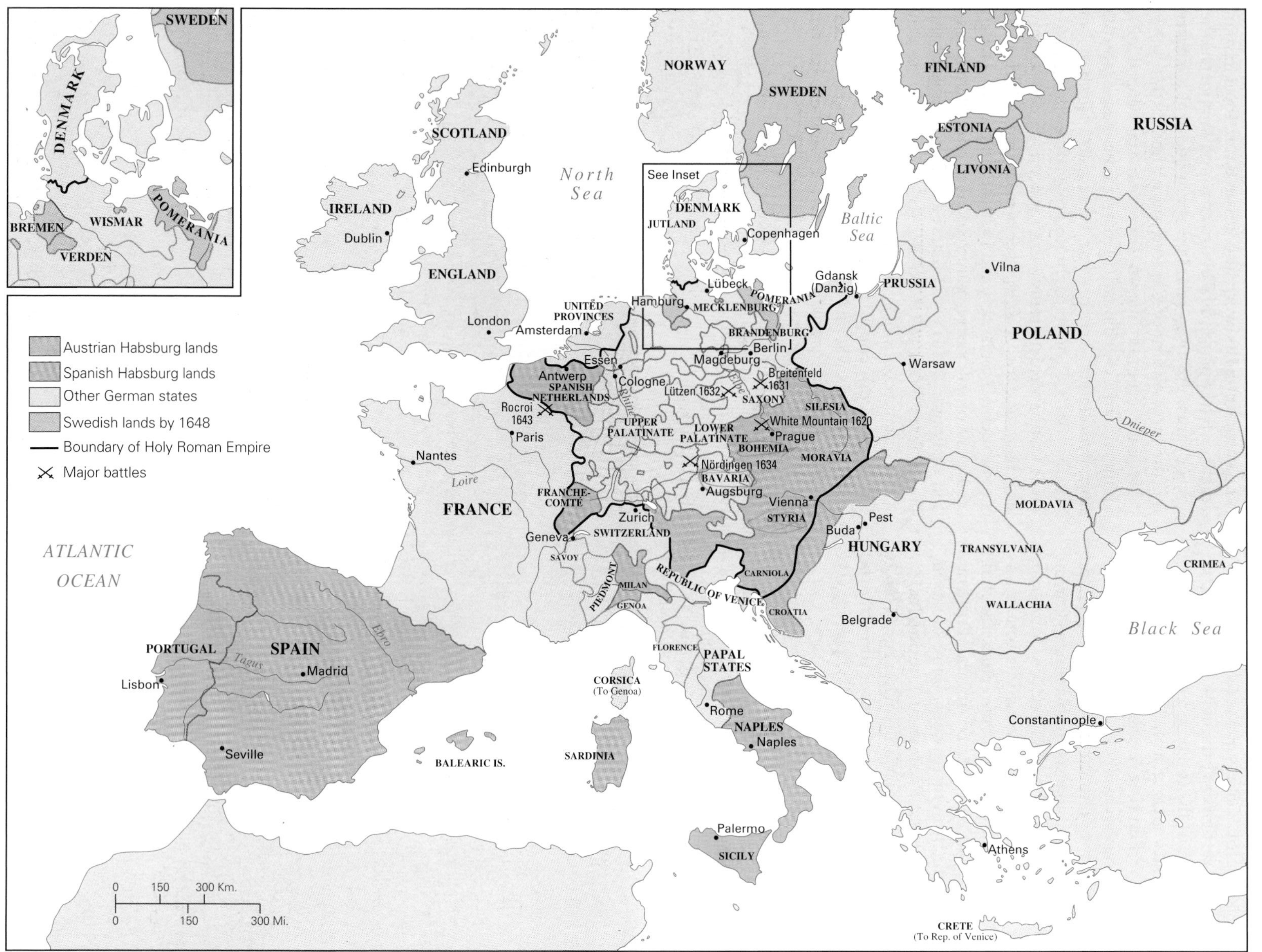

MAP 15.2 Europe in 1648 Which country emerged from the Thirty Years' War as the strongest European power? What dynastic house was that country's major rival in the early modern period?

headed by Frederick, the elector of the Palatinate. The Bohemians fought for religious liberty and independence from Habsburg rule. In 1620 Frederick was defeated by Catholic forces at the Battle of the White Mountain. Ferdinand, recently elected Holy Roman emperor as Ferdinand II, followed up his victories by wiping out Protestantism in Bohemia through forcible conversions and the activities of militant Jesuit missionaries. Within ten years, Bohemia was completely Catholic.

The second, or Danish, phase of the war (1625–1629)—so called because of the participation of King Christian IV of Denmark (r. 1588–1648), the ineffective leader of the Protestant cause—witnessed additional Catholic victories. The Catholic imperial army led by Albert of Wallenstein scored smashing victories. It swept through Silesia, north through Schleswig and Jutland to the Baltic, and east into Pomerania. Wallenstein, who had made himself indispensable to the emperor Ferdinand, was an unscrupulous opportunist who used his vast riches to build an army loyal only to himself. The general seemed interested more in carving out an empire for himself than in aiding the Catholic cause. He quarreled with the Catholic League, and soon the Catholic forces were divided. Religion was eclipsed as a basic issue of the war.

The year 1629 marked the peak of Habsburg power. The Jesuits persuaded the emperor to issue the Edict of Restitution, whereby all Catholic properties lost to Protestantism since 1552 were to be restored and only Catholics and Lutherans (not Calvinists, Hussites, or other sects) were to be allowed to practice their faiths. When Wallenstein began ruthless enforcement of the edict, Protestants throughout Europe feared collapse of the balance of power in north-central Europe.

The third, or Swedish, phase of the war (1630–1635) began with the arrival in Germany of the Swedish king Gustavus Adolphus (r. 1594–1632). The ablest administrator of his day and a devout Lutheran, Gustavus Adolphus intervened to support the oppressed Protestants within the empire. Cardinal Richelieu, the chief minister of King Louis XIII of France (r. 1610–1643), subsidized the Swedes, hoping to weaken Habsburg power in Europe. In 1631, with a small but well-disciplined army equipped with superior muskets, Gustavus Adolphus won a brilliant victory at Breitenfeld. Again in 1632 he was victorious at Lützen, though he was fatally wounded in the battle.

The participation of the Swedes in the Thirty Years' War proved decisive for the future of Protestantism and later German history. When Gustavus Adolphus landed on German soil, he headed a Baltic empire under Swedish influence. The Swedish victories ended the Habsburg ambition of uniting all the German states under imperial authority.

The death of Gustavus Adolphus in 1632, followed by the defeat of the Swedes at the Battle of Nördlingen in 1634, prompted the French to enter the war on the side of the Protestants. Thus began the French, or international, phase of the Thirty Years' War (1635–1648). For almost a century, French foreign policy had been based on opposition to the Habsburgs because a weak empire divided into scores of independent principalities enhanced France's international stature. In 1635 Cardinal Richelieu declared war on Spain and again sent financial and military assistance to the Swedes and the German Protestant princes. The war dragged on. French, Dutch, and Swedes, supported by Scots, Finns, and German mercenaries, burned, looted, and destroyed German agriculture and commerce. The Thirty Years' War lasted so long because neither side had the resources to win a quick, decisive victory. Finally, in October 1648, peace was achieved.

The treaties signed at Münster and Osnabrück, commonly called the **Peace of Westphalia**, marked a turning point in European political, religious, and social history. Conflicts fought over religious faiths ended. The treaties recognized the sovereign, independent authority of more than three hundred German princes; each would govern his territory and make war and peace. Since the time of Frederick II Hohenstaufen (see pages 337–338), Germany had followed a pattern of state building different from that of France and England: the imperial power (the emperor) had shared authority with the princes. After the Peace of Westphalia, the Habsburg emperors' power was severely limited, but the Holy Roman Empire continued to function as a federation.

The independence of the United Provinces of the Netherlands was acknowledged. Political divisions within the empire, Germany's weak frontiers, and the acquisition of the province of Alsace increased France's size and prestige. Sweden received a large cash indemnity and jurisdiction over German territories along the Baltic Sea. The powerful Swedish presence in northeastern Germany subsequently posed a major threat to the future kingdom of Brandenburg-Prussia. The treaties also denied the papacy the right to participate in German religious affairs—a restriction symbolizing the reduced role of the church in European politics.

In religion, the Westphalian treaties stipulated that the Augsburg agreement of 1555 should stand permanently. The sole modification was that Calvinism, along with Catholicism and Lutheranism, would become a legally permissible creed. The north German states remained Protestant; the south German states, Catholic.

Germany After the Thirty Years' War

The Thirty Years' War was a disaster for the German economy and society, probably the most destructive event in German history before the twentieth century. Perhaps one-third of the urban residents and two-fifths of the inhabitants of rural areas died. Entire areas of Germany were depopulated, partly by military actions, partly by disease—typhus, dysentery, bubonic plague, and syphilis accompanied the movements of armies—and partly by the thousands of refugees who fled to safer areas.

In the late sixteenth and early seventeenth centuries, all Europe experienced an economic crisis primarily caused by the influx of silver from South America. Because the Thirty Years' War was fought on German soil, these economic difficulties were badly aggravated in the empire. Scholars still cannot estimate the value of losses in agricultural land and livestock, in trade and commerce. The trade of southern cities such as Augsburg, already hard hit by the shift in transportation routes from the Mediterranean to the Atlantic, was virtually destroyed by the fighting in the south. Meanwhile, towns such as Lübeck, Hamburg, and Bremen in the north and Essen in the Ruhr area actually prospered because of the many refugees they attracted. The destruction of land and foodstuffs, compounded by the flood of Spanish silver, brought on a severe price rise. During and after the war, inflation was worse in Germany than anywhere else in Europe.

Agricultural areas suffered catastrophically. The population decline caused a rise in the value of labor, and owners of great estates had to pay more for agricultural workers. Farmers who needed only small amounts of capital to restore their lands started over again. Many small farmers, however, lacked the revenue to rework their holdings and had to become day laborers. Nobles and landlords bought up many small holdings and acquired great estates. In some parts of Germany, especially east of the Elbe River in areas such as Mecklenburg and Pomerania, peasants' loss of land led to the rise of a new serfdom.[7] Thus the Thirty Years' War contributed to the legal and economic decline of the largest segment of German society.

Discovery, Reconnaissance, and Expansion

Historians have variously called the period from 1450 to 1650 the "Age of Discovery," the "Age of Reconnaissance," and the "Age of Expansion." All three labels are appropriate. The Age of Discovery refers to the era's phenomenal advances in geographical knowledge and technology. In 1350 it took as long to sail from the eastern end of the Mediterranean to the western end as it had taken a thousand years earlier. Even in the fifteenth century, Europeans knew little more about the earth's surface than the Romans had. By 1650, however, Europeans had made an extensive reconnaissance—or preliminary exploration—and had sketched fairly accurately the physical outline of the whole earth. Much of the geographical information they had gathered was tentative and not fully understood—hence the appropriateness of the term the Age of Reconnaissance.

The designation of the era as the Age of Expansion refers to the migration of Europeans to other parts of the world. This colonization resulted in political control of much of South and North America; coastal regions of Africa, India, China, and Japan; and many Pacific islands. This political hegemony was accompanied by economic exploitation, religious domination, and the introduction of European patterns of social and intellectual life. Indeed, the sixteenth-century expansion of European society launched a new age in world history.

Overseas Exploration and Conquest

The outward expansion of Europe began with the Viking voyages across the Atlantic in the ninth and tenth centuries. Under Eric the Red and Leif Ericson, the Vikings discovered Greenland and the eastern coast of North America. The Vikings also made permanent settlements in, and a legal imprint on, Iceland, Ireland, England, Normandy, and Sicily (see pages 255–259). The Crusades of the eleventh through thirteenth centuries were another phase in Europe's attempt to explore and exploit peoples on the periphery of the continent. But the lack of a strong territorial base, superior Muslim military strength, and sheer misrule combined to make the Crusader kingdoms short-lived. In the mid-fifteenth century, Europe seemed ill-prepared for further international ventures, and by 1450 a grave new threat had appeared in the East—the Ottoman Turks.

Combining excellent military strategy with efficient administration of their conquered territories, the Turks had subdued most of Asia Minor and begun to settle on the western side of the Bosporus. The Muslim Ottoman Turks under Sultan Mohammed II (r. 1451–1481) captured Constantinople in 1453, pressed northwest into the Balkans, and by the early sixteenth century controlled the eastern Mediterranean. The Turkish menace badly frightened Europeans. In France in the fifteenth and sixteenth centuries, twice as many books were printed about the Turkish threat as about the American discoveries. Yet

Catalan Atlas, 1375 Abraham Cresques and his son Yehuda, Jews living in Palma on the island of Majorca (at the time, almost all the best mapmakers were Jewish), produced this atlas for Peter IV of Aragon. Consulting Marco Polo's manuscripts and interviewing Arabic seamen and European travelers, the Cresques aimed to produce a world map showing the various peoples inhabiting it. The atlas consists of twelve leaves mounted on boards to be folded like a screen. Primitive by modern standards, the atlas was at the time a masterpiece of empirical evidence. *(Bibliothèque Nationale, Paris)*

these centuries witnessed a fantastic continuation, on a global scale, of European expansion.

Political centralization in Spain, France, and England helps explain those countries' outward push. In the fifteenth century, Isabella and Ferdinand had consolidated their several kingdoms to achieve a more united Spain. The Catholic rulers revamped the Spanish bureaucracy and humbled the Muslims and the Jews. The Spanish monarchy was stronger than before and in a position to support foreign ventures; it could bear the costs and dangers of exploration. But Portugal, situated on the extreme southwestern edge of the European continent, got a head start on the rest of Europe. Still insignificant as a European land power despite its recently secured frontiers, Portugal sought greatness in the unknown world overseas.

Portugal's taking of Ceuta, an Arab city in northern Morocco, in 1415 marked the beginning of European exploration and control of overseas territory. The objectives of Portuguese policy included the historic Iberian crusade to Christianize Muslims and to find gold, an overseas route to the spice markets of India, and the mythical Christian ruler of Ethiopia, Prester John.

In the early phases of Portuguese exploration, Prince Henry (1394–1460), called "the Navigator" because of the school he established for the study of geography and navigation and for the annual expeditions he sent down the western coast of Africa, played the leading role. In the fifteenth century, most of the gold that reached Europe came from the Sudan in West Africa and from the Akan peoples living near the area of present-day Ghana.

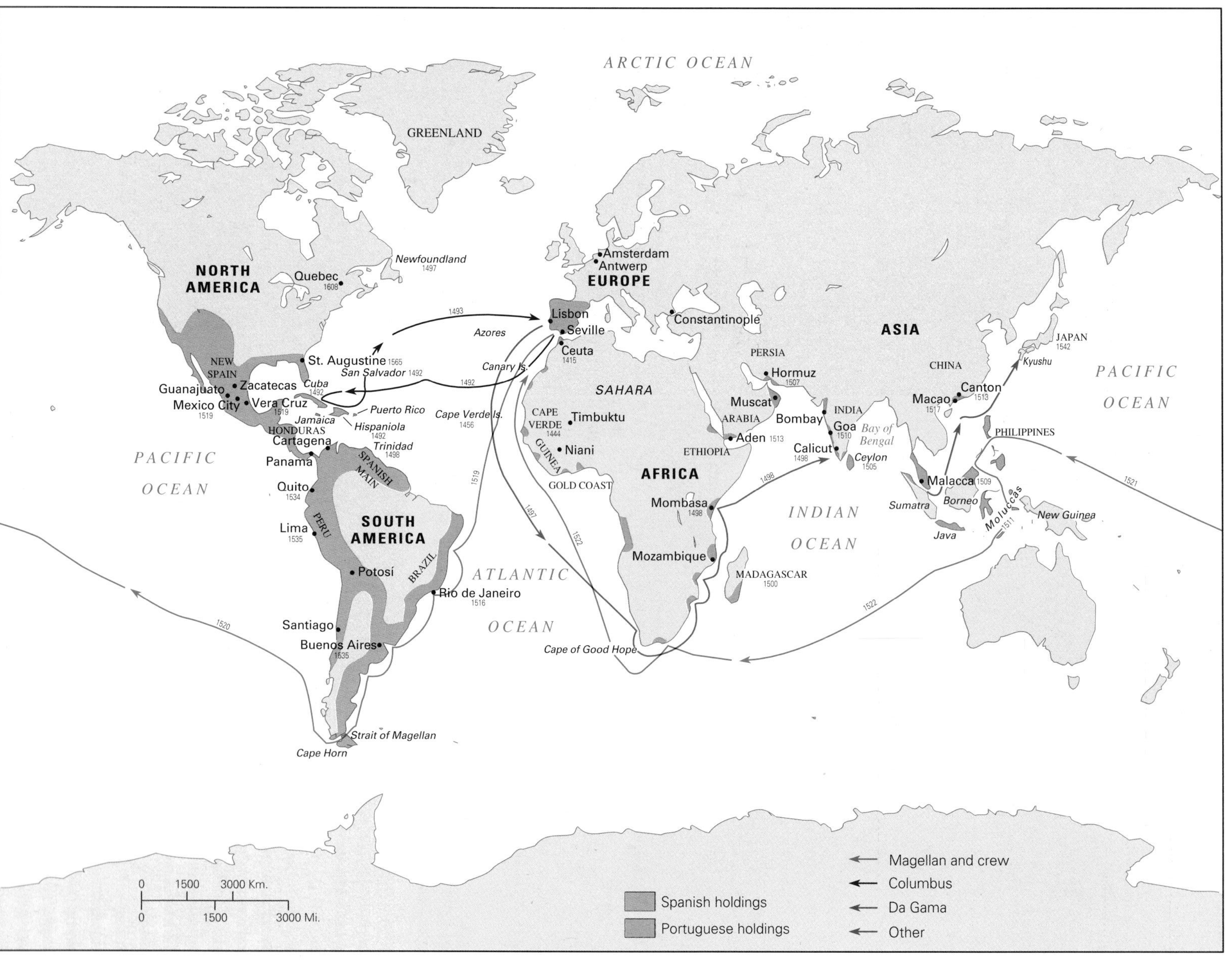

MAP 15.3 Overseas Exploration and Conquest, Fifteenth and Sixteenth Centuries The voyages of discovery marked another phase in the centuries-old migrations of European peoples. Consider the major contemporary significance of each of the three voyages depicted on the map.

Muslim caravans brought the gold from the African cities of Niani and Timbuktu and carried it north across the Sahara to Mediterranean ports. Then the Portuguese muscled in on this commerce in gold. Prince Henry's carefully planned expeditions succeeded in reaching Guinea, and under King John II (r. 1481–1495) the Portuguese established trading posts and forts on the Guinea coast and penetrated into the continent all the way to Timbuktu (see Map 15.3). Portuguese ships transported gold to Lisbon, and by 1500 Portugal controlled the flow of gold to Europe. The golden century of Portuguese prosperity had begun.

Still the Portuguese pushed farther south down the west coast of Africa. In 1487 Bartholomew Diaz rounded the Cape of Good Hope at the southern tip, but storms and a threatened mutiny forced him to turn back. On a later expedition (1497–1499), the Portuguese mariner Vasco da Gama reached India and returned to Lisbon loaded with spices and samples of Indian cloth. King Manuel (r. 1495–1521) promptly dispatched thirteen ships under the command of Pedro Alvares Cabral, assisted by Diaz, to set up trading posts in India. On April 22, 1500, the coast of Brazil in South America was sighted and claimed for the Crown of Portugal. Cabral then proceeded south and east around the Cape of Good Hope and reached India. Half the fleet was lost on the return voyage, but the six spice-laden vessels that dropped anchor in Lisbon harbor in July 1501 more than paid for the entire expedition. Thereafter, convoys were sent out every March. Lisbon became the entrance port for Asian goods into Europe—but this was not accomplished without a fight.

For centuries the Muslims had controlled the rich spice trade of the Indian Ocean, and they did not surrender it willingly. Portuguese commercial activities were accompanied by the destruction or seizure of strategic Muslim coastal forts, which later served Portugal as both trading posts and military bases. Alfonso de Albuquerque, whom the Portuguese crown appointed as governor of India (1509–1515), decided that these bases, not inland territories, should control the Indian Ocean. Accordingly, his cannon blasted open the ports of Calicut, Ormuz, Goa, and Malacca, the vital centers of Arab domination of South Asian trade. This bombardment laid the foundation for Portuguese imperialism in the sixteenth and seventeenth centuries: a strange way to bring Christianity to "those who were in darkness." As one scholar wrote about the opening of China to the West, "while Buddha came to China on white elephants, Christ was borne on cannon balls."[8]

In March 1493, between the voyages of Diaz and da Gama, Spanish ships under a triumphant Genoese mariner named Christopher Columbus (1451–1506), in the service of the Spanish crown, entered Lisbon harbor. Spain also had begun the quest for an empire.

Technological Stimuli to Exploration

Technological developments were the key to Europe's remarkable outreach. By 1350 *cannon*—iron or bronze guns that fired iron or stone balls—had been fully developed in western Europe. These pieces of artillery emitted frightening noises and great flashes of fire and could batter down fortresses and even city walls. Sultan Mohammed II's siege of Constantinople in 1453 provides a classic illustration of the effectiveness of cannon fire.

Constantinople had very strong walled fortifications. The sultan secured the services of a Western technician, who built fifty-six small cannon and a gigantic gun that could hurl stone balls weighing about eight hundred pounds. The gun could be moved only by several hundred oxen and loaded and fired only by about a hundred men working together. This awkward but powerful weapon breached the walls of Constantinople, which cracked on the second day of the bombardment. Lesser cannon finished the job.

Early cannon posed serious technical difficulties. Iron cannon were cheaper than bronze to construct, but they were difficult to cast effectively and were liable to crack and injure artillerymen. Bronze guns, made of copper and tin, were less subject than iron to corrosion, but they were very expensive. All cannon were extraordinarily difficult to move, required considerable time for reloading, and were highly inaccurate. They thus proved inefficient for land warfare. However, they could be used at sea.

The mounting of cannon on ships and improved techniques of shipbuilding gave impetus to European expansion. Since ancient times, most seagoing vessels had been narrow, open boats called *galleys,* propelled largely by manpower. Slaves or convicts who had been sentenced to the galleys manned the oars of the ships that sailed the Mediterranean, and both cargo ships and warships carried soldiers for defense. Though well suited to the placid and thoroughly explored waters of the Mediterranean, galleys could not withstand the rough winds and uncharted shoals of the Atlantic. The need for sturdier craft, as well as population losses caused by the Black Death, forced the development of a new style of ship that would not require soldiers for defense or much manpower to sail.

In the course of the fifteenth century, the Portuguese developed the *caravel,* a small, light, three-masted sailing ship. Though somewhat slower than the galley, the caravel held more cargo and was highly maneuverable. When

Nocturnal An instrument for determining the hour of night at sea by finding the progress of certain stars around the polestar (center aperture). *(National Maritime Museum, London)*

fitted with cannon, it could dominate larger vessels, such as the round ships commonly used as merchantmen. The substitution of wind power for manpower and artillery fire for soldiers signaled a great technological advance and gave Europeans navigational and fighting ascendancy over the rest of the world.[9]

Other fifteenth-century developments in navigation helped make possible the conquest of the Atlantic. The **magnetic compass** enabled sailors to determine their direction and position at sea. The **astrolabe**, an instrument developed by Muslim navigators in the twelfth century and used to determine the altitude of the sun and other celestial bodies, permitted mariners to plot their *latitude,* or position north or south of the equator. Steadily improved maps and sea charts gave information about distance, sea depths, and general geography.

The Explorers' Motives

The expansion of Europe was not motivated by demographic pressures. The Black Death had caused serious population losses from which Europe had not recovered in 1500. Few Europeans immigrated to North or South America in the sixteenth century. Half of those who did sail to America died en route; half of those who reached the New World eventually returned to their homeland. Why, then, did explorers brave the Atlantic and Pacific Oceans, risking their lives to discover new continents and spread European culture?

The reasons are varied and complex. People of the sixteenth century were still basically medieval in the sense that their attitudes and values were shaped by religion and expressed in religious terms. In the late fifteenth century, crusading fervor remained a basic part of the Portuguese and Spanish national ideal. The desire to Christianize Muslims and pagan peoples played a central role in European expansion. Queen Isabella of Spain, for example, showed a fanatical zeal for converting the Muslims to Christianity, and she concentrated her efforts on the Muslims in Granada. After the abortive crusading attempts of the thirteenth century, rulers realized full well that they lacked the material resources to mount the full-scale assault on Islam necessary for victory. Crusading impulses thus shifted from the Muslims to the pagan peoples of Africa and the Americas.

Moreover, after the reconquista, enterprising young men of the Spanish upper classes found their economic and political opportunities severely limited. As a study of the Castilian city of Ciudad Real shows, the ancient aristocracy controlled the best agricultural land and monopolized urban administrative posts. Great merchants and a few nobles (surprisingly, since Spanish law forbade participation by nobles in commercial ventures) dominated the textile and leather-glove manufacturing industries. Consequently, many ambitious men immigrated to the Americas to seek their fortunes.[10]

Government sponsorship and encouragement of exploration also accounted for the results of the various voyages. Mariners and explorers could not as private individuals afford the massive sums needed to explore mysterious oceans and control remote continents. The strong financial support of Prince Henry the Navigator led to Portugal's phenomenal success in the spice trade. Even the grudging and modest assistance of Isabella and Ferdinand eventually brought untold riches—and complicated problems—to Spain. The Dutch in the seventeenth century, through such government-sponsored trading companies as the Dutch East India Company, reaped enormous wealth, and although the Netherlands was a small country in size, it dominated the European economy in 1650.

Scholars have frequently described the European discoveries as a manifestation of Renaissance curiosity about the physical universe—the desire to know more about the geography and peoples of the world. Cosmography, natural history, and geography aroused enormous interest among educated people in the fifteenth and sixteenth centuries. Just as science fiction and speculation about life on other planets excite readers today, quasi-scientific literature about Africa, Asia, and the Americas captured the imaginations of literate Europeans. Fernández de

Oviedo's ***General History of the Indies*** (1547), a detailed eyewitness account of plants, animals, and peoples, was widely read.

Spices were another important incentive for voyages of discovery. Introduced into western Europe by the Crusaders in the twelfth century, nutmeg, mace, ginger, cinnamon, and pepper added flavor and variety to the monotonous diet of Europeans. Spices were also used in the preparation of medicinal drugs and incense for religious ceremonies. In the late thirteenth century, Venetian Marco Polo (1254?–1324?), the greatest of medieval travelers, had visited the court of the Chinese emperor. The widely publicized account of his experiences in *Travels* (ca 1298) stimulated the trade in spices between Asia and Italy. The Venetians came to hold a monopoly of that trade in western Europe.

Spices were grown in India and China, shipped across the Indian Ocean to ports on the Persian Gulf, and then transported by Arabs across the Arabian Desert to Mediterranean ports. But the rise of the Ming Dynasty in China in the late fourteenth century resulted in the expulsion of foreigners. And the steady penetration of the Ottoman Turks into the eastern Mediterranean forced Europeans to seek a new route to the Asian spice markets.

The basic reason for European exploration and expansion, however, was the quest for material profit. Mariners and explorers frankly admitted this. As Bartholomew Diaz put the matter, his motives were "to serve God and His Majesty, to give light to those who were in darkness and to grow rich as all men desire to do." When Vasco da Gama reached the port of Calicut, India, in 1498, a native asked what the Portuguese wanted. Da Gama replied, "Christians and spices."[11] The bluntest of the Spanish conquistadors, Hernando Cortés announced as he prepared to conquer Mexico, "I have come to win gold, not to plow the fields like a peasant."[12] A sixteenth-

Pepper Harvest To break the monotony of a bland diet, Europeans had a passion for pepper, which—along with cinnamon, cloves, nutmeg, and ginger—was the main object of the Asian trade. Since one kilo of pepper cost 2 grams of silver at the place of production in the East Indies, 10 to 14 grams of silver in Alexandria, Egypt, 14 to 18 grams in Venice, and 20 to 30 grams at the markets of northern Europe, we can appreciate the fifteenth-century expression "as dear as pepper." Here natives fill vats, while the dealer tastes a peppercorn for pungency. *(Bibliothèque Nationale, Paris/ Bridgeman Art Library International Ltd)*

century diplomat, Ogier Gheselin de Busbecq, summed up this paradoxical attitude well: in expeditions to the Indies and the Antipodes, he said, "religion supplies the pretext and gold the motive."[13]

Spanish and Portuguese explorers carried the fervent Catholicism and missionary zeal of the Iberian Peninsula to the New World, and once in America they urged home governments to send clerics. At bottom, however, wealth was the driving motivation.

The Problem of Christopher Columbus

The year 1992, which marked the quincentenary of Columbus's first voyages to the Americas, spawned an enormous amount of discussion about the significance of his voyages. Journalists, scholars, amateurs, and polemicists debated Columbus's accomplishments and failures. Until the 1980s, however, most writers would have generally agreed with Harvard historian Samuel Eliot Morison in his 1942 biography of the explorer:

> *The whole history of the Americas stems from the Four Voyages of Columbus; today a score of independent nations and dominions unite in homage to Columbus, the stout-hearted son of Genoa, who carried Christian civilization across the Ocean Sea.*[14]

In 1942, the Western Powers believed they were engaged in a life-and-death struggle to defend "Christian civilization" against the evil of fascism.

In contrast to this lavish praise, Columbus has recently undergone severe criticism. He enslaved and sometimes killed the Indians he encountered. He was a cruel and ineffective governor of Spain's Caribbean colony. Moreover, he did not discover the continents: others—Africans and Europeans—had been there before him. And not only did he not discover the continents; he also misunderstood what he had found. In short, he was a fool who did not know what was going on around him. Some have criticized him because he abandoned the mother of his illegitimate son. Other writers have faulted Columbus as an opportunistic adventurer who loved the trappings of grand titles. Some claim he was the originator of European exploitation of the non-European world; he destroyed the paradise that had been the New World.[15] Because these judgments rest on social and ethical standards that did not exist in Columbus's world, responsible scholars consider them ahistorical.

Using the evidence of his journal (sea log) and letters, let us ask three basic questions. First, what kind of man was Columbus, and what forces or influences shaped him? Second, in sailing westward from Europe, what were his goals? Third, did he achieve his goals, and what did he make of his discoveries?

The central feature in the character of Christopher Columbus is that he was a deeply religious man. He began the *Journal* of his voyage to the Americas in the form of a letter to Ferdinand and Isabella of Spain:

> *On 2 January in the year 1492, when your Highnesses had concluded their war with the Moors who reigned in Europe, I saw your Highnesses banners victoriously raised on the towers of the Alhambra, the citadel of the city, and the Moorish king come out of the city gates and kiss the hands of your Highnesses and the prince, My Lord. And later in that same month, on the grounds of information I had given your Highnesses concerning the lands of India . . . your Highnesses decided to send me, Christopher Columbus, to see these parts of India and the princes and peoples of those lands and consider the best means for their conversion.*[16]

Thus he had witnessed the Spanish reconquest of Granada and shared fully in the religious and nationalistic fervor surrounding that event. Just seven months separated Isabella and Ferdinand's entry into Granada on January 2 and Columbus's departure westward on August 3, 1492. In his mind, the two events were clearly linked. Long after Europeans knew something of Columbus's discoveries in the Caribbean, they nevertheless considered the restoration of Muslim Granada to Christian hands as Ferdinand and Isabella's greatest achievement; for the reconquest the Spanish pope Alexander VI rewarded them in 1494 with the title "Most Catholic Kings." Like the Spanish rulers and most Europeans of his age, Columbus understood Christianity as a missionary religion that should be carried to places and peoples where it did not exist. Although Columbus certainly had material and secular goals, first and foremost, as he wrote in 1498, he believed he was a divine agent: "God made me the messenger of the new heaven and the new earth of which he spoke in the Apocalypse of St. John . . . and he showed me the post where to find it."[17]

Columbus was also very knowledgeable about the sea. He was familiar with such fifteenth-century Portuguese navigational developments as *portolans*—written descriptions of the courses along which ships sailed, showing bays, coves, capes, ports, and the distances between these places—and the use of the magnetic needle as a nautical instrument. Columbus had spent years consulting geographers, mapmakers, and navigators. And, as he implied in his *Journal,* he had acquired not only theoretical but also practical experience: "I have spent twenty-three years at sea and have not left it for any length of time worth mentioning, and I have seen everything from east to west [meaning he had been to England] and I have been to Guinea [north and west Africa]."[18] Although some of Columbus's geographical theories, such as his measurement of the distance from Portugal to Japan at 2,760 miles, when it is actually 12,000, proved inaccurate, his successful thirty-three-day voyage to the Caribbean owed a great deal to his seamanship and his knowledge of the accurate use of instruments.

What was the object of this first voyage? He gave the answer in the very title of the expedition, "The Enterprise of the Indies." He wanted to find a direct ocean route to Asia that would provide the opportunity for a greatly expanded trade in which Spain would participate. Two recent scholars have written, "If Columbus had not sailed westward in search of Asia, someone else would have done so. The time was right for such a bold undertaking." Someone else might have done so, but the fact remains that Columbus, displaying a characteristic Renaissance curiosity and restless drive, actually did it.

How did Columbus interpret what he had found, and in his mind did he achieve what he had set out to do? His mind had been formed by the Bible and the geographical writings of classical authors, as had the minds of most educated people of his times. Thus as people have often done in every age, Columbus ignored the evidence of his eyes and described what he wanted to see in the Caribbean as an idyllic paradise, a peaceful garden of Eden. (See the feature "Listening to the Past: Columbus Describes His First Voyage" on pages 526–527.) When accounts of his travels were published, Europeans' immediate fascination with this image of the New World meant that Columbus's propaganda created an instant myth. But having sensed that he had not found the spice markets and bazaars of Asia, Columbus shifted his goal from establishing trade with the (East) Indians and Chinese to establishing the kind of trade the Portuguese then conducted with Africa and with the Atlantic islands. That meant setting up some form of government in the islands, and Columbus had little interest in or capacity for governing. In 1496 he had forcibly subjugated the island of Hispaniola, enslaved the Indians, and laid the basis for a system of land grants tied to the Indians' labor service. Borrowing practices and institutions from reconquest Spain and the Canary Islands, Columbus laid the foundation for Spanish imperial administration. In all of this, Columbus was very much a man of his times. He never understood, however, that the scale of his discoveries created problems of trade, settlers, governmental bureaucracy, and, from a twenty-first-century perspective, the rights of native peoples.[19]

Later Explorers

News of Columbus's first voyage rapidly spread across Europe. On April 1, 1493, a printer in Barcelona published in Spanish Columbus's letter describing what he believed he had found. By the end of that month, the letter had been translated into Latin and published in Rome as *De Insulis Inventis* (On the Discoveries of the Islands). Within a year, printers in Paris, Basel, Antwerp, and Venice had brought out six more Latin editions, which were soon followed by translations in German and Tuscan, the dialect of the Florentines. In a 1503 letter, Florentine navigator Amerigo Vespucci (1454–1512), in whose honor America was named, wrote, "Those new regions which we found and explored with the fleet . . . we may rightly call a New World." This letter, titled *Mundus Novus* (The New World), was the first document to describe America as a continent separate from Asia. Some scholars today try to avoid the terms *discovery* and *New World,* lest they be considered Eurocentric, but the use of those words rests on a tradition begun by the early explorers themselves.

The Caribbean islands—the West Indies—represented to zealous Spanish missionaries millions of Indian natives for conversion to Christianity. Hispaniola, Cuba, and Puerto Rico also offered gold. Forced labor and starvation in the Spaniards' gold mines rapidly killed off the Indians. Even more, diseases brought by Europeans, against which the long-isolated Indians had no immunity, had a devastating effect on the native people. When Columbus arrived in 1492, the population of Hispaniola stood at approximately 100,000; in 1570, 300 people survived. Indian slaves from the Bahamas and black Africans from Guinea were then imported to do the mining.

The search for precious metals determined the direction of Spanish exploration and expansion into South America. When it became apparent that placer mining (in which ore is separated from soil by panning) in the Caribbean islands was slow and the rewards were slim, new routes to the East and new sources of gold and silver were sought.

In 1519 Spanish ruler Charles V commissioned Ferdinand Magellan (1480–1521) to find a direct route to the spices of the Moluccas off the southeast coast of Asia. Magellan sailed southwest across the Atlantic to Brazil and proceeded south around Cape Horn into the Pacific Ocean (see Map 15.3). He crossed the Pacific, sailing west, to the Malay Archipelago, which he called the "Western Isles." (Some of these islands were conquered in the 1560s and named the "Philippines" for Philip II of Spain.)

Yanhuitlan Codex The Mixtec people in southern Mexico, having assimilated and reinterpreted European forms, possessed an advanced and sophisticated culture. About 1550, Mesoamerican scholars of the Mixtec produced this codex (manuscript), which shows those they considered leaders of colonial society: from left, Indian *caciques* (leaders, chiefs); a Dominican friar of the order charged with converting the region; and Spanish administrators. *(Academia de Bella Artes, Puebla. Courtesy, Library of Congress)*

Though Magellan was killed, the expedition continued, returning to Spain in 1522 from the east by way of the Indian Ocean, the Cape of Good Hope, and the Atlantic. Terrible storms, mutiny, starvation, and disease haunted this voyage. Nevertheless, it verified the theory that the earth was round and brought information about the vastness of the Pacific. Magellan also proved that the earth was much larger than Columbus had estimated.

In the West Indies, the slow recovery of gold, the shortage of a healthy labor force, and sheer restlessness speeded up Spain's search for wealth. In 1519, the year Magellan departed on his worldwide expedition, a brash and determined Spanish adventurer named Hernando Cortés (1485–1547) crossed from Hispaniola to mainland Mexico with six hundred men, seventeen horses, and ten cannon. Within three years, Cortés had taken captive the Aztec emperor Montezuma, conquered the fabulously rich Aztec Empire, and founded Mexico City as the capital of New Spain. The subjugation of northern Mexico took longer, but between 1531 and 1550 the Spanish gained control of Zacatecas and Guanajuato, where rich silver veins were soon tapped.

Another Spanish conquistador, Francisco Pizarro (1470–1541), repeated Cortés's feat in Peru. Between 1531 and 1536, with even fewer resources, Pizarro crushed the Inca Empire in western South America and established the Spanish viceroyalty of Peru, with its center at Lima. In 1545 the Spanish opened at Potosí in the Peruvian highlands what became the richest silver mines in the New World.

Between 1525 and 1575, the riches of the Americas poured into the Spanish port of Seville and the Portuguese capital of Lisbon. For all their new wealth, however, Lisbon and Seville did not become important trading centers. It was the Flemish city of Antwerp, controlled by the Spanish Habsburgs, that developed into the great entrepôt for overseas bullion and Portuguese spices and served as the commercial and financial capital of the entire European world (see page 493).

By the end of the sixteenth century, Amsterdam had overtaken Antwerp as the financial capital of Europe. The Dutch had also embarked on foreign exploration and conquest. The Dutch East India Company, founded in 1602, became the major organ of Dutch imperialism and within a few decades expelled the Portuguese from Ceylon and other East Indian islands. By 1650 the Dutch West India Company had successfully intruded on the Spanish possessions in the Americas, in the process gaining control of much of the African and American trade.

English and French explorations lacked the immediate, sensational results of those of the Spanish and Portuguese. In 1497 John Cabot, a Genoese merchant living in London, sailed for Brazil but discovered Newfoundland. The next year he returned and explored the New England coast and perhaps as far south as Delaware. Since these expeditions found no spices or gold, King Henry VII lost interest in exploration. Between 1534 and 1541, Frenchman Jacques Cartier made several voyages and explored the St. Lawrence region of Canada, but the first permanent French settlement, at Quebec, was not founded until 1608.

The Economic Effects of Spain's Discoveries in the New World

The sixteenth century has been called the **Golden Century of Spain.** The influence of Spanish armies, Spanish Catholicism, and Spanish wealth was felt all over Europe. This greatness rested largely on the influx of precious metals from the New World. The mines at Zacatecas and Guanajuato in Mexico and Potosí in Peru poured out huge quantities of precious metals. To protect this treasure from French and English pirates, armed convoys transported it each year to Spain. Between 1503 and 1650, 16 million kilograms of silver and 185,000 kilograms of gold entered the port of Seville.

Meanwhile, Spain was experiencing a steady population increase, creating a sharp rise in the demand for food and goods. Spanish colonies in the Americas also represented a demand for products. Because Spain had expelled some of its best farmers and business people, the Jews in 1492 and the Muslims in the sixteenth and seventeenth centuries, the Spanish economy suffered and could not meet the new demands. Prices rose and with them the costs of manufacturing cloth and other goods. As a result, Spanish products could not compete in the international market with cheaper products made elsewhere. The textile industry was badly hurt. Prices spiraled upward faster than the government could levy taxes to dampen the economy. (Higher taxes would have cut the public's buying power; with fewer goods sold, prices would have come down.)

Did the flood of American silver bullion cause the inflation? Scholars have long debated this question. Prices rose most steeply before 1565, but bullion imports reached their peak between 1580 and 1620. Thus there is no direct correlation between silver imports and the inflation rate. Did the substantial population growth accelerate the inflation rate? Perhaps: when the population pressure declined after 1600, prices gradually stabilized. One fact is certain: the **price revolution** severely strained government budgets. Several times between 1557 and 1647, Philip II and his successors were forced to repudiate the state debt, which in turn undermined confidence in the government. By the seventeenth century, the economy was a shambles, and Spanish predominance was over.

As Philip II paid his armies and foreign debts with silver bullion, the Spanish inflation was transmitted to the rest of Europe. Between 1560 and 1600, much of Europe experienced large price increases. Prices doubled and in some cases quadrupled, and wages did not keep pace with prices. Spain suffered most severely, but all European countries were affected. People who lived on fixed incomes, such as the continental nobles, were badly hurt because their money bought less. Those who owed fixed sums of money, such as the middle class, prospered: in a time of rising prices, debts had less value each year. Food costs rose most sharply, and the poor fared worst of all.

Colonial Administration

Columbus, Cortés, and Pizarro claimed the lands they had "discovered" for the Crown of Spain. How were these lands to be governed? According to the Spanish theory of absolutism, the Crown was entitled to exercise full authority over all imperial lands. In the sixteenth century, the Crown divided its New World territories into four **viceroyalties,** or administrative divisions: New Spain, which consisted of Mexico, Central America, and present-day California, Arizona, New Mexico, and Texas, with the capital at Mexico City; Peru, originally all the lands in continental South America, later reduced to the territory of modern Peru, Chile, Bolivia, and Ecuador, with the viceregal seat at Lima; New Granada, including present-day Venezuela, Colombia, Panama, and, after 1739, Ecuador, with Bogotá as its administrative center; and La Plata, consisting of Argentina, Uruguay, and Paraguay, with Buenos Aires as the capital. Within each territory, the viceroy, or imperial governor, exercised broad military and civil authority as the direct representative of the sovereign in Madrid. The viceroy presided over the *audiencia,* a board of twelve to fifteen judges that served as his advisory council and the highest judicial body. The enlightened Spanish king Charles III (r. 1759–1788) introduced the system of *intendants.* These royal officials possessed broad military, administrative, and financial authority within their intendancy and were responsible not to the viceroy but to the monarchy in Madrid.

From the early sixteenth century to the beginning of the nineteenth, the Spanish monarchy acted on the mercantilist principle that the colonies existed for the financial benefit of the home country. The mining of gold and silver was always the most important industry in the colonies. The Crown claimed the **quinto,** one-fifth of all precious metals mined in South America. Gold and silver yielded the Spanish monarchy 25 percent of its total income. In return, it shipped manufactured goods to the Americas and discouraged the development of native industries.

The Portuguese governed their colony of Brazil in a similar manner. After the union of the Crowns of Portugal and Spain in 1580, Spanish administrative forms were introduced. Local officials called *corregidores* held judicial and military powers. Mercantilist policies placed severe restrictions on Brazilian industries that might compete with those of Portugal. In the seventeenth century, the use of black slave labor made possible the cultivation of coffee and cotton, and in the eighteenth century Brazil led the world in the production of sugar. The unique feature of colonial Brazil's culture and society was its thoroughgoing intermixture of Indians, whites, and blacks.

Changing Attitudes

What were the cultural consequences of the religious wars and of the worldwide discoveries? What impact did the discoveries and wars have on Europeans' attitudes? The clash of traditional religious and geographical beliefs with the new knowledge provided by explorers—combined with decades of devastation and disorder within Europe—bred confusion, uncertainty, and insecurity. Geographical evidence based on verifiably scientific proofs contradicted the evidence of the Scriptures and of the classical authors.

The age of religious wars was one of extreme and violent contrasts. It was a deeply religious period in which people fought passionately for their beliefs; 70 percent of the books printed dealt with religious subjects. Yet the times saw the beginnings of religious skepticism. Europeans explored new continents, partly with the missionary aim of Christianizing the peoples they encountered. Yet the Spanish, Portuguese, Dutch, and English proceeded to dominate and enslave the Indians and blacks they found. While Europeans indulged in gross sensuality, the social status of women declined. The exploration of new continents reflected deep curiosity and broad intelligence, yet Europeans believed in witches and burned thousands at the stake. Sexism, racism, and skepticism had all originated in ancient times. But late in the sixteenth century, they began to take on their familiar modern forms.

The Status of Women

Did new ideas about women appear in this period? Theological and popular literature on marriage in Reformation Europe helps answer this question (see pages 466, 472). These manuals emphasized the qualities expected of each partner. A husband was obliged to provide for the material welfare of his wife and children. He was directed to protect his family while remaining steady and self-controlled. Especially was a husband and father to rule his household firmly but justly. But he was not to behave as a tyrant, a guideline counselors repeated frequently. A wife should be a mature person, a good household manager, and a subservient and faithful spouse. The husband also owed fidelity, and both Protestant and Catholic moralists rejected the double standard of sexual morality as a threat to family unity. Counselors believed that marriage should be based on mutual respect and trust. While they discouraged impersonal unions arranged by parents, they did not think romantic attachments—based on physical attraction and emotional love—a sound basis for an enduring relationship.

Moralists held that the household was a woman's first priority. She might assist in her own or her husband's business and do charitable work. Involvement in social or public activities, however, was inappropriate because it distracted the wife from her primary responsibility, her household. If women suffered under their husbands' yokes, writers explained that submission was the punishment they had inherited from Eve, penance for man's fall, like the pain of childbearing. Moreover, they said, a woman's lot was no worse than a man's: he had to earn the family's bread by the sweat of his brow.[20]

Catholics viewed marriage as a sacramental union, which, validly entered into, could not be dissolved. Protestants saw marriage as a contract, whereby each partner promised the other support, companionship, and the sharing of mutual goods. Protestants recognized a mutual right to divorce and remarriage for various reasons, including adultery and irreparable breakdown.[21] Society in the early modern period was patriarchal. While women neither lost their identity nor lacked meaningful work, the pervasive assumption was that men ruled. Leading students of the Lutherans, Catholics, French Calvinists, and English Puritans tend to concur that there was no amelioration in women's definitely subordinate status.

There were some remarkable success stories, however. Elizabeth Hardwick, the orphaned daughter of an obscure English country squire, made four careful marriages, each of which brought her more property and carried her higher up the social ladder. She managed her estates, amounting to more than 100,000 acres, with a degree of business sense rare in any age. The two great mansions she built, Chatsworth and Hardwick, stand today as monuments to her acumen. Having established several aristocratic dynasties, she died in 1608, past her eightieth year, one of the richest people in England.[22]

Artists' drawings of plump, voluptuous women and massive, muscular men revealed the contemporary standards of physical beauty. It was a sensual age that gloried in the delights of the flesh. Some people, such as humanist poet Aretino, found sexual satisfaction with both sexes. Reformers and public officials simultaneously condemned and condoned sexual "sins." The oldest profession had many practitioners, and when in 1566 Pope Pius IV expelled all the prostitutes from Rome, so many people left and the city suffered such a loss of revenue that in less than a month the pope was forced to rescind the order. Scholars debated Saint Augustine's notion that whores served a useful social function by preventing worse sins. Prostitution was common because poverty forced women and young men into it. Since the later Middle Ages, licensed houses of prostitution had been common in urban centers (see page 398). The general public took the matter for granted. Consequently, civil authorities in both Catholic and Protestant countries licensed houses of public prostitution. These establishments were intended, however, for the convenience of single men, and some Protestant cities, such as Geneva and Zurich, installed officials in the brothels with the express purpose of preventing married men from patronizing them.

Moralists naturally railed against prostitution. For example, Melchior Ambach, the Lutheran editor of many tracts against adultery and whoring, wrote in 1543 that if "houses of women" for single and married men were allowed, why not provide a "house of boys" for women who lacked husbands to service them? "Would whoring be any worse for the poor, needy female sex?"[23] Ambach, of course, was not being serious: by treating infidelity from the perspective of female, rather than male, customers, he was still insisting that prostitution destroyed the family and society.

Single women of the middle and working classes in the sixteenth and seventeenth centuries worked in many occupations and professions—as domestic servants, butchers, shopkeepers, nurses, goldsmiths, midwives, and workers in the weaving and printing industries. Married women normally assisted in their husbands' businesses. And what became of the thousands of women who left convents and nunneries during the Reformation? This question concerns primarily women of the upper classes, who formed the dominant social group in the religious houses of late medieval Europe.

Luther and the Protestant reformers believed that celibacy had no scriptural basis, that young girls were forced by their parents into convents, and that once there they were bullied by men into staying. Therefore, reformers favored the suppression of women's religious houses and encouraged ex-nuns to marry. Marriage, the reformers maintained, not only gave women emotional and sexual satisfaction, but also freed them from clerical domination, cultural deprivation, and sexual repression.[24] Consequently, these women apparently passed from clerical domination to subservience to husbands.

If some nuns in the Middle Ages lacked a genuine religious vocation and if some religious houses witnessed financial mismanagement and moral laxness, convents nevertheless provided women of the upper classes with scope for their literary, artistic, medical, or administrative talents if they could not or would not marry. With the closing of convents, marriage became virtually the only occupation for upper-class Protestant women. This helps explain why Anglicans, Calvinists, and Lutherans established communities of religious women, such as the Lutheran one at Kaiserwerth in the Rhineland, in the eighteenth and nineteenth centuries.[25]

The Great European Witch-hunt

The great European witch scare reveals something about contemporary attitudes toward women. The period of the religious wars witnessed a startling increase in the phenomenon of witch-hunting, whose prior history was long but sporadic. "A **witch**," according to Chief Justice Coke of England, "was a person who hath conference with the Devil to consult with him or to do some act." This definition by the highest legal authority in England demonstrates that educated as well as ignorant people believed in witches. Witches were thought to be individuals who could mysteriously injure other people or animals—by causing a person to become blind or impotent, for instance, or by preventing a cow from giving milk. Belief in witches predated Christianity. For centuries, tales had circulated about old women who made nocturnal travels on greased broomsticks to *sabbats,* or assemblies of witches, where they participated in sexual orgies and feasted on the flesh of infants. In the popular imagination, witches had definite characteristics. The vast majority were married women or widows between fifty and seventy years old, crippled or bent with age, with pockmarked skin. They often practiced midwifery or folk medicine, and most had sharp tongues and were quick to scold.

Religious reformers' extreme notions of the Devil's powers and the insecurity created by the religious wars contributed to the growth of belief in witches. The idea

Hans Baldung Grien (1484/5–1545): Witches' Sabbat (1510) Trained by the great German graphic artist and painter Albrecht Dürer at Nuremberg, Baldung (as he was known) in this woodcut combines learned and stereotypical beliefs about witches: they traveled at night on broomsticks, met at sabbats (or assemblies), feasted on infants (in dish held high), concocted strange potions, and possessed an aged and debauched sensuality. *(Germanisches Nationalmuseum Nürnberg)*

developed that witches made pacts with the Devil in return for the power to work mischief on their enemies. Since pacts with the Devil meant the renunciation of God, witchcraft was considered heresy. Persecution for witchcraft had actually begun in the later fourteenth century, when witchcraft was declared heresy. The century between 1560 and 1660, when mainstream Protestantism and Tridentine Catholicism had begun to settle into definite confessional blocs, saw witch-hunting on an unprecedented and virulent scale, touching every part of Europe from Iceland to Russia.

Fear of witches took a terrible toll on innocent lives in parts of Europe. In southwestern Germany, 3,229 witches were executed between 1561 and 1670, most by burning. The communities of the Swiss Confederation tried 8,888 persons between 1470 and 1700 and executed 5,417 of them as witches. In all the centuries before 1500, witches in England had been suspected of causing perhaps "three deaths, a broken leg, several destructive storms and some bewitched genitals." Yet between 1559 and 1736, witches were thought to have caused thousands of deaths, and in that period almost 1,000 witches were executed in England.[26]

Historians and anthropologists have offered a variety of explanations for the great European witch-hunt. Some scholars maintain that charges of witchcraft were a means of accounting for inexplicable misfortunes. Just as the English in the fifteenth century had blamed their military failures in France on Joan of Arc's witchcraft, so in the seventeenth century the English Royal College of Physicians attributed undiagnosable illnesses to witchcraft. Some scholars hold that in small communities, which typically insisted on strict social conformity, charges of witchcraft were a means of attacking and eliminating the nonconformist; witches, in other words, served the collective need for scapegoats. The evidence of witches' trials, some writers suggest, shows that women were not accused because they harmed or threatened their neighbors; rather, their communities believed such women worshiped the Devil, engaged in wild sexual activities with him, and ate infants. Other scholars argue the exact opposite: that people were tried and executed as witches because their neighbors feared their evil powers. Finally, there is the theory that the unbridled sexuality attributed to witches was a psychological projection on the part of their accusers resulting from Christianity's repression of sexuality.

Though these different hypotheses exist, scholars still cannot fully explain the phenomenon. The exact reasons for the persecution of women as witches probably varied from place to place. Nevertheless, given the broad strand of misogyny (hatred of women) in Western religion, the long-held belief in the susceptibility of women (so-called weaker vessels) to the Devil's allurements, and the pervasive seventeenth-century belief about women's multiple and demanding orgasms and thus their sexual insatiability, it is not difficult to understand why women were accused of all sorts of mischief and witchcraft. Charges of witchcraft provided a legal basis for the execution of tens of thousands of women. As the most important capital crime for women in early modern times, witchcraft has considerable significance for the history and status of women.[27] Witch-hunting declined only in the late eighteenth century, as fear of the Devil and his powers of malevolent sorcery waned among the educated ruling classes.

European Slavery and the Origins of American Racism

Since ancient times, victors in battle have enslaved conquered peoples. In the later Middle Ages, slavery was deeply entrenched in southern Italy, Sicily, Crete, and Iberia. The bubonic plague, famines, and other epidemics created a severe shortage of agricultural and domestic workers throughout Europe, encouraging Italian merchants to buy slaves from the Balkans, Thrace, southern Russia, and central Anatolia for sale in the West. In 1364 the Florentine government allowed the unlimited importation of slaves so long as they were not Christians. Between 1414 and 1423, at least ten thousand slaves were sold in Venice alone. The slave trade represented one aspect of Italian business enterprise during the Renaissance: where profits were lucrative, papal threats of excommunication failed to stop Genoese slave traders (see page 438). The Genoese set up colonial stations in the Crimea and along the Black Sea, and according to an international authority on slavery, these outposts were "virtual laboratories" for the development of slave plantation agriculture in the New World.[28] This form of slavery had nothing to do with race; almost all slaves were white. How, then, did black African slavery enter the European picture and take root in South and then North America?

In 1453 the Ottoman capture of Constantinople halted the flow of white slaves from the Black Sea region and the Balkans. Mediterranean Europe, cut off from its traditional source of slaves, had no alternative source for slave labor but sub-Saharan Africa. The centuries-old trans-Saharan trade was greatly stimulated by the existence of a ready market in the vineyards and sugar plantations of Sicily and Majorca. By the later fifteenth century, the Mediterranean had developed an "American" form of slavery before the discovery of America.

African Slave and Indian Woman A black slave approaches an Indian prostitute. Unable to explain what he wants, he points with his finger; she eagerly grasps for the coin. The Spanish caption above moralizes on the black man using stolen money—yet the Spaniards ruthlessly expropriated all South American mineral wealth. *(New York Public Library)*

(See the feature "Individuals in Society: Juan de Pareja.") Because slavery was sanctioned by the Bible and the ancient philosophers, few people thought it morally wrong.

Meanwhile, the Genoese and other Italians had colonized the Canary Islands in the eastern Atlantic. Prince Henry the Navigator's sailors (see page 503) discovered the Madeira Islands and made settlements there. In this stage of European expansion, "the history of slavery became inextricably tied up with the history of sugar." Though it was an expensive luxury that only the affluent could afford, population increases and monetary expansion in the fifteenth century led to an increasing demand for sugar. Resourceful Italians provided the capital, cane, and technology for sugar cultivation on plantations in southern Portugal, Madeira, and the Canary Islands. Meanwhile, in the period 1490 to 1530, the port of Lisbon saw between three hundred and two thousand black slaves arrive annually (see Map 15.4). From Lisbon, where African slaves performed most of the manual labor and constituted 10 percent of the city's population, slaves were transported to the sugar plantations of Madeira, the Azores, and the Cape Verde Islands. Sugar and the small Atlantic islands gave New World slavery its distinctive shape. Columbus himself, who spent a decade in Madeira, brought sugar plants on his voyages to "the Indies."[29]

As already discussed, European expansion across the Atlantic led to the economic exploitation of the Americas. In the New World, the major problem settlers faced was a shortage of labor. As early as 1495, the Spanish solved the problem by enslaving the native Indians. In the next two centuries, the Portuguese, Dutch, and English followed suit.

Although the Aztecs of Mexico and the Incas of Peru had various forms of servile labor, including domestic, agricultural, and industrial slavery, before European intrusion, native American peoples were not accustomed to the harshness of Spanish exploitation. They could not endure panning for gold for twelve hours a day in the broiling sun. The Indians died "like fish in a bucket," one Spanish settler reported.[30] In 1515 a Spanish missionary, Bartolomé de las Casas (1474–1566), who had seen the evils of Indian slavery, urged the future emperor Charles V to end Indian slavery and to import blacks from Africa. Church law did not strictly forbid black slavery, and Las Casas thought blacks could better survive under South American conditions. Charles agreed, and in 1518 the African slave trade began. (When the blacks arrived, Las Casas immediately regretted his suggestion.) Columbus's introduction of sugar plants, moreover, stimulated the need for black slaves; and the experience and model of plantation slavery in Portugal and the Atlantic islands encouraged the establishment of a similar agricultural pattern in the New World.

In Africa, where slavery was entrenched (as it was in the Islamic world, southern Europe, and China), African kings and dealers sold black slaves to European merchants who participated in the transatlantic trade. The Portuguese brought the first slaves to Brazil; by 1600, 4,000 were being imported annually. After its founding in 1621, the Dutch West India Company, with the full support of the government of the United Provinces, transported thousands of Africans to Brazil and the

Individuals in Society

Juan de Pareja

A marginal person is one who lives outside the mainstream of the dominant society, who is not fully assimilated into or accepted by that society, but from whose life and experience we learn about the values and ideals of the dominant group. Such a person was the Spanish religious and portrait painter Juan de Pareja.

Pareja was born in Antequera, an agricultural region and the old center of Muslim culture near Seville in southern Spain. Of his parents we know nothing. Because a rare surviving document calls him a "mulatto," one of his parents must have been white and the other must have had some African blood. The Spanish word *mulatto* derives from the Arabic *muwallad,* a person of mixed race, and some scholars, using religion to describe ethnic category, speak of Pareja's "Muslim descent." The region from which he came makes that possible, but we do not know whether he actually believed in or practiced Islam.

In 1630 Pareja applied to the mayor of Seville for permission to travel to Madrid to visit his brother and "to perfect his art." The document lists his occupation as "a painter in Seville." Since it mentions no other name, it is reasonable to assume that Pareja arrived in Madrid a free man. Sometime between 1630 and 1648, however, he came into the possession of the artist Diego Velázquez (1599–1660); Pareja became a slave.

In the twelfth century, Muslim slaves helped build the cathedral of Saint James at Santiago de Compostela, one of the great shrines of medieval Christendom. During the long wars of the reconquista, Muslims and Christians captured each other in battle and used the defeated as slaves. The fifteenth and sixteenth centuries had seen a steady flow of sub-Saharan Africans into the Iberian peninsula. Thus early modern Spain was a slaveholding society.

How did Velázquez acquire Pareja? By purchase? As a gift? Had Pareja fallen into debt, or committed some crime, and thereby lost his freedom? We do not know. Velázquez, the greatest Spanish painter of the seventeenth century, had a large studio with many assistants. Pareja was set to grinding powders to make colors and to preparing canvases. He must have demonstrated ability because, when Velázquez went to Rome in 1648, he chose Pareja to accompany him.

In 1650, as practice for a portrait of Pope Innocent X, Velázquez painted Pareja. That same year, Velázquez signed the document that gave Pareja his freedom, to become effective in 1654. From 1654 until his death, Pareja worked in Madrid as an independent painter. Although he received recognition for his work, only one painting survives: *The Calling of Saint Matthew,* signed and dated 1661 (see page 522). Modern art historians dispute its merit. Some believe it shows a forceful baroque energy and considerable originality; others consider it derivative of Velázquez.

Velázquez, Juan de Pareja *(1650).* (The Metropolitan Museum of Art, Fletcher Fund, Rogers Fund, and Bequest of Miss Adelaide Milton de Groot (1876–1967), by exchange, supplemented by gifts from friends of the Museum, 1971. [1971.86]. Photograph © 1986 The Metropolitan Museum of Art)

What does the public career of this seventeenth-century marginal person tell us about the man and his world? After living in Seville and Madrid, he traveled widely, visiting Genoa, Venice, Rome, and Naples. Travel may have broadened him, producing a cosmopolitan man. Pareja's career suggests that a person of talent and ability could rise in Spanish society, despite the social and religious barriers that existed at the time. Jonathan Brown, the leading authority on Velázquez, describes Pareja's appearance in Velázquez's portrait as "self-confident." A more enthusiastic student writes, "The Metropolitan is probably the greatest museum in the world . . . and this [Velázquez's portrait of Pareja] is its greatest painting. . . . The man was technically a slave. . . . However, we can see from Velázquez's painting that the two were undeniably equals. That steady look of self-controlled power can even make us wonder which of the two had a higher opinion of himself."

Questions for Analysis

1. Since slavery was an established institution in Spain, speculate on Velázquez's possible reasons for giving Pareja his freedom.
2. What issues of cultural diversity might Pareja have faced in seventeenth-century Spain?

Sources: Jonathan Brown, *Velázquez: Painter and Courtier* (New Haven, Conn.: Yale University Press, 1986); *Grove Dictionary of Art* (New York: Macmillan, 2000); *Sister Wendy Beckett's 1000 Masterpieces* (New York: Dorling Kindersley Inc., 1999).

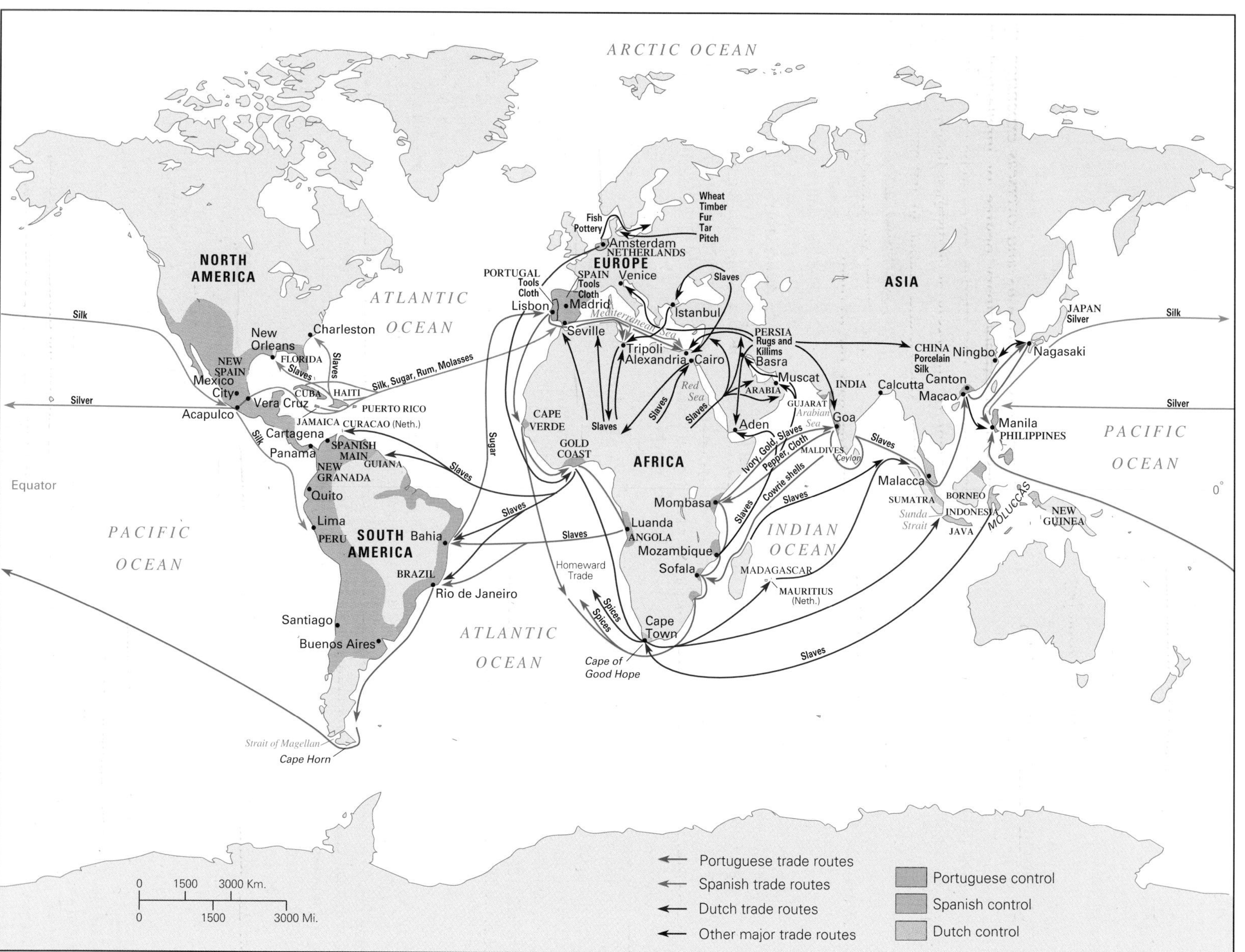

MAP 15.4 The Worldwide Slave Trade By the mid-seventeenth century, trade in spices, silk, sugar, and slaves linked all parts of the globe. The trans-Atlantic trade in African peoples was one aspect of global commerce, one facet of worldwide slavery.

Caribbean. In the late seventeenth century, with the chartering of the Royal African Company, the English got involved. Thereafter, large numbers of African blacks poured into the West Indies and North America. In 1790 there were 757,181 blacks in a total U.S. population of 3,929,625. When the first census was taken in Brazil in 1798, blacks numbered about 2 million in a total population of 3.25 million.

Settlers brought to the Americas the racial attitudes they had absorbed in Europe. Settlers' beliefs and attitudes toward blacks derived from two basic sources: Christian theological speculation (see page 440) and Arab ideas. In the sixteenth and seventeenth centuries, the English, for example, were extremely curious about Africans' lives and customs, and slavers' accounts were extraordinarily popular. Travel literature depicted Africans as savages because of their eating habits, morals, clothing, and social customs; as barbarians because of their language and methods of war; and as heathens because they were not Christian (virtually the identical language with which the English described the Irish—see page 406). Africans were believed to possess a potent sexuality. One seventeenth-century observer considered Africans "very lustful and impudent, . . . (for a Negroes hiding his members, their extraordinary greatness) is a token of their lust." African women were considered sexually aggressive, with a "temper hot and lascivious."[31]

"At the time when Columbus sailed to the New World, Islam was the largest world religion, and the only world religion that showed itself capable of expanding rapidly in areas as far apart and as different from each other as Senegal [in northwest Africa], Bosnia [in the Balkans], Java, and the Philippines."[32] Medieval Arabic literature emphasized blacks' physical repulsiveness, mental inferiority, and primitivism. In contrast to civilized peoples from the Mediterranean to China, some Arab writers absurdly claimed, sub-Saharan blacks were the only peoples who had produced no sciences or stable states. Though black kings, the Muslim historian Khaldun alleged, sold their subjects without even a pretext of crime or war, the victims bore no resentment because they gave no thought to the future and had "by nature few cares and worries; dancing and rhythm are for them inborn."[33] It is easy to see how such ridiculous myths developed into the classic stereotypes used to justify black slavery in South and North America in the seventeenth, eighteenth, and nineteenth centuries. Medieval Christians and Arabs had similar notions of blacks as primitive people ideally suited to enslavement. Perhaps centuries of commercial contacts between Middle Eastern and Mediterranean peoples had familiarized the latter with Arab racial attitudes. The racial beliefs that the Portuguese, Spanish, Dutch, and English brought to the New World, however, derived primarily from Christian theological speculation.

Literature and Art

The age of religious wars and overseas expansion also witnessed an extraordinary degree of intellectual and artistic ferment. This effervescence can be seen in the development of the essay as a distinct literary genre; in other prose, poetry, and drama; in art; and in music. In many ways, literature, the visual arts, music, and the drama of the period mirrored the social and cultural conditions that gave rise to them.

The Essay: Michel de Montaigne

Decades of religious fanaticism, bringing famine, civil anarchy, and death, led both Catholics and Protestants to doubt that any one faith contained absolute truth. The late sixteenth and seventeenth centuries witnessed the beginning of modern skepticism. Skepticism is a school of thought founded on doubt that total certainty or definitive knowledge is ever attainable. The skeptic is cautious and critical and suspends judgment. Perhaps the finest representative of early modern skepticism is Frenchman Michel de Montaigne (1533–1592).

Montaigne descended from a bourgeois family that had made a fortune selling salted herring and wine and in 1477 had purchased the title and property of Montaigne in Gascony; his mother came from a Jewish family that had been forced to flee Spain. Montaigne received a classical education, studied law, and secured a judicial appointment in 1554. He condemned the ancient nobility of the sword for being more concerned with war and sports than with the cultivation of the mind.

At the age of thirty-eight, Montaigne resigned his judicial post, retired to his estate, and devoted the rest of his life to study, contemplation, and an effort to understand himself. His wealth provided him with the leisure time to do so. A humanist, he believed that the object of life was to "know thyself," for self-knowledge teaches men and women how to live in accordance with nature and God. Montaigne developed a new literary genre, the essay—from the French *essayer,* meaning "to test or try"—to express his thoughts and ideas.

Montaigne's *Essays* provides insight into the mind of a remarkably civilized man. From the ancient authors, especially the Roman Stoic Seneca, Montaigne acquired a sense of calm, patience, tolerance, and broad-mindedness. Montaigne had grown up during the French civil wars, perhaps the worst kind of war. Religious ideology had set family against family, even brother against brother. He wrote:

In this controversy . . . France is at present agitated by civil wars, the best and soundest side is undoubtedly that which maintains both the old religion and the old government of the country. However, among the good men who follow that side . . . we see many whom passion drives outside the bounds of reason, and makes them sometimes adopt unjust, violent, and even reckless courses.[34]

Though he remained a Catholic, Montaigne possessed a detachment, an independence, an openness of mind, and a willingness to look at all sides of a question. As he wrote, "I listen with attention to the judgment of all men; but so far as I can remember, I have followed none but my own. Though I set little value upon my own opinion, I set no more on the opinions of others."

Montaigne's essay "On Cannibals" reflects the impact of overseas discoveries on Europeans' consciousness. His tolerant mind rejected the notion that one culture is superior to another:

I long had a man in my house that lived ten or twelve years in the New World, discovered in these latter days, and in that part of it where Villegaignon landed [Brazil]. . . .

I find that there is nothing barbarous and savage in [that] nation, . . . excepting, that every one gives the title of barbarism to everything that is not in use in his own country. As, indeed, we have no other level of truth and reason, than the example and idea of the opinions and customs of the place wherein we live.[35]

Montaigne's rejection of dogmatism, his secularism, and his skepticism thus represented a basic change. In his own time and throughout the seventeenth century, few would have agreed with him. The publication of his ideas, however, anticipated a basic shift in attitudes. Montaigne inaugurated an era of doubt. "Wonder," he said, "is the foundation of all philosophy, research is the means of all learning, and ignorance is the end."[36]

Elizabethan and Jacobean Literature

In addition to the essay as a literary genre, the period fostered remarkable creativity in other branches of literature. England, especially in the latter part of Elizabeth's reign and in the first years of her successor, James I (r. 1603–1625), witnessed remarkable literary expression. The terms *Elizabethan* and *Jacobean* (referring to the reign of James) are used to designate the English music, poetry, prose, and drama of this period. The poetry of Sir Philip Sidney (1554–1586), such as *Astrophel* and *Stella,* strongly influenced later poetic writing. The *Faerie Queene* of Edmund Spenser (1552–1599) endures as one of the greatest moral epics in any language. The rare poetic beauty of the plays of Christopher Marlowe (1564–1593), such as *Tamburlaine* and *The Jew of Malta,* paved the way for the work of Shakespeare. Above all, the immortal dramas of William Shakespeare (1564–1616) and the stately prose of the Authorized, or King James, Bible marked the Elizabethan and Jacobean periods as the golden age of English literature.

William Shakespeare, the son of a successful glove manufacturer who rose to the highest municipal office in the Warwickshire town of Stratford-on-Avon, chose a career on the London stage. By 1592 he had gained recognition as an actor and playwright. Between 1599 and 1603, Shakespeare performed in Lord Chamberlain's Company and became co-owner of the Globe Theatre, which after 1603 presented his plays.

Shakespeare's genius lay in the originality of his characterizations, the diversity of his plots, his understanding of human psychology, and his unexcelled gift for language. Shakespeare was a Renaissance man in his deep appreciation for classical culture, individualism, and humanism. Such plays as *Julius Caesar, Pericles,* and *Antony and Cleopatra* deal with classical subjects and figures. Several of his comedies have Italian Renaissance settings. The nine history plays, including *Richard II, Richard III,* and *Henry IV,* enjoyed the greatest popularity among Shakespeare's contemporaries. Written during the decade after the defeat of the Spanish Armada, the history plays express English national consciousness. Lines such as these from *Richard II* reflect this sense of national greatness with unparalleled eloquence:

This royal Throne of Kings, this sceptre'd Isle,
This earth of Majesty, this seat of Mars,
This other Eden, demi-paradise,
This fortress built by Nature for herself,
Against infection and the hand of war:
This happy breed of men, this little world,
This precious stone, set in the silver sea,
Which serves it in the office of a wall,
Or as a moat defensive to a house,
Against the envy of less happier Lands,
This blessed plot, this earth, this Realm, this England.

Shakespeare's later plays, above all the tragedies *Hamlet, Othello,* and *Macbeth,* explore an enormous range of

Titus Andronicus With classical allusions, fifteen murders and executions, a Gothic queen who takes a black lover, and incredible violence, this early Shakespearean tragedy (1594) was a melodramatic thriller that enjoyed enormous popularity with the London audience. Modern critics believe that it foreshadowed *King Lear* with its emphasis on suffering and madness. *(The Folger Shakespeare Library)*

human problems and are open to an almost infinite variety of interpretations. *Othello,* which nineteenth-century historian Thomas Macaulay called "perhaps the greatest work in the world," portrays an honorable man destroyed by a flaw in his own character and the satanic evil of his supposed friend Iago. *Macbeth*'s central theme is exorbitant ambition. Shakespeare analyzes the psychology of sin in the figures of Macbeth and Lady Macbeth, whose mutual love under the pressure of ambition leads to their destruction. The central figure in *Hamlet,* a play suffused with individuality, wrestles with moral problems connected with revenge and with the human being's relationship to life and death. The soliloquy in which Hamlet debates suicide is perhaps the most widely quoted passage in English literature:

To be, or not to be: that is the question:
Whether 'tis nobler in the mind to suffer
The slings and arrows of outrageous fortune,
Or to take arms against a sea of troubles,
And by opposing end them?

Hamlet's sad cry "There is nothing either good or bad but thinking makes it so" expresses the anguish and uncertainty of modern life. *Hamlet* has always enjoyed great popularity because in the title character's many-faceted personality people have seen an aspect of themselves.

Shakespeare's dynamic language bespeaks his extreme sensitivity to the sounds and meanings of words. Perhaps no phrase better summarizes the reason for his immortality than this line from *Antony and Cleopatra:* "Age cannot wither [him], nor custom stale/ [his] infinite variety."

Another great masterpiece of the Jacobean period was the Authorized Bible. At a theological conference in 1604, a group of Puritans urged James I to support a new translation of the Bible. The king in turn assigned the task to a committee of scholars, who published their efforts in 1611. Divided into chapters and verses, the Authorized

Juan de Pareja: The Calling of Saint Matthew Using rich but subdued colors, Pareja depicts the biblical text (Mark 2:13–17), with Jesus in traditional first-century dress and the other figures, arranged around a table covered with an oriental carpet, in seventeenth-century apparel. Matthew, at Jesus' right hand, seems surprised by the "call." Pareja, following a long tradition (see, for example, page 428), includes himself (*standing, rear center*). *(Museo Nacional del Prado, Madrid/The Bridgeman Art Library International Ltd)*

Version is actually a revision of earlier Bibles more than an original work. Yet it provides a superb expression of the mature English vernacular in the early seventeenth century. Consider Psalm 37:

Fret not thy selfe because of evill doers, neither bee thou envious against the workers of iniquitie.
For they shall soone be cut downe like the grasse; and wither as the greene herbe.
Trust in the Lord, and do good, so shalt thou dwell in the land, and verely thou shalt be fed.
Delight thy selfe also in the Lord; and he shall give thee the desires of thine heart.

The Authorized Version, so called because it was produced under royal sponsorship—it had no official ecclesiastical endorsement—represented the Anglican and Puritan desire to encourage laypeople to read the Scriptures. It quickly achieved great popularity and displaced all earlier versions. British settlers carried this Bible to the North American colonies, where it became known as the King James Bible. For centuries the King James Bible has had a profound influence on the language and lives of English-speaking peoples.

Baroque Art and Music

Throughout European history, the cultural tastes of one age have often seemed quite unsatisfactory to the next. So it was with the baroque. The term **baroque** itself may have come from the Portuguese word for an "odd-shaped, imperfect pearl" and was commonly used by late-eighteenth-century art critics as an expression of scorn for what they considered an overblown, unbalanced style. The hostility of these critics, who also scorned the Gothic style of medieval cathedrals in favor of a classicism inspired by antiquity and the Renaissance, has long since passed. Specialists now agree that the triumphs of the baroque marked one of the high points in the history of Western culture.

The early development of the baroque is complex, but most scholars stress the influence of Rome and the revitalized Catholic church of the later sixteenth century. The papacy and the Jesuits encouraged the growth of an intensely emotional, exuberant art. These patrons wanted artists to go beyond the Renaissance focus on pleasing a small, wealthy, cultural elite. They wanted artists to appeal to the senses and thereby touch the souls and kindle the faith of ordinary churchgoers while proclaiming the power and confidence of the reformed Catholic church. In addition to this underlying religious emotionalism, the baroque drew its sense of drama, motion, and ceaseless striving from the Catholic Reformation. The interior of the famous Jesuit Church of Jesus in Rome—the Gesù—combined all these characteristics in its lavish, shimmering, wildly active decorations and frescoes.

Taking definite shape in Italy after 1600, the baroque style in the visual arts developed with exceptional vigor in Catholic countries—in Spain and Latin America, Austria, southern Germany, and Poland. Yet baroque art was more than just "Catholic art" in the seventeenth century and the first half of the eighteenth. True, neither Protestant England nor the Netherlands ever came fully under the spell of the baroque, but neither did Catholic France. And Protestants accounted for some of the finest examples of baroque style, especially in music. The baroque style spread partly because its tension and bombast spoke to an agitated age, which was experiencing great violence and controversy in politics and religion.

In painting, the baroque reached maturity early with Peter Paul Rubens (1577–1640), the most outstanding and representative of baroque painters. Studying in his native Flanders and in Italy, where he was influenced by masters of the High Renaissance such as Michelangelo, Rubens developed his own rich, sensuous, colorful style, which was

Rubens: The Horrors of War With enormous intellectual and physical energy, as well as a large studio of assistants, Peter Paul Rubens was incredibly productive, the most influential figure in baroque art in northern Europe. In this dynamic allegory from 1638, Venus tries to restrain Mars (holding the torch); he is followed by disease and famine. The shrieking lady at left, clad in black, represents miserable Europe. *(Palazzo Pitti/The Bridgeman Art Library International Ltd)*

characterized by animated figures, melodramatic contrasts, and monumental size. Although Rubens excelled in glorifying monarchs such as Queen Mother Marie de' Medici of France, he was also a devout Catholic. Nearly half of his pictures treat Christian subjects. Yet one of Rubens's trademarks was fleshy, sensual nudes, who populate his canvases as Roman goddesses, water nymphs, and remarkably voluptuous saints and angels.

Rubens was enormously successful. To meet the demand for his work, he established a large studio and hired many assistants to execute his rough sketches and gigantic murals. Sometimes the master artist added only the finishing touches. Rubens's wealth and position—on occasion he was given special diplomatic assignments by the Habsburgs—affirmed that distinguished artists continued to enjoy the high social status they had won in the Renaissance.

In music, the baroque style reached its culmination almost a century later in the dynamic, soaring lines of the endlessly inventive Johann Sebastian Bach (1685–1750), one of the greatest composers the Western world has ever produced. Organist and choirmaster of several Lutheran churches across Germany, Bach was equally at home writing secular concertos and sublime religious cantatas. Bach's organ music, the greatest ever written, combined the baroque spirit of invention, tension, and emotion in an unforgettable striving toward the infinite. Unlike Rubens, Bach was not fully appreciated in his lifetime, but since the early nineteenth century his reputation has grown steadily.

Summary

European expansion and colonization took place against a background of religious conflict and rising national consciousness. Though the medieval religious framework had broken down, people still thought largely in religious terms. Europeans explained what they did politically and economically in terms of religious doctrine. Religious ideology served as a justification for a variety of goals, such as the French nobles' opposition to the Crown and the Dutch struggle for political and economic independence from Spain. In Germany, religious hatred and foreign ambition led to the Thirty Years' War. After 1648 the divisions between Protestant and Catholic tended to become permanent. Religious skepticism and racial attitudes were harbingers of developments to come. The essays of Montaigne, the plays of Marlowe and Shakespeare, the King James Bible, and the splendors of baroque art remain classic achievements of the Western cultural heritage.

In the sixteenth and seventeenth centuries, Europeans for the first time gained access to large parts of the globe. European peoples had the intellectual curiosity, driving ambition, and scientific technology to attempt feats that were as difficult and expensive then as going to the moon is today. Exploration and exploitation contributed to a more sophisticated standard of living, in the form of spices and Asian luxury goods, and to a terrible international inflation resulting from the influx of South American silver and gold. Governments, the upper classes, and the peasantry were badly hurt by the resulting inflation. Meanwhile, the middle class of bankers, shippers, financiers, and manufacturers prospered for much of the seventeenth century.

Key Terms

- Treaty of Cateau-Cambrésis
- Huguenots
- Saint Bartholomew's Day massacre
- politiques
- Edict of Nantes
- bourse
- Union of Utrecht
- Escorial
- Spanish Armada
- Protestant Union
- Peace of Westphalia
- magnetic compass
- astrolabe
- *General History of the Indies*
- Golden Century of Spain
- price revolution
- viceroyalties
- quinto
- witch
- baroque

Notes

1. J. H. Hale, "War and Public Opinion in the Fifteenth and Sixteenth Centuries," *Past and Present* 22 (July 1962): 18–32.
2. Quoted in J. L. Motley, *The Rise of the Dutch Republic* (Philadelphia: David McKay, 1898), 1.109.
3. Quoted in P. Smith, *The Age of the Reformation* (New York: Henry Holt, 1951), p. 248.
4. H. Kamen, *Philip of Spain* (New Haven, Conn.: Yale University Press, 1997), pp. 76–78; the quotations are on pp. 77 and 76, respectively.
5. Quoted ibid., p. 235.
6. G. Parker, *The Grand Strategy of Philip II* (New Haven, Conn.: Yale University Press, 2000), pp. 115–122; the quotation is on p. 119.
7. H. Kamen, "The Economic and Social Consequences of the Thirty Years' War," *Past and Present* 39 (April 1968): 44–61.
8. Quoted in C. M. Cipolla, *Guns, Sails, and Empires: Technological Innovation and the Early Phases of European Expansion, 1400–1700* (New York: Minerva Press, 1965), pp. 115–116.
9. J. H. Parry, *The Age of Reconnaissance* (New York: Mentor Books, 1963), chaps. 3 and 5.
10. See C. R. Phillips, *Ciudad Real, 1500–1750: Growth, Crisis, and Readjustment in the Spanish Economy* (Cambridge, Mass.: Harvard University Press, 1979), pp. 103–104, 115.
11. Quoted in Cipolla, *Guns, Sails, and Empires,* p. 132.

12. Quoted in F. H. Littell, *The Macmillan Atlas: History of Christianity* (New York: Macmillan, 1976), p. 75.
13. Quoted in Cipolla, *Guns, Sails, and Empires,* p. 133.
14. S. E. Morison, *Admiral of the Ocean Sea: A Life of Christopher Columbus* (Boston: Little, Brown, 1942), p. 339.
15. T. K. Rabb, "Columbus: Villain or Hero," *The Princeton Alumni Weekly,* October 14, 1992, p. 13.
16. J. M. Cohen, ed. and trans., *The Four Voyages of Christopher Columbus* (New York: Penguin Books, 1969), p. 37.
17. Quoted in R. L. Kagan, "The Spain of Ferdinand and Isabella," in *Circa 1492: Art in the Age of Exploration,* ed. J. A. Levenson (Washington, D.C.: National Gallery of Art, 1991), p. 60.
18. Quoted in F. Maddison, "Tradition and Innovation: Columbus' First Voyage and Portuguese Navigation in the Fifteenth Century," in *Circa 1492: Art in the Age of Exploration,* ed. J. A. Levenson (Washington, D.C.: National Gallery of Art, 1991), p. 69.
19. See W. D. Phillips and C. R. Phillips, *The Worlds of Christopher Columbus* (Cambridge: Cambridge University Press, 1992), p. 273.
20. This passage is based heavily on S. Ozment, *When Fathers Ruled: Family Life in Reformation Europe* (Cambridge, Mass.: Harvard University Press, 1983), pp. 50–99.
21. Ibid., pp. 85–92.
22. See D. Durant, *Bess of Hardwick: Portrait of an Elizabethan Dynasty* (London: Weidenfeld & Nicolson, 1977).
23. Quoted in Ozment, *When Fathers Ruled,* p. 56.
24. Ibid., pp. 9–14.
25. See F. Biot, *The Rise of Protestant Monasticism* (Baltimore: Helicon Press, 1968), pp. 74–78.
26. N. Cohn, *Europe's Inner Demons: An Enquiry Inspired by the Great Witch-hunt* (New York: Basic Books, 1975), pp. 253–254; K. Thomas, *Religion and the Decline of Magic* (New York: Charles Scribner's Sons, 1971), pp. 450–455.
27. See E. W. Monter, "The Pedestal and the Stake: Courtly Love and Witchcraft," in *Becoming Visible: Women in European History,* ed. R. Bridenthal and C. Koonz (Boston: Houghton Mifflin, 1977), pp. 132–135; and A. Fraser, *The Weaker Vessel* (New York: Random House, 1985), pp. 100–103.
28. C. Verlinden, *The Beginnings of Modern Colonization,* trans. Y. Freccero (Ithaca, N.Y.: Cornell University Press, 1970), pp. 5–6, 80–97.
29. This section leans heavily on D. B. Davis, *Slavery and Human Progress* (New York: Oxford University Press, 1984), pp. 54–62; the quotation is on p. 58.
30. Quoted in D. P. Mannix, with M. Cowley, *Black Cargoes: A History of the Atlantic Slave Trade* (New York: Viking Press, 1968), p. 5.
31. Quoted ibid., p. 19.
32. See P. Brown, "Understanding Islam," *New York Review of Books,* February 22, 1979, pp. 30–33.
33. Quoted in Davis, *Slavery and Human Progress,* pp. 43–44.
34. D. M. Frame, trans., *The Complete Works of Montaigne* (Stanford, Calif.: Stanford University Press, 1958), pp. 175–176.
35. C. Cotton, trans., *The Essays of Michel de Montaigne* (New York: A. L. Burt, 1893), pp. 207, 210.
36. Ibid., p. 523.

Suggested Reading

For the religious wars, in addition to the references in the Suggested Reading for Chapter 14 and the Notes to this chapter, see H. Kamen, *The Iron Century: Social Change in Europe, 1550–1660* (1971), a fundamental work; and G. Huppert, *After the Black Death: A Social History of Early Modern Europe* (1986), a lucidly written and highly recommended work for students. P. Roberts, *A City in Conflict: Troyes During the French Wars of Religion* (1996), provides a fascinating account of the bitter divisions the religious conflicts created among neighbors in one important French city. J. H. M. Salmon, *Society in Crisis: France in the Sixteenth Century* (1975), traces the fate of French institutions during the civil wars. A. N. Galpern, *The Religions of the People in Sixteenth-Century Champagne* (1976), is a useful case study in religious anthropology, and W. A. Christian, Jr., *Local Religion in Sixteenth-Century Spain* (1981), traces the attitudes and practices of ordinary Spanish people.

A cleverly illustrated introduction to the Low Countries is K. H. D. Kaley, *The Dutch in the Seventeenth Century* (1972). For Spanish military operations in the Low Countries, see G. Parker, *The Army of Flanders and the Spanish Road, 1567–1659: The Logistics of Spanish Victory and Defeat in the Low Countries' Wars* (1972), and the more recent R. A. Stradling, *The Armada of Flanders: Spanish Maritime Policy and European War, 1568–1668* (1992). G. Parker, *Spain and the Netherlands, 1559–1659: Ten Studies* (1979), contains useful essays, of which students may especially want to consult "Why Did the Dutch Revolt Last So Long?" For the later phases of the Dutch-Spanish conflict, see J. I. Israel, *The Dutch Republic and the Hispanic World, 1606–1661* (1982), which treats the struggle in global perspective. Similarly, Geoffrey Parker, *The Grand Strategy of Philip II* (2000), treats Philip's attempts to rule a global empire with vivid documentation; serious students of many facets of the period will have to consult this book because it explores the aims and strategies of Philip's allies and enemies as well.

The starting point for the study of England's great ruler is W. MacCaffrey, *Elizabeth I* (1993). N. Jones, *The Birth of the Elizabethan Age* (1993), brings to life the concerns of the English people. S. Frye, *Elizabeth I: The Competition for Representation* (1996), uses feminist analysis to describe the way Elizabeth built her public image and used her authority. C. Erickson, *The First Elizabeth* (1983), gives a psychologically resonant portrait, and C. Haight, *Elizabeth I* (1988), and J. E. Neale, *Queen Elizabeth I* (1957), remain helpful.

Nineteenth- and early-twentieth-century historians described the defeat of the Spanish Armada as a great victory for Protestantism, democracy, and capitalism, which those scholars tended to link together. More recent historians have treated the event in terms of its contemporary significance. H. Kamen, *Philip of Spain* (1971), offers a fine revisionist portrait of the ruler at the center of late-sixteenth-century international affairs. A. W. Lovett, *Early Habsburg Spain, 1517–1598* (1986), discusses many facets of Spanish culture as well as giving a provocative portrait of Philip II. G. Mattingly, *The Armada* (1959), gives the diplomatic and political background. The best recent account of the Spanish

(continued on page 528)

Listening to the Past

Columbus Describes His First Voyage

On his return voyage to Spain in January 1493, Christopher Columbus composed a letter intended for wide circulation and had copies of it sent ahead to Isabella and Ferdinand and others when the ship docked at Lisbon. Because the letter sums up Columbus's understanding of his achievements, it is considered the most important document of his first voyage. Remember that his knowledge of Asia rested heavily on Marco Polo's Travels, *published around 1298.*

Since I know that you will be pleased at the great success with which the Lord has crowned my voyage, I write to inform you how in thirty-three days I crossed from the Canary Islands to the Indies, with the fleet which our most illustrious sovereigns gave me. I found very many islands with large populations and took possession of them all for their Highnesses; this I did by proclamation and unfurled the royal standard. No opposition was offered.

I named the first island that I found "San Salvador," in honour of our Lord and Saviour who has granted me this miracle. . . . When I reached Cuba, I followed its north coast westwards, and found it so extensive that I thought this must be the mainland, the province of Cathay.* . . . From there I saw another island eighteen leagues eastwards which I then named "Hispaniola."† . . .

Hispaniola is a wonder. The mountains and hills, the plains and meadow lands are both fertile and beautiful. They are most suitable for planting crops and for raising cattle of all kinds, and there are good sites for building towns and villages. The harbours are incredibly fine and there are many great rivers with broad channels and the majority contain gold.‡ The trees, fruits and plants are very different from those of Cuba. In Hispaniola there are many spices and large mines of gold and other metals. . . .§

The inhabitants of this island, and all the rest that I discovered or heard of, go naked, as their mothers bore them, men and women alike. A few of the women, however, cover a single place with a leaf of a plant or piece of cotton which they weave for the purpose. They have no iron or steel or arms and are not capable of using them, not because they are not strong and well built but because they are amazingly timid. All the weapons they have are canes cut at seeding time, at the end of which they fix a sharpened stick, but they have not the courage to make use of these, for very often when I have sent two or three men to a village to have conversation with them a great number of them have come out. But as soon as they saw my men all fled immediately, a father not even waiting for his son. And this is not because we have harmed any of them; on the contrary, wherever I have gone and been able to have conversation with them, I have given them some of the various things I had, a cloth and other articles, and received nothing in exchange. But they have still remained incurably timid. True, when they have been reassured and lost their fear, they are so ingenuous and so liberal with all their possessions that no one who has not seen them would believe it. If one asks for anything they have they never say no. On the contrary, they offer a share to anyone with demonstrations of heartfelt affection, and they are immediately content with any small thing, valuable or valueless,

*Cathay is the old name for China. In the log-book and later in this letter Columbus accepts the native story that Cuba is an island which they can circumnavigate in something more than twenty-one days, yet he insists here and later, during the second voyage, that it is in fact part of the Asiatic mainland.

†Hispaniola is the second largest island of the West Indies; Haiti occupies the western third of the island, the Dominican Republic the rest.

‡This did not prove to be true.

§These statements are also inaccurate.

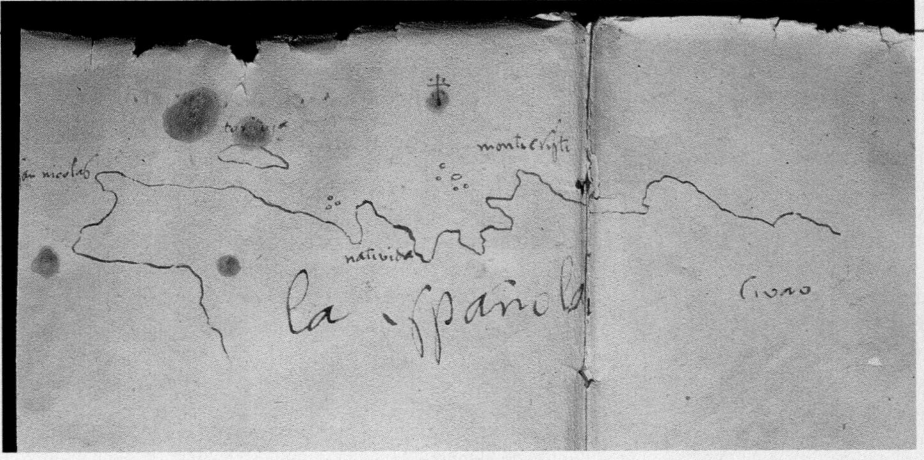

Columbus's map of Hispaniola. Would this small vague sketch of Hispaniola (now Haiti and the Dominican Republic) have been of much use to explorers after Columbus? *(Col. Duke of Alba, Madrid/Institut Amatller d'Art Hispanic)*

that is given them. I forbade the men to give them bits of broken crockery, fragments of glass or tags of laces, though if they could get them they fancied them the finest jewels in the world.

I hoped to win them to the love and service of their Highnesses and of the whole Spanish nation and to persuade them to collect and give us of the things which they possessed in abundance and which we needed. They have no religion and are not idolaters; but all believe that power and goodness dwell in the sky and they are firmly convinced that I have come from the sky with these ships and people. In this belief they gave me a good reception everywhere, once they had overcome their fear; and this is not because they are stupid—far from it, they are men of great intelligence, for they navigate all those seas, and give a marvellously good account of everything—but because they have never before seen men clothed or ships like these. . . .

In all these islands the men are seemingly content with one woman, but their chief or king is allowed more than twenty. The women appear to work more than the men and I have not been able to find out if they have private property. As far as I could see whatever a man had was shared among all the rest and this particularly applies to food. . . . In another island, which I am told is larger than Hispaniola, the people have no hair. Here there is a vast quantity of gold, and from here and the other islands I bring Indians as evidence.

In conclusion, to speak only of the results of this very hasty voyage, their Highnesses can see that I will give them as much gold as they require, if they will render me some very slight assistance; also I will give them all the spices and cotton they want. . . . I will also bring them as much aloes as they ask and as many slaves, who will be taken from the idolaters. I believe also that I have found rhubarb and cinnamon and there will be countless other things in addition. . . .

So all Christendom will be delighted that our Redeemer has given victory to our most illustrious King and Queen and their renowned kingdoms, in this great matter. They should hold great celebrations and render solemn thanks to the Holy Trinity with many solemn prayers, for the great triumph which they will have, by the conversion of so many peoples to our holy faith and for the temporal benefits which will follow, for not only Spain, but all Christendom will receive encouragement and profit.

This is a brief account of the facts.

Written in the caravel off the Canary Islands.||

15 February 1493

At your orders
THE ADMIRAL

Questions for Analysis

1. How did Columbus explain the success of his voyage?
2. What was Columbus's view of the native Americans he met?
3. Evaluate his statements that the Caribbean islands possessed gold, cotton, and spices.
4. Why did Columbus cling to the idea that he had reached Asia?

||Actually, Columbus was off Santa Maria in the Azores.

Source: J. M. Cohen, ed. and trans., *The Four Voyages of Christopher Columbus* (Penguin Classics, 1958), pp. 115–123.

Armada is G. Parker and C. Martin, *The Spanish Armada* (1988). Significant aspects of Portuguese culture are treated in A. Hower and R. Preto-Rodas, eds., *Empire in Transition: The Portuguese World in the Time of Camões* (1985).

R. G. Asch, *The Thirty Years War: The Holy Roman Empire and Europe* (1997), is an important revisionist study with valuable material on the role of war finance in domestic and international aspects of the conflict. G. Parker, *The Thirty Years' War* (1984), is important but densely written. A variety of opinions on the causes and results of the war are given in T. K. Rabb's anthology, *The Thirty Years' War* (1981). Also see J. V. Polisensky, "The Thirty Years' War and the Crises and Revolutions of Sixteenth Century Europe," *Past and Present* 39 (1968), and M. Roberts, "Queen Christina and the General Crisis of the Seventeenth Century," *Past and Present* 22 (1962), which treats the overall significance of Swedish participation.

A good starting point for the study of European society in the age of exploration is J. A. Levenson's anthology *Circa 1492: Art in the Age of Exploration* (1991), which treats geographical, nautical, political, and humanistic developments in a worldwide context. Parry, cited in the Notes, which addresses the causes and consequences of the voyage of discovery, and J. H. Parry, *The Discovery of South America* (1979), which examines Europeans' reactions to the maritime discoveries and the whole concept of discovery, are still valuable. The urbane studies of C. M. Cipolla, including the one cited in the Notes, *Clocks and Culture, 1300–1700* (1967), *Cristofano and the Plague: A Study in the History of Public Health in the Age of Galileo* (1973), and *Public Health and the Medical Profession in the Renaissance* (1976), present fascinating material on technological and sociological developments in a lucid style. The work of W. D. Phillips and C. R. Phillips, cited in the Notes, is strongly recommended. The advanced student should consult F. Braudel, *Civilization and Capitalism, 15th–18th Century,* vol. 1: *The Structures of Everyday Life* (1981); vol. 2: *The Wheels of Commerce* (1982); and vol. 3: *The Perspective of the World* (1984). These fat volumes combine vast erudition, a global perspective, and remarkable illustrations.

On witches and witchcraft, see, in addition to the titles by Cohn and Thomas cited in the Notes, J. B. Russell, *Witchcraft in the Middle Ages* (1976) and *Lucifer: The Devil in the Middle Ages* (1984); R. Kieckhefer, *European Witch Trials: Their Foundations in Popular and Learned Culture, 1300–1500* (1976), which places the subject within the social context; H. C. E. Midelfort, *Witch Hunting in Southwestern Germany: The Social and Intellectual Foundations* (1972), a sensitive and informed work; E. W. Monter, *Witchcraft in France and Switzerland* (1976), which discusses the subject with wit and wisdom; C. Ginzburg, *The Night Battle: Witchcraft and Agrarian Cults in the Sixteenth and Seventeenth Centuries* (1983), for small Italian communities; J. C. Baroja, *The World of Witches* (1964), for Spain; and G. R. Quaife, *Godly Zeal and Furious Rage: The Witch in Early Modern Europe* (1987), an excellent and lucidly written synthesis.

For women, marriage, and the family, see L. Stone, *The Family, Sex, and Marriage in England, 1500–1800* (1977), a controversial work; D. Underdown, "The Taming of the Scold," and S. Amussen, "Gender, Family, and the Social Order," in *Order and Disorder in Early Modern England,* ed. A. Fletcher and J. Stevenson (1985); A. Macfarlane, *Marriage and Love in England: Modes of Reproduction, 1300–1848* (1986); C. R. Boxer, *Women in Iberian Expansion Overseas, 1415–1815* (1975), a helpful study of women's role in overseas migration; S. M. Wyntjes, "Women in the Reformation Era," in *Becoming Visible: Women in European History,* ed. R. Bridenthal and C. Koonz (1977), a quick survey of conditions in different countries; A. Clark, *The Working Life of Women in the Seventeenth Century* (1968); K. M. Wilson, ed., *Women Writers of the Renaissance and Reformation* (1987); M. J. M. Ezell, *The Patriarch's Wife: Literary Evidence and the History of the Family* (1987); and L. Pollock, *A Lasting Relationship: Parents and Children over Three Centuries* (1987). Ozment's work listed in the Notes is a seminal study concentrating on Germany and Switzerland.

As background to slavery and racism in North and South America, students should see J. L. Watson, ed., *Asian and African Systems of Slavery* (1980), a valuable collection of essays, as well as the works by Davis and by Mannix and Cowley mentioned in the Notes: Davis shows how slavery was viewed as a progressive force in the expansion of the Western world, and Mannix and Cowley provide a hideously fascinating account of the slave trade. For North American conditions, interested students should consult W. D. Jordan, *The White Man's Burden: Historical Origins of Racism in the United States* (1974). The excellent essays in G. M. Frederickson, *The Arrogance of Race: Historical Perspectives on Slavery, Racism, and Social Inequality* (1988), stress the social and economic circumstances associated with the rise of plantation slavery. For Caribbean and South American developments, see F. P. Bowser, *The African Slave in Colonial Peru* (1974); J. S. Handler and F. W. Lange, *Plantation Slavery in Barbados: An Archeological and Historical Investigation* (1978); and R. E. Conrad, *Children of God's Fire: A Documentary History of Black Slavery in Brazil* (1983).

The leading authority on Montaigne is D. M. Frame; see his *Montaigne's Discovery of Man* (1955) and his translation listed in the Notes. For baroque art, see V. L. Tapié, *The Age of Grandeur: Baroque Art and Architecture* (1961), a standard work; and J. Montagu, *Roman Baroque Sculpture: The Industry of Art* (1985), an original and entertaining study.

Peter Paul Rubens, Ceiling of the Banqueting House, Whitehall Palace, London (1635). King James I is raised by the allegorical figures of Justice, Religion, and Truth into the dazzling light of heaven, perhaps a fitting memorial for the advocate of the divine right of kings. *(Whitehall, London/The Bridgeman Art Library International Ltd.)*

chapter

16 Absolutism and Constitutionalism in Western Europe (ca 1589–1715)

chapter outline

- Absolutism
- Constitutionalism

The seventeenth century was a period of revolutionary transformation. That century witnessed agricultural and manufacturing crises that had profound political consequences. A colder and wetter climate throughout most of the period meant a shorter farming season. Grain yields declined. In an age when cereals constituted the bulk of the diet for most people everywhere, smaller harvests led to food shortages and starvation. Food shortages in turn meant population decline or stagnation. Industry also suffered. While the evidence does not permit broad generalizations, it appears that the output of woolen textiles, one of the most important manufactures, declined sharply in the first half of the century. This economic crisis was not universal: it struck various sections of Europe at different times and to different degrees. In the middle decades of the century, Spain, France, Germany, and England all experienced great economic difficulties; but these years saw the golden age of the Netherlands.

Meanwhile, governments increased their spending, primarily for state armies; in the seventeenth century, armies grew larger than they had been since the time of the Roman Empire. To pay for these armies, governments taxed. The greatly increased burden of taxation, falling on a population already existing at a subsistence level, triggered revolts. Peasant revolts were extremely common;[1] in France, urban disorders were so frequent an aspect of the social and political landscape as to be "a distinctive feature of life."[2]

Princes struggled to free themselves from the restrictions of custom, powerful social groups, or competing institutions. Spanish and French monarchs gained control of the major institution in their domains, the Roman Catholic church. Rulers of England and some of the German principalities set up national churches. In the German Empire, the Peace of Westphalia placed territorial sovereignty in the princes' hands. The kings of France, England, and Spain claimed the basic loyalty of their subjects. Monarchs made laws, to which everyone within their borders was subject. These powers added up to something close to **sovereignty.**

A state may be termed *sovereign* when it possesses a monopoly over the instruments of justice and the use of force within clearly defined boundaries. In a sovereign state, no system of courts, such as ecclesiastical tribunals, competes with state courts in the dispensation of justice; and private armies, such as those of feudal lords, present no threat to royal authority because the state's army is stronger. Royal law touches all persons within the country.

Sovereignty had been evolving during the late sixteenth century. Most seventeenth-century governments now needed to address the problem of *which* authority within the state would possess sovereignty—the Crown or privileged groups. In the period between roughly 1589 and 1715, two basic patterns of government emerged in Europe: absolute monarchy and the constitutional state. Almost all subsequent European governments have been modeled on one of these patterns.

- How did these forms of government differ from the feudal and dynastic monarchies of earlier centuries?
- In what sense were these forms "modern"?
- What social and economic factors limited absolute monarchs?
- Which Western countries most clearly illustrate the new patterns of political organization?
- Why is the seventeenth century considered the "golden age of the Netherlands"?

This chapter will explore these questions.

Absolutism

In the *absolutist* state, sovereignty is embodied in the person of the ruler. Absolute kings claimed to rule by divine right, meaning they were responsible to God alone. (Medieval kings governed "by the grace of God," but invariably they acknowledged that they had to respect and obey the law.) Absolute monarchs in the seventeenth and eighteenth centuries had to respect the fundamental laws of the land, though they claimed to rule by divine right.

Absolute rulers tried to control competing jurisdictions, institutions, or interest groups in their territories. They regulated religious sects. They abolished the liberties long held by certain areas, groups, or provinces. Absolute kings also secured the cooperation of the one class that historically had posed the greatest threat to monarchy, the nobility. Medieval governments, restrained by the church, the feudal nobility, and their own financial limitations, had been able to exert none of these controls.

In some respects, the key to the power and success of absolute monarchs lay in how they solved their financial problems. Medieval kings frequently had found temporary financial support through bargains with the nobility: the nobility agreed to an ad hoc grant of money in return for freedom from future taxation. In contrast, the absolutist solution was the creation of new state bureaucracies that directed the economic life of the country in the interests of the king, either forcing taxes ever higher or devising alternative methods of raising revenue.

Bureaucracies were composed of career officials appointed by and solely accountable to the king. The backgrounds of these civil servants varied. Absolute monarchs sometimes drew on the middle class, as in France, or utilized members of the nobility, as in Spain and eastern Europe. Where there was no middle class or an insignificant one, as in Austria, Prussia, Spain, and Russia, the government of the absolutist state consisted of an interlocking elite of monarchy, aristocracy, and bureaucracy.

Royal agents in medieval and Renaissance kingdoms had used their public offices and positions to benefit themselves and their families. In England, for example, Crown servants from Thomas Becket to Thomas Wolsey had treated their high offices as their private property and reaped considerable profit from them. The most striking difference between seventeenth-century bureaucracies and their predecessors was that seventeenth-century civil servants served the state as represented by the king. Bureaucrats recognized that the offices they held were public, or state, positions. The state paid them salaries to handle revenues that belonged to the Crown, and they were not supposed to use their positions for private gain. Bureaucrats gradually came to distinguish between public duties and private property.

Absolute monarchs also maintained permanent standing armies. Medieval armies had been raised by feudal lords for particular wars or campaigns, after which the troops were disbanded. In the seventeenth century, monarchs alone recruited and maintained armies—in peacetime as well as wartime. Kings deployed their troops both inside and outside the country in the interests of the monarchy. Armies became basic features of absolutist, and modern, states. Absolute rulers also invented new methods of compulsion. They concerned themselves with the private lives of potentially troublesome subjects, often through the use of secret police.

The word **absolutism** was coined only in 1830, two centuries after the developments it attempts to classify occurred. Some scholars today deny that absolute monarchy was a stage in the evolution of the modern state between medieval feudal monarchies and the constitutional governments of recent centuries. As one student of early modern France writes, "I believe the prevailing historiographical concept of 'absolute monarchy' is a myth promulgated by the royal government and legitimized by historians."[3] Such historians prefer the term *administra-*

1575 1605 1635 1665 1695 1725

Political/Military

- 1589–1610 Henry IV in France
- 1642–1649 English civil war ends with execution of Charles I
- 1643–1715 Louis XIV in France
- 1653–1658 Military rule in England under Oliver Cromwell
- 1660 Restoration of English monarchy under Charles II
- 1688–1689 Glorious Revolution in England
- 1701–1713 War of the Spanish Succession
- 1713 Peace of Utrecht

Social/Economic

- 1602 Dutch East India Company founded
- 1665–1683 Jean-Baptiste Colbert applies mercantilism to France

Intellectual/Religious

- 1594–1665 Life of painter Nicholas Poussin
- 1598 Edict of Nantes
- 1635 Birth of French Academy
- 1670 Charles II agrees to re-Catholicize England in secret agreement with Louis XIV
- 1685 Edict of Nantes revoked

tive monarchy, by which they mean that the French state in the seventeenth century became stronger in that it could achieve more of its goals, it was centralized from Paris, and its administrative bureaucracy greatly expanded. Although the administrative monarchy interfered in many aspects of the private individual's daily life, it did not have the consent of the governed, and it especially lacked the idea of the rule of law—law made by a representative body—the administrative monarchy was actually limited, or checked, in ways that traditional interpretations of absolute monarchy did not consider.[4]

The rule of absolute monarchs was not all-embracing because they lacked the financial and military resources and the technology to make it so. Thus the absolutist state was not the same as a totalitarian state. **Totalitarianism** is a twentieth-century phenomenon; it seeks to direct all facets of a state's culture—art, education, religion, the economy, and politics—in the interests of the state. By definition, totalitarian rule is *total* regulation. By twentieth-century standards, the ambitions of absolute monarchs were quite limited: each sought the exaltation of himself or herself as the embodiment of the state. Whether or not Louis XIV of France actually said, *"L'état, c'est moi!"* (I am the state!), the remark expresses his belief that he personified the French nation. Yet the absolutist state did foreshadow recent totalitarian regimes in two fundamental respects: in the glorification of the state over all other aspects of the culture and in the use of war and an expansionist foreign policy to divert attention from domestic ills. All of this is best illustrated by the experience of France, aptly known as the model of absolute monarchy.

The Foundations of French Absolutism: Henry IV, Sully, and Richelieu

In 1589 Henry IV (see page 493) inherited an enormous mess. Civil wars had wracked France since 1561. Catastrophically poor harvests meant that all across France peasants lived on the verge of starvation, fighting off wolves and bands of demobilized soldiers. Some provinces, such as Burgundy, suffered almost complete depopulation. Commercial activity had fallen to one-third its 1580 level. Nobles, officials, merchants, and peasants wanted peace, order, and stability. "Henri le Grand" (Henry the Great), as the king was called, promised "a chicken in every pot" and inaugurated a remarkable recovery. Henry may have been the first French ruler since Louis IX, in the thirteenth century, genuinely to care about his people, and he was the only king whose statue the Paris crowd did not tear down in the Revolution of 1789.

Henry converted to Catholicism and sought better relations with the pope. He tried to gain Protestant confidence by issuing the Edict of Nantes in 1598 (see pages 541–542) and by appointing the devout Protestant Maximilien de Béthune, duke of Sully, as his chief minister. Aside from a short, successful war with Savoy in 1601, Henry kept France at peace. Maintaining that "if we are without compassion for the people, they must succumb and we all perish with them," Henry sharply lowered taxes on the overburdened peasants. In compensation for the lost revenues, in 1602–1604 he introduced the *paulette,* an annual fee paid by royal officials to guarantee heredity in their offices.

Sully proved to be an effective administrator. He combined the indirect taxes on salt, sales, and transit and leased their collection to financiers. Although the number of taxes declined, revenues increased because of the revival of trade.[5] One of the first French officials to appreciate the possibilities of overseas trade, Sully subsidized the Company for Trade with the Indies. He started a country-wide highway system and even dreamed of an international organization for the maintenance of peace.

In only twelve years, Henry IV and Sully restored public order in France and laid the foundations for economic prosperity. By the standards of the time, Henry IV's government was progressive and promising. His murder in 1610 by a crazed fanatic led to a severe crisis.

After the death of Henry IV, the queen-regent Marie de' Medici headed the government for the child-king Louis XIII (r. 1610–1643), but in fact feudal nobles and princes of the blood dominated the political scene. In 1624 Marie de' Medici secured the appointment of Armand Jean du Plessis—Cardinal Richelieu (1585–1642)—to the council of ministers. It was a remarkable appointment. The next year, Richelieu became president of the council, and after 1628 he was first minister of the French crown. Richelieu used his strong influence over King Louis XIII to exalt the French monarchy as the embodiment of the French state. One of the greatest servants of that state, Richelieu set in place the cornerstone of French absolutism, and his work served as the basis for France's cultural hegemony of Europe in the later seventeenth century.

Richelieu's policy was the total subordination of all groups and institutions to the French monarchy. The French nobility, with its selfish and independent interests, had long constituted the foremost threat to the centralizing goals of the Crown and to a strong national state. Therefore, Richelieu sought to curb the power of the nobility. In 1624 he succeeded in reshuffling the royal council, eliminating potential power brokers. Thereafter Richelieu dominated the council in an unprecedented way. He leveled castles, long the symbol of feudal independence, and crushed aristocratic conspiracies with quick executions. For example, when the duke of Montmorency, the first peer of France and godson of Henry IV, became involved in a revolt, he was summarily beheaded.

The constructive genius of Cardinal Richelieu is best reflected in the administrative system he established. He extended the use of the royal commissioners called intendants. France was divided into thirty-two *généralités* (districts), in each of which after 1634 a royal intendant held a commission to perform specific tasks, often financial but also judicial and policing. Intendants transmitted information from local communities to Paris and delivered royal orders from the capital to their généralités. Almost always recruited from the newer judicial nobility, the *noblesse de robe,* intendants were appointed directly by the monarch, to whom they were solely responsible. They could not be natives of the districts where they held authority; thus they had no vested interest in their localities. The intendants recruited men for the army, supervised the collection of taxes, presided over the administration of local law, checked up on the local nobility, and regulated economic activities—commerce, trade, the guilds, marketplaces—in their districts. They were to use their power for two related purposes: to enforce royal orders in the généralités of their jurisdiction and to weaken the power and influence of the regional nobility. As the intendants' power increased under Richelieu, so did the power of the centralized French state.

In 1598 Henry IV's lawyers had drawn up the "Law of Concord." It had been published as the Edict of Nantes to create a temporary and provisional situation of religious toleration in order to secure not the permanent coexistence of two religions (the Calvinist, Reformed, or Huguenot faith and Roman Catholicism), but "religious and civil concord"—that is, the confessional reunification of all French people under the king's religion, Roman Catholicism. The Edict of Nantes named 150 towns throughout France; the king granted Protestants the right to practice their faith in those towns, and he gave the towns 180,000 écus to support the maintenance of their military garrisons. Huguenots numbered perhaps 10 percent of the total French population, most of them concentrated in the southwest. In 1627 Louis XIII, with the unanimous consent of the royal council, decided to end Protestant military and political independence, because, he said, it constituted "a state within a state." According to Louis, Huguenots demanded freedom of conscience, but they did not allow Catholics to worship in their cities, which he interpreted as *political* disobedience.[6]

Attention focused on La Rochelle, fourth largest of the French Atlantic ports and a major commercial center with strong ties to the northern Protestant states of Holland and England. Louis intended to cut off English aid, and he personally supervised the siege of La Rochelle. The city fell in October 1628. Its municipal government was suppressed, and its walled fortifications were destroyed. Although Protestants retained the right of public worship, the king reinstated the Catholic liturgy, and Cardinal Richelieu himself celebrated the first Mass. The military fall of La Rochelle weakened the influence of aristocratic adherents of Calvinism and was one step in the evolution of a unified French state.

Louis XIII, Richelieu, and later Louis XIV also faced serious urban protests. Real or feared unemployment, high food prices, grain shortages, new taxes, and what ordinary townspeople perceived as oppressive taxation all triggered domestic violence. Major insurrections occurred at Dijon

Procession of the Catholic League In response to what many French Catholics considered the monarchy's laxness in crushing heresy, nobles, burghers, and friars formed groups or leagues to fight Protestantism at the local level. The resulting chaos, with armed private citizens indiscriminately firing guns, is illustrated in this scene, probably in Paris. *(Musée des Beaux-Arts, Valenciennes/Giraudon/Art Resource, NY)*

in 1630 and 1668, at Bordeaux in 1635 and 1675, at Montpellier in 1645, at Lyons in 1667–1668 and 1692, and at Amiens in 1685, 1695, 1704, and 1711. Sometimes rumor and misinformation sparked these riots. In any case, they were all characterized by deep popular anger, a vocabulary of violence, and what a recent historian calls "the culture of retribution"—that is, the punishment of royal "outsiders," officials who attempted to announce or to collect taxes. These officials often were seized, beaten, and hacked to death. For example, in 1673 Louis XIV's imposition of new taxes on legal transactions, tobacco, and pewterware provoked a major uprising in Bordeaux.

Municipal and royal authorities responded feebly. They lacked the means of strong action. They feared that stern repressive measures, such as sending in troops to fire on crowds, would create martyrs and further inflame the situation, while forcible full-scale military occupation of a city would be very expensive. Thus authorities allowed the crowds to "burn themselves out," as long as they did not do too much damage. Royal edicts were suspended, prisoners were released, and discussions were initiated. By the end of the century, municipal governments were better integrated into the national structure, and local authorities had the prompt military support of the Paris government. Those who publicly opposed government policies and taxes received swift and severe punishment.[7]

French foreign policy under Richelieu was aimed at the destruction of the fence of Habsburg territories that surrounded France. Consequently, Richelieu supported the Habsburgs' enemies. In 1631 he signed a treaty with the Lutheran king Gustavus Adolphus promising French support against the Catholic Habsburgs in what has been called the Swedish phase of the Thirty Years' War (see page 501). French influence became an important factor in the political future of the German Empire. Richelieu acquired for France extensive rights in Alsace in the east and Arras in the north.

Richelieu's efforts at centralization extended even to literature. In 1635 he gave official recognition to a group of philologists who were interested in grammar and rhetoric. Thus was born the French Academy. With Richelieu's encouragement, the French Academy began the preparation of a dictionary to standardize the French language; it was completed in 1694. The French Academy survives as a prestigious society, and its membership now includes people outside the field of literature.

All of these new policies, especially war, cost money. In his *Political Testament*, Richelieu wrote, "I have always said that finances are the sinews of the state." He meant that revenues determine a government's ability to inaugurate and enforce policies and programs. A state secures its revenues through taxation. But the political and economic structure of France greatly limited the government's ability to tax. Seventeenth-century France remained "a collection of local economies and local societies dominated by local elites." The rights of some assemblies in some provinces, such as Brittany, to vote their own taxes; the hereditary exemption from taxation of many wealthy members of the nobility and the middle class; and the royal pension system drastically limited the government's power to tax.

Richelieu and, later, Louis XIV temporarily solved their financial problems by securing the cooperation of local elites. The central government shared the proceeds of tax revenue with local powers. It never gained all the income it needed. Because the French monarchy could not tax at will, it never completely controlled the financial system. In practice, therefore, French absolutism was limited.[8]

In building the French state, Richelieu believed he had to resort to drastic measures against persons and groups within France and to conduct a tough anti-Habsburg foreign policy. He knew also that his approach sometimes seemed to contradict traditional Christian teaching. As a priest and bishop, how did he justify his policies? He developed his own **raison d'état** (reason of state): "Where the interests of the state are concerned, God absolves actions which, if privately committed, would be a crime."[9]

Richelieu's successor as chief minister and then regent for the boy-king Louis XIV was Cardinal Jules Mazarin (1602–1661). He continued Richelieu's centralizing policies, but his attempts to increase royal revenues led to the civil wars of 1648–1653 known as the **Fronde**.

The word *fronde* means "slingshot" or "catapult," and a *frondeur* was originally a street urchin who threw mud at the passing carriages of the rich. But the Fronde originated in the provinces, not Paris, and the term *frondeur* came to be applied to anyone who opposed the policies of the government. Many individuals and groups did so. Influential segments of the nobility resented the increased power of the monarchy under Louis XIII and what they perceived as their diminished role in government. Mazarin could not control them as Richelieu had done. Royal bureaucrats, judges in the parlements, and intendants who considered their positions the means to social and economic advancement felt that they were being manipulated by the Crown and their interests ignored.[10] The state's financial situation steadily weakened because entire regions of France refused to pay taxes. The French defeat of Spanish armies at Rocroi in 1643 marked the final collapse of Spanish military power in Europe; the victory also led the French people to believe that because peace was at hand, taxes were unnecessary. When a desperate government devised new taxes, the Parlement of Paris rejected them. Popular rebellions led by aristocratic factions broke out in the provinces and spread to Paris.[11] As rebellion continued, civil order broke down completely. A vast increase in the state bureaucracy, representing an expansion of royal power, and new means of extracting money from working people incurred the bitter opposition of peasants and urban artisans. Violence continued intermittently for the next twelve years.

The conflicts of the Fronde had three significant results for the future. First, it became apparent that the government would have to compromise with the bureaucrats and social elites that controlled local institutions and constituted the state bureaucracy. These groups were already largely exempt from taxation, and Louis XIV confirmed their privileged social status. Second, the French economy was badly disrupted and would take years to rebuild. Third, the Fronde had a traumatic effect on the young Louis XIV. The king and his mother were frequently threatened and sometimes treated as prisoners by aristocratic factions. On one occasion, a mob broke into the royal bedchamber to make sure the king was actually there; it succeeded in giving him a bad fright. Louis never forgot such humiliations. The period of the Fronde formed the cornerstone of his political education and of his conviction that the sole alternative to anarchy was absolute monarchy. The personal rule of Louis XIV represented the culmination of the process of centralization, but it also witnessed the institutionalization of procedures that would ultimately undermine the absolute monarchy.

The Absolute Monarchy of Louis XIV

According to the court theologian Bossuet, the clergy at the coronation of Louis XIV in Reims Cathedral asked God to cause the splendors of the French court to fill all who beheld it with awe. God subsequently granted that prayer. In the reign of Louis XIV (r. 1643–1715), the longest in European history, the French monarchy reached the peak of absolutist development. In the magnificence of his court, in the brilliance of the culture that he presided over and that permeated all of Europe, and in his remarkably long life, the "Sun King" dominated his age. No wonder scholars have characterized the second half of the seventeenth century as the "Grand Century," the "Age of Magnificence," and, echoing the eighteenth-century philosopher Voltaire, the "Age of Louis XIV."

In old age, Louis claimed that he had grown up learning very little, but recent historians think he was being modest. True, he knew little Latin and only the rudiments of arithmetic and thus by Renaissance standards was not well educated. Nevertheless, he learned to speak Italian and Spanish fluently, he spoke and wrote elegant French, and he knew some French history and more European geography than the ambassadors accredited to his court. He imbibed the devout Catholicism of his mother, Anne of Austria, and throughout his long life scrupulously performed his religious duties. (Beginning in 1661, Louis attended Mass daily, but rather than paying attention to the liturgy, he said his rosary—to the scorn of his courtiers, who considered this practice "rustic.") Religion, Anne, and Mazarin all taught Louis that God had established kings as his rulers on earth. The royal coronation consecrated Louis to God's service, and he was certain—to use Shakespeare's phrase—that there was a divinity that doth hedge a king. Though kings were a race apart, they could not do as they pleased: they had to obey God's laws and rule for the good of the people.

Louis's education was more practical than formal. Under Mazarin's instruction, he studied state papers as they arrived, and he attended council meetings and sessions at which French ambassadors were dispatched abroad and foreign ambassadors received. He learned by direct experience and gained professional training in the work of government. Above all, the misery he suffered during the Fronde gave him an eternal distrust of the nobility and a profound sense of his own isolation. Accordingly, silence, caution, and secrecy became political tools for the achievement of his goals. His characteristic answer to requests of all kinds became the enigmatic *"Je verrai"* (I shall see).

Louis grew up with an absolute sense of his royal dignity. Contemporaries considered him tall (he was actually five feet five inches) and distinguished in appearance but inclined to heaviness because of the gargantuan meals in which he indulged. Louis XIV was a consummate actor, and his "terrifying majesty" awed all who saw him. He worked extremely hard and succeeded in being "every moment and every inch a king." Because he so relished the role of monarch, historians have had difficulty distinguishing the man from the monarch.

Historians have often said that Louis XIV introduced significant government innovations, the greatest of which was "the complete domestication of the nobility." By this phrase scholars mean that he exercised complete control over the powerful social class that historically had opposed the centralizing goals of the French monarchy. Recent research has suggested that notions of "domestication" represent an exaggeration. What Louis XIV actually achieved was the cooperation of the nobility. Throughout France the nobility agreed to participate in

Luca Giordano: The Pasta Eater In the seventeenth century, rich people carried a fork when they dined out, but its use spread very slowly from Italy and came into common use only about 1750. A German preacher damned the fork as a diabolical luxury: "God would not have given us fingers if he wanted us to use forks." So, if King Louis XIV could eat chicken stew with his fingers without spilling it, how can we fault this Neapolitan workingman for enjoying his pasta without a fork? *(The Art Museum, Princeton University Museum purchase, John Maclean Magie and Gertrude Magie Fund. Photo: Bruce White)*

projects that both exalted the monarchy and reinforced the aristocrats' ancient prestige. Thus the relationship between the Crown and the nobility constituted collaboration rather than absolute control.

In the province of Languedoc, for example, Louis and his agents persuaded the notables to support the construction of the Canal des Deux Mers, a waterway linking the Mediterranean Sea and the Atlantic Ocean. Royal encouragement for the manufacture of luxury draperies in Languedocian towns likewise tied provincial business people to national goals, although French cloths subsequently proved unable to compete with cheaper Dutch ones. Above all, in the campaign for the repression of the Huguenots, the interests of the monarchy and nobility coincided (see page 541). Through mutual collaboration, the nobility and the king achieved goals that neither could have won without the other. For his part, Louis won increased military taxation from the Estates of Languedoc. In return, Louis graciously granted the nobility and dignitaries privileged social status and increased access to his person, which meant access to the enormous patronage the king had to dispense. French government rested on the social and political structure of seventeenth-century France, a structure in which the nobility historically exercised great influence. In this respect, therefore, French absolutism was not so much modern as the last phase of a historical feudal society.[12]

Louis XIV installed his royal court at Versailles, a small town ten miles from Paris. He required all the great nobility of France, at the peril of social, political, and sometimes economic disaster, to come live at Versailles for at least part of the year. Today Versailles stands as the best surviving museum of a vanished society on earth. In the seventeenth century, it became a model of rational order, the center of France, and the perfect symbol of the king's power. (See the feature "Listening to the Past: The Court at Versailles" on pages 562–563.)

Louis XIII had begun Versailles as a hunting lodge, a retreat from a queen he did not like. His son's architects, Le Nôtre and Le Vau, turned what the duke of Saint-Simon called "the most dismal and thankless of sights" into a veritable paradise. Wings were added to the original building to make the palace U-shaped. Everywhere at Versailles the viewer had a sense of grandeur, vastness, and elegance. Enormous staterooms became display galleries for inlaid tables, Italian marble statuary, Gobelin tapestries woven at the state factory in Paris, silver ewers, and beautiful (if uncomfortable) furniture. If genius means attention to detail, Louis XIV and his designers had it: the decor was perfected down to the last doorknob and keyhole. In the gigantic Hall of Mirrors, later to reflect so much of German as well as French history, hundreds of candles illuminated the domed ceiling, where allegorical paintings celebrated the king's victories.

The art and architecture of Versailles served as fundamental tools of state policy under Louis XIV. The king used architecture to overawe his subjects and foreign visitors. Versailles was seen as a reflection of French genius. Thus the Russian tsar Peter the Great imitated Versailles in the construction of his palace, Peterhof, as did the Prussian emperor Frederick the Great in his palace at Potsdam outside Berlin.

As in architecture, so too in language. Beginning in the reign of Louis XIV, French became the language of polite society and the vehicle of diplomatic exchange.

Hall of Mirrors, Versailles The grandeur and elegance of the Sun King's reign are reflected in the Hall of Mirrors, where the king's victories were celebrated in paintings on the domed ceiling. Hundreds of candles lit up the dome. *(Michael Holford)*

French also gradually replaced Latin as the language of international scholarship and learning. The wish of other kings to ape the courtly style of Louis XIV and the imitation of French intellectuals and artists spread the language all over Europe. The royal courts of Sweden, Russia, Poland, and Germany all spoke French. In the eighteenth century, the great Russian aristocrats were more fluent in French than in Russian. In England the first Hanoverian king, George I, spoke fluent French and only halting English. France inspired a cosmopolitan European culture in the late seventeenth century, and that culture was inspired by the king. The French today revere Louis XIV as one of their greatest national heroes because of the culture that he inspired and symbolized.

Against this background of magnificent splendor, Saint-Simon writes, Louis XIV

> *reduced everyone to subjection, and brought to his court those very persons he cared least about. Whoever was old enough to serve did not dare demur. It was still another device to ruin the nobles by accustoming them to equality and forcing them to mingle with everyone indiscriminately. . . .*
>
> *Louis XIV took great pains to inform himself on what was happening everywhere, in public places, private homes, and even on the international scene. . . . Spies and informers of all kinds were numberless.*[13]

Though this passage was written by one of Louis's severest critics, all agree that the king used court ceremonials to undermine the power of the great nobility. By excluding the highest nobles from his councils, he weakened their ancient right to advise the king and to participate in government; they became mere instruments of royal policy. Operas, fetes, balls, gossip, and trivia occupied the nobles' time and attention. Through painstaking attention to detail and precisely calculated showmanship, Louis XIV reduced the major threat to his power. He separated power from status and grandeur: he secured the nobles' cooperation, and the nobles enjoyed the status and grandeur in which they lived.

In government Louis utilized several councils of state, which he personally attended, and the intendants, who acted for the councils throughout France. A stream of questions and instructions flowed between local districts and Versailles, and under Louis XIV a uniform and centralized administration was imposed on the country. In 1685 France was the strongest and most highly centralized state in Europe.

Councilors of state came from the recently ennobled or the upper middle class. Royal service provided a means of social mobility. These professional bureaucrats served the state in the person of the king, but they did not share power with him. Louis stated that he chose bourgeois

The Spider and the Fly In reference to the insect symbolism (*upper left*), the caption on the lower left side of this illustration states, "The noble is the spider, the peasant the fly." The other caption (*upper right*) notes, "The more people have, the more they want. The poor man brings everything—wheat, fruit, money, vegetables. The greedy lord sitting there ready to take everything will not even give him the favor of a glance." This satirical print summarizes peasant grievances. *(New York Public Library)*

officials because he wanted "people to know by the rank of the men who served him that he had no intention of sharing power with them."[14] If great ones were the king's advisers, they would seem to share the royal authority; professional administrators from the middle class would not.

Throughout his long reign and despite increasing financial problems, he never called a meeting of the Estates General. The nobility therefore had no means of united expression or action. Nor did Louis have a first minister; he kept himself free from worry about the inordinate power of a Richelieu. Louis's use of spying and terror—a secret police force, a system of informers, and the practice of opening private letters—foreshadowed some of the devices of the modern state. French government remained highly structured, bureaucratic, centered at Versailles, and responsible to Louis XIV.

Financial and Economic Management Under Louis XIV: Colbert

Finance was the grave weakness of Louis XIV's absolutism. An expanding professional bureaucracy, the court of Versailles, and extensive military reforms (see page 543) cost a great amount of money. The French method of collecting taxes consistently failed to produce enough revenue. Tax farmers, agents who purchased from the Crown the right to collect taxes in a particular district, pocketed the difference between what they raked in and what they handed over to the state. Consequently, the tax farmers profited, while the government got far less than the people paid. In addition, by an old agreement between the Crown and the nobility, the king could freely tax the common people provided he did not tax the nobles. The nobility thereby relinquished a role in government: since nobles did not pay taxes, they could not legitimately claim a say in how taxes were spent. Louis, however, lost enormous potential revenue. The middle classes, moreover, secured many tax exemptions. With the rich and prosperous classes exempt, the tax burden fell heavily on those least able to pay, the poor peasants.

The king named Jean-Baptiste Colbert (1619–1683), the son of a wealthy merchant-financier of Reims, as controller general of finances. Colbert came to manage the entire royal administration and proved himself a financial genius. Colbert's central principle was that the wealth and the economy of France should serve the state. He did not invent the system called "mercantilism," but he rigorously applied it to France.

Mercantilism is a collection of governmental policies for the regulation of economic activities, especially commercial activities, by and for the state. In seventeenth- and eighteenth-century economic theory, a nation's international power was thought to be based on its wealth, specifically its gold supply. Because, mercantilist theory held, resources were limited, state intervention was needed to secure the largest part of a limited resource. To accumulate gold, a country always had to sell more goods abroad than it bought. Colbert believed that a successful economic policy meant more than a favorable balance of trade, however. He insisted that the French sell abroad and buy *nothing* back. France should be self-sufficient, able to produce within its borders everything the subjects of the French king needed. Consequently, the outflow of gold would be halted, debtor states would pay in bullion, and with the wealth of the nation increased, its power and prestige would be enhanced.

Colbert attempted to accomplish self-sufficiency through state support for both old industries and newly created ones. He subsidized the established cloth industries at Abbeville, Saint-Quentin, and Carcassonne. He granted special royal privileges to the rug and tapestry industries at Paris, Gobelin, and Beauvais. New factories at Saint-Antoine in Paris manufactured mirrors to replace Venetian imports. Looms at Chantilly and Alençon competed with lacemaking at Bruges in the Spanish Netherlands, and foundries at Saint-Étienne made steel and firearms that reduced Swedish imports. To ensure a high-quality finished product, Colbert set up a system of state inspection and regulation. To ensure order within every industry, he compelled all craftsmen to organize into guilds, and within every guild he gave the masters absolute power over their workers. Colbert encouraged skilled foreign craftsmen and manufacturers to immigrate to France, and he gave them special privileges. To improve communications, he built roads and canals, the most famous, the Canal des Deux Mers. To protect French goods, he abolished many domestic tariffs and enacted high foreign tariffs, which prevented foreign products from competing with French ones.

Colbert's most important work was the creation of a powerful merchant marine to transport French goods. He gave bonuses to French shipowners and shipbuilders and established a method of maritime conscription, arsenals, and academies for the training of sailors. In 1661 France possessed 18 unseaworthy vessels; by 1681 it had 276 frigates, galleys, and ships of the line.

Colbert hoped to make Canada—rich in untapped minerals and some of the best agricultural land in the world—part of a vast French empire. He gathered four thousand peasants from western France and shipped them to Canada, where they peopled the province of Quebec. (In 1608, one year after the English arrived at Jamestown, Virginia, Sully had established the city of Quebec, which became the capital of French Canada.) Subsequently, the Jesuit Jacques Marquette and the merchant Louis Joliet sailed down the Mississippi River and took possession of the land on both sides as far south as present-day Arkansas. In 1684 the French explorer Robert La Salle continued down the Mississippi to its mouth and claimed vast territories and the rich delta for Louis XIV. The area was called, naturally, "Louisiana."

How successful were Colbert's policies? His achievement in the development of manufacturing was prodigious. The textile industry, especially in woolens, expanded enormously, and "France . . . had become in 1683 the leading nation of the world in industrial productivity."[15] The commercial classes prospered, and between 1660 and 1700 their position steadily improved. The national economy, however, rested on agriculture. Although French peasants did not become serfs, as did the peasants of eastern Europe, they were mercilessly taxed. After 1685 other hardships afflicted them: poor harvests, continuing deflation of the currency, and fluctuation in the price of grain. Many peasants emigrated. With the decline in population and thus in the number of taxable people (the poorest), the state's resources fell. A totally inadequate tax base and heavy expenditure for war in the later years of Louis's reign made Colbert's goals unattainable.

The Revocation of the Edict of Nantes

The absolutist state also attempted to control religion.

We now see with the proper gratitude what we owe to God . . . for the best and largest part of our subjects of the so-called reformed religion have embraced Catholicism, and now that, to the extent that the execution of the Edict of Nantes remains useless, we have judged that we can do nothing better to wipe out the memory of the troubles, of the confusion, of the evils that the progress of this false religion has caused our kingdom . . . than to revoke entirely the said Edict.[16]

Thus in 1685 Louis XIV revoked the Edict of Nantes, by which his grandfather Henry IV had granted liberty of conscience to French Huguenots. The new law ordered the destruction of churches, the closing of schools, the Catholic baptism of Huguenots, and the exile of Huguenot pastors who refused to renounce their faith. Why? There had been so many mass conversions during previous years (many of them forced) that Madame de Maintenon, Louis's second wife, could say that "nearly all the Huguenots were converted." Some Huguenots had emigrated. Richelieu had already deprived French Calvinists of political rights. Why, then, did Louis, by revoking the edict, persecute some of his most loyal and industrially skilled subjects, force others to flee abroad, and provoke the outrage of Protestant Europe?

First, the French monarchy had never intended religious toleration to be permanent (see page 534); religious pluralism was not a seventeenth-century ideal. Although recent scholarship has convincingly shown that Louis XIV was basically tolerant, he considered religious unity politically necessary to realize his goal of "one king, one law, one faith." He hated division within the realm and insisted that religious unity was essential to his royal dignity and to the security of the state.

Second, while France in the early years of Louis's reign permitted religious liberty, it was not a popular policy. Aristocrats had long petitioned Louis to crack down on Protestants. But the revocation was solely the king's decision, and it won him enormous praise. "If the flood of congratulation means anything, it . . . was probably the one act of his reign that, at the time, was popular with the majority of his subjects."[17]

While contemporaries applauded Louis XIV, later scholars damned him for the adverse impact that revocation of the Edict of Nantes had on the economy and foreign affairs. Tens of thousands of Huguenot craftsmen, soldiers, and business people emigrated, depriving France of their skills and tax revenues and carrying their bitterness to Holland, England, Prussia, and Cape Town in southern Africa. Modern scholarship has greatly modified this picture, however. While Huguenot settlers in northern Europe aggravated Protestant hatred for Louis, the revocation of the Edict of Nantes had only minor and scattered effects on French economic development.[18]

French Classicism

Scholars characterize the art and literature of the age of Louis XIV as **French classicism**. By this they mean that the artists and writers of the late seventeenth century imitated the subject matter and style of classical antiquity, that their work resembled that of Renaissance Italy, and that French art possessed the classical qualities of discipline, balance, and restraint. Classicism was the official style of Louis's court. In painting, however, French classicism had already reached its peak before 1661, the beginning of the king's personal government.

Nicholas Poussin (1594–1665) is generally considered the finest example of French classicist painting. Poussin spent all but eighteen months of his creative life in Rome because he found the atmosphere in Paris uncongenial. Deeply attached to classical antiquity, he believed that the highest aim of painting was to represent noble actions in a logical and orderly, but not realistic, way. His masterpiece, *The Rape of the Sabine Women*, exhibits these qualities. Its subject is an incident in Roman history; the figures of people and horses are ideal representations, and the emotions expressed are studied, not spontaneous. Even the buildings are exact architectural models of ancient Roman structures.

Poussin, whose paintings still had individualistic features, did his work before 1661. After Louis's accession to power, the principles of absolutism molded the ideals of French classicism. Individualism was not allowed, and artists' efforts were directed to the glorification of the state as personified by the king. Precise rules governed all aspects of culture, with the goal of formal and restrained perfection.

Contemporaries said that Louis XIV never ceased playing the role of grand monarch on the stage of his court. If the king never fully relaxed from the pressures and intrigues of government, he did enjoy music and theater and used them as a backdrop for court ceremonials. Louis favored Jean-Baptiste Lully (1632–1687), whose orchestral works combined lively animation with the restrained austerity typical of French classicism. Lully also composed court ballets, and his operatic productions achieved a powerful influence throughout Europe. Louis supported François Couperin (1668–1733), whose harpsichord and organ works possessed the regal grandeur the king loved, and Marc-Antoine Charpentier (1634–1704), whose solemn religious music entertained him at meals. Charpentier received a pension for the *Te Deums,* hymns of thanksgiving, he composed to celebrate French military victories.

Louis XIV loved the stage, and in the plays of Molière and Racine his court witnessed the finest achievements in the history of the French theater. When Jean-Baptiste Poquelin (1622–1673), the son of a prosperous tapestry maker, refused to join his father's business and entered the theater, he took the stage name "Molière." As playwright, stage manager, director, and actor, Molière produced comedies that exposed the hypocrisies and follies of society through brilliant caricature. *Tartuffe* satirized the religious hypocrite, *Le Bourgeois Gentilhomme* (The Bourgeois Gentleman) attacked the social parvenu, and *Les Femmes Savantes* (The Learned Women) mocked the fashionable pseudo-intellectuals of the day. In structure Molière's plays followed classical models, but they were based on careful social observation. Molière made the bourgeoisie the butt of his ridicule; he stopped short of criticizing the nobility, reflecting the policy of his royal patron.

While Molière dissected social mores, his contemporary Jean Racine (1639–1699) analyzed the power of love. Racine based his tragic dramas on Greek and Roman legends, and his persistent theme was the conflict of good and evil. Several plays—*Andromaque, Bérénice, Iphigénie,* and *Phèdre*—bear the names of women and deal with the power of passion in women. Louis preferred *Mithridate* and *Britannicus* because of the "grandeur" of their themes. For simplicity of language, symmetrical structure, and calm restraint, the plays of Racine represent the finest examples of French classicism. His tragedies and Molière's comedies are still produced today.

Louis XIV's Wars

On his deathbed, Louis XIV is reputed to have said, "I have gone to war too lightly and pursued it for vanity's sake." Perhaps he never actually said this. If he did, perhaps it was part of the confessional style of the time, which required that a penitent exaggerate his sins.[19] In any case, the course of Louis's reign suggests that he acted according to his observation that "the character of

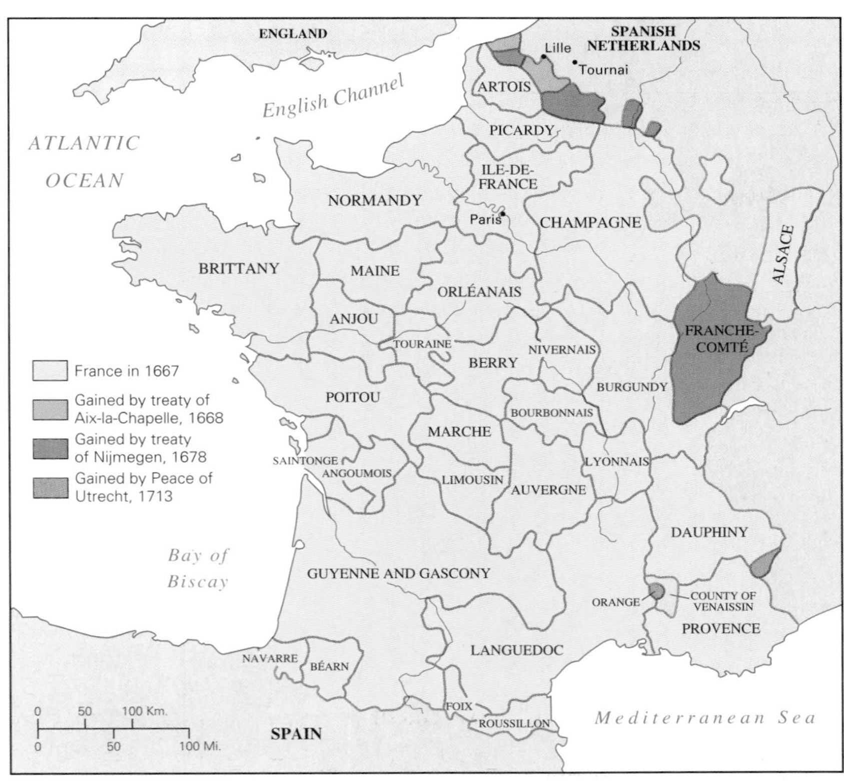

MAP 16.1 The Acquisitions of Louis XIV, 1668–1713 The desire for glory and the weakness of his German neighbors encouraged Louis's expansionist policy, but he paid a high price for his acquisitions.

a conqueror is regarded as the noblest and highest of titles." In pursuit of the title of "conqueror," he kept France at war for thirty-three of the fifty-four years of his personal rule.

It is an axiom of history that war or the preparation for war is always a government's greatest expense. In 1635, when Richelieu became first minister of Louis XIII, the French army consisted of 25,000 men. In 1659, at the time of the Treaty of the Pyrenees, which ended the war with Spain, the army theoretically was composed of 250,000 men. In 1666 Louis appointed François le Tellier (later marquis de Louvois) secretary of state for war. Under the king's watchful eye, Louvois created a professional army that was modern in the sense that the French state, rather than private nobles, employed the soldiers. The king himself took command and directly supervised all aspects and details of military affairs.

Louvois utilized several methods in recruiting troops: dragooning, in which press gangs seized men off the streets, often drunks, bums, and criminals (this method was not popular); conscription; and, after 1688, lottery. Louvois also recruited regiments of foreign mercenaries. Under the strict direction of Jean Martinet (d. 1672), whose name became a byword in the French and English languages for absolute adherence to the rules, the foreign and native-born soldiers were turned into a tough, obedient military machine. A commissariat was established to feed the troops, taking the place of the ancient method of living off the countryside. An ambulance corps was designed to look after the wounded. Uniforms and weapons were standardized. A rational system of training and promotion was imposed. All this added up to a military revolution. A new military machine now existed that gave one national state, France, the potential to dominate the affairs of the continent for the first time in European history.

Louis continued on a broader scale the expansionist policy begun by Cardinal Richelieu. In 1667, using a dynastic excuse, he invaded Flanders, part of the Spanish Netherlands, and Franche-Comté in the east. In consequence, he acquired twelve towns, including the important commercial centers of Lille and Tournai (see Map 16.1). Five years later, Louis personally led an army of over 100,000 men into Holland, and the Dutch ultimately saved themselves only by opening the dikes and flooding the countryside. This war, which lasted six years and eventually involved the Holy Roman Empire and Spain, was concluded by the Treaty of Nijmegen (1678). Louis gained additional Flemish towns and all of Franche-Comté.

Encouraged by his successes, by the weakness of the German Empire, and by divisions among the other European powers, Louis continued his aggression. In 1681 he seized the city of Strasbourg, and three years later he

MAP 16.2 Europe in 1715 The series of treaties commonly called the Peace of Utrecht (April 1713–November 1715) ended the War of the Spanish Succession and redrew the map of Europe. A French Bourbon king succeeded to the Spanish throne on the understanding that the French not attempt to unite the French and Spanish crowns. France surrendered to Austria the Spanish Netherlands (later Belgium), then in French hands, and France recognized the Hohenzollern rulers of Prussia. Spain ceded Gibraltar to Great Britain, for which it has been a strategic naval station ever since. Spain also granted to Britain the *asiento,* the contract for supplying African slaves to America.

sent his armies into the province of Lorraine. At that moment, the king seemed invincible. In fact, Louis had reached the limit of his expansion. The wars of the 1680s and 1690s brought him no additional territories.

Louis attempted to support an army of 200,000 men in several different theaters of war against the great nations of Europe, the powerful Bank of Amsterdam, and (after 1694) the Bank of England. This task far exceeded French resources, given the very inequitable system of taxation. The military revolution involving the reform and great expansion of the army required funding that the state could not meet. Claude Le Peletier, Colbert's successor as minister of finance, resorted to the devaluation of the currency (which hurt those who hoarded coins) and the old device of selling offices, tax exemptions, and titles of nobility. To raise revenue for the war effort, on December 14, 1689, Louis published a declaration ordering that all the nation's silverware be handed over to the mint. Setting an example, Louis sent off the silver furniture of Versailles. The royal apartments and the Hall of Mirrors looked like a house repossessed by sheriffs.[20] This action did little good. None of these measures produced enough revenue. So the weight of taxation fell on the already-overburdened peasants. They expressed their frustrations in widespread revolts that hit all parts of France in the 1690s.

A series of bad harvests between 1688 and 1694 brought catastrophe. Cold, wet summers reduced the harvests by an estimated one-third to two-thirds. The price of wheat skyrocketed. The result was widespread starvation, and in many provinces the death rate rose to several times the normal figure. Parish registers reveal that France buried at least one-tenth of its population in those years, perhaps 2 million in 1693 to 1694 alone. Rising grain prices, new taxes for war on top of old ones, a slump in manufacturing and thus in exports, and the constant nuisance of pillaging troops—all these meant great suffering for the French people. France wanted peace at any price. Louis XIV granted a respite for five years while he prepared for the conflict later known as the War of the Spanish Succession (1701–1713).

This war, provoked by the territorial disputes of the previous century, also involved the dynastic question of the succession to the Spanish throne. It was an open secret in Europe that the king of Spain, Charles II (r. 1665–1700), was mentally defective and sexually impotent. In 1698 the European powers, including France, agreed by treaty to partition, or divide, the vast Spanish possessions between the king of France and the Holy Roman emperor, who were Charles II's brothers-in-law. When Charles died in 1700, however, his will left the Spanish crown and the worldwide Spanish empire to Philip of Anjou, Louis XIV's grandson. While the will specifically rejected union of the French and Spanish crowns, Louis was obviously the power in France, not his seventeen-year-old grandson. Louis reneged on the treaty and accepted the will.

The Dutch and the English would not accept French acquisition of the Spanish Netherlands and of the rich trade with the Spanish colonies. The union of the Spanish and French crowns, moreover, would have totally upset the European balance of power. Claiming that he was following both Spanish national interests and French dynastic and national interests, Louis presented Philip of Anjou to the Spanish ambassador saying, "You may salute him as your king." After a Mass of thanksgiving, the Spanish ambassador was heard to say, "What rapture! The Pyrenees no longer exist."[21] The possibility of achieving this goal provoked the long-anticipated crisis.

In 1701 the English, Dutch, Austrians, and Prussians formed the Grand Alliance against Louis XIV. They claimed that they were fighting to prevent France from becoming too strong in Europe, but during the previous half century, overseas maritime rivalry among France, Holland, and England had created serious international tension. The secondary motive of the allied powers was to check France's expanding commercial power in North America, Asia, and Africa. In the ensuing series of conflicts, two great soldiers dominated the alliance against France: Eugene, prince of Savoy, representing the Holy Roman Empire, and Englishman John Churchill, subsequently duke of Marlborough. Eugene and Churchill inflicted a severe defeat on Louis in 1704 at Blenheim in Bavaria. Marlborough followed with another victory at Ramillies near Namur in Brabant.

The war was finally concluded at Utrecht in 1713, where the principle of partition was applied. Louis's grandson, Philip, remained the first Bourbon king of Spain on the understanding that the French and Spanish crowns would never be united. France surrendered Newfoundland, Nova Scotia, and the Hudson Bay territory to England, which also acquired Gibraltar, Minorca, and control of the African slave trade from Spain. The Dutch gained little because Austria received the former Spanish Netherlands (see Map 16.2).

The **Peace of Utrecht** had important international consequences. It represented the balance-of-power principle in operation, setting limits on the extent to which any one power—in this case, France—could expand. The treaty completed the decline of Spain as a great power. It vastly expanded the British Empire. And it gave European powers experience in international cooperation.

Tiepolo: The Triumph of Spain This painting is from the ceiling of the Royal Palace in Madrid. Arguably the greatest Italian painter of the eighteenth century, Giovanni Tiepolo depicted the Spanish Empire as the self-assured champion of Christian cultural values in Europe and America. Completed in 1764, a century after the empire had gone into irrevocable decline, this piece represents only an illusion of grandeur. *(Palacio Real de Madrid/The Bridgeman Art Library International Ltd)*

The Peace of Utrecht marked the end of French expansionist policy. In Louis's thirty-five-year quest for military glory, his main territorial acquisition was Strasbourg. Even revisionist historians, who portray the aging monarch as responsible in negotiation and moderate in his demands, acknowledge "that the widespread misery in France during the period was in part due to royal policies, especially the incessant wars."[22] To raise revenue for the wars, forty thousand additional offices had been sold, thus increasing the number of families exempt from future taxation. In 1714 France hovered on the brink of financial bankruptcy. Louis had exhausted the country without much compensation. It is no wonder that when he died on September 1, 1715, Saint-Simon wrote, "Those . . . wearied by the heavy and oppressive rule of the King and his ministers, felt a delighted freedom. . . . Paris . . . found relief in the hope of liberation. . . . The provinces . . . quivered with delight . . . [and] the people, ruined, abused, despairing, now thanked God for a deliverance which answered their most ardent desires."[23]

The Decline of Absolutist Spain in the Seventeenth Century

Spanish absolutism and greatness had preceded those of the French. In the sixteenth century, Spain (or, more precisely, the kingdom of Castile) had developed the standard features of absolute monarchy: a permanent bureaucracy staffed by professionals employed in the various councils of state, a standing army, and national taxes, the *servicios*, which fell most heavily on the poor.

France depended on financial and administrative unification within its borders; Spain had developed an international absolutism on the basis of silver bullion from Peru. Spanish gold and silver, armies, and glory had dominated the continent for most of the sixteenth century, but by the 1590s the seeds of disaster were sprouting. The lack of a strong middle class, largely the result of the expulsion of the Jews and Moors (see page 448), the agricultural crisis and population decline, the failure to invest in productive enterprises, the intellectual isolation and psychological malaise—all combined to reduce Spain, by 1715, to a second-rate power.

The fabulous and seemingly inexhaustible flow of silver from Mexico and Peru, together with the sale of cloth, grain, oil, and wine to the colonies, greatly enriched Spain. In the early seventeenth century, however, the Dutch and English began to trade with the Spanish colonies, cutting into the revenues that had gone to Spain. Mexico and Peru themselves developed local industries, further lessening their need to buy from Spain. Between 1610 and 1650, Spanish trade with the colonies fell 60 percent.

At the same time, the native Indians and African slaves who worked the South American silver mines, under conditions that would have shamed the ancient Egyptian pharaohs, suffered frightful epidemics of disease. Moreover, the lodes started to run dry. Consequently, the quantity of metal produced for Spain steadily declined. But in Madrid royal expenditures constantly exceeded income. The remedies applied in the face of a mountainous state debt and declining revenues were devaluation of the coinage and declarations of bankruptcy. In 1596, 1607,

1627, 1647, and 1680, Spanish kings found no solution to the problem of an empty treasury other than to cancel the national debt. Given the frequency of cancellation, public confidence in the state deteriorated.

Spain, in contrast to the other countries of western Europe, had only a tiny middle class. Public opinion, taking its cue from the aristocracy, condemned moneymaking as vulgar and undignified. Those with influence or connections sought titles of nobility and social prestige. Thousands entered economically unproductive professions or became priests, monks, and nuns: there were said to be nine thousand monasteries in the province of Castile alone. The flood of gold and silver had produced severe inflation, pushing the costs of production in the textile industry higher and higher to the point that Castilian cloth could not compete in colonial and international markets. Many businessmen found so many obstacles in the way of profitable enterprise that they simply gave up.[24]

Spanish aristocrats, attempting to maintain an extravagant lifestyle they could no longer afford, increased the rents on their estates. High rents and heavy taxes in turn drove the peasants from the land. Agricultural production suffered, and the peasants departed for the large cities, where they swelled the ranks of unemployed beggars.

Their most Catholic majesties, the kings of Spain, had no solutions to these dire problems. If one can discern personality from pictures, the portraits of Philip III (r. 1598–1622), Philip IV (r. 1622–1665), and Charles II (r. 1665–1700) hanging in the Prado, the Spanish national museum in Madrid, reflect the increasing weakness of the dynasty. Their faces—the small, beady eyes; the long noses; the jutting Habsburg jaws; the pathetically stupid expressions—tell a story of excessive inbreeding and decaying monarchy. The Spanish kings all lacked force of character. Philip III, a pallid, melancholy, and deeply pious man "whose only virtue appeared to reside in a total absence of vice," handed the government over to the lazy duke of Lerma, who used it to advance his personal and familial wealth. Philip IV left the management of his several kingdoms to Gaspar de Guzmán, count-duke of Olivares.

Olivares was an able administrator. He did not lack energy and ideas; he devised new sources of revenue. But he clung to the grandiose belief that the solution to Spain's difficulties rested in a return to the imperial tradition. Unfortunately, the imperial tradition demanded the revival of war with the Dutch at the expiration of a twelve-year truce in 1622 and a long war with France over Mantua (1628–1659). Spain thus became embroiled in the Thirty Years' War. These conflicts, on top of an empty treasury, brought disaster.

In 1640 Spain faced serious revolts in Catalonia and Portugal; in 1643 the French inflicted a crushing defeat on a Spanish army at Rocroi in what is now Belgium. By the Treaty of the Pyrenees of 1659, which ended the French-Spanish wars, Spain was compelled to surrender extensive territories to France. This treaty marked the end of Spain as a great power.

Peeter Snayers: Spanish Troops (detail) The long wars that Spain fought over Dutch independence, in support of Habsburg interests in Germany, and against France left the country militarily exhausted and financially drained by the mid-1600s. Here Spanish troops—thin, emaciated, and probably unpaid—straggle away from battle. *(Museo Nacional del Prado, Madrid. Photo: José Baztan y Alberto Otero)*

Seventeenth-century Spain was the victim of its past. It could not forget the grandeur of the sixteenth century and look to the future. The bureaucratic councils of state continued to function as symbols of the absolute Spanish monarchy. But because those councils were staffed by aristocrats, it was the aristocracy that held the real power. Spanish absolutism had been built largely on slave-produced gold and silver. When the supply of bullion decreased, the power and standing of the Spanish state declined.

The most cherished Spanish ideals were military glory and strong Roman Catholic faith. In the seventeenth century, Spain lacked the finances and the manpower to fight the expensive wars in which it got involved. Spain also ignored the new mercantile ideas and scientific methods because they came from heretical nations, Holland and England. The incredible wealth of South America destroyed what remained of the Spanish middle class and created contempt for business and manual labor.

The decadence of the Habsburg dynasty and the lack of effective royal councilors also contributed to Spanish failure. Spanish leaders seemed to lack the will to reform. Pessimism and fatalism permeated national life. In the reign of Philip IV, a royal council was appointed to plan the construction of a canal linking the Tagus and Manzanares Rivers in Spain. After interminable debate, the committee decided that "if God had intended the rivers to be navigable, He would have made them so."

In the brilliant novel ***Don Quixote,*** Spanish writer Miguel de Cervantes (1547–1616) produced one of the great masterpieces of world literature. *Don Quixote* delineates the whole fabric of sixteenth-century Spanish society. The main character, Don Quixote, lives in a world of dreams, traveling about the countryside seeking military glory. From the title of the book, the English language has borrowed the word *quixotic*. Meaning "idealistic but impractical," the term characterizes seventeenth-century Spain. As a leading scholar has written, "The Spaniard convinced himself that reality was what he felt, believed, imagined. He filled the world with heroic reverberations. Don Quixote was born and grew."[25]

Constitutionalism

The seventeenth century saw the appearance of the constitutional state. While France and, later, Prussia, Russia, and Austria solved the question of sovereignty with the absolutist state, England and Holland evolved toward the constitutional state. What is constitutionalism? Is it identical to democracy?

Constitutionalism is the limitation of government by law. Constitutionalism also implies a balance between the authority and power of the government, on the one hand, and the rights and liberties of the subjects, on the other.

A nation's constitution may be written or unwritten. It may be embodied in one basic document, occasionally revised by amendment or judicial decision, like the Constitution of the United States. Or it may be partly written and partly unwritten and include parliamentary statutes, judicial decisions, and a body of traditional procedures and practices, like the English, Canadian, and Dutch constitutions. Whether written or unwritten, a constitution gets its binding force from the government's acknowledgment that it must respect that constitution—that is, that the state must govern according to the laws. Likewise, in a constitutional state, the people look on the laws and the constitution as the protectors of their rights, liberties, and property.

Modern constitutional governments may take either a republican or a monarchical form. In a constitutional republic, the sovereign power resides in the electorate and is exercised by the electorate's representatives. In a constitutional monarchy, a king or queen serves as the head of state and possesses some residual political authority, but again the ultimate, or sovereign, power rests in the electorate.

A constitutional government is not, however, quite the same as a democratic government. In a complete democracy, *all* the people have the right to participate either directly or indirectly (through their elected representatives) in the government of the state. Democratic government, therefore, is intimately tied up with the *franchise* (the vote). Most men could not vote until the late nineteenth century. Even then, women—probably the majority in Western societies—lacked the franchise; they gained the right to vote only in the twentieth century. Consequently, although constitutionalism developed in the seventeenth century, full democracy was achieved only in recent times.

The Decline of Royal Absolutism in England (1603–1649)

In 1588 Queen Elizabeth I of England exercised very great personal power; by 1689 the English monarchy was severely circumscribed. Change in England was anything but orderly. Seventeenth-century England displayed little political stability. It executed one king and experienced a bloody civil war; experimented with military dictatorship, then restored the son of the murdered king; and finally, after a bloodless revolution, established constitutional monarchy. Political stability came only in the 1690s. How do we account for the fact that after such a violent and tumultuous century, England laid the foundations for constitutional monarchy? What combination of political, socioeconomic, and religious factors brought on a civil war in 1642–1649 and then the constitutional settlement of 1688–1689?

The extraordinary success of Elizabeth I had rested on her political shrewdness and flexibility, her careful management of finances, her wise selection of ministers, her clever manipulation of Parliament, and her sense of royal dignity and devotion to hard work. The aging queen had always refused to discuss the succession. After her Scottish cousin James Stuart succeeded her as James I (r. 1603–1625), Elizabeth's strengths seemed even greater than they actually had been.

King James was well educated, learned, and, with thirty-five years' experience as king of Scotland, politically shrewd. But he was not as interested in displaying the majesty and mystique of monarchy as Elizabeth had been. He also lacked the common touch. Urged to wave at the crowds who waited to greet their new ruler, James complained that he was tired and threatened to drop his breeches "so they can cheer at my arse." The new king failed to live up to the role expected of him in England. Moreover, James, in contrast to Elizabeth, was a poor judge of character, and in a society already hostile to the Scots and concerned about proper spoken English, James's Scottish accent was a disadvantage.[26]

James was devoted to the theory of the divine right of kings. He expressed his ideas about divine right in his essay "The Trew Law of Free Monarchy." According to James I, a monarch has a divine (or God-given) right to his authority and is responsible only to God. Rebellion is the worst of political crimes. If a king orders something evil, the subject should respond with passive disobedience but should be prepared to accept any penalty for noncompliance.

He went so far as to lecture the House of Commons: "There are no privileges and immunities which can stand against a divinely appointed King." This notion, implying total royal jurisdiction over the liberties, persons, and properties of English men and women, formed the basis of the Stuart concept of absolutism. Such a view ran directly counter to the long-standing English idea that a person's property could not be taken away without due process of law. James's expression of such views before the English House of Commons constituted a grave political mistake.

The House of Commons guarded the state's pocketbook, and James and later Stuart kings badly needed to open that pocketbook. Elizabeth had left James a sizable royal debt. Through prudent management, the debt could have been gradually reduced, but James I looked on all revenues as a happy windfall to be squandered on a lavish court and favorite courtiers. In reality, the extravagance displayed in James's court as well as the public flaunting of his male lovers weakened respect for the monarchy.

Elizabeth had also left her Stuart successors a House of Commons that appreciated its own financial strength and intended to use that strength to acquire a greater say in the government of the state. The knights and burgesses who sat at Westminster in the late sixteenth and early seventeenth centuries wanted a voice in royal expenditures, religious reform, and foreign affairs. Essentially, the Commons wanted sovereignty.

Profound social changes had occurred since the sixteenth century. The English House of Commons during the reigns of James I and his son Charles I (r. 1625–1649) was very different from the assembly Henry VIII had manipulated into passing his Reformation legislation. The dissolution of the monasteries and the sale of monastic land had enriched many people. Agricultural techniques such as the draining of wasteland and the application of fertilizers had improved the land and its yield. In the seventeenth century, old manorial common land was enclosed and turned into sheep runs, breeding was carefully supervised, and the size of the flocks increased. In these activities, as well as in the renting and leasing of parcels of land, precise accounts were kept.

Many people invested in commercial ventures at home, such as the expanding cloth industry, and through partnerships and joint stock companies engaged in foreign enterprises. Many also made prudent marriages. These developments led to a great deal of social mobility. Both in commerce and in agriculture, the English in the late sixteenth and early seventeenth centuries were capitalists, investing their profits to make more money. Though the international inflation of the period hit everywhere, in England commercial and agricultural income rose faster than prices. Wealthy country gentry, rich city merchants, and financiers invested abroad.

The typical pattern was for the commercially successful to set themselves up as country gentry, thus creating an elite group that possessed a far greater proportion of land and of the national wealth in 1640 than had been the case in 1540. Small wonder that in 1640 someone could declare in the House of Commons, probably accurately, "We could buy the House of Lords three times over." Increased wealth had also produced a better-educated and more articulate House of Commons. Many members had acquired at least a smattering of legal knowledge, which they used to search for medieval precedents from which to argue against the king. The class that dominated the Commons wanted political power corresponding to its economic strength.

In England, unlike France, there was no social stigma attached to paying taxes. Members of the House of Commons were willing to tax themselves provided they had some say in the expenditure of those taxes and in the formulation of state policies. The Stuart kings, however, considered such ambitions intolerable presumption and a threat to their divine-right prerogative. Consequently, at every Parliament between 1603 and 1640, bitter squabbles erupted between the Crown and the wealthy, articulate, and legally minded Commons. Charles I's attempt to govern without Parliament (1629–1640) and to finance his government by arbitrary nonparliamentary levies, brought the country to a crisis.

Religious Issues

An issue graver than royal extravagance and Parliament's desire to make law also disturbed the English and embittered relations between the king and the House of Commons. That problem was religion. In the early seventeenth century, increasing numbers of English people felt dissatisfied with the Church of England established by Henry VIII and reformed by Elizabeth. Many **Puritans** (see page 476) believed that the Reformation had not gone far enough. They wanted to "purify" the Anglican church of Roman Catholic elements—elaborate vestments and ceremonials, bishops, the position of the altar in the church, even the giving and wearing of wedding rings.

It is very difficult to establish what proportion of the English population was Puritan. According to the present scholarly consensus, the dominant religious groups in the early seventeenth century were Calvinist; their more zealous members were Puritans. It also seems clear that many English people were attracted by the socioeconomic implications of John Calvin's theology. Calvinism emphasized hard work, sobriety, thrift, competition, and postponement of pleasure, and it tended to link sin and poverty with weakness and moral corruption. These attitudes fit in precisely with the economic approaches and practices of many (successful) business people and farmers. These values have frequently been called the "Protestant ethic," "middle-class ethic," or "capitalist ethic." While it is hazardous to identify capitalism with Protestantism—there were many successful Catholic capitalists, for example—the "Protestant virtues" represented the prevailing values of members of the House of Commons.

Puritans wanted to abolish bishops in the Church of England, and when James I said, "No bishop, no king," he meant that the bishops were among the chief supporters of the throne. He was no Puritan, but he was Calvinist (see page 470) in doctrine. Yet James and his son Charles I both gave the impression of being sympathetic to Roman Catholicism. Charles supported the policies of William Laud (1573–1645), archbishop of Canterbury, who tried to impose elaborate ritual and rich ceremonials on all churches. Laud insisted on complete uniformity of church services and enforced that uniformity through an ecclesiastical court called the "Court of High Commission." People believed the country was being led back to Roman Catholicism. In 1637 Laud attempted to impose two new elements on church organization in Scotland: a new prayer book, modeled on the Anglican *Book of Common Prayer,* and bishoprics, which the Presbyterian Scots firmly rejected. The Scots therefore revolted. To finance an army to put down the Scots, King Charles was compelled to summon Parliament in November 1640.

Charles I was an intelligent man, but contemporaries found him deceitful, dishonest, and treacherous. Therefore, they did not trust him. For eleven years, Charles had ruled without Parliament, financing his government through extraordinary stopgap levies considered illegal by most English people. For example, the king revived a medieval law requiring coastal districts to help pay the cost of ships for defense, but he levied the tax, called "ship money," on inland as well as coastal counties. When the issue was tested in the courts, the judges, having been suborned, decided in the king's favor.

Most members of Parliament believed that such taxation without consent amounted to arbitrary and absolute despotism. Consequently, they were not willing to trust the king with an army. Accordingly, this Parliament, called the "Long Parliament" because it sat from 1640 to 1660, proceeded to enact legislation that limited the power of the monarch and made arbitrary government impossible.

In 1641 the Commons passed the Triennial Act, which compelled the king to summon Parliament every three years. The Commons impeached Archbishop Laud and abolished the Court of High Commission. It went further and threatened to abolish the institution of episcopacy. King Charles, fearful of a Scottish invasion—the original reason for summoning Parliament—accepted these measures. Understanding and peace were not achieved, however, partly because radical members of the Commons pushed increasingly revolutionary propositions, partly because Charles maneuvered to rescind those he had already approved. An uprising in Ireland precipitated civil war.

Ever since Henry II had conquered Ireland in 1171, English governors had mercilessly ruled the land, and

Puritan Occupations These twelve engravings depict typical Puritan occupations and show that the Puritans came primarily from the artisan and lower middle classes. The governing classes and peasants adhered to the traditions of the Church of England.

English landlords had ruthlessly exploited the Irish people. The English Reformation had made a bad situation worse: because the Irish remained Catholic, religious differences became united with economic and political oppression. Without an army, Charles I could neither come to terms with the Scots nor put down the Irish rebellion, and the Long Parliament remained unwilling to place an army under a king it did not trust. Charles thus instigated military action against parliamentary forces. He recruited an army drawn from the nobility and its cavalry staff, the rural gentry, and mercenaries. The parliamentary army was composed of the militia of the city of London, country squires with business connections, and men with a firm belief in the spiritual duty of serving.

The English civil war (1642–1649) tested whether sovereignty in England was to reside in the king or in Parliament. The civil war did not resolve that problem, however, although it ended in 1649 with the execution of King Charles on the charge of high treason—a severe blow to the theory of divine-right monarchy. The period between 1649 and 1660, called the "Interregnum" because it separated two monarchical periods, witnessed England's solitary experience of military dictatorship.

Puritanical Absolutism in England: Cromwell and the Protectorate

The problem of sovereignty was vigorously debated in the middle years of the seventeenth century. In *Leviathan,* English philosopher and political theorist Thomas Hobbes (1588–1679) maintains that sovereignty is ultimately derived from the people, who transfer it to the monarchy by implicit contract. The power of the ruler is absolute, but kings do not hold their power by divine right. This view pleased no one.

When Charles I was beheaded on January 30, 1649, the kingship was abolished. A commonwealth, or **republican government,** was proclaimed. Theoretically, legislative power rested in the surviving members of Parliament, and executive power was lodged in a council of state. In fact, the army that had defeated the royal forces controlled the government, and Oliver Cromwell controlled the army. Though called the "Protectorate," the rule of Cromwell (1653–1658) constituted military dictatorship.

The army had prepared a constitution, the Instrument of Government (1653), that invested executive power in a lord protector (Cromwell) and a council of state. The instrument provided for triennial parliaments and gave

Parliament the sole power to raise taxes. But after repeated disputes, Cromwell tore the document up. He continued the standing army and proclaimed quasi-martial law. He divided England into twelve military districts, each governed by a major general. The major generals acted through the justices of the peace though sometimes overrode them. On the issue of religion, Cromwell favored toleration, and the Instrument of Government gave all Christians, except Roman Catholics, the right to practice their faith. Toleration meant state protection of many different Protestant sects, however, and most English people had no enthusiasm for such a notion; the idea was far ahead of its time. As for Irish Catholicism, Cromwell identified it with sedition. In 1649 he crushed a rebellion at Drogheda in Ireland with merciless savagery, leaving a legacy of Irish hatred for England that has not yet subsided. The state rigorously censored the press, forbade sports, and kept the theaters closed in England.

Cromwell's regulation of the nation's economy had features typical of seventeenth-century absolutism. The lord protector's policies were mercantilist, similar to those Colbert established in France. Cromwell enforced a Navigation Act (1651) requiring that English goods be transported on English ships. The navigation act was a great boost to the development of an English merchant marine and brought about a short but successful war with the commercially threatened Dutch. Cromwell also welcomed the immigration of Jews because of their skills, and they began to return to England after four centuries of absence.

Military government collapsed when Cromwell died in 1658. Fed up with military rule, the English longed for a return to civilian government, restoration of the common law, and social stability. Moreover, the strain of creating a community of puritanical saints proved too psychologically exhausting. Government by military dictatorship was an unfortunate experiment that the English

Cartoon of 1649: "The Royall Oake of Brittayne" Chopping down this tree signifies the end of royal authority, stability, the Magna Carta (see page 343), and the rule of law. As pigs graze (representing the unconcerned common people), being fattened for slaughter, Oliver Cromwell, with his feet in hell, quotes Scripture. This is a royalist view of the collapse of Charles I's government and the rule of Cromwell. *(Courtesy of the Trustees of the British Museum)*

never forgot or repeated. By 1660 they were ready to restore the monarchy.

The Restoration of the English Monarchy

The Restoration of 1660 re-established the monarchy in the person of Charles II (r. 1660–1685), eldest son of Charles I. At the same time, both houses of Parliament were restored, together with the established Anglican church, the courts of law, and the system of local government through justices of the peace. The Restoration failed to resolve two serious problems, however. What was to be the attitude of the state toward Puritans, Catholics, and dissenters from the established church? And what was to be the constitutional position of the king—that is, what was to be the relationship between the king and Parliament?

About the first of these issues, Charles II, a relaxed, easygoing, and sensual man, was basically indifferent. He was not interested in doctrinal issues. Members of Parliament were, and they enacted a body of laws that sought to compel religious uniformity. Those who refused to receive the Eucharist of the Church of England could not vote, hold public office, preach, teach, attend the universities, or even assemble for meetings, according to the Test Act of 1673. But these restrictions could not be enforced. When the Quaker William Penn held a meeting of his Friends and was arrested, the jury refused to convict him.

In politics Charles II was determined "not to set out in his travels again," which meant that he intended to get along with Parliament. Charles II's solution to the problem of the relationship between the king and the House of Commons had profound importance for later constitutional development. Generally good rapport existed between the king and the strongly royalist Parliament that had restored him. This rapport was due largely to the king's appointment of a council of five men who served both as his major advisers and as members of Parliament, thus acting as liaison agents between the executive and the legislature. This body—known as the "Cabal" from the names of its five members (Clifford, Arlington, Buckingham, Ashley-Cooper, and Lauderdale)—was an ancestor of the later cabinet system (see page 554). Although its members sometimes disagreed and intrigued among themselves, it gradually came to be accepted that the Cabal was answerable in Parliament for the decisions of the king. This development gave rise to the concept of ministerial responsibility: royal ministers must answer to the Commons.

Harmony between the Crown and Parliament rested on the understanding that Charles would summon frequent parliaments and that Parliament would vote him sufficient revenues. But Parliament did not grant him an adequate income. Accordingly, in 1670 Charles entered into a secret agreement with Louis XIV. The French king would give Charles 200,000 pounds annually, and in return Charles would relax the laws against Catholics, gradually re-Catholicize England, support French policy against the Dutch, and convert to Catholicism himself.

When the details of this secret treaty leaked out, a great wave of anti-Catholic fear swept England. This fear was compounded by a crucial fact: although Charles had produced several bastards, he had no legitimate children. It therefore appeared that his brother and heir, James, duke of York, who had publicly acknowledged his Catholicism, would inaugurate a Catholic dynasty. A combination of hatred for the French absolutism embodied in Louis XIV, hostility to Roman Catholicism, and fear of a permanent Catholic dynasty produced virtual hysteria. The Commons passed an exclusion bill denying the succession to a Roman Catholic, but Charles quickly dissolved Parliament, and the bill never became law.

James II (r. 1685–1688) did succeed his brother. Almost at once the worst English anti-Catholic fears, already aroused by Louis XIV's revocation of the Edict of Nantes, were realized. In direct violation of the Test Act, James appointed Roman Catholics to positions in the army, the universities, and local government. When these actions were tested in the courts, the judges, whom James had appointed, decided for the king. The king was suspending the law at will and appeared to be reviving the absolutism of his father and grandfather. He went further. Attempting to broaden his base of support with Protestant dissenters and nonconformists, James issued a declaration of indulgence granting religious freedom to all.

Two events gave the signals for revolution. First, seven bishops of the Church of England petitioned the king that they not be forced to read the declaration of indulgence because of their belief that it was an illegal act. They were imprisoned in the Tower of London but subsequently acquitted amid great public enthusiasm. Second, in June 1688 James's second wife produced a male heir. A Catholic dynasty seemed ensured. The fear of a Roman Catholic monarchy supported by France and ruling outside the law prompted a group of eminent persons to offer the English throne to James's Protestant daughter, Mary, and her Dutch husband, Prince William of Orange. In December 1688 James II, his queen, and their infant son fled to France and became pensioners of Louis XIV. Early in 1689, William and Mary were crowned king and queen of England.

The Triumph of England's Parliament: Constitutional Monarchy and Cabinet Government

The English call the events of 1688 to 1689 the "Glorious Revolution." The revolution was indeed glorious in the sense that it replaced one king with another with a minimum of bloodshed. It also represented the destruction, once and for all, of the idea of divine-right monarchy. William and Mary accepted the English throne from Parliament and in so doing explicitly recognized the supremacy of Parliament. The revolution of 1688 established the principle that sovereignty, the ultimate power in the state, was divided between king and Parliament and that the king ruled with the consent of the governed.

The men who brought about the revolution quickly framed their intentions in the Bill of Rights, the cornerstone of the modern British constitution. The basic principles of the Bill of Rights were formulated in direct response to Stuart absolutism. Law was to be made in Parliament; once made, it could not be suspended by the Crown. Parliament had to be called at least every three years. Both elections to and debate in Parliament were to be free in the sense that the Crown was not to interfere in them (this aspect of the bill was widely disregarded in the eighteenth century). Judges would hold their offices "during good behavior," a provision that ensured the independence of the judiciary. No longer could the Crown get the judicial decisions it wanted by threats of removal. There was to be no standing army in peacetime—a limitation designed to prevent the repetition of Cromwellian military government. The Bill of Rights granted "that the subjects which are Protestants may have arms for their defense suitable to their conditions and as allowed by law,"[27] meaning that Catholics could not possess firearms because the Protestant majority feared them. Additional legislation granted freedom of worship to Protestant dissenters and nonconformists and required that the English monarch always be Protestant.

The Glorious Revolution found its best defense in political philosopher John Locke's ***Second Treatise of Civil Government*** (1690). Locke (1632–1704) maintained that people set up civil governments to protect life, liberty, and property. A government that oversteps its proper function—protecting the natural rights of life, liberty, and property—becomes a tyranny. (By "natural" rights, Locke meant rights basic to all men because all have the ability to reason.) Under a tyrannical government, the people have the natural right to rebellion. Such rebellion can be avoided if the government carefully respects the rights of citizens and if people zealously defend their liberty. Recognizing the close relationship between economic and political freedom, Locke linked economic liberty and private property with political freedom; his defense of property included a justification for a narrow franchise. Locke served as the great spokesman for the liberal English revolution of 1688 to 1689 and for representative government. His idea that there are natural or universal rights equally valid for all peoples and societies was especially popular in colonial America.

The events of 1688 to 1689 did not constitute a *democratic* revolution. The revolution placed sovereignty in Parliament, and Parliament represented the upper classes. The great majority of English people acquired no say in their government. The English revolution established a constitutional monarchy; it also inaugurated an age of aristocratic government, which lasted at least until 1832 and in many ways until 1928, when women received full voting rights.

In the course of the eighteenth century, the **cabinet system** of government evolved. The term *cabinet* derives from the small private room in which English rulers consulted their chief ministers. In a cabinet system, the leading ministers, who must have seats in and the support of a majority of the House of Commons, formulate common policy and conduct the business of the country. During the administration of one royal minister, Sir Robert Walpole, who led the cabinet from 1721 to 1742, the idea developed that the cabinet was responsible to the House of Commons. The Hanoverian king George I (r. 1714–1727) normally presided at cabinet meetings throughout his reign, but his son and heir, George II (r. 1727–1760), discontinued the practice. The influence of the Crown in decision making accordingly declined. Walpole enjoyed the favor of the monarchy and of the House of Commons and came to be called the king's first, or "prime," minister. In the English cabinet system, both legislative power and executive power are held by the leading ministers, who form the government.

The Dutch Republic in the Seventeenth Century

In the late sixteenth century, the seven northern provinces of the Netherlands fought for and won their independence from Spain as the Republic of United Provinces of the Netherlands—an independence that was confirmed by the Peace of Westphalia ending the Thirty Years' War in 1648 (see pages 501–502). The seventeenth century witnessed an unparalleled flowering of Dutch scientific, artistic, and literary achievement. In this period, often called the "golden age of the Netherlands," Dutch ideas and attitudes played a profound role in shaping a new and modern world-view. At the same time, the

Jan Vermeer: The Art of Painting or The Artist's Studio In a typically Dutch interior—black and white marble floor, brass chandelier, map of Holland on the wall—an artist paints an allegory of Clio, the Muse of History (often shown holding a book and a trumpet). The Muses, nine goddesses of Greek mythology, were thought to inspire the arts. Considered the second-greatest Dutch painter (after Rembrandt), Vermeer (1632–1675) was a master of scenes of everyday life, but he probably meant his work to be understood on more than one level. *(Kunsthistorisches Museum, Vienna/Art Resource, NY)*

United Provinces was another model of the development of the modern constitutional state.

Within each province, an oligarchy of wealthy merchants called "regents" handled domestic affairs in the local Estates. The provincial Estates held virtually all the power. A federal assembly, or **States General,** handled matters of foreign affairs, such as war. But the States General did not possess sovereign authority since all issues had to be referred back to the local Estates for approval. The States General appointed a representative, the **stadholder,** in each province. As the highest executive there, the stadholder carried out ceremonial functions and was responsible for defense and good order. The sons of William the Silent, Maurice and William Louis, held the office of stadholder in all seven provinces. As members of the House of Orange, they were closely identified with Dutch patriotism. The regents in each province jealously guarded local independence and resisted efforts at centralization. Nevertheless, Holland, which had the largest navy and the most wealth, dominated the republic and the States General. Significantly, the Estates assembled at Holland's capital, The Hague.

The government of the United Provinces fit none of the standard categories of seventeenth-century political organization. The Dutch were not monarchical but fiercely republican. The government was controlled by wealthy merchants and financiers. Though rich, their values were not aristocratic but strongly middle-class. The Dutch republic was not a strong federation but a confederation—that is, a weak union of strong provinces. The provinces were a temptation to powerful neighbors, yet the Dutch resisted the long Spanish effort at reconquest and withstood both French and English attacks in the second half of the century.

The political success of the Dutch rested on the phenomenal commercial prosperity of the Netherlands. The moral and ethical bases of that commercial wealth were thrift, frugality, and religious toleration. John Calvin had written, "From where do the merchant's profits come except from his own diligence and industry?" This attitude encouraged a sturdy people who had waged a centuries-old struggle against the sea.

Alone of all European peoples in the seventeenth century, the Dutch practiced religious toleration. Peoples of

Jan Steen: The Christening Feast As the mother, surrounded by midwives, rests in bed (*rear left*) and the father proudly displays the swaddled child, thirteen other people, united by gestures and gazes, prepare the celebratory meal. Very prolific, Steen was a master of warm-hearted domestic scenes. In contrast to the order and cleanliness of many seventeenth-century Dutch genre paintings, Steen's more disorderly portrayals gave rise to the epithet "a Jan Steen household," meaning an untidy house. *(Wallace Collection, London/The Bridgeman Art Library International Ltd)*

all faiths were welcome within their borders. Although there is scattered evidence of anti-Semitism, Jews enjoyed a level of acceptance and absorption in Dutch business and general culture unique in early modern Europe. (See the feature "Individuals in Society: Glückel of Hameln.") The urbanity of Dutch society allowed a rare degree of religious freedom. As long as business people conducted their religion in private, the government did not interfere with them.

Toleration paid off: it attracted a great deal of foreign capital and investment. Deposits at the Bank of Amsterdam were guaranteed by the city council, and in the middle years of the century, the bank became Europe's best source of cheap credit and commercial intelligence and the main clearing-house for bills of exchange. People of all races and creeds traded in Amsterdam, at whose docks on the Amstel River five thousand ships were berthed. Joost van den Vondel, the poet of Dutch imperialism, exulted:

God, God, the Lord of Amstel cried, hold every conscience free;
And Liberty ride, on Holland's tide, with billowing sails to sea,
And run our Amstel out and in; let freedom gird the bold,
And merchant in his counting house stand elbow deep in gold.[28]

The fishing industry was the cornerstone of the Dutch economy. For half the year, from June to December, fishing fleets combed the dangerous English coast and the North Sea and raked in tiny herring. Profits from herring stimulated shipbuilding, and even before 1600 the Dutch were offering the lowest shipping rates in Europe. The Dutch merchant marine was the largest in Europe. In 1650 contemporaries estimated that the Dutch had sixteen thousand merchant ships, half the European total. All the wood for these ships had to be imported: the Dutch bought whole forests from Norway. They also bought entire vineyards from French growers before the grapes were harvested. They controlled the Baltic grain trade, buying entire wheat and rye crops in Poland, east Prussia, and Swedish Pomerania. Because the Dutch dealt in bulk, nobody could undersell them. Foreign merchants coming to Amsterdam could buy anything from precision lenses for the microscope (recently invented by Dutchman Anton van Leeuwenhoek) to mus-

Individuals in Society

Glückel of Hameln

In 1690 a Jewish widow in the small German town of Hameln* in Lower Saxony sat down to write her autobiography. She wanted to distract her mind from the terrible grief she felt over the death of her husband and to provide her twelve children with a record "so you will know from what sort of people you have sprung, lest today or tomorrow your beloved children or grand-children came and know naught of their family." Out of her pain and heightened consciousness, Glückel (1646–1724) produced an invaluable source for scholars.

She was born in Hamburg two years before the end of the Thirty Years' War. In 1649 the merchants of Hamburg expelled the Jews, who moved to nearby Altona, then under Danish rule. When the Swedes overran Altona in 1657–1658, the Jews returned to Hamburg "purely at the mercy of the Town Council." Glückel's narrative proceeds against a background of the constant difficulties (harassment) to which Jews were subjected—special papers, permits, bribes—and in Hameln she wrote, "And so it has been to this day and, I fear, will continue in like fashion."

When Glückel was "barely twelve," her father betrothed her to Chayim Hameln. She married at age fourteen. She describes him as "the perfect pattern of the pious Jew," a man who stopped his work every day for study and prayer, fasted, and was scrupulously honest in his business dealings. Only a few years older than Glückel, Chayim earned his living dealing in precious metals and in making small loans on pledges (articles held on security). This work required his constant travel to larger cities, markets, and fairs, often in bad weather, always over dangerous roads. Chayim consulted his wife about all his business dealings. As he lay dying, a friend asked if he had any last wishes. "None," he replied. "My wife knows everything. She shall do as she has always done." For thirty years, Glückel had been his friend, full business partner, and wife. They had thirteen children, twelve of whom survived their father, eight then unmarried. As Chayim had foretold, Glückel succeeded in launching the boys in careers and in providing dowries for the girls.

Glückel's world was her family, the Jewish community of Hameln, and the Jewish communities into which her children married. Social and business activities took her to Amsterdam, Baiersdorf, Bamberg, Berlin, Cleves, Danzig, Metz, and Vienna, so her world was not a narrow or provincial one. She took great pride that Prince Frederick of Cleves, later king of Prussia, danced at the wedding of her eldest daughter. The rising prosperity of Chayim's businesses allowed the couple to maintain up to six servants. Jews, however, lived on the margins of Christian society, and traditional sociological categories cannot be applied to them.

Gentleness and deep mutual devotion seem to pervade Rembrandt's The Jewish Bride. (Rijksmuseum-Stichting Amsterdam)

Glückel was deeply religious, and her culture was steeped in Jewish literature, legends, and mystical and secular works. Above all, she relied on the Bible. Her language, heavily sprinkled with scriptural references, testifies to a rare familiarity with the basic book of Western civilization. The Scriptures were her consolation, the source of her great strength in a hostile world.

Students who would learn about business practices, the importance of the dowry in marriage, childbirth, the ceremony of bris, birthrates, family celebrations, even the meaning of life can gain a good deal from the memoirs of this extraordinary woman, who was, in the words of one of her descendants, the poet Heinrich Heine, "the gift of a world to me."

Questions for Analysis

1. Consider the ways in which Glückel of Hameln was an ordinary woman of her times.
2. How was Glückel's life affected by the broad events and issues of the seventeenth century?

*Town immortalized by the Brothers Grimm. In 1284 the town contracted with the Pied Piper to rid it of rats and mice; he lured them away by playing his flute. When the citizens refused to pay, he charmed away their children in revenge.

Source: The Memoirs of Glückel of Hameln, trans. M. Lowenthal (New York: Schocken Books, 1977).

kets for an army of five thousand. Although Dutch cities became famous for their exports—diamonds and linens from Haarlem, pottery from Delft—Dutch wealth depended less on exports than on transport.

In 1602 a group of the regents of Holland formed the **Dutch East India Company,** a joint stock company. The investors each received a percentage of the profits proportional to the amount of money they had put in. Within half a century, the Dutch East India Company had cut heavily into Portuguese trading in East Asia. The Dutch seized the Cape of Good Hope, Ceylon, and Malacca and established trading posts in each place. In the 1630s, the Dutch East India Company was paying its investors about a 35 percent annual return on their investments. The Dutch West India Company, founded in 1621, traded extensively with Latin America and Africa (see Map 16.3).

Trade and commerce brought the Dutch prodigious wealth. In the seventeenth century, the Dutch enjoyed the highest standard of living in Europe, perhaps in the world. Amsterdam and Rotterdam built massive granaries where the surplus of one year could be stored against possible shortages the next. Thus, excepting the 1650s, when bad harvests reduced supplies, food prices fluctuated very little. By the standards of Cologne, Paris, or London, salaries were high for all workers—except women, but even women's wages were high when compared with those of women in other parts of Europe. All classes of society, including unskilled laborers, ate well. The low price of bread meant that, compared to other places in Europe, a higher percentage of the worker's income could be spent on fish, cheese, butter, vegetables, even meat. A scholar has described the Netherlands as "an island of plenty in a sea of want." Consequently, the Netherlands experienced very few of the food riots that characterized the rest of Europe.[29]

Although the initial purpose of the Dutch East and West India Companies was commercial—the import of spices and silks to Europe—the Dutch found themselves involved in the imperialist exploitation of parts of East Asia and Latin America, with great success. In 1652 the Dutch founded Cape Town on the southern tip of Africa as a fueling station for ships planning to cross the Pacific. But war with France and England in the 1670s hurt the United Provinces. The long War of the Spanish Succession—in which the Dutch prince William of Orange utilized, as King William III of England, English wealth in the Dutch fight against Louis XIV—was a costly drain on Dutch labor and financial resources. The peace signed in 1713 to end the war marked the beginning of Dutch economic decline.

Room from Het Scheepje (The Little Ship) A retired sea captain who became a successful brewer in Haarlem owned the house (adjacent to his brewery) that included this room. The brass chandelier, plates, tiles, Turkish rug on the table (probably from Transylvania in the Ottoman Empire), oak mantelpiece, and paneling make this a superb example of a Dutch domestic interior during the Golden Age. A bed, built into the wall paneling, was warmed at night by coals in the pan hanging by the fireplace. *(Room from Het Scheepje, Haarlem, The Netherlands, early 17th century. Philadelphia Museum of Art, Gift of Edward W. Bok. 1928-66-1)*

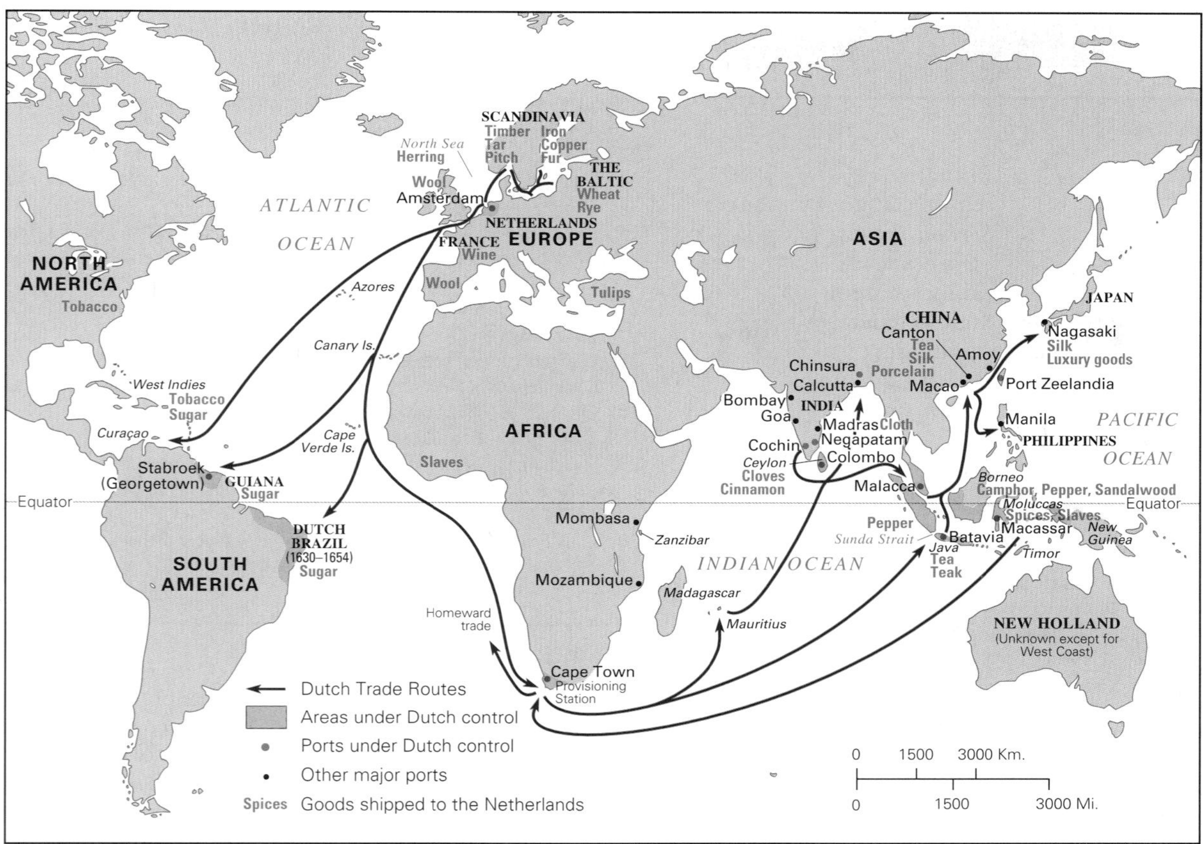

MAP 16.3 Seventeenth-Century Dutch Commerce Dutch wealth rested on commerce, and commerce depended on the huge Dutch merchant marine, manned by perhaps forty-eight thousand sailors. The fleet carried goods from all parts of the globe to the port of Amsterdam.

Summary

According to Thomas Hobbes, the central drive in every human is "a perpetual and restless desire of Power, after Power, that ceaseth only in Death." The seventeenth century solved the problem of sovereign power in two fundamental ways: absolutism and constitutionalism. The France of Louis XIV witnessed the emergence of the fully absolutist state. The king commanded all the powers of the state: judicial, military, political, and, to a great extent, ecclesiastical. France developed a centralized bureaucracy, a professional army, and a state-directed economy, all of which Louis personally supervised. For the first time in history, all the institutions and powers of the national state were effectively controlled by a single person. The king saw himself as the representative of God on earth, and it has been said that "to the seventeenth century imagination God was a sort of image of Louis XIV."[30]

As Louis XIV personifies absolutism, so Stuart England exemplifies the evolution of the first modern constitutional state. The conflicts between Parliament and the first two Stuart rulers, James I and Charles I, tested where sovereign power would rest in the state. The resulting civil war did not solve the problem. The Instrument of Government provided for a balance of government authority and recognition of popular rights; as such, the Instrument has been called the first modern constitution. Unfortunately, it lacked public support. James II's absolutist tendencies brought on the Glorious Revolution of 1688 to 1689, and the people who made that revolution settled three basic issues. Sovereign power was divided between king and Parliament, with Parliament enjoying the greater share. Government was to be based on the rule of law. And the liberties of English people were made explicit in written form in the Bill of Rights.

The models of governmental power established by seventeenth-century England and France strongly influenced other states then and ever since. As American novelist William Faulkner wrote, "The past isn't dead; it's not even past."

Key Terms

sovereignty
absolutism
totalitarianism
raison d'état
Fronde
mercantilism
French classicism
Peace of Utrecht
Don Quixote
constitutionalism
Puritans
republican government
Second Treatise of Civil Government
cabinet system
States General
stadholder
Dutch East India Company

Notes

1. G. Parker and L. M. Smith, "Introduction," and N. Steensgaard, "The Seventeenth Century Crisis," in *The General Crisis of the Seventeenth Century,* ed. G. Parker and L. M. Smith (London: Routledge & Kegan Paul, 1985), pp. 1–53, esp. p. 12.
2. See W. Beik, *Urban Protest in Seventeenth-Century France: The Culture of Retribution* (New York: Cambridge University Press, 1997), p. 1.
3. J. B. Collins, *The State in Early Modern France* (Cambridge, England: Cambridge University Press, 1995), p. 1.
4. Ibid., p. 3.
5. Ibid., pp. 22–26.
6. See M. Turchetti, "The Edict of Nantes," in *The Oxford Encyclopedia of the Reformation,* ed. H. J. Hillerbrand, vol. 3 (New York: Oxford University Press, 1996), pp. 126–128.
7. See Beik, *Urban Protest,* chaps. 1, 2, 3, and 11.
8. J. B. Collins, *Fiscal Limits of Absolutism: Direct Taxation in Early Seventeenth-Century France* (Berkeley and Los Angeles: University of California Press, 1988), pp. 1, 3–4, 215–222.
9. Quoted in J. H. Elliott, *Richelieu and Olivares* (Cambridge: Cambridge University Press, 1984), p. 135; and in W. F. Church, *Richelieu and Reason of State* (Princeton, N.J.: Princeton University Press, 1972), p. 507.
10. D. Parker, *The Making of French Absolutism* (New York: St. Martin's Press, 1983), pp. 146–148.
11. Collins, *The State in Early Modern France,* pp. 65–78.
12. See W. Beik, *Absolutism and Society in Seventeenth-Century France: State Power and Provincial Aristocracy in Languedoc* (Cambridge: Cambridge University Press, 1985), pp. 279–302.
13. S. de Gramont, ed., *The Age of Magnificence: Memoirs of the Court of Louis XIV by the Duc de Saint Simon* (New York: Capricorn Books, 1964), pp. 141–145.
14. Quoted in J. Wolf, *Louis XIV* (New York: W. W. Norton, 1968), p. 146.
15. Quoted in A. Trout, *Jean-Baptiste Colbert* (Boston: Twayne, 1978), p. 128.
16. Quoted in Wolf, *Louis XIV,* p. 394.
17. Ibid.
18. See W. C. Scoville, *The Persecution of the Huguenots and French Economic Development: 1680–1720* (Berkeley and Los Angeles: University of California Press, 1960).
19. F. Bluche, *Louis XIV,* trans. M. Greengrass (Oxford: Basil Blackwell, 1990), p. 607.
20. Ibid., p. 458.
21. Quoted in ibid., p. 519.
22. W. F. Church, *Louis XIV in Historical Thought: From Voltaire to the Annales School* (New York: W. W. Norton, 1976), p. 92.
23. Quoted in Gramont, *The Age of Magnificence,* p. 183.
24. J. H. Elliott, *Imperial Spain, 1469–1716* (New York: Mentor Books, 1963), pp. 306–308.
25. B. Bennassar, *The Spanish Character: Attitudes and Mentalities from the Sixteenth to the Nineteenth Century,* trans. B. Keen (Berkeley and Los Angeles: University of California Press, 1979), p. 125.
26. For a revisionist interpretation, see J. Wormald, "James VI and I: Two Kings or One?" *History* 62 (June 1983): 187–209.
27. C. Stephenson and G. F. Marcham, *Sources of English Constitutional History* (New York: Harper & Row, 1937), p. 601.
28. Quoted in D. Maland, *Europe in the Seventeenth Century* (New York: Macmillan, 1967), pp. 198–199.
29. S. Schama, *The Embarrassment of Riches: An Interpretation of Dutch Culture in the Golden Age* (New York: Alfred A. Knopf, 1987), pp. 165–170; quotation is on p. 167.
30. C. J. Friedrich and C. Blitzer, *The Age of Power* (Ithaca, N.Y.: Cornell University Press, 1957), p. 112.

Suggested Reading

Students who wish to explore the problems presented in this chapter in greater depth will easily find a rich and exciting literature. The following surveys all provide good background material: H. Kamen, *The Iron Century: Social Change in Europe, 1550–1660* (1971); G. Parker, *Europe in Crisis, 1598–1618* (1980), a sound introduction to the social, economic, and religious tensions of the period; and R. S. Dunn, *The Age of Religious Wars, 1559–1715* (1979), which examines the period from the perspective of the confessional strife between Protestants and Catholics but contains material on absolutism and constitutionalism.

For the period of Louis XIII, Richelieu, and the Fronde, see L. Moote, *Louis XIII: The Just* (1989), an important biography; J. Bergin, *Richelieu: Power and the Pursuit of Wealth* (1989), a detailed study of how Richelieu used his various offices to acquire great wealth for himself and his family; and O. Ranum, *The Fronde* (1994), probably the best work in English on the Fronde. Two important studies of French local administration are J. B. Collins, *Classes, Estates, and Order in Early Modern Brittany* (1994), and R. Schneider, *Public Life in Toulouse, 1463–1789* (1989). Those with facility in French might tackle P. Goubert, *Mazarin* (1991), for his administration. K. Norberg, *Rich and Poor in Grenoble, 1600–1815* (1985), provides an interesting case study of the wretched conditions of the poor, while W. Beik, *Urban Protest in Seventeenth-Century France* (1997), explores the cultural significance of the widespread incidence of urban violence.

The very important work of P. K. Monod, *The Power of Kings: Monarchy and Religion in Europe, 1589–1715* (1999), provides a broad comparative study of the changes in monarchical authority and power and of the shift from medieval ideas of sacred kingship to "modern" ideas of the rational state.

Louis XIV and his age have predictably attracted the attention of many scholars. Bluche, although hagiographical, is an almost definitive study, and Wolf remains valuable; both are cited in the Notes. The excellent work of P. Burke, *The Fabrication of Louis XIV* (1992), explores the images or representations of the king in stone, bronze, paint, plays, operas, and rituals. For the court of Louis XIV, see also K. A. Hoffmann, *Society of Pleasures: Interdisciplinary Readings in Pleasure and Power During the Reign of Louis XIV* (1997), a sophisticated study of the uses of pleasure as a political tool; R. Chartier, *The Cultural Origins of the French Revolution* (1991); and J. F. Solnon, *La Cour de France* (1987). The advanced student will want to consult the excellent historiographical analysis by Church mentioned in the Notes. Perhaps the best works of the Annales school on the period are P. Goubert, *Louis XIV and Twenty Million Frenchmen* (1972), and his heavily detailed *The Ancien Régime: French Society, 1600–1750,* 2 vols. (1969–1973), which contains invaluable material on the lives and work of ordinary people. For the French economy and financial conditions, see R. Bonney, *The King's Debts: Finance and Politics in France, 1589–1661* (1981), and the works of Trout and Scoville listed in the Notes. Scoville's book is a significant contribution to revisionist history. For Louis XIV's foreign policy and wars, see P. Sonnino, *Louis XIV and the Origins of the Dutch Wars* (1988), and H. Kamen, *The War of Succession in Spain, 1700–1715* (1969). R. Hatton, *Europe in the Age of Louis XIV* (1979), is a well-illustrated survey of many aspects of seventeenth-century European culture. O. Ranum, *Paris in the Age of Absolutism* (1968), describes the geographical, political, economic, and architectural significance of the cultural capital of Europe, whereas V. L. Tapie, *The Age of Grandeur: Baroque Art and Architecture* (1960), emphasizes the relationship between art and politics and has excellent illustrations.

For Spain and Portugal, in addition to the works in the Notes, see H. Kamen, *Spain in the Later Seventeenth Century, 1665–1700* (1980); M. Defourneaux, *Daily Life in Spain in the Golden Age* (1976), highly useful for an understanding of ordinary people and of Spanish society; and C. R. Phillips, *Ciudad Real, 1500–1750: Growth, Crisis, and Readjustment in the Spanish Economy* (1979), a significant case study. A. Pagden, *Spanish Imperialism and the Political Imagination* (1990), explores Spanish ideas of empire, primarily in Italy and the Americas, and shows that the failure to revise ideas to meet changing circumstances led to the empire's decline.

The following works offer solid material on English political and social issues of the seventeenth century: J. P. Kenyon, *Stuart England* (1978), and K. Wrightson, *English Society, 1580–1680* (1982). Perhaps the most comprehensive treatments of Parliament are C. Russell, *Crisis of Parliaments, 1509–1660* (1971), and *Parliaments and English Politics, 1621–1629* (1979). On the background of the English civil war, L. Stone, *The Crisis of the Aristocracy* (1965) and *The Causes of the English Revolution* (1972), are standard works; both B. Manning, *The English People and the English Revolution* (1976), and D. Underdown, *Revel, Riot, and Rebellion* (1985), discuss the extent of popular involvement; Underdown's is the more sophisticated treatment. For English intellectual currents, see J. O. Appleby, *Economic Thought and Ideology in Seventeenth-Century England* (1978), and C. Hill, *Intellectual Origins of the English Revolution* (1966). M. J. Braddick, *The Nerves of State: Taxation and the Financing of the English State, 1558–1714* (1996), surveys the evolution of parliamentary taxation as the means of financing state expenses, especially military ones. S. Porter, ed., *London and the Civil War* (1996), treats the city's choice of allegiance and contribution to the war effort.

C. Durston and J. Eales, eds., *The Culture of English Puritanism, 1560–1700* (1996), provides a revisionist definition of the term *Puritan* and explores topics such as Sabbatarianism and iconoclasm. For the several shades of Protestant sentiment in the early seventeenth century, see P. Collinson, *The Religion of Protestants* (1982). C. M. Hibbard, *Charles I and the Popish Plot* (1983), is an important reference work for several religious issues.

For women, see R. Thompson, *Women in Stuart England and America* (1974), and A. Fraser, *The Weaker Vessel* (1985). For Cromwell and the Interregnum, see C. Firth, *Oliver Cromwell and the Rule of the Puritans in England* (1956); C. Hill, *God's Englishman* (1972); and A. Fraser, *Cromwell, the Lord Protector* (1973).

For the Restoration and the Glorious Revolution, see R. Hutton, *Charles II: King of England, Scotland and Ireland* (1989), and A. Fraser, *Royal Charles: Charles II and the Restoration* (1979), two highly readable biographies; R. Ollard, *The Image of the King: Charles I and Charles II* (1980), which examines the nature of monarchy; J. Miller, *James II: A Study in Kingship* (1977); J. Childs, *The Army, James II, and the Glorious Revolution* (1980); J. R. Jones, *The Revolution of 1688 in England* (1972); and L. G. Schwoerer, *The Declaration of Rights, 1689* (1981), a fine assessment of that fundamental document. For the continuation of an older system during the rise of the Whigs and Tories, see B. Hill, *The Early Parties and Politics in Britain, 1688–1832* (1996).

On Holland, the starting point for serious study is Schama, mentioned in the Notes, a brilliant and beautifully illustrated achievement. J. L. Price, *Culture and Society in the Dutch Republic During the Seventeenth Century* (1974), is a sound scholarly work. R. Boxer, *The Dutch Seaborne Empire* (1980), and the appropriate chapters of the Maland work cited in the Notes are useful for Dutch overseas expansion and the reasons for Dutch prosperity. The following works focus on the economic and cultural life of the leading Dutch city: V. Barbour, *Capitalism in Amsterdam in the Seventeenth Century* (1950), and D. Regin, *Traders, Artists, Burghers: A Cultural History of Amsterdam in the Seventeenth Century* (1977). J. M. Montias, *Artists and Artisans in Delft: A Socio-economic Study of the Seventeenth Century* (1982), examines another major city. The leading statesmen of the period may be studied in these biographies: H. H. Rowen, *John de Witt, Grand Pensionary of Holland, 1625–1672* (1978); S. B. Baxter, *William the III and the Defense of European Liberty, 1650–1702* (1966); and J. den Tex, *Oldenbarnevelt,* 2 vols. (1973).

Many facets of the lives of ordinary French, Spanish, English, and Dutch people are discussed in P. Burke, *Popular Culture in Early Modern Europe* (1978), a provocative study.

Listening to the Past

The Court at Versailles

Although the Duc de Saint-Simon (1675–1755) was a soldier, courtier, and diplomat, his enduring reputation rests on his Memoirs *(1788), an eyewitness account of the personality and court of Louis XIV. A nobleman of ancient lineage, Saint-Simon resented Louis's "domestication" of the nobility and his promotion of the bourgeoisie.* The Memoirs, *excerpted here, remains a monument of French literature and an indispensable historical source, partly for its portrait of the court at Versailles.*

Very early in the reign of Louis XIV the Court was removed from Paris, never to return. The troubles of the minority had given him a dislike to that city; his enforced and surreptitious flight from it still rankled in his memory; he did not consider himself safe there, and thought cabals would be more easily detected if the Court was in the country, where the movements and temporary absences of any of its members would be more easily noticed. . . . No doubt that he was also influenced by the feeling that he would be regarded with greater awe and veneration when no longer exposed every day to the gaze of the multitude.

His love-affair with Mademoiselle de la Vallière, which at first was covered as far as possible with a veil of mystery, was the cause of frequent excursions to Versailles. . . . The visits of Louis XIV becoming more frequent, he enlarged the *château* by degrees till its immense buildings afforded better accommodation for the Court than was to be found at St. Germain, where most of the courtiers had to put up with uncomfortable lodgings in the town. The Court was therefore removed to Versailles in 1682, not long before the Queen's death. The new building contained an infinite number of rooms for courtiers, and the King liked the grant of these rooms to be regarded as a coveted privilege.

He availed himself of the frequent festivities at Versailles, and his excursions to other places, as a means of making the courtiers assiduous in their attendance and anxious to please him; for he nominated beforehand those who were to take part in them, and could thus gratify some and inflict a snub on others. He was conscious that the substantial favours he had to bestow were not nearly sufficient to produce a continual effect; he had therefore to invent imaginary ones, and no one was so clever in devising petty distinctions and preferences which aroused jealousy and emulation. The visits to Marly later on were very useful to him in this way; also those to Trianon [Marly and Trianon were small country houses], where certain ladies, chosen beforehand, were admitted to his table. It was another distinction to hold his candlestick at his *coucher;* as soon as he had finished his prayers he used to name the courtier to whom it was to be handed, always choosing one of the highest rank among those present. . . .

Not only did he expect all persons of distinction to be in continual attendance at Court, but he was quick to notice the absence of those of inferior degree; at his *lever* [formal rising from bed in the morning], his *coucher* [preparations for going to bed], his meals, in the gardens of Versailles (the only place where the courtiers in general were allowed to follow him), he used to cast his eyes to right and left; nothing escaped him, he saw everybody. If any one habitually living at Court absented himself he insisted on knowing the reason; those who came there only for flying visits had also to give a satisfactory explanation; any one who seldom or never appeared there was certain to incur his displeasure. If asked to bestow a favour on such persons he would reply haughtily: "I do not know him"; of such as rarely presented themselves he would say, "He is a man I never see"; and from these judgements there was no appeal.

He always took great pains to find out what was going on in public places, in society, in private

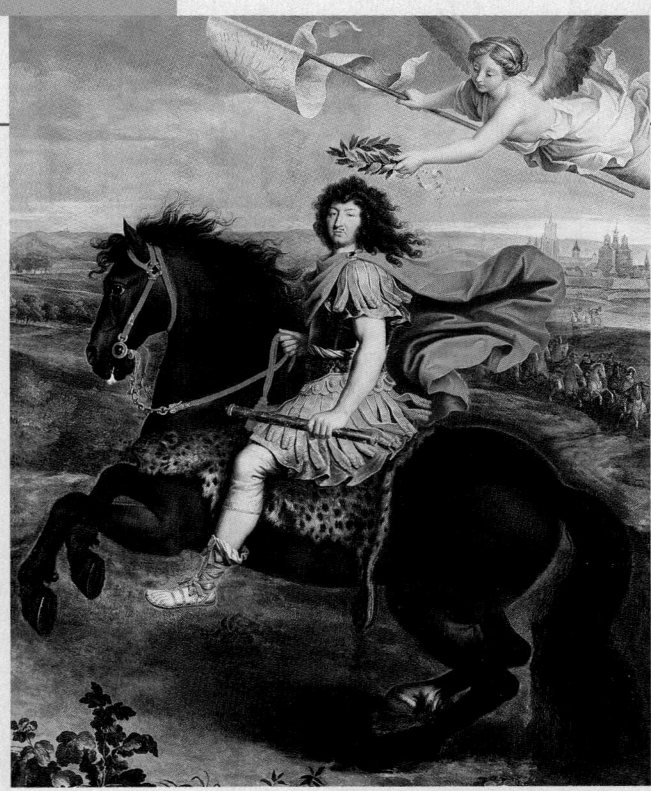

Painting of Louis XIV by Mignard Pierre (1612–1695). *(Galleria Sabauda, Turin/ Scala/Art Resource, NY)*

houses, even family secrets, and maintained an immense number of spies and tale-bearers. These were of all sorts; some did not know that their reports were carried to him; others did know it; there were others, again, who used to write to him directly, through channels which he prescribed; others who were admitted by the backstairs and saw him in his private room. Many a man in all ranks of life was ruined by these methods, often very unjustly, without ever being able to discover the reason; and when the King had once taken a prejudice against a man, he hardly ever got over it. . . .

No one understood better than Louis XIV the art of enhancing the value of a favour by his manner of bestowing it; he knew how to make the most of a word, a smile, even of a glance. If he addressed any one, were it but to ask a trifling question or make some commonplace remark, all eyes were turned on the person so honored; it was a mark of favour which always gave rise to comment. . . .

He loved splendour, magnificence, and profusion in all things, and encouraged similar tastes in his Court; to spend money freely on equipages [the king's horse carriages] and buildings, on feasting and at cards, was a sure way to gain his favour, perhaps to obtain the honour of a word from him. Motives of policy had something to do with this; by making expensive habits the fashion, and, for people in a certain position, a necessity, he compelled his courtiers to live beyond their income, and gradually reduced them to depend on his bounty for the means of subsistence. This was a plague which, once introduced, became a scourge to the whole country, for it did not take long to spread to Paris, and thence to the armies and the provinces; so that a man of any position is now estimated entirely according to his expenditure on his table and other luxuries. This folly, sustained by pride and ostentation, has already produced widespread confusion; it threatens to end in nothing short of ruin and a general overthrow.

Questions for Analysis

1. How would you define the French court? Why did Louis XIV move it to Versailles?
2. By what means did Louis control the nobility at Versailles? Why did he use those particular means?
3. Consider the role of ritual and ceremony in some modern governments, such as the U.S. government. How does it compare to Louis XIV's use of ceremony, as portrayed by Saint-Simon?
4. Saint-Simon faulted Louis for encouraging the nobles' extravagance. Is that a justifiable criticism?

Source: F. Arkwright, ed., *The Memoirs of the Duke de Saint-Simon,* vol. 5 (New York: Brentano's, n.d.), pp. 271–274, 276–278.

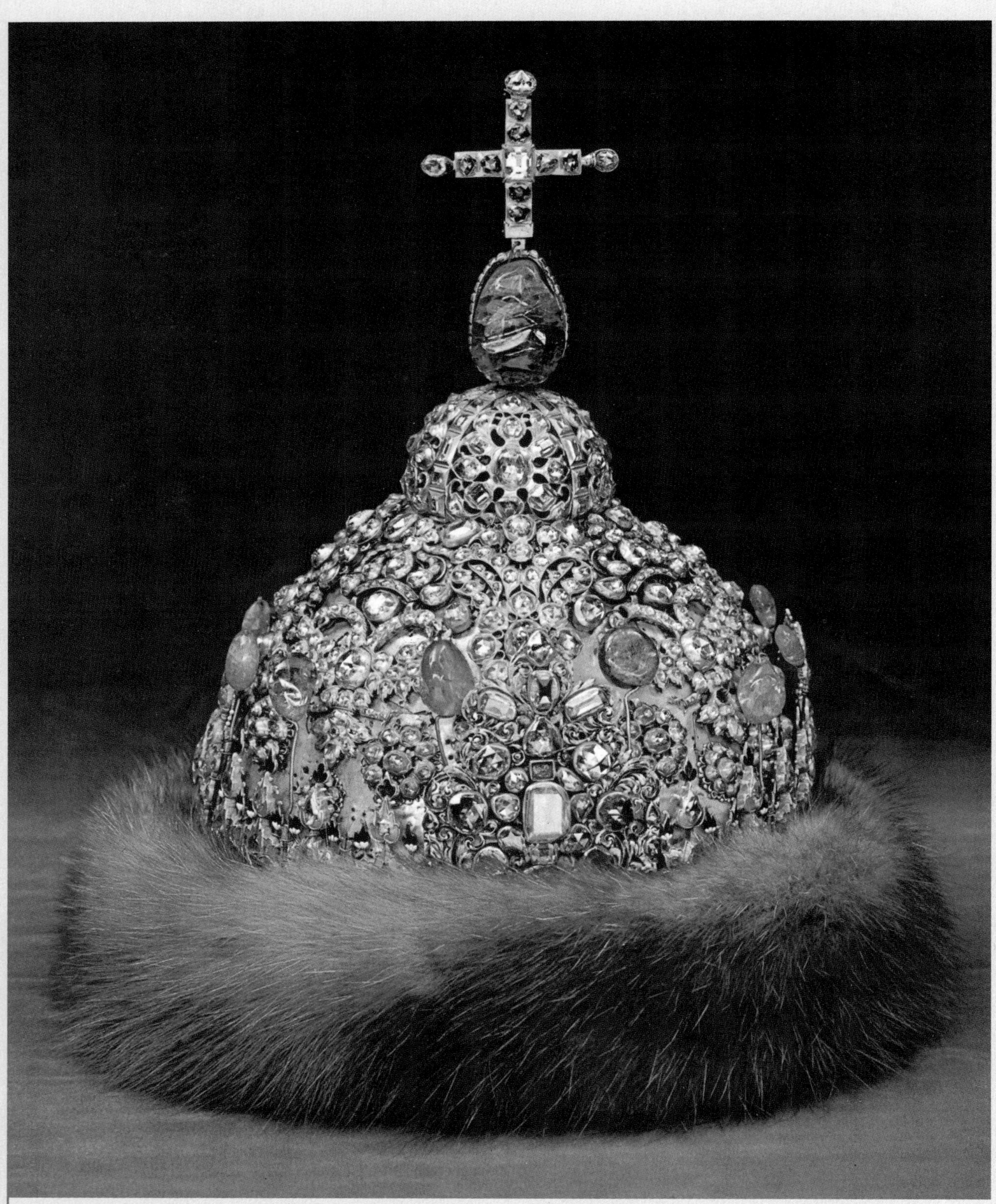

Peter the Great's magnificent new crown, created for his coronation in 1682 with his half-brother Ivan. *(State Museum of the Kremlin, Moscow/Sovfoto)*

chapter

17 Absolutism in Eastern Europe to 1740

chapter outline

- Lords and Peasants in Eastern Europe
- The Rise of Austria and Prussia
- The Development of Russia
- Absolutism and Baroque Architecture

The seventeenth century witnessed a struggle between constitutionalism and absolutism in eastern Europe, as it did in western Europe (see Chapter 16). But with the notable exception of the kingdom of Poland, monarchical absolutism was triumphant in eastern Europe; constitutionalism was decisively defeated. Absolute monarchies emerged in Austria, Prussia, and Russia. This development had significance for at least two reasons. First, these three monarchies exercised enormous influence until 1918, and they created an authoritarian tradition that lasted into the late twentieth century in eastern Europe. Second, the absolute monarchs of eastern Europe had a powerful impact on culture, encouraging a flowering of the baroque style in architecture and the arts.

Although the monarchs of eastern Europe were greatly impressed by Louis XIV and his model of royal absolutism, their states differed in several important ways from that of their French counterpart. Louis XIV built French absolutism on the foundation of a well-developed medieval monarchy and a strong royal bureaucracy. And when Louis XIV came to the throne, the powers of the nobility were already somewhat limited, the French middle class was relatively strong, and the peasants were generally free from serfdom. Eastern absolutism rested on a very different social reality: a powerful nobility, a weak middle class, and an oppressed peasantry composed of serfs.

These different conditions raise three questions:

- Why did the basic structure of society in eastern Europe move away from that of western Europe in the early modern period?
- How and why did the rulers of Austria, Prussia, and Russia, each in a different social environment, manage to build powerful absolute monarchies that proved more durable than that of Louis XIV?
- How did the absolute monarchs' interaction with artists and architects contribute to the splendid achievements of baroque culture?

These are the questions that this chapter will explore.

Lords and Peasants in Eastern Europe

When absolute monarchy took shape in eastern Europe in the seventeenth century, it built on social and economic foundations laid between roughly 1400 and 1650. In those years, the princes and the landed nobility of eastern Europe—with the major exception of the Ottoman rulers in the Balkans—rolled back the gains made by the peasantry during the High Middle Ages and reimposed a harsh serfdom on the rural masses. The nobility also reduced the importance of the towns and the middle classes. This process differed profoundly from developments in western Europe, where peasants won greater freedom and the urban capitalistic middle class continued its rise.

The Medieval Background

Between roughly 1400 and 1650, nobles and rulers re-established **serfdom** in the eastern lands of Bohemia, Silesia, Hungary, eastern Germany, Poland, Lithuania, and Russia. The east—the land east of the Elbe River in Germany, which historians often call "East Elbia"—gained a certain social and economic unity in the process. But eastern peasants lost their rights and freedoms. They became bound first to the land they worked and then, by degrading obligations, to the lords they served.

This development was a tragic reversal of trends in the High Middle Ages. The period from roughly 1050 to 1300 had been a time of general economic expansion characterized by the growth of trade, towns, and population. Expansion also meant clearing the forests and colonizing the frontier beyond the Elbe River. Anxious to attract German settlers to sparsely populated lands, the rulers and nobles of eastern Europe had offered potential newcomers economic and legal incentives. Large numbers of incoming settlers obtained land on excellent terms and gained much greater personal freedom. These benefits were also gradually extended to the local Slavic populations, even those of central Russia. Thus by 1300 a very general improvement in peasant conditions had occurred in eastern Europe; serfdom had all but disappeared. Peasants bargained freely with their landlords and moved about as they pleased. Opportunities and improvements east of the Elbe had a positive impact on western Europe, where the weight of serfdom was also reduced between 1100 and 1300. Thus fundamental social and economic developments moved in the same direction throughout Europe in the High Middle Ages, reinforcing a cultural and religious unity stretching all across Europe.

After about 1300, however, as Europe's population and economy both declined grievously, mainly because of the Black Death, the east and the west went in different directions. In both east and west, a many-sided landlord reaction occurred as lords sought to solve their tough economic problems by more heavily exploiting the peasantry. Yet this reaction generally failed in the west. In many western areas by 1500, almost all of the peasants were free, and in the rest of western Europe serf obligations had declined greatly. East of the Elbe, however, the landlords won. By 1500 eastern peasants were well on their way to becoming serfs again.

Throughout eastern Europe, as in western Europe, the drop in population and prices in the fourteenth and fifteenth centuries caused severe labor shortages and hard times for the nobles. Yet rather than offer better economic and legal terms to keep old peasants and attract new ones, eastern landlords used political and police power to turn the tables on peasants. They did this in two ways.

First, the lords made their kings and princes issue laws that restricted or eliminated the peasants' precious, time-honored right of free movement. Thus a peasant could no longer leave to take advantage of better opportunities elsewhere without the lord's permission, and the lord had no reason to make such concessions. In Prussian territories by 1500, the law required that runaway peasants be hunted down and returned to their lords; a runaway servant was to be nailed to a post by one ear and given a knife to cut himself loose. Until the middle of the fifteenth century, medieval Russian peasants had been free to move wherever they wished and seek the best landlord. Thereafter this freedom was gradually curtailed, so that by 1497 a Russian peasant had the right to move only during a two-week period after the fall harvest. Eastern peasants were losing their status as free and independent men and women.

Second, lords steadily took more and more of their peasants' land and imposed heavier and heavier labor obligations. Instead of being independent farmers paying reasonable, freely negotiated rents, peasants tended to become forced laborers on the lords' estates. By the early 1500s, lords in many territories could command their peasants to work for them without pay as many as six days a week.

The gradual erosion of the peasantry's economic position was bound up with manipulation of the legal system. The local lord was also the local prosecutor, judge, and jailer. As a matter of course, he ruled in his own favor in disputes with his peasants. There were no independent royal officials to provide justice or uphold the common law.

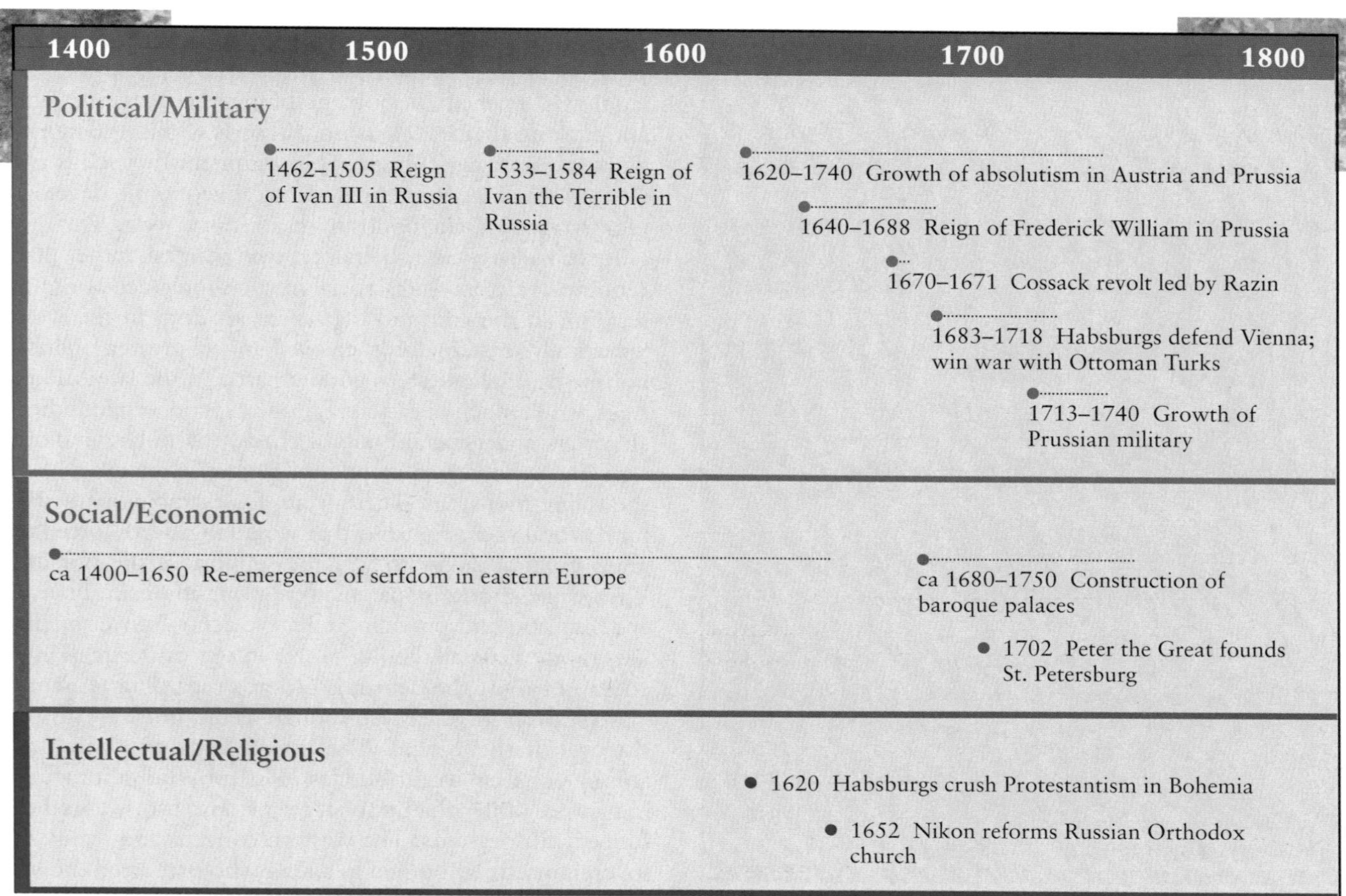

The Consolidation of Serfdom

Between 1500 and 1650, the social, legal, and economic conditions of peasants in eastern Europe continued to decline. Free peasants lost their freedom and became serfs. In Poland, for example, nobles gained complete control over their peasants in 1574, after which they could legally inflict the death penalty on their serfs whenever they wished. In Prussia in 1653, peasants were assumed to be tied to their lords in **hereditary subjugation**—bound to their lords from one generation to the next as well as to the land.

In Russia the right of peasants to move from a given estate was "temporarily" suspended in the 1590s and permanently abolished in 1603. In 1649 a new law code completed the process. The Russian tsar lifted the nine-year time limit on the recovery of runaways, who were to be returned to their lords whenever they were caught. Moreover, the new law code set no limits on the lords' authority over their peasants. Although the political development of the various eastern states differed, the legal re-establishment of permanent hereditary serfdom had become the common fate of peasants in the east by the middle of the seventeenth century.

This consolidation of serfdom was accompanied by the growth of estate agriculture, particularly in Poland and eastern Germany. In the sixteenth century, European economic expansion and population growth resumed after the great declines of the late Middle Ages. Prices for agricultural commodities also rose sharply as gold and silver flowed in from the New World. Thus Polish and German lords had powerful economic incentives to increase the production of their estates. And they did.

Lords seized more and more peasant land for their own estates and then demanded and received ever more unpaid serf labor on those enlarged estates. Even when the estates were inefficient and technically backward, as they generally were, the great Polish nobles and middle-

Estonia in the 1660s The Estonians were conquered by German military nobility in the Middle Ages and reduced to serfdom. The German-speaking nobles ruled the Estonian peasants with an iron hand, and Peter the Great reaffirmed their domination when Russia annexed Estonia (see Map 17.3 on page 578). *(Mansell Collection/TimePix)*

rank German lords squeezed sizable, cheap, and thus very profitable surpluses out of their impoverished peasants. Surpluses in wheat and timber were easily sold to big foreign merchants, who exported them to the growing cities of the west. Thus the poor east helped feed the wealthier west.

The re-emergence of serfdom in eastern Europe in the early modern period was clearly a momentous human development, and historians have advanced a variety of explanations for it. Some scholars have stressed the economic interpretation. Agricultural depression and population decline in the fourteenth and fifteenth centuries led to a severe labor shortage, they have argued, and thus eastern landlords naturally tied their precious peasants to the land. With the return of prosperity and the development of export markets in the sixteenth century, the landlords finished the job, grabbing the peasants' land and making them work as unpaid serfs within the framework of estate agriculture. This argument by itself is not very convincing, for almost identical economic developments "caused" the opposite result in the west.

It seems fairly clear, therefore, that political, rather than economic, factors were crucial in the simultaneous rise of serfdom in the east and decline of serfdom in the west. Specifically, eastern lords enjoyed much greater political power than their western counterparts. In the late Middle Ages, when much of eastern Europe experienced innumerable wars and general political chaos, the noble landlord class greatly increased its political power at the expense of the ruling monarchs. There were, for example, many disputed royal successions, so that weak kings were forced to grant political favors to win the support of the nobility. Thus while strong monarchs were rising in Spain, France, and England and providing effective central government, kings were generally losing power in the east. Such kings could not resist the demands of lords regarding peasants.

Moreover, most eastern monarchs did not want to resist even if they could. The typical king was only first among equals in the noble class. He, too, thought mainly in private, rather than public, terms. He, too, wanted to squeeze his peasants. The western concept and reality of sovereignty, as embodied in a king who protected the interests of all his people, was not well developed in eastern Europe before 1650.

The political power of the peasants was also weaker in eastern Europe and declined steadily after about 1400. Although there were occasional bloody peasant uprisings against the oppression of the landlords, they never succeeded. Nor did eastern peasants effectively resist day-by-day infringements on their liberties by their landlords. Part of the reason was that the lords, rather than the kings, ran the courts—one of the important concessions nobles extorted from weak monarchs.

Similarly, with the approval of weak kings, the landlords systematically undermined the medieval privileges of the towns and the power of the urban classes. Instead of selling products to local merchants in the towns, as required in the Middle Ages, the landlords sold directly to big foreign capitalists. For example, Dutch ships sailed up the rivers of Poland and eastern Germany to the loading docks of the great estates, completely short-circuiting the local towns. Moreover, "town air" no longer "made people free," for the eastern towns had lost their medieval right of refuge and were now compelled to return runaways to their lords. The population of the towns and the importance of the urban middle classes declined greatly. These developments both reflected and promoted the supremacy of noble landlords in most of eastern Europe in the sixteenth century.

Subsequently, in the eighteenth century, travelers and writers from western Europe became increasingly aware of real and even imagined differences that they observed in eastern Europe. Developing their ideas of refined society and gradual progress (see Chapter 18), westerners portrayed eastern Europe as being more "barbaric" and less "civilized" than their homelands.[1] Thus they expanded eastern Europe's undeniably harsher social and economic conditions to encompass a very debatable cultural and moral inferiority.

The Rise of Austria and Prussia

Despite the strength of the nobility and the weakness of many monarchs before 1600, strong kings did begin to emerge in many lands in the course of the seventeenth century. War and the threat of war aided rulers greatly in their attempts to build absolute monarchies. There was also an endless struggle for power, as eastern rulers not only fought one another but also battled with armies of invaders from Asia. In this atmosphere of continual wartime emergency, monarchs reduced the political power of the landlord nobility. Cautiously leaving the nobles the unchallenged masters of their peasants, the would-be absolutist monarchs of eastern Europe gradually gained and monopolized political power in three key areas. First, they imposed and collected permanent taxes without consent. Second, they maintained permanent standing armies, which policed the country in addition to fighting abroad. Third, they conducted relations with other states as they pleased.

As with all general historical developments, there were important variations on the absolutist theme in eastern Europe. The royal **absolutism** created in Prussia was stronger and more effective than that established in Austria. This advantage gave Prussia a thin edge over Austria in the struggle for power in east-central Europe in the eighteenth century. That edge had great long-term political significance, for it was a rising Prussia that unified the German people in the nineteenth century and imposed on them a militaristic Prussian stamp.

Austria and the Ottoman Turks

Like all the other peoples and rulers of central Europe, the Habsburgs of Austria emerged from the brutal Thirty Years' War, which lasted from 1618 to 1648, impoverished and exhausted. Their efforts to root out Protestantism in the German lands and to turn the weak Holy Roman Empire into a real state had failed utterly. The Habsburgs did remain the hereditary emperors of the ancient Holy Roman Empire, which was inhabited mainly by German-speakers and was more accurately called the German Empire. Real power in the German Empire lay in the hands of a bewildering variety of three hundred separate political jurisdictions, which included independent cities, small principalities, medium-size states such as Bavaria and Saxony, and some (but not all) of the territories of Prussia and the Habsburgs.

Defeat in central Europe opened new vistas for the Habsburgs. They were forced to turn inward and eastward in an attempt to fuse their diverse holdings into a strong unified state. An important step in this direction had actually been taken in Bohemia during the Thirty Years' War. Protestantism had been strong among the Czechs, a Slavic people concentrated in Bohemia. Indeed, the lesser Czech nobility was largely Protestant in 1600 and had considerable political power because it dominated the **Bohemian Estates**—the representative body of the different estates, or legal orders, in Bohemia. In 1618 the Bohemian Estates had risen up in defense of Protestant rights. This revolt was crushed in 1620 at the Battle of the White Mountain, a momentous turning point in Czech history. The victorious Habsburg king, Ferdinand II (r. 1619–1637), drastically reduced the power of the Bohemian Estates. Ferdinand also confiscated the landholdings of many Protestant nobles and gave them to a few great Catholic nobles who had remained loyal and to a motley band of aristocratic soldiers of fortune who had nothing in common with the Czech-speaking peasants. After 1650 a large portion of the Bohemian nobility was of recent foreign origin and owed everything to the Habsburgs.

With the help of this new nobility, the Habsburgs established strong direct rule over reconquered Bohemia. The condition of the enserfed peasantry worsened substantially: three days per week of unpaid labor—the *robot*—became the norm, and a quarter of the serfs worked for their lords every day but Sundays and religious holidays. Protestantism was also stamped out, in the course of which a growing unity of religion was brought about. The reorganization of Bohemia was a giant step toward absolutism.

After the Thirty Years' War, Ferdinand III (r. 1637–1657) centralized the government in the hereditary German-speaking provinces, most notably Austria, Styria, and the Tyrol, which formed the core area of the Habsburg holdings. For the first time, Ferdinand III's reign saw the creation of a permanent standing army ready to

The Battle of Mohács, 1526 The *Süleymanname* (Book of Suleiman), a biography, contains these fascinating illustrations of the great Ottoman victory at Mohács, which enabled the Turks to add Hungary to their expanding empire. In the right panel, Suleiman in a white turban sits on a black horse surrounded by his personal guard, while his janissary soldiers fire their muskets and cannon at the enemy. In the left panel, the Europeans are in disarray, in contrast to the Turks' discipline and order. *(Topkapi Saray Museum)*

put down any internal opposition. The Habsburg monarchy was then ready to turn toward the plains of Hungary, which had long been divided and fought over by the Habsburgs and the Ottoman Turks.

The Ottomans had come out of Central Asia as conquering warriors, settled in Anatolia, in present-day Turkey, and created one of history's greatest military empires. At their peak in the middle of the sixteenth century under Sultan Suleiman the Magnificent (r. 1520–1566), they ruled the most powerful empire in the world. Their possessions stretched from western Persia across North Africa and up into the heart of central Europe (see Map 17.1). Followers of Islam, the Ottoman Turks were old and determined foes of the Catholic Habsburgs. Their armies had almost captured Vienna in 1529, and for more than 150 years thereafter the Ottomans ruled the many different ethnic groups living in the Balkans, almost all of Hungary, and part of southern Russia.

The Ottoman Empire was originally built on a fascinating and very non-European conception of state and society. There was an almost complete absence of private landed property. All the agricultural land of the empire was the personal hereditary property of the **sultan,** who exploited the land as he saw fit according to Ottoman political theory. There was therefore no security of landholding and no hereditary nobility. The sultan also

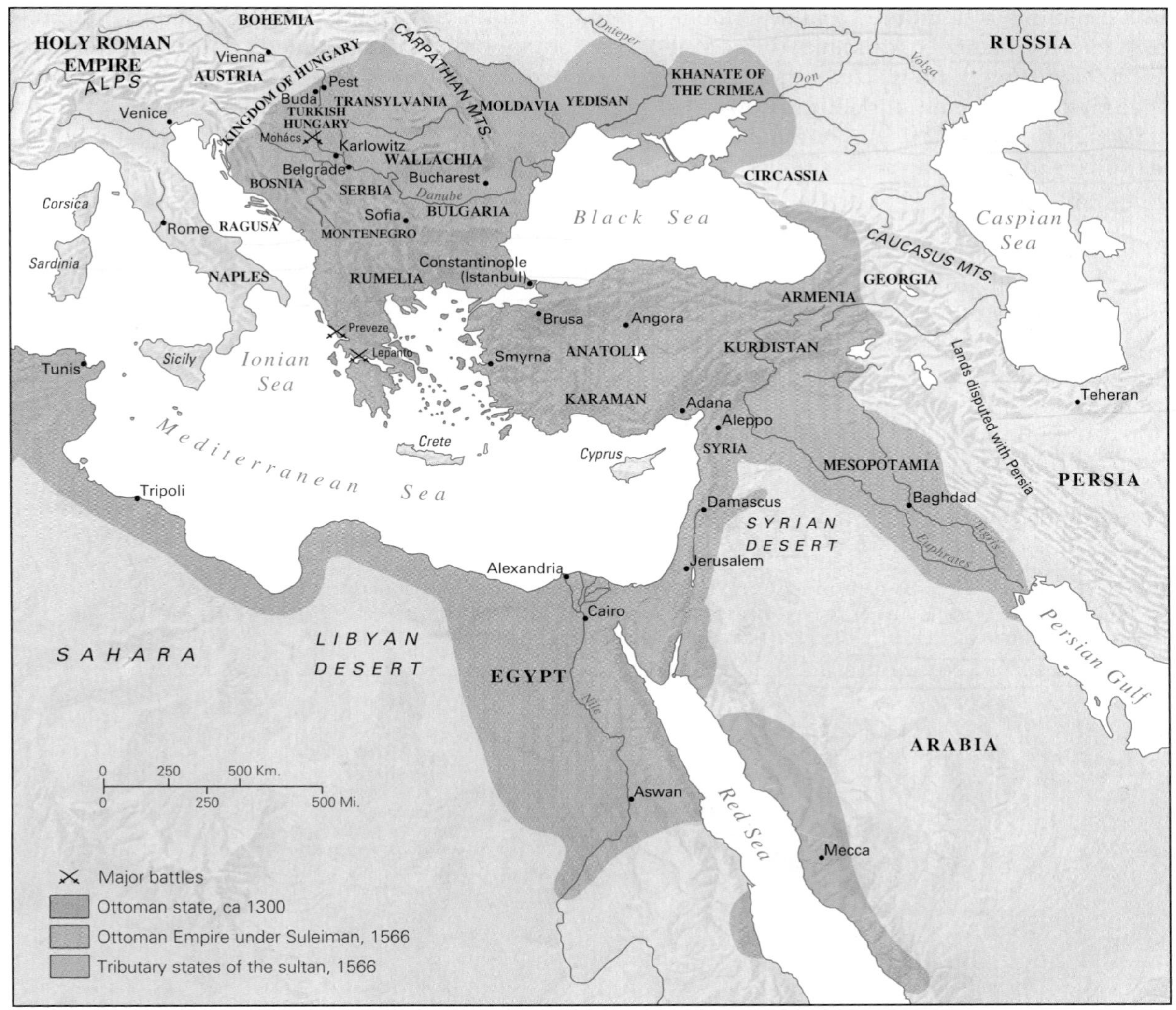

MAP 17.1 The Ottoman Empire at Its Height, 1566 The Ottomans, like their great rivals the Habsburgs, rose to rule a vast dynastic empire encompassing many different peoples and ethnic groups. The army and the bureaucracy served to unite the disparate territories into a single state under an absolutist ruler.

defended peasant communities from greedy officials, so that peasants could afford to pay their taxes and support the state.

The top ranks of the bureaucracy were staffed by the sultan's slave corps. Every year the sultan levied a "tax" of one to three thousand male children on the conquered Christian populations in the Balkans. These and other slaves were raised in Turkey as Muslims and trained to fight and to administer. The most talented slaves rose to the top of the bureaucracy; the less fortunate formed the brave and skillful core of the sultan's army, the so-called janissary corps.

As long as the Ottoman Empire expanded, the system worked well. As the sultan won more territory, he could impose his slave tax on larger populations. Moreover, he could amply reward loyal and effective servants by letting them draw a carefully defined income from conquered Christian peasants on a strictly temporary basis. For a long time, Christian peasants in eastern Europe were economically exploited less by the Muslim Turks than by

Christian nobles, and they were not reduced to serfdom. Nor were they forced to convert to Islam. After about 1570, however, the powerful, centralized Ottoman system slowly began to disintegrate as the Turks' western advance was stopped. Temporary Muslim landholders became hard-to-control permanent oppressors. Weak sultans left the glory of the battlefield for the delights of the harem, and the army lost its dedication and failed to keep up with European military advances.

Yet in the late seventeenth century, under vigorous reforming leadership, the Ottoman Empire succeeded in marshaling its forces for one last mighty attack on the Habsburgs. A huge Turkish army surrounded Vienna and laid siege to it in 1683. After holding out against great odds for two months, the city was relieved at the last minute by a mixed force of Habsburg, Saxon, Bavarian, and Polish troops, and the Ottomans were forced to retreat. Soon the retreat became a rout. As Russian and Venetian allies attacked on other fronts, the Habsburgs conquered almost all of Hungary and Transylvania (part of present-day Romania) by 1699 (see Map 17.2).

The Turkish wars and this great expansion strengthened the Habsburg army and promoted some sense of unity in the Habsburg lands. But Habsburg efforts to create a fully developed, highly centralized, absolutist state were only partly successful.

The Habsburg state was composed of three separate and distinct territories—the old "hereditary provinces" of Austria, the kingdom of Bohemia, and the kingdom of Hungary. These three parts were tied together primarily by their common ruler, the Habsburg monarch. Each part had its own laws and political life, for the noble-

MAP 17.2 The Growth of Austria and Brandenburg-Prussia to 1748 Austria expanded to the southwest into Hungary and Transylvania at the expense of the Ottoman Empire. It was unable to hold the rich German province of Silesia, however, which was conquered by Brandenburg-Prussia.

dominated Estates continued to exist in each territory, though with reduced powers. The Habsburgs themselves were well aware of the fragility of the union they had forged. In 1713 Charles VI (r. 1711–1740) proclaimed the so-called **Pragmatic Sanction,** which stated that the Habsburg possessions were never to be divided and were always to be passed intact to a single heir, who might be female since Charles was the last of all Habsburg males. Charles spent much of his reign trying to get this principle accepted by the various branches of the Habsburg family, by the three different Estates of the realm, and by the states of Europe. His fears turned out to be well founded.

The Hungarian nobility, despite its reduced strength, effectively thwarted the full development of Habsburg absolutism. Time and again throughout the seventeenth century, Hungarian nobles—the most numerous in Europe, making up 5 to 7 percent of the Hungarian population—rose in revolt against Vienna's attempts to impose absolute rule. They never triumphed decisively, but neither were they ever crushed, as the Czech nobility had been in 1620.

The Hungarians resisted because many of them remained Protestants, especially in the area long ruled by the more tolerant Turks, and hated the heavy-handed attempts of the conquering Habsburgs to re-Catholicize everyone. Moreover, until 1683 the lords of Hungary had a powerful military ally in Turkey. Finally, the Hungarian nobility, and even part of the Hungarian peasantry, had become attached to a national ideal long before most of the other peoples of eastern Europe did so. Hungarian nobles were determined to maintain as much independence and local control as possible. Thus when the Habsburgs were bogged down in the War of the Spanish Succession (see page 545), the Hungarians rose in one last patriotic rebellion under Prince Francis Rákóczy in 1703. Rákóczy and his forces were eventually defeated, but this time the Habsburgs had to accept a definitive compromise. Charles VI restored many of the traditional privileges of the Hungarian aristocracy in return for Hungarian acceptance of hereditary Habsburg rule. Thus Hungary, unlike Austria or Bohemia, never came close to being fully integrated into a centralized, absolute Habsburg state.

Prussia in the Seventeenth Century

After 1400 the eastern German princes lost political power and influence, while a revitalized landed nobility became the undisputed ruling class. The Hohenzollern family, which ruled through its senior and junior branches as the imperial electors of Brandenburg and the dukes of Prussia, had little real princely power.

Nothing suggested that the Hohenzollern family and its princely territories would ever play an important role in European or even German affairs. The **elector of Brandenburg**'s right to help choose the Holy Roman emperor with six other electors bestowed prestige, but the elector had no military strength whatsoever. Moreover, Brandenburg, the area around Berlin and the elector's power base, was completely cut off from the sea (see Map 17.2). Brandenburg lacked defensible natural frontiers, and the land was poor, a combination of sand and swamp. Contemporaries contemptuously called Brandenburg the "sand-box of the Holy Roman Empire."[2]

Moreover, the territory of the elector's cousin, the duke of Prussia, was totally separated from Brandenburg and was part of Poland. Prussia had originally been conquered in the thirteenth century by the Germanic order of Teutonic Knights as part of a larger struggle between German conquerors and the indigenous Slavic populations. However, by 1600 Prussia's German-speaking peasants had much in common with Polish peasants in other provinces, for both ethnic groups had seen most of their freedoms reduced or revoked by their noble landlords. (Poland's numerous lesser nobility also dominated the Polish state, which was actually a constitutional republic headed by an elected king who had little real power.) In 1618 the junior branch of the Hohenzollern family died out, and Prussia reverted to the elector of Brandenburg.

The elector of Brandenburg was a helpless spectator in the Thirty Years' War, his territories alternately ravaged by Swedish and Habsburg armies. Population fell drastically, and many villages disappeared. Yet the devastation of Brandenburg and Prussia prepared the way for Hohenzollern absolutism because foreign armies dramatically weakened the political power of the Estates—the representative assemblies of the realm. This weakening of the Estates helped the very talented young elector Frederick William (r. 1640–1688), later known as the "Great Elector," to ride roughshod over traditional representative rights and to take a giant step toward royal absolutism. This constitutional struggle, often unjustly neglected by historians, was the most crucial in Prussian history for hundreds of years, until that of the 1860s.

When he came to power in 1640, the twenty-year-old Great Elector was determined to unify his three quite separate provinces and add to them by diplomacy and war. These provinces were Brandenburg itself; Prussia, inherited in 1618; and completely separate, scattered holdings along the Rhine in western Germany, inherited in 1614 (see Map 17.2). Each of the three provinces was

Molding the Prussian Spirit Discipline was strict and punishment brutal in the Prussian army. This scene, from an eighteenth-century book used to teach schoolchildren in Prussia, shows one soldier being flogged while another is being beaten with canes as he walks between rows of troops. The officer on horseback proudly commands. *(University of Illinois Library, Champaign)*

inhabited by Germans, but each had its own Estates, whose power had increased until about 1600 as the power of the rulers declined. Although the Estates had not met regularly during the chaotic Thirty Years' War, they still had the power of the purse in their respective provinces. Taxes could not be levied without their consent. The Estates of Brandenburg and Prussia were dominated by the nobility and the landowning classes, known as the **Junkers.** But this was also the case in most European countries that had representative bodies, including the English Parliament before and after the civil war. Had the Estates successfully resisted the absolutist demands of the Great Elector, they, too, might have evolved toward more broadly based constitutionalism.

The struggle between the Great Elector and the provincial Estates was long, complicated, and intense. After the Thirty Years' War, representatives of the nobility zealously reasserted the right of the Estates to vote taxes, a right the Swedish armies of occupation had simply ignored. Yet first in Brandenburg in 1653 and then in Prussia between 1661 and 1663, the Great Elector eventually had his way.

To pay for the permanent standing army he first established in 1660, Frederick William forced the Estates to accept the introduction of permanent taxation without consent. The power of the Estates declined rapidly thereafter, for the Great Elector had both financial independence and superior force. The state's total revenue tripled during his reign. The size of the army leaped about tenfold. In 1688 a population of one million was supporting a peacetime standing army of thirty thousand.

In accounting for the Great Elector's fateful triumph, two factors appear central. First, as in the formation of every absolutist state, war was a decisive factor. The ongoing struggle between Sweden and Poland for control of the Baltic after 1648 and the wars of Louis XIV in western Europe created an atmosphere of permanent crisis. The wild Tartars of the Crimea in southern Russia swept through Prussia in the winter of 1656 to 1657, killing and carrying off as slaves more than fifty thousand people, according to an old estimate. This invasion softened up the Estates and strengthened the urgency of the Great Elector's demands for more money for more soldiers.

Second, the nobility had long dominated the government through the Estates, but it was unwilling to join the representatives of the towns in a consistent common front and was focused on its own rights and privileges. When, therefore, the Great Elector reconfirmed these privileges in 1653 and after, even while reducing the political power of the Estates, the nobility growled but did not bite. It accepted a compromise whereby the bulk of the new taxes fell on towns and royal authority stopped at the landlords' gates. The elector could and did use naked force to break the liberties of the towns. The main leader of the urban opposition in the key city of Königsberg, for example, was simply arrested and imprisoned for life without trial.

The Consolidation of Prussian Absolutism

By the time of his death in 1688, the Great Elector had created a single state out of scattered principalities. But his new creation was still small and fragile. All the leading states of Europe had many more people, and strong monarchy was still a novelty. Moreover, the Great Elector's successor, Elector Frederick III, "the Ostentatious" (r. 1688–1713), was weak of body and mind, and he focused on imitating the style of Louis XIV, building an expensive palace and cultivating the arts. His main political accomplishment was winning a prestigious royal title and being crowned King Frederick I in 1701 as a reward for aiding the Holy Roman emperor in the War of the Spanish Succession.

This tendency toward luxury-loving, petty tyranny was completely reversed by Frederick William I, "the Soldiers' King" (r. 1713–1740). A crude, dangerous psychoneurotic, Frederick William I was nevertheless the most talented reformer ever produced by the Hohenzollern family. It was he who truly established Prussian absolutism and gave it a unique character. It was he who created the best army in Europe, for its size, and it was he who infused strict military values into a whole society. In the words of a famous historian of Prussia:

> *For a whole generation, the Hohenzollern subjects were victimized by a royal bully, imbued with an obsessive bent for military organization and military scales of value. This left a deep mark upon the institutions of Prussiandom and upon the molding of the "Prussian spirit."*[3]

Frederick William's attachment to the army and military life was intensely emotional. He had, for example, a bizarre, almost pathological love for tall soldiers, whom he credited with superior strength and endurance. Like some fanatical modern-day basketball coach in search of a championship team, he sent his agents throughout Prussia and all of Europe to trick, buy, and kidnap top recruits. Neighboring princes sent him their giants as gifts to win his gratitude. Prussian mothers told their sons, "Stop growing or the recruiting agents will get you."[4]

Profoundly militaristic in temperament, Frederick William always wore an army uniform, and he lived the highly disciplined life of the professional soldier. He began his work by five or six in the morning; at ten he almost always went to the parade ground to drill or inspect his troops. A man of violent temper, Frederick William personally punished the most minor infractions on the spot: a missing button off a soldier's coat quickly provoked a savage beating with a heavy walking stick.

Frederick William's love of the army was also based on a hardheaded conception of the struggle for power and a dog-eat-dog view of international politics. Years later he summed up his life's philosophy in his instructions to his son: "A formidable army and a war chest large enough to make this army mobile in times of need can create great respect for you in the world, so that you can speak a word like the other powers."[5] This unshakable belief that the welfare of king and state depended on the army above all else reinforced Frederick William's passion for the soldier's life.

The cult of military power provided the rationale for a great expansion of royal absolutism in Prussia. As the ruthless king himself put it: "I must be served with life and limb, with house and wealth, with honour and conscience, everything must be committed except eternal salvation—that belongs to God, but all else is mine."[6] To make good these extraordinary demands, Frederick William created a strong centralized bureaucracy. Meanwhile the last traces

A Prussian Giant Grenadier Frederick William I wanted tall, handsome soldiers. He dressed them in tight bright uniforms to distinguish them from the peasant population from which most soldiers came. He also ordered several portraits of his favorites from his court painter, J. C. Merk. Grenadiers wore the miter cap instead of an ordinary hat so that they could hurl their heavy grenades unimpeded by a broad brim. *(The Royal Collection © Her Majesty Queen Elizabeth II)*

of the parliamentary Estates and local self-government vanished.

The king's grab for power brought him into considerable conflict with the noble landowners, the Junkers. In his early years, he even threatened to destroy them; yet, in the end, the Prussian nobility was not destroyed but enlisted—into the army. Responding to a combination of threats and opportunities, the Junkers became the officer caste. A new compromise had been worked out whereby the proud nobility imperiously commanded the peasantry in the army as well as on the estates.

Coarse and crude, penny-pinching and hard-working, Frederick William achieved results. Above all, he built a first-rate army, although he had only third-rate resources. The standing army increased from thirty-eight thousand to eighty-three thousand during his reign. Prussia, twelfth in Europe in population, had the fourth largest army by 1740. Moreover, soldier for soldier, the Prussian army became the best in Europe, astonishing foreign observers with its precision, skill, and discipline. For the next two hundred years, Prussia and then Prussianized Germany would usually win the crucial military battles.

Frederick William and his ministers also built an exceptionally honest and conscientious bureaucracy, which not only administered the country but also tried with some success to develop the country economically. Finally, like the miser he was known to be, living very frugally off the income of his own landholdings, the king loved his "blue boys" so much that he hated to "spend" them. This most militaristic of kings was, paradoxically, almost always at peace.

Nevertheless, the Prussian people paid a heavy and lasting price for the obsessions of their royal drillmaster. Civil society became rigid and highly disciplined. Prussia became the "Sparta of the North"; unquestioning obedience was the highest virtue. As a Prussian minister later summed up, "To keep quiet is the first civic duty."[7] Thus the policies of Frederick William I combined with harsh peasant bondage and Junker tyranny to lay the foundations for probably the most militaristic country of modern times.

The Development of Russia

One of the favorite parlor games of nineteenth-century Russian (and non-Russian) intellectuals was debating whether Russia was a Western, European or a non-Western, Asiatic society. This question was particularly fascinating because it was unanswerable. To this day Russia differs fundamentally from the West in some basic ways, though Russian history has paralleled that of the West in other aspects.

Certainly Russian developments in the early medieval period had important parallels with those in the West. The eastern Slavs were converted by missionaries from the Byzantine Empire to Orthodox Christianity, which became the state religion of the powerful Kievan principality, in the territory of present-day Ukraine. **Eastern Orthodoxy** rejects the authority of the pope, but this is the main difference in religious and moral beliefs dividing it from Roman Catholicism. Also in the mainstream of European medieval civilization was the loose but real political unification of the eastern Slavic territories under a single prince and a single dynasty in the eleventh century. So, too, was the typical feudal division of the land-based society into a **boyard nobility** and a commoner peasantry. After the death of Great Prince Iaroslav the Wise (r. 1019–1054), the Kievan principality disintegrated into competing political units. But similar fragmentations of central authority occurred in many European kingdoms at various points in the Middle Ages, and a strong native ruler might have emerged in Russia eventually to resume the centralizing work of earlier Kievan monarchs.

Such was not the case, however. Brutally conquered and subjugated by a foreign invader, Russia created a system of rule that was virtually unknown in the West. Thus the differences between Russia and the West became striking and profound in the long period from about 1250 until 1700. And when absolute monarchy triumphed under the rough guidance of Peter the Great in the early eighteenth century, it was a quite different type of absolute monarchy from that of France or even Prussia.

The Mongol Yoke and the Rise of Moscow

Like the Germans and the Italians, the eastern Slavs might have emerged from the Middle Ages weak and politically divided had it not been for the Mongol conquest of the Kievan principality. Nomadic tribes from present-day Mongolia, the Mongols were temporarily unified in the thirteenth century by Chinggis Khan (1162–1227), one of history's greatest conquerors. In five years his armies subdued all of China. His successors then turned westward, smashing everything in their path and reaching the plains of Hungary victorious before they pulled back in 1242. The Mongol army—the Golden Horde—was savage in the extreme, often slaughtering entire populations of cities before burning them to the ground. En route to Mongolia in 1245, Archbishop John of Plano Carpini, the papal ambassador to Mongolia, passed through Kiev, which the Mongols had sacked in 1242, and wrote an unforgettable eyewitness account:

The Mongols went against Russia and enacted a great massacre in the Russian land. They destroyed towns and fortresses and killed people. They besieged Kiev, which had been the capital of Russia, and after a long siege they took it and killed the inhabitants of the city. For this reason, when we passed through that land, we found lying in the field countless heads and bones of dead people; for this city had been extremely large and very populous, whereas now it has been reduced to nothing: barely two hundred houses stand there, and those people are held in the harshest slavery.[8]

Having devastated and conquered, the Mongols ruled the eastern Slavs for more than two hundred years, the so-called **Mongol Yoke.** They built their capital of Saray on the lower Volga (see Map 17.3). They forced all the bickering Slavic princes to submit to their rule and to give them tribute and slaves. If the conquered peoples rebelled, the Mongols were quick to punish with death and destruction. Thus the Mongols unified the eastern Slavs, for the Mongol khan was acknowledged by all as the supreme ruler.

The Mongol unification completely changed the internal political situation. Although the Mongols conquered, they were quite willing to use local princes as obedient servants and tax collectors. Therefore, they did not abolish the title of "great prince," bestowing it instead on the prince who served them best and paid them most handsomely.

Beginning with Alexander Nevsky in 1252, the previously insignificant princes of Moscow became particularly adept at serving the Mongols. They loyally put down popular uprisings and collected the khan's harsh taxes. By way of reward, the princes of Moscow emerged as hereditary great princes. Eventually the Muscovite princes were able to destroy their princely rivals and even replace the khan as supreme ruler.

One of the more important Muscovite princes was Ivan I (r. 1328–1341), popularly known as "Ivan Moneybags." Extremely stingy, Ivan I built up a large personal fortune and increased his influence by loaning money to less frugal princes to pay their Mongol taxes. Ivan's most serious rival was the prince of Tver, who joined his people in 1327 in a revolt against Mongol oppression. Appointed commander of a large Russian-Mongol army, Ivan laid waste to Tver and its lands. For this proof of devotion, the Mongols made Ivan the general tax collector for all the Slavic lands they had subjugated and named him great prince.

In the next hundred-odd years, the great princes of Moscow significantly increased their holdings. Then, in the

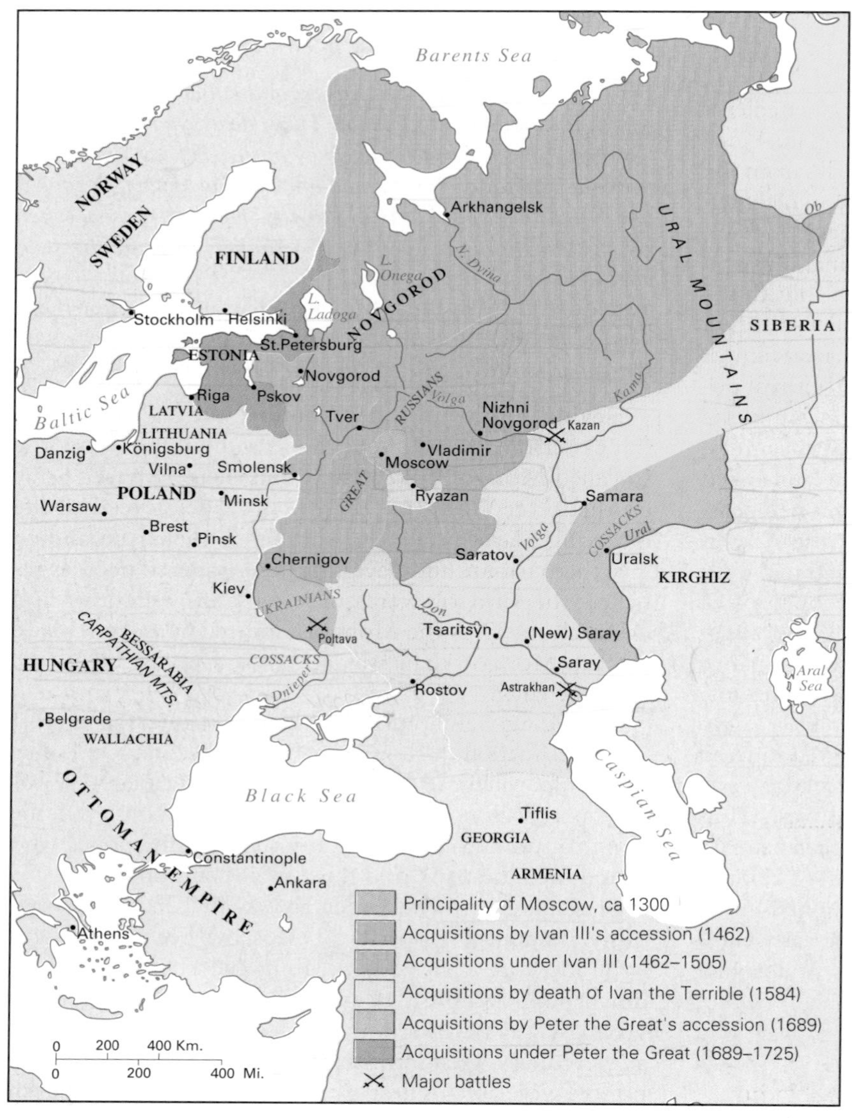

MAP 17.3 The Expansion of Russia to 1725 After the disintegration of the Kievan state and the Mongol conquest, the princes of Moscow and their descendants gradually extended their rule over an enormous territory. Ivan the Terrible acquired more territory than Peter the Great.

reign of Ivan III (r. 1462–1505), the process of gathering in the territories around Moscow was largely completed. Of the principalities that Ivan III purchased and conquered, the large, rich merchant republic of Novgorod was most crucial (see Map 17.3). Thus the princes of Moscow defeated all rivals to win complete princely authority.

Not only was the prince of Moscow the *unique* ruler, he was the *absolute* ruler, the autocrat, the *tsar*—the Slavic contraction for "caesar," with all its connotations. This imperious conception of absolute power and **autocracy** was powerfully reinforced by two developments. First, about 1480 Ivan III felt strong enough to stop acknowledging the khan as his supreme ruler. There is good evidence to suggest that Ivan and his successor saw themselves as khans, exercising unrestrained and unpredictable power.

Second, after the fall of Constantinople to the Turks in 1453, the tsars saw themselves as the heirs of both the caesars and Orthodox Christianity, the one true faith. All the other kings of Europe were heretics; only the tsars were rightful and holy rulers. The idea was promoted by Orthodox churchmen, who spoke of "holy Russia" as the "Third Rome." As the monk Pilotheus stated, "Two Romes have fallen, but the third stands, and a fourth there will not be."[9] Ivan's marriage to the daughter of

Collecting Taxes in Russia Ivan I, known as Ivan Moneybags and pictured here at the center, zealously served his Mongol masters. This work by an unknown artist shows the great prince's agents beating peasants into paying the heavy Mongol tax, a portion of which Ivan skimmed off to increase his own wealth and power. *(Novosti)*

the last Byzantine emperor further enhanced the aura of an imperial inheritance of Moscow.

As peasants had begun losing their freedom of movement in the fifteenth century, so had the noble boyars begun losing power and influence. For example, when Ivan III conquered the principality of Novgorod in the 1480s, he confiscated fully 80 percent of the land, executing the previous owners or resettling them nearer Moscow. He then kept more than half of the confiscated land for himself and distributed the remainder to members of a newly emerging **service nobility,** who held the tsar's land on the explicit condition that they serve in the tsar's army.

Tsar and People to 1689

The rise of the new service nobility accelerated under Ivan IV (r. 1533–1584), the famous "Ivan the Terrible." Having ascended the throne at age three, Ivan suffered insults and neglect at the hands of the haughty boyars after his mother mysteriously died, possibly poisoned, when he was just eight. At age sixteen he suddenly pushed aside his hated boyar advisers. In an awe-inspiring ceremony complete with gold coins pouring down on his head, he majestically crowned himself and officially took the august title of tsar for the first time.

Selecting the beautiful and kind Anastasia of the popular Romanov family for his wife and queen, the young tsar soon declared war on the remnants of Mongol power. He defeated the faltering khanates of Kazan and Astrakhan between 1552 and 1556, adding vast new territories to Russia. In the course of these wars, Ivan virtually abolished the old distinction between hereditary boyar private property and land granted temporarily for service. All nobles, old and new, had to serve the tsar in order to hold any land.

The process of transforming the entire nobility into a service nobility was completed in the second part of Ivan

Ivan the Terrible Ivan IV, the first to take the title Tsar of Russia, executed many Muscovite boyars and their peasants and servants. His ownership of all the land, trade, and industry restricted economic development. *(National Museum, Copenhagen, Denmark)*

the Terrible's reign. In 1557 Ivan turned westward, and for the next twenty-five years Muscovy waged an exhausting, unsuccessful war primarily against the large Polish-Lithuanian state, which joined Poland with much of Ukraine in the sixteenth century. Quarreling with the boyars over the war and blaming them for the sudden death of his beloved Anastasia in 1560, the increasingly cruel and demented Ivan turned to strike down all who stood in his way.

Above all, he struck down the ancient Muscovite boyars with a reign of terror. Leading boyars, their relatives, and even their peasants and servants were executed en masse by a special corps of unquestioning servants. Dressed in black and riding black horses, they were forerunners of the modern dictator's secret police. Large estates were confiscated, broken up, and reapportioned to the lower service nobility. The great boyar families were severely reduced. The newer, poorer, more nearly equal service nobility, still less than 0.5 percent of the total population, was totally dependent on the autocrat.

Ivan also took giant strides toward making all commoners servants of the tsar. His endless wars and demonic purges left much of central Russia depopulated. As the service nobles demanded more from the remaining peasants, more and more peasants fled toward the wild, recently conquered territories to the east and south. There they formed free groups and outlaw armies known as **Cossacks**, who maintained a precarious independence beyond the tsar's reach. The solution to the problem of peasant flight was to complete the tying of the peasants to the land and to the noble landholders, who were bound in turn to serve the tsar.

In the time of Ivan the Terrible, urban traders and artisans were also bound to their towns and jobs so that the tsar could tax them more heavily. Ivan assumed that the tsar owned Russia's trade and industry, just as he owned all the land. The urban classes had no security in their work or property, and even the wealthiest merchants were basically dependent agents of the tsar. If a new commercial activity became important and profitable, it was often taken over by the tsar and made a royal monopoly. Royal monopolization and service obligations checked the growth of the Russian middle classes and stood in sharp contrast to developments in western Europe, where the capitalist middle classes were gaining strength and security in their private property.

Ivan the Terrible's system of autocracy and compulsory service struck foreign observers forcibly. Sigismund Herberstein, a German traveler to Russia, wrote in 1571: "All the people consider themselves to be *kholops,* that is, slaves of their Prince." At the same time, Jean Bodin, the French thinker who did so much to develop the modern concept of sovereignty, concluded that Russia's political system was fundamentally different from those of all other European monarchies and comparable only to that of the Ottoman Empire. In both the Ottoman Empire and Russia, "the prince is become lord of the goods and persons of his subjects . . . governing them as a master of a family does his slaves."[10] The Mongol inheritance weighed heavily on Russia.

As has so often occurred in Russia, the death of an iron-fisted tyrant—in this case, Ivan the Terrible in 1584—ushered in an era of confusion and violent struggles for power. Events were particularly chaotic after Ivan's son, Theodore, died in 1598 without an heir. The years 1598 to 1613 were aptly called the "Time of Troubles."

The close relatives of the deceased tsar intrigued against and murdered one another, alternately fighting and welcoming the invading Swedes and Poles, who even occupied Moscow. Most serious for the cause of autocracy, there was a great social upheaval. Cossack bands, led by a

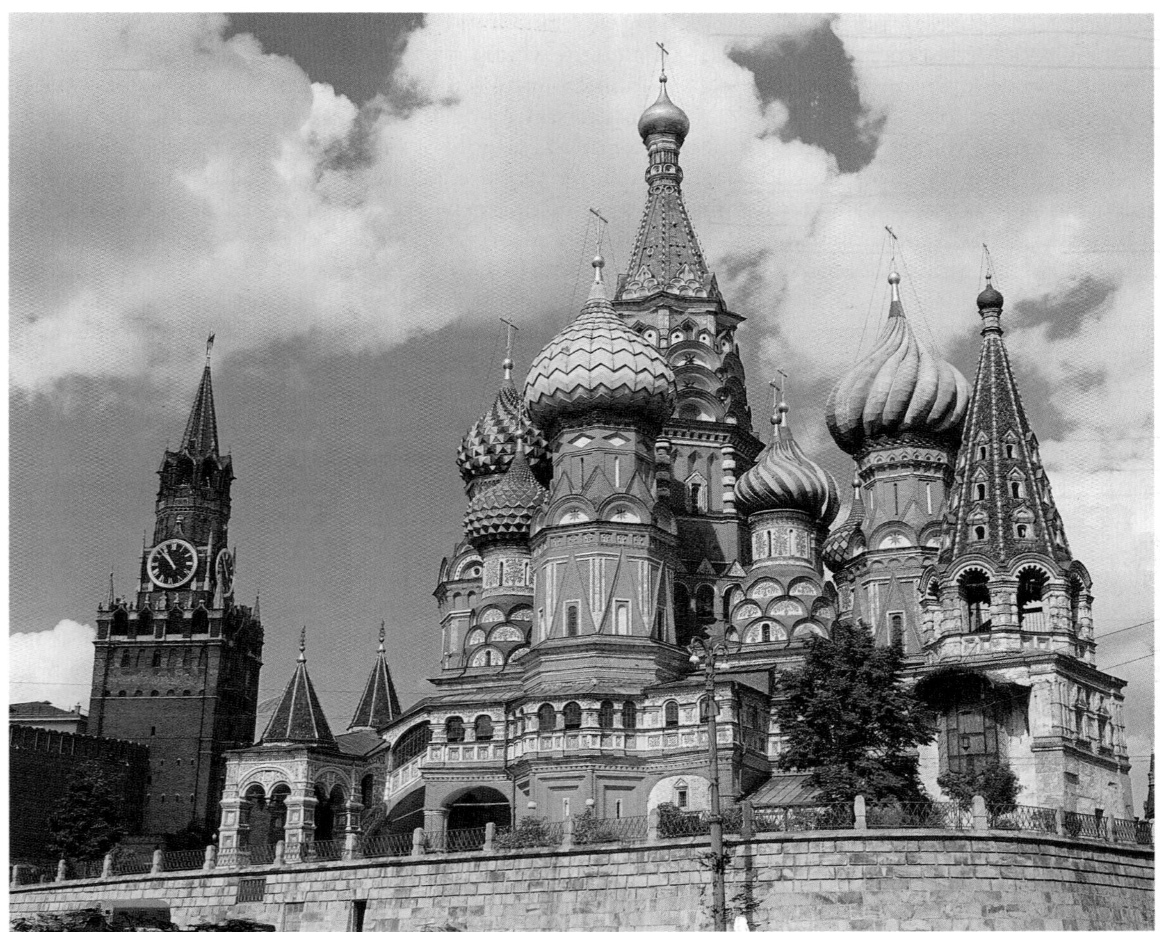

Saint Basil's Cathedral, Moscow With its sloping roofs and colorful onion-shaped domes, Saint Basil's is a striking example of powerful Byzantine influences on Russian culture. According to tradition, an enchanted Ivan the Terrible blinded the cathedral's architects to ensure that they would never duplicate their fantastic achievement, which still dazzles the beholder in today's Red Square. *(George Holton/Photo Researchers)*

former slave named Ivan Bolotnikov, marched northward, rallying peasants and slaughtering nobles and officials. The mass of Cossacks and peasants called for the "true tsar," who would restore their freedom of movement, reduce their heavy taxes, and lighten the yoke imposed by the landlords.

This social explosion from below brought the nobles, big and small, to their senses. They put aside their quarrels and finally crushed the Cossack rebellion at the gates of Moscow. In 1613 the nobles elected Ivan the Terrible's sixteen-year-old grandnephew, Michael Romanov, the new hereditary tsar. Then they rallied around him in the face of common internal and external threats. Michael's election was a real restoration, and his reign saw the gradual re-establishment of tsarist autocracy. (See the feature "Listening to the Past: A Foreign Traveler in Russia" on pages 590–591.) Thus while peasants were completely enserfed in 1649, Ivan's heavy military obligations on the nobility were relaxed considerably. In the long reign of Michael's successor, the pious Alexis (r. 1645–1676), this asymmetry of obligations was accentuated.

The result was a second round of mass upheaval and protest. In the later seventeenth century, the unity of the Russian Orthodox church was torn apart by a great split. The initiating event was the religious reforms introduced in 1652 by the patriarch Nikon, a dogmatic purist who wished to bring "corrupted" Russian practices of worship into line with the Greek Orthodox model. The self-serving church hierarchy quickly went along, but the intensely religious common people resisted. They saw Nikon as the Antichrist, who was stripping them of the only thing they had—the true religion of "holy Russia."

Great numbers left the church and formed illegal communities of "Old Believers," who were hunted down and persecuted. As many as twenty thousand people burned themselves alive, singing the "hallelujah" in their chants three times rather than twice, as Nikon had demanded. After the great split, the Russian masses were alienated from the established church, which became dependent on the state for its authority.

Again the Cossacks revolted against the state, which was doggedly trying to catch up with them on the frontiers and reduce them to serfdom. Under Stenka Razin they moved up the Volga River in 1670 and 1671, attracting a great army of urban poor and peasants, killing landlords and government officials, and proclaiming freedom from oppression. This rebellion to overthrow the established order was finally defeated by the government. (See the feature "Individuals in Society: Stenka Razin, Russian Rebel.") In response, the thoroughly scared upper classes tightened the screws of serfdom even further. Holding down the peasants, and thereby maintaining the tsar, became almost the principal obligation of the nobility until 1689.

The Reforms of Peter the Great

It is now possible to understand the reforms of Peter the Great (r. 1682–1725) and his kind of monarchical absolutism. Contrary to some historians' assertions, Peter was interested primarily in military power, not in some grandiose westernization plan. A giant for his time, at six feet seven inches, and possessing enormous energy and willpower, Peter was determined to redress the defeats the tsar's armies had occasionally suffered in their wars with Poland and Sweden since the time of Ivan the Terrible.

Peter was equally determined to continue the tsarist tradition of territorial expansion. After a long war, Russia had gained a large mass of Ukraine from weak and decentralized Poland in 1667 (see Map 17.3), and it completed the conquest of Siberia in the seventeenth century. After the seventeen-year-old Peter overturned the regency in 1689, the thirty-six years of his personal rule knew only one year of peace.

When Peter took control in 1689, the heart of his army still consisted of cavalry made up of boyars and service nobility. Foot soldiers played a secondary role, and the whole army served on a part-time basis. The Russian army was lagging behind the professional standing armies being formed in Europe in the seventeenth century. The core of such armies was a highly disciplined infantry that fired and refired muskets as it fearlessly advanced, until it charged with bayonets fixed. Such a large, permanent army would be enormously expensive, and thus Peter's military moves were cautious in the 1690s.

Maintaining an existing Russian alliance with Austria and Poland against the Ottoman Empire, Peter campaigned first against Turkish forts and Tartar vassals on the Black Sea. Learning from early mistakes, he conquered Azov in 1696. Fascinated by weapons and foreign technology, the confident tsar then led a group of 250 Russian officials and young nobles on an eighteen-month tour of western European capitals. Traveling unofficially as an ordinary Russian to avoid formal ceremonies, Peter worked with his hands at various crafts and met with foreign kings and experts. He was particularly impressed with the growing power of the Dutch and the English and considered how Russia could profit from their example.

Returning to Russia, Peter entered into a secret alliance with Denmark and the elector of Saxony, who was also the elected king of Poland, to wage a sudden war of aggression against Sweden. Sweden was then a leading power in northern Europe. Despite the country's small population and limited agricultural resources, Swedish rulers in the seventeenth century had developed a strong absolutist state and built an excellent standing army. Expanding beyond Sweden, they held substantial territory in northern Germany, Finland, and Estonia. Yet these possessions were scattered and appeared vulnerable. Above all, Peter and his allies believed that their combined forces could win easy victories because Sweden was in the hands of a new and inexperienced king. They were mistaken.

Eighteen-year-old Charles XII (1697–1718) surprised Peter when he showed daring military genius. Defeating Denmark quickly in 1700, Charles turned on Russia. In a blinding snowstorm, his well-trained professional army attacked and routed unsuspecting Russians besieging the Swedish fortress of Navra on the Baltic coast. Peter and the survivors fled in panic to Moscow. It was, for the Russians, a grim beginning to the long and brutal Great Northern War, which lasted from 1700 to 1721.

Suffering defeat and faced with a military crisis, the energetic Peter responded with a long series of practical but far-reaching measures designed to increase state power, strengthen his armies, and gain victory. In essence, Peter's solution was to tighten up Muscovy's old service

Individuals in Society

Stenka Razin, Russian Rebel

The Don Cossack Stenka Razin led the largest peasant rebellion in Europe in the seventeenth century, a century rich in peasant revolt. Who was this Cossack leader who challenged Moscow, this outlaw who grew into a social revolutionary?

Descended from fugitives who fled to the turbulent southern frontier in search of freedom, Razin epitomized the old Cossack spirit of liberty and self-rule. Sharing the Cossack love of fighting and adventure, Razin also felt great sympathy for northern "have-nots" who had lost out and could not escape their fate. Why this was so remains a mystery. His family belonged to the Cossack establishment, which had settled the lower Don Valley long ago and received annual payments from the tsar in return for friendship and defense. One folk story tells of a hatred kindled by a Russian prince who unjustly hanged an older brother leading a Cossack detachment in Poland. True or not, rebel leaders like Razin have often come from comfortable backgrounds. As Paul Avrich notes, "Seldom have the oppressed themselves led the way, but rather those who have been aroused by their suffering and degradation."*

Whatever his motivation, Stenka Razin was a born leader. A striking personality with violent emotions, he was also shrewd and generous. He understood the lower classes and how to move them. The crowds called him a magician—a magician who hated the privileged and whom they felt compelled to follow.

Razin was a seasoned warrior of about forty years of age when in 1667 he led his first campaign. With an armed band of poor and rootless Cossacks, recent fugitives living upstream from the well-settled Cossacks, Razin sailed down the Volga River and seized a rich convoy of Russian merchant ships. He reportedly told survivors they were free to go or join him as free Cossacks. "I have come to fight only the boyars and the wealthy lords. As for the poor and the plain folk, I shall treat them as brothers."† Moving on to plunder Persian commerce on the Caspian Sea, Razin's forces returned home loaded with booty, which they divided equally according to Cossack custom. Gaining immense popularity and responding to threats from Moscow, Razin and his movement changed. The gang of outlaws became a rebel army.

In early 1670, Razin marched north with seven thousand Don Cossacks. His leaflets proclaimed that he was entering Russia "to establish the Cossack way, so that all men will be equal." Shrewdly blaming treacherous nobles and officials, and not the divinely appointed tsar, for the exploitation of the people, Razin's agents infiltrated the fortified towns along the Volga. Some towns resisted, but many threw open their gates, as the urban poor rose up against the "traitors and bloodsuckers." Peasants joined the revolt, killing lords and burning manor houses.

Stenka Razin in Cossack dress, from a contemporary engraving. (Novosti)

Frightened but unified, Russia's tiny elite mobilized all its strength. In late 1670, crack cavalry units of service nobility finally repulsed the swollen, ill-equipped army of the poor at Simbirsk on the upper Volga. The insurgents had to retreat. Fighting until the end, Razin was captured, hideously tortured, and chopped into pieces on the execution block. His followers and sympathizers were slaughtered with ferocious cruelty.

A fearless leader in the struggle against tsarist absolutism, Stenka Razin nurtured a myth of rebellion that would inspire future generations with dreams of freedom. He became Russia's most celebrated folk hero. He lived in story and song, an immortal superman who would someday ride out of the forest and deliver the people from oppression.

Questions for Analysis

1. What did Stenka Razin do? Why did his rebellion inspire future generations?
2. How would you interpret Razin? Was he a great hero, a common criminal, or something else?

*Paul Avrich, *Russian Rebels, 1600–1800* (New York: Schocken Books, 1972), p. 67. This account is based on Avrich's masterful study.

†Quoted ibid., p. 70.

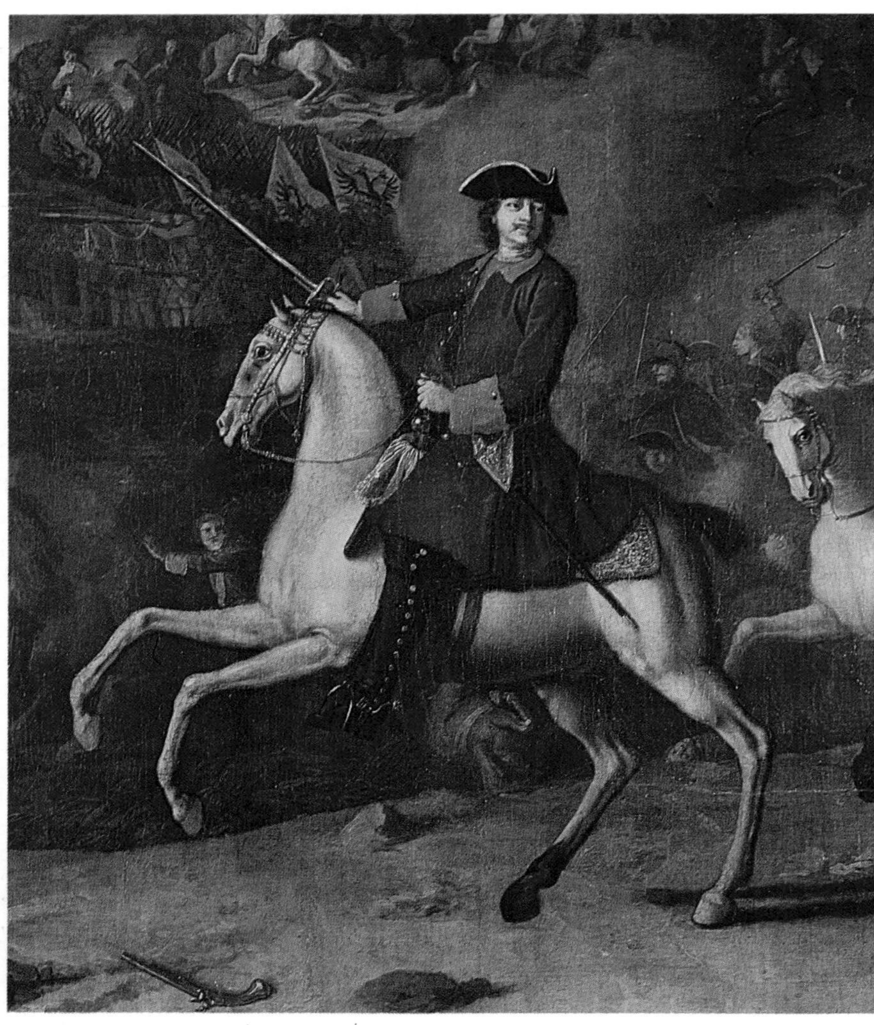

Peter the Great This painting by Louis Karavack celebrates the power and determination of Russia's famous ruler. Most appropriately, it shows him imperiously leading his armies into battle. Peter waged war almost continually throughout his long reign, and the desire to build a large modern army motivated many of his reforms. *(Hermitage, Leningrad/Novosti)*

system and really make it work. Every nobleman, great or small, was once again required to serve in the army or in the civil administration—for life. Since a more modern army and government required skilled technicians and experts, Peter created schools and even universities to produce them. One of his most hated reforms required five years of compulsory education away from home for every young nobleman. Peter established an interlocking military-civilian bureaucracy with fourteen ranks, and he decreed that all had to start at the bottom and work toward the top. Some people of non-noble origins rose to high positions in this embryonic meritocracy. Drawing on his experience abroad, Peter searched out talented foreigners and placed them in his service. These measures gradually combined to make the army and government more powerful and efficient.

Peter also greatly increased the service requirements of the commoners. In the wake of the disaster at Navra, he established a regular standing army of more than 200,000 soldiers, made up mainly of peasants commanded by officers from the nobility. In addition, special forces of Cossacks and foreigners numbered more than 100,000. The departure of a drafted peasant boy was celebrated by his family and village almost like a funeral, as indeed it was, since the recruit was drafted for life. The peasantry also served with its taxes, which increased threefold during Peter's reign. Serfs were arbitrarily assigned to work in the growing number of factories and mines. Most of these industrial enterprises were directly or indirectly owned by the state, and they were worked almost exclusively for the military. In general, Russian serfdom became more oppressive under the reforming tsar.

The constant warfare of Peter's reign consumed 80 to 85 percent of all revenues and brought only modest territorial expansion. Yet the Great Northern War with Sweden was crowned in the end by Russian victory. Mobilizing superior resources and a much larger population, Peter's new war machine crushed the smaller army of Sweden's Charles XII in Ukraine at Poltava in 1709, one of the most significant battles in Russian history. The war dragged on until 1721, but Sweden never really regained the offensive, and Russia eventually annexed Estonia and much of present-day Latvia (see Map 17.3), lands that had never before been under Russian rule. Russia became the dominant power on the Baltic Sea and very much a European Great Power. If victory or defeat is the ultimate historical criterion, Peter's reforms were a success.

There were other important consequences of Peter's reign. Because of his feverish desire to use modern technology to strengthen the army, many Westerners and Western ideas flowed into Russia for the first time. A new class of educated Russians began to emerge. At the same time, vast numbers of Russians, especially among the poor and weak, hated Peter's massive changes. The split between the enserfed peasantry and the educated nobility thus widened, even though all were caught up in the demands of the sovereign.

A new idea of state interest, as distinct from the tsar's personal interests, began to take hold. Peter himself claimed time and again to be serving the common good. For the first time, a Russian tsar attached explanations to his decrees in an attempt to gain the confidence and support of the populace. Yet as before, the tsar alone decided what the common good was. Here was a source of future tension between tsar and people.

Thus Peter built on the service obligations of old Muscovy. His monarchical absolutism was truly the culmination of the long development of a unique Russian civilization. Yet the creation of a more modern army and state introduced much that was new and Western to that civilization. This development paved the way for Russia to move much closer to the European mainstream in its thought and institutions during the Enlightenment, especially under Catherine the Great.

Absolutism and Baroque Architecture

The rise of royal absolutism in eastern Europe had many consequences. Nobles served their powerful rulers in new ways, while the great inferiority of the urban middle classes and the peasants was reconfirmed. Armies became larger and more professional, while taxes rose and authoritarian traditions were strengthened. Nor was this all. Royal absolutism also interacted with baroque culture and art, baroque music and literature. Inspired in part by Louis XIV of France, the great and not-so-great rulers called on the artistic talent of the age to glorify their power and magnificence. This exaltation of despotic rule was particularly striking in the lavish masterpieces of architecture.

Palaces and Power

Baroque culture and art grew out of the revitalized Catholic church of the later sixteenth century. The papacy and the Jesuits especially encouraged an emotional, exuberant art, which appealed to the senses of churchgoers and proclaimed the confidence and power of the Catholic Reformation. The baroque style then spread throughout Europe in the seventeenth century, for dramatic baroque palaces symbolized the age of absolutist power, as soaring Gothic cathedrals had expressed the idealized spirit of the High Middle Ages.

By 1700 palace building had become a veritable obsession for the rulers of central and eastern Europe. Their baroque palaces were clearly intended to overawe the people with the monarch's strength. The great palaces were also visual declarations of equality with Louis XIV and were therefore modeled after Versailles to a greater or lesser extent. One such palace was Schönbrunn, an enormous Viennese Versailles begun in 1695 by Emperor Leopold to celebrate Austrian military victories and Habsburg might. Charles XI of Sweden, having reduced the power of the aristocracy, ordered the construction in 1693 of his Royal Palace, which dominates the center of Stockholm to this day.

Petty princes in the German lands also contributed mightily to the palace-building mania. Frederick the Great of Prussia noted that every descendant of a princely family "imagines himself to be something like Louis XIV. He builds his Versailles, has his mistresses, and maintains his army."[11] The not-very-important elector-archbishop of Mainz, the ruling prince of that city, confessed apologetically that "building is a craze which costs much, but every fool likes his own hat."[12]

In central and eastern Europe, the favorite noble servants of royalty became extremely rich and powerful, and they, too, built grandiose palaces in the capital cities. These palaces were in part an extension of the monarch, for they surpassed the buildings of less favored nobles and showed all the high road to fame and fortune. Take, for example, the palaces of Prince Eugene of Savoy, a French nobleman who became Austria's most famous military hero. It was Eugene who led the Austrian army, smashed the Turks, fought Louis XIV to a standstill, and generally guided the triumph of absolutism in Austria. Rewarded with great wealth by his grateful royal employer, Eugene called on the leading architects of the day, J. B. Fischer von Erlach and Johann Lukas von Hildebrandt, to consecrate his glory in stone and fresco. Fischer built Eugene's Winter (or Town) Palace in Vienna, and he and Hildebrandt collaborated on the prince's Summer Palace on the city's outskirts (see accompanying illustration).

Palaces like those of Prince Eugene were magnificent examples of the baroque style. They expressed the baroque delight in bold, sweeping statements, which were intended to provide a dramatic emotional experience. To create this experience, baroque masters dissolved the traditional artistic frontiers: the architect permitted the painter and the artisan to cover a building's undulating surfaces with wildly colorful paintings, graceful sculptures, and fanciful carvings. Space was used in a highly original way to blend everything together in a total environment. These techniques shone in all their glory in the churches of southern Germany and in the colossal halls of royal palaces. Artistic achievement and political statement reinforced each other.

Prince Eugene's Summer Palace, Vienna The prince's summer residence featured two baroque gems, the Lower Belvedere and the lovely Upper Belvedere, completed in 1722 and shown here. The building's interior is equally stunning, with crouching giants serving as pillars and a magnificent great staircase. Art and beauty convey a feeling of immense prestige and power. *(Erich Lessing/Art Resource, NY)*

Royal Cities

Absolute monarchs and baroque architects were not content with fashioning ostentatious palaces. They remodeled existing capital cities, or even built new ones, to reflect royal magnificence and the centralization of political power. Karlsruhe, founded in 1715 as the capital city of a small German principality, is one extreme example. There broad, straight avenues radiated out from the palace so that all roads—like all power—were focused on the ruler. More typically, the monarch's architects added new urban areas alongside the old city; these areas then became the real heart of the expanding capital.

The distinctive features of these new additions were their broad avenues, their imposing government buildings, and their rigorous mathematical layout. Along these major thoroughfares nobles built elaborate baroque townhouses; stables and servants' quarters were built on the alleys behind. Wide avenues also facilitated the rapid movement of soldiers through the city to quell any disturbance (the king's planners had the needs of the military constantly in mind). Under the arcades along the avenues appeared smart and very expensive shops, the first department stores, with plate-glass windows and fancy displays.

The new avenues brought reckless speed to European cities all across the continent. Whereas everyone had walked through the narrow, twisting streets of the medieval town, the high and mighty now raced down the broad boulevards in their elegant carriages. A social gap opened between the wealthy riders and the gaping, dodging pedestrians. "Mind the carriages!" wrote one eighteenth-century observer in Paris:

> *Here comes the black-coated physician in his chariot, the dancing master in his coach, the fencing master in his surrey—and the Prince behind six horses at the gallop as if he were in the open country. . . . The threatening wheels of the overbearing rich drive as rapidly as ever over stones stained with the blood of their unhappy victims.*[13]

Speeding carriages on broad avenues, an endless parade of power and position: here were the symbols and substance of the baroque city.

The Growth of St. Petersburg

No city illustrates better than St. Petersburg the close ties among politics, architecture, and urban development in this period. In 1700, when the Great Northern War between Russia and Sweden began, the city did not exist. There was only a small Swedish fortress on one of the waterlogged islands at the mouth of the Neva River, where it flows into the Baltic Sea. In 1702 Peter the Great's armies seized this desolate outpost. Within a year the reforming tsar had decided to build a new city there and to make it, rather than ancient Moscow, his capital.

Since the first step was to secure the Baltic coast, military construction was the main concern for the next eight years. A mighty fortress was built on Peter Island, and a port and shipyards were built across the river on the mainland as a Russian navy came into being. The land was swampy and uninhabited, the climate damp and unpleasant. But Peter cared not at all: for him the inhospitable northern marshland was a future metropolis, gloriously bearing his name.

After the decisive Russian victory at Poltava in 1709 greatly reduced the threat of Swedish armies, Peter moved into high gear. In one imperious decree after another, he ordered his people to build a city that would equal any in the world. Such a city had to be Western and baroque, just as Peter's army had to be Western and permanent. From such a new city, his "window on Europe," Peter also believed it would be easier to reform the country militarily and administratively.

These general political goals matched Peter's architectural ideas, which had been influenced by his travels in western Europe. First, Peter wanted a comfortable, "modern" city. Modernity meant broad, straight, stone-paved avenues; houses built in a uniform line and not haphazardly set back from the street; large parks; canals for drainage; stone bridges; and street lighting. Second, all building had to conform strictly to detailed architectural regulations set down by the government. Finally, each social group—the nobility, the merchants, the artisans, and so on—was to live in a certain section of town. In short, the city and its population were to conform to a carefully defined urban plan of the baroque type.

Peter used the traditional but reinforced methods of Russian autocracy to build his modern capital. The creation of St. Petersburg was just one of the heavy obligations he dictatorially imposed on all social groups in Russia. The peasants bore the heaviest burdens. Just as the government drafted peasants for the army, it also drafted twenty-five thousand to forty thousand men each summer to labor in St. Petersburg for three months without pay. Every ten to fifteen peasant households had to furnish one such worker each summer and then pay a special tax in order to feed that worker in St. Petersburg.

Peasants hated this forced labor in the capital, and each year one-fourth to one-third of those sent risked brutal punishment and ran away. Many peasant construction

St. Petersburg, ca 1760 Rastrelli's remodeled Winter Palace, which housed the royal family until the Russian Revolution of 1917, stands on the left along the Neva River. The Navy Office with its famous golden spire and other government office buildings are nearby and across the river. Russia became a naval power and St. Petersburg a great port. *(Michael Holford)*

workers died each summer from hunger, sickness, and accidents. Thus beautiful St. Petersburg was built on the shoveling, carting, and paving of a mass of conscripted serfs.

Peter also drafted more privileged groups to his city, but on a permanent basis. Nobles were summarily ordered to build costly stone houses and palaces in St. Petersburg and to live in them most of the year. The more serfs a noble possessed, the bigger his dwelling had to be. Merchants and artisans were also commanded to settle and build in St. Petersburg. These nobles and merchants were then required to pay for the city's avenues, parks, canals, embankments, pilings, and bridges, all of which were very costly in terms of both money and lives because they were built on a swamp. The building of St. Petersburg was, in truth, an enormous direct tax levied on the wealthy, which in turn forced the peasantry to do most of the work. No wonder so many Russians hated Peter's new city.

Yet the tsar had his way. By the time of his death in 1725, there were at least six thousand houses and numerous impressive government buildings in St. Petersburg. Under the remarkable women who ruled Russia throughout most of the eighteenth century, St. Petersburg blossomed fully as a majestic and well-organized city, at least in its wealthy showpiece sections. Peter's youngest daughter, the quick-witted Elizabeth (r. 1741–1762), named as her chief architect Bartolomeo Rastrelli, who had come to Russia from Italy as a boy of fifteen in 1715. Combining Italian and Russian traditions into a unique, wildly colorful St. Petersburg style, Rastrelli built many palaces for the nobility and all the larger government buildings erected during Elizabeth's reign. He also rebuilt the Winter Palace as an enormous, aqua-colored royal residence, now the Hermitage Museum. There Elizabeth established a flashy, luxury-loving, and slightly crude court, which Catherine the Great in turn made truly imperial. All the while St. Petersburg grew rapidly, and its almost 300,000 inhabitants in 1782 made it one of the world's largest cities. Peter and his successors had created out of nothing a magnificent and harmonious royal city, which unmistakably proclaimed the power of Russia's rulers and the creative potential of the absolutist state.

Summary

From about 1400 to 1650, social and economic developments in eastern Europe increasingly diverged from those in western Europe. In the east, peasants and townspeople lost precious freedoms, while the nobility increased its power and prestige. It was within this framework of resurgent serfdom and entrenched nobility that Austrian and Prussian monarchs fashioned absolutist states in the seventeenth and early eighteenth centuries.

These monarchs won absolutist control over standing armies, permanent taxes, and legislative bodies. But they did not question underlying social and economic relationships. Indeed, they enhanced the privileges of the nobility, which furnished the leading servitors for enlarged armies and growing state bureaucracies.

In Russia the social and economic trends were similar, but the timing of political absolutism was different. Mongol conquest and rule were a crucial experience, and a harsh, indigenous tsarist autocracy was firmly in place by the reign of Ivan the Terrible in the sixteenth century. More than a century later, Peter the Great succeeded in tightening up Russia's traditional absolutism and modernizing it by reforming the army, the bureaucracy, and the defense industry. In Russia and throughout eastern Europe, war and the needs of the state in time of war weighed heavily in the triumph of absolutism.

Triumphant absolutism interacted spectacularly with the arts. Baroque art, which had grown out of the Catholic Reformation's desire to move the faithful and exalt the true faith, admirably suited the secular aspirations of eastern European rulers. They built grandiose baroque palaces, monumental public squares, and even whole cities to glorify their power and majesty. Thus baroque art attained magnificent heights in eastern Europe, symbolizing the ideal and harmonizing with the reality of imperious royal absolutism.

Key Terms

- serfdom
- hereditary subjugation
- absolutism
- Bohemian Estates
- sultan
- Pragmatic Sanction
- elector of Brandenburg
- Junkers
- Eastern Orthodoxy
- boyard nobility
- Mongol Yoke
- autocracy
- service nobility
- Cossacks
- baroque

Notes

1. See L. Wolff, *Inventing Eastern Europe: The Map of Civilization on the Mind of the Enlightenment* (Stanford, Calif.: Stanford University Press, 1994).
2. Quoted in F. L. Carsten, *The Origins of Prussia* (Oxford: Clarendon Press, 1954), p. 175.
3. H. Rosenberg, *Bureaucracy, Aristocracy, and Autocracy: The Prussian Experience, 1660–1815* (Boston: Beacon Press, 1966), p. 38.
4. Quoted in R. Ergang, *The Potsdam Fuhrer: Frederick William I, Father of Prussian Militarism* (New York: Octagon Books, 1972), pp. 85, 87.
5. Ibid., p. 43.
6. Quoted in R. A. Dorwart, *The Administrative Reforms of Frederick William I of Prussia* (Cambridge, Mass.: Harvard University Press, 1953), p. 226.
7. Quoted in Rosenberg, *Bureaucracy, Aristocracy, and Autocracy,* p. 40.
8. Quoted in N. V. Riasanovsky, *A History of Russia* (New York: Oxford University Press, 1963), p. 79.
9. Quoted in I. Grey, *Ivan III and the Unification of Russia* (New York: Collier Books, 1967), p. 42.
10. Both quoted in R. Pipes, *Russia Under the Old Regime* (New York: Charles Scribner's Sons, 1974), pp. 65, 85.
11. Quoted in Ergang, *The Potsdam Fuhrer,* p. 13.
12. Quoted in J. Summerson, in *The Eighteenth Century: Europe in the Age of Enlightenment,* ed. A. Cobban (New York: McGraw-Hill, 1969), p. 80.
13. Quoted in L. Mumford, *The Culture of Cities* (New York: Harcourt Brace Jovanovich, 1938), p. 97.

Suggested Reading

All of the books cited in the Notes are recommended. Carsten's is the best study on early Prussian history, and Rosenberg's is a masterful analysis of the social context of Prussian absolutism. In addition to Ergang's work, an exciting and critical biography of ramrod Frederick William I, there is G. Ritter, *Frederick the Great* (1968), a more sympathetic study of the talented son by one of Germany's most famous conservative historians. G. Craig, *The Politics of the Prussian Army, 1640–1945* (1964), expertly traces the great

(continued on page 592)

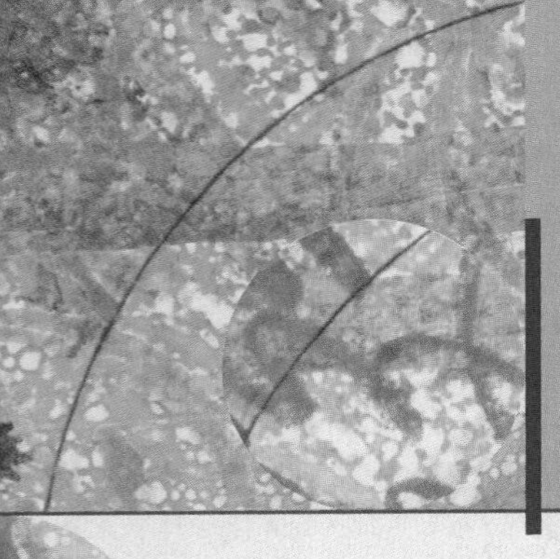

Listening to the Past

A Foreign Traveler in Russia

Russia in the seventeenth century remained a remote and mysterious land for western and even central Europeans, who had few direct contacts with the tsar's dominion. Knowledge of Russia came mainly from occasional travelers who had visited Muscovy and sometimes wrote accounts of what they had seen.

The most famous of these accounts was by the German Adam Olearius (ca 1599–1671), who was sent to Moscow by the duke of Holstein on three diplomatic missions in the 1630s. These missions ultimately proved unsuccessful, but they provided Olearius with a rich store of information for his Travels in Moscovy, *from which the following excerpts are taken. Published in German in 1647 and soon translated into several languages (but not Russian), Olearius's unflattering but well-informed study played a major role in shaping European ideas about Russia.*

The government of the Russians is what political theorists call a "dominating and despotic monarchy," where the sovereign, that is, the tsar or the grand prince who has obtained the crown by right of succession, rules the entire land alone, and all the people are his subjects, and where the nobles and princes no less than the common folk—townspeople and peasants—are his serfs and slaves, whom he rules and treats as a master treats his servants. . . .

If the Russians be considered in respect to their character, customs, and way of life, they are justly to be counted among the barbarians. . . . The vice of drunkenness is so common in this nation, among people of every station, clergy and laity, high and low, men and women, old and young, that when they are seen now and then lying about in the streets, wallowing in the mud, no attention is paid to it, as something habitual. If a cart driver comes upon such a drunken pig whom he happens to know, he shoves him onto his cart and drives him home, where he is paid his fare. No one ever refuses an opportunity to drink and to get drunk, at any time and in any place, and usually it is done with vodka. . . .

The Russians being naturally tough and born, as it were, for slavery, they must be kept under a harsh and strict yoke and must be driven to do their work with clubs and whips, which they suffer without impatience, because such is their station, and they are accustomed to it. Young and half-grown fellows sometimes come together on certain days and train themselves in fisticuffs, to accustom themselves to receiving blows, and, since habit is second nature, this makes blows given as punishment easier to bear. Each and all, they are slaves and serfs. . . .

Because of slavery and their rough and hard life, the Russians accept war readily and are well suited to it. On certain occasions, if need be, they reveal themselves as courageous and daring soldiers. . . .

Although the Russians, especially the common populace, living as slaves under a harsh yoke, can bear and endure a great deal out of love for their masters, yet if the pressure is beyond measure, then it can be said of them: "Patience, often wounded, finally turned into fury." A dangerous indignation results, turned not so much against their sovereign as against the lower authorities, especially if the people have been much oppressed by them and by their supporters and have not been protected by the higher authorities. And once they are aroused and enraged, it is not easy to appease them. Then, disregarding all dangers that may ensue, they resort to every kind of violence and behave like madmen. . . . They own little; most of them have no feather beds; they lie on cushions, straw, mats, or their clothes; they sleep on benches and, in winter, like the non-Germans [i.e., natives] in Livonia, upon the oven,

The brutality of serfdom is shown in this illustration from Olearius's *Travels in Muscovy. (University of Illinois Library, Champaign)*

which serves them for cooking and is flat on the top; here husband, wife, children, servants, and maids huddle together. In some houses in the countryside we saw chickens and pigs under the benches and the ovens. . . .

Russians are not used to delicate food and dainties; their daily food consists of porridge, turnips, cabbage, and cucumbers, fresh and pickled, and in Moscow mostly of big salt fish which stink badly, because of the thrifty use of salt, yet are eaten with relish. . . .

The Russians can endure extreme heat. In the bathhouse they stretch out on benches and let themselves be beaten and rubbed with bunches of birch twigs and wisps of bast (which I could not stand); and when they are hot and red all over and so exhausted that they can bear it no longer in the bathhouse, men and women rush outdoors naked and pour cold water over their bodies; in winter they even wallow in the snow and rub their skin with it as if it were soap; then they go back into the hot bathhouse. And since bathhouses are usually near rivers and brooks, they can throw themselves straight from the hot into the cold bath. . . .

Generally noble families, even the small nobility, rear their daughters in secluded chambers, keeping them hidden from outsiders; and a bridegroom is not allowed to have a look at his bride until he receives her in the bridal chamber. Therefore some happen to be deceived, being given a misshapen and sickly one instead of a fair one, and sometimes a kinswoman or even a maidservant instead of a daughter; of which there have been examples even among the highborn. No wonder therefore that often they live together like cats and dogs and that wife-beating is so common among Russians. . . .

In the Kremlin and in the city there are a great many churches, chapels, and monasteries, both within and without the city walls, over two thousand in all. This is so because every nobleman who has some fortune has a chapel built for himself, and most of them are of stone. The stone churches are round and vaulted inside. . . . They allow neither organs nor any other musical instruments in their churches, saying: Instruments that have neither souls nor life cannot praise God. . . .

In their churches there hang many bells, sometimes five or six, the largest not over two hundredweights. They ring these bells to summon people to church, and also when the priest during mass raises the chalice. In Moscow, because of the multitude of churches and chapels, there are several thousand bells, which during the divine service create such a clang and din that one unaccustomed to it listens in amazement.

Questions for Analysis

1. In what ways were all social groups in Russia similar, according to Olearius?
2. How did Olearius characterize the Russians in general? What supporting evidence did he offer for his judgment?
3. Does Olearius's account help explain Stenka Razin's rebellion? In what ways?
4. On the basis of these representative passages, why do you think Olearius's book was so popular and influential in central and western Europe?

Source: G. Vernadsky and R. T. Fisher, Jr., eds., *A Source Book for Russian History from Early Times to 1917*, vol. 1 (New Haven: Yale University Press, 1972), pp. 249–251.

influence of the military on the Prussian state over three hundred years. A. Corvisier, *Armies and Societies in Europe, 1494–1789* (1979), places military organization in a broad social framework. A good general account is provided in D. McKay and H. Scott, *The Rise of the Great Powers, 1648–1815* (1983). J. Gagliardo, *Germany Under the Old Regime, 1600–1790* (1991), is an impressive survey of developments in all the German states and provides an excellent bibliography. M. Hughes, *Early Modern Germany, 1477–1802* (1992), is also recommended. R. J. Evans, *The Making of the Habsburg Empire, 1550–1700* (1979), is an impressive achievement. C. Ingrao, *The Habsburg Monarchy, 1618–1815* (1994), is a superior synthesis with an up-to-date bibliography. J. Stoye, *The Siege of Vienna* (1964), is a fascinating account of the last great Ottoman offensive, which is also treated in the interesting study by P. Coles, *The Ottoman Impact on Europe, 1350–1699* (1968).

The Austro-Ottoman conflict is a theme of L. S. Stavrianos, *The Balkans Since 1453* (1977), and D. McKay's fine biography, *Prince Eugene of Savoy* (1978). On the Balkans, also see T. Stoianovich, *Balkan Worlds: The First and Last Europe* (1994), and the innovative M. Todorova, *Imaging the Balkans* (1997). M. Pinson, ed., *The Muslims of Bosnia-Herzegovina: Their Historic Development from the Middle Ages to the Dissolution of Yugoslavia* (1993), is a good introduction.

On eastern European peasants and serfdom, D. Chirot, ed., *The Origins of Backwardness in Eastern Europe: Economics and Politics from the Middle Ages Until the Twentieth Century* (1989), is a wide-ranging introduction, which may be compared with J. Blum, "The Rise of Serfdom in Eastern Europe," *American Historical Review* 62 (July 1957): 807–836. Wolfe, cited in the Notes, argues provocatively that the French philosophes of the eighteenth century were the first to divide Europe into a backward east and a more advanced west. E. Levin, *Sex and Society in the World of the Orthodox Slavs, 900–1700* (1989), carries family history to eastern Europe. R. Mousnier, *Peasant Uprisings in Seventeenth-Century France, Russia, and China* (1970), is a fine comparative study. Another valuable comparative study, analyzing the political struggle between rulers and nobles in Poland, Hungary, Latvia, Moldavia, and Ukraine, is O. Subtelny, *Domination in Eastern Europe* (1986). Also see L. and M. Frey, *Societies in Upheaval: Insurrections in France, Hungary and Spain in the Early Eighteenth Century* (1989). J. Blum, *Lord and Peasant in Russia from the Ninth to the Nineteenth Century* (1961), provides a good look at conditions in rural Russia, and P. Avrich, *Russian Rebels, 1600–1800* (1972), treats some of the violent peasant upheavals those conditions produced. R. Hellie, *Enserfment and Military Change in Muscovy* (1971), is outstanding, as is A. Yanov's provocative *Origins of Autocracy: Ivan the Terrible in Russian History* (1981). In addition to the fine surveys by Pipes and Riasanovsky cited in the Notes, J. Billington, *The Icon and the Axe* (1970), is a stimulating history of early Russian intellectual and cultural developments, such as the great split in the church. M. Raeff, *Origins of the Russian Intelligentsia* (1966), skillfully probes the mind of the Russian nobility in the eighteenth century. James Cracraft, ed., *Peter the Great Transforms Russia,* 3d ed. (1991), groups interpretive essays by leading scholars, and B. Lincoln, *Sunlight at Midnight: St. Petersburg and the Rise of Modern Russia* (2001), captures the spirit of Peter's new northern capital. B. H. Sumner, *Peter the Great and the Emergence of Russia* (1962), is a fine brief introduction. These works may be compared with the brilliant biography by Russia's greatest prerevolutionary historian, V. Klyuchevsky, *Peter the Great* (English trans., 1958), and with N. Riasanovsky, *The Image of Peter the Great in Russian History and Thought* (1985). G. Vernadsky and R. Fisher, eds., *A Source Book of Russian History from Early Times to 1917,* 3 vols. (1972), is an invaluable, highly recommended collection of documents and contemporary writings. S. Baron, ed., *The Travels of Olearius in Seventeenth-Century Russia* (1967), is also highly recommended.

R. Harbison, *Reflections on the Baroque* (2001), is a well-illustrated and imaginative integration of ideas and the arts, while G. Hersey, *Architecture and Geometry in the Age of the Baroque* (2001), explores the link between architecture and scientific thinking. Also recommended on art and architecture are E. Hempel, *Baroque Art and Architecture in Central Europe* (1965); G. Hamilton, *The Art and Architecture of Russia* (1954); and N. Pevsner, *An Outline of European Architecture,* 6th ed. (1960). J. Cracraft has written an outstanding two-volume study of the artistic and cultural transformation associated with Peter the Great, *The Petrine Revolution in Russian Architecture* (1988) and *The Petrine Revolution in Russian Imagery* (1997).

Voltaire, the renowned Enlightenment thinker, leans forward on the left to exchange ideas and witty conversation with Frederick the Great, king of Prussia. *(Bildarchiv Preussischer Kulturbesitz)*

chapter

18 Toward a New World-view

chapter outline

- The Scientific Revolution
- The Enlightenment
- The Enlightenment and Absolutism

Most people are not philosophers, but they nevertheless have a basic outlook on life, a more or less coherent **world-view.** At the risk of oversimplification, one may say that the world-view of medieval and early modern Europe was primarily religious and theological. Not only did Christian or Jewish teachings form the core of people's spiritual and philosophical beliefs, but religious teachings also permeated all the rest of human thought and activity. Political theory relied on the divine right of kings, for example, and activities ranging from marriage and divorce to business and eating habits were regulated by churches and religious doctrines.

In the course of the eighteenth century, this religious and theological world-view underwent a fundamental transformation among the European upper and comfortable classes. Economically secure and increasingly well educated, these privileged groups of preindustrial Europe interacted with talented writers and as a result often came to see the world primarily in secular and scientific terms. And while few individuals abandoned religious beliefs altogether, the role of churches and religious thinking in earthly affairs and in the pursuit of knowledge was substantially reduced. Among many in the aristocracy and solid middle classes, a new critical, scientific, and very "modern" world-view took shape.

- Why did this momentous change occur?
- How did this new world-view affect the way people thought about society and human relations?
- What impact did this new way of thinking have on political developments and monarchical absolutism?

This chapter will focus on these questions.

The Scientific Revolution

The foremost cause of the change in world-view was the scientific revolution. Modern science—precise knowledge of the physical world based on the union of experimental observations with sophisticated mathematics—crystallized in the seventeenth century. Whereas science had been secondary and subordinate in medieval intellectual life, it became independent and even primary for many educated people in the eighteenth century.

The emergence of modern science was a development of tremendous long-term significance. A noted historian has even said that the scientific revolution of the late sixteenth and seventeenth centuries "outshines everything since the rise of Christianity and reduces the Renaissance and Reformation to the rank of mere episodes, mere internal displacements, within the system of medieval Christendom." The scientific revolution was "the real origin both of the modern world and the modern mentality."[1] This statement is an exaggeration, but not much of one. Of all the great civilizations, only that of the West developed modern science. With the scientific revolution Western society began to acquire its most distinctive traits.

Though historians agree that the scientific revolution was enormously important, they approach it in quite different ways. Some scholars believe that the history of scientific achievement in this period had its own basic "internal" logic and that "nonscientific" factors had quite limited significance. These scholars write brilliant, often highly technical, intellectual studies, but they neglect the broader historical context. Other historians stress "external" economic, social, and religious factors, brushing over the scientific developments themselves. Historians of science now realize that these two approaches need to be brought together. Therefore, let us examine the milestones on the fateful march toward modern science first and then search for the nonscientific influences along the route.

Scientific Thought in 1500

Since developments in astronomy and physics were at the heart of the scientific revolution, one must begin with the traditional European conception of the universe and movement within it. In the early 1500s, traditional European ideas about the universe were still based primarily on the ideas of Aristotle, the great Greek philosopher of the fourth century B.C. These ideas had gradually been recovered during the Middle Ages and then brought into harmony with Christian doctrines by medieval theologians. According to this revised Aristotelian view, a motionless earth was fixed at the center of the universe. Around it moved ten separate transparent crystal spheres. In the first eight spheres were embedded, in turn, the moon, the sun, the five known planets, and the fixed stars. Then followed two spheres added during the Middle Ages to account for slight changes in the positions of the stars over the centuries. Beyond the tenth sphere was heaven, with the throne of God and the souls of the saved. Angels kept the spheres moving in perfect circles.

Aristotle's views, suitably revised by medieval philosophers, also dominated thinking about physics and motion on earth. Aristotle had distinguished sharply between the world of the celestial spheres and that of the earth—the sublunar world. The spheres consisted of a perfect, incorruptible "quintessence," or fifth essence. The sublunar world, however, was made up of four imperfect, changeable elements. The "light" elements (air and fire) naturally moved upward, while the "heavy" elements (water and earth) naturally moved downward. These natural directions of motion did not always prevail, however, for elements were often mixed together and could be affected by an outside force such as a human being. Aristotle and his followers also believed that a uniform force moved an object at a constant speed and that the object would stop as soon as that force was removed.

Aristotle's ideas about astronomy and physics were accepted with minor revisions for two thousand years, and with good reason. First, they offered an understandable, commonsense explanation for what the eye actually saw. Second, Aristotle's science as interpreted by Christian theologians fit neatly with Christian doctrines. It established a home for God and a place for Christian souls. It put human beings at the center of the universe and made them the critical link in a "great chain of being" that stretched from the throne of God to the most lowly insect on earth. Thus science was primarily a branch of theology, and it reinforced religious thought. At the same time, medieval "scientists" were already providing closely reasoned explanations of the universe, explanations they felt were worthy of God's perfect creation.

The Copernican Hypothesis

The desire to explain and thereby glorify God's handiwork led to the first great departure from the medieval system. This departure was the work of the Polish clergyman and astronomer Nicolaus Copernicus (1473–1543). As a young man, Copernicus studied church law and astronomy in various European universities. He saw how professional astronomers still depended for their most accurate calculations on the work of Ptolemy, the last great ancient astronomer, who had lived in Alexandria in the second century A.D. Ptolemy's achievement had been to work out complicated rules to explain the minor irregularities in the movement of the planets. These rules enabled stargazers and astrologers to track the planets with greater precision. Many people then (and now) believed

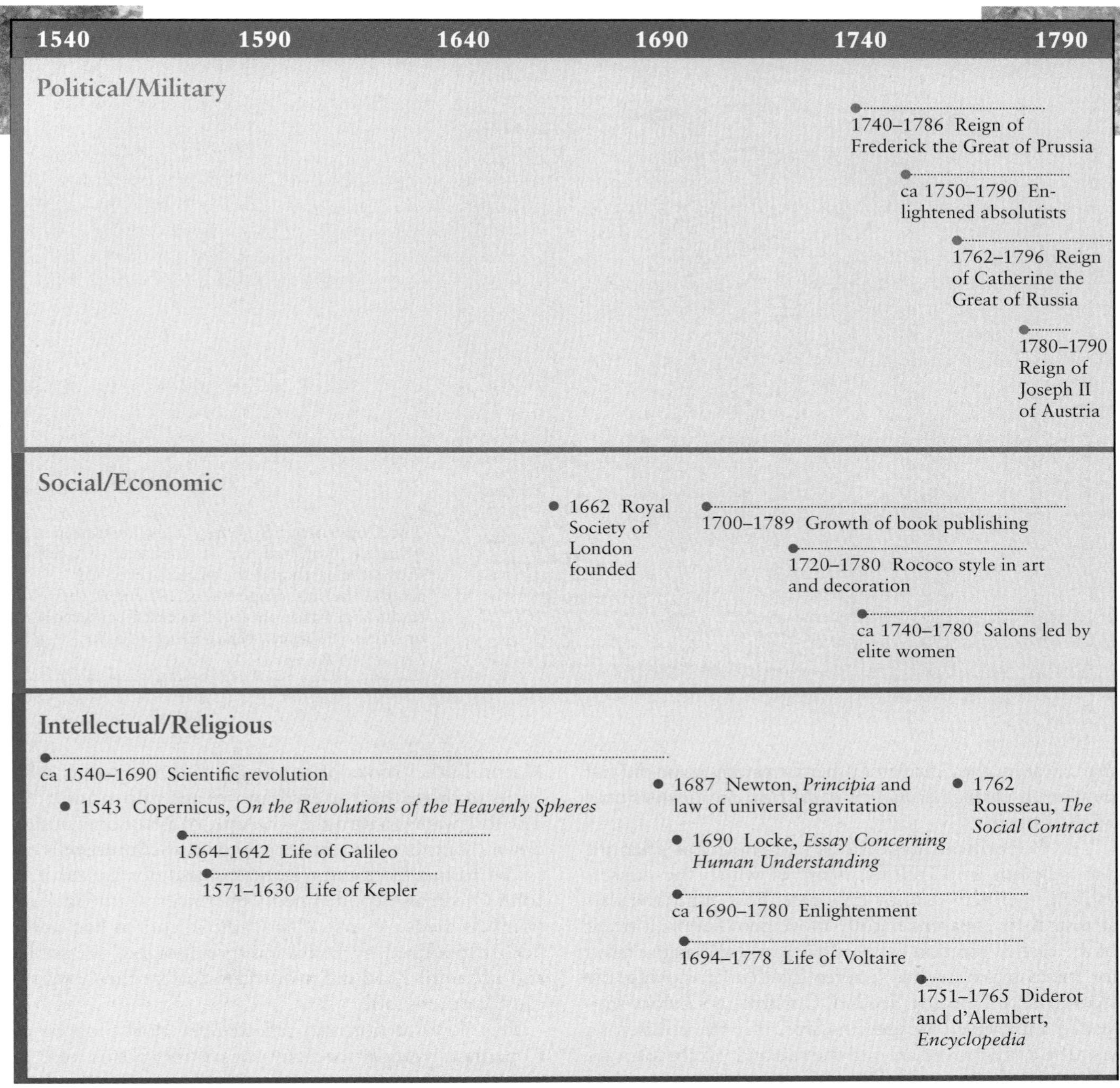

that the changing relationships between planets and stars influenced and even determined the future.

The young Copernicus was uninterested in astrology and felt that Ptolemy's cumbersome and occasionally inaccurate rules detracted from the majesty of a perfect Creator. He preferred an old Greek idea being discussed in Renaissance Italy: that the sun, rather than the earth, was at the center of the universe. Finishing his university studies and returning to a church position in East Prussia, Copernicus worked on his hypothesis from 1506 to 1530. Never questioning the Aristotelian belief in crystal spheres or the idea that circular motion was most perfect and divine, Copernicus theorized that the stars and planets, including the earth, revolved around a fixed sun. Yet Copernicus was a cautious

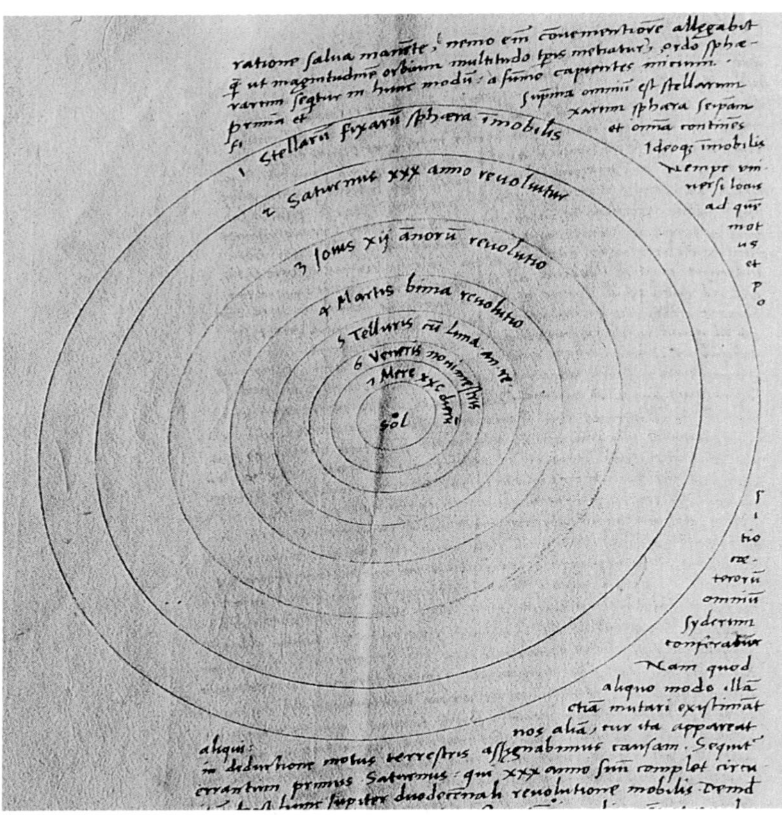

The Copernican System This illustration from the published text of Copernicus's treatise shows the earth and the planets revolving around the sun. Copernicus challenged the traditional astronomy and its earth-centered universe. *(Collegium Maius, Cracow/Erich Lessing/Art Resource, NY)*

man. Fearing the ridicule of other astronomers, he did not publish his *On the Revolutions of the Heavenly Spheres* until 1543, the year of his death.

The **Copernican hypothesis** had enormous scientific and religious implications, many of which the conservative Copernicus did not anticipate. First, it put the stars at rest, their apparent nightly movement simply a result of the earth's rotation. Thus it destroyed the main reason for believing in crystal spheres capable of moving the stars around the earth. Second, Copernicus's theory suggested a universe of staggering size. If in the course of a year the earth moved around the sun and yet the stars appeared to remain in the same place, then the universe was unthinkably large or even infinite. Finally, by characterizing the earth as just another planet, Copernicus destroyed the basic idea of Aristotelian physics—that the earthly world was quite different from the heavenly one. Where, then, was the realm of perfection? Where were heaven and the throne of God?

The Copernican hypothesis quickly brought sharp attacks from religious leaders, especially Protestants. Hearing of Copernicus's work even before it was published, Martin Luther spoke of him as the "new astrologer who wants to prove that the earth moves and goes round. . . . The fool wants to turn the whole art of astronomy upside down." Luther noted that "as the Holy Scripture tells us, so did Joshua bid the sun stand still and not the earth."[2] John Calvin also condemned Copernicus. Catholic reaction was milder at first. The Catholic church had never been hypnotized by literal interpretations of the Bible, and not until 1616 did it officially declare the Copernican hypothesis false.

This slow reaction also reflected the slow progress of Copernicus's theory for many years. Other events were almost as influential in creating doubts about traditional astronomical ideas. In 1572 a new star appeared and shone very brightly for almost two years. The new star, which was actually a distant exploding star, made an enormous impression on people. It seemed to contradict the idea that the heavenly spheres were unchanging and therefore perfect. In 1577 a new comet suddenly moved through the sky, cutting a straight path across the supposedly impenetrable crystal spheres. It was time, as a typical scientific writer put it, for "the radical renovation of astronomy."[3]

From Brahe to Galileo

One astronomer who agreed was Tycho Brahe (1546–1601). Born into a leading Danish noble family and earmarked for a career in government, Brahe was at an early age tremendously impressed when a partial eclipse of the sun occurred exactly as expected. It seemed to him "something divine that men could know the motions of the stars so accurately that they were able a long time beforehand to predict their places and relative positions."[4] Completing his studies abroad and returning to Denmark, Brahe established himself as Europe's leading astronomer with his detailed observations of the new star of 1572. Aided by generous grants from the king of Denmark, Brahe built the most sophisticated observatory of his day. For twenty years he meticulously observed the stars and planets with the naked eye. An imposing man who had lost a piece of his nose in a duel and replaced it with a special bridge of gold and silver alloy, a noble who exploited his peasants arrogantly and approached the heavens humbly, Brahe's great contribution was his mass of data. His limited understanding of mathematics prevented him, however, from making much sense out of his data. Part Ptolemaic, part Copernican, he believed that all the planets revolved around the sun and that the entire group of sun and planets revolved in turn around the earth-moon system.

It was left to Brahe's brilliant young assistant, Johannes Kepler (1571–1630), to go much further. Kepler was a medieval figure in many ways. Coming from a minor German noble family and trained for the Lutheran ministry, he long believed that the universe was built on mystical mathematical relationships and a musical harmony of the heavenly bodies. Working and reworking Brahe's mountain of observations in a staggering sustained effort after the Dane's death, this brilliant mathematician eventually went beyond mystical intuitions.

Kepler formulated three famous laws of planetary motion. First, building on Copernican theory, he demonstrated in 1609 that the orbits of the planets around the sun are elliptical rather than circular. Second, he demonstrated that the planets do not move at a uniform speed in their orbits. Third, in 1619 he showed that the time a planet takes to make its complete orbit is precisely related to its distance from the sun. Kepler's contribution was monumental. Whereas Copernicus had speculated, Kepler proved mathematically the precise relations of a sun-centered (solar) system. His work demolished the old system of Aristotle and Ptolemy, and in his third law he came close to formulating the idea of universal gravitation.

While Kepler was unraveling planetary motion, a young Florentine named Galileo Galilei (1564–1642) was challenging all the old ideas about motion. Like so many early scientists, Galileo was a poor nobleman first marked for a religious career. However, he soon became fascinated by mathematics. A brilliant student, Galileo became a professor of mathematics in 1589 at age twenty-five. He proceeded to examine motion and mechanics in a new way. Indeed, his great achievement was the elaboration and consolidation of the **experimental method.** That is, rather than speculate about what might or should happen, Galileo conducted controlled experiments to find out what actually *did* happen.

In his famous acceleration experiment, he showed that a uniform force—in this case, gravity—produced a uniform acceleration. Here is how Galileo described his path-breaking method and conclusion in his *Two New Sciences:*

A piece of wooden moulding . . . was taken; on its edge was cut a channel a little more than one finger in breadth. Having made this groove very straight, smooth and polished, and having lined it with parchment, also as smooth and polished as possible, we rolled along it a hard, smooth and very round bronze ball. . . . Noting . . . the time required to make the descent . . . we now rolled the ball only one-quarter the length of the channel; and having measured the time of its descent, we found it precisely one-half of the former. . . . In such experiments [over many distances], repeated a full hundred times, we always found that the spaces traversed were to each other as the squares of the times, and that this was true for all inclinations of the plane.[5]

With this and other experiments, Galileo also formulated the **law of inertia.** Rest was not the natural state of objects. Rather, an object continues in motion forever unless stopped by some external force. Aristotelian physics was in a shambles.

In the tradition of Brahe, Galileo also applied the experimental method to astronomy. On hearing details about the invention of the telescope in Holland, Galileo made one for himself and trained it on the heavens. He quickly discovered the first four moons of Jupiter, which clearly suggested that Jupiter could not possibly be embedded in any impenetrable crystal sphere. This discovery provided new evidence for the Copernican theory, in which Galileo already believed.

Galileo then pointed his telescope at the moon. He wrote in 1610 in *Siderus Nuncius:*

I feel sure that the moon is not perfectly smooth, free from inequalities, and exactly spherical, as a large school of philosophers considers with regard to the moon and the

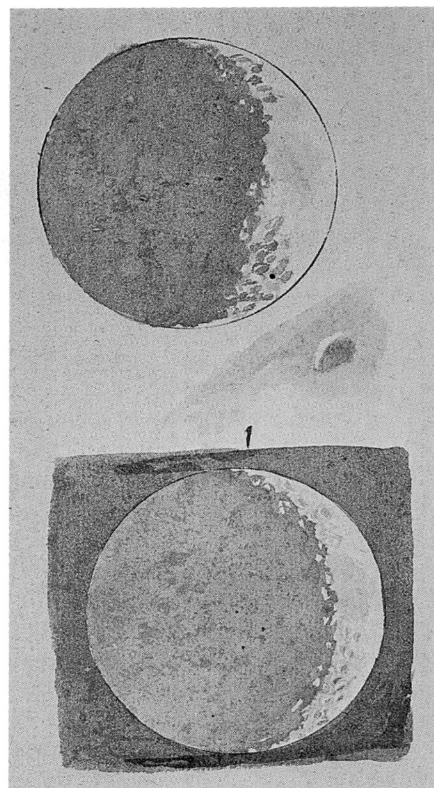

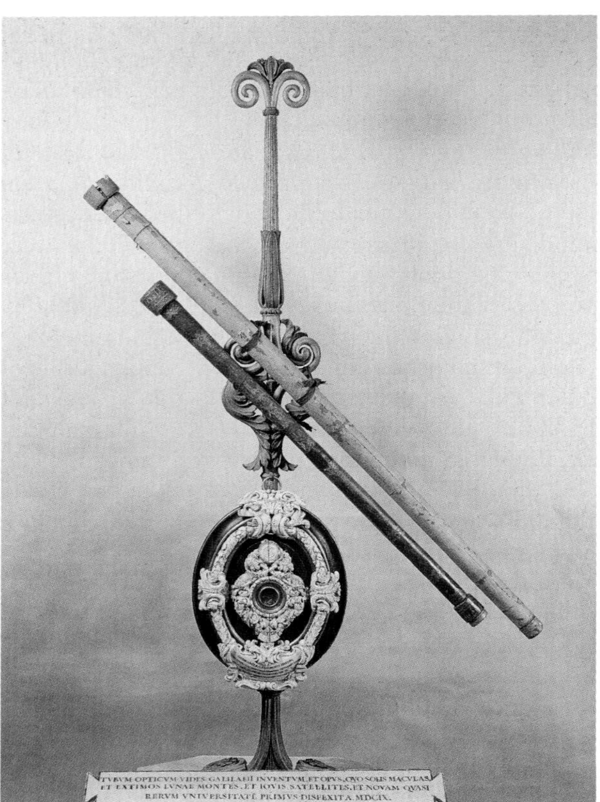

Galileo's Paintings of the Moon When Galileo published the results of his telescopic observations of the moon, he added these paintings to illustrate the marvels he had seen. Galileo made two telescopes, which are shown here. The larger one magnifies fourteen times, the smaller twenty times. *(Biblioteca Nazionale Centrale, Florence/Art Resource, NY; Museum of Science, Florence/Art Resource, NY)*

other heavenly bodies. On the contrary, it is full of inequalities, uneven, full of hollows and protuberances, just like the surface of the earth itself, which is varied. . . . The next object which I have observed is the essence or substance of the Milky Way. By the aid of a telescope anyone may behold this in a manner which so distinctly appeals to the senses that all the disputes which have tormented philosophers through so many ages are exploded by the irrefutable evidence of our eyes, and we are freed from wordy disputes upon the subject. For the galaxy is nothing else but a mass of innumerable stars planted together in clusters.[6]

Reading these famous lines, one feels a crucial corner in Western civilization being turned. The traditional religious and theological world-view, which rested on determining and accepting the proper established authority, was beginning to give way in certain fields to a critical, modern scientific method. This new method of learning and investigating was the greatest accomplishment of the entire scientific revolution, for it proved capable of great extension. A historian investigating documents of the past, for example, is not so different from a Galileo studying stars and rolling balls.

Galileo was employed in Florence by the Medici grand dukes of Tuscany, and his work eventually aroused the ire of some theologians. The issue was presented in 1624 to Pope Urban VIII, who permitted Galileo to write about different possible systems of the world as long as he did not presume to judge which one actually existed. After the publication in Italian of his widely read *Dialogue on the Two Chief Systems of the World* in 1632, which openly lampooned the traditional views of Aristotle and Ptolemy and defended those of Copernicus, Galileo was tried for heresy by the papal Inquisition. Imprisoned and threatened with torture, the aging Galileo recanted, "renouncing and cursing" his Copernican errors. Of minor importance in the development of science, Galileo's trial later became for some writers the perfect symbol of the inherent conflict between religious belief and scientific knowledge.

Newton's Synthesis

The accomplishments of Kepler, Galileo, and other scientists had taken effect by about 1640. The old astronomy and physics were in ruins, and several fundamental breakthroughs had been made. The new findings had not, however, been fused together in a new synthesis, a single explanatory system that would comprehend motion both on earth and in the skies. That synthesis, which prevailed until the twentieth century, was the work of Isaac Newton (1642–1727).

Newton was born into lower English gentry and attended Cambridge University. A genius who spectacularly united the experimental and theoretical-mathematical sides of modern science, Newton was also fascinated by alchemy. He sought the elixir of life and a way to change base metals into gold and silver. Not without reason did the twentieth-century economist John Maynard Keynes call Newton the "last of the magicians." Newton was also intensely religious. He was far from being the perfect rationalist so endlessly eulogized by writers in the eighteenth and nineteenth centuries.

Of his intellectual genius and incredible powers of concentration there can be no doubt, however. Arriving at some of his most basic ideas about physics in 1666 at age twenty-four, but unable to prove these theories mathematically, he attained a professorship and studied optics for many years. In 1684 Newton returned to physics for eighteen extraordinarily intensive months. For weeks on end he seldom left his room except to read his lectures. His meals were sent up, but he usually forgot to eat them, his mind fastened like a vise on the laws of the universe. He opened the third book of his immortal *Mathematical Principles of Natural Philosophy,* published in Latin in 1687 and generally known as the *Principia,* with these lines:

In the preceding books I have laid down the principles of philosophy [that is, science]. . . . These principles are the laws of certain motions, and powers or forces, which chiefly have respect to philosophy. . . . It remains that from the same principles I now demonstrate the frame of the System of the World.

Newton made good his grandiose claim. His towering accomplishment was to integrate in a single explanatory system the astronomy of Copernicus, as corrected by Kepler's laws, with the physics of Galileo and his predecessors. Newton did this by means of a set of mathematical laws that explain motion and mechanics. These laws of dynamics are complex, and it took scientists and engineers two hundred years to work out all their implications. Nevertheless, the key feature of the Newtonian synthesis was the **law of universal gravitation.** According to this law, every body in the universe attracts every other body in the universe in a precise mathematical relationship, whereby the force of attraction is proportional to the quantity of matter of the objects and inversely proportional to the square of the distance between them. The whole universe—from Kepler's elliptical orbits to Galileo's rolling balls—was unified in one majestic system.

Isaac Newton This portrait suggests the depth and complexity of the great genius. Is the powerful mind behind those piercing eyes thinking of science or of religion, or perhaps of both? *(Scala/Art Resource, NY)*

Causes of the Scientific Revolution

With a charming combination of modesty and self-congratulation, Newton once wrote, "If I have seen further [than others], it is by standing on the shoulders of Giants."[7] Surely the path from Copernicus to Newton confirms the "internal" view of the scientific revolution as a product of towering individual genius. The problems of science were inherently exciting, and solution of those problems was its own reward for inquisitive, high-powered minds. Yet there were certainly broader causes as well.

First, the long-term contribution of medieval intellectual life and medieval universities to the scientific revolution was much more considerable than historians unsympathetic to the Middle Ages once believed. By the thirteenth century, permanent universities with professors and large student bodies had been established in western Europe to train the lawyers, doctors, and church leaders that society required. By 1300 philosophy had taken its place alongside law, medicine, and theology. Medieval philosophers developed a limited but real independence from theologians and a sense of free inquiry. They nobly pursued a body of knowledge and tried to arrange it meaningfully by means of abstract theories.

Within this framework, science was able to emerge as a minor but distinct branch of philosophy. In the fourteenth and fifteenth centuries, leading universities established new professorships of mathematics, astronomy, and physics (natural philosophy) within their faculties of philosophy. Although the prestige of the new fields was low among both professors and students, rational, critical thinking was applied to scientific problems by a permanent community of scholars. And an outlet existed for the talents of a Galileo or a Newton: all the great pathfinders either studied or taught at universities.

Second, the Renaissance also stimulated scientific progress. The recovery of the finest works of Greek mathematics—a byproduct of Renaissance humanism's ceaseless search for the knowledge of antiquity—greatly improved European mathematics well into the early seventeenth century. The recovery of more texts also showed that classical mathematicians had their differences; Europeans were thus forced to resolve, if possible, these ancient controversies by means of their own efforts. Finally, the Renaissance pattern of patronage, especially in Italy, was often scientific as well as artistic and humanistic. Various rulers and wealthy business people supported scientific investigations, as the Medicis of Florence supported those of Galileo.

The navigational problems of long sea voyages in the age of overseas expansion were a third factor in the scientific revolution. Ship captains on distant shores needed to be able to chart their positions as accurately as possible so that reliable maps could be drawn and the risks of international trade reduced. As early as 1484, the king of Portugal appointed a commission of mathematicians to perfect tables to help seamen find their latitude. This resulted in the first European navigation manual.

The problem of fixing longitude was much more difficult. In England the government and the great capitalistic trading companies turned to science and scientific education in an attempt to solve this pressing practical problem. When the famous Elizabethan financier Sir Thomas Gresham left a large amount of money to establish Gresham College in London, he stipulated that three of the college's seven professors had to concern themselves exclusively with scientific subjects. The professor of astronomy was directed to teach courses on the science of navigation. A seventeenth-century popular ballad took note of the new college's calling:

This college will the whole world measure
Which most impossible conclude,
And navigation make a pleasure
By finding out the longitude.[8]

At Gresham College scientists had, for the first time in history, an important, honored role in society. They enjoyed close ties with top officials of the Royal Navy and with leading merchants and shipbuilders. Gresham College became the main center of scientific activity in England in the first half of the seventeenth century. The close tie between practical men and scientists also led to the establishment in 1662 of the Royal Society of London, which published scientific papers and sponsored scientific meetings.

Navigational problems were also critical in the development of many new scientific instruments, such as the telescope, barometer, thermometer, pendulum clock, microscope, and air pump. Better instruments, which permitted more accurate observations, often led to important new knowledge. Galileo with his telescope was by no means unique.

Better instruments were part of a fourth factor in the scientific revolution, the development of better ways of obtaining knowledge about the world. Two important thinkers, Francis Bacon (1561–1626) and René Descartes (1596–1650), represented key aspects of this improvement in scientific methodology.

The English politician and writer Francis Bacon was the greatest early propagandist for the new experimental method. Rejecting the Aristotelian and medieval method of using speculative reasoning to build general theories, Bacon argued that new knowledge had to be pursued through empirical, experimental research. The researcher who wants to learn more about leaves or rocks should not speculate about the subject but rather collect a multitude of specimens and then compare and analyze them, he said. General principles will then emerge. Bacon's contribution was to formalize the empirical method, which had already been used by Brahe and Galileo, into the general theory of inductive reasoning known as **empiricism.**

Bacon claimed that the empirical method would result not only in more knowledge but also in highly practical, useful knowledge. According to Bacon, scientific discoveries like those so avidly sought at Gresham College would bring about much greater control over the physical environment and make people rich and nations powerful. Thus Bacon helped provide a radically new and effective justification for private and public support of scientific inquiry.

The French philosopher René Descartes was a true genius who made his first great discovery in mathematics. As a twenty-three-year-old soldier serving in the Thirty Years' War, he experienced on a single night in 1619 a life-changing intellectual vision. Descartes saw that there was a perfect correspondence between geometry and algebra and that geometrical, spatial figures could be expressed as algebraic equations and vice versa. A major step forward in the history of mathematics, Descartes's discovery of analytic geometry provided scientists with an important new tool.

Descartes's greatest achievement was to develop his initial vision into a whole philosophy of knowledge and science. He decided it was necessary to doubt everything that could reasonably be doubted and then, as in geometry, to use deductive reasoning from self-evident principles to ascertain scientific laws. Descartes's reasoning ultimately reduced all substances to "matter" and "mind"—that is, to the physical and the spiritual. His view of the world as consisting of two fundamental entities is known as **Cartesian dualism.** Descartes was a profoundly original and extremely influential thinker.

Bacon's inductive experimentalism and Descartes's deductive, mathematical reasoning are combined in the modern scientific method, which began to crystallize in

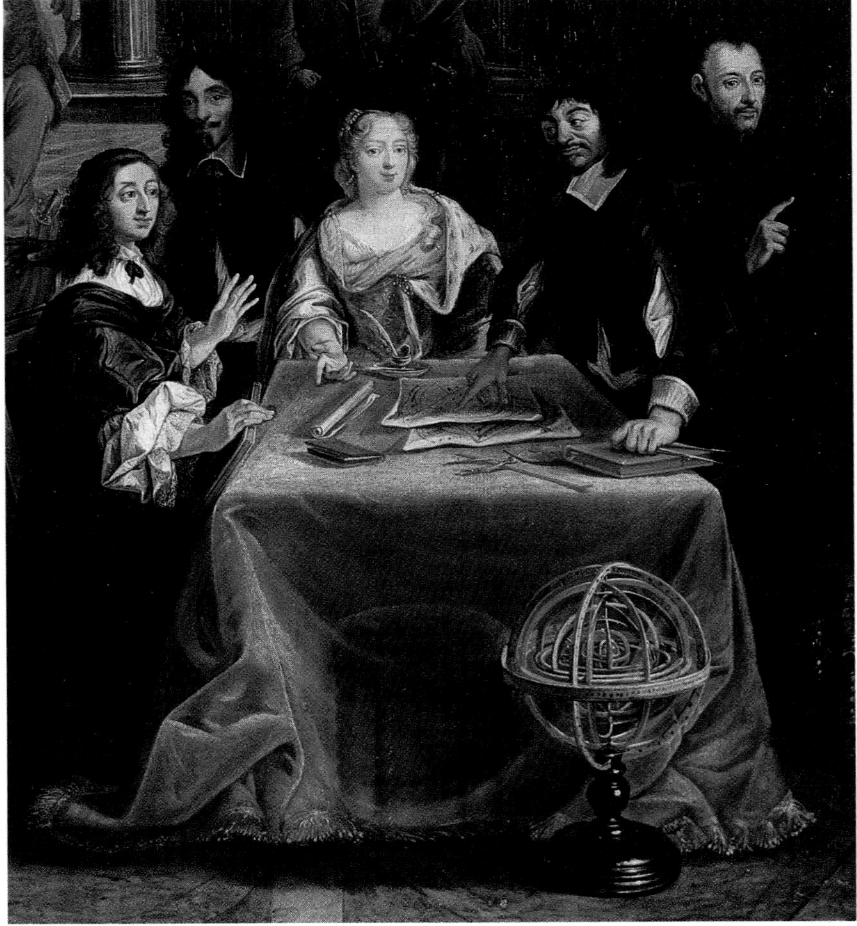

Descartes in Sweden Queen Christina of Sweden encouraged art and science, and she invited many foreign artists and scholars to visit her court. She speaks here with French mathematician and philosopher René Descartes in 1649. The daughter of Protestant hero Gustavus Adolphus, Christina rejected marriage, abdicated in 1654, converted to Catholicism, and died in Rome. *(Versailles/Bulloz)*

The Observatory at Nuremberg The quest for scientific knowledge in the seventeenth century was already an expensive undertaking that required teamwork and government support, as this encyclopedic illustration suggests. Nuremberg was a historic center of commerce and culture in southern Germany, and its observatory played a pioneering role in early astronomical advance. *(Kunstsammlungen der Veste Coburg)*

the late seventeenth century. Neither man's extreme approach was sufficient by itself. Bacon's inability to appreciate the importance of mathematics and his obsession with practical results clearly showed the limitations of antitheoretical empiricism. Likewise, some of Descartes's positions—he believed, for example, that it was possible to deduce the whole science of medicine from first principles—demonstrated the inadequacy of rigid, dogmatic rationalism. Thus the modern scientific method has joined precise observations and experimentalism with the search for general laws that may be expressed in rigorously logical, mathematical language.

Finally, there is the question of the role of religion in the development of science. Just as some historians have argued that Protestantism led to the rise of capitalism, others have concluded that Protestantism was a fundamental factor in the rise of modern science. Protestantism, particularly in its Calvinist varieties, supposedly made scientific inquiry a question of individual conscience and not of religious doctrine. The Catholic church, in contrast, supposedly suppressed scientific theories that conflicted with its teachings and thus discouraged scientific progress.

The truth of the matter is more complicated. *All* religious authorities—Catholic, Protestant, and Jewish—opposed the Copernican system to a greater or lesser extent until about 1630, by which time the scientific revolution was definitely in progress. The Catholic church was initially less hostile than Protestant and Jewish religious leaders, and Italian scientists played a crucial role in scientific progress right up to the trial of Galileo in 1633. Thereafter, the Counter-Reformation church became more hostile to science, a change that helped account for the decline of science in Italy (but not in Catholic France) after 1640. At the same time, Protestant countries such as the Netherlands and Denmark became quite "proscience," especially if the country lacked a strong religious authority capable of imposing religious orthodoxy on scientific questions.

This was certainly the case with Protestant England after 1630. English religious conflicts became so intense that the authorities could not impose religious unity on anything, including science. Significantly, the forerunners of the Royal Society agreed to discuss only "neutral" scientific questions so as not to come to blows over closely related religious and political disputes. The work of Bacon's many followers during Oliver Cromwell's commonwealth helped solidify the neutrality and independence of science. Bacon advocated the experimental approach precisely because it was open-minded and independent of any preconceived religious or philosophical ideas. Neutral and useful, science became an accepted part of life and developed rapidly in England after about 1640.

Some Consequences of the Scientific Revolution

The rise of modern science had many consequences, some of which are still unfolding. First, it went hand in hand with the rise of a new and expanding social group—the international scientific community. Members of this community were linked together by common interests and shared values as well as by journals and the learned scientific societies founded in many countries in the later seventeenth and the eighteenth centuries. Expansion of knowledge was the primary goal of this community, and scientists' material and psychological rewards depended on their success in this endeavor. Thus science became quite competitive, and even more scientific advance was inevitable.

Second, the scientific revolution introduced not only new knowledge about nature but also a new and revolutionary way of obtaining such knowledge—the modern scientific method. In addition to being both theoretical and experimental, this method was highly critical, and it differed profoundly from the old way of getting knowledge about nature. It refused to base its conclusions on tradition and established sources, on ancient authorities and sacred texts.

The scientific revolution had few consequences for economic life and the living standards of the masses until the late eighteenth century at the very earliest. True, improvements in the techniques of navigation facilitated overseas trade and helped enrich leading merchants. But science had relatively few practical economic applications, and the hopes of the early Baconians were frustrated. The close link between theoretical, or pure, science and applied technology, which we take for granted today, simply did not exist in the eighteenth century. Thus the scientific revolution of the seventeenth century was first and foremost an intellectual revolution. For more than a hundred years its greatest impact was on how people thought and believed.

The Enlightenment

The scientific revolution was the single most important factor in the creation of the new world-view of the eighteenth-century **Enlightenment.** This world-view, which has played a large role in shaping the modern mind, grew out of a rich mix of ideas. These ideas were diverse and often conflicting, for the talented (and not-so-talented) writers who espoused them competed vigorously for the attention of a growing public of well-educated but fickle readers, who remained a small minority of the population. Despite this diversity, three central concepts stand at the core of Enlightenment thinking.

The most important and original idea of the Enlightenment was that the methods of natural science could and should be used to examine and understand all aspects of life. This was what intellectuals meant by *reason,* a favorite word of Enlightenment thinkers. Nothing was to be accepted on faith. Everything was to be submitted to the rational, critical, scientific way of thinking. This **rationalism** often brought the Enlightenment into a head-on conflict with established churches, which rested their beliefs on the special authority of the Bible and Christian theology. A second important Enlightenment concept was that the scientific method was capable of discovering the laws of human society as well as those of nature. Thus was social science born. Its birth led to the third key idea, that of **progress.** Armed with the proper method of discovering the laws of human existence, Enlightenment thinkers believed that it was at least possible for human beings to create better societies and better people. Their belief was strengthened by some modest improvements in economic and social life during the eighteenth century.

The Enlightenment was therefore profoundly secular. It revived and expanded the Renaissance concentration on worldly explanations. In the course of the eighteenth century, the Enlightenment had a profound impact on the thought and culture of the urban middle classes and the aristocracy. It did not, however, have much appeal for the urban poor and the peasants, who were preoccupied with the struggle for survival and who often resented the Enlightenment attack on traditional popular beliefs (see Chapters 19 and 20).

The Emergence of the Enlightenment

Loosely united by certain key ideas, the European Enlightenment was a broad intellectual and cultural movement that gained strength gradually and did not reach its maturity until about 1750. Yet it was the generation that came of age between the publication of Newton's *Principia* in 1687 and the death of Louis XIV in 1715 that tied the crucial knot between the scientific revolution and a new outlook on life. Talented writers of that generation popularized hard-to-understand scientific achievements for the educated elite.

The most famous and influential popularizer was a versatile French man of letters, Bernard de Fontenelle (1657–1757). He set out to make science witty and entertaining for a broad nonscientific audience—as easy to read as a novel. This was a tall order, but Fontenelle largely succeeded. His most famous work, *Conversations on the Plurality of Worlds* (1686), begins with two elegant figures walking in the gathering shadows of a large park. One is a woman, a sophisticated aristocrat, and the other is her friend, perhaps even her lover. They gaze at the stars, and their talk turns to a passionate discussion of . . . astronomy! He confides that "each star may well be a different world," then gently stresses how error is giving way to truth. At one point he explains:

> *There came on the scene . . . one Copernicus, who made short work of all those various circles, all those solid skies, which the ancients had pictured to themselves. . . . Fired with the noble zeal of a true astronomer, he took the earth and spun it very far away from the center of the universe, where it had been installed, and in that center he put the sun, which had a far better title to the honor.*[9]

Rather than despair at this dismissal of traditional understanding, Fontenelle's lady rejoices in the knowledge that the human mind is capable of making great progress.

Popularizing Science The frontispiece illustration of Fontenelle's *Conversations on the Plurality of Worlds* invites the reader to share the pleasures of astronomy with an elegant lady and an entertaining teacher. The drawing shows the planets revolving around the sun. *(By permission of the Syndics of Cambridge University Library)*

This concept of progress was essentially a creation of the later seventeenth century. Medieval and Reformation thinkers had been concerned primarily with sin and salvation. The humanists of the Renaissance had emphasized worldly matters, but they had looked backward. They had believed it might be possible to equal the magnificent accomplishments of the ancients, but they did not ask for more. Fontenelle and like-minded writers had come to believe that at least in science and mathematics, their era had gone far beyond antiquity. Progress, at least intellectual progress, was very possible.

Fontenelle and other writers of his generation were also instrumental in bringing science into conflict with religion. This was a major innovation because many seventeenth-century scientists, both Catholic and Protestant, believed that their work exalted God. They did not draw antireligious implications from their scientific findings. The greatest scientist of them all, Isaac Newton, was a devout, if unorthodox, Christian who saw all of his studies as directed toward explaining God's message.

Fontenelle, in contrast, was skeptical about absolute truth and cynical about the claims of organized religion. Since such unorthodox views could not be stated openly in an absolute monarchy like Louis XIV's France, Fontenelle made his point through subtle editorializing about science. His depiction of the cautious Copernicus as a self-conscious revolutionary was typical. In *Eulogies of Scientists,* Fontenelle exploited with endless variations the fundamental theme of rational, progressive scientists versus prejudiced, reactionary priests.

The progressive and antireligious implications that writers such as Fontenelle drew from the scientific revolution reflected a very real crisis in European thought at the end of the seventeenth century. This crisis had its roots in several intellectual uncertainties and dissatisfactions, of which the demolition of Aristotelian-medieval science was only one.

A second uncertainty involved the whole question of religious truth. The destructive wars of religion that culminated in the Thirty Years' War (1618–1648) had been fought, in part, because religious freedom was an intolerable idea in Europe in the early seventeenth century. Both Catholics and Protestants had believed that religious truth was absolute and therefore worth fighting and dying for. Most Catholics and Protestants also believed that a strong state required unity in religious faith. Yet the disastrous results of the many attempts to impose such religious unity, such as Louis XIV's brutal expulsion of the French Huguenots in 1685, led some people to ask if ideological conformity in religious matters was really necessary. Others skeptically asked if religious truth could ever be known with absolute certainty and concluded that it could not.

The most famous of these skeptics was Pierre Bayle (1647–1706), a French Huguenot who despised Louis XIV and found refuge in the Netherlands. A teacher by profession and a crusading journalist by inclination, Bayle took full advantage of the toleration and intellectual freedom of his adopted land. He critically examined the religious beliefs and persecutions of the past in his *Historical and Critical Dictionary,* written in French and published in the Netherlands in 1697. Demonstrating that human beliefs had been extremely varied and very often mistaken, Bayle concluded that nothing can ever be known beyond all doubt. In religion as in philosophy, humanity's best hope was open-minded toleration. Bayle's **skepticism** was very influential. Reprinted frequently in the Netherlands and in England, his four-volume *Dictionary* was found in more private libraries of eighteenth-century France than any other book.

The rapidly growing travel literature on non-European lands and cultures was a third cause of uncertainty. In the wake of the great discoveries, Europeans were learning that the peoples of China, India, Africa, and the Americas all had their own very different beliefs and customs. Europeans shaved their faces and let their hair grow. Turks shaved their heads and let their beards grow. In Europe a man bowed before a woman to show respect. In Siam a man turned his back on a woman when he met her because it was disrespectful to look directly at her. Countless similar examples discussed in the travel accounts helped change the perspective of educated Europeans. They began to look at truth and morality in relative, rather than absolute, terms. If anything was possible, who could say what was right or wrong?

A fourth cause and manifestation of European intellectual turmoil was John Locke's epoch-making *Essay Concerning Human Understanding*. Published in 1690—the same year Locke published his famous *Second Treatise of Civil Government* (see page 554)—Locke's essay brilliantly set forth a new theory about how human beings learn and form their ideas. In doing so, he rejected the prevailing view of Descartes, who had held that all people are born with certain basic ideas and ways of thinking. Locke insisted that all ideas are derived from experience. The human mind at birth is like a blank tablet, or **tabula rasa,** on which the environment writes the individual's understanding and beliefs. Human development is therefore determined by education and social institutions, for good or for evil. Locke's *Essay Concerning Human Understanding* passed through many editions and translations. It was, along with Newton's *Principia,* one of the dominant intellectual inspirations of the Enlightenment.

The Philosophes and the Public

By the time Louis XIV died in 1715, many of the ideas that would soon coalesce into the new world-view had been assembled. Yet Christian Europe was still strongly attached to its traditional beliefs, as witnessed by the powerful revival of religious orthodoxy in the first half of the eighteenth century (see pages 681–683). By the outbreak of the American Revolution in 1775, however, a large portion of western Europe's educated elite had embraced many of the new ideas. This acceptance was the work of one of history's most influential groups of intellectuals, the **philosophes.** It was the philosophes who proudly and effectively proclaimed that they, at long last, were bringing the light of knowledge to their ignorant fellow creatures in an Age of Enlightenment.

Philosophe is the French word for "philosopher," and it was in France that the Enlightenment reached its highest development. There were at least three reasons for this. First, French was the international language of the educated classes in the eighteenth century, and the education of the rich and the powerful across Europe often lay in the hands of French tutors espousing Enlightenment ideas. France's cultural leadership was reinforced by the fact that it was still the wealthiest and most populous country in Europe.

Second, after the death of Louis XIV, French absolutism and religious orthodoxy remained strong, but not too strong. Critical books were often banned by the censors, and their authors were sometimes jailed or exiled—but not tortured or burned. Intellectual radicals battled against powerful opposition in France, but they did not face the overwhelming restraints generally found in eastern and east-central Europe.

Third, the French philosophes were indeed philosophers, asking fundamental philosophical questions about the meaning of life, God, human nature, good and evil, and cause and effect. But in the tradition of Bayle and Fontenelle, they were not content with abstract arguments or ivory-tower speculations. They were determined to reach and influence all the French (and European) economic and social elites, many of which were joined together in the eighteenth-century concept of the educated or enlightened public, or simply **the public.**

As a wealth of recent scholarship has shown, the public was quite different from the great majority of the population, which was known as the common people, or simply "the people." French philosophe Jean le Rond d'Alembert (1717–1783) characteristically made a sharp distinction between "the truly enlightened public" and "the blind and noisy multitude."[10] A leading scholar has even concluded that the differences between the upper and comfortable middling groups that made up the French public were "insignificant" in comparison with the great gulf between the public and the common people.[11] Above all, the philosophes believed that the great majority of the common people were doomed to superstition and confusion because they lacked the money and leisure to look beyond their bitter struggle with grinding poverty (see pages 630–633).

Suspicious of the people but intensely committed to reason, reform, and slow, difficult progress, the great philosophes and their imitators were not free to write as they wished, since it was illegal in France to criticize openly either church or state. Their most radical works had to circulate in manuscript form. Knowing that direct attacks would probably be banned or burned, the philosophes wrote novels and plays, histories and philosophies, dictionaries and encyclopedias, all filled with satire and double meanings to spread their message to the public.

One of the greatest philosophes, the baron de Montesquieu (1689–1755), brilliantly pioneered this approach in *The Persian Letters,* an extremely influential social satire published in 1721. Montesquieu's work consisted of amusing letters supposedly written by Persian travelers, who see European customs in unique ways and thereby cleverly criticize existing practices and beliefs.

Having gained fame by using wit as a weapon against cruelty and superstition, Montesquieu settled down on his family estate to study history and politics. His interest was partly personal, for, like many members of the high French nobility, he was dismayed that royal absolutism had triumphed in France under Louis XIV. But Montesquieu was also inspired by the example of the physical sciences, and he set out to apply the critical method to the problem of government in *The Spirit of Laws* (1748). The result was a complex comparative study of republics, monarchies, and despotisms—a great pioneering inquiry in the emerging social sciences.

Showing that forms of government were shaped by history, geography, and customs, Montesquieu focused on the conditions that would promote liberty and prevent tyranny. He argued that despotism could be avoided if there was a **separation of powers,** with political power divided and shared by a variety of classes and legal estates holding unequal rights and privileges. A strong, independent upper class was especially important, according to Montesquieu, because in order to prevent the abuse of power, "it is necessary that by the arrangement of things, power checks power." Admiring greatly the English balance of power among the king, the houses of Parliament, and the independent courts, Montesquieu believed that in France the thirteen high courts—the *parlements*—were frontline defenders of liberty against royal despotism. Apprehensive about the uneducated poor, Montesquieu was clearly no democrat, but his theory of separation of powers had a great impact on France's wealthy, well-educated elite. The constitutions of the young United States in 1789 and of France in 1791 were based in large part on this theory.

The most famous and in many ways most representative philosophe was François Marie Arouet, who was known by the pen name Voltaire (1694–1778). In his long career, this son of a comfortable middle-class family wrote more than seventy witty volumes, hobnobbed with kings and queens, and died a millionaire because of shrewd business speculations. His early career, however, was turbulent. In 1717 Voltaire was imprisoned for eleven months in the Bastille in Paris for insulting the regent of France. In 1726 a barb from his sharp tongue led a great French nobleman to have him beaten and arrested. This experience made a deep impression on Voltaire. All his life he struggled against legal injustice and unequal treatment before the law. Released from prison after promising to leave the country, Voltaire lived in England for three years and came to share Montesquieu's enthusiasm for English institutions.

Returning to France and soon threatened again with prison in Paris, Voltaire had the great fortune of meeting Gabrielle-Emilie Le Tonnelier de Breteuil, marquise du Châtelet (1706–1749), an intellectually gifted woman from the high aristocracy with a passion for science. Inviting Voltaire to live in her country house at Cirey in Lorraine and becoming his long-time companion (under the eyes of her tolerant husband), Madame du Châtelet studied physics and mathematics and published scientific articles and translations.

Perhaps the finest representative of a small number of elite Frenchwomen and their scientific accomplishments during the Enlightenment, Madame du Châtelet suffered nonetheless because of her gender. Excluded on principle from the Royal Academy of Sciences and from stimulating interchange with other scientists because she was a woman, she depended on private tutors for instruction and became uncertain of her ability to make important scientific discoveries. Madame du Châtelet therefore concentrated on spreading the ideas of others, and her translation with an accompanying commentary of Newton's *Principia* into French for the first (and only) time was her greatest work. But she, who had patiently explained Newton's complex mathematical proofs to Europe's foremost philosophe, had no doubt that women's limited scientific contributions in the past were due to limited and unequal education. She once wrote that if she were a ruler, "I would reform an abuse which cuts off, so to speak, half the human race. I would make women participate in all the rights of humankind, and above all in those of the intellect."[12]

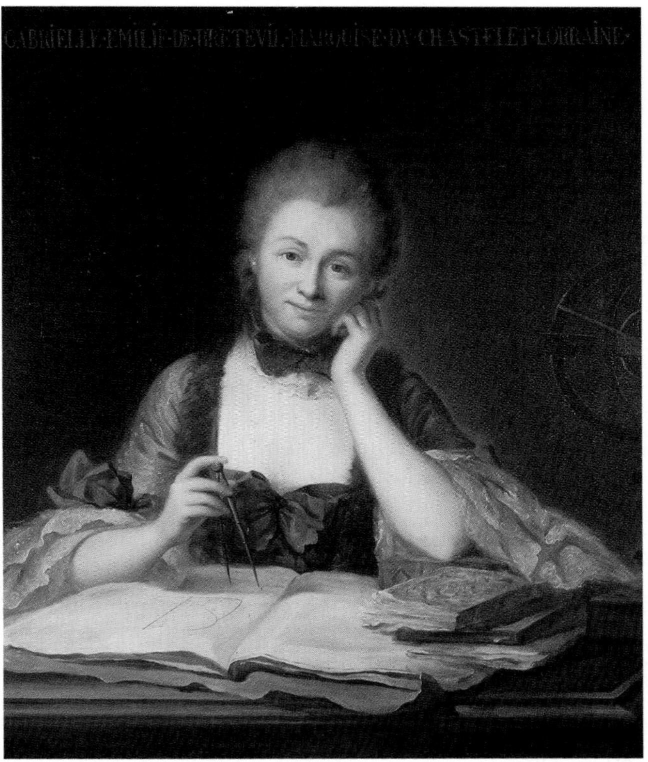

Madame du Châtelet was fascinated by the new world system of Isaac Newton. She helped to spread Newton's ideas in France by translating his *Principia* and by influencing Voltaire, her companion for fifteen years until her death. *(Giraudon/Art Resource, NY)*

While living at Cirey, Voltaire wrote various works praising England and popularizing English scientific progress. Newton, he wrote, was history's greatest man, for he had used his genius for the benefit of humanity. "It is," wrote Voltaire, "the man who sways our minds by the prevalence of reason and the native force of truth, not they who reduce mankind to a state of slavery by force and downright violence . . . that claims our reverence and admiration."[13] In the true style of the Enlightenment, Voltaire mixed the glorification of science and reason with an appeal for better individuals and institutions.

Yet like almost all of the philosophes, Voltaire was a reformer, not a revolutionary, in social and political matters.

He was eventually appointed royal historian in 1743, and his *Age of Louis XIV* portrayed Louis as the dignified leader of his age. Voltaire also began a long correspondence with Frederick the Great and, after the death of his beloved Emilie, accepted Frederick's invitation to come brighten up the Prussian court in Berlin. The two men later quarreled, but Voltaire always admired Frederick as a free thinker and an enlightened monarch.

Unlike Montesquieu, Voltaire pessimistically concluded that the best one could hope for in the way of government was a good monarch, since human beings "are very rarely worthy to govern themselves." Nor did he believe in social and economic equality in human affairs. The idea of making servants equal to their masters was "absurd and impossible." The only realizable equality, Voltaire thought, was that "by which the citizen only depends on the laws which protect the freedom of the feeble against the ambitions of the strong."[14]

Voltaire's philosophical and religious positions were much more radical. In the tradition of Bayle, Voltaire's voluminous writings challenged, often indirectly, the Catholic church and Christian theology at almost every point. Though he was considered by many devout Christians to be a shallow blasphemer, Voltaire's religious views were influential and quite typical of the mature Enlightenment. Voltaire clearly believed in God, but his was a distant, deistic God, the great Clockmaker who built an orderly universe and then stepped aside and let it run. Above all, Voltaire and most of the philosophes hated all forms of religious intolerance, which they believed often led to fanaticism and savage, inhuman action. Simple piety and human kindness—as embodied in Christ's great commandments to "love God and your neighbor as yourself"—were religion enough, even Christianity enough, as may be seen in Voltaire's famous essay on religion. (See the feature "Listening to the Past: Voltaire on Religion" on pages 626–627.)

The ultimate strength of the French philosophes lay in their number, dedication, and organization. The philosophes felt keenly that they were engaged in a common undertaking that transcended individuals. Their greatest and most representative intellectual achievement was, quite fittingly, a group effort—the seventeen-volume *Encyclopedia: The Rational Dictionary of the Sciences, the Arts, and the Crafts,* edited by Denis Diderot (1713–1784) and Jean le Rond d'Alembert. Diderot and d'Alembert made a curious pair. Diderot began his career as a hack writer, first attracting attention with a skeptical tract on religion that was quickly burned by the judges of Paris. D'Alembert was one of Europe's leading scientists and mathematicians, the orphaned and illegitimate son of celebrated aristocrats. From different circles and with different interests, the two men set out to find coauthors who would examine the rapidly expanding whole of human knowledge. Even more fundamentally, they set out to teach people how to think critically and objectively about all matters. As Diderot said, he wanted the *Encyclopedia* to "change the general way of thinking."[15]

The editors of the *Encyclopedia* had to conquer innumerable obstacles. After the appearance in 1751 of the first volume, which dealt with such controversial subjects as atheism, the soul, and blind people (all words beginning with *a* in French), the government temporarily banned publication. The pope later placed the work on the Catholic church's index of forbidden works and pronounced excommunication on all who read or bought it. The timid publisher watered down some of the articles in the last ten volumes without the editors' consent in an attempt to appease the authorities. Yet Diderot's unwavering belief in the importance of his mission held the encyclopedists together for fifteen years, and the enormous work was completed in 1765. Hundreds of thousands of articles by leading scientists, famous writers, skilled workers, and progressive priests treated every aspect of life and knowledge.

Not every article was daring or original, but the overall effect was little short of revolutionary. Science and the industrial arts were exalted, religion and immortality questioned. Intolerance, legal injustice, and out-of-date social institutions were openly criticized. More generally, the writers of the *Encyclopedia* showed that human beings could use the process of reasoning to expand human knowledge. The encyclopedists were convinced that greater knowledge would result in greater human happiness, for knowledge was useful and made possible economic, social, and political progress. The *Encyclopedia* was widely read, especially in less expensive reprint editions published in Switzerland, and it was extremely influential in France and throughout western Europe as well. It summed up the new world-view of the Enlightenment.

The Later Enlightenment

After about 1770, the harmonious unity of the philosophes and their thought began to break down. As the new world-view became increasingly accepted by the educated public, some thinkers sought originality by exaggerating certain Enlightenment ideas to the exclusion of others. These latter-day philosophes often built rigid, dogmatic systems.

In his *System of Nature* (1770) and other works, the wealthy German-born but French-educated Baron Paul

Illustrating the *Encyclopedia:* "The Print Shop" Diderot wanted to present all valid knowledge—that is, knowledge based on reason and the senses and not on tradition and authority. This plate, one of 3,000 detailed illustrations accompanying the 70,000 essays in the *Encyclopedia,* shows (*from left to right*) compositors setting type, arranging lines, and blocking down completed forms. Printed sheets dry above. *(Division of Rare & Manuscript Collections, Cornell University Library)*

d'Holbach (1723–1789) argued that human beings were machines completely determined by outside forces. Free will, God, and immortality of the soul were foolish myths. D'Holbach's aggressive atheism and determinism, which were coupled with deep hostility toward Christianity and all other religions, dealt the unity of the Enlightenment movement a severe blow. Deists such as Voltaire, who believed in God but not in established churches, were repelled by the inflexible atheism they found in the *System of Nature*. They saw in it the same dogmatic intolerance they had been fighting all their lives.

D'Holbach published his philosophically radical works anonymously in the Netherlands to avoid possible prosecution in France, and in his lifetime he was best known to the public as the generous patron and witty host of writers and intellectuals. At his twice-weekly dinner parties, an inner circle of regulars who knew the baron's secret exchanged ideas with aspiring philosophes and distinguished visitors. One of the most important was Scottish philosopher David Hume (1711–1776), whose carefully argued skepticism had a powerful long-term influence.

Building on Locke's teachings on learning, Hume argued that the human mind is really nothing but a bundle of impressions. These impressions originate only in sense experiences and our habits of joining these experiences together. Since our ideas ultimately reflect only our sense experiences, our reason cannot tell us anything about questions that cannot be verified by sense experience (in the form of controlled experiments or mathematics), such as the origin of the universe or the existence of God. Paradoxically, Hume's rationalistic inquiry ended up undermining the Enlightenment's faith in the power of reason.

Another French aristocrat, Marie-Jean Caritat, the marquis de Condorcet (1743–1794), transformed the Enlightenment belief in gradual, hard-won progress into fanciful utopianism. In his *Progress of the Human Mind,* written in 1793 during the French Revolution (see Chapter 21), Condorcet hypothesized and tracked nine stages of human progress that had already occurred and predicted that the tenth would bring perfection. Ironically, Condorcet wrote this work while fleeing for his life. Caught and condemned by revolutionary extremists, he preferred death by his own hand to the blade of the guillotine.

Other thinkers and writers after about 1770 began to attack the Enlightenment's faith in reason, progress, and moderation. The most famous of these was the Swiss Jean-Jacques Rousseau (1712–1778), a brilliant and difficult thinker, an appealing but neurotic individual. Born into a poor family of watchmakers in Geneva, Rousseau went to Paris and was greatly influenced by Diderot and Voltaire. Always extraordinarily sensitive and suspicious, Rousseau came to believe that his philosophe friends and the women of the Parisian salons were plotting against him. In the mid-1750s, he broke with them personally and intellectually, living thereafter as a lonely outsider with his uneducated common-law wife and going in his own highly original direction.

Like other Enlightenment thinkers, Rousseau was passionately committed to individual freedom. Unlike them, however, he attacked rationalism and civilization as destroying, rather than liberating, the individual. Warm, spontaneous feeling had to complement and correct cold intellect. Moreover, the basic goodness of the individual and the unspoiled child had to be protected from the cruel refinements of civilization. These ideas greatly influenced the early romantic movement (see pages 766–770), which rebelled against the culture of the Enlightenment in the late eighteenth century. They also had a powerful impact on the development of child psychology and modern education.

Rousseau's contribution to political theory in *The Social Contract* (1762) was equally significant. His contribution was based on two fundamental concepts: the general will and popular sovereignty. According to Rousseau, the **general will** is sacred and absolute, reflecting the common interests of all the people, who have displaced the monarch as the holder of sovereign power. The general will is not necessarily the will of the majority, however. At times the general will may be the authentic, long-term needs of the people as correctly interpreted by a farseeing minority. Little noticed before the French Revolution, Rousseau's concept of the general will appealed greatly to democrats and nationalists after 1789. The concept has also been used since 1789 by many dictators claiming that they, rather than some momentary majority of the voters, represent the general will and thus the true interests of democracy and the sovereign masses.

Urban Culture and Public Opinion

The writings and press campaigns of the philosophes were part of a profound cultural transformation. The object of impressive ongoing research and scholarly debate in recent years, this transformation had several interrelated aspects.

Of great importance, the European market for books grew dramatically in the eighteenth century. In Germany the number of new titles appearing annually grew substantially and at an accelerating rate, from roughly six hundred new titles in 1700 to about eleven hundred in 1764 and about twenty-six hundred in 1780. Well-studied France, which was indicative of general European trends, witnessed an explosive growth in book consumption. A modest increase in literacy was partly responsible, as the popular classes bought more penny tracts and escapist stories (see pages 669–671). Yet the solid middle class, the clergy, and the aristocracy accounted for most of the change. The number of books in the hands of these privileged groups increased eightfold to tenfold between the 1690s and the 1780s, when the private library of the typical noble contained more than three hundred volumes. Moreover, a much more avid French reader purchased a totally transformed product. The number of religious and devotional books published legally in Paris declined precipitously, from one-half of the total in the 1690s to one-tenth of the total in the 1780s. History and law held constant, while the proportion of legally published books treating the arts and sciences surged.

Even these figures understate the shift in French taste because France's unpredictable but pervasive censorship caused many books to be printed abroad and then smuggled back into the country for "under-the-cloak" sale. Experts believe that perhaps the majority of French books produced between 1750 and 1789 came from publishing companies located outside France. These publishers, located primarily in the Netherlands and Switzerland but also in England and a few small west German principalities, also smuggled forbidden books in French and other languages into the absolutist states of central, southern, and eastern Europe. The recently discovered catalogues of some of these foreign publishers reveal a massive presence of the famous French philosophes, reaffirming the philosophes' central role in the spread of critical secular attitudes.

The illegal book trade in France also featured an astonishing growth of scandalmongering denunciations of high political figures and frankly pornographic works. These literary forms frequently came together in scathing pornographic accounts of the moral and sexual depravity

Selling Books, Promoting Ideas This appealing bookshop with its intriguing ads for the latest works offers to put customers "Under the Protection of Minerva," the Roman goddess of wisdom. Large packets of books sit ready for shipment to foreign countries. Book consumption surged in the eighteenth century. *(Musée des Beaux-Arts, Dijon/Art Resource, NY)*

of the French court, allegedly mired in luxury, perversion, and adultery. A favorite theme was the way that some beautiful but immoral aristocratic women used their sexual charms to gain power over weak rulers and high officials, thereby corrupting the process of government. Spurred by repeated royal directives, the French police did its best to stamp out this underground literature, but new slanders kept cropping up, like the wild tabloid fantasies at checkout counters in today's supermarkets.

Reading more books on many more subjects, the educated public in France and throughout Europe increasingly approached reading in a new way. The result was what some German scholars have called a "reading revolution." The old style of reading in Europe had been centered on sacred texts, full of authority, inspiring reverence and teaching earthly duty and obedience to God. Reading had been patriarchal and communal, with the father of the family slowly reading the text aloud and the audience savoring each word. Now reading involved many texts, which were constantly changing and commanded no special respect. Reading became individual, silent, and rapid. The well-educated classes were reading insatiably, skeptically, and carelessly. Subtle but profound, the reading revolution was closely linked to the rise of a critical world-view.

As the reading public developed, it joined forces with the philosophes to call for the autonomy of the printed word. Immanuel Kant (1724–1804), a professor in East Prussia and the greatest German philosopher of the age, argued in 1784 that if serious thinkers were granted the freedom to exercise their reason publicly in print, then enlightenment would almost surely follow. Kant suggested that Prussia's Frederick the Great was an enlightened monarch precisely because he permitted such freedom of the press.

Outside of Prussia, the Netherlands, and Great Britain, however, the philosophes and the public resorted to discussion and social interchange in order to circumvent censorship and create an autonomous cultural sphere. Indeed, sparkling conversation in private homes spread Enlightenment ideas to Europe's upper middle class and aristocracy. Paris set the example, and other French and European cities followed. In Paris a number of talented and often rich women presided over regular social gatherings of the great and near-great in their elegant private drawing rooms, or **salons.** There they encouraged a d'Alembert and a Fontenelle to exchange witty, uncensored observations on literature, science, and philosophy with great aristocrats, wealthy middle-class financiers, high-ranking officials, and noteworthy foreigners. Thus talented hostesses brought the various French elites together and mediated the public's freewheeling examination of Enlightenment thought.

Elite women also exercised an unprecedented feminine influence on artistic taste. Soft pastels, ornate interiors, sentimental portraits, and starry-eyed lovers protected by hovering cupids were all hallmarks of the style they favored. This style, known as rococo, was popular throughout Europe in the eighteenth century. It has been argued that feminine influence in the drawing room went hand in hand with the emergence of polite society and the general attempt to civilize a rough military nobility. Similarly, some philosophes championed greater rights and expanded education for women, claiming that the position and treatment of women were the best indicators of a society's level of civilization and decency.[16] To be sure, for these male philosophes greater rights for women did not mean equal rights, and the philosophes were not particularly disturbed by the fact that elite women remained legally subordinate to men in economic and political affairs. Elite women lacked many rights, but so did most men.

One of the most famous salons was that of Madame Geoffrin, the unofficial godmother of the *Encyclopedia*. Having lost her parents at an early age, the future Madame Geoffrin was married at fifteen by her well-meaning grandmother to a rich and boring businessman of forty-eight. After dutifully raising her children, Madame

Enlightenment Culture was elegant, intellectual, and international. Here the seven-year-old Austrian child prodigy Wolfgang Amadeus Mozart (1756–1791) plays his own composition at an "English tea" given by the Princess de Conti near Paris. Mozart's phenomenal creative powers lasted a lifetime and he produced a vast range of symphonies, operas, and chamber music. *(Réunion des Musées Nationaux/Art Resource, NY)*

Geoffrin broke out of her gilded cage. With the aid of an aristocratic neighbor and in spite of her husband's loud protests, she developed a twice-weekly salon that counted Fontenelle and Montesquieu among its regular guests. Inheriting a large fortune after her husband's death, Madame Geoffrin gave the encyclopedists generous financial aid and helped save their enterprise from collapse. Corresponding with the king of Sweden and Catherine the Great of Russia, Madame Geoffrin remained her own woman, a practicing Christian who would not tolerate attacks on the church in her house.

The salons seem to have functioned as informal schools where established hostesses bonded with younger women and passed skills on to them. One talented young woman who received such help was Julie de Lespinasse. Eventually forming her own highly informal salon and attracting the keenest minds in France and Europe, Lespinasse epitomized the skills of the Enlightenment hostess. As one philosophe wrote:

> *She could unite the different types, even the most antagonistic, sustaining the conversation by a well-aimed phrase, animating and guiding it at will. . . . Politics, religion, philosophy, news: nothing was excluded. Her circle met daily from five to nine. There one found men of all ranks in the State, the Church, and the Court, soldiers and foreigners, and the leading writers of the day.*[17]

As this passage suggests, the salons created an independent cultural realm freed from religious dogma and political censorship. There a diverse but educated public could debate issues and form its own ideas, its own *public opinion*. And all who were educated and civilized had equal rights in the elaboration of this new and powerful force. Thus the salons graciously united members of the intellectual, economic, and social elites. In such an atmosphere, the philosophes, the French nobility, and the prosperous middle classes intermingled and increasingly influenced one another. Thinking critically about almost any question became fashionable and flourished alongside hopes for human progress through greater knowledge and enlightened public opinion.

The Enlightenment and Absolutism

How did the Enlightenment influence political developments? To this important question there is no easy answer. On the one hand, the French philosophes and kindred spirits in most continental countries were primarily interested in converting people to critical, scientific thinking and were not particularly concerned with politics. On the other hand, such thinking naturally led to political criticism and interest in political reform as both possible and desirable. Some Enlightenment thinkers, led by the nobleman Montesquieu, argued for curbs on monarchical power in order to promote liberty.

Until the American Revolution, however, most Enlightenment thinkers outside of England and the Netherlands believed that political change could best come from above—from the ruler—rather than from below, especially in central and eastern Europe. Royal absolutism was a fact of life, and the kings and queens of Europe's leading states clearly had no intention of giving up their great power. Therefore, the philosophes and their sympathizers realistically concluded that a benevolent absolutism offered the best opportunities for improving society. Critical thinking was turning the art of good government into an exact science. It was necessary only to educate and "enlighten" the monarch, who could then make good laws and promote human happiness. Enlightenment thinkers also turned toward rulers because rulers seemed to be listening, treating them with respect and seeking their advice. Finally, the philosophes distrusted "the people." They believed that the common people were deluded by superstitions and driven by violent passions, little children in need of firm parental guidance.

Encouraged and instructed by the philosophes, many absolutist rulers of the later eighteenth century tried to govern in an "enlightened" manner. Yet the actual programs and accomplishments of these rulers varied greatly. It is necessary to examine the evolution of monarchical absolutism at close range before trying to form any overall judgment regarding the Enlightenment's effect and the meaning of what historians have often called the **enlightened absolutism** of the later eighteenth century.

Enlightenment teachings inspired European rulers in small as well as large states in the second half of the eighteenth century. Absolutist princes and monarchs in several west German and Italian states, as well as in Scandinavia, Spain, and Portugal, proclaimed themselves more enlightened. A few smaller states were actually the most successful in making reforms, perhaps because their rulers were not overwhelmed by the size and complexity of their realms. Denmark, for example, carried out an extensive and progressive land reform in the 1780s that practically abolished serfdom and gave Danish peasants secure tenure on their farms. Yet by far the most influential of the new-style monarchs were in Prussia, Russia, and Austria, and they deserve primary attention.

Frederick the Great of Prussia

Frederick II (r. 1740–1786), commonly known as Frederick the Great, built masterfully on the work of his father, Frederick William I (see pages 575–576). This was somewhat surprising, for, like many children with tyrannical parents, he rebelled against his family's wishes in his early years. Rejecting the crude life of the barracks, Frederick embraced culture and literature, even writing poetry and fine prose in French, a language his father detested. After trying unsuccessfully to run away in 1730 at age eighteen, he was virtually imprisoned and compelled to watch as his companion in flight was beheaded at his father's command. Yet like many other rebellious youths, Frederick eventually reached a reconciliation with his father, and by the time he came to the throne ten years later, Frederick was determined to use the splendid army that his father had left him.

Therefore, when the ruler of Austria, Charles VI, also died in 1740 and his young and charismatic daughter, Maria Theresa, inherited the Habsburg dominions, Frederick suddenly and without warning invaded her rich, mainly German province of Silesia. This action defied solemn Prussian promises to respect the Pragmatic Sanction, which guaranteed Maria Theresa's succession. Maria Theresa's ethnically diverse army was no match for Prussian precision. In 1742, as other greedy powers were falling on her lands in the general European War of the Austrian Succession (1740–1748), she was forced to cede almost all of Silesia to Prussia (see Map 17.2 on page 572). In one stroke Prussia doubled its population to six million people. Now Prussia unquestionably towered above all the other German states and stood as a European Great Power.

Though successful in 1742, Frederick had to spend much of his reign fighting against great odds to save Prussia from total destruction. Maria Theresa was determined to regain Silesia, and when the ongoing competition between Britain and France for colonial empire brought another great conflict in 1756 (see page 647), Austria fashioned an aggressive alliance with France and Russia. During the Seven Years' War (1756–1763), the aim of the alliance was to conquer Prussia and divide up its territory. Frederick led his army brilliantly, striking repeatedly at vastly superior forces invading from all sides. At times he believed all was lost, but he fought on with stoic courage. In the end, he was miraculously saved: Peter III came to the Russian throne in 1762 and called off the attack against Frederick, whom he greatly admired.

In the early years of his reign, Frederick II had kept his enthusiasm for Enlightenment culture strictly separated from a brutal concept of international politics. He wrote:

> *Of all States, from the smallest to the biggest, one can safely say that the fundamental rule of government is the principle of extending their territories. . . . The passions of rulers have no other curb but the limits of their power. Those are the fixed laws of European politics to which every politician submits.*[18]

But the terrible struggle of the Seven Years' War tempered Frederick and brought him to consider how more humane policies for his subjects might also strengthen the state.

Thus Frederick went beyond a superficial commitment to Enlightenment culture for himself and his circle. He tolerantly allowed his subjects to believe as they wished in religious and philosophical matters. He promoted the advancement of knowledge, improving his country's schools and permitting scholars to publish their findings. Moreover, Frederick tried to improve the lives of his subjects more directly. As he wrote his friend Voltaire, "I must enlighten my people, cultivate their manners and morals, and make them as happy as human beings can be, or as happy as the means at my disposal permit." The legal system and the bureaucracy were Frederick's primary tools. Prussia's laws were simplified, torture of prisoners was abolished, and judges decided cases quickly and impartially. Prussian officials became famous for their hard work and honesty. After the Seven Years' War ended in 1763, Frederick's government energetically promoted the reconstruction of agriculture and industry in his war-torn country. Frederick himself set a good example. He worked hard and lived modestly, claiming that he was "only the first servant of the state." Thus Frederick justified monarchy in terms of practical results and said nothing of the divine right of kings.

Frederick's dedication to high-minded government went only so far, however. He never tried to change Prussia's existing social structure. True, he condemned serfdom in the abstract, but he accepted it in practice and did not even free the serfs on his own estates. He accepted and extended the privileges of the nobility, which he saw as his primary ally in the defense and extension of his realm. The Junker nobility remained the backbone of the army and the entire Prussian state.

Nor did Frederick listen to thinkers like Moses Mendelssohn (1729–1786), who urged that Jews be given freedom and civil rights. (See the feature "Individuals in Society: Moses Mendelssohn and the Jewish Enlightenment.") As in other German states, Jews in Prussia remained an oppressed group. The vast majority were confined to tiny, overcrowded ghettos, were excluded by

Individuals in Society

Moses Mendelssohn and the Jewish Enlightenment

In 1743 a small, humpbacked Jewish boy with a stammer left his poor parents in Dessau in central Germany and walked eighty miles to Berlin, the capital of Frederick the Great's Prussia. According to one story, when the boy reached the Rosenthaler Gate, the only one through which Jews could pass, he told the inquiring watchman that his name was Moses and that he had come to Berlin "to learn." The watchman laughed and waved him through. "Go Moses, the sea has opened before you."* Embracing the Enlightenment and seeking a revitalization of Jewish religious thought, Moses Mendelssohn did point his people in a new and uncharted direction.

Turning in Berlin to a learned rabbi he had previously known in Dessau, the young Mendelssohn studied Jewish law and eked out a living copying Hebrew manuscripts in a beautiful hand. But he was soon fascinated by an intellectual world that had been closed to him in the Dessau ghetto. There, like most Jews throughout central Europe, he had spoken Yiddish—a mixture of German, Polish, and Hebrew. Now, working mainly on his own, he mastered German; learned Latin, Greek, French, and English; and studied mathematics and Enlightenment philosophy. Word of his exceptional abilities spread in Berlin's Jewish community (1,500 of the city's 100,000 inhabitants). He began tutoring the children of a wealthy Jewish silk merchant, and he soon became the merchant's clerk and later his partner. But his great passion remained the life of the mind and the spirit, which he avidly pursued in his off hours.

Gentle and unassuming in his personal life, Mendelssohn was a bold thinker. Reading eagerly in Western philosophy since antiquity, he was, as a pious Jew, soon convinced that Enlightenment teachings need not be opposed to Jewish thought and religion. Indeed, he concluded that reason could complement and strengthen religion, although each would retain its integrity as a separate sphere.† Developing his idea in his first great work, "On the Immortality of the Soul" (1767), Mendelssohn used the neutral setting of a philosophical dialogue between Socrates and his followers in ancient Greece to argue that the human soul lived forever. In refusing to bring religion and critical thinking into conflict, he was strongly influenced by contemporary German philosophers who argued similarly on behalf of Christianity. He reflected the way the German Enlightenment generally supported established religion, while the French Enlightenment attacked it. This was the most important difference in Enlightenment thinking between the two countries.

Lavater (right) *attempts to convert Mendelssohn, in a painting by Moritz Oppenheim of an imaginary encounter.* (Collection of the Judah L. Magnes Museum, Berkeley)

Mendelssohn's treatise on the human soul captivated the educated German public, which marveled that a Jew could have written a philosophical masterpiece. In the excitement, a Christian zealot named Lavater challenged Mendelssohn in a pamphlet to accept Christianity or to demonstrate how the Christian faith was not "reasonable." Replying politely but passionately, the Jewish philosopher affirmed that all his studies had only strengthened him in the faith of his fathers, although he certainly did not seek to convert anyone not born into Judaism. Rather, he urged toleration in religious matters. He spoke up courageously for his fellow Jews and decried the oppression they endured, and he continued to do so for the rest of his life.

Orthodox Jew and German philosophe, Moses Mendelssohn serenely combined two very different worlds. He built a bridge from the ghetto to the dominant culture over which many Jews would pass, including his novelist daughter Dorothea and his famous grandson, the composer Felix Mendelssohn.

Questions for Analysis

1. How did Mendelssohn seek to influence Jewish religious thought in his time?
2. How do Mendelssohn's ideas compare with those of the French Enlightenment?

*H. Kupferberg, *The Mendelssohns: Three Generations of Genius* (New York: Charles Scribner's Sons, 1972), p. 3.

†D. Sorkin, *Moses Mendelssohn and the Religious Enlightenment* (Berkeley: University of California Press, 1996), pp. 8ff.

law from most business and professional activities, and could be ordered out of the kingdom at a moment's notice. A very few Jews in Prussia did manage to succeed and obtain the right of permanent settlement, usually by performing some special service for the state. But they were the exception, and Frederick firmly opposed any general emancipation for the Jews, as he did for the serfs.

Catherine the Great of Russia

Catherine the Great of Russia (r. 1762–1796) was one of the most remarkable rulers who ever lived, and the French philosophes adored her. Catherine was a German princess from Anhalt-Zerbst, a totally insignificant principality sandwiched between Prussia and Saxony. Her father commanded a regiment of the Prussian army, but her mother was related to the Romanovs of Russia, and that proved to be Catherine's chance.

Peter the Great had abolished the hereditary succession of tsars so that he could name his successor and thus preserve his policies. This move opened a period of palace intrigue and a rapid turnover of rulers until Peter's youngest daughter, Elizabeth, came to the Russian throne in 1741. A shrewd but crude woman—one of her official lovers was an illiterate shepherd boy—Elizabeth named her nephew Peter heir to the throne and chose Catherine to be his wife in 1744. It was a mismatch from the beginning. The fifteen-year-old Catherine was intelligent and attractive; her husband was stupid and ugly, his face badly scarred by smallpox. Ignored by her childish husband, Catherine carefully studied Russian, endlessly read writers such as Bayle and Voltaire, and made friends at court. Soon she knew what she wanted. "I did not care about Peter," she wrote in her *Memoirs,* "but I did care about the crown."[19]

As the old empress Elizabeth approached death, Catherine plotted against her unpopular husband. She selected as her new lover a tall, dashing young officer named Gregory Orlov, who with his four officer brothers commanded considerable support among the soldiers stationed in St. Petersburg. When Peter came to the throne in 1762, his decision to withdraw Russian troops from the coalition against Prussia alienated the army. At the end of six months, Catherine and her military conspirators deposed Peter III in a palace revolution. Then the Orlov brothers murdered him. The German princess became empress of Russia.

Catherine had drunk deeply at the Enlightenment well. Never questioning the common assumption that absolute monarchy was the best form of government, she set out to rule in an enlightened manner. She had three main goals. First, she worked hard to bring the sophisticated culture of western Europe to backward Russia. To do so, she imported Western architects, sculptors, musicians, and intellectuals. She bought masterpieces of Western art in wholesale lots and patronized the philosophes. An enthusiastic letter writer, she corresponded extensively with Voltaire and praised him as the "champion of the human race." When the French government banned the *Encyclopedia,* she offered to publish it in St. Petersburg. She sent money to Diderot when he needed it. With these and countless similar actions, Catherine won good press in the West for herself and for her country. Moreover, this intellectual ruler, who wrote plays and loved good talk, set the tone for the entire Russian nobility. Peter the Great westernized Russian armies, but it was Catherine who westernized the thinking of the Russian nobility.

Catherine's second goal was domestic reform, and she began her reign with sincere and ambitious projects. Better laws were a major concern. In 1767 she appointed a special legislative commission to prepare a new law code. No new unified code was ever produced, but Catherine did restrict the practice of torture and allowed limited religious toleration. She also tried to improve education and strengthen local government. The philosophes applauded these measures and hoped more would follow.

Such was not the case. In 1773 a common Cossack soldier named Emelian Pugachev sparked a gigantic uprising of serfs, very much as Stenka Razin had done a century earlier (see page 583). Proclaiming himself the true tsar, Pugachev issued "decrees" abolishing serfdom, taxes, and army service. Thousands joined his cause, slaughtering landlords and officials over a vast area of southwestern Russia. Pugachev's untrained hordes eventually proved no match for Catherine's noble-led regular army. Betrayed by his own company, Pugachev was captured and savagely executed.

Pugachev's rebellion was a decisive turning point in Catherine's domestic policy. On coming to the throne, she had condemned serfdom in theory, but Pugachev's rebellion put an end to any illusions she might have had about reforming the system. The peasants were clearly dangerous, and her empire rested on the support of the nobility. After 1775 Catherine gave the nobles absolute control of their serfs. She extended serfdom into new areas, such as Ukraine. In 1785 she formalized the nobility's privileged position, freeing nobles forever from taxes and state service. Under Catherine the Russian nobility attained its most exalted position, and serfdom entered its most oppressive phase.

Catherine's third goal was territorial expansion, and in this respect she was extremely successful. Her armies

Pugachev and Catherine This haunting portrait of Pugachev has been painted over an existing portrait of empress Catherine the Great, who seems to be peeking over the rebel leader's head. Painting from life in 1773, the artist may have wanted to represent Pugachev's legitimacy as Catherine's rightful successor. *(From* Pamiatniki Kul'tury, *No. 32, 1961)*

subjugated the last descendants of the Mongols, the Crimean Tartars, and began the conquest of the Caucasus. Her greatest coup by far was the partition of Poland (see Map 18.1). By 1700 Poland had become a weak and decentralized republic with an elected king (page 573), and Poland's fate in the late eighteenth century demonstrated the dangers of failing to build a strong absolutist state. All important decisions continued to require the unanimous agreement of all nobles elected to the Polish Diet, which meant that nothing could ever be done to strengthen the state. When, between 1768 and 1772, Catherine's armies scored unprecedented victories against the Turks and thereby threatened to disturb the balance of power between Russia and Austria in eastern Europe, Frederick of Prussia obligingly came forward with a deal. He proposed that Turkey be let off easily and that Prussia, Austria, and Russia each compensate itself by taking a gigantic slice of Polish territory. Catherine jumped at the chance. The first partition of Poland took place in 1772. Two more partitions, in 1793 and 1795, gave all three powers more Polish territory, and the ancient republic of Poland simply vanished from the map.

Expansion helped Catherine keep the nobility happy, for it provided her with vast new lands to give to her faithful servants and her many lovers. On all the official royal favorites she lavished large estates with many serfs, as if to make sure there were no hard feelings when her interest cooled. Until the end this remarkable woman—who always believed that, in spite of her domestic setbacks, she was slowly civilizing Russia—kept her zest for life. Fascinated by a new twenty-two-year-old flame when she was a roly-poly grandmother in her sixties, she happily reported her good fortune to a favorite former lover: "I have come back to life like a frozen fly; I am gay and well."[20]

MAP 18.1 The Partition of Poland and Russia's Expansion, 1772–1795 Though all three of the great eastern absolutist states profited from the division of large but weak Poland, Catherine's Russia gained the most. Russia's European border moved far to the west, and the Russian empire became a leading actor in European politics.

The Austrian Habsburgs

In Austria two talented rulers did manage to introduce major reforms, although traditional power politics was more important than Enlightenment teachings. One was Joseph II (r. 1780–1790), a fascinating individual. For an earlier generation of historians, he was the "revolutionary emperor," a tragic hero whose lofty reforms were undone by the landowning nobility he dared to challenge. More recent scholarship has revised this romantic interpretation and stressed how Joseph II continued the state-building work of his mother, the empress Maria Theresa (1740–1780), a remarkable but old-fashioned absolutist.

Emerging from the long War of the Austrian Succession in 1748 with only the serious loss of Silesia, Maria Theresa and her closest ministers were determined to introduce reforms that would make the state stronger and more efficient. Three aspects of these reforms were most important. First, Maria Theresa introduced measures aimed at limiting the papacy's political influence in her realm. Second, a whole series of administrative reforms strengthened the central bureaucracy, smoothed out some provincial differences, and revamped the tax system, taxing even the lands of nobles without special exemptions. Third, the government sought to improve the lot of the agricultural population, cautiously reducing the power of lords over their hereditary serfs and their partially free peasant tenants.

Coregent with his mother from 1765 onward and a strong supporter of change, Joseph II moved forward rapidly when he came to the throne in 1780. He con-

Maria Theresa The empress and her husband pose with eleven of their sixteen children at Schönbrunn palace in this family portrait by court painter Martin Meytens (1695–1770). Joseph, the heir to the throne, stands at the center of the star pattern. Wealthy women often had very large families, in part because they seldom nursed their babies as poor women usually did. *(Réunion des Musées Nationaux/Art Resource, NY)*

trolled the established Catholic church even more closely in an attempt to ensure that it produced better citizens. He granted religious toleration and civic rights to Protestants and Jews—a radical innovation that impressed his contemporaries. In even more spectacular peasant reforms, Joseph abolished serfdom in 1781, and in 1789 he decreed that all peasant labor obligations be converted into cash payments. This ill-conceived measure was violently rejected not only by the nobility but also by the peasants it was intended to help since their primitive barter economy was woefully lacking in money. When a disillusioned Joseph died prematurely at forty-nine, the entire Habsburg empire was in turmoil. His brother Leopold II (r. 1790–1792) was forced to cancel Joseph's radical edicts in order to re-establish order. Peasants once again were required to do forced labor for their lords.

Absolutism in France

The Enlightenment's influence on political developments in France was complex. The monarchy maintained its absolutist claims, and some philosophes, such as Voltaire, believed that the king was still the best source of needed reform. At the same time, discontented nobles and learned judges drew on thinkers such as Montesquieu for liberal arguments. They sought with some success to limit the king's power, as France diverged from the absolutist states just considered.

When Louis XIV finally died in 1715, to be succeeded by his five-year-old great-grandson, Louis XV (r. 1715–1774), the Sun King's elaborate system of absolutist rule was challenged in a general reaction. Favored by the duke of Orléans (1674–1723), who governed as regent until 1723, the nobility made a strong comeback.

Most important, in 1715 the duke restored to the high courts of France—the parlements—the ancient right to evaluate royal decrees publicly in writing before they were registered and given the force of law. The restoration of this right to evaluate, which had been suspended under Louis XIV, was a fateful step. The high court judges had originally come from the middle class. By the eighteenth century, however, these middle-class judges had risen to become hereditary nobles, thereby attaining the high social status that middle-class officials wanted. Moreover, these judicial positions became essentially private property, passed down from father to son. By allowing this well-entrenched and increasingly aristocratic group to evaluate the king's decrees before they became law, the duke of Orléans sanctioned a counterweight to absolute power.

These implications became clear when the heavy expenses of the War of the Austrian Succession plunged France into financial crisis. In 1748 Louis XV appointed a finance minister who decreed a 5 percent income tax on every individual regardless of social status. Exemption from most taxation had long been a hallowed privilege of the nobility, and other important groups—the clergy, the large towns, and some wealthy bourgeoisie—had also gained special tax advantages over time. The result was a vigorous protest from many sides, led by the influential Parlement of Paris. The monarchy retreated; the new tax was dropped.

Following the disastrously expensive Seven Years' War, the conflict re-emerged. The government tried to maintain emergency taxes after the war ended. The Parlement of Paris protested and even challenged the basis of royal authority, claiming that the king's power had to be limited to protect liberty. Once again the government caved in and withdrew the wartime taxes in 1764. The judicial opposition then asserted that the king could not levy taxes without the consent of the Parlement of Paris acting as the representative of the entire nation.

Indolent and sensual by nature, more interested in his many mistresses than in affairs of state, Louis XV finally roused himself for a determined defense of his absolutist inheritance. "The magistrates," he angrily told the Parlement of Paris in a famous face-to-face confrontation, "are my officers. . . . In my person only does the sovereign power rest."[21] In 1768 Louis appointed a tough career official named René de Maupeou as chancellor and ordered him to crush the judicial opposition.

Maupeou abolished the existing parlements and exiled the vociferous members of the Parlement of Paris to the provinces. He created a new and docile parlement of royal officials, and he began once again to tax the privileged groups. A few philosophes applauded these measures: the sovereign was using his power to introduce badly needed reforms that had been blocked by a self-serving aristocratic elite. Most philosophes and educated public opinion as a whole sided with the old parlements, however, and there was widespread criticism of "royal despotism." The illegal stream of scandalmongering, pornographic attacks on the king and his court became a torrent, and some scholars now believe these lurid denunciations ate away at the foundations of royal authority, especially among the common people in turbulent Paris. The king was being stripped of the sacred aura of God's anointed on earth and was being reinvented in the popular imagination as a loathsome degenerate. Yet the monarchy's power was still great enough for Maupeou simply to ride over the opposition, and Louis XV would probably have prevailed—if he had lived to a very ripe old age.

But Louis XV died in 1774. The new king, Louis XVI (r. 1774–1792), was a shy twenty-year-old with good intentions. Taking the throne, he is reported to have said, "What I should like most is to be loved."[22] The eager-to-please monarch decided to yield in the face of such strong criticism from so much of France's educated elite. He dismissed Maupeou and repudiated the strong-willed minister's work. All the old parlements were reinstated, as enlightened public opinion cheered and anticipated moves toward more representative government. But such moves were not forthcoming. Instead, a weakened but unreformed monarchy faced a judicial opposition that claimed to speak for the entire French nation. Increasingly locked in stalemate, the country was drifting toward renewed financial crisis and political upheaval.

The Overall Influence of the Enlightenment

Having examined the evolution of monarchical absolutism in four leading states, we can begin to look for meaningful generalizations and evaluate the overall influence of Enlightenment thought on politics.

France clearly diverged from its eastern neighbors in its political development in the eighteenth century. The French monarch's capacity to govern in a truly absolutist manner declined substantially. The political resurgence of the French nobility after 1715 and the growth of judicial opposition drew crucial support from educated public opinion, which increasingly made the liberal critique of unregulated royal authority its own.

The situation in eastern and east-central Europe was different. The liberal critique of absolute monarchy remained an intellectual curiosity, and proponents of reform from above held sway. Moreover, despite differences, the leading eastern European monarchs of the later eighteenth century all claimed that they were acting on the principles of the Enlightenment. The philosophes generally agreed with this assessment and cheered them on. Beginning in the mid-nineteenth century, historians developed the idea of a common "enlightened despotism" or "enlightened absolutism," and they canonized Frederick, Catherine, and Joseph as its most outstanding examples. More recent research has raised doubts about this old interpretation and has led to a fundamental revaluation.

There is general agreement that these absolutists, especially Catherine and Frederick, did encourage and spread the cultural values of the Enlightenment. Perhaps this was their greatest achievement. Skeptical in religion and intensely secular in basic orientation, they unabashedly accepted the here and now and sought their happiness in the enjoyment of it. At the same time, they were proud of their intellectual accomplishments and good taste, and they supported knowledge, education, and the arts. No wonder the philosophes felt these monarchs were kindred spirits.

Historians also agree that the absolutists believed in change from above and tried to enact needed reforms. Yet the results of these efforts brought only very modest improvements, and the life of the peasantry remained very hard in the eighteenth century. Thus some historians have concluded that these monarchs were not really sincere in their reform efforts. Others disagree, arguing that powerful nobilities blocked the absolutists' genuine commitment to reform. (The old interpretation of Joseph II as the tragic revolutionary emperor forms part of this argument.)

The emerging answer to this controversy is that the later eastern absolutists were indeed committed to reform but that humanitarian objectives were of quite secondary importance. Above all, the absolutists wanted reforms that would strengthen the state and allow them to compete militarily with their neighbors. Modern scholarship has therefore stressed how Catherine, Frederick, and Joseph were in many ways simply continuing the state building of their predecessors, reorganizing armies and expanding bureaucracies to raise more taxes and troops. The reason for this continuation was simple. The international political struggle was brutal, and the stakes were high. First Austria under Maria Theresa and then Prussia under Frederick the Great had to engage in bitter fighting to escape dismemberment, while decentralized Poland was coldly divided and eventually liquidated.

Yet in this drive for more state power, the later absolutists were also innovators, and the idea of an era of enlightened absolutism retains a certain validity. Sharing the Enlightenment faith in critical thinking and believing that knowledge meant power, these absolutists really were more enlightened than their predecessors because they put state-building reforms in a new, broader perspective. Above all, the later absolutists considered how more humane laws and practices could help their populations become more productive and satisfied and thus able to contribute more substantially to the welfare of the state. It was from this perspective that they introduced many of their most progressive reforms, tolerating religious minorities, simplifying legal codes, and promoting practical education.

The primacy of state over individual interests also helps explain some puzzling variations in social policies. For example, Catherine the Great took measures that worsened the peasants' condition because she looked increasingly to the nobility as her natural ally and sought to strengthen it. Frederick the Great basically favored the status quo, limiting only the counterproductive excesses of his trusted nobility against its peasants. Joseph II believed that greater freedom for peasants was the means to strengthen his realm, and he acted accordingly. Each enlightened absolutist sought greater state power, but each believed a different policy would attain it.

The eastern European absolutists of the later eighteenth century combined old-fashioned state building with the culture and critical thinking of the Enlightenment. In doing so, they succeeded in expanding the role of the state in the life of society. Unlike the successors of Louis XIV, they perfected bureaucratic machines that were to prove surprisingly adaptive and capable of enduring into the twentieth century.

Summary

This chapter has focused on the complex development of a new world-view in Western civilization. This new view was essentially critical and secular, drawing its inspiration from the scientific revolution and crystallizing in the Enlightenment.

Decisive breakthroughs in astronomy and physics in the seventeenth century, which demolished the imposing medieval synthesis of Aristotelian philosophy and Christian theology, had only limited practical consequences despite the expectations of scientific enthusiasts. Yet the impact of new scientific knowledge on intellectual life became great. Interpreting scientific findings and Newtonian laws in an antitraditional, antireligious manner, the French philosophes of the Enlightenment extolled the superiority of rational, critical thinking. This new method, they believed, promised not just increased knowledge but even the discovery of the fundamental laws of human society. Although they reached different conclusions when they turned to social and political realities, they did stimulate absolute monarchs to apply reason to statecraft and the search for useful reforms. Above all, the philosophes succeeded in shaping an emerging public opinion and spreading their radically new world-view. These were momentous accomplishments.

Key Terms

world-view
Copernican hypothesis
experimental method
law of inertia
law of universal gravitation
empiricism
Cartesian dualism
Enlightenment
rationalism
progress
skepticism
tabula rasa
philosophes
the public
separation of powers
general will
salons
enlightened absolutism

Notes

1. H. Butterfield, *The Origins of Modern Science* (New York: Macmillan, 1951), p. viii.
2. Quoted in A. G. R. Smith, *Science and Society in the Sixteenth and Seventeenth Centuries* (New York: Harcourt Brace Jovanovich, 1972), p. 97.
3. Quoted in Butterfield, *The Origins of Modern Science,* p. 47.
4. Quoted in Smith, *Science and Society,* p. 100.
5. Ibid., pp. 115–116.
6. Ibid., p. 120.
7. A. R. Hall, *From Galileo to Newton, 1630–1720* (New York: Harper & Row, 1963), p. 290.
8. Quoted in R. K. Merton, *Science, Technology and Society in Seventeenth-Century England,* rev. ed. (New York: Harper & Row, 1970), p. 164.
9. Quoted in P. Hazard, *The European Mind, 1680–1715* (Cleveland: Meridian Books, 1963), pp. 304–305.
10. Quoted in R. Chartier, *The Cultural Origins of the French Revolution* (Durham, N.C.: Duke University Press, 1991), p. 27.
11. J. Bosher, *The French Revolution* (New York: W. W. Norton, 1988), p. 31.
12. L. Schiebinger, *The Mind Has No Sex? Women in the Origins of Modern Science* (Cambridge, Mass.: Harvard University Press, 1989), p. 64.
13. Quoted in L. M. Marsak, ed., *The Enlightenment* (New York: John Wiley & Sons, 1972), p. 56.
14. Quoted in G. L. Mosse et al., eds., *Europe in Review* (Chicago: Rand McNally, 1964), p. 156.
15. Quoted in P. Gay, "The Unity of the Enlightenment," *History* 3 (1960): 25.
16. See E. Fox-Genovese, "Women in the Enlightenment," in *Becoming Visible: Women in European History,* 2d ed., ed. R. Bridenthal, C. Koonz, and S. Stuard (Boston: Houghton Mifflin, 1987), esp. pp. 252–259, 263–265.
17. Quoted in G. P. Gooch, *Catherine the Great and Other Studies* (Hamden, Conn.: Archon Books, 1966), p. 149.
18. Quoted in L. Krieger, *Kings and Philosophers, 1689–1789* (New York: W. W. Norton, 1970), p. 257.
19. Quoted in Gooch, *Catherine the Great,* p. 15.
20. Ibid., p. 53.
21. Quoted in R. R. Palmer, *The Age of Democratic Revolution,* vol. 1 (Princeton, N.J.: Princeton University Press, 1959), pp. 95–96.
22. Quoted in G. Wright, *France in Modern Times,* 4th ed. (New York: W. W. Norton, 1987), p. 34.

Suggested Reading

The first three authors cited in the Notes—Butterfield, Smith, and Hall—have written excellent general interpretations of the scientific revolution. These may be compared with S. Shapin, *The Scientific Revolution* (2001), which is concise and well informed with an eye for the dramatic, and with M. Jacob, *The Cultural Meaning of the Scientific Revolution* (1988). The older study of England by Merton, mentioned in the Notes, also analyzes ties between science and the larger community. Schiebinger, cited in the Notes, provides a brilliant analysis of how the new science gradually excluded women interested in science, a question completely neglected in older studies. A. Debus, *Man and Nature in the Renaissance* (1978), is good on the Copernican revolution. D. Sobel, *Longitude: The True Story of a Lone Genius Who Solved the Greatest Scientific Problem of His Day* (1995), is an engrossing biography that became a bestseller. M. Boas, *The Scientific Renaissance, 1450–1630* (1966), is especially insightful about the influence of magic on science. S. Drake, *Galileo* (1980), is a good short biography. T. Kuhn, *The Structure of Scientific Revolutions* (1962), is a challenging, much-discussed attempt to understand major breakthroughs in scientific thought over time. E. Andrade, *Sir Isaac Newton* (1958), is a good brief biography, which may be compared with R. Westfall, *Never at Rest: A Biography of Isaac Newton* (1993), and F. Manuel, *The Religion of Isaac Newton* (1974).

Hazard, listed in the Notes, is a classic study of the formative years of Enlightenment thought. R. Reill and E. Wilson, *Encyclopedia of the Enlightenment* (1996), is particularly helpful on culture and the leading philosophes. M. Jacob, *The Enlightenment: A Brief History with Documents* (2000), is also recommended. Important studies from the cultural perspective include D. Goodman, *The Republic of Letters: A Cultural History of the Enlightenment* (1994), and A. Farge, *Subversive Worlds: Public Opinion in Eighteenth Century France* (1994). D. Roche, *France in the Enlightenment* (1998), is a distinguished scholar's bustling panorama of life and thought, action and wit. P. Gay has written several major studies on the Enlightenment: *Voltaire's Politics* (1959) and *The Party of Humanity* (1971) are two of the best. J. Sklar, *Montesquieu* (1987), is an engaging biography. I. Wade, *The Structure and Form of the French Enlightenment* (1977), is a major synthesis. F. Baumer, *Religion and the Rise of Skepticism* (1969), and H. Payne, *The Philosophes and the People* (1976), are important studies. D. Van Kley, *The Religious Origins of the French Revolution* (1996), is a stimulating reinterpretation. The changing attitudes of the educated public are imaginatively analyzed by R. Chartier, *The Cultural Origins of the French Revolution* (1991) and *French Historical Studies* (Fall 1992). R. Danton, *The Literary Underground of the Old Regime* (1982), provides a fascinating glimpse of low-life publishing. On women, see the stimulating study by Fox-Genovese cited in the Notes, as well as the collected work by N. Davis and A. Farge, eds., *A History of Women: Renaissance and Enlightenment Paradoxes* (1993). More specialized studies include E. Goldsmith and D. Goodman, eds., *Going Public: Women and Publishing in Early Modern France* (1995); S. Spencer, ed., *French Women and the Age of Enlightenment* (1984); and K. Rogers, *Feminism in Eighteenth-Century England* (1982). J. Landes, *Women and the Public Sphere in the Age of the French Revolution* (1988), is a fascinating and controversial study of women and politics. L. Wolff, *Inventing Eastern Europe: The Map of Civilization on the Mind of the Enlightenment* (1994), is recommended. Above all, one should read some of the philosophes and let them speak for themselves. Two good anthologies are C. Brinton, ed., *The Portable Age of Reason* (1956), and F. Manuel, ed., *The Enlightenment* (1951). Voltaire's most famous and very amusing novel, *Candide,* is highly recommended, as is S. Gendzier, ed., *Denis Diderot: The Encyclopedia: Selections* (1967).

In addition to the works mentioned in the Suggested Reading for Chapters 16 and 17, the monarchies of Europe are carefully analyzed in H. Scott, *Enlightened Absolutism* (1990); C. Tilly, ed., *The Formation of National States in Western Europe* (1975); and J. Gagliardo, *Enlightened Despotism* (1967), all of which have useful bibliographies. M. Anderson, *Historians and Eighteenth-Century Europe* (1979), is a valuable introduction to modern scholarship, and C. Behrens, *Society, Government, and the Enlightenment: The Experience of Eighteenth-Century France and Prussia* (1985), is a stimulating comparative study. J. Black, *Eighteenth-Century Europe, 1700–1789* (1990), is a fine survey, and E. Le Roy Ladurie, *The Ancien Régime* (1996), is an impressive synthesis by a well-known French historian. J. Lynch, *Bourbon Spain, 1700–1808* (1989), and R. Herr, *The Eighteenth-Century Revolution in Spain* (1958), skillfully analyze the impact of Enlightenment thought in Spain. Important works on Austria include C. Macartney, *Maria Theresa and the House of Austria* (1970); D. Beales, *Joseph II* (1987); and T. Blanning, *Joseph II and Enlightened Absolutism* (1970). There are several fine works on Russia. J. Alexander, *Catherine the Great: Life and Legend* (1989), is the best biography of the famous ruler, which may be compared with the empress's own story, *The Memoirs of Catherine the Great,* ed. D. Maroger (1961). I. de Madariaga, *Russia in the Age of Catherine the Great* (1981), and P. Dukes, *The Making of Russian Absolutism, 1613–1801* (1982), are strongly recommended. Two excellent works on Moses Mendelssohn are the brilliant study by D. Sorkin, *Moses Mendelssohn and the Religious Enlightenment* (1996), and the popular biography of the family by H. Kupferberg, *The Mendelssohns: Three Generations of Genius* (1972). J. Israel, *European Jewry in the Age of Mercantilism, 1550–1750* (1985), is recommended.

The musical and artistic culture of the time may be approached through A. Cobban, ed., *The Eighteenth Century* (1969), a richly illustrated work with excellent essays; and C. B. Behrens, *The Ancien Régime* (1967). T. Crow, *Painters and Public Life in Eighteenth-Century Paris* (1985), examines artists and cultural politics. C. Rosen, *The Classical Style: Haydn, Mozart, Beethoven* (1972), brilliantly synthesizes music and society, as did Mozart himself in his great opera *The Marriage of Figaro,* where the count is the buffoon and his servant the hero.

Listening to the Past

Voltaire on Religion

Voltaire was the most renowned and probably the most influential of the French philosophes. His biting, satirical novel Candide *(1759) is still widely assigned in college courses, and his witty yet serious* Philosophical Dictionary *remains a source of pleasure and stimulation. The* Dictionary *consists of a series of essays on topics ranging from Adam to Zoroaster, from certainty to circumcision. The following passage is taken from the essay on religion.*

Voltaire began writing the Philosophical Dictionary *in 1752, at the age of fifty-eight, after arriving at the Prussian court in Berlin. Frederick the Great applauded Voltaire's efforts, but Voltaire put the project aside after leaving Berlin, and the first of several revised editions was published anonymously in 1764. It was an immediate, controversial success. Snapped up by an "enlightened" public, it was denounced by religious leaders as a threat to the Christian community and was burned in Geneva and Paris.*

I meditated last night; I was absorbed in the contemplation of nature; I admired the immensity, the course, the harmony of those infinite globes which the vulgar do not know how to admire.

I admired still more the intelligence which directs these vast forces. I said to myself: "One must be blind not to be dazzled by this spectacle; one must be stupid not to recognize its author; one must be mad not to worship the Supreme Being. What tribute of worship should I render Him? Should not this tribute be the same in the whole of space, since it is the same Supreme Power which reigns equally in all space?

"Should not a thinking being who dwells on a star in the Milky Way offer Him the same homage as a thinking being on this little globe of ours? Light is the same for the star Sirius as for us; moral philosophy must also be the same. If a feeling, thinking animal on Sirius is born of a tender father and mother who have been occupied with his happiness, he owes them as much love and care as we owe to our parents. If someone in the Milky Way sees a needy cripple, and if he can aid him and does not do so, then he is guilty toward all the globes.

"Everywhere the heart has the same duties: on the steps of the throne of God, if He has a throne; and in the depths of the abyss, if there is an abyss."

I was deep in these ideas when one of those genii who fill the spaces between the worlds came down to me. I recognized the same aerial creature who had appeared to me on another occasion to teach me that the judgments of God are different from our own, and how a good action is preferable to a controversy.

The genie transported me into a desert all covered with piles of bones. . . . He began with the first pile. "These," he said, "are the twenty-three thousand Jews who danced before a calf, together with the twenty-four thousand who were killed while fornicating with Midianitish women. The number of those massacred for such errors and offences amounts to nearly three hundred thousand.

"In the other piles are the bones of the Christians slaughtered by each other because of metaphysical disputes. They are divided into several heaps of four centuries each. One heap would have mounted right to the sky; they had to be divided."

"What!" I cried, "brothers have treated their brothers like this, and I have the misfortune to be of this brotherhood!"

"Here," said the spirit, "are the twelve million native Americans killed in their own land because they had not been baptized."

An impish Voltaire, by the French sculptor Houdon. *(Courtesy of Board of Trustees of the Victoria & Albert Museum)*

"My God! . . . Why assemble here all these abominable monuments to barbarism and fanaticism?"

"To instruct you. . . . Follow me now." [The genie takes Voltaire to the "heroes of humanity, who tried to banish violence and plunder from the world," and tells Voltaire to question them.]

[At last] I saw a man with a gentle, simple face, who seemed to me to be about thirty-five years old. From afar he looked with compassion upon those piles of whitened bones, through which I had been led to reach the sage's dwelling place. I was astonished to find his feet swollen and bleeding, his hands likewise, his side pierced, and his ribs laid bare by the cut of the lash. "Good God!" I said to him, "is it possible for a just man, a sage, to be in this state? I have just seen one who was treated in a very hateful way, but there is no comparison between his torture and yours. Wicked priests and wicked judges poisoned him; is it by priests and judges that you were so cruelly assassinated?"

With great courtesy he answered, "Yes."

"And who were these monsters?"

"They were hypocrites."

"Ah! that says everything; I understand by that one word that they would have condemned you to the cruelest punishment. Had you then proved to them, as Socrates did, that the Moon was not a goddess, and that Mercury was not a god?"

"No, it was not a question of planets. My countrymen did not even know what a planet was; they were all arrant ignoramuses. Their superstitions were quite different from those of the Greeks."

"Then you wanted to teach them a new religion?"

"Not at all; I told them simply: 'Love God with all your heart and your neighbor as yourself, for that is the whole of mankind's duty.' Judge yourself if this precept is not as old as the universe; judge yourself if I brought them a new religion." . . .

"But did you say nothing, do nothing that could serve them as a pretext?"

"To the wicked everything serves as pretext."

"Did you not say once that you were come not to bring peace, but a sword?"

"It was a scribe's error; I told them that I brought peace and not a sword. I never wrote anything; what I said can have been changed without evil intention."

"You did not then contribute in any way by your teaching, either badly reported or badly interpreted, to those frightful piles of bones which I saw on my way to consult with you?"

"I have only looked with horror upon those who have made themselves guilty of all these murders."

. . . [Finally] I asked him to tell me in what true religion consisted.

"Have I not already told you? Love God and your neighbor as yourself."

"Is it necessary for me to take sides either for the Greek Orthodox Church or the Roman Catholic?"

"When I was in the world I never made any difference between the Jew and the Samaritan."

"Well, if that is so, I take you for my only master." Then he made a sign with his head that filled me with peace. The vision disappeared, and I was left with a clear conscience.

Questions for Analysis

1. Why did Voltaire believe in a Supreme Being? Does this passage reflect the influence of Isaac Newton's scientific system? If so, how?
2. Was Voltaire trying to entertain or teach, or do both? Was he effective? Why or why not?
3. If Voltaire was trying to convey serious ideas about religion and morality, what were those ideas? What was he attacking?
4. If a person today thought and wrote like Voltaire, would that person be called a defender or a destroyer of Christianity? Why?

Source: F. M. Arouet de Voltaire, *Oeuvres complètes,* vol. 8, trans. J. McKay (Paris: Firmin-Didot, 1875), pp. 188–190.

The East India Dock, London (detail), by Samuel Scott, a painting infused with the spirit of maritime expansion. *(© The Board of Trustees of the Victoria & Albert Museum)*

chapter

19 The Expansion of Europe in the Eighteenth Century

chapter outline

- Agriculture and the Land
- The Beginning of the Population Explosion
- The Growth of Cottage Industry
- Building the Atlantic Economy

The world of absolutism and aristocracy, a combination of raw power and elegant refinement, was a world apart from that of the common people. For the overwhelming majority of the population in the eighteenth century, life remained a struggle with poverty and uncertainty, with the landlord and the tax collector. In 1700 peasants on the land and artisans in their shops lived little better than had their ancestors in the Middle Ages. Only in science and thought, and there only among a few intellectual elites and their followers, had Western society succeeded in going beyond the great achievements of the High Middle Ages, achievements that in turn owed so much to Greece and Rome.

Everyday life was a struggle because European societies, despite their best efforts, still could not produce very much by modern standards. Ordinary men and women might work like their beasts in the fields, and they often did, but there was seldom enough good food, warm clothing, and decent housing. Life went on; history went on. The wars of religion ravaged Germany in the seventeenth century; Russia rose to become a Great Power; the state of Poland simply disappeared; monarchs and nobles continually jockeyed for power and wealth. In 1700 or even 1750, the idea of progress, of substantial improvement in the lives of great numbers of people, was still only the dream of a small elite in fashionable salons.

Yet the economic basis of European life was beginning to change. In the course of the eighteenth century, the European economy emerged from the long crisis of the seventeenth century, responded to challenges, and began to expand once again. Population resumed its growth, while colonial empires developed and colonial elites prospered. Some areas were more fortunate than others. The rising Atlantic powers—Holland, France, and, above all, England—and their colonies led the way. The expansion of agriculture and industry, trade and population, marked the beginning of a surge comparable to that of the eleventh- and twelfth-century springtime of European civilization. But this time, broadly based expansion was not cut short. This time the response to new challenges led toward one of the most influential developments in human history, the Industrial Revolution, considered in Chapter 22.

- What were the causes of this renewed surge?
- Why were the fundamental economic underpinnings of European society beginning to change, and what were the dimensions of these changes?
- How did these changes affect people and their work?

These are the questions this chapter will address.

Agriculture and the Land

At the end of the seventeenth century, the economy of Europe was agrarian, as it had been for several hundred years. With the possible exception of Holland, at least 80 percent of the people of all western European countries drew their livelihoods from agriculture. In eastern Europe the percentage was considerably higher.

Men and women lavished their attention on the land, plowing fields and sowing seed, reaping harvests and storing grain. The land repaid these efforts, year after year yielding up the food and most of the raw materials for industry that made life possible. Yet the land was stingy. Even in a rich agricultural region such as the Po Valley in northern Italy, every bushel of wheat sown yielded on average only five or six bushels of grain at harvest during the seventeenth century. The average French yield in the same period was somewhat less. Such yields were barely more than those attained in fertile, well-watered areas in the thirteenth century or in ancient Greece. By modern standards, output was distressingly low.

If the land was stingy, it was also capricious. In most regions of Europe in the sixteenth and seventeenth centuries, harvests were poor, or even failed completely, every eight or nine years. The vast majority of the population, which lived off the land, might survive a single bad harvest by eating less and drawing on their reserves of grain. But when the land's caprices combined with persistent bad weather—too much rain rotting the seed or drought withering the young stalks—the result was catastrophic. Meager grain reserves were soon exhausted, and the price of grain soared. Provisions from other areas with better harvests were hard to obtain.

In such crisis years, which periodically stalked Europe in the seventeenth and even into the early eighteenth century, a terrible tightening knot in the belly forced people to use substitutes—the **famine foods** of a desperate population. People gathered chestnuts and stripped bark in the forests, they cut dandelions and grass, and they ate these substitutes to escape starvation. Even cannibalism occurred in the seventeenth century.

Such unbalanced and inadequate food in famine years made people weak and extremely susceptible to illness and epidemics. Eating material unfit for human consumption, such as bark or grass, resulted in dysentery and intestinal ailments of many kinds. Influenza and smallpox preyed with particular savagery on populations weakened by famine. In famine years the number of deaths soared far above normal. A third of a village's population might disappear in a year or two. Indeed, the 1690s were as dismal as many of the worst periods of earlier times. One county in Finland, probably typical of the entire country, lost fully 28 percent of its inhabitants in 1696 and 1697. In preindustrial Europe the harvest was the real king, and the king was seldom generous and often cruel.

To understand why Europeans produced barely enough food in good years and occasionally agonized through years of famine throughout the later seventeenth century, one must follow the plowman, his wife, and his children into the fields to observe their battle for food and life. There the ingenious pattern of farming that Europe had developed in the Middle Ages, a pattern that allowed fairly large numbers of people to survive but could never produce material abundance, was still dominant.

The Open-Field System

The greatest accomplishment of medieval agriculture was the **open-field system** of village farming developed by European peasants. That system divided the land to be cultivated by the peasants of a given village into several large fields, which were in turn cut up into long, narrow strips. The fields were open, and the strips were not enclosed into small plots by fences or hedges. An individual peasant family—if it was fortunate—held a number of strips scattered throughout the various large fields. The land of those who owned but did not till, primarily the nobility, the clergy, and wealthy townspeople, was also in scattered strips. Peasants farmed each large field as a community, with each family following the same pattern of plowing, sowing, and harvesting in accordance with tradition and the village leaders.

The ever-present problem was exhaustion of the soil. When the community planted wheat year after year in a field, the nitrogen in the soil was soon depleted, and crop failure was certain. Since the supply of manure for fertilizer was limited, the only way for the land to recover its life-giving fertility was for a field to lie fallow for a period of time. In the early Middle Ages, a year of fallow was alternated with a year of cropping, but three-year rotations were introduced, especially on more fertile lands. This

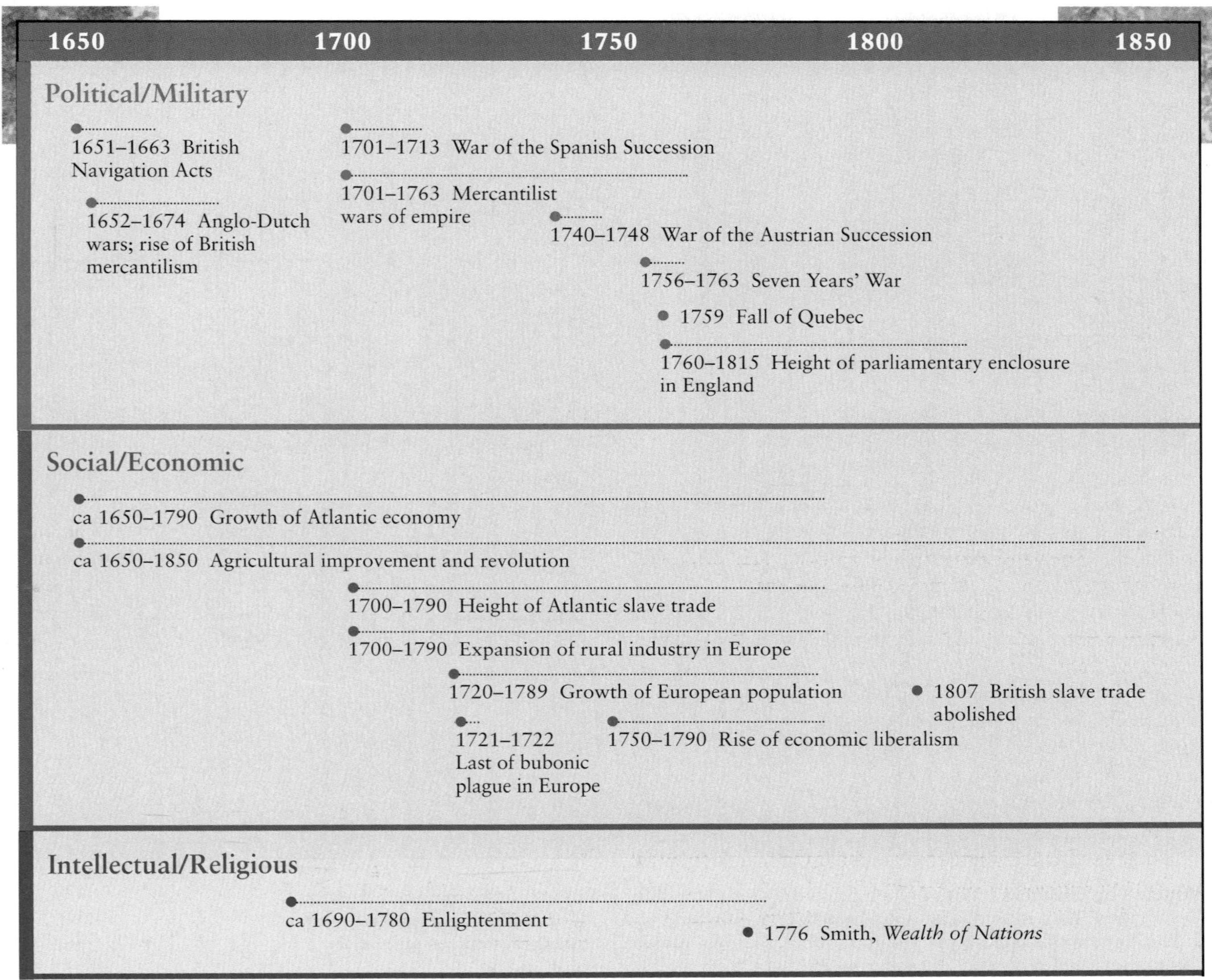

system permitted a year of wheat or rye to be followed by a year of oats or beans and only then by a year of fallow.

Traditional village rights reinforced the traditional pattern of farming. In addition to rotating field crops in a uniform way, villages maintained open meadows for hay and natural pasture. These lands were **common lands**, set aside primarily for the draft horses and oxen so necessary in the fields, but open to the cows and pigs of the village community as well. After the harvest, the men and women of the village also pastured their animals on the wheat or rye stubble. In many places such pasturing followed a brief period, also established by tradition, for the gleaning of grain. Poor women would go through the fields picking up the few single grains that had fallen to the ground in the course of the harvest. The subject of a great nineteenth-century painting, *The Gleaners* by Jean François Millet (see page 632), this backbreaking work by hard-working but impoverished women meant quite literally the slender margin of survival for some people in the winter months.

In the age of absolutism and nobility, state and landlord continued to levy heavy taxes and high rents as a matter of course. In so doing, they stripped the peasants of much of their meager earnings. The level of exploitation varied.

Millet: The Gleaners Poor French peasant women search for grains and stalks that the harvesters (*background*) have missed. The open-field system seen here could still be found in parts of Europe in 1857, when this picture was painted. Millet is known for his great paintings expressing social themes. *(Réunion des Musées Nationaux/Art Resource, NY)*

Generally speaking, the peasants of eastern Europe were worst off. As we saw in Chapter 17, they were serfs bound to their lords in hereditary service. In much of eastern Europe, there were few limitations on the amount of forced labor the lord could require, and five or six days of unpaid work per week on the lord's land were not uncommon. Well into the nineteenth century, individual Russian serfs and serf families were regularly sold with and without land.

Social conditions were better in western Europe. Peasants were generally free from serfdom. In France, western Germany, and the Low Countries, they owned land and could pass it on to their children. Yet life in the village was unquestionably hard, and poverty was the great reality for most people. For the Beauvais region of France at the beginning of the eighteenth century, it has been carefully estimated that in good years and bad only a tenth of the peasants could live satisfactorily off the fruits of their landholdings. Owning considerably less than half of the land, the peasants of this region had to pay heavy royal taxes, the church's tithe, and dues to the lord, as well as set aside seed for the next season. Left with only half of their crop for their own use, these peasants had to toil and till for others and seek work for wages in a variety of jobs. It was a constant scramble for a meager living. And this was in a rich agricultural region in a country where peasants were comparatively well-off. The privileges of Europe's ruling elites weighed heavily on the people of the land.

The Agricultural Revolution

One possible way for European peasants to improve their difficult position was to take land from those who owned but did not labor. Yet the social and political conditions that enabled the ruling elites to squeeze the peasants were ancient and deeply rooted, and powerful forces stood ready to crush any protest. Only with the coming of the French Revolution were European peasants, mainly in France, able to improve their position by means of radical mass action.

Technological progress offered another possibility. The great need was for new farming methods that would enable Europeans to produce more and eat more. Uncultivated fields were the heart of the matter. If peasants (and their noble landlords) could replace the idle fallow with crops, they could increase the land under cultivation by 50 percent. So remarkable were the possibilities and the results that historians have often spoken of the progressive elimination of the fallow, which occurred gradually throughout Europe from the mid-seventeenth century on, as an **agricultural revolution**. This agricultural revolution, which took longer than historians used to believe, was a great milestone in human development.

Because grain crops exhaust the soil and make fallowing necessary, the secret to eliminating the fallow lies in alternating grain with certain nitrogen-storing crops. Such crops not only rejuvenate the soil even better than fallowing but also give more produce. The most important of these land-reviving crops are peas and beans, root crops such as turnips and potatoes, and clovers and grasses. In the eighteenth century, peas and beans were old standbys; turnips, potatoes, and clover were newcomers to the fields. As the eighteenth century went on, the number of crops that were systematically rotated grew. New patterns of organization allowed some farmers to develop increasingly sophisticated patterns of **crop rotation** to suit different kinds of soils. For example, farmers in French Flanders near Lille in the late eighteenth century used a ten-year rotation, alternating a number of grain, root, and hay crops in a given field on a ten-year schedule. Continual experimentation led to more scientific farming.

Improvements in farming had multiple effects. The new crops made ideal feed for animals. Because peasants and larger farmers had more fodder, hay, and root crops for the winter months, they could build up their small herds of cattle and sheep. More animals meant more meat and better diets for the people. More animals also meant more manure for fertilizer and therefore more grain for bread and porridge. The vicious cycle in which few animals meant inadequate manure, which meant little grain and less fodder, which led to fewer animals, and so on, could certainly be broken.

Advocates of the new crop rotations, who included an emerging group of experimental scientists, some government officials, and a few big landowners, believed that new methods were scarcely possible within the traditional framework of open fields and common rights. A farmer who wanted to experiment with new methods would have to get all the landholders in a village to agree to the plan, and advocates of improvement maintained that this would be difficult, if not impossible, given peasant caution and the force of tradition. Therefore, they argued that innovating agriculturalists needed to enclose and consolidate their scattered holdings into compact, fenced-in fields in order to farm more effectively. In doing so, the innovators also needed to enclose their individual shares of the natural pasture, the common. According to proponents of this idea, known as **enclosure**, a revolution in village life and organization was the necessary price of technical progress.

That price seemed too high to many poor rural people, who held small, inadequate holdings or very little land at all. Common rights were precious to these poor peasants. The rights to glean and to graze a cow on the common, to gather firewood in the lord's forest and pick berries in the marsh, were vital because they helped poor peasants retain a modicum of independence and status and avoid falling into the growing group of landless, "proletarian" wage workers. Thus when the small landholders and the village poor could effectively oppose the enclosure of the open fields and the common pasture, they did so. Moreover, in many countries they usually found allies among the larger, predominately noble landowners, who were also wary of enclosure because it required large investments and posed risks for them as well. Only powerful social and political pressures could overcome such combined opposition.

The old system of unenclosed open fields and the new system of continuous rotation coexisted in Europe for a long time. It could also be found in much of France and Germany in the early years of the nineteenth century because peasants there had successfully opposed efforts to introduce the new techniques in the late eighteenth century. Indeed, until the end of the eighteenth century, the promise of the new system was extensively realized only in the Low Countries and in England.

Hendrick Sorgh: Vegetable Market, 1662 The wealth and well-being of the industrious, capitalistic Dutch shine forth in this winsome market scene. The market woman's baskets are filled with delicious fresh produce that ordinary citizens can afford—eloquent testimony to the responsive, enterprising character of Dutch agriculture. *(Historisch Museum, Rotterdam)*

The Leadership of the Low Countries and England

The new methods of the agricultural revolution originated in the Low Countries. The vibrant, dynamic, middle-class society of seventeenth-century republican Holland was the most advanced in Europe in many areas of human endeavor (see pages 554–559). In shipbuilding and navigation, in commerce and banking, in drainage and agriculture, the people of the Low Countries, especially the Dutch, provided models the jealous English and French sought to copy or to cripple.

By the middle of the seventeenth century, intensive farming was well established throughout much of the Low Countries. Enclosed fields, continuous rotation, heavy manuring, and a wide variety of crops—all these innovations were present. Agriculture was highly specialized and commercialized. The same skills that grew turnips produced flax to be spun into linen for clothes and tulip bulbs to lighten the heart with their beauty. The fat cattle of Holland, so beloved by Dutch painters, gave the most milk in Europe. Dutch cheeses were already world renowned.

One reason for early Dutch leadership in farming was that the Low Countries were one of the most densely populated areas in Europe. In order to feed themselves and provide employment, the Dutch were forced at an early date to seek maximum yields from their land and to increase the cultivated area through the steady draining of marshes and swamps.

The pressure of population was connected with the second cause, the growth of towns and cities in the Low Countries. Stimulated by commerce and overseas trade, Amsterdam grew from 30,000 inhabitants to 200,000 in its golden seventeenth century. The growth of urban population provided Dutch peasants with good markets for all they could produce and allowed each region to specialize in what it did best. Thus the Dutch could develop their potential, and the Low Countries became "the

Mecca of foreign agricultural experts who came . . . to see Flemish agriculture with their own eyes, to write about it and to propagate its methods in their home lands."[1]

The English were the best students. Drainage and water control were one subject in which they received instruction. Large parts of seventeenth-century Holland had once been sea and sea marsh, and the efforts of centuries had made the Dutch the world's leaders in the skills of drainage. In the first half of the seventeenth century, Dutch experts made a great contribution to draining the extensive marshes, or fens, of wet and rainy England.

The most famous of these Dutch engineers, Cornelius Vermuyden, directed one large drainage project in Yorkshire and another in Cambridgeshire. In the Cambridge fens, Vermuyden and his Dutch workers eventually reclaimed forty thousand acres, which were then farmed intensively in the Dutch manner. Swampy wilderness was converted into thousands of acres of some of the best land in England. On such new land, where traditions and common rights were not yet firmly established, farmers introduced new crops and new rotations fairly easily.

Dutch experience was also important to Viscount Charles Townsend (1674–1738), one of the pioneers of English agricultural improvement. This powerful lord learned about turnips and clover while serving as English ambassador to Holland. In the 1710s, he was using these crops in the sandy soil of his large estates in Norfolk in eastern England. When Lord Charles retired from politics in 1730 and returned to Norfolk, it was said that he spoke of turnips, turnips, and nothing but turnips. This led some wit to nickname his lordship "Turnip" Townsend. But Townsend had the last laugh. Draining extensively, manuring heavily, and sowing crops in regular rotation without fallowing, the farmers who leased Townsend's lands produced larger crops. They and he earned higher incomes. Those who had scoffed reconsidered. By 1740 agricultural improvement in various forms had become something of a craze among the English aristocracy.

Jethro Tull (1674–1741), part crank and part genius, was another important English innovator. A true son of the early Enlightenment, Tull adopted a critical attitude toward accepted ideas about farming and tried to develop better methods through empirical research. He was especially enthusiastic about using horses, rather than slower-moving oxen, for plowing. He also advocated sowing seed with drilling equipment rather than scattering it by hand. Drilling distributed seed in an even manner and at the proper depth. There were also improvements in livestock, inspired in part by the earlier successes of English country gentlemen in breeding ever-faster horses for the races and fox hunts that were their passions. Selective breeding of ordinary livestock was a marked improvement over the old pattern, which has been graphically described as little more than "the haphazard union of nobody's son with everybody's daughter."

Selective Breeding New breeding practices meant bigger livestock and more meat on English tables. This gigantic champion, one of the new improved shorthorn breed, was known as the Newbus Ox. Such great fat beasts were pictured in the press and praised by poets. ***(Institute of Agricultural History and Museum of English Rural Life, University of Reading)***

By the mid-eighteenth century, English agriculture was in the process of a long but radical transformation. The eventual result was that by 1870 English farmers were producing 300 percent more food than they had produced in 1700, although the number of people working the land had increased by only 14 percent. This great surge of agricultural production provided food for England's rapidly growing urban population. It was a tremendous achievement.

The Cost of Enclosure

What was the cost of technical progress in England, and to what extent did its payment result in social injustice? Scholars agree that the impetus for enclosing the fields came mainly from the powerful ruling class, the English aristocracy. Owning large estates, the aristocracy benefited directly from higher yields that could support higher rents, and it was able and ready to make expensive investments in the new technology. Beyond these certainties, there are important differences of interpretation among historians. Many historians stress the initiative and enterprise of the big English landowners, which they contrast with the inertia and conservatism of continental landowners, big and small. These historians also assert that the open fields were enclosed fairly, with both large and small owners receiving their fair share after the strips had been surveyed and consolidated.

Other historians argue that fairness was more apparent than real. The large landowners controlled Parliament, which made the laws. They had Parliament pass hundreds of "enclosure acts," each of which authorized the fencing of open fields in a given village and the division of the common land in proportion to one's property in the open fields. The heavy legal and surveying costs of enclosure were also divided among the landowners. This meant that many peasants who had small holdings had to sell out to pay their share of the expenses. Similarly, landless cottagers lost their age-old access to the common pasture without any compensation whatsoever. This dealt landless families a serious blow because it deprived women of the means to raise animals for market and earn vital income. In the spirited words of one critical historian, "Enclosure (when all the sophistications are allowed for) was a plain enough case of class robbery, played according to the fair rules of property and law laid down by a Parliament of property owners and lawyers."[2]

In assessing these conflicting interpretations, one must put eighteenth-century developments in a longer historical perspective. In the first place, as much as half of English farmland was already enclosed by 1750. A great wave of enclosure of English open fields into sheep pastures had already occurred in the sixteenth and early seventeenth centuries, dispossessing many English peasants in order to produce wool for the textile industry. In the later seventeenth and early eighteenth centuries, many open fields were enclosed fairly harmoniously by mutual agreement among all classes of landowners in English villages. Thus parliamentary enclosure, the great bulk of which occurred after 1760 and particularly during the Napoleonic wars early in the nineteenth century, only completed a process that was in full swing. Nor did an army of landless cottagers and farm laborers appear only in the last years of the eighteenth century. Much earlier, and certainly by 1700 because of the early enclosures for sheep runs, there were perhaps two landless agricultural workers in England for every independent farmer. In 1830, after the enclosures were complete, the proportion of landless laborers was not substantially greater.

By 1700 a highly distinctive pattern of landownership and production existed in England. At one extreme were a few large landowners; at the other, a large mass of landless cottagers who labored mainly for wages and who could graze only a pig or a cow on the village common. In between stood two other groups: small, independent peasant farmers who owned their own land and prosperous tenant farmers who rented land from the big landowners, hired wage laborers, and sold their output on a cash market. Yet the small, independent English peasant farmers had been declining in number since the early enclosures, and in the eighteenth century they could not compete with the rising group of profit-minded, market-oriented tenant farmers.

These tenant farmers, many of whom had formerly been independent owners, were the key to mastering the new methods of farming. Well financed by the large landowners, the tenant farmers fenced fields, built drains, and improved the soil with fertilizers. Such improvements actually increased employment opportunities for wage workers in some areas. So did new methods of farming, for land was farmed more intensively without the fallow, and new crops such as turnips required more care and effort. Thus enclosure did not force people off the land and into the towns by eliminating jobs, as has sometimes been claimed.

At the same time, by eliminating common rights and greatly reducing the access of poor men and women to the land, the eighteenth-century enclosure movement marked the completion of two major historical developments in England—the rise of market-oriented estate agriculture and the emergence of a landless rural proletariat. By 1815 a tiny minority of wealthy English (and Scottish) landowners held most of the land and pursued profits aggressively, leasing their holdings through agents at competitive prices to middle-size farmers, who relied on landless laborers for their workforce. These landless laborers may have lived as well in 1800 as their predecessors had in 1700 in strictly economic terms. But they had lost that bit of independence and self-respect that common rights had provided and were completely dependent on cash wages. In no other European country had this **proletarianization**—this transformation of large numbers of small peasant farmers into landless rural wage earners—gone so far. And England's village poor found the cost of change heavy and unjust.

The Beginning of the Population Explosion

Another factor that affected the existing order of life and forced economic changes in the eighteenth century was the remarkable growth of European population, the beginning of the "population explosion." This explosion continued in Europe until the twentieth century, by which time it was affecting nonwestern areas of the globe. What caused the growth of population, and what did the challenge of more mouths to feed and more hands to employ do to the European economy?

Limitations on Population Growth

Many commonly held ideas about population in the past are wrong. One such mistaken idea is that people always married young and had large families. A related error is that population was always growing too fast. On the contrary, until 1700 the total population of Europe grew slowly much of the time, and it followed an irregular cyclical pattern (see Figure 19.1).

The cyclical pattern of European population growth had a great influence on many aspects of social and economic life over time, although striking local and regional differences often make generalization difficult. As we have seen, the terrible ravages of the Black Death caused a sharp drop in population and prices after 1350 and also created a labor shortage throughout Europe (see page 566). Lords in eastern Europe responded to this labor shortage by reversing the trend toward personal freedom and gradually reinstituting serfdom. This landlord reaction failed in western Europe, however, where serf obligations had declined or even disappeared by 1500.

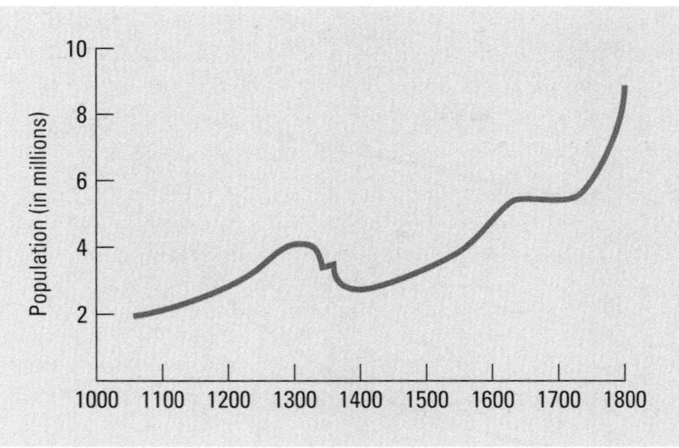

FIGURE 19.1 The Growth of Population in England, 1000–1800 England is a good example of both the uneven increase of European population before 1700 and the third great surge of growth, which began in the eighteenth century. *(Source: E. A. Wrigley,* Population and History. *Copyright © 1969 by McGraw-Hill. Reprinted by permission of The McGraw-Hill Companies.)*

Moreover, the era of labor shortages and low food prices after the Black Death resulted in an increased standard of living for peasants and artisans. Some economic historians calculate that for those common people in western Europe who managed to steer clear of warfare and of power struggles within the ruling class, the later Middle Ages was an era of exceptional well-being.

But peasant and artisan well-being was eroded in the course of the sixteenth century. The second great surge of population growth (see Figure 19.1) outstripped the growth of agricultural production after about 1500. There was less food per person, and food prices rose more rapidly than wages, a development intensified by the inflow of precious metals from the Americas and a general, if uneven, European price revolution. The result was a substantial decline in living standards for the great majority of people throughout Europe. This decline especially aggravated the plight of both the urban and the rural poor. By 1600 the pressure of population on resources was severe in much of Europe, and widespread poverty was an undeniable reality.

For this reason, population growth slowed and stopped in seventeenth-century Europe. Births and deaths, fertility and mortality, were in a crude but effective balance. The birthrate—annual births as a proportion of the population—was fairly high but was far lower than it would have been if all women between ages fifteen and forty-five had been having as many children as

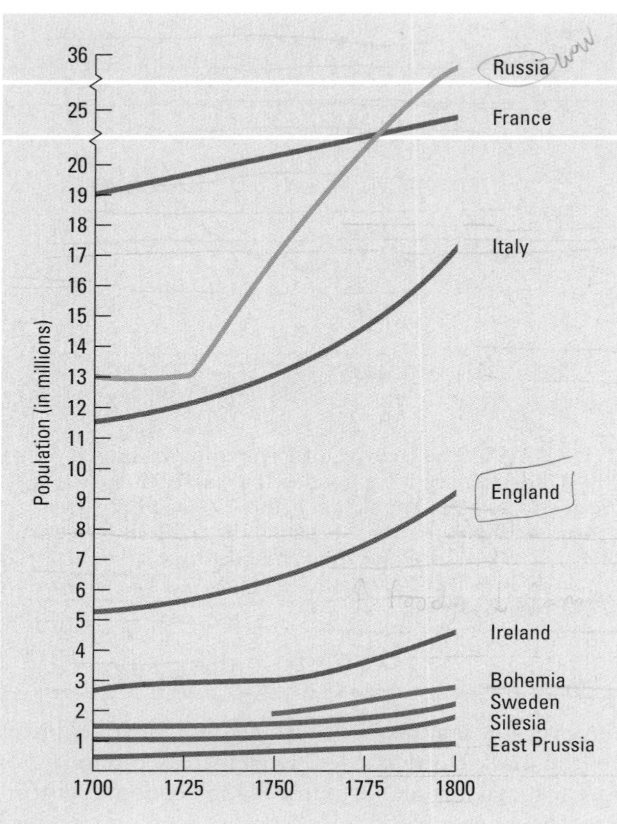

FIGURE 19.2 The Increase of Population in Europe in the Eighteenth Century France's large population continued to support French political and intellectual leadership. Russia emerged as Europe's most populous state because natural increase was complemented by growth from territorial expansion.

biologically possible. The death rate in normal years was also high, though somewhat lower than the birthrate. As a result, the population grew modestly in normal years at a rate of perhaps 0.5 to 1 percent, or enough to double the population in 70 to 140 years. This is, of course, a generalization encompassing many different patterns. In areas such as Russia and colonial New England, where there was a great deal of frontier to be settled, the annual rate of natural increase, not counting in-migration, might well have exceeded 1 percent. In a country such as France, where the land had long been densely settled, the rate of increase might have been less than 0.5 percent.

Although population growth of even 1 percent per year is fairly modest by the standards of some African and Latin American countries today, it will produce a very large increase over a long period. An annual increase of even 1 percent will result in sixteen times as many people in three hundred years. Such gigantic increases simply did not occur in agrarian Europe before the eighteenth century. In certain abnormal years and tragic periods—the Black Death was only the most extreme and extensive example—many more people died than were born. Total population fell sharply, even catastrophically. A number of years of modest growth would then be necessary to make up for those who had died in an abnormal year. Such savage increases in deaths occurred periodically in the seventeenth century on a local and regional scale, and these demographic crises combined with birthrates far below the biological potential to check the growth of population until after 1700.

The grim reapers of demographic crisis were famine, epidemic disease, and war. Famine, the inevitable result of poor farming methods and periodic crop failures, was particularly murderous because it was accompanied by disease. With a brutal one-two punch, famine stunned and weakened a population, and disease finished it off. Disease could also ravage the population independently of famine.

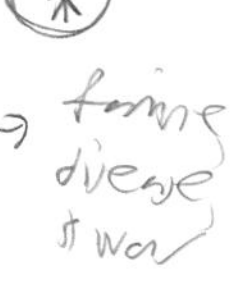

War was another scourge. The indirect effects were more harmful than the organized killing. War spread disease. Soldiers and camp followers passed venereal disease throughout the countryside to scar and kill. Armies requisitioned scarce food supplies and disrupted the agricultural cycle. The Thirty Years' War witnessed all possible combinations of distress. In the German states, the number of inhabitants declined by more than *two-thirds* in some large areas and by at least one-third almost everywhere else.

The New Pattern of the Eighteenth Century

In the eighteenth century, the population of Europe began to grow markedly. This increase in numbers occurred in all areas of Europe, western and eastern, northern and southern, dynamic and stagnant. Growth was especially dramatic after about 1750 (see Figure 19.2).

Although it is certain that Europe's population grew greatly, it is less clear why. Because population grew throughout Europe, it is best to look first for general factors. What caused fewer people to die or, possibly, more babies to be born? In some areas some women did have more babies than before because new opportunities for employment in rural industry allowed them to marry at an earlier age, as we shall see (see pages 662–666). But the basic cause for Europe as a whole was a decline in mortality—fewer deaths.

Bubonic Plague in Marseilles, 1721 In this gruesome scene, people are trying to flee the plague-ridden port by ship, but most are prevented from doing so by measures to quarantine the disease. The wharf is littered with the bodies of the dead and dying. Ominous black clouds represent the stench of the polluted air. *(Courtesy of the Trustees of the British Museum)*

The bubonic plague mysteriously disappeared. Following the Black Death in the fourteenth century, plagues had remained a part of the European experience, striking again and again with savage force, particularly in towns. As late as 1721, a ship from Syria and the Levant, where plague was ever present, brought the disease to Marseilles. In a few weeks, forty thousand of the city's ninety thousand inhabitants died. The epidemic swept southern France, killing one-third, one-half, even three-fourths of those in the larger towns. Once again an awful fear swept across Europe. But the epidemic passed, and that was the last time plague fell on western and central Europe. Stricter measures of quarantine in Mediterranean ports and along the Austrian border with Turkey helped, as human carriers of plague were carefully isolated. Chance and plain good luck were more important, however.

It is now understood that bubonic plague is, above all, a disease of rats. More precisely, it is the black rat that spreads major epidemics, for the black rat's flea is the principal carrier of the plague bacillus. After 1600, for reasons unknown, a new rat of Asiatic origin—the brown, or wander, rat—began to drive out and eventually eliminate its black competitor. In the words of one authority, "This revolution in the animal kingdom must have gone far to break the lethal link between rat and man."[3] Although the brown rat also contracts the plague, another kind of flea is its main parasite. That flea carries the plague poorly and, for good measure, has little taste for human blood.

Advances in medical knowledge did not contribute much to reducing the death rate in the eighteenth century. The most important advance in preventive medicine in this period was inoculation against smallpox. This great improvement was long confined mainly to England and probably did little to reduce deaths throughout Europe until the latter part of the century. However, improvements in the water supply and sewerage, which were frequently promoted by strong absolutist monarchies, resulted in somewhat better public health and helped reduce such diseases as typhoid and typhus in some urban areas of western Europe. Improvements in water supply and the drainage of swamps also reduced Europe's large insect population. Filthy flies and mosquitoes played a major role in spreading serious epidemics and also in transmitting common diseases, especially those striking children and young adults. Thus early public health measures helped the decline in mortality that began with the disappearance of plague and continued into the early nineteenth century.

Human beings also became more successful in their efforts to safeguard the supply of food and protect against famine. The eighteenth century was a time of considerable canal and road building in western Europe. These advances in transportation, which were also among the more positive aspects of strong absolutist states, lessened the impact of local crop failure and famine. Emergency supplies could be brought in, and localized starvation became less frequent. Wars became more gentlemanly and less destructive than in the seventeenth century and spread fewer epidemics. New foods, particularly the potato from South America, were introduced. In short, population grew in the eighteenth century primarily because years of abnormal death rates were less catastrophic. Famines, epidemics, and wars continued to occur, but their severity moderated.

The growth of population in the eighteenth century cannot be interpreted as a sign of human progress, however. As we have seen, serious population pressures on resources were in existence by 1600 and continued throughout the seventeenth century. Thus renewed population growth in the eighteenth century maintained or even increased the imbalance between the number of people and the economic opportunities available to them. There was only so much land available, and tradition slowed the adoption of better farming methods. Therefore, agriculture could not provide enough work for the rapidly growing labor force, and poor people in the countryside had to look for new ways to make a living.

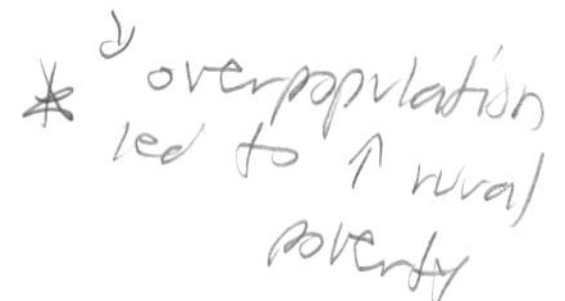

Building a Royal Highway in France An expanding system of all-weather roads improved French communications, promoted trade, and facilitated relief in time of famine. This majestic painting by Claude-Joseph Vernet (1714–1789) captures the spirit of the Enlightenment's cautious optimism and its faith in hard-won progress. *(Giraudon/The Bridgeman Art Library International Ltd)*

The Growth of Cottage Industry

The growth of population increased the number of rural workers with little or no land, and this in turn contributed to the development of industry in rural areas. The poor in the countryside increasingly needed to supplement their earnings from agriculture with other types of work, and capitalists from the city were eager to employ them, often at lower wages than urban workers usually commanded. Manufacturing with hand tools in peasant cottages and work sheds grew markedly in the eighteenth century. Rural industry became a crucial feature of the European economy.

To be sure, peasant communities had always made some clothing, processed some food, and constructed some housing for their own use. But in the High Middle Ages, peasants did not produce manufactured goods on a large scale for sale in a market. Industry in the Middle Ages was dominated and organized by urban craft guilds and urban merchants, who jealously regulated handicraft production and sought to maintain it as an urban monopoly. By the eighteenth century, however, the pressures of rural poverty and the need to employ landless proletarians were overwhelming the efforts of urban artisans to maintain their traditional control over industrial production. A new system was expanding lustily.

The new system has had many names. It has often been called **cottage industry** or "domestic industry" to distinguish it from the factory industry that came later. In recent years, some scholars have preferred to speak of "protoindustrialization," by which they usually mean a stage of rural industrial development with wage workers and hand tools that necessarily preceded the emergence of large-scale factory industry. The focus on protoindustrialization has been quite valuable because it has sparked renewed interest in Europe's early industrial development and shown again that the mechanized factories grew out of a vibrant industrial tradition. However, the evolving concept of protoindustrialization also has different versions, some of which are rigid and unduly deterministic. Thus the phrase **putting-out system**, widely used by contemporaries to describe the key features of eighteenth-century rural industry, still seems a more appropriate term for the new form of industrial production.

The Weaver's Repose This painting by Decker Cornelis Gerritz (1594–1637) captures the pleasure of release from long hours of toil in cottage industry. The loom realistically dominates the cramped living space and the family's modest possessions. *(Musées Royaux des Beaux-Arts, Brussels. Copyright A.C.I.)*

The Putting-Out System

The two main participants in the putting-out system were the merchant capitalist and the rural worker. The merchant loaned, or "put out," raw materials to several cottage workers, who processed the raw materials in their own homes and returned the finished product to the merchant. For example, a merchant would provide raw wool, and the workers would spin and weave the wool into cloth. The merchant then paid the outworkers for their work by the piece and proceeded to sell the finished product. There were endless variations on this basic relationship. Sometimes rural workers would buy their own materials and work as independent producers before they sold to the merchant. Sometimes several workers toiled together to perform a complicated process in a workshop. The relative importance of earnings from the land and from industry varied greatly for handicraft workers, although industrial wages usually became more important for a given family with time. In all cases, however, the putting-out system was a kind of capitalism. Merchants needed large amounts of capital, which they held in the form of goods being worked up and sold in distant markets. They sought to make profits and increase the capital in their businesses.

The putting-out system grew because it had competitive advantages. Underemployed labor was abundant, and poor peasants and landless laborers would work for low wages. Since production in the countryside was unregulated, workers and merchants could change procedures and experiment as they saw fit. Because they did not need to meet rigid guild standards, which maintained quality but discouraged the development of new methods, cottage industry became capable of producing many kinds of goods. Textiles; all manner of knives, forks, and housewares; buttons and gloves; clocks; and musical instruments could be produced quite satisfactorily in the countryside. Luxury goods for the rich, such as exquisite tapestries and fine porcelain, demanded special training, close supervision, and centralized workshops. Yet such goods were as exceptional as those who used them. The skills of rural industry were sufficient for everyday articles.

Rural manufacturing did not spread across Europe at an even rate. It appeared first in England and developed most successfully there, particularly for the spinning and weaving of woolen cloth. By 1500 half of England's textiles were being produced in the countryside. By 1700 English industry was generally more rural than urban and heavily reliant on the putting-out system. Continental countries developed rural industry more slowly.

In France at the time of Louis XIV, Colbert had revived the urban guilds and used them as a means to control the cities and collect taxes (see pages 540–541). But the pressure of rural poverty proved too great. In 1762 the special privileges of urban manufacturing were severely restricted in France, and the already developing rural industries were given free rein from then on. The royal government in France had come to believe that the best way to help the poor in the countryside was to encourage the growth of cottage manufacturing. Governments in Germany and the Low Countries also gradually reduced the power of guilds in the countryside. (See the feature "Listening to the Past: The Decline of the Guilds" on pages 658–659.) Thus the latter part of the eighteenth century witnessed a remarkable expansion of rural industry in certain densely populated regions of continental Europe (see Map 19.1). The pattern established in England was spreading to the continent.

The Textile Industry

Throughout most of history until at least the nineteenth century, the industry that has employed the most people has been textiles. The making of linen, woolen, and, eventually, cotton cloth was the typical activity of cottage workers engaged in the putting-out system. A look inside the cottage of the English rural textile worker illustrates a way of life as well as an economic system.

The rural worker lived in a small cottage with tiny windows and little space. Indeed, the worker's cottage was often a single room that served as workshop, kitchen, and bedroom. There were only a few pieces of furniture, of which the weaver's loom was by far the largest and most important. That loom had changed somewhat in the early eighteenth century, when John Kay's invention of the flying shuttle enabled the weaver to throw the shuttle back and forth between the threads with one hand. Aside from that improvement, however, the loom was as it had been for much of history. In the cottage there were also spinning wheels, tubs for dyeing cloth and washing raw wool, and carding pieces to comb and prepare the raw material.

These different pieces of equipment were necessary because cottage industry was first and foremost a family enterprise. All the members of the family helped in the work, so that "every person from seven to eighty (who retained their sight and who could move their hands) could earn their bread," as one eighteenth-century English observer put it.[4] While the women and children prepared the raw material and spun the thread, the man of the house wove the cloth. There was work for everyone, even the

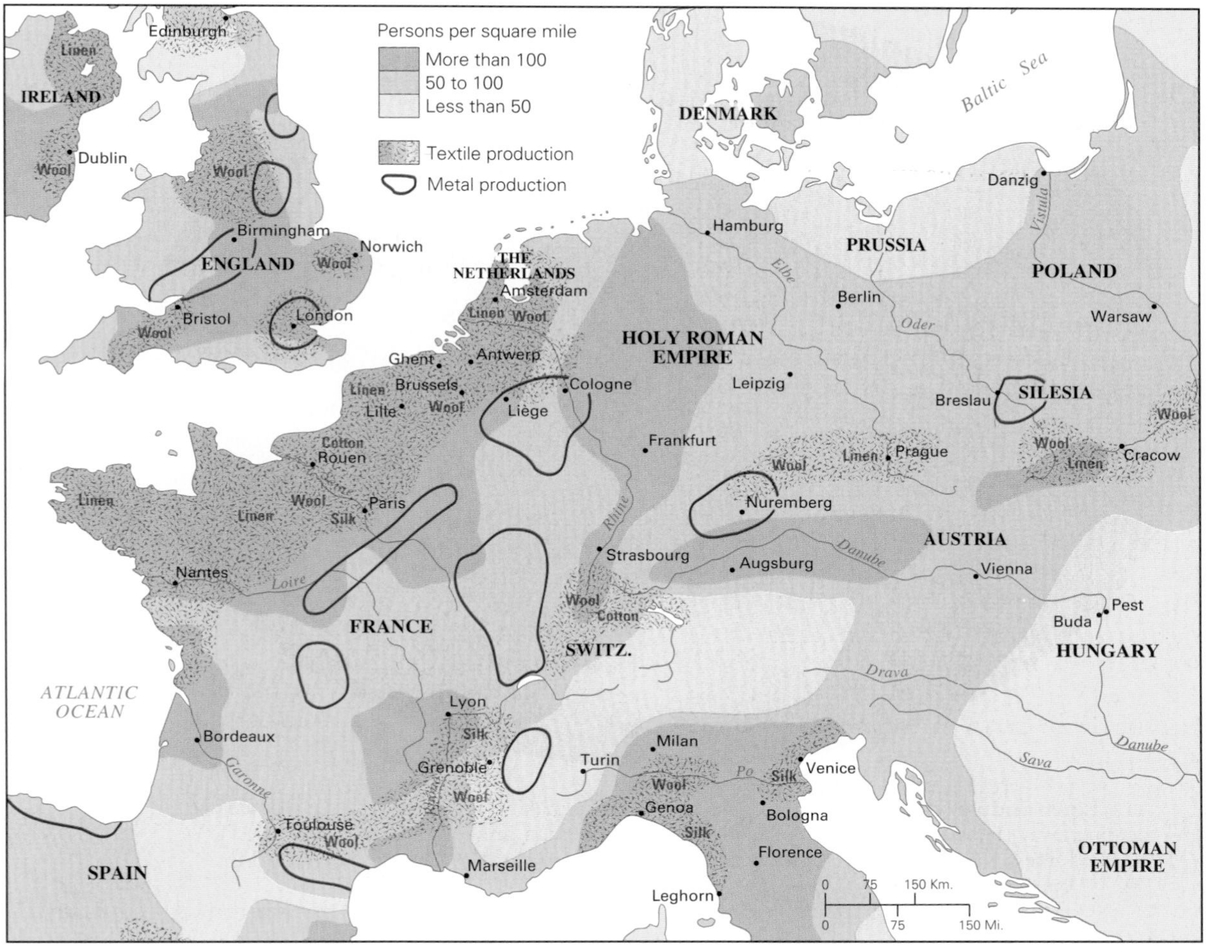

MAP 19.1 Industry and Population in Eighteenth-Century Europe The growth of cottage manufacturing in rural areas helped country people to increase their income and contributed to increases in the population. This putting-out system began in England, and much of the work was in the textile industry. Cottage industry was also strong in the Low Countries—modern-day Belgium and Holland.

youngest, which encouraged cottage workers to marry early and have large families. After the dirt was beaten out of the raw cotton, it had to be thoroughly cleaned with strong soap in a tub, where a child's tiny feet functioned like the agitator in a washing machine. George Crompton, the son of Samuel Crompton, who in 1784 invented the mule for cotton spinning, recalled that "soon after I was able to walk I was employed in the cotton manufacture. . . . My mother tucked up my petticoats about my waist, and put me into the tub to tread upon the cotton at the bottom."[5] Slightly older children and aged relatives carded and combed the cotton or wool so that the mother and the older daughter she had taught could spin it into thread. Each member had a task. The very young and very old worked in the family unit as a matter of course.

There was always a serious imbalance in this family enterprise: the work of four or five spinners was needed to keep one weaver steadily employed. Therefore, the wife and the husband had to constantly find more thread and more spinners. Widows and unmarried women—those "spinsters" who spun for their living—were recruited by the wife. Or perhaps the weaver's son went off on horseback to seek thread. The need for more thread might even lead the weaver and his wife to

The Linen Industry in Ireland Many steps went into making textiles. Here the women are beating away the woody part of the flax plant so that the man can comb out the soft part. The combed fibers will then be spun into thread and woven into cloth by this family enterprise. *(Mary Evans Picture Library)*

become small capitalist employers. At the end of the week when they received the raw wool or cotton from the merchant manufacturer, they would put out some of this raw material to other cottages. The following week they would return to pick up the thread and pay for the spinning, which would help keep the weaver busy for a week until the merchant came for the finished cloth.

Relations between workers and employers were often marked by sharp conflict. An English popular song written about 1700, called "The Clothier's Delight, or the Rich Men's Joy and the Poor Men's Sorrow," has the merchant boasting of the countless tricks he uses to "beat down wages":

We heapeth up riches and treasure great store
Which we get by griping and grinding the poor.
And this is a way for to fill up our purse
Although we do get it with many a curse.[6]

There were constant disputes over the weights of materials and the quality of the cloth. Merchants accused workers of stealing raw materials, and weavers complained that merchants delivered underweight bales. Suspicions abounded.

There was another problem, at least from the merchant capitalist's point of view. Rural labor was cheap, scattered, and poorly organized. For these reasons it was hard to control. Cottage workers tended to work in spurts. After they got paid on Saturday afternoon, the men in particular tended to drink and relax for two or three days. Indeed, Monday was called "holy Monday" because inactivity was so religiously observed. By the end of the week, the weaver was probably working feverishly to make his quota. But if he did not succeed, there was little the merchant could do. When times were good and the merchant could easily sell everything produced, the weaver and his family did fairly well and were particularly inclined to loaf—to the dismay of the capitalist. Thus the putting-out system in the textile industry had definite shortcomings from the employer's point of view. Ambitious merchant capitalists therefore intensified their search for ways to produce more efficiently and to squeeze still more work out of "undisciplined" cottage workers.

Building the Atlantic Economy

In addition to agricultural improvement, population pressure, and growing cottage industry, the expansion of Europe in the eighteenth century was characterized by the growth of world trade. Spain and Portugal revitalized their empires and began drawing more wealth from renewed development. Yet once again the countries of northwestern Europe—the Netherlands, France, and, above all, Great Britain—benefited most. Great Britain, which was formed in 1707 by the union of England and Scotland in a single kingdom, gradually became the leading maritime power. Thus the British played the critical role in building a fairly unified Atlantic economy, which offered remarkable opportunities for them and their colonists.

Mercantilism and Colonial Wars

Britain's commercial leadership in the eighteenth century had its origins in the mercantilism of the seventeenth century (see page 540). European **mercantilism** was a system of economic regulations aimed at increasing the power of the state. As practiced by a leading advocate such as Colbert under Louis XIV, mercantilism aimed particularly at creating a favorable balance of foreign trade in order to increase a country's stock of gold. A country's gold holdings served as an all-important treasure chest, to be opened periodically to pay for war in a violent age.

Early English mercantilists shared these views. What distinguished English mercantilism was the unusual idea that government economic regulations could and should serve the private interests of individuals and groups as well as the public needs of the state. As Josiah Child, a very wealthy brewer and director of the East India Company, put it, in the ideal economy "Profit and Power ought jointly to be considered."[7] By contrast, in France and other continental countries, seventeenth-century mercantilists generally put the needs of the state first, and they seldom saw a possible union of public and private interests for a common good.

The result of the English desire to increase both military power and private wealth was the mercantile system of the **Navigation Acts**. Oliver Cromwell established the first of these laws in 1651, and the restored monarchy of Charles II extended them further in 1660 and 1663; these Navigation Acts were not seriously modified until 1786. The acts required that most goods imported from Europe into England and Scotland be carried on British-owned ships with British crews or on ships of the country producing the article. Moreover, these laws gave British merchants and shipowners a virtual monopoly on trade with British colonies. The colonists were required to ship their products on British (or American) ships and to buy almost all of their European goods from Britain. It was believed that these economic regulations would help British merchants and workers as well as colonial plantation owners and farmers. And the emerging British Empire would develop a shipping industry with a large number of tough, experienced, deep-water seamen, who could be drafted when necessary into the Royal Navy to protect the island nation and its colonial possessions.

The Navigation Acts were a form of economic warfare. Their initial target was the Dutch, who were far ahead of the English in shipping and foreign trade in the mid-seventeenth century (see page 554). The Navigation Acts, in conjunction with three Anglo-Dutch wars between 1652 and 1674, did seriously damage Dutch shipping and commerce. The thriving Dutch colony of New Amsterdam was seized in 1664 and renamed "New York." By the late seventeenth century, the Netherlands was falling behind England in shipping, trade, and colonies.

Thereafter France stood clearly as England's most serious rival in the competition for overseas empire. Rich in natural resources, endowed with a population three or four times that of England, and allied with Spain, continental Europe's leading military power was already building a powerful fleet and a worldwide system of rigidly monopolized colonial trade. Thus from 1701 to 1763, Britain and France were locked in a series of wars to decide, in part, which nation would become the leading maritime power and claim the lion's share of the profits of Europe's overseas expansion (see Map 19.2).

The first round was the War of the Spanish Succession (see page 545), which started when Louis XIV declared his willingness to accept the Spanish crown willed to his grandson. Besides upsetting the continental balance of power, a union of France and Spain threatened to encircle and destroy the British colonies in North America (see Map 19.2). Defeated by a great coalition of states after twelve years of fighting, Louis XIV was forced in the Peace of Utrecht (1713) to cede Newfoundland, Nova Scotia, and the Hudson Bay territory to Britain. Spain was compelled to give Britain control of its West African

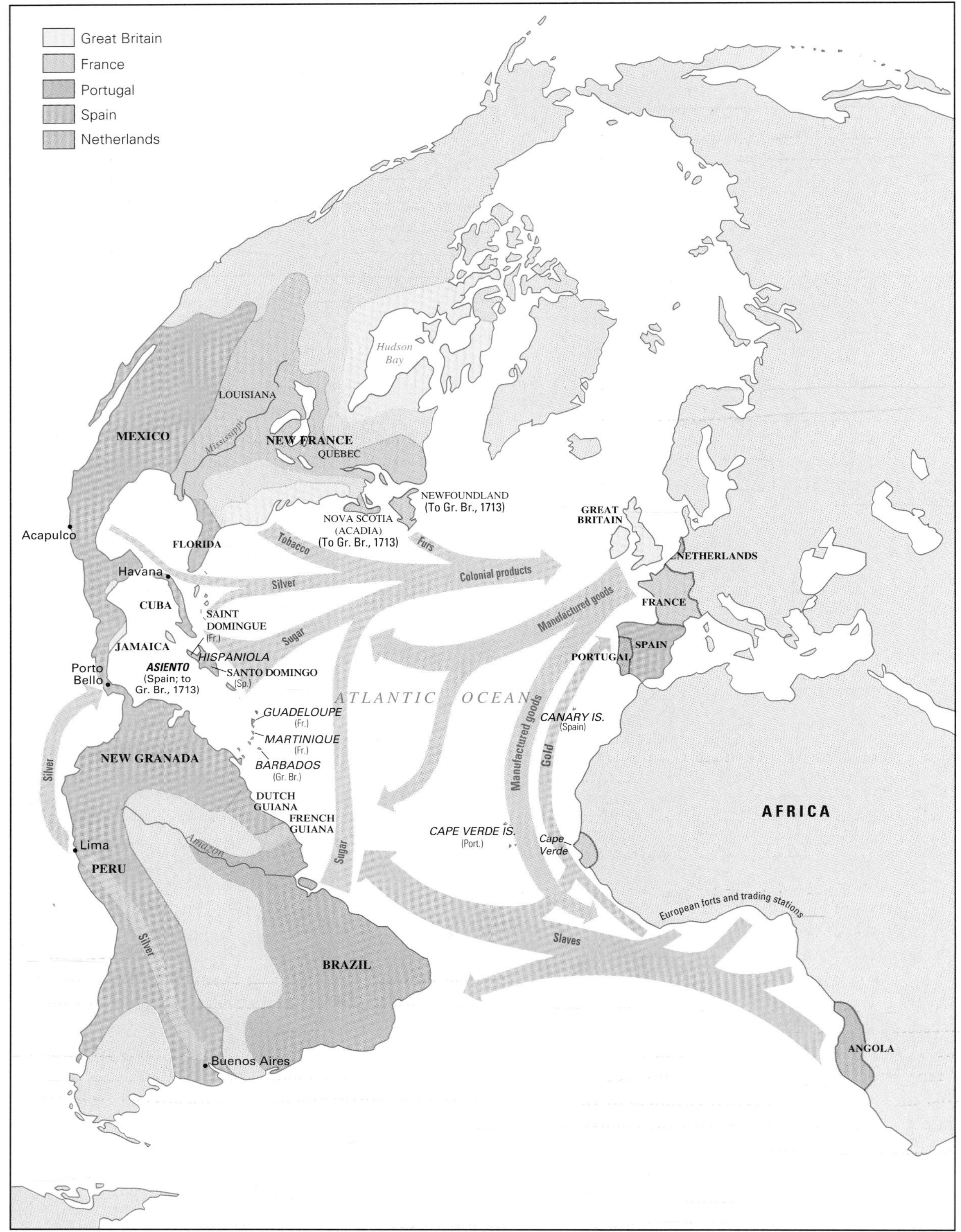

MAP 19.2 The Atlantic Economy in 1701 The growth of trade encouraged both economic development and military conflict in the Atlantic basin. Four continents were linked together by the exchange of goods and slaves.

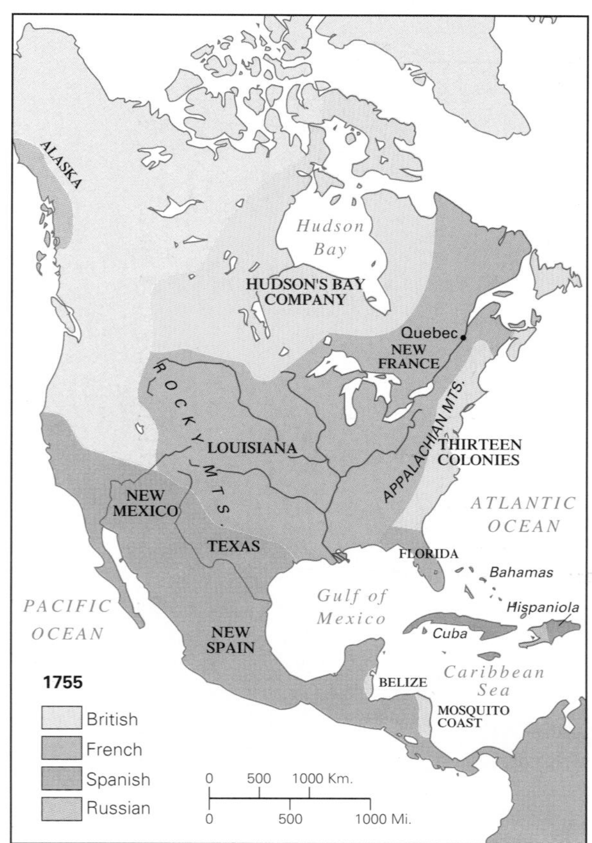

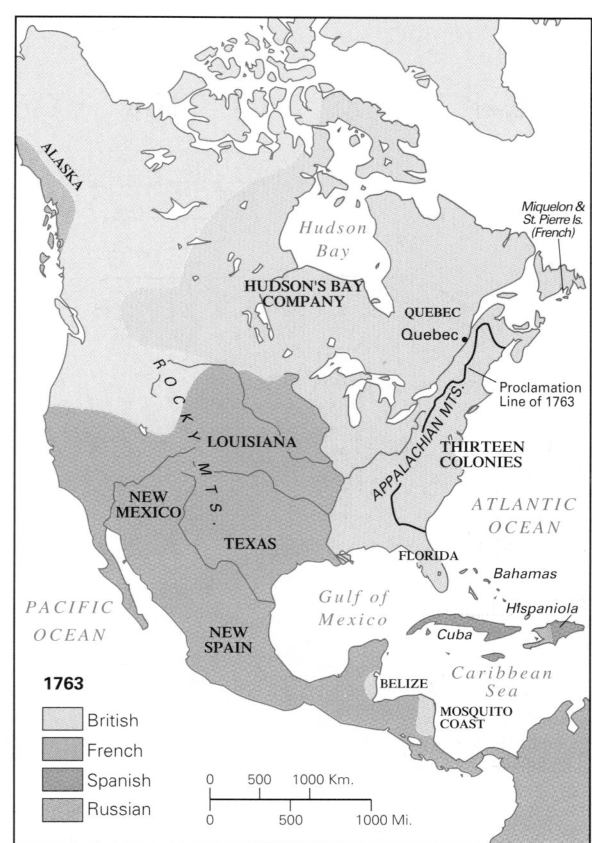

MAP 19.3 European Claims in North America Before and After the Seven Years' War (1756–1763) France lost its vast claims in North America, though the British government then prohibited colonists from settling west of the Appalachian Mountains in 1763. The British had raised taxes on themselves and the colonists to pay for the war, and they wanted to avoid costly conflicts with native Americans living in the newly conquered territory.

slave trade—the so-called *asiento*—and to let Britain send one ship of merchandise into the Spanish colonies annually, through Porto Bello on the Isthmus of Panama.

France was still a mighty competitor. The War of the Austrian Succession (1740–1748), which started when Frederick the Great of Prussia seized Silesia from Austria's Maria Theresa (see page 616), gradually became a world war that included Anglo-French conflicts in India and North America. The war ended with no change in the territorial situation in North America.

This inconclusive standoff helped set the stage for the Seven Years' War (1756–1763). In central Europe, Austria's Maria Theresa sought to win back Silesia and crush Prussia, thereby re-establishing the Habsburgs' traditional leadership in German affairs. She almost succeeded (see page 616), but Prussia survived with its boundaries intact.

Inconclusive in Europe, the Seven Years' War was the decisive round in the Franco-British competition for colonial empire. The fighting began in North America. The population of New France was centered in Quebec and along the St. Lawrence River. But French soldiers and Canadian fur traders had also built forts and trading posts along the Great Lakes, through the Ohio country, and down the Mississippi to New Orleans (see Map 19.3). Allied with many native American tribes, the French built more forts in 1753 in what is now western Pennsylvania to protect their claims. The following year, a Virginia force attacked a small group of French soldiers, and soon the war to conquer Canada was on.

Although the inhabitants of New France were greatly outnumbered—Canada counted 55,000 inhabitants, as opposed to 1.2 million in the thirteen English colonies—

The Taking of Quebec City The French successfully defended their capital from British attack in 1690 and again in 1711. But in 1759 British troops landed, scaled the cliffs in the dead of the night, and defeated the French on the Plains of Abraham above Quebec, as this print shows. The battle gave Britain a decisive victory in the long struggle for empire in North America. *(Courtesy of the Royal Ontario Museum, Toronto, Canada)*

French and Canadian forces under the experienced marquis de Montcalm fought well and scored major victories until 1758. Then, led by their new chief minister, William Pitt, whose grandfather had made a fortune in India, the British diverted men and money from the war in Europe, which remained nevertheless the main focus for the French court at Versailles. The British concentrated instead on the struggle for empire, using superior sea power to destroy the French fleet and choke off French commerce around the world. In 1759 a combined British naval and land force laid siege to fortress Quebec. After four long months, they finally defeated Montcalm's army in a dramatic battle that sealed the fate of France in North America.

British victory on all colonial fronts was ratified in the Treaty of Paris (1763). France lost all its possessions on the mainland of North America. Canada and all French territory east of the Mississippi River passed to Britain, and France ceded Louisiana to Spain as compensation for Spain's loss of Florida to Britain. France also gave up most of its holdings in India, opening the way to British dominance on the subcontinent. By 1763 British naval power, built in large part on the rapid growth of the British shipping industry after the passage of the Navigation Acts, had triumphed decisively. Britain had realized its goal of monopolizing a vast trading and colonial empire for its exclusive benefit.

Land and Labor in British America

As Britain built its empire in North America, it secured an important outlet for surplus population, so that migration abroad limited poverty in England, Scotland, and northern Ireland. The settlers also benefited, for they shared in the rights of European conquest and had privileged access to virtually free and unlimited land. Thus the situation in the American colonies contrasted sharply with that in the British Isles, where land was already highly concentrated in the hands of the nobility and gentry in 1700. White settlers who came to the colonies as free men and women, as indentured servants pledged to work seven years for their passage, or as prisoners and convicts could obtain their own farms on easy terms as soon as they had their personal freedom. And unlike the great majority of European peasants, American farmers could keep most of what they produced.

Cheap land and tremendous demand for scarce labor power were also critical factors in the growth of slavery in the British colonies. The Spanish and the Portuguese had introduced slavery into the Americas in the sixteenth century. In the seventeenth century, the Dutch aggressively followed their example and transported thousands of Africans, first to Brazil and then to the Caribbean. There slaves worked on sugar plantations that normally earned large profits for plantation owners and European traders. Most slaves came from Africa because native Americans were not accustomed to any form of forced labor and died in large numbers when enslaved.

As England adopted mercantilist policies after 1650, big investors also established valuable sugar plantations in the Caribbean and brought slave laborers from Africa to work them. The small white farmers, who had settled the islands and grew tobacco, generally sold out and migrated to the mainland colonies. Black slaves then became the overwhelming majority of the population in Britain's Caribbean colonies. By 1700 the pattern of plantations based on slave exploitation had spread to the Virginia lowlands, which British indentured servants were carefully avoiding, and by 1730 the large plantations there were worked entirely by black slaves. The exploitation of slave labor permitted an astonishing tenfold increase in tobacco production between 1700 and 1774 and created a wealthy aristocratic planter class in Maryland and Virginia. In 1790, when the U.S. population was approaching 4 million, blacks accounted for almost 20 percent of the total.

Slavery was uncommon in New England and the middle colonies, and in the course of the eighteenth century these areas began to export ever more foodstuffs, primarily to the West Indies. There the owners of the sugar plantations came to depend on the mainland colonies for grain and dried fish to feed their slaves. The plantation owners, whether they grew tobacco in Virginia and Maryland or sugar in the West Indies, had the exclusive privilege of supplying the British Isles with their products. Thus white colonists, too, had their place in the protective mercantile system of the Navigation Acts.

The abundance of almost free land resulted in a rapid increase in the colonial population in the eighteenth century. In a mere three-quarters of a century after 1700, the white population of the mainland colonies multiplied a staggering ten times, as immigrants arrived and colonial couples raised large families.

Rapid population growth did not reduce the white settlers to poverty. On the contrary, agricultural development resulted in fairly high standards of living, and on the eve of the American Revolution white men and women in the mainland British colonies probably had the highest average income and standard of living in the world.[8] There was also an unusual degree of economic equality by European standards. Few white people were extremely rich, and few were extremely poor. Thus it is clear just how much the colonists benefited from hard work and the mercantile system created by the Navigation Acts.

The Growth of Foreign Trade

Britain and especially England, its most important part, also profited greatly from the mercantile system. Above all, the rapidly growing and increasingly wealthy agricultural populations of the mainland colonies provided an expanding market for English manufactured goods. This situation was extremely fortunate, for England in the eighteenth century was gradually losing, or only slowly expanding, its sales to many of its traditional European markets. In the Americas merchant capitalists and manufacturers found new and exciting opportunities for profit and wealth.

Since the late Middle Ages, England had relied very heavily on the sale of woolen cloth in foreign markets. Indeed, as late as 1700, woolen cloth was the only important manufactured good exported from England, and fully 90 percent of it was sold to Europeans. In the course of the eighteenth century, the states of continental Europe were trying to develop their own cottage textile industries in an effort to deal with rural poverty and overpopulation. They adopted protectionist, mercantilist policies to exclude competing goods from abroad. By 1773 England was selling only about two-thirds as much woolen cloth to northern and western Europe as it had in 1700.

As trade with Europe stagnated, protected colonial markets came to the rescue. The markets of the Atlantic economy led the way (see Figure 19.3). English exports of manufactured goods to the Atlantic economy—primarily the mainland colonies of North America and the West Indian sugar islands, with an important assist from West Africa and Latin America—soared from £500,000 to £4.0 million. Sales to other colonies—Ireland and India—also rose substantially in the eighteenth century.

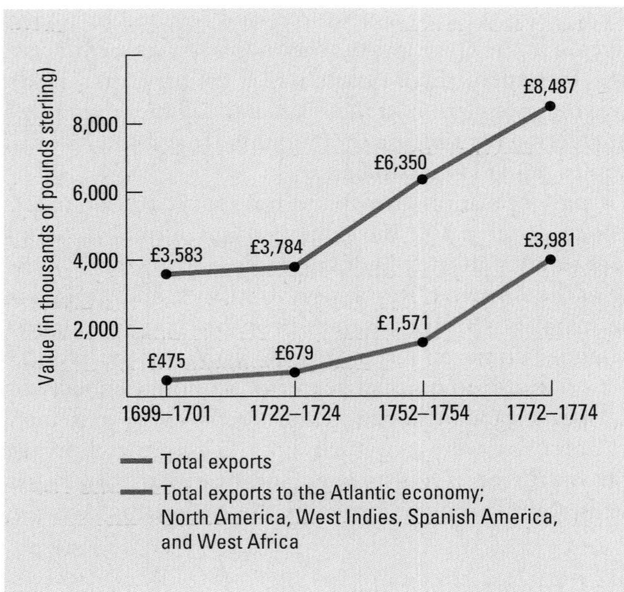

FIGURE 19.3 Exports of English Manufactured Goods, 1700–1774 While trade between England and Europe stagnated after 1700, English exports to Africa and the Americas boomed and greatly stimulated English economic development. *(Source: R. Davis, "English Foreign Trade, 1700–1774,"* Economic History Review, *2d ser., 15 (1962): 302–303.)*

English exports became much more balanced and diversified. To America and Africa went large quantities of metal items—axes to frontier settlers, firearms, chains to slave owners. There were also clocks and coaches, buttons and saddles, china and furniture, musical instruments and scientific equipment, and a host of other things. By 1750 half the nails made in England were going to the colonies. Foreign trade became the bread and butter of some industries.

Thus the mercantilist system formed in the seventeenth century to attack the Dutch and to win power and profit for England achieved remarkable success in the eighteenth century. The English concentrated in their hands much of the trade flowing through the growing Atlantic economy. Of great importance, the pressure of demand from three continents on the cottage industry of one medium-size country heightened the efforts of English merchant capitalists to find new and improved ways to produce more goods. By the 1770s England stood on the threshold of the epoch-making industrial changes that will be described in Chapter 22.

The Atlantic Slave Trade

Although the trade in African people was a worldwide phenomenon, the **Atlantic slave trade** became the most extensive and significant portion of it. In the words of a leading historian, by 1700 "it was impossible to imagine the Atlantic system without slavery and the slave trade."[9]

The forced migration of millions of Africans—so cruel, unjust, and tragic—remained a key element in the Atlantic system and western European economic expansion throughout the eighteenth century. Indeed, the brutal trade intensified dramatically after 1700, and especially after 1750. According to one authoritative estimate, European traders purchased and shipped 6.13 million African slaves across the Atlantic between 1701 and 1800—fully 52 percent of the estimated total of 11.7 million Africans transported between 1450 and 1900, not including an additional 10 to 15 percent who died in procurement and transit.[10] By the peak decade of the 1780s, shipments of black men and women averaged about 80,000 per year, in an attempt to satisfy the constantly rising demand for labor power—and slave owner profits—in the Americas.

Intensification of the slave trade resulted in fundamental changes in its organization. Before 1700 European states waged costly wars with one another through monopolist trading companies, in hopes of controlling slave exports from Africa. European agents in fortified trading posts tapped into traditional African networks and markets for slaves, who were mainly captives taken in battles between African states, plus some Africans punished with slavery by local societies or secured through small-scale raiding. After 1700, as Britain became the undisputed leader in the slave trade, European governments and ship captains of different nationalities cut back on fighting between themselves and concentrated on commerce. They generally adopted the shore method of trading, which was less expensive. Thus European ships sent boats ashore or invited African dealers to bring traders and slaves out to their ships. This method allowed ships to move easily along the coast from market to market and to depart more quickly for the Americas.

Increasing demand resulted in rising prices for African slaves in the eighteenth century. Some African merchants and rulers who controlled exports profited, and some Africans secured foreign products that they found appealing because of price or quality. But generally such economic returns did not spread very far. The negative consequences of the expanding slave trade predominated.

Wars between Africans to obtain salable captives increased, and leaders purchased more guns and gunpowder and bought relatively fewer textiles and consumer goods. The kingdom of Dahomey, which entered the slave trade in the eighteenth century and made it a royal monopoly, built up its army, attacked far into the interior, and profited greatly as a major supplier of slaves. More common perhaps was the experience of the kingdom of the Congo in central Africa, where the perpetual Portuguese search for slaves undermined the monarchy, destroyed political unity, and led to constant disorder. All along Africa's western coast small-scale raiding for slaves also spread far into the interior. There kidnappers seized and enslaved men and women like Olaudah Equiano and his sister, whose tragic separation, exile, and exploitation personified the full horror and inhumanity of the Atlantic slave trade. (See the feature "Individuals in Society: Olaudah Equiano.") Africans who committed crimes had traditionally paid fines, but because of the urgent demand for slaves many misdemeanors became punishable by sale to slave dealers. Finally, while the population of Europe (and Asia) grew very substantially in the eighteenth century, that of Africa stagnated or possibly declined.

Until 1700, and perhaps even 1750, almost all Europeans considered the African slave trade a legitimate business activity. But shiploads of African slaves were never landed in northwestern Europe, partly because cheap labor abounded there. Blacks did arrive in England (and France) as personal slaves, but if a slave ran away, the courts and the poor often supported the slave, not the slave owner. Runaways merged into London's growing population of free and escaped blacks; unions between blacks and whites were not uncommon. In 1772 a high court ruling, though limited in scope, "clearly doomed the slave status in England."[11]

After 1775, a much broader campaign to abolish slavery developed in Britain, and according to some recent scholarship, between 1788 and 1792 it grew into the first peaceful mass political movement based on the mobilization of public opinion in British history. British women

City of Luanda, Angola Founded by the Portuguese in 1575, Luanda was a center of the huge slave trade to Brazil. In this eighteenth-century print, offices and warehouses line the streets, and slaves (*right foreground*) are dragged to the ships for transportation to America. *(Miriam and Ira D. Wallach Division of Art, Prints and Photographs. The New York Public Library, Astor, Lenox, and Tilden Foundation)*

A Slave Ship and Its Victims This 1827 lithograph of slaves in a ship's hold bound for Brazil depicts the "scene of horror almost inconceivable" that Equiano encountered in crossing the Atlantic. Inhuman overcrowding of slaves resulted in shocking death rates. The man on the right will be thrown overboard. *(Houghton Library, Harvard University)*

played a critical role in this mass movement. They denounced the immorality of human bondage and stressed the cruel and sadistic treatment of female slaves and slave families. These attacks put the defenders of slavery on the defensive. In 1807 Parliament abolished the British slave trade, although slavery continued for years in British colonies and the Americas.

Revival in Colonial Latin America

When the last Spanish Habsburg, the feeble-minded Charles II, died in 1700 (see page 545), Spain's vast empire lay ready for dismemberment. Yet in one of those striking reversals with which history is replete, Spain revived. The empire held together and even prospered, while a European-oriented landowning aristocracy enhanced its position in colonial society.

Spain recovered in part because of better leadership. Louis XIV's grandson, who took the throne as Philip V (r. 1700–1746), brought new men and fresh ideas with him from France and rallied the Spanish people to his Bourbon dynasty in the long War of the Spanish Succession. When peace was restored, a series of reforming ministers reasserted royal authority, overhauling state finances and strengthening defense.

Revitalization in Madrid had positive results in the colonies. They succeeded in defending themselves from numerous British attacks and even increased in size. Spain received Louisiana from France in 1763, and missionaries and ranchers extended Spanish influence all the way to northern California.

Political success was matched by economic improvement. After declining markedly in the seventeenth century, silver mining recovered greatly, and in 1800 Spanish

Individuals in Society

Olaudah Equiano

The slave trade was a mass migration involving millions of human beings. It was also the sum of individual lives spent partly or entirely in slavery. Although most of those lives remain hidden to us, Olaudah Equiano (1745–1797) is an important exception.

Equiano was born in Benin (modern Nigeria) of Ibo ethnicity. His father, one of the village elders (or chieftains), presided over a large household that included "many slaves," prisoners captured in local wars. All people, slave and free, shared in the cultivation of family lands. One day, when all the adults were in the fields, two strange men and a woman broke into the family compound, kidnapped the eleven-year-old boy and his sister, tied them up, and dragged them into the woods. Brother and sister were separated and Olaudah was sold several times to various dealers before reaching the coast. As it took six months to walk there, his home must have been far inland.

The slave ship and the strange appearance of the white crew terrified the boy. Much worse was the long voyage from Benin to Barbados in the Caribbean, as Equiano later recounted. "The stench of the [ship's] hold . . . became absolutely pestilential . . . [and] brought on a sickness among the slaves, of which many died. . . . The shrieks of the women and the groans of the dying rendered the whole a scene of horror almost inconceivable." Placed on deck with the sick and dying, Equiano saw two and then three of his "enchained countrymen" escape somehow through the nettings and jump into the sea, "preferring death to such a life of misery."*

Equiano's new owner, an officer in the Royal Navy, took him to England and saw that the lad received some education. Engaged in bloody action in Europe for almost four years as a captain's boy in the Seven Years' War, Equiano hoped that his loyal service and Christian baptism would help to secure his freedom. He also knew that slavery was generally illegal in England. But his master deceived him. Docking in London, he and his accomplices forced a protesting and heartbroken Equiano onto a ship bound for the Caribbean.

There he was sold to Robert King, a Quaker merchant from Philadelphia who dealt in sugar and rum. Equiano developed his mathematical skills, worked hard to please as a clerk in King's warehouse, and became first mate on one of King's ships. Allowed to trade on the side for his own profit, Equiano amassed capital, repaid King his original purchase price, and received his deed of manumission at the age of twenty-one. King urged his talented former slave to stay on as a business partner, but Equiano hated the limitations and dangers of black freedom in the colonies—he was almost kidnapped back into slavery while loading a ship in Georgia—and could think only of England. Settling in London, Equiano studied, worked as a hairdresser, and went to sea periodically as a merchant seaman. He developed his ardent Christian faith and became a leading member of London's sizable black community.

Olaudah Equiano, in an engraving from his autobiography. (National Portrait Gallery, Smithsonian Institution)

Equiano loathed the brutal slavery and the vicious exploitation that he saw in the West Indies and Britain's mainland colonies. A complex and sophisticated man, he also respected the integrity of Robert King and admired British navigational and industrial technologies. He encountered white oppressors and made white friends. He once described himself as "almost an Englishman." In the 1780s he joined with white and black activists in the antislavery campaign. He wrote his *Interesting Narrative,* a well-documented autobiographical indictment of slavery. Above all, he urged Christians to live by the principles they professed and to treat blacks equally as free human beings and children of God. With the success of his widely read book, he carried his message to large audiences across Britain and Ireland and inspired the growing movement to abolish slavery.

Questions for Analysis

1. What aspects of Olaudah Equiano's life as a slave were typical? What aspects were atypical?
2. Describe Equiano's culture and personality. What aspects are most striking? Why?

*Olaudah Equiano, *The Interesting Narrative of the Life of Olaudah Equiano Written by Himself,* ed. with an introduction by Robert J. Allison (Boston: Bedford Books, 1995), pp. 56–57. Recent scholarship has re-examined Equiano's life and thrown some details of his identity into question.

Forming the Mexican People This painting by an unknown eighteenth-century artist presents a naive but sympathetic view of interracial unions and marriages in colonial Mexico. On the left, the union of a Spanish man and a native American woman has produced a racially mixed mestizo. The handsome group on the right features a mestizo woman and a Spaniard with their little daughter. *(Private Collection/Banco Nacional de Mexico)*

America accounted for half of the world's silver production. Silver mining also encouraged food production for large mining camps and gave the **Creoles**—people of Spanish blood born in America—the means to purchase more and more European luxuries and manufactured goods. A class of wealthy Creole merchants arose to handle this flourishing trade, which often relied on smuggled goods from Great Britain.

Rivaling the officials dispatched from Spain, Creole estate owners controlled much of the land and strove to become a genuine European aristocracy. Estate owners believed that work in the fields was the proper occupation of an impoverished peasantry. The defenseless native Americans suited their needs. As the indigenous population recovered in numbers, slavery and periodic forced labor gave way to widespread **debt peonage** from 1600 on. Under this system, a planter or rancher would keep the estate's Christianized, increasingly Hispanicized Indians in perpetual debt bondage by periodically advancing food, shelter, and a little money. Debt peonage was a form of serfdom.

The large middle group in Spanish colonies consisted of racially mixed **mestizos**, the offspring of Spanish men and Indian women. The most talented mestizos realistically aspired to join the Creoles, for enough wealth and power could make one considered white. Thus by the end of the colonial era, roughly 20 percent of the population was classified as white and about 30 percent as mestizo. Pure-blooded Indians accounted for most of the remainder, but some black slaves were found in every part of Spanish America. Great numbers of blacks went in chains to work the enormous sugar plantations of Portuguese Brazil, and about half the Brazilian population in the early nineteenth century was of African origin. The people of Brazil intermingled sexually and culturally, and the population grew to include every color in the racial rainbow. South America occupied an important place in the expanding Atlantic economy.

Adam Smith and Economic Liberalism

Although mercantilist policies strengthened both the Spanish and British colonial empires in the eighteenth century, a strong reaction against mercantilism ultimately set in. Creole merchants chafed at regulations imposed from Madrid. Small English merchants complained loudly about the injustice of handing over exclusive trading rights to great trading combines such as the East India Company. Wanting a bigger position in overseas commerce, independent merchants in many countries began campaigning against "monopolies" and calling for "free trade."

The general idea of freedom of enterprise in foreign trade was persuasively developed by Scottish professor of philosophy Adam Smith (1723–1790). Smith, whose *Inquiry into the Nature and Causes of the Wealth of Nations* (1776) established the basis for modern economics, was highly critical of eighteenth-century mercantilism. Mercantilism, he said, meant a combination of stifling government regulations and unfair privileges for state-approved monopolies and government favorites. Far preferable was free competition, which would best protect consumers from price gouging and give all citizens a fair and equal right to do what they did best. In keeping with the "system of natural liberty" that he advocated, Smith argued that government should limit itself to "only three duties." It should provide a defense against foreign invasion, maintain civil order with courts and police protection, and sponsor certain indispensable public works and institutions that could never adequately profit private investors.

Often lampooned in the nineteenth and twentieth centuries as a mouthpiece for business interests, Smith was one of the Enlightenment's most original and characteristic thinkers. He relied on the power of reason to unlock the secrets of the secular world, and he believed that he spoke for truth, not for special interests. Thus unlike many disgruntled merchant capitalists, Smith applauded the modest rise in real wages of British workers in the eighteenth century and went on to say, "No society can surely be flourishing and happy, of which the far greater part of the members are poor and miserable." Quite realistically, Smith concluded that employers were "always and everywhere in a sort of tacit, but constant and uniform combination, not to raise the wages of labour above their actual rate" and sometimes entered "into particular combinations to sink the wages even below this rate."[12]

Adam Smith Appointed professor at Glasgow University at age twenty-seven, Smith established an international reputation with his first book. He then became the well-paid tutor of a rich young lord and traveled widely before publishing *The Wealth of Nations,* the point of departure for modern economics. *(Special Collections/Glasgow University Library)*

Yet Smith did not call for more laws and more police power to force people into proper economic behavior. Instead, he made the pursuit of self-interest in a competitive market the source of an underlying and previously unrecognized harmony, a harmony that would result in gradual progress.

According to Smith:

[Every individual generally] neither intends to promote the public interest, nor knows how much he is promoting it. . . . He is in this case, as in many cases, led by an invisible hand

to promote an end which was no part of his intention. Nor is it always the worse for society that it was not part of it. I have never known much good done by those who affected to trade for the public good.[13]

The "invisible hand" of free competition for one and for all disciplined the greed of selfish individuals and provided the most effective means of increasing the wealth of both rich and poor.

Smith's provocative work had a great international impact. Going through eight editions in English and translated into several languages within twenty years, it quickly emerged as the classic argument for **economic liberalism** and unregulated capitalism.

Summary

While some European intellectual elites and parts of the educated public were developing a new view of the world in the eighteenth century, Europe as a whole was experiencing a gradual but far-reaching expansion. As agriculture began showing signs of modest improvement across the continent, first the Low Countries and then England launched changes that gradually revolutionized agriculture. Plague disappeared, and the populations of all countries grew significantly, thereby encouraging the growth of wage labor, cottage industry, and merchant capitalism.

Europeans also continued their overseas expansion, fighting for empire and profit and, in particular, consolidating their hold on the Americas. A revived Spain and its Latin American colonies participated fully in this expansion. As in agriculture and cottage industry, however, England and its empire proved most successful. The English concentrated much of the growing Atlantic trade in their hands, a development that challenged and enriched English industry and intensified interest in new methods of production and in an emerging economic liberalism. Thus by the 1770s, England was approaching an economic breakthrough as fully significant as the great political upheaval destined to develop shortly in neighboring France.

Key Terms

- famine foods
- open-field system
- common lands
- agricultural revolution
- crop rotation
- enclosure
- proletarianization
- cottage industry
- putting-out system
- mercantilism
- Navigation Acts
- Atlantic slave trade
- Creoles
- debt peonage
- mestizos
- economic liberalism

Notes

1. B. H. Slicher van Bath, *The Agrarian History of Western Europe, A.D. 500–1850* (New York: St. Martin's Press, 1963), p. 240.
2. E. P. Thompson, *The Making of the English Working Class* (New York: Vintage Books, 1966), p. 218.
3. Quoted in E. E. Rich and C. H. Wilson, eds., *The Cambridge Economic History of Europe,* vol. 4 (Cambridge: Cambridge University Press, 1967), p. 85.
4. Quoted in I. Pinchbeck, *Women Workers and the Industrial Revolution, 1750–1850* (New York: F. S. Crofts, 1930), p. 113.
5. Quoted in S. Chapman, *The Lancashire Cotton Industry* (Manchester, England: Manchester University Press, 1903), p. 13.
6. Quoted in P. Mantoux, *The Industrial Revolution in the Eighteenth Century* (New York: Harper & Row, 1961), p. 75.
7. Quoted in C. Wilson, *England's Apprenticeship, 1603–1763* (London: Longmans, Green, 1965), p. 169.
8. G. Taylor, "America's Growth Before 1840," *Journal of Economic History* 24 (December 1970): 427–444.
9. Seymour Drescher, "Free Labor vs. Slave Labor: The British and Caribbean Cases," in *Terms of Labor: Slavery, Serfdom, and Free Labor,* ed. Stanley L. Engerman (Stanford, Calif.: Stanford University Press, 1999), pp. 52–53.
10. P. E. Lovejoy, *Transformations in Slavery: A History of Slavery in Africa* (Cambridge: Cambridge University Press, 1983), p. 19.
11. Seymour Drescher, *Capitalism and Antislavery: British Mobilization in Comparative Perspective* (London: Macmillan, 1986), p. 38.
12. R. Heilbroner, ed., *The Essential Adam Smith* (New York: W. W. Norton, 1986), p. 196.
13. Ibid., p. 265.

Suggested Reading

The work by Slicher van Bath listed in the Notes is a wide-ranging general introduction to the gradual transformation of European agriculture. J. Blum, *The End of the Old Order in Rural Europe* (1978), is an impressive comparative study. J. de Vries, *The Dutch Rural Economy in the Golden Age, 1500–1700* (1974), examines the causes of early Dutch leadership in farming, while J. de Vries and A. van der Woude, *The First Modern Economy: Success, Failure, and Perseverance of the Dutch Economy, 1500–1815* (1997), is a masterful extension of that investigation. M. Overton, *Agricultural Revolution in England* (1996), and A. Kussmaul, *A General View of the Rural Economy of England, 1538–1840* (1989), chart the path of agricultural progress in England. J. Neeson, *Commoners: Common Right, Enclosure and Social Change, 1700–1820* (1993), stresses popular resistance to enclosure and the losses it brought for the common people. J. Gargliardo, *From Pariah to Patriot: The Changing Image of the German Peasant, 1770–1840* (1969), examines the development of reforms designed to improve the lot of the peasantry in Germany. R. Forster, *The Nobility of Toulouse in the Eighteenth Century* (1960), and A. Goodwin, ed., *The European Nobility in the Eighteenth Century* (1967), are excellent studies on aristocrats in different countries. E. Le Roy Ladurie,

The Peasants of Languedoc (1976), a brilliant and challenging study of rural life in southern France for several centuries, complements J. Goody et al., eds., *Family and Inheritance: Rural Society in Western Europe, 1200–1800* (1976). Important, more recent studies on population and disease include M. Oldstone, *Viruses, Plagues, and History* (1998), and C. Cipolla, *Miasmas and Disease: Public Health and Environment in the Pre-Industrial Age* (1992). P. Allen, *The Wages of Sin: Sex and Disease, Past and Present* (2000), tells the long, sad story of sexually transmitted diseases with compassion. J. Brewer and R. Porter, eds., *Consumption and the World of Goods* (1993), is a fascinating collection of studies and reflects the growing historical interest in consumption as well as production. O. Hufton deals vividly and sympathetically with rural migration, work, women, and much more in *The Poor in Eighteenth-Century France* (1974).

S. Ogilvie and M. Cerman, eds., *European Proto-industrialization* (1996), is a stimulating, up-to-date survey of several countries by leading scholars. An ambitious re-examination with extensive bibliographical references, M. Gutman, *Toward the Modern Economy: Early Modern Industry in Europe, 1500–1800* (1988), highlights the creativity of rural industry, as does J. Goodman and K. Honeyman, *Gainful Pursuits: The Making of Industrial Europe, 1600–1914* (1988). D. Landes, *The Unbound Prometheus* (1969), places more emphasis on the growing limitations of cottage production, as does S. Ogilvie, *State Corporatism and Proto-Industry: The Württemberg Black Forest, 1580–1797* (1997), which stresses the long life and intense conservatism of rural guilds in southern Germany. D. Hefter, ed., *European Women and Industrial Craft* (1995); G. Gullickson, *Spinners and Weavers of Auffay: Rural Industry and the Sexual Division of Labor in a French Village, 1750–1850* (1986); and M. Sonenscher, *The Hatters of Eighteenth-Century France* (1987), are all valuable.

Two excellent multivolume series, one edited by Rich and Wilson and mentioned in the Notes, and the other edited by C. Cipolla, *The Fontana Economic History of Europe,* cover the sweep of economic developments from the Middle Ages to the present and have extensive bibliographies. So does R. Cameron, *A Concise Economic History of the World* (1989), which deals mainly with Europe. F. Braudel, *Civilization and Capitalism, Fifteenth–Eighteenth Centuries* (1981, 1984), is a monumental and highly recommended three-volume synthesis. In the area of trade and colonial competition, V. Barbour, *Capitalism in Amsterdam* (1963), and C. R. Boxer, *The Dutch Seaborne Empire* (1970), are very interesting on Holland. R. Herr, *The Eighteenth-Century Revolution in Spain* (1958), studies economic policy and colonial revival. J. Brewer, *The Sinews of Power: War, Money, and the English State, 1688–1783* (1989), looks at English victories, whereas G. Parker, *The Military Revolution: Military Technology in the Rise of the West* (1988), a masterful, beautifully illustrated work, explores the roots of European power and conquest. J. Black, *Cambridge Illustrated Atlas of Warfare: Renaissance to Revolution, 1492–1792* (1996), surveys war in a global perspective with dramatic pictures and outstanding maps. D. K. Fieldhouse, *The Colonial Empires* (1971), and R. Davies, *The Rise of Atlantic Economies* (1973), are valuable works on the struggle for empire. For slavery, see especially H. Klein, *The Atlantic Slave Trade* (1999), an excellent short synthesis, as well as the works by Drescher and Lovejoy cited in the Notes. C. Midgley, *Women Against Slavery: The British Campaigns, 1780–1870* (1992), examines the major role of women abolitionists in Britain. J. Lamb, V. Smith, and N. Thomas, eds., *Exploration and Exchange: A South Seas Anthology, 1680–1900* (2001), is a collection of narratives by European visitors and a pleasure for the reader. W. J. Eccles, *France in America,* rev. ed. (1990), is outstanding and supersedes F. Parkman, *France and England in North America,* a multivolume classic and a famous example of nineteenth-century romantic history.

Listening to the Past

The Decline of the Guilds

The growth of unregulated rural manufacturing in the eighteenth century put pressure on the guilds and contributed to their decline. Guilds, also known as trade corporations, were organized in a medieval hierarchy of masters (employers), journeymen (day workers), and apprentices, and they claimed that their rules guaranteed fair wages, high-quality goods, and community values. However, both French philosophes and liberal European officials increasingly disagreed. The first excerpt, from a 1776 law abolishing French guilds by the reform minister Jacques Turgot, is an important example of the liberal critique in action. The law was repealed when Turgot fell from office, but in 1791 French revolutionaries passed a similar measure. The second excerpt, from a letter by a Prussian official, explains what it meant "to work free" and testifies to the growth of the putting-out system alongside the guilds in the German states.

Edict Abolishing the Guilds in France

In nearly all the towns of our Kingdom the practice of different arts and crafts is concentrated in the hands of a small number of masters, united in a corporation, who alone have the exclusive right to manufacture and sell particular articles; so that those of our subjects who, through wish or necessity intend to practise in these fields, must have attained the mastership, to which they are admitted only after very long tests which are as difficult as they are useless, and after having satisfied rules or manifold exactions, which absorb part of the funds they need to set up in business or even to exist. . . .

God, in giving man needs, by making work necessary, has made the right to work a universal prerogative, and this is the first, the most sacred and the most indefeasible of all rights.

We regard it as one of the first duties of our law, and one of the acts most worthy of our charity, to free our subjects from all attacks against the inalienable right of mankind. Consequently, we wish to abolish these arbitrary institutions, which do not allow the poor man to earn his living; which reject a sex whose weakness has given it more needs and fewer resources, and which seem, in condemning it to an inevitable misery, to support seduction and debauchery; which destroy emulation and industry and nullify the talents of those whose circumstances have excluded them from membership of a corporation; which deprive the State and the arts of all the knowledge brought to them by foreigners; which retard the progress of these arts through the innumerable difficulties encountered by inventors with whom different corporations dispute the right to exploit their discoveries . . . which, by the huge expenses artisans are obliged to sustain to obtain the right to work, by their various exactions and frequent fines for alleged illegalities, by all kinds of expenditure, waste and interminable law suits, resulting from the respective claims of all these corporations on the extent of their exclusive privileges, burden industry with an oppressive tax, which bears heavily on the people, and is without benefit to the State; which finally, by the facility they provide for members of corporations to combine to force the poorest members to submit to the laws of the rich, become an instrument of privilege and encourage developments, the effect of which is to raise above their natural level the price of those goods which are most essential for the people.

Breakdown of the Guilds in Germany

Following the repeated complaint of the woollen and worsted weaver named Ast, calling himself a manufacturer of woollen materials, about the runaway apprentice Leder, Your Majesty demanded on 10th and 21st inst. to be informed what the term "to work free" means. It is well known that the [free] woollen and worsted weavers in Germany and abroad are without a guild, that is to say, do not belong to a company which is governed by certain rules or privileges, but follow their trade as woollen and worsted weavers without regulation. For in an organized trade with its own Charter within which it has to operate and which has an assessor appointed whose task it is to see that it is observed, no apprentice may be taken on, unless he first proves by his birth certificate or patent of legitimacy that he was born in wedlock, or legitimized by royal patent. Further, according to the rules of apprenticeship, no apprentice may be given his freedom until his years of apprenticeship are ended according to the registry, and his master declares before the assembled trade when his indenture as journeyman is made out that he has an adequate knowledge of his craft. Similarly, no one can achieve the rights of mastership without having completed two years as journeyman as laid down, and produced the appropriate masterpiece.

All these regulations are omitted in the case of free weavers. For there are really no masters, journeymen and apprentices among them; but if a weaver is able and has resources to set up looms, he sets on workers, usually lads or those who have some knowledge of the trade, who may call themselves apprentices or journeymen, but are not recognized and esteemed as such by those within the guild, since the employer has not produced a masterpiece, the journeymen and apprentices have no indentures or birth certificates, they have no privileges, no assessor, and thus live without a regulation. Such a woollen or worsted weaver will then be called a "free worker." . . .

If such woollen weavers, who have mostly been attracted into the country by the large manufacturers, want to set up here on their own, although they have not been properly brought up within their company, and cannot be accepted as masters, they can receive permission, for themselves only, "to work free." Many of the weavers working "free" have felt the disadvantages of exclusion from their guild, so that some years ago, after some long-drawn-out disputes between the organized and unorganized weavers, they were granted the concession, on certain prescribed conditions, to be accepted as members of their guilds, whereby the number of unorganized ones has been much reduced, except for the large manufacturers and their workers, who are largely still unorganized.

A German brush maker and guild member shows a customer his wares. *(The Fotomas Index/The Bridgeman Art Library International Ltd)*

Such outsiders as have risen to the level of manufacturers, by which it is meant that they man several, perhaps many, looms with unorganized workers, have never been granted this concession, but have, as the term goes, "worked free"; and since they cannot become masters and therefore are not allowed to use the term of master, have termed themselves woollen manufacturers, in order to distinguish themselves from the other excluded, but minor, weavers.

Questions for Analysis

1. How did Turgot justify the abolition of French guilds? Do you think his reasons are valid? Why?
2. How were woolen weavers and their employers organized in Prussia?
3. Do guilds—and modern-day unions—help or hurt workers? Defend your position.

Source: S. Pollard and C. Holmes, eds., *Documents of European Economic History,* vol. 1: *The Process of Industrialization, 1750–1870* (New York: St. Martin's Press, 1968), pp. 53, 55–56.

Market in Piazza San Carlo, Turin (detail), by Michele Graneri (1736–1778). *(Museo Civico, Turin/Madeline Grimaldi)*

chapter

20 The Changing Life of the People

chapter outline

- Marriage and the Family
- Children and Education
- Food and Medical Practice
- Religion and Popular Culture

The discussion of agriculture and industry in the last chapter showed the common people at work, straining to make ends meet within the larger context of population growth, gradual economic expansion, and ferocious political competition. Yet the world of work was only part of life. That life was embedded in a rich complex of family organization, community practices, everyday experiences, and collective attitudes.

In recent years, historians have intensively studied all these aspects of popular life. The challenge has been formidable because regional variations abounded and the common people left few written records. Yet despite many ongoing debates among specialists, imaginative research has resulted in major findings and much greater knowledge. It is now possible to follow the common people beyond the world of work and ask, "What about the rest of the human experience?"

- What changes occurred in marriage and the family in the course of the eighteenth century?
- What was life like for children, and how did attitudes toward children evolve?
- What did people eat, and how did changes in diet and medical care affect people's lives?
- What were the patterns of popular religion and culture? How did these patterns come into contact—and conflict—with the critical world-view of the educated public and thereby widen the cultural divide between rich and poor in the era of the Enlightenment?

Such questions help us better understand how the peasant masses and urban poor really lived in western Europe before the age of revolution opened at the end of the eighteenth century. These questions will be the focus of this chapter.

Marriage and the Family

The basic unit of social organization is the family. It is within the structure of the family that human beings love, mate, and reproduce themselves. It is primarily the family that teaches the child, imparting values and customs that condition an individual's behavior for a lifetime. The family is also an institution woven into the web of history. It evolves and changes, assuming different forms in different times and places.

Extended and Nuclear Families

In many traditional Asian and African societies, the typical family has often been an **extended family.** A newly married couple, instead of establishing a home, will go to live with either the bride's or the groom's family. The wife and husband raise their children while living under the same roof with their own brothers and sisters, who may also be married. The family is a big, three- or four-generation clan, headed by a patriarch or perhaps a matriarch, and encompassing everyone from the youngest infant to the oldest grandparent.

Extended families, it is often said, provide security for adults and children in traditional agrarian peasant economies. Everyone has a place within the extended family, from cradle to grave. Sociologists have frequently assumed that the extended family gives way to the conjugal, or nuclear, family with the advent of industrialization and urbanization. In a society characterized by nuclear families, couples establish their own households when they marry, and they raise their children apart from their parents. A similar process has indeed been occurring in much of Asia and Africa in recent times. And since Europe was once agrarian and preindustrial, it has often been believed that the extended family must also have prevailed in Europe before being destroyed by the Industrial Revolution.

In recent years, innovative historians, analyzing previously neglected parish registers of births, deaths, and marriages, have greatly increased knowledge about the details of family life for the great majority of people before the nineteenth century. It seems clear that the extended, three-generation family was a great rarity in western and central Europe by 1700. Indeed, the extended family may never have been common in Europe, although it is hard to know about the early Middle Ages because fewer records survive. When young European couples married, they normally established their own households and lived apart from their parents. When a three-generation household came into existence, it was usually a parent who moved in with a married child rather than a newly married couple moving in with either set of parents.

Most people did not marry young in the seventeenth and early eighteenth centuries. The average person, who was neither rich nor aristocratic, married surprisingly late, many years after reaching adulthood and many more after beginning to work. In one well-studied, apparently typical English village, both men and women married for the first time at an average age of twenty-seven or older in the seventeenth and eighteenth centuries. A similar pattern existed in early-eighteenth-century France. Moreover, a substantial portion of men and women never married at all.

The custom of late marriage combined with a nuclear-family household was a distinctive characteristic of European society. It seems likely that the aggressive dynamism and creativity that have characterized European society were due in large part to the pattern of marriage and family. This pattern of marriage normally joined a mature man and a mature woman—two adults who had already experienced a great deal of life and could transmit self-reliance and real skills to the next generation.

Why was marriage delayed? The main reason was that couples normally could not marry until they could support themselves economically. The land was still the main source of income. The peasant son often needed to wait until his father's death to inherit the family farm and marry his sweetheart. Similarly, the peasant daughter and her family needed to accumulate a small dowry to help her fiancé buy land or build a house.

There were also laws and community controls to temper impetuous love and physical attraction. In some areas, couples needed the legal permission or tacit approval of the local lord or landowner in order to marry. In Austria and Germany, there were legal restrictions on marriage, and well into the nineteenth century poor couples had particular difficulty securing the approval of local officials. These officials believed that freedom to marry for the lower classes would mean more landless paupers, more abandoned children, and more money for welfare. Village elders often agreed. Thus prudence, law, and custom combined to postpone the march to the altar. This pattern helped society maintain some kind of balance between the number of people and the available economic resources.

Work Away from Home

Many young people worked within their families until they could start their own households. Boys plowed and wove; girls spun and tended the cows. Many others left

1700 | 1725 | 1750 | 1775 | 1800 | 1825

Political/Military

- 1740–1780 Reign of Maria Theresa in Austria
- 1740–1786 Reign of Frederick the Great in Prussia
- 1775–1783 American Revolution
- 1789–1799 French Revolution
- 1799–1815 Napoleonic era

Social/Economic

- 1720–1780 Government-run foundling homes established
- 1750–1850 Illegitimacy explosion
- 1757 Madame du Coudray, *Manual on the Art of Childbirth*
- 1796 Jenner performs first smallpox vaccination

Intellectual/Religious

- 1717 Attendance at elementary schools mandatory in Prussia
- 1750–1790 Wesley preaches revival in England
- 1762 Rousseau advocates child care in *Emile*
- 1763 Louis XV orders Jesuits out of France

home temporarily to work elsewhere. In the towns, a lad might be apprenticed to a craftsman for seven or fourteen years to learn a trade. During that time, he would not be permitted to marry. In most trades, he earned little and worked hard, but if he was lucky, he might eventually be admitted to a guild and establish his economic independence. More often, the young man would drift from one tough job to another: hired hand for a small farmer, wage laborer on a new road, carrier of water in a nearby town. He was always subject to economic fluctuations, and unemployment was a constant threat.

Girls also temporarily left their families to work, at an early age and in large numbers. The range of opportunities open to them was more limited, however. Service in another family's household was by far the most common job, and even middle-class families often sent their daughters into service. Thus a few years away from home as a servant were often a normal part of growing up.

The legions of young servant girls worked hard but had little real independence. Sometimes the employer paid the girl's wages directly to her parents. Constantly under the eye of her mistress, the servant girl found her tasks were many—cleaning, shopping, cooking, caring for the baby. Often the work was endless, for there were no laws to limit exploitation. Rarely were girls so brutalized that they snapped under the strain of such treatment like Varka—the Russian servant girl in Chekhov's chilling story "Sleepy"—who, driven beyond exhaustion, finally quieted her mistress's screaming child by strangling it in its cradle. But court records are full of complaints by servant girls of physical mistreatment by their mistresses. There were many others like the fifteen-year-old English girl in the early eighteenth century who told the judge that her mistress had not only called her "very opprobrious names, as Bitch, Whore and the like," but also "beat her without provocation and beyond measure."[1]

Chardin: The Kitchen Maid Lost in thought as she pauses in her work, perhaps this young servant is thinking about her village and loved ones there. Chardin was one of eighteenth-century France's greatest painters, and his scenes from everyday life provide valuable evidence for the historian. *(Samuel H. Kress Collection. Photograph © 2002 Board of Trustees, National Gallery of Art, Washington, 1738, oil on canvas, 18⅛ × 14¾)*

There was also the pressure of seducers and sexual attack. In theory, domestic service offered protection and security within a new family for a young girl leaving home. But in practice, she was often the easy prey of a lecherous master or his sons or friends. Indeed, "the evidence suggests that in all European countries, from Britain to Russia, the upper classes felt perfectly free to exploit sexually girls who were at their mercy."[2] If the girl became pregnant, she was quickly fired and thrown out in disgrace to make her own way. Prostitution and petty thievery were often the harsh consequences of unwanted pregnancy. "What are we?" exclaimed a bitter Parisian prostitute. "Most of us are unfortunate women, without origins, without education, servants and maids for the most part."[3]

Premarital Sex and Community Controls

Did the plight of some former servant girls mean that late marriage in preindustrial Europe went hand in hand with premarital sex and many illegitimate children? For most of western and central Europe until at least 1750, the answer seems to have been no. English parish registers seldom listed more than one bastard out of every twenty children baptized. Some French parishes in the seventeenth century had extraordinarily low rates of illegitimacy, with less than 1 percent of the babies born out of wedlock. Illegitimate babies were apparently a rarity, at least as far as the official church records are concerned.

At the same time, premarital sex was clearly commonplace. In one well-studied English village, 33 percent of all first children were conceived before the couple was married, and many were born within three months of the marriage ceremony. In the mid-eighteenth century, 20 percent of the women in the French village of Auffay, in Normandy, were pregnant when they got married, although only 2 percent of all babies in the village were born to unwed mothers. No doubt many of these French and English couples were already betrothed, or at least "going steady," before they entered into an intimate relationship, and pregnancy simply set the marriage date once and for all.

But the combination of very low rates of illegitimate birth with large numbers of pregnant brides also reflected the powerful **community controls** of the traditional village, particularly the open-field village, with its pattern of cooperation and common action. That spirit of common action was rapidly mobilized by the prospect of an unwed (and therefore poor) mother with an illegitimate child, a condition inevitably viewed as a grave threat to the economic, social, and moral stability of the closely knit community. Irate parents and anxious village elders, indignant priests and authoritative landlords, all combined to pressure any young people who wavered about marriage in the face of unexpected pregnancy. These controls meant in the countryside that premarital sex was not entered into lightly and that it was generally limited to those contemplating marriage.

The concerns of the village and the family weighed heavily on most aspects of a couple's life, both before and after marriage. One leading authority describes the traditional French peasant household in these terms:

> *The individuality of the couple, or rather, its tendency towards individuality, was crushed by the family institutions, and also by the social pressures exercised by the village community as a whole, and by the neighborhood in particular. Anything that might endanger the [couple's] household*

might also prejudice the village community, and the community reacted, occasionally violently, to punish those who contravened the rules. The intrusion of the community into every aspect of family life was very noticeable.[4]

Whereas uninvolved individuals today are inclined to stay out of the domestic disputes and marital scandals of their neighbors, the people in peasant communities gave such affairs the loudest and most unfavorable publicity, either at the time of the event or during the Carnival season (see page 683). Relying on degrading public rituals, the young men of the village would typically gang up on the person they wanted to punish and force him or her to sit astride a donkey facing backward and holding up the donkey's tail. They would parade the overly brutal spouse-beating husband (or wife), or the couple whose adultery had been discovered, all around the village, loudly proclaiming the offender's misdeeds with scorn and ridicule. The donkey ride and similar colorful humiliations ranging from rotten vegetables splattered on the doorstep to obscene and insulting midnight serenades were common punishments throughout much of Europe. They epitomized the community's far-reaching effort to police personal behavior and maintain community standards.

Community controls did not extend to family planning, however. Once a couple married, it generally had several children. Birth control within marriage was not unknown in western and central Europe before the nineteenth century, but it was primitive and quite undependable. The most common method was *coitus interruptus*—withdrawal by the male before ejaculation. The French, who were apparently early leaders in contraception, were using this method extensively to limit family size by the end of the eighteenth century.

Mechanical and other means of contraception were also used in the eighteenth century, but mainly by certain sectors of the urban population. The "fast set" of London used the "sheath" regularly, although primarily to protect against venereal disease, not pregnancy. Prostitutes used various contraceptive techniques to prevent pregnancy, and such information was available in large towns if a person really sought it.

New Patterns of Marriage and Illegitimacy

In the second half of the eighteenth century, the pattern of late marriage and few births out of wedlock began to change and break down. The number of illegitimate births soared between about 1750 and 1850 as much of Europe experienced an **illegitimacy explosion**. In Frankfurt, Germany, for example, illegitimate births rose steadily from about 2 percent of all births in the early 1700s to a peak of about 25 percent around 1850. In Bordeaux, France, 36 percent of all babies were being born out of wedlock by 1840. Small towns and villages experienced less startling climbs, but increases from a range of 1 to 3 percent initially to 10 to 20 percent between 1750 and 1850 were commonplace. Fewer young women were abstaining from premarital intercourse, and, more important, fewer young men were marrying the women they got pregnant. Thus a profound sexual and cultural transformation took place.

Historians are still debating the meaning of this transformation, but two interrelated ideas dominate most interpretations. First, the growth of cottage industry created new opportunities for earning a living, opportunities not tied to the land. Cottage industry tended to develop in areas where the land was poor in quality and divided into small, inadequate holdings. As cottage industry took hold in such areas, population grew rapidly because young people attained greater independence and did not have to wait to inherit a farm in order to get married and have children. A scrap of ground for a garden and a cottage for the loom and spinning wheel could be quite enough for a modest living. A contemporary observer of an area of rapidly growing cottage industry in Switzerland at the end of the eighteenth century described these changes:

The increased and sure income offered by the combination of cottage manufacture with farming hastened and multiplied marriages and encouraged the division of landholdings, while enhancing their value; it also promoted the expansion and embellishment of houses and villages.[5]

Cottage workers married not only at an earlier age but also for different reasons. Nothing could be so businesslike, so calculating, as a peasant marriage that was often dictated by the needs of the couple's families. After 1750, however, courtship became more extensive and freer as cottage industry grew. It was easier to yield to the attraction of the opposite sex and fall in love. Members of the older generation were often highly critical of the lack of responsibility they saw in the early marriages of the poor, the union of "people with only two spinning wheels and not even a bed." But such scolding did not stop cottage workers from marrying for love rather than for economic considerations as they blazed a path that factory workers would follow in the nineteenth century.

Second, the needs of a growing population sent many young villagers to towns and cities in search of temporary or permanent employment. Mobility in turn encouraged new sexual and marital relationships, which were less subject to village tradition and resulted in more illegitimate births. Yet

David Allan: The Penny Wedding (1795) The spirited merry-making of a peasant wedding was a popular theme of European artists. In rural Scotland "penny weddings" like this one were common: guests paid a fee for the food and fun; the money left over went to the newlyweds to help them get started. Music, dancing, feasting, and drinking characterized these community parties, which led the Presbyterian church to oppose them and hasten their decline. *(National Galleries of Scotland)*

most young women in urban areas found work only as servants or textile workers. Poorly paid, insecure, and with little possibility of truly independent, "liberated" lives, they looked mainly to marriage and family life as an escape from hard work and as the foundation of a satisfying life.

Promises of marriage from a man of the working girl's own class often led to sex, which was widely viewed as part of serious courtship. In one medium-size French city in 1787 to 1788, the great majority of unwed mothers stated that sexual intimacy had followed promises of marriage. Their sisters in rural Normandy reported again and again that they had been "seduced in anticipation of marriage."[6] Many soldiers, day laborers, and male servants were no doubt sincere in their proposals. But their lives were also insecure, and many hesitated to take on the heavy economic burdens of wife and child.

Thus it became increasingly difficult for a woman to convert pregnancy into marriage, and in a growing number of cases the intended marriage did not take place. The romantic, yet practical, dreams and aspirations of many young workingmen and workingwomen in towns and villages were frustrated by low wages, inequality, and changing economic and social conditions. Old patterns of marriage and family were breaking down among the common people. Only in the late nineteenth century would more stable patterns reappear.

Children and Education

In the traditional framework of agrarian Europe, women married late but then began bearing children rapidly. If a woman married before she was thirty, and if both she and her husband lived to forty-five, the chances were roughly one in two that she would give birth to six or more children. The newborn child entered a dangerous world. Infant mortality was high. One in five was sure to die, and one in three was quite likely to in the poorer areas. Newborn children were very likely to catch mysterious infectious diseases of the chest and stomach, and many babies died of dehydration brought about by a bad bout of ordinary diarrhea. Even in rich families, little could be done for an ailing child. Childhood itself was dangerous because of adult indifference, neglect, and even abuse.

Schools and formal education played only a modest role in the lives of ordinary children, and many boys and many more girls never learned to read. Nevertheless, basic literacy was growing among the popular classes, whose reading habits have been intensively studied in recent years. Attempting to peer into the collective attitudes of the common people and compare them with those of the book-hungry cultivated public, historians have produced some fascinating insights.

Child Care and Nursing

Women of the lower classes generally breast-fed their infants and for a much longer period than is customary today. Breast-feeding decreases the likelihood of pregnancy for the average woman by delaying the resumption of ovulation. By nursing their babies, women limited their fertility and spaced their children—from two to three years apart. If a newborn baby died, nursing stopped and a new life could be created. Nursing also saved lives: the breast-fed infant received precious immunity-producing substances with its mother's milk and was more likely to survive than when it was given any artificial food. In many areas of Russia, where the common practice was to give a new child a sweetened (and germ-laden) rag to suck on for its subsistence, half the babies did not survive the first year.

In contrast to the laboring poor, the women of the aristocracy and upper middle class seldom nursed their own children. The upper-class woman felt that breast-feeding was crude, common, and undignified. Instead, she hired a wet nurse to suckle her child. The urban mother of more modest means—the wife of a shopkeeper or an artisan—also commonly used a wet nurse in order to facilitate full-time work in the shop.

Wet-nursing was a very widespread and flourishing business in the eighteenth century, a dismal business within the framework of the putting-out system. The traffic was in babies rather than in wool and cloth, and two or three years often passed before the wet-nurse worker finished her task. The great French historian Jules Michelet described with compassion the plight of the wet nurse, who was still going to the homes of the rich in early-nineteenth-century France:

> *People do not know how much these poor women are exploited and abused, first by the vehicles which transport them (often barely out of their confinement), and afterward by the employment offices which place them. Taken as nurses on the spot, they must send their own child away, and consequently it often dies. They have no contact with the family that hires them, and they may be dismissed at the first caprice of the mother or doctor. If the change of air and place should dry up their milk, they are discharged without any compensation.*[7]

Other observers noted the flaws of wet-nursing. It was a common belief that with her milk a nurse passed her bad traits to a baby. When the child turned out poorly, it was assumed that "the nurse had changed it." Many observers charged that nurses were often negligent and greedy. They claimed that there were large numbers of **killing nurses** with whom no child ever survived. The nurse let the child die quickly so that she could take another child and another fee.

Foundlings and Infanticide

In the ancient world it was not uncommon to allow or force newborn babies, particularly girl babies, to die when there were too many mouths to feed. To its great and eternal credit, the early medieval church, strongly influenced by Jewish law, denounced **infanticide** as a pagan practice and insisted that every human life was sacred. The willful destruction of newborn children became a crime punishable by death. And yet, as the previous reference to killing nurses suggests, direct and indirect methods of eliminating unwanted babies did not disappear. There were, for example, many cases of "overlaying"—parents rolling over and suffocating the child placed between them in their bed. Such parents claimed they had been drunk and had acted unintentionally. In Austria in 1784, suspicious authorities made it illegal for parents to take children under five into bed with them.

The young woman who could not provide for a child had few choices. Abortions were illegal, dangerous, and apparently rare. Rather, the distraught mother could bundle up her newborn baby and leave it on the doorstep of a church, so that her child might at least be baptized. In the late seventeenth century, Saint Vincent de Paul was so distressed by the number of babies brought to the steps of Notre Dame in Paris that he established a home for foundlings. Others followed his example. In England the government acted on a petition calling for a foundling hospital "to prevent the frequent murders of poor, miserable infants at birth" and "to suppress the inhuman custom of exposing newborn children to perish in the streets."

In much of Europe in the eighteenth century, foundling homes emerged as a favorite charity of the rich and powerful. Great sums were spent on them. In the early nineteenth century the foundling home in St. Petersburg had twenty-five thousand children in its care and was receiving five thousand new babies a year. At their best, foundling homes in the eighteenth century were a good example of Christian charity and social concern in an age of great poverty and inequality.

Yet the foundling home was no panacea. By the 1770s, one-third of all babies born in Paris were being immediately abandoned to the foundling home by their mothers. Fully one-third of all those foundlings were abandoned by married couples, a powerful commentary on the standard of living among the working poor, for whom an additional mouth to feed often meant tragedy.

Abandoned Children At this French foundlings' home a desperate, secretive mother could give up her baby without any questions, day or night. She placed her child on the revolving table and the nun on duty took it in. Similar practices existed in many countries. *(Jean-Loup Charmet)*

Furthermore, great numbers of babies entered the foundling homes, but few left. Even in the best of these homes, 50 percent of the babies normally died within a year. In the worst, fully 90 percent did not survive. They succumbed to long journeys over rough roads, the intentional and unintentional neglect of their wet nurses, and the customary childhood illnesses. So great was the carnage that some contemporaries called the foundling hospitals "legalized infanticide."

Attitudes Toward Children

What were the more typical circumstances of children's lives? Did the treatment of foundlings reflect the attitudes of normal parents? Although some scholars argue otherwise, it seems that the young child was often of minor concern to its parents and to society in the eighteenth century. This indifference toward children was found in all classes; rich children were by no means exempt. The practice of using wet nurses, who were casually selected and often negligent, is one example of how even the rich and the prosperous put the child out of sight and out of mind. One French moralist, writing in 1756 about how to improve humanity, observed that "one blushes to think of loving one's children." It has been said that the English gentleman of the period "had more interest in the diseases of his horses than of his children."[8]

Feelings toward children were greatly influenced by the terrible frequency of death among children of all classes. Doctors and clergymen urged parents not to become too emotionally involved with their children, who were so unlikely to survive. Mothers especially did not always heed such warnings, but the risk of emotional devastation was very real for them. The great eighteenth-century English historian Edward Gibbon (1737–1794) wrote that "the death of a new born child before that of its parents may seem unnatural but it is a strictly probable event, since of any given number the greater part are extinguished before the ninth year, before they possess the faculties of the mind and the body." Gibbon's father named all his boys Edward after himself, hoping that at least one of them would survive to carry his name. His prudence was not misplaced. Edward the future historian and eldest survived. Five brothers and sisters who followed him all died in infancy.

The medical establishment was seldom interested in the care of children. One contemporary observer quoted a famous doctor as saying that "he never wished to be called to a young child because he was really at a loss to know what to offer for it." The best hope for children was often treatment by women healers and midwives, who helped many women deliver their babies and provided advice on child care. Nevertheless, children were still caught in a vicious circle: they were neglected because they were very likely to die, and they were likely to die because they were neglected.

Emotional detachment from children often shaded off into abuse. When parents and other adults did turn toward children, it was normally to discipline and control them. The novelist Daniel Defoe (1659–1731), who was always delighted when he saw very young children working hard in cottage industry, coined the axiom "Spare the rod and spoil the child." He meant it. So did Susannah Wesley (1669–1742), mother of John Wesley, the founder of Methodism. According to her, the first task of a parent toward her children was "to conquer the will, and bring them to an obedient temper." She reported that her babies were "taught to fear the rod, and to cry softly; by which means they escaped the abundance of correction they might otherwise have had, and that most odious noise of the crying of children was rarely heard in the house."[9]

It was hardly surprising that when English parish officials dumped their paupers into the first factories late in the eighteenth century, the children were beaten and brutalized (see pages 744–746). That was part of the child-rearing pattern—considerable indifference, on the one hand, and strict physical discipline, on the other—that prevailed throughout most of the eighteenth century.

From the middle of the century, this pattern came under increasing attack and began to change. Critics, led by Jean-Jacques Rousseau in 1762 in his famous and influential treatise *Emile* (see the feature "Listening to the Past: Gender Constructions and Education for Girls" on pages 686–687), called for greater love and tenderness toward children and proposed imaginative new teaching methods that also constructed rigid gender differences. In addition to supporting foundling homes to discourage infanticide and urging wealthy women to nurse their own babies, these new voices ridiculed the practice of swaddling: wrapping youngsters in tight-fitting clothes and blankets was generally believed to form babies properly by "straightening them out." By the end of the eighteenth century, small children were often being dressed in simpler, more comfortable clothing, allowing much greater freedom of movement. More parents expressed a delight in the love and intimacy of the child and found real pleasure in raising their offspring. These changes were part of the general growth of humanitarianism and cautious optimism about human potential that characterized the eighteenth-century Enlightenment.

Schools and Popular Literature

The role of schools and formal education outside the home was also growing more important. The aristocracy and the rich had led the way in the sixteenth century with special colleges, often run by Jesuits. But schools charged specifically with elementary education of the children of the common people usually did not appear until the seventeenth century. These schools specialized in boys and girls from seven to twelve, who were taught basic literacy and religion.

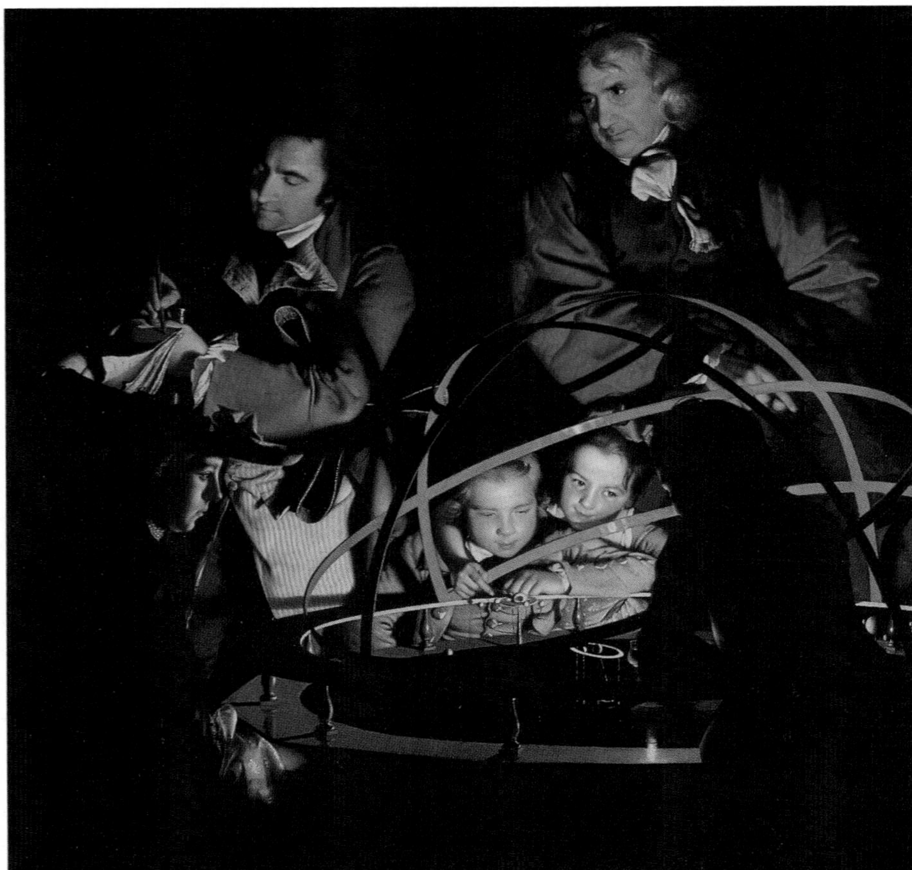

Cultivating the Joy of Discovery This English painting by Joseph Wright of Derby (1734–1797) reflects new attitudes toward child development and education, which advocated greater freedom and direct experience. The children rapturously watch a planetarium, which illustrates the movements and positions of the planets in the solar system. Wise teachers stand by, letting the children learn at their own pace. *(Derby Museum & Art Gallery/The Bridgeman Art Library International Ltd)*

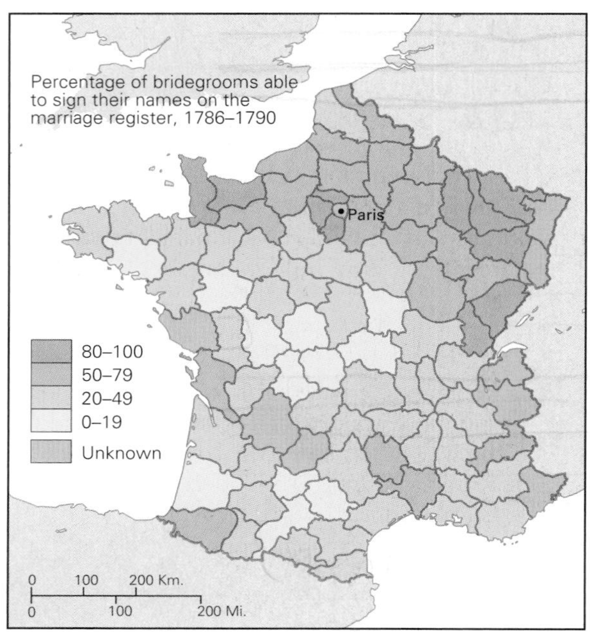

MAP 20.1 Literacy in France on the Eve of the French Revolution Literacy rates increased but still varied widely between and within states in eighteenth-century Europe. Northern France was clearly ahead of southern France.

Scholars generally agree that the religious struggle unleashed by the Protestant and Catholic Reformations served as the catalyst in promoting popular literacy between 1500 and 1800. Both Protestant and Catholic reformers pushed reading as a means of instilling their teachings more effectively. Thus literacy was often highest in border areas, such as eastern France, which were open to outside influences and to competition for believers from different churches. The growth of popular education quickened in the eighteenth century, but there was no revolutionary acceleration, and many common people received no formal education.

Prussia led the way in the development of universal education, inspired by the old Protestant idea that every believer should be able to read and study the Bible in the quest for personal salvation and by the new idea of a population capable of effectively serving the state. As early as 1717, Prussia made attendance at elementary schools compulsory, and more Protestant German states, such as Saxony and Württemberg, followed in the eighteenth century. Religious motives were also extremely important elsewhere. From the middle of the seventeenth century, Presbyterian Scotland was convinced that the path to salvation lay in careful study of the Scriptures, and it established an effective network of parish schools for rich and poor alike. The Church of England and the dissenting congregations established "charity schools" to instruct the children of the poor, and in 1682 France began setting up Christian schools to teach the catechism and prayers as well as reading and writing. France did less well than the Habsburg state, the only Catholic land to promote elementary education enthusiastically in the eighteenth century. Some elementary education was becoming a reality, and schools were of growing significance in the life of the child.

The result of these efforts was a remarkable growth in basic literacy between 1600 and 1800. Whereas in 1600 only one male in six was barely literate in France and Scotland, and one in four in England, by 1800 almost nine out of ten Scottish males, two out of three French males (see Map 20.1), and more than half of English males were literate. In all three countries, the bulk of the jump occurred in the eighteenth century. Women were also increasingly literate, although they lagged behind men in most countries.

The growth in literacy promoted a growth in reading, and historians have carefully examined what the common people read in an attempt to discern what they were thinking. One thing seems certain: the major philosophical works of the Enlightenment had little impact on peasants and workers, who could neither afford nor understand those favorites of the book-hungry educated public.

Although the Bible remained the overwhelming favorite, especially in Protestant countries, the staple of popular literature was short pamphlets known as chapbooks. Printed on the cheapest paper available, many chapbooks dealt with religious subjects. They featured Bible stories, prayers, devotions, and the lives of saints and exemplary Christians. Promising happiness after death, devotional literature was also intensely practical. It gave the believer moral teachings and a confidence in God that helped in daily living.

Entertaining, often humorous stories formed a second element of popular literature. Fairy tales, medieval romances, fictionalized history, and fantastic adventures—these were some of the delights that filled the peddler's pack as he approached a village. Both heroes and villains possessed superhuman powers in this make-believe world, a world of danger and magic, of fairy godmothers and evil trolls. But the good fairies always triumphed over the evil ones in the story's marvelous resolution.

The significance of these entertaining stories for the peasant reader is debated. Many scholars see them reflecting a desire for pure escapism and a temporary flight

A Peasant Family Reading the Bible Praised by the philosophe Diderot for its moralistic message, this engraving of a painting by Jean-Baptiste Greuze (1725–1805) does capture the power of sacred texts and the spoken word. The peasant patriarch reads aloud from the massive family Bible and the close-knit circle of absorbed listeners concentrates on every word. Only the baby is distracted. *(Bibliothèque Nationale, Paris/Giraudon/Art Resource, NY)*

from harsh everyday reality. Others see these tales reflecting ancient folk wisdom and counseling prudence in a world full of danger and evil, where wolves dress up like grandmothers and eat Little Red Riding Hoods.

Finally, some popular literature was highly practical, dealing with rural crafts, household repairs, useful plants, and similar matters. Much of such lore was stored in almanacs. With calendars listing secular, religious, and astrological events mixed in with agricultural schedules, bizarre bits of information, and jokes, the almanac was universal, noncontroversial, and highly appreciated, even by many in the comfortable classes. "Anyone who could would read an almanac."[10]

In general, however, the reading of the common people had few similarities with that of educated elites. Popular literature was simple and practical, both as devotional self-help and as how-to instruction. It was also highly escapist, not unlike the mass of inexpensive paperbacks sold in drugstores today. Neither the practical nor the escapist elements challenged the established order. Rather, the common people were apparently content with works that reinforced traditional values and did not foster social or religious criticism. These results fit well with the modest educational objectives of rulers and educated elites. They believed that carefully limited instruction stressing religion and morals was useful to the masses but that too much study would only disorient them and foster discontent.

Food and Medical Practice

As we saw in Chapter 19, the European population increased rapidly in the eighteenth century. Plague and starvation gradually disappeared, and Europeans lived longer. What were the characteristics of diets and nutrition in this era of improving health and longevity? Although medical practice played only a small part, what was it like in the eighteenth century? What does a comparison of rich and poor reveal?

Diets and Nutrition

At the beginning of the eighteenth century, ordinary men and women depended on grain as fully as they had in the past. Bread was quite literally the staff of life. Peasants in the Beauvais region of France ate two pounds of bread a day, washing it down with water, green wine, beer, or a little skim milk. Their dark bread was made from a mixture of roughly ground wheat and rye—the standard flour of the common people. The poor also ate grains in soup and gruel. In rocky northern Scotland, for example, people depended on oatmeal, which they often ate half-cooked so that it would swell in their stomachs and make them feel full.

Little wonder, then, that an adequate supply of grain and an affordable price of bread loomed large in the popular imagination. Even peasants normally needed to buy some grain for food, and, in full accord with landless laborers and urban workers, they believed in the old medieval idea of the **just price.** That is, they believed that prices should be "fair," protecting both consumers and producers and imposed by government decree if necessary.

In the later eighteenth century, this traditional, moral view of prices and the economy clashed repeatedly with the emerging free-market philosophy of unregulated supply and demand, which was increasingly favored by government officials, large landowners, and economists led by Adam Smith (see page 655). In years of poor harvests and soaring prices, this clash often resulted in food riots and popular disturbances. Peasants and workers would try to stop wagons loaded with grain from leaving their region, or they would seize grain held by speculators and big merchants accused of hoarding and rigging the market. (Usually the tumultuous crowd paid what it

An English Food Riot Nothing infuriated ordinary women and men more than the idea that merchants and landowners were withholding grain from the market in order to push high prices even higher. In this cartoon an angry crowd hands out rough justice to a rich farmer accused of hoarding. *(Courtesy of the Trustees of the British Museum)*

considered to be a fair price for what it took.) Governments were keenly aware of the problem of adequate grain supplies, and they would sometimes try to control prices to prevent unrest in crisis years.

The rural and urban poor also ate a fair quantity of vegetables. Indeed, vegetables were considered "poor people's food." Peas and beans were probably the most common; grown as field crops in much of Europe since the Middle Ages, they were eaten fresh in late spring and summer. Dried, they became the basic ingredients in the soups and stews of the long winter months. In most regions, other vegetables appeared in season on the tables of the poor, primarily cabbages, carrots, and wild greens. Fruit was uncommon and limited to the summer months.

The common people of Europe loved meat and eggs, but they seldom ate their fill. Indeed, the poor ate less meat in 1700 than in 1500 because their general standard of living had declined as the population surged in the sixteenth century (see page 637) and meat became more expensive. In the eighteenth century, the beginnings of agricultural transformation (see page 633) increased per capita meat consumption only in Britain and the Low Countries. Moreover, in most European countries harsh game laws deprived the poor of the right to hunt and eat game such as rabbits, deer, and partridges. Only nobles and large landowners could legally kill game. Few laws were more bitterly resented—or more frequently broken—by ordinary people than those governing hunting. When the poor did eat meat—on a religious holiday or at a wedding or other festive occasion—it was most likely lamb or mutton. Sheep could survive on rocky soils and did not compete directly with humans for the slender resources of grain.

Milk was rarely drunk. Perhaps because some individuals do suffer seriously from dairy allergies, it was widely believed that milk caused sore eyes, headaches, and a variety of ills, except among the very young and very old. Milk was used primarily to make cheese and butter, which did not spoil as milk did and which the poor liked but could afford only occasionally. Medical and popular opinion considered whey, the watery liquid left after milk was churned, "an excellent temperate drink."

The diet of the rich—aristocrats, officials, and the comfortable bourgeoisie—was traditionally quite different from that of the poor. The upper classes were rapacious carnivores, and a truly elegant dinner consisted of one rich meat after another. Three separate meat courses might be followed by three fish courses laced with piquant sauces and complemented with sweets, cheeses, and nuts of all kinds. Fruits and vegetables were not often found on the tables of the rich.

There was also an enormous amount of overdrinking among the rich. The English squire, for example, who loved to hunt with his hounds, loved to drink with a similar passion. He became famous as the "four-bottle man." Sometimes he ended the evening under the table in a drunken stupor, but very often he did not. The wine and the meat were consumed together in long hours of sustained excess, permitting the gentleman and his guests to drink enormous quantities without getting stupefyingly drunk.

The diet of small traders, master craftsmen, minor bureaucrats—the people of the towns and cities—was generally less monotonous than that of the peasantry. The markets, stocked by market gardens on the outskirts, provided a substantial variety of meats, vegetables, and fruits, although bread and beans still formed the bulk of such families' diets.

There were also regional dietary differences in 1700. Generally speaking, northern, Atlantic Europe ate better than southern, Mediterranean Europe. The poor of England and the Netherlands probably ate best of all. Contemporaries on both sides of the Channel often contrasted the English citizen's consumption of meat with the French peasant's greater dependence on bread and vegetables.

The Impact of Diet on Health

How were the poor and the rich served by their quite different diets? At first glance, the diet of the laboring poor, relying as it did on grains and vegetables, might seem low in protein. However, the whole-grain wheat or rye flour used in eighteenth-century bread retained most of the bran—the ground-up husk—and the all-important wheat germ, which contains higher proportions of some minerals, vitamins, and good-quality proteins than does the rest of the grain. In addition, the field peas and beans contained protein that complemented the proteins in whole-grain bread. The proteins in whey, cheese, and eggs, which the poor ate at least occasionally, also supplemented the bread and vegetables.

The basic bread-and-vegetables diet of the poor *in normal times* was adequate. But a key dietary problem was getting enough green vegetables (or milk) to ensure adequate supplies of vitamins A and C. A severe deficiency of vitamin C produces scurvy, a disease that leads to rotting gums, swelling of the limbs, and great weakness. Before the season's first vegetables, many people experienced shortages of vitamin C and suffered from mild cases of scurvy. (Scurvy was an acute problem for sailors on long voyages and by the end of the sixteenth century was being controlled on ships by a daily ration of lime juice.)

Royal Interest in the Potato Frederick the Great of Prussia, shown here supervising cultivation of the potato, used his influence and position to promote the new food on his estates and throughout Prussia. Peasants could grow potatoes with the simplest hand tools, but it was backbreaking labor, as this painting by R. Warthmüller suggests. *(Private Collection, Hamburg/AKG London)*

The practice of gorging on meat, sweets, and spirits caused the rich their own nutritional problems. Because of their great disdain for fresh vegetables, they, too, were very often deficient in vitamins A and C. Gout was a common affliction of the overfed and underexercised rich. No wonder they were often caricatured as dragging their flabby limbs and bulging bellies to the table to stuff their swollen cheeks and poison their livers. People of moderate means, who could afford some meat and dairy products with fair regularity but who had not abandoned the bread and vegetables of the poor, were best off from a nutritional standpoint.

Patterns of food consumption changed rather markedly as the century progressed. More varied diets associated with new methods of farming were confined largely to the Low Countries and England, but a new food—the potato—came to the aid of the poor everywhere. Introduced into Europe from the Americas—along with corn, squash, tomatoes, and many other useful plants—the humble potato is actually an excellent food. Containing a good supply of carbohydrates, calories, and vitamins A and C, the potato offset the lack of vitamins from green vegetables in the poor person's winter and early-spring diet, and it provided a much higher caloric yield than grain for a given piece of land.

For some desperately poor peasants the potato replaced grain as the primary food in the eighteenth century. This happened first in Ireland, where English (Protestant) repression and exploitation forced large numbers of poor (Catholic) peasants to live off tiny scraps of rented ground. Elsewhere in Europe, potatoes took hold more slowly because many people did not like them. Thus, potatoes were first fed to pigs and livestock, and there was even debate over whether they were fit for humans. In Germany the severe famines caused by the Seven Years' War settled the matter: potatoes were edible and not just "famine food." By the end of the century, the potato had become an important dietary supplement in much of Europe.

There was also a general growth of market gardening, and a greater variety of vegetables appeared in towns and cities. In the course of the eighteenth century, the large towns and cities of maritime Europe began to receive semitropical fruits, such as oranges and lemons, from Portugal and the West Indies, although they were not cheap.

Bread also began to change, most noticeably for the English and for the comfortable groups on the European continent. Rising incomes and new tastes led to a shift from whole-grain black or brown bread to "bread as white as snow" and started a decline in bread's nutritional value. The high-roughage bran and some of the dark but high-vitamin germ were increasingly sifted out by millers. This foretold further "improvements" in the nineteenth century, which would leave bread perfectly white and greatly reduced in nutritional value.

Another sign of nutritional decline was the growing consumption of sugar. Initially a luxury, sugar dropped rapidly in price as slave-based production increased in the Americas and the sweetener was much more widely used in the eighteenth century. This development probably led to an increase in cavities and to other ailments as well, although the greater or lesser poverty of the laboring poor still protected most of them from the sugar-tooth virus of the rich and well-to-do.

Medical Practitioners

Although sickness, pain, and disease—intractable challenges built into the human condition—permeated the European experience in the eighteenth century, medical science played a very small part in improving the health of most people. Yet the Enlightenment's growing focus on discovering the laws of nature and on human problems did give rise to a great deal of research and experimentation. The century also saw a remarkable rise in the number of medical practitioners. Therefore, when significant breakthroughs in knowledge came in the middle and late nineteenth century, they could be rapidly evaluated and diffused.

Care of the sick in the eighteenth century was the domain of several competing groups: faith healers, apothecaries (or pharmacists), physicians, surgeons, and midwives. Both men and women were prominent in the healing arts, as had been the case since the Middle Ages. But by 1700 the range of medical activities open to women was severely restricted, because women were generally denied admission to medical colleges male practitioners dominated and lacked the diplomas necessary for practice as physicians and surgeons. In the course of the eighteenth century, the position of women as midwives and healers further eroded.

Faith healers remained active. They and their patients believed that demons and evil spirits caused disease by lodging in people and that the proper treatment was to exorcise, or drive out, the offending devil. This demonic view of disease was strongest in the countryside, where popular belief placed great faith in the healing power of religious relics, prayer, and the laying on of hands. Faith healing was particularly effective in the treatment of mental disorders such as hysteria and depression, where the link between attitude and illness is most direct.

In the larger towns and cities, apothecaries sold a vast number of herbs, drugs, and patent medicines for every conceivable "temperament and distemper." Their prescriptions were incredibly complex—a hundred or more drugs might be included in a single prescription—and often very expensive. Some of the drugs and herbs undoubtedly worked. For example, strong laxatives were given to the rich for their constipated bowels, and regular **purging** of the bowels was considered essential for good health and the treatment of illness. In fact, only bloodletting was more effective in speeding patients to their graves. In the countryside, people often turned to midwives and women healers for herbs and folk remedies.

Physicians, who were invariably men, were apprenticed in their teens to a practicing physician for several years of on-the-job training. This training was then rounded out with hospital work or some university courses. Because such prolonged training was expensive, physicians continued to come mainly from prosperous families, and they usually concentrated on urban patients from similar social backgrounds. They had little contact with urban workers and less with peasants.

Physicians in the eighteenth century were increasingly willing to experiment with new methods, but time-honored practices lay heavily on them. Physicians, like apothecaries, laid great stress on purging. And bloodletting was still considered a medical cure-all. It was the way "bad blood," the cause of illness, was removed and the balance of humors necessary for good health was restored.

Surgeons, in contrast to physicians, made considerable medical and social progress in the eighteenth century. Long considered as ordinary male artisans comparable to butchers and barbers, surgeons began studying anatomy seriously and improved their art. With endless opportunities to practice, army surgeons on gory battlefields led the way. They learned that a soldier with an extensive wound, such as a shattered leg or arm, could perhaps be saved if the surgeon could obtain above the wound a flat surface that could be cauterized with fire. Thus if a soldier (or a civilian) had a broken limb and the bone stuck out, the surgeon amputated so that the remaining stump could be cauterized and the likelihood of death reduced.

The eighteenth-century surgeon (and patient) labored in the face of incredible difficulties. Almost all operations were performed without any painkiller, for the anesthesias of the day were hard to control and were believed too dangerous for general use. The terrible screams of people whose limbs were being sawed off echoed across battlefields and through hospitals. Many patients died from the agony and shock of such operations. Surgery was also performed in the midst of filth and dirt, for there simply was no knowledge of bacteriology and the nature of infection. The simplest wound treated by a surgeon could fester and lead to death.

Teaching Midwives This plate from Madame du Coudray's text for midwives, *Manual on the Art of Childbirth,* illustrates "another incorrect method of delivery." The caption tells the midwife that she should have rotated the baby within the womb to face the mother's back, so that the chin does not catch on the pubis bone and dislocate the jaw. *(Rare Books Division, Countway [Francis A.] Library of Medicine)*

Cette Planche réprésente encore une fauße manœuvre en préférant de tirer l'enfant la face en devant plutôt que de lui avoir tourné par derri-
ère, ce qui donne lieu au menton de l'enfant de s'accrocher sur les os Pubis èt en continuant de le tirer dans cette position la tête se renversant
en arrière la machoire peut se luxer, d'ailleurs l'occiput par ce renverse-
ment appuyant sur l'os Sacrum, il est impoßible de faire paßer la tête
dans le détroit du petit baßin, il faut donc en repoußant l'enfant un
peu en haut lui retourner la face en arrière.

Midwives, who were a special object of suspicion and persecution in the witch-hunt craze of the sixteenth and seventeenth centuries, continued to deliver the overwhelming majority of babies throughout the eighteenth century. The typical midwife was an older, often widowed woman of modest social origins and long professional experience. Trained initially by another woman practitioner, the midwife primarily assisted in labor and delivering babies. But the midwife also treated female problems, such as irregular menstrual cycles, breast-feeding difficulties, sterility, and venereal disease, and she ministered to small children.

The midwife orchestrated labor and birth in a woman's world, where friends and relatives offered the pregnant woman assistance and encouragement in the familiar surroundings of her own home. Excluded by tradition and modesty, the male surgeon (and the husband) rarely entered this world, because most births, then as now, were normal and spontaneous. Following the invention of the forceps, which might help in an exceptionally difficult birth, surgeon-physicians used their monopoly over this and other instruments to seek lucrative new business. Attacking midwives as ignorant and dangerous, they persuaded growing numbers of wealthy women of the superiority of their services and sought to undermine faith in midwives.

Recent research suggests that women practitioners successfully defended much but not all of their practice in the eighteenth century. In France one enterprising Parisian midwife secured royal financing for her campaign to teach better birthing techniques to village midwives, which reinforced the position of women practitioners. (See the feature "Individuals in Society: Madame du Coudray, the Nation's Midwife.") In northern Italy, state and church pressures led to major changes in midwife training and certification, but women remained dominant in the birthing trade. It appears that midwives generally lost no more babies than male doctors, who were still summoned to treat nonelite women only when a life-threatening situation required surgery.

While ordinary physicians were bleeding, apothecaries purging, surgeons sawing, faith healers praying, and midwives assisting, the leading medical thinkers were attempting to pull together and assimilate all the information and misinformation they had been accumulating. The attempt was ambitious: to systematize medicine around simple, basic principles, as Newton had done in physics. But the schools of thought resulting from such speculation and theorizing did little to improve medical care.

Individuals in Society

Madame du Coudray, the Nation's Midwife

In 1751 a highly esteemed Parisian midwife left the capital for a market town in central France. Having accepted an invitation to instruct local women in the skills of childbirth, Madame Angelique Marguerite Le Boursier du Coudray soon demonstrated a marvelous ability to teach students and win their respect. The thirty-six-year-old midwife found her mission: she would become the nation's midwife.

For eight years Madame du Coudray taught young women from the impoverished villages of Auvergne. In doing so, she entered into the world of unschooled midwives, typically solid matrons with several children who relied on traditional birthing practices and folk superstitions. Trained in Paris through a rigorous three-year apprenticeship and imbued with an Enlightenment faith in the power of knowledge, du Coudray had little sympathy for these village midwives. Many peasant mothers told her about their difficult deliveries and their many uterine "infirmities," which they attributed to "the ignorance of the women to whom they had recourse, or to that of some inexperienced village [male] surgeons."* Du Coudray agreed. Botched deliveries by incompetents resulted in horrible deformities and unnecessary deaths.

Determined to raise standards, Madame du Coudray saw that her unlettered pupils learned through the senses, not through books. Thus she made, possibly for the first time in history, a life-size obstetrical model—a "machine"—out of fabric and stuffing for use in her classes. "I had . . . the students maneuver in front of me on a machine . . . which represented the pelvis of a woman, the womb, its opening, its ligaments, the conduit called the vagina, the bladder, and *rectum intestine*. I added a [toy] child of natural size, whose joints were flexible enough to be able to be put in different positions." Now du Coudray could demonstrate the problems of childbirth, and each student could practice on the model in the "lab session."

As her reputation grew, Madame du Coudray sought to reach a national audience. In 1757 she wrote and had published the first of several editions of her *Manual on the Art of Childbirth*. Handsomely and effectively illustrated (see page 676), the *Manual* incorporated her hands-on teaching method and served as a text and reference for students and graduates. In 1759 the government authorized Madame du Coudray to carry her instruction "throughout the realm" and promised financial support. Her reception was not always warm, for she was a self-assured and demanding woman, who could anger old midwives, male surgeons, and skeptical officials. But aided by servants, a niece, and her husband, this inspired and indefatigable woman took her course from town to town until her retirement in 1784. Typically her students were young peasant women on tiny stipends, who came into town from surrounding villages for two to three months of instruction. Classes met mornings and afternoons six days a week, with ample time to practice on the mannequin. After a recuperative break, Madame du Coudray and her entourage moved on.

Madame du Coudray in 1769, at the height of her importance. (Rare Books Division, Countway [Francis A.] Library of Medicine)

Teaching thousands of fledgling midwives, Madame du Coudray may well have contributed to the decline in infant mortality and to the increase in population occurring in France in the eighteenth century—an increase she and her royal supporters fervently desired. Certainly she spread better knowledge about childbirth from the educated elite to the common people.

Questions for Analysis

1. How do you account for Madame du Coudray's remarkable success?
2. Does Madame du Coudray's career reflect tensions between educated elites and the common people? If so, how?

*Quotes are from Nina Gelbart, *The King's Midwife: A History and Mystery of Madame du Coudray* (Berkeley: University of California Press, 1998), pp. 60–61. This definitive biography is excellent.

Hospital Life Patients crowded into hospitals like this one in Hamburg in 1746 had little chance of recovery. A priest by the window administers last rites, while in the center a surgeon coolly saws off the leg of a man who has received no anesthesia. *(Germanisches Nationalmuseum, Nuremberg)*

Hospitals and Medical Experiments

Hospitals were terrible places throughout most of the eighteenth century. There was no isolation of patients. Operations were performed in a patient's bed. Nurses were old, ignorant, greedy, and often drunk women. Fresh air was considered harmful, and infections of every kind were rampant. Diderot's article in the *Encyclopedia* on the Hôtel-Dieu in Paris, the "richest and most terrifying of all French hospitals," vividly describes normal conditions of the 1770s:

> *Imagine a long series of communicating wards filled with sufferers of every kind of disease who are sometimes packed three, four, five or even six into a bed, the living alongside the dead and dying, the air polluted by this mass of unhealthy bodies, passing pestilential germs of their afflictions from one to the other, and the spectacle of suffering and agony on every hand. That is the Hôtel-Dieu.*
>
> *The result is that many of these poor wretches come out with diseases they did not have when they went in, and often pass them on to the people they go back to live with. Others are half-cured and spend the rest of their days in an invalidism as hard to bear as the illness itself; and the rest perish, except for the fortunate few whose strong constitutions enable them to survive.*[11]

No wonder the poor of Paris hated hospitals and often saw confinement there as a plot to kill paupers.

In the last years of the century, the humanitarian concern already reflected in Diderot's description of the Hôtel-Dieu led to a movement for hospital reform throughout western Europe. Efforts were made to improve ventilation and eliminate filth on the grounds that bad air caused disease. The theory was wrong, but the results were beneficial, since the spread of infection was somewhat reduced.

Mental hospitals, too, were incredibly savage institutions. The customary treatment for mental illness was bleeding and cold water, administered more to maintain discipline than to effect a cure. Violent persons were chained to the wall and forgotten. A breakthrough of sorts occurred in the 1790s when William Tuke founded the first humane sanatorium in England. In Paris an innovative warden, Philippe Pinel, took the chains off the mentally disturbed in 1793 and tried to treat them as patients rather than as prisoners.

In the eighteenth century, all sorts of wildly erroneous ideas about mental illness circulated. One was that moonlight caused madness, a belief reflected in the word *lunatic*—someone harmed by lunar light. Another mid-eighteenth-century theory, which lasted until at least 1914, was that masturbation caused madness, not to mention acne, epilepsy, and premature ejaculation. Thus parents, religious institutions, and schools waged relentless war on masturbation by males, although they were uninterested in female masturbation.

In the second half of the eighteenth century, medicine in general turned in a more practical and experimental direction. Some of the experimentation was creative quackery involving the recently discovered phenomenon of electricity. One magnificent quack in London promoted sleep on a cure-all Celestial Bed, which was lavishly decorated with magnets and electrical devices. A single night on the bed cost a small fortune. Because so many expensive treatments were worthless or harmful, the common people were probably much less deprived by their reliance on faith healers and folk medicine than one might think.

Experimentation and the intensified search for solutions to human problems led to some real advances in medicine after 1750, however. The eighteenth century's greatest medical triumph was the conquest of smallpox. With the progressive decline of bubonic plague, smallpox became the most terrible of the infectious diseases, and it is estimated that 60 million Europeans died of it in the eighteenth century. Fully 80 percent of the population was stricken at some point in life.

The first step in the conquest of this killer in Europe came in the early eighteenth century. An English aristocrat whose beauty had been marred by the pox, Lady Mary Wortley Montagu, learned about the long-established practice of **smallpox inoculation** in the Muslim lands of western Asia while her husband was serving as British ambassador to the Ottoman Empire. She had her own son successfully inoculated with the pus from a smallpox victim and was instrumental in spreading the practice in England after her return in 1722. But inoculation was risky and widely condemned because about one person in fifty died from it. In addition, people who had been inoculated were infectious and often spread the disease.

Subsequent success in reducing the risks of inoculation and in finding cheaper methods led to something approaching mass inoculation in England in the 1760s. On the continent, the well-to-do were also inoculated, beginning with royal families and then spreading to the middle classes. By the later years of the century, smallpox inoculation was playing some part in the decline of the death rate and the general increase in European population.

The final breakthrough against smallpox came at the end of the century. Edward Jenner (1749–1823), a talented country doctor, noted that in the English countryside there was a long-standing belief that dairy maids who had contracted cowpox did not get smallpox. Cowpox produces sores on the cow's udder and on the hands of the milker. The sores resemble those of smallpox, but the disease is mild and not contagious.

For eighteen years Jenner practiced a kind of Baconian science, carefully collecting data on protection against smallpox by cowpox. Finally, in 1796 he performed his first vaccination on a young boy using matter taken from a milkmaid with cowpox. Performing more successful vaccinations, Jenner published his findings in 1798. The new method of treatment spread rapidly, and smallpox soon declined to the point of disappearance in Europe and then throughout the world. Jenner eventually received prizes totaling £30,000 from the British government for his great discovery, a fitting recompense for a man who made an enormous gift to humanity and helped lay the foundation for the science of immunology in the nineteenth century.

Religion and Popular Culture

Though the critical spirit of the Enlightenment spread among the educated elite in the eighteenth century, the majority of ordinary men and women remained firmly committed to the Christian religion, especially in rural areas. Religious faith promised salvation and eternal life, and it gave comfort and courage in the face of sorrow and death. Religion also remained strong because it was usually embedded in local traditions, everyday social experience, and popular culture.

Yet the popular religion of village Europe was everywhere enmeshed in a larger world of church hierarchies and state power. These powerful outside forces sought to regulate religious life at the local level. Their efforts created tensions that helped set the scene for a vigorous religious revival in Germany and England. Similar tensions arose in Catholic countries, where powerful elites criticized and attacked popular religious practices that their increasingly rationalistic minds deemed foolish and superstitious.

The Anti-Jesuit Campaign This print denounces the Jesuit order and the two Jesuit priests involved in 1758 in an unsuccessful plot to assassinate the king of Portugal. A long separate caption accuses the treacherous priests, seated lower left and right of the unsuspecting king, of "trampling underfoot Religion, the Gospel, and Kings." *(Editions Robert Laffont)*

The Institutional Church

As in the Middle Ages, the local parish church remained the basic religious unit all across Europe. Still largely coinciding with the agricultural village, the parish fulfilled many needs. The parish church was the focal point of religious devotion, which went far beyond sermons and Holy Communion. The parish church organized colorful processions and pilgrimages to local shrines. Even in Protestant countries, where such activities were severely restricted, congregations gossiped and swapped stories after services, and neighbors came together in church for baptisms, marriages, funerals, and special events. Thus the parish church was woven into the very fabric of community life.

Moreover, the local church had important administrative tasks. Priests and parsons were truly the bookkeepers of agrarian Europe, and it is because parish registers were so complete that historians have learned so much about population and family life. Parishes also normally distributed charity to the destitute, looked after orphans, and provided whatever primary education was available for the common people.

The many tasks of the local church were usually the responsibility of a resident priest or pastor, a full-time professional working with assistants and lay volunteers. All clerics—whether Roman Catholic, Protestant, Greek Orthodox, or Russian Orthodox—also shared the fate of middlemen in a complicated institutional system. Charged most often with ministering to poor peasants, the priest or parson was the last link in a powerful church-state hierarchy that was everywhere determined to control religion down to the grassroots. However, the regulatory framework of belief, which went back at least to the fourth century when Christianity became the official religion of the Roman Empire, had undergone important changes since 1500.

The Protestant Reformation had burst forth as a culmination of medieval religiosity and a desire to purify Christian belief. Martin Luther, the most influential of the early reformers, preached that all men and women were saved from their sins and God's damnation only by personal faith in Jesus Christ. The individual could reach God directly, without need of priestly intermediaries.

As the Reformation gathered force, with peasant upheaval and doctrinal competition, German princes and monarchs in northern Europe put themselves at the head of official churches in their territories. Protestant authorities, with generous assistance from state-certified theologians like Luther, then proceeded to regulate their "territorial churches" strictly, selecting personnel and imposing detailed rules. They joined with Catholics to crush the Anabaptists, who, with their belief in freedom of conscience and separation of church and state, had become the real revolutionaries. Thus the Reformation, initially so radical in its rejection of Rome and its stress on individual religious experience, eventually resulted in a bureaucratization of the church and local religious life in Protestant Europe.

The Reformation era also increased the practical power of Catholic rulers over "their" churches, but it was only in the eighteenth century that some Catholic monarchs began to impose striking reforms. These reforms, which had their counterparts in Orthodox Russia, had a very "Protestant" aspect. They increased state control over the Catholic church, making it less subject to papal influence.

Spain, a deeply Catholic country with devout rulers, nevertheless took firm control of ecclesiastical appointments. Papal proclamations could not even be read in Spanish churches without prior approval from the government. Spain also asserted state control over the Spanish Inquisition, which pursued heresy as an independent agency under Rome's direction and went far toward creating a "national" Catholic church, as France had done earlier.

A more striking indication of state power and papal weakness was the fate of the Society of Jesus, or **Jesuits.** The well-educated Jesuits were extraordinary teachers, missionaries, and agents of the papacy. In many Catholic countries, the Jesuits exercised tremendous political influence, since individual members held high government positions and Jesuit colleges formed the minds of Europe's Catholic nobility. Yet by playing politics so effectively, the Jesuits eventually elicited a broad coalition of enemies. Bitter controversies led Louis XV to order the Jesuits out of France in 1763 and confiscate their property. France and Spain then pressured Rome to dissolve the Jesuits completely. In 1773 a reluctant pope caved in, although the order was revived after the French Revolution.

Some Catholic rulers also believed that the clergy in monasteries and convents should make a more practical contribution to social and religious life. Austria, a leader in controlling the church (see page 620) and promoting primary education, showed how far the process could go. Whereas Maria Theresa sharply restricted entry into "unproductive" orders, Joseph II recalled the radical initiatives of the Protestant Reformation. In his Edict on Idle Institutions, Joseph abolished contemplative orders, henceforth permitting only orders that were engaged in teaching, nursing, or other practical work. The state also expropriated the dissolved monasteries and used their wealth for charitable purposes and higher salaries for ordinary priests.

Protestant Revival

In their attempt to recapture the vital core of the Christian religion, the Protestant reformers had rigorously suppressed all the medieval practices that they considered nonessential or erroneous. For example, they had taken very seriously the commandment "Thou shalt not make any graven image" (Exodus 20:4), and their radical reforms had reordered church interiors. Relics and crucifixes had been permanently removed from crypt and altar, while stained-glass windows had been smashed and walls and murals covered with whitewash. Processions and pilgrimages, saints and shrines—all such practices had been eliminated because they were not founded on Scripture. Such revolutionary changes had often troubled ordinary churchgoers, but by the late seventeenth century the vast reforms of the Reformation had been completed and thoroughly routinized in most Protestant churches.

Indeed, official Protestant churches had generally settled into a smug complacency. In the Reformation heartland, one concerned German minister wrote that the Lutheran church "had become paralyzed in forms of dead doctrinal conformity" and badly needed a return to its original inspiration.[12] This voice was one of many that would prepare and then guide a powerful Protestant revival, which was largely successful because it answered the intense but increasingly unsatisfied needs of common people.

The Protestant revival began in Germany. It was known as **Pietism,** and three aspects helped explain its powerful appeal. First, Pietism called for a warm, emotional religion that everyone could experience. Enthusiasm—in prayer, in worship, in preaching, in life itself—was the key concept. "Just as a drunkard becomes full of wine, so must the congregation become filled with spirit," declared one exuberant writer. Another said simply, "The heart must burn."[13]

Second, Pietism reasserted the earlier radical stress on the priesthood of all believers, thereby reducing the large gulf between the official clergy and the Lutheran laity. Bible reading and study were enthusiastically extended to all classes, and this provided a powerful spur for popular education as well as individual religious development (see page 670). Finally, Pietists believed in the practical power of Christian rebirth in everyday affairs. Reborn Christians were expected to lead good, moral lives and come from all social classes.

Pietism had a major impact on John Wesley (1703–1791), who served as the catalyst for popular religious revival in England. Wesley came from a long line of ministers, and when he went to Oxford University to prepare for the clergy, he mapped a fanatically earnest "scheme of religion." Like some students during final-exam period, he organized every waking moment. After becoming a teaching fellow at Oxford, he organized a Holy Club for similarly minded students, who were soon known contemptuously as **Methodists** because they were so methodical in their devotion. Yet like the young Luther, Wesley remained intensely troubled about his own salvation, even after his ordination as an Anglican priest in 1728.

Wesley's anxieties related to grave problems of the faith in England. The Church of England was shamelessly used by the government to provide favorites with high-paying jobs and sinecures. Building of churches practically stopped while the population grew, and in many parishes there was a grave shortage of pews. Services and sermons had settled into an uninspiring routine. That the properly purified religion had been separated from local customs and

A Midsummer Afternoon with a Methodist Preacher (detail) This painting by de Loutherbourg suggests in a humorous manner how Wesley and his followers took their optimistic Christianity to the people of England. Methodist ministers championed open-air preaching and weeklong revivals. *(National Gallery of Canada, Ottawa)*

social life was symbolized by church doors that were customarily locked on weekdays. Moreover, the skepticism of the Enlightenment was making inroads among the educated classes, and deism was becoming popular. Some bishops and church leaders acted as if they believed that doctrines such as the Virgin Birth were little more than particularly elegant superstitions.

Spiritual counseling from a sympathetic Pietist minister from Germany prepared Wesley for a mystical, emotional "conversion" in 1738. He described this critical turning point in his *Journal:*

> *In the evening I went to a [Christian] society in Aldersgate Street where one was reading Luther's preface to the Epistle to the Romans. About a quarter before nine, while he was describing the change which God works in the heart through faith in Christ, I felt my heart strangely warmed. I felt I did trust in Christ, Christ alone for salvation; and an assurance was given me that he had taken away my sins, even mine, and saved me from the law of sin and death.*[14]

Wesley's emotional experience resolved his intellectual doubts. Moreover, he was convinced that any person, no matter how poor or uneducated, might have a similarly heartfelt conversion and gain the same blessed assurance.

Wesley took the good news to the people, traveling some 225,000 miles by horseback and preaching more than forty thousand sermons in fifty years. Since existing churches were often overcrowded and the church-state establishment was hostile, Wesley preached in open fields. People came in large numbers. Of critical importance was Wesley's rejection of Calvinist predestination—the doctrine of salvation granted only to a select few. Expanding on earlier Dutch theologians' views, he preached that *all* men and women who earnestly sought salvation might be saved. It was a message of hope and joy, of free will and universal salvation.

Wesley's ministry won converts, formed Methodist cells, and eventually resulted in a new denomination. And as Wesley had been inspired by Pietist revival in Germany, so evangelicals in the Church of England and the old dissenting groups now followed Wesley's example, giving impetus to an even broader awakening among the lower classes. In Protestant countries, religion remained a vital force in the lives of the people.

Catholic Piety

Religion also flourished in Catholic Europe around 1700, but there were important differences with Protestant practice. First of all, the visual contrast was striking; baroque art had lavished rich and emotionally exhilarating figures and images on Catholic churches, just as Protestants had removed theirs. From almost every indication, people in Catholic Europe remained intensely religious. More than 95 percent of the population probably attended church for Easter Communion, the climax of the Catholic church year.

The tremendous popular strength of religion in Catholic countries reflected religion's integral role in community life and popular culture. Thus although Catholics reluctantly confessed their sins to priests, they enthusiastically joined together in religious festivals to celebrate the passage of the liturgical year. In addition to the great processional days—such as Palm Sunday, the joyful re-enactment of Jesus' triumphal entry into Jerusalem—each parish had its own saints' days, processions, and pilgrimages. Led by its priest, a congregation might march around the village or across the countryside to a local shrine or chapel. Before each procession or feast day, the priest explained its religious significance to kindle group piety. But processions were also folklore and tradition, an escape from work, and a form of recreation. A holiday atmosphere sometimes reigned on longer processions, with drinking and dancing and couples disappearing into the woods.

Indeed, devout Catholics held many religious beliefs that were marginal to the Christian faith, often of obscure or even pagan origin. On the Feast of Saint Anthony, for example, priests were expected to bless salt and bread for farm animals to protect them from disease. One saint's relics could help cure a child of fear, and there were healing springs for many ailments. The ordinary person combined a strong Christian faith with a wealth of time-honored superstitions.

Inspired initially by the fervor of the Catholic Counter-Reformation and then to some extent by the critical rationalism of the Enlightenment, parish priests and Catholic hierarchies sought increasingly to "purify" popular religious practice. Thus one parish priest in France lashed out at his parishioners, claiming that they were "more superstitious than devout . . . and sometimes appear as baptized idolators."[15] French priests particularly denounced the "various remnants of paganism" found in popular bonfire ceremonies during Lent, in which young men, "yelling and screaming like madmen," tried to jump over the bonfires in order to help the crops grow and protect themselves from illness. One priest saw rational Christians regressing into pagan animals—"the triumph of Hell and the shame of Christianity."[16]

In contrast with Protestant reformers, who had already used the power of the territorial state to crush such practices, many Catholic priests and hierarchies preferred a compromise between theological purity and the people's piety, perhaps realizing that the line between divine truth and mere superstition is not easily drawn. Thus the severity of the attack on popular Catholicism varied widely by country and region. Where authorities pursued purification vigorously, as in Austria under Joseph II, pious peasants saw only an incomprehensible attack on the true faith and drew back in anger. Their reaction dramatized the growing tension between the attitudes of educated elites and the common people.

Leisure and Recreation

The combination of religious celebration and popular recreation seen in festivals and processions was most strikingly displayed at **Carnival,** a time of reveling and excess in Catholic and Mediterranean Europe. Carnival preceded Lent—the forty days of fasting and penitence before Easter—and for a few exceptional days in February or March, a wild release of drinking, masquerading, and dancing reigned. Moreover, a combination of plays, processions, and rowdy spectacles turned the established order upside down. Peasants became nobles, fools turned into philosophers, and the rich were humbled. These once-a-year rituals gave people a much-appreciated chance to release their pent-up frustrations and aggressions before life returned to the usual pattern of leisure and recreation.

That pattern featured socializing in groups, for despite the spread of literacy, the culture of the common people was largely oral rather than written. In the cold, dark winter months, families gathered around the fireplace to talk, sing, tell stories, do craftwork, and keep warm. In some parts of Europe, women would gather together in groups in someone's cottage to chat, sew, spin, and laugh. Sometimes a few young men would be invited so that the daughters (and mothers) could size up potential suitors in a supervised atmosphere. A favorite recreation of men was drinking and talking with buddies in public places, and it was a sorry village that had no tavern. In addition to old favorites such as beer and wine, the common people turned with gusto toward cheap and potent hard liquor, which fell in price because of improved techniques for distilling grain in the eighteenth century.

Towns and cities offered a wide range of amusements. Many of these had to be paid for because the eighteenth century saw a sharp increase in the commercialization of leisure-time activities—a trend that continues to this day. Urban fairs featured prepared foods, acrobats, freak shows, open-air performances, optical illusions, and the like. Such entertainments attracted a variety of social classes. So did the growing number of commercial, profit-oriented spectator sports. These ranged from traveling circuses and horse races to boxing matches and bullfights. Modern sports heroes, such as brain-bashing heavyweight champions and haughty matadors, made their appearance on the historical scene.

Blood sports, such as bullbaiting and cockfighting, remained popular with the masses. In bullbaiting the bull, usually staked on a chain in the courtyard of an inn, was attacked by ferocious dogs for the amusement of the innkeeper's clients. Eventually the maimed and tortured animal was slaughtered by a butcher and sold as meat. In cockfighting two roosters, carefully trained by their owners and armed with razor-sharp steel spurs, slashed and clawed each other in a small ring until the victor won—and the loser died. An added attraction of cockfighting was that the screaming spectators could bet on the lightning-fast combat and its uncertain outcome.

In trying to place the vibrant popular culture of the common people in broad perspective, historians have stressed the growing criticism levied against it by the educated elites in the second half of the eighteenth century. These elites, which had previously shared the popular enthusiasm for religious festivals, Carnival, drinking in taverns, blood sports, and the like, now tended to see only superstition, sin, disorder, and vulgarity.[17] The resulting attack on popular culture, which had its more distant origins in the Protestant clergy's efforts to eliminate frivolity and superstition, was intensified as an educated public embraced the critical world-view of the Enlightenment. This shift in cultural attitudes drove a wedge between the common people and the educated public. The mutual hostility that this separation engendered played an important role in the emergence of sharp class conflict in the era of the French and the Industrial Revolutions.

Summary

In the current generation, imaginative research has greatly increased the specialist's understanding of ordinary life and social patterns in the past. The human experience as recounted by historians has become richer and more

Cockfighting in England This engraving by William Hogarth (1697–1764) satirizes the popular taste for blood sports, which Hogarth despised and lampooned in his famous *Four Stages of Cruelty*. The central figure in the wildly excited gathering is a blind nobleman, who actually existed and seldom missed a fight. Note the steel spurs on the birds' legs. *(Courtesy of Trustees of the British Museum)*

meaningful, and many mistaken ideas have fallen by the wayside. This has been particularly true of eighteenth-century, predominately agrarian Europe, which combined a fascinating mixture of continuity and change.

To summarize, the life of the people remained primarily rural and oriented toward the local community. Tradition, routine, and well-established codes of behavior framed much of the everyday experience of the typical villager. Thus just as the three-field agricultural cycle and its pattern of communal rights had determined traditional patterns of grain production, so did community values in the countryside strongly encourage a late age of marriage, a low rate of illegitimate births, and a strict attitude toward children. Patterns of recreation and leisure, from churchgoing and religious festivals to sewing and drinking in groups within an oral culture, also reflected and reinforced community ties and values. Many long-standing ideas and beliefs, ranging from obscure religious customs to support for fair prices, remained strong forces and sustained continuity in popular life.

Yet powerful forces also worked for change. Many of these came from outside and above, from the aggressive capitalists, educated elites, and government officials discussed in the last two chapters. Closely knit villages began to lose control over families and marital practices, as could be seen in the earlier, more romantic marriages of cottage workers and in the beginning of the explosion in illegitimate births. Although the new, less rigorous attitudes toward children that were emerging in elite culture did not reach the people, the elite belief in the usefulness of some education did result in growing popular literacy. The grain-based diet became more varied with the grudging acceptance of the potato, and the benefits of the spectacular conquest of smallpox began to reach the common people in the late eighteenth century. Finally, the common people found that their beliefs and customs were being increasingly attacked by educated elites, who thought they knew better. The popular reaction to these attacks generally remained muted in the eighteenth century, but the common people and their advocates would offer vigorous responses and counterattacks in the revolutionary era.

Key Terms

- extended family
- community controls
- illegitimacy explosion
- wet-nursing
- killing nurses
- infanticide
- just price
- purging
- smallpox inoculation
- Jesuits
- Pietism
- Methodists
- Carnival
- blood sports

Notes

1. Quoted in J. M. Beattie, "The Criminality of Women in Eighteenth-Century England," *Journal of Social History* 8 (Summer 1975): 86.
2. W. L. Langer, "Infanticide: A Historical Survey," *History of Childhood Quarterly* 1 (Winter 1974): 357.
3. Quoted in R. Cobb, *The Police and the People: French Popular Protest, 1789–1820* (Oxford: Clarendon Press, 1970), p. 238.
4. M. Segalen, *Love and Power in the Peasant Family: Rural France in the Nineteenth Century* (New York: Basil Blackwell, 1983), p. 41. The passage as cited here has been edited to the past tense.
5. Quoted in D. S. Landes, ed., *The Rise of Capitalism* (New York: Macmillan, 1966), pp. 56–57.
6. G. Gullickson, *Spinners and Weavers of Auffay: Rural Industry and the Sexual Division of Labor in a French Village, 1750–1850* (Cambridge: Cambridge University Press, 1986), p. 186. See also L. A. Tilly, J. W. Scott, and M. Cohen, "Women's Work and European Fertility Patterns," *Journal of Interdisciplinary History* 6 (Winter 1976): 447–476.
7. J. Michelet, *The People,* trans. with an introduction by J. P. McKay (Urbana: University of Illinois Press, 1973; original publication, 1846), pp. 38–39.
8. Quoted in B. W. Lorence, "Parents and Children in Eighteenth-Century Europe," *History of Childhood Quarterly* 2 (Summer 1974): 1–2.
9. Ibid., pp. 13, 16.
10. E. Kennedy, *A Cultural History of the French Revolution* (New Haven, Conn.: Yale University Press, 1989), p. 47.
11. Quoted in R. Sand, *The Advance to Social Medicine* (London: Staples Press, 1952), pp. 86–87.
12. Quoted in K. Pinson, *Pietism as a Factor in the Rise of German Nationalism* (New York: Columbia University Press, 1934), p. 13.
13. Ibid., pp. 43–44.
14. Quoted in S. Andrews, *Methodism and Society* (London: Longmans, Green, 1970), p. 327.
15. Quoted in I. Woloch, *Eighteenth-Century Europe: Tradition and Progress, 1715–1789* (New York: W. W. Norton, 1982), p. 292.
16. Quoted in T. Tackett, *Priest and Parish in Eighteenth-Century France* (Princeton, N.J.: Princeton University Press, 1977), p. 214.
17. Woloch, *Eighteenth-Century Europe,* pp. 220–221; see also pp. 214–220 for this section.

Suggested Reading

Among general introductions to the history of the family, women, and children, J. Casey, *The History of the Family* (1989), is recommended. A. Imhof, *Lost Worlds: How Our European Ancestors Coped with Everyday Life and Why Life Is So Hard Today* (1996), sheds new light on family ties and attitudes toward death, which may be compared with P. Laslett, *The World We Have Lost* (1965), a pioneering investigation of England before the Industrial Revolution. R. Rudolph, ed., *The European Peasant Family and Society: Historical Studies* (1995), considers patterns of marriage and family dynamics. L. Stone, *The Family, Sex and Marriage in*

(continued on page 688)

Listening to the Past

Gender Constructions and Education for Girls

Emile, or On Education (1762), by Jean-Jacques Rousseau, is one of history's most original and influential books. Sometimes called a declaration of rights for children, it pleads for the humane treatment of children and lambasts widespread indifference and harsh discipline.

Rousseau's long, rambling work, part novel and part philosophical treatise, also had a powerful impact on theories of education. Emile *argues that education must shield the unspoiled child from the corrupting influences of civilization and allow the child to develop naturally and spontaneously. Children should learn what they—not their teachers—find interesting and useful.*

As this selection shows, Rousseau constructed sharp gender divisions. Girls and boys were basically equal as human beings, but sex made them both similar and different, intended by their natures for different occupations. Whereas Emile would eventually tackle academic subjects, Sophie, his future wife, would receive only lessons in household management, good mothering, and wifely obedience. The idea of educating girls and boys to operate "naturally" in their "separate spheres" would flourish in the nineteenth century.

Sophie ought to be a woman as Emile is a man—that is to say, she ought to have everything which suits the constitution of her species and her sex in order to fill her place in the physical and moral order. Let us begin, then, by examining the similarities and the differences of her sex and ours.

In everything not connected with sex, woman is man. She has the same organs, the same needs, the same faculties. The machine is constructed in the same way; its parts are the same; the one functions as does the other; the form is similar; and in whatever respect one considers them, the difference between them is only one of more or less.

In everything connected with sex, woman and man are in every respect related and in every respect different. The difficulty of comparing them comes from the difficulty of determining what in their constitutions is due to sex and what is not. . . .

There is no parity between the two sexes in regard to the consequences of sex. The male is male only at certain moments. The female is female her whole life or at least during her whole youth. Everything constantly recalls her sex to her; and, to fulfill its functions well, she needs a constitution which corresponds to it. She needs care during her pregnancy; she needs rest at the time of childbirth; she needs a soft and sedentary life to suckle her children; she needs patience and gentleness, a zeal and an affection that nothing can rebuff in order to raise her children. She serves as the link between them and their father; she alone makes him love them and give them the confidence to call them his own. How much tenderness and care is required to maintain the union of the whole family! . . .

Once it is demonstrated that man and woman are not and ought not to be constituted in the same way in either character or temperament, it follows that they ought not to have the same education. In following nature's directions, man and woman ought to act in concert, but they ought not to do the same things. The goal of their labors is common, but their labors themselves are different, and consequently so are the tastes directing them. . . .

All the faculties common to the two sexes are not equally distributed between them; but taken together, they balance out. Woman is worth more as woman and less as man. Wherever she makes use of her rights, she has the advantage. Wherever she wants to usurp ours, she remains beneath us. . . .

To cultivate man's qualities in women and to neglect those which are proper to them is obviously to work to their detriment. . . . Believe me, judicious mother, do not make a decent man of your daughter, as though you would give nature the lie. Make a decent woman of her, and be sure that as a result she will be worth more for herself and for us.

Does it follow that she ought to be raised in ignorance of everything and limited to the housekeeping functions alone? Will man turn his companion into his servant? . . . Surely not. It is not thus that nature has spoken in giving women such agreeable and nimble minds. On the contrary, nature wants them to think, to judge, to love, to know, to cultivate their minds as well as their looks. These are the weapons nature gives them to take the place of the strength they lack and to direct others. They ought to learn many things but only those that are suitable for them to know. . . .

The children of both sexes have many common entertainments, and that ought to be so. Is this not also the case when they are grown up? They also have particular tastes which distinguish them. Boys seek movement and noise: drums, boots, little carriages. Girls prefer what presents itself to sight and is useful for ornamentation: mirrors, jewels, dresses, particularly dolls. The doll is the special entertainment of this sex. . . .

Observe a little girl spending the day around her doll. . . . [S]he puts all her coquetry into it. She will not always leave it there. She awaits the moment when she will be her own doll. . . .

This is a very definite primary taste. You have only to follow and regulate it. It is certain that the little girl would want with all her heart to know how to adorn her doll, to make its bracelets, its scarf, its flounce, its lace. . . . In this way there emerges the reason for the first lessons she is given. They are not tasks prescribed to her, they are kindnesses done for her. In fact, almost all little girls learn to read and write with repugnance. But as for holding a needle, that they always learn gladly. They imagine themselves to be grown up and think with pleasure that these talents will one day be useful for adorning themselves.

Once this first path is opened, it is easy to follow. Sewing, embroidery, and lacemaking come by themselves. Tapestry is not much to their taste. . . .

Whatever humorists may say, good sense belongs equally to the two sexes. Girls are generally more docile than boys, and one should even use more authority with them, as I shall say a little later. But it does not follow that anything ought to be demanded from them whose utility they cannot see. The art of mothers is to show them the utility of everything they prescribe to them, and that is all the easier since intelligence is more precocious in girls than in boys. This rule banishes—for their sex as well as for ours—not only idle studies which lead to no good and do not even make those who have pursued them more attractive to others, but even those which are not useful at their age and whose usefulness for a more advanced age the child cannot foresee. If I do not want to push a boy to learn to read, all the more I do not want to force girls to before making them well aware of what the use of reading is. In the way this utility is ordinarily showed to them, we follow our own idea far more than theirs. After all, where is the necessity for a girl to know how to read and write so early? Will she so soon have a household to govern? There are very few girls who do abuse this fatal science more than they make good use of it. And all of them have too much curiosity not to learn it—without our forcing them to do so—when they have the leisure and the occasion. Perhaps girls ought to learn to do arithmetic before anything, for nothing presents a more palpable utility at all times, requires longer practice, and is so exposed to error as calculation. If the little girl were to get cherries for her snack only by doing an arithmetical operation, I assure you that she would soon know how to calculate.

Jean-Jacques Rousseau (1712–1778), portrayed as a gentle teacher and a pensive philosopher. *(The Granger Collection, New York)*

Questions for Analysis

1. What similarities and differences between women/girls and men/boys does Rousseau see? In your opinion, which appear more important to Rousseau? Why?
2. Were Rousseau's views on gender differences and education reactionary or progressive?

Source: Jean-Jacques Rousseau, *Emile, or On Education,* trans. Alan Bloom.

England, 1500–1800 (1977), is a provocative general interpretation, and L. Tilly and J. Scott, *Women, Work and Family* (1978), remains an excellent introduction. Two valuable works on women, both with good bibliographies, are M. Boxer and J. Quataert, eds., *Connecting Spheres: Women in the Western World, 1500 to the Present* (1987), and R. Bridenthal, C. Koonz, and S. Stuard, eds., *Becoming Visible: Women in European History,* 2d ed. (1987). P. Aries, *Centuries of Childhood: A Social History of Family Life* (1962), is a famous pioneering study, which may be compared with the more recent synthesis by H. Cunningham, *Children and Childhood in Western Society Since 1500* (1995). J. Henderson and R. Walls, eds., *Poor Women and Children in the European Past* (1994), considers abandonment, illegitimacy, orphanages, and other topics in this chapter. E. Shorter, *The Making of the Modern Family* (1975), is a lively, controversial interpretation, which should be compared with the excellent study by M. Segalen, *Love and Power in the Peasant Family: Rural France in the Nineteenth Century* (1983). A. MacFarlane, *The Family Life of Ralph Josselin* (1970), is a brilliant re-creation of the intimate family circle of a seventeenth-century English clergyman who kept a detailed diary; MacFarlane's *Origins of English Individualism: The Family, Property and Social Transition* (1978) is a major work. L. Pollack, *Forgotten Children: Parent-Child Relations from 1500 to 1900* (1983), is a general introduction. B. Lorence-Kot, *Child-Rearing and Reform: A Study of Nobility in Eighteenth-Century Poland* (1985), stresses the harshness of parental discipline. Various aspects of sexual relationships are treated imaginatively by M. Foucault, *The History of Sexuality* (1981), and R. Wheaton and T. Hareven, eds., *Family and Sexuality in French History* (1980).

L. Moch, *Moving Europeans: Migration in Western Europe Since 1650* (1992), offers a rich, human, and highly recommended account of the movements of millions of ordinary people. J. Burnett, *A History of the Cost of Living* (1969), has a great deal of interesting information about what people spent their money on in the past. J. C. Drummond and A. Wilbraham, *The Englishman's Food: A History of Five Centuries of English Diet,* 2d ed. (1958), remains a valuable and fascinating introduction. J. Knyveton, *Diary of a Surgeon in the Year 1751–1752* (1937), gives a contemporary's unforgettable picture of both eighteenth-century medicine and social customs, as does M. Romsey, *Professional and Popular Medicine in France, 1770–1830: The Social World of Medical Practice* (1988). Good introductions to the evolution of medical practices are B. Ingles, *History of Medicine* (1965); Roy Porter, ed., *The Cambridge Illustrated History of Medicine* (1996); and A. Digby, *Making a Medical Living: Doctors and Patients in the English Market for Medicine, 1720–1991* (1994). M. Lindemann, *Health and Healing in Eighteenth-Century Germany* (1996), is a wide-ranging synthesis. H. Marland, ed., *The Art of Midwifery: Early Modern Midwives in Europe* (1993), discusses developments in several countries and complements L. Ulrich, *A Midwife's Tale: The Life of Martha Ballard, Based on Her Diary, 1785–1812* (1990), a superb reconstruction. W. Boyd, *History of Western Education* (1966), is a standard survey, whereas R. Houston, *Literacy in Early Modern Europe: Culture and Education, 1500–1800* (1988), is brief and engaging.

The study of popular culture is expanding. Among older studies, M. George, *London Life in the Eighteenth Century* (1965), is a delight, whereas D. Roche, *The People of Paris: An Essay in Popular Culture in the Eighteenth Century* (1987), presents an unforgettable portrait of the Paris poor. I. Woloch, *Eighteenth-Century Europe: Tradition and Progress, 1715–1789* (1982), includes a survey of popular culture and a good bibliography. E. Kennedy, *A Cultural History of the French Revolution* (1989), beautifully captures rural and urban attitudes in France before and during the French Revolution. R. Malcolmson, *Popular Recreation in English Society, 1700–1850* (1973), provides a colorful account of boxers, bettors, bullbaiting, and more. L. Hunt, *The New Cultural History* (1989), provides an engaging discussion of conceptual issues. G. Rude, *The Crowd in History, 1730–1848* (1964), is an influential effort to see politics and popular protest from below. An important series edited by R. Forster and O. Ranuum considers neglected social questions such as diet, abandoned children, and deviants, as does P. Burke's excellent study, *Popular Culture in Early Modern Europe* (1978). J. Gillis, *For Better, for Worse: Marriage in Britain Since 1500* (1985), and R. Philips, *Untying the Knot: A Short History of Divorce* (1991), are good introductions to institutional changes.

Good works on religious life include J. Delumeau, *Catholicism Between Luther and Voltaire: A New View of the Counter-Reformation* (1977); B. Semmel, *The Methodist Revolution* (1973); and J. Bettey, *Church and Community: The Parish Church in English Life* (1979).

The Planting of a Liberty Tree, by Pierre Antoine Leseur.
(Giraudon/Art Resource, NY)

chapter

21 The Revolution in Politics, 1775–1815

chapter outline

- Liberty and Equality
- The American Revolutionary Era, 1775–1789
- The French Revolution, 1789–1791
- World War and Republican France, 1791–1799
- The Napoleonic Era, 1799–1815

The last years of the eighteenth century were a time of great upheaval. A series of revolutions and revolutionary wars challenged the old order of monarchs and aristocrats. The ideas of freedom and equality, ideas that have not stopped shaping the world since that era, flourished and spread. The revolutionary era began in North America in 1775. Then in 1789 France, the most influential country in Europe, became the leading revolutionary nation. It established first a constitutional monarchy, then a radical republic, and finally a new empire under Napoleon. The armies of France also joined forces with patriots and radicals abroad in an effort to establish new governments based on new principles throughout much of Europe. The world of modern domestic and international politics was born.

- What caused this era of revolution?
- What were the ideas and objectives of the men and women who rose up violently to undo the established system?
- What were the gains and losses for privileged groups and for ordinary people in a generation of war and upheaval?

These are the questions underlying this chapter's examination of the revolutionary era.

Liberty and Equality

Two ideas fueled the revolutionary period in both America and Europe: **liberty and equality.** What did eighteenth-century politicians and other people mean by liberty and equality, and why were those ideas so radical and revolutionary in their day?

The call for liberty was first of all a call for individual human rights. Even the most enlightened monarchs customarily claimed that it was their duty to regulate what people wrote and believed. Liberals of the revolutionary era protested such controls from on high. They demanded freedom to worship according to the dictates of their consciences, an end to censorship, and freedom from arbitrary laws and from judges who simply obeyed orders from the government. The Declaration of the Rights of Man, issued at the beginning of the French Revolution, proclaimed, "Liberty consists in being able to do anything that does not harm another person." In the context of the monarchical and absolutist forms of government then dominating Europe, this was a truly radical idea.

The call for liberty was also a call for a new kind of government. Revolutionary liberals believed that the people had **sovereignty**—that is, that the people alone had the authority to make laws limiting an individual's freedom of action. In practice, this system of government meant choosing legislators who represented the people and were accountable to them.

Equality was a more ambiguous idea. Eighteenth-century liberals argued that, in theory, all citizens should have identical rights and civil liberties and that the nobility had no right to special privileges based on the accident of birth. However, liberals accepted some well-established distinctions.

First, most eighteenth-century liberals were *men* of their times, and they generally shared with other men the belief that equality between men and women was neither practical nor desirable. Women played an important political role in the French Revolution at several points, but the men of the French Revolution limited formal political rights—the right to vote, to run for office, to participate in government—to men.

Second, liberals never believed that everyone should be equal economically. Quite the contrary. As Thomas Jefferson wrote in an early draft of the American Declaration of Independence (before he changed "property" to the more noble-sounding "happiness"), everyone was equal in "the pursuit of property." Jefferson and other liberals certainly did not expect equal success in that pursuit. Great differences in wealth and income between rich and poor were perfectly acceptable to liberals. The essential point was that everyone should legally have an equal chance.

In eighteenth-century Europe, however, such equality of opportunity was a truly revolutionary idea. Society was still legally divided into groups with special privileges, such as the nobility and the clergy, and groups with special burdens, such as the peasantry. And in most countries, various middle-class groups—professionals, business people, townspeople, and craftsmen—enjoyed privileges that allowed them to monopolize all sorts of economic activity. Liberals criticized not economic inequality itself but this kind of economic inequality based on legal distinctions for different social groups.

Although the ideas of liberty and equality—the central ideas of classical liberalism—had deep roots in Western history dating back to ancient Greece and the Judeo-Christian tradition, classical liberalism first crystallized at the end of the seventeenth century and during the Enlightenment of the eighteenth century. Liberal ideas reflected the Enlightenment's stress on human dignity, personal liberty, and human happiness on earth and its faith in science, rationality, and progress.

Certain English and French thinkers were mainly responsible for joining the Enlightenment's concern for personal freedom and legal equality to a theoretical justification of liberal self-government. The two most important were John Locke and the baron de Montesquieu. Locke maintained that England's long political tradition rested on "the rights of Englishmen" and on representative government through Parliament. He argued that if a government oversteps its proper function of protecting the natural rights of life, liberty, and private property, it becomes a tyranny. Montesquieu was also inspired by English constitutional history. He, too, believed that powerful "intermediary groups"—such as the judicial nobility of which he was a proud member—offered the best defense of liberty against despotism.

The belief that representative institutions could defend their liberty and interests appealed powerfully to well-educated, prosperous, middle-class groups, which historians have traditionally labeled as the **bourgeoisie.** Yet liberal ideas about individual rights and political freedom also appealed to much of the hereditary nobility, at least in western Europe and as formulated by Montesquieu. **Representative government** did not mean democracy, which liberal thinkers tended to equate with mob rule. Rather, they envisioned voting for representatives as being restricted to those who owned property—those with "a stake in society." England had shown the way. After 1688 it had combined a parliamentary system and considerable individual liberty with a restricted franchise and unquestionable aristocratic pre-eminence. In the course of the eighteenth century, many leading French nobles, led by high-ranking noble judges, who were inspired by the doctrines of Montesquieu, were increasingly eager to follow the English example. Thus eighteenth-century liberalism in western Europe found broad support among the prosperous, well-educated elites in both the nobility and the bourgeoisie.

What liberalism lacked from the beginning was strong popular support, for at least two reasons. First, for common people, the great questions were not theoretical and political but immediate and economic; getting enough to eat was a crucial challenge. Second, some of the traditional practices and institutions that liberals wanted to abolish were dear to peasants and urban workers. Comfortable elites had already come into conflict with the

1770	1780	1790	1800	1810	1820

Political/Military

- 1773 Boston Tea Party
- 1775–1783 American Revolution
- 1789 Ratification of U.S. Constitution
- 1789 Storming of the Bastille
- 1789–1799 French Revolution
- 1793–1794 Robespierre's Reign of Terror
- 1793 Execution of Louis XVI
- 1794 Robespierre deposed and executed
- 1794–1799 Thermidorian reaction
- 1799–1815 Napoleonic era
- 1812 Napoleon invades Russia
- 1814–1815 Napoleon defeated and exiled

Social/Economic

- 1786–1789 Financial crisis in France
- 1789 Feudalism abolished in France
- 1793–1794 Economic controls to help poor in France

Intellectual/Religious

- 1775 Paine, *Common Sense*
- 1790 Burke, *Reflections on the Revolution in France*
- 1792 Wollstonecraft, *A Vindication of the Rights of Woman*

people in the eighteenth century over the enclosure of common lands and the regulation of food prices. This conflict would sharpen in the revolutionary era as differences in outlook and well-being led to many misunderstandings and disappointments for both groups.

The American Revolutionary Era, 1775–1789

The era of liberal political revolution began in the New World. The thirteen mainland colonies of British North America revolted against their home country and then succeeded in establishing a new, unified government.

Americans have long debated the meaning of their revolution. Some have even questioned whether it was a real revolution, as opposed to a war for independence. According to some scholars, the Revolution was conservative and defensive in that its demands were for the traditional liberties of English citizens; Americans were united against the British, but otherwise they were a satisfied people, not torn by internal conflict. Other scholars have argued that, on the contrary, the American Revolution was quite radical. It split families between patriots and Loyalists and divided the country. It achieved goals that were as fully advanced as those obtained by the French in their great Revolution a few years later.

How does one reconcile these positions? Both contain large elements of truth. The American revolutionaries did believe that they were demanding only the traditional rights of English men and women. But those traditional rights were liberal rights, and in the American context they had very strong democratic and popular overtones. Thus the American Revolution was fought in the name of established ideals that were still quite radical in the context of the times. And in founding a government firmly based on liberal principles, the Americans set an example that had a forceful impact on Europe and sped up political development there.

The Origins of the Revolution

The American Revolution had its immediate origins in a squabble over increased taxes. The British government had fought and decisively won the Seven Years' War (see pages 647–648) on the strength of its professional army and navy. The American colonists had furnished little real aid. The high cost of the war to the British, however, had led to a doubling of the British national debt. Anticipating further expense defending its recently conquered western lands from native American uprisings, the British government in London set about reorganizing the empire with a series of bold, largely unprecedented measures. Breaking with tradition, the British decided to maintain a large army in North America after peace was restored in 1763 and to tax the colonies directly. In 1765 the government pushed through Parliament the Stamp Act, which levied taxes on a long list of commercial and legal documents, diplomas, pamphlets, newspapers, almanacs, dice, and playing cards. A stamp glued to each article indicated the tax had been paid.

Toward Revolution in Boston The Boston Tea Party was only one of many angry confrontations between British officials and Boston patriots. On January 27, 1774, an angry crowd seized a British customs collector and then tarred and feathered him. This French engraving of 1784 commemorates the defiant and provocative action. *(The Granger Collection, New York)*

This effort to increase taxes as part of a tightening up of the empire seemed perfectly reasonable to the British. Heavier stamp taxes had been collected in Great Britain for two generations, and Americans were being asked only to pay a share of their own defense costs. Moreover, Americans had been paying only very low local taxes. The Stamp Act would have doubled taxes to about 2 shillings per person per year, whereas the British paid the highest taxes in the Western world—26 shillings per person. The colonists protested the Stamp Act vigorously and violently, however, and after their rioting and boycotts against British goods, Parliament reluctantly repealed the new tax.

As the fury over the Stamp Act revealed, much more was involved than taxes. The key questions were political. To what extent could the home government refashion the empire and reassert its power while limiting the authority of colonial legislatures and their elected representatives? Accordingly, who should represent the colonies, and who had the right to make laws for Americans? The British government replied that Americans were represented in Parliament, albeit indirectly (like most British people themselves), and that the absolute supremacy of Parliament throughout the empire could not be questioned. Many Americans felt otherwise. As John Adams put it, "A Parliament of Great Britain can have no more rights to tax the colonies than a Parliament of Paris." Thus imperial reorganization and parliamentary supremacy came to appear as grave threats to Americans' existing liberties and time-honored institutions.

Americans had long exercised a great deal of independence. In British North America, unlike England and Europe, no powerful established church existed, and personal freedom in questions of religion was taken for granted. The colonial assemblies made the important laws, which were seldom overturned by the home government. The right to vote was much more widespread than in England. In many parts of colonial Massachusetts, for example, as many as 95 percent of the adult males could vote.

Moreover, greater political equality was matched by greater social and economic equality. Neither a hereditary nobility nor a hereditary serf population existed, although the slavery of the Americas consigned blacks to a legally oppressed caste. Independent farmers were the largest group in the country and set much of its tone. In short, the colonial experience had slowly formed a people who felt themselves separate and distinct from the home country, and the controversies over taxation intensified those feelings.

In 1773 the dispute over taxes and representation flared up again. The British government had permitted the financially hard-pressed East India Company to ship its tea from China directly to its agents in the colonies rather than through London middlemen who sold to independent merchants in the colonies. Thus the company secured a vital monopoly on the tea trade, and colonial merchants were suddenly excluded from a lucrative business. The colonists were quick to protest.

In Boston men disguised as Indians had a rowdy "tea party" and threw the company's tea into the harbor. This led to extreme measures. The so-called Coercive Acts closed the port of Boston, curtailed local elections and town meetings, and greatly expanded the royal governor's power. County conventions in Massachusetts protested vehemently and urged that the acts be "rejected as the attempts of a wicked administration to enslave America." Other colonial assemblies joined in the denunciations. In September 1774, the First Continental Congress met in Philadelphia, where the more radical members argued successfully against concessions to the Crown. Compromise was also rejected by the British Parliament, and in April 1775 fighting began at Lexington and Concord.

Independence

The fighting spread, and the colonists moved slowly but inevitably toward open rebellion and a declaration of independence. The uncompromising attitude of the British government and its use of German mercenaries went a long way toward dissolving long-standing loyalties to the home country and rivalries among the separate colonies. *Common Sense* (1775), a brilliant attack by the recently arrived English radical Thomas Paine (1737–1809), also mobilized public opinion in favor of independence. A runaway bestseller with sales of 120,000 copies in a few months, Paine's tract ridiculed the idea of a small island ruling a great continent. In his call for freedom and republican government, Paine expressed Americans' growing sense of separateness and moral superiority.

On July 4, 1776, the Second Continental Congress adopted the Declaration of Independence. Written by Thomas Jefferson, the Declaration of Independence boldly listed the tyrannical acts committed by George III (r. 1760–1820) and confidently proclaimed the natural rights of mankind and the sovereignty of the American states. Sometimes called the world's greatest political editorial, the Declaration of Independence in effect universalized the traditional rights of English people and made them the rights of all mankind. It stated that "all men are created equal. . . . They are endowed by their Creator with certain unalienable rights. . . . Among these are life, liberty, and the pursuit of happiness." No other American political document has ever caused such excitement, either at home or abroad.

Many American families remained loyal to Britain; many others divided bitterly. After the Declaration of Independence, the conflict often took the form of a civil war pitting patriot against Loyalist. The Loyalists tended to be wealthy and politically moderate. Many patriots, too, were wealthy—individuals such as John Hancock and George Washington—but willingly allied themselves with farmers and artisans in a broad coalition. This coalition harassed the Loyalists and confiscated their property to help pay for the American war effort. The broad social base of the revolutionaries tended to make the liberal revolution democratic. State governments extended the right to vote to many more men (but not to any women) in the course of the war and re-established themselves as republics.

On the international scene, the French sympathized with the rebels and supplied guns and gunpowder from the beginning. The French wanted revenge for the humiliating defeats of the Seven Years' War. By 1777 French volunteers were arriving in Virginia, and a dashing young nobleman, the marquis de Lafayette (1757–1834), quickly became one of Washington's most trusted generals. In 1778 the French government offered a formal alliance to the American ambassador in Paris, Benjamin Franklin, and in 1779 and 1780 the Spanish and Dutch declared war on Britain. Catherine the Great of Russia helped organize the League of Armed Neutrality in order to protect neutral shipping rights, which Britain refused to recognize.

Thus by 1780 Great Britain was engaged in an imperial war against most of Europe as well as the thirteen colonies. In these circumstances, and in the face of severe reverses in India, in the West Indies, and at Yorktown in Virginia, a new British government decided to cut its losses. American negotiators in Paris were receptive. They feared that France wanted a treaty that would bottle up the new United States east of the Allegheny Mountains and give British holdings west of the Alleghenies to

The Signing of the Declaration of Independence, July 4, 1776 John Trumbull's famous painting shows the dignity and determination of America's revolutionary leaders. An extraordinarily talented group, they succeeded in rallying popular support without losing power to more radical forces in the process. *(The Granger Collection, New York)*

France's ally, Spain. Thus the American negotiators deserted their French allies and accepted the extraordinarily favorable terms Britain offered.

By the Treaty of Paris of 1783, Britain recognized the independence of the thirteen colonies and ceded all its territory between the Allegheny Mountains and the Mississippi River to the Americans. Out of the bitter rivalries of the Old World, the Americans snatched dominion over a vast territory.

Framing the Constitution

The liberal program of the American Revolution was consolidated by the federal Constitution, the Bill of Rights, and the creation of a national republic. Assembling in Philadelphia in the summer of 1787, the delegates to the Constitutional Convention were determined to end the period of economic depression, social uncertainty, and very weak central government that had followed independence. The delegates thus decided to grant the federal, or central, government important powers: regulation of domestic and foreign trade, the right to tax, and the means to enforce its laws.

Strong rule would be placed squarely in the context of representative self-government. Senators and congressmen would be the lawmaking delegates of the voters, and the president of the republic would be an elected official. The central government would operate in Montesquieu's framework of **checks and balances.** The executive, legislative, and judicial branches would systematically balance one another. The power of the federal government would in turn be checked by the powers of the individual states.

checks & balances.

When the results of the secret deliberations of the Constitutional Convention were presented to the states for ratification, a great public debate began. The opponents of the proposed constitution—the Antifederalists—charged that the framers of the new document had taken too much power from the individual states and made the federal government too strong. Moreover, many Antifederalists feared for the personal liberties and individual freedoms for which they had just fought. In order to overcome these objections, the Federalists solemnly promised to spell out these basic freedoms as soon as the new Constitution was adopted. The result was the first ten amendments to the Constitution, which the first Congress passed shortly after it met in New York in March 1789. These amendments formed an effective bill of rights to safeguard the individual. Most of them—trial by jury, due process of law, right to assemble, freedom from unreasonable search—had their origins in English law and the English Bill of Rights of 1689. Other rights—the freedoms of speech, the press, and religion—reflected natural-law theory and the American experience.

The American Constitution and the Bill of Rights exemplified the great strengths and the limits of what came to be called **classical liberalism.** Liberty meant individual freedoms and political safeguards. Liberty also meant representative government but did not necessarily mean democracy, with its principle of one person, one vote. Equality—slaves excepted—meant equality before the law, not equality of political participation or wealth. The radicalism of liberal revolution in America was primarily legal and political, *not* economic or social.

The Revolution's Impact on Europe

Hundreds of books, pamphlets, and articles analyzed and romanticized the American upheaval. Thoughtful Europeans noted, first of all, its enormous long-term implications for international politics. A secret report by the Venetian ambassador to Paris in 1783 stated what many felt: "If only the union of the Provinces is preserved, it is reasonable to expect that, with the favorable effects of time, and of European arts and sciences, it will become the most formidable power in the world."[1] More generally, American independence fired the imaginations of those aristocrats who were uneasy with their hereditary privileges and those commoners who yearned for legal equality. Many Europeans believed that the world was advancing and that America was leading the way.

Europeans who dreamed of a new era were fascinated by the political lessons of the American Revolution. The Americans had begun with a revolutionary defense against tyrannical oppression, and they had been victorious. They had then shown how rational beings could assemble together to exercise sovereignty and write a permanent constitution—a new social contract. All this gave greater reality to the concepts of individual liberty and representative government and reinforced one of the primary ideas of the Enlightenment: that a better world was possible.

The French Revolution, 1789–1791

No country felt the consequences of the American Revolution more directly than France. Hundreds of French officers served in America and were inspired by the experience. The most famous of these, the young and impressionable marquis de Lafayette, left home as a great aristocrat determined only to fight France's traditional foe, England. He returned with a love of liberty and firm republican convictions. French intellectuals and publicists engaged in passionate analysis of the federal Constitution as well as the constitutions of the various states of the new United States. The American Revolution undeniably hastened upheaval in France.

Yet the French Revolution did not mirror the American example. It was more radical and more complex, more influential and more controversial, more loved and more hated. For Europeans and most of the rest of the world, it was the great revolution of the eighteenth century, *the* revolution that opened the modern era in politics.

The Breakdown of the Old Order

Like the American Revolution, the French Revolution had its immediate origins in the financial difficulties of the government. The efforts of Louis XV's ministers to raise taxes had been thwarted by the high courts, led by the Parlement of Paris, which was strengthened in its opposition by widespread popular support (see page 622). When renewed efforts to reform the tax system met a similar fate in 1776, the government was forced to finance all of its enormous expenditures during the American war with borrowed money. As a result, the national debt and the annual budget deficit soared. By the 1780s, fully 50 percent of France's annual budget went for ever-increasing interest payments on the ever-increasing debt. Another 25 percent went to maintain the military, while 6 percent was absorbed by the costly and extravagant king and his court at Versailles. Less than 20 percent of

The Three Estates In this political cartoon from 1789 a woman of the third estate struggles under the burden of a nun and an aristocrat. The third estate is being represented in a new way as the true nation, oppressed by the parasitic clergy and nobility. *(Musée Carnavalet/Photo Bulloz)*

the entire national budget was available for the productive functions of the state, such as transportation and general administration. This was an impossible financial situation.

One way out would have been for the government to declare partial bankruptcy, forcing its creditors to accept greatly reduced payments on the debt. The powerful Spanish monarchy had regularly repudiated large portions of its debt in earlier times, and France had done likewise after an attempt to establish a French national bank had ended in financial disaster in 1720. Yet by the 1780s, the French debt was being held by an army of aristocratic and bourgeois creditors, and the French monarchy, though absolute in theory, had become too weak for such a drastic and unpopular action.

Nor could the king and his ministers, unlike modern governments, print money and create inflation to cover their deficits. Unlike England and Holland, which had far larger national debts relative to their populations, France had no central bank, no paper currency, and no means of creating credit. French money was good gold coin. Therefore, when a depressed economy and a lack of public confidence made it increasingly difficult for the government to obtain new gold loans in 1786, it had no alternative but to try increasing taxes. And since France's tax system was unfair and out-of-date, increased revenues were possible only through fundamental reforms. Such reforms, which would affect all groups in France's complex and fragmented society, opened a Pandora's box of social and political demands. Thus historians have usually looked to social forces and social relationships in their efforts to understand the Revolution, as we shall now see.

Legal Orders and Social Realities

As in the Middle Ages, France's 25 million inhabitants were still legally divided into three orders, or **estates**—the clergy, the nobility, and everyone else. As the nation's first estate, the clergy numbered about 100,000 and had important privileges. It owned about 10 percent of the land and paid only a "voluntary gift," rather than regular taxes, to the government every five years. Moreover, the church levied a tax (the tithe) on landowners, which averaged somewhat less than 10 percent. Much of the church's income was actually drained away from local parishes by political appointees and worldly aristocrats at the top of the church hierarchy—to the intense dissatisfaction of the poor parish priests.

The second legally defined estate consisted of some 400,000 noblemen and noblewomen—the descendants of "those who fought" in the Middle Ages. The nobles owned outright about 25 percent of the land in France, and they, too, were taxed very lightly. Moreover, nobles continued to enjoy certain **manorial rights,** or privileges of lordship, that dated back to medieval times and allowed them to tax the peasantry for their own profit. This was done by means of exclusive rights to hunt and fish, village monopolies on baking bread and pressing grapes for wine, fees for justice, and a host of other "useful privileges." In addition, nobles had "honorific privileges," such as the right to precedence on public occasions and the right to wear a sword. These rights conspicuously proclaimed the nobility's legal superiority and exalted social position.

Everyone else was a commoner, legally a member of the third estate. A few commoners—prosperous merchants or lawyers and officials—were well educated and rich, and might even buy up manorial rights as profitable investments. Many more commoners were urban artisans and unskilled day laborers. The vast majority of the third estate consisted of the peasants and agricultural workers in the countryside. Thus the third estate was a conglomeration of vastly different social groups united only by their shared legal status as distinct from the nobility and clergy.

In discussing the long-term origins of the French Revolution, historians have long focused on growing tensions between the nobility and the comfortable members of the third estate, usually known as the *bourgeoisie,* or middle class. A dominant historical interpretation, which held sway for at least two generations, maintained that the bourgeoisie was basically united by economic position and class interest. Aided by the general economic expansion discussed in Chapter 19, the middle class grew rapidly in the eighteenth century, tripling to about 2.3 million persons, or about 8 percent of France's population. Increasing in size, wealth, culture, and self-confidence, this rising bourgeoisie became progressively exasperated by archaic "feudal" laws restraining the economy and by the pretensions of a reactionary nobility, which was closing ranks against middle-class needs and aspirations. As a result, the French bourgeoisie eventually rose up to lead the entire third estate in a great social revolution, a revolution that destroyed feudal privileges and established a capitalist order based on individualism and a market economy.

In recent years, a flood of new research has challenged these accepted views. Above all, revisionist historians have questioned the existence of a growing social conflict between a progressive capitalistic bourgeoisie and a reactionary feudal nobility in eighteenth-century France. Instead, these historians see both bourgeoisie and nobility as highly fragmented, riddled with internal rivalries. The great nobility, for example, was profoundly separated from the lesser nobility by differences in wealth, education, and world-view. Differences within the bourgeoisie—between wealthy financiers and local lawyers, for example—were no less profound. Rather than standing as unified blocs against each other, nobility and bourgeoisie formed two parallel social ladders increasingly linked together at the top by wealth, marriage, and Enlightenment culture.

Revisionist historians stress three developments in particular. First, the nobility remained a fluid and relatively open order. Throughout the eighteenth century, substantial numbers of successful commoners continued to seek and obtain noble status through government service and purchase of expensive positions conferring nobility. Second, key sections of the nobility were no less liberal than the middle class, and until revolution actually began, both groups generally supported the judicial opposition to the government led by the Parlement of Paris. Third, the nobility and the bourgeoisie were not really at odds in the economic sphere. Both looked to investment in land and government service as their preferred activities, and the ideal of the merchant capitalist was to gain enough wealth to retire from trade, purchase estates, and live nobly as a large landowner. At the same time, wealthy nobles often acted as aggressive capitalists, investing especially in mining, metallurgy, and foreign trade.

The revisionists have clearly shaken the belief that the bourgeoisie and the nobility were inevitably locked in growing conflict before the Revolution. But in stressing the similarities between the two groups, especially at the top, revisionists have also reinforced the view, long maintained by historians, that the Old Regime had ceased to correspond with social reality by the 1780s. Legally, society was still based on rigid orders inherited from the Middle Ages. In reality, France had already moved far toward being a society based on wealth and education, where an emerging elite that included both aristocratic and bourgeois notables was frustrated by a bureaucratic monarchy that continued to claim the right to absolute power.

The Formation of the National Assembly

The Revolution was under way by 1787, though no one could have realized what was to follow. Spurred by a depressed economy and falling tax receipts, Louis XVI's minister of finance revived old proposals to impose a general tax on all landed property as well as to form provincial assemblies to help administer the tax, and he convinced the king to call an assembly of notables to gain support for the idea. The assembled notables, who were mainly important noblemen and high-ranking clergy, were not in favor of it. In return for their support, they demanded that control over all government spending be given to the provincial assemblies. When the government refused, the notables responded that such sweeping tax changes required the approval of the Estates General, the representative body of all three estates, which had not met since 1614.

Facing imminent bankruptcy, the king tried to reassert his authority. He dismissed the notables and established new taxes by decree. In stirring language, the judges of the Parlement of Paris promptly declared the royal initiative null and void. When the king tried to exile the judges, a tremendous wave of protest swept the country. Frightened investors also refused to advance more loans to the state. Finally in July 1788, a beaten Louis XVI bowed to public opinion and called for a spring session of the Estates General. Absolute monarchy was collapsing.

What would replace it? Throughout the unprecedented election campaign of 1788 and 1789, that question excited France. All across the country, clergy, nobles, and commoners came together in their respective orders to draft petitions for change and to elect their respective delegates to the Estates General. The local assemblies of the clergy showed considerable dissatisfaction with the church hierarchy, and two-thirds of the delegates were chosen from among the poorer parish priests, who were commoners by birth. The nobles were politically divided. A conservative majority was drawn from the poorer and more numerous provincial nobility, but fully one-third of the nobility's representatives were liberals committed to major changes.

As for the third estate, there was great popular participation in the elections. Almost all male commoners twenty-five years of age or older had the right to vote. However, voting required two stages, which meant that most of the representatives finally selected by the third estate were well-educated, prosperous members of the middle class. Most of them were not businessmen but lawyers and government officials. Social status and prestige were matters of particular concern to this economic elite. There were no delegates elected from the great mass of laboring poor—the peasants and urban artisans.

The petitions for change coming from the three estates showed a surprising degree of consensus on most issues. There was general agreement that royal absolutism should give way to constitutional monarchy, in which laws and taxes would require the consent of the Estates General meeting regularly. All agreed that individual liberties would have to be guaranteed by law, that the economic position of the parish clergy would have to be improved, and that economic development required reforms. The striking similarities in the grievance petitions of the clergy, nobility, and third estate reflected the broad commitment of France's educated elite to liberalism.

Yet an increasingly bitter quarrel undermined this consensus during the intense electoral campaign: *how* would the Estates General vote, and precisely *who* would lead in the political reorganization that was generally desired? The Estates General of 1614 had sat as three separate houses. Any action had required the agreement of at least two branches, a requirement that had virtually guaranteed control by the nobility and the clergy. Immediately after the victory over the king, the aristocratic Parlement of Paris, mainly out of respect for tradition but partly out of a desire to enhance the nobility's political position, ruled that the Estates General should once again sit separately. The ruling was quickly denounced by some middle-class intellectuals, who demanded instead a single assembly dominated by the third estate to ensure fundamental reforms. Reflecting increased political competition and a growing hostility toward aristocratic aspirations, the abbé Emmanuel Joseph Sieyès argued in 1789 in his famous pamphlet *What Is the Third Estate?* that the nobility was a tiny, overprivileged minority and that the neglected third estate constituted the true strength of the French nation. When the government agreed that the third estate should have as many delegates as the clergy and the nobility combined, but then rendered this act meaningless by upholding voting by separate order, middle-class leaders saw fresh evidence of an aristocratic conspiracy.

In May 1789, the twelve hundred delegates of the three estates paraded in medieval pageantry through the streets of Versailles to an opening session resplendent with feudal magnificence. The estates were almost immediately deadlocked. Delegates of the third estate refused to transact any business until the king ordered the clergy and nobility to sit with them in a single body. Finally, after a six-week war of nerves, a few parish priests began to go over to the third estate, which on June 17 voted to call itself the "National Assembly." On June 20, the delegates of the third estate, excluded from their hall because of "repairs," moved to a large indoor tennis court. There they swore the famous Oath of the Tennis Court, pledging not to disband until they had written a new constitution.

The king's actions were then somewhat contradictory. On June 23, he made a conciliatory speech urging reforms to a joint session, and four days later he ordered the three estates to meet together. At the same time, the vacillating and indecisive monarch apparently followed the advice of relatives and court nobles, who urged him to dissolve the Estates General by force. The king called an army of eighteen thousand troops toward Versailles, and on July 11 he dismissed his finance minister and his other more liberal ministers. Faced with growing opposition since 1787, Louis XVI had resigned himself to bankruptcy. Now he belatedly sought to reassert his historic "divine right" to rule. The middle-class delegates and their allies from the liberal nobility had done their best, but they were resigned to being disbanded at bayonet point. One third-estate delegate reassured a worried colleague, "You won't hang—you'll only have to go back home."[2]

The Revolt of the Poor and the Oppressed

While the educated delegates of the third estate pressed for symbolic equality with the nobility and clergy in a single legislative body at Versailles, economic hardship gripped the common people of France in a tightening vise. Grain was the basis of the diet of ordinary people in the eighteenth century, and in 1788 the harvest had been extremely poor. The price of bread began to soar.

The Oath of the Tennis Court This painting, based on an unfinished work by Jacques-Louis David (1748–1825), enthusiastically celebrates the revolutionary rupture of June 20, 1789. Locked out of their assembly hall at Versailles and joined by some sympathetic priests, the delegates of the third estate have moved to an indoor tennis court and are swearing never to disband until they have written a new constitution and put France on a firm foundation. *(Réunion des Musées Nationaux/Art Resource, NY)*

In Paris, where bread was regularly subsidized by the government in an attempt to prevent popular unrest, the price rose to 4 sous. The poor could scarcely afford to pay 2 sous per pound, for even at that price a laborer with a wife and three children had to spend half of his wages to buy the family's bread.

Harvest failure and high bread prices unleashed a classic economic depression of the preindustrial age. With food so expensive and with so much uncertainty, the demand for manufactured goods collapsed. Thousands of artisans and small traders were thrown out of work. By the end of 1789, almost half of the French people would be in need of relief. One person in eight was a pauper living in extreme want. In Paris perhaps 150,000 of the city's 600,000 people were without work in July 1789.

Against this background of poverty and ongoing political crisis, the people of Paris entered decisively onto the revolutionary stage. They believed in a general, though ill-defined, way that the economic distress had human causes. They believed that they should have steady work and enough bread at fair prices to survive. Specifically, they feared that the dismissal of the king's moderate finance minister would put them at the mercy of aristocratic landowners and grain speculators. Rumors that the king's troops would sack the city began to fill the air. Angry crowds formed, and passionate voices urged action. On July 13, the people began to seize arms for the defense of the city as the king's armies moved toward Paris, and on July 14 several hundred people marched to the Bastille to search for weapons and gunpowder.

A medieval fortress with walls ten feet thick and eight great towers each one hundred feet high, the Bastille had long been used as a prison. It was guarded by eighty retired soldiers and thirty Swiss mercenaries. The governor of the fortress-prison refused to hand over the powder, panicked, and ordered his men to fire, killing ninety-eight people attempting to enter. Cannon were brought to batter the main gate, and fighting continued until the prison surrendered. The governor of the prison was later hacked to death, and his head and that of the mayor of Paris, who had been slow to give the crowd arms, were stuck on pikes and paraded through the streets. The next day a committee of citizens appointed the marquis de Lafayette commander of the city's armed forces. Paris was lost to the king, who was forced to recall the finance minister and disperse his troops. The popular uprising had broken the power monopoly of the royal army and thereby saved the National Assembly.

As the delegates resumed their long-winded and inconclusive debates at Versailles, the countryside sent them a radical and unmistakable message. Throughout France, peasants began to rise in spontaneous, violent, and effective insurrection against their lords, ransacking manor houses and burning feudal documents that recorded the peasants' obligations. Neither middle-class landowners, who often owned manors and village monopolies, nor the larger, more prosperous farmers were spared. In some areas, peasants reinstated traditional village practices, undoing recent enclosures and reoccupying old common lands. Peasants seized forests, and taxes went unpaid. Fear of vagabonds and outlaws—called the **Great Fear** by contemporaries—seized the countryside and fanned the flames of rebellion. The long-suffering peasants were doing their best to free themselves from manorial rights and exploitation.

Faced with chaos, yet afraid to call on the king to restore order, some liberal nobles and middle-class dele-

Storming the Bastille This representation by an untrained contemporary artist shows civilians and members of the Paris militia—the "conquerors of the Bastille"—on the attack. This successful action had enormous practical and symbolic significance, and July 14 has long been France's most important national holiday. *(Musée Carnavalet/Photo Hubert Josse—JLJ)*

gates at Versailles responded to peasant demands with a surprise maneuver on the night of August 4, 1789. The duke of Aiguillon, also notably one of France's greatest noble landowners, declared that

in several provinces the whole people forms a kind of league for the destruction of the manor houses, the ravaging of the lands, and especially for the seizure of the archives where the title deeds to feudal properties are kept. It seeks to throw off at last a yoke that has for many centuries weighted it down.[3]

He urged equality in taxation and the elimination of feudal dues. In the end, all the old exactions imposed on the peasants—serfdom where it still existed, exclusive hunting rights for nobles, fees for justice, village monopolies, the right to make peasants work on the roads, and a host of other dues—were abolished, generally without compensation. Though a clarifying law passed a week later was less generous, the peasants ignored the "fine print." They never paid feudal dues again. Thus the French peasantry, which already owned about 30 percent of all the land, achieved an unprecedented victory in the early days of revolutionary upheaval. Henceforth, the French peasants would seek mainly to protect and consolidate their revolutionary triumph. As the Great Fear subsided in the countryside, they became a force for order and stability.

A Limited Monarchy

The National Assembly moved forward. On August 27, 1789, it issued the Declaration of the Rights of Man, which stated, "Men are born and remain free and equal in rights." The declaration also maintained that mankind's natural rights are "liberty, property, security, and resistance to oppression" and that "every man is presumed innocent until he is proven guilty." As for law, "it is an expression of the general will; all citizens have the right to concur personally or through their representatives in its formation. . . . Free expression of thoughts and opinions is one of the most precious rights of mankind: every citizen may therefore speak, write, and publish freely." In short, this clarion call of the liberal revolutionary ideal guaranteed equality before the law, representative government for a sovereign people, and individual freedom. This revolutionary credo, only two pages long, was propagandized throughout France and Europe and around the world.

Moving beyond general principles to draft a constitution proved difficult. The questions of how much power the king should retain and whether he could permanently veto legislation led to another deadlock. Once again the decisive answer came from the poor—in this instance, the poor women of Paris.

Women customarily bought the food and managed the poor family's slender resources. In Paris great numbers of women also worked for wages, often within the putting-out system, making garments and luxury items destined for an aristocratic and international clientele. Immediately after the fall of the Bastille, many of France's great court nobles began to leave Versailles for foreign lands, so that a plummeting demand for luxuries intensified the general economic crisis; international markets also declined. The church was no longer able to give its traditional grants of food and money to the poor. Increasing unemployment and hunger put tremendous pressure on household managers, and the result was another popular explosion.

On October 5 some seven thousand desperate women marched the twelve miles from Paris to Versailles to demand action. A middle-class deputy looking out from the Assembly saw "multitudes arriving from Paris including fishwives and bullies from the market, and these people wanted nothing but bread." This great crowd invaded the Assembly, "armed with scythes, sticks and pikes." One tough old woman directing a large group of younger women defiantly shouted into the debate, "Who's that talking down there? Make the chatterbox shut up. That's not the point: the point is that we want bread."[4] Hers was the genuine voice of the people, essential to any understanding of the French Revolution.

The women invaded the royal apartments, slaughtered some of the royal bodyguards, and furiously searched for the queen, Marie Antoinette, who was widely despised for her frivolous and supposedly immoral behavior. "We are going to cut off her head, tear out her heart, fry her liver, and that won't be the end of it," they shouted, surging through the palace in a frenzy. It seems likely that only the intervention of Lafayette and the National Guard saved the royal family. But the only way to calm the disorder was for the king to go and live in Paris, as the crowd demanded.

The next day, the king, the queen, and their son left for Paris in the midst of a strange procession. The heads of two aristocrats, stuck on pikes, led the way. They were followed by the remaining members of the royal bodyguard, unarmed and mocked by fierce men holding sabers and pikes. A mixed and victorious multitude surrounded the carriage of the captured royal family, hurling crude insults at the queen. There was drinking and eating among the women, who had clearly emerged as a major element in the Parisian revolutionary crowd.[5]

The National Assembly followed the king to Paris, and the next two years, until September 1791, saw the consolidation of the liberal revolution. Under middle-class leadership, the National Assembly abolished the French nobility as a legal order and pushed forward with the creation of a

constitutional monarchy, which Louis XVI reluctantly agreed to accept in July 1790. In the final constitution, the king remained the head of state, but all lawmaking power was placed in the hands of the National Assembly, elected by the economic upper half of French males.

New laws broadened women's rights to seek divorce, to inherit property, and to obtain financial support from fathers for illegitimate children. But women were not allowed to vote or hold political office for at least two reasons. First, the great majority of comfortable, well-educated males in the National Assembly believed that women should be limited to child rearing and domestic duties and should leave politics and most public activities to men, as Rousseau had advocated in his influential *Emile* (see pages 686–687). Second, the delegates to the National Assembly were convinced that political life in absolutist France had been profoundly corrupt and that a prime example of this corruption was the way that some talented but immoral aristocratic women had used their sexual charms to manipulate weak rulers and their ministers. Thus delegates argued that excluding women from politics would help create the civic virtue that had been missing: pure, home-focused wives would raise the high-minded sons needed to govern the nation.

The National Assembly replaced the complicated patchwork of historic provinces with eighty-three departments of approximately equal size. The jumble of weights and measures that varied from province to province was reformed, leading to the introduction of the simple, uniform metric system in 1793. The National Assembly promoted the liberal concept of economic freedom. Monopolies, guilds, and workers combinations were prohibited, and barriers to trade within France were abolished in the name of economic liberty. Thus the National Assembly applied the critical spirit of the Enlightenment to reform France's laws and institutions completely.

The Assembly also imposed a radical reorganization on the country's religious life. It granted religious freedom to the tiny minority of French Jews and Protestants. Of greater impact, it then nationalized the Catholic church's property and abolished monasteries as useless relics of a distant past. The government used all former church property as collateral to guarantee a new paper currency, the *assignats,* and then sold these properties in an attempt to put the state's finances on a solid footing. Although the church's land was sold in large blocks, peasants eventually purchased much when it was subdivided. These purchases strengthened their attachment to the new revolutionary order in the countryside.

The religious reorganization of France brought the new government into conflict with the Catholic church and many sincere Christians, especially in the countryside. Many delegates to the National Assembly, imbued with the rationalism and skepticism of the eighteenth-century philosophes, harbored a deep distrust of popular piety and "superstitious religion." Thus they established a national church, with priests chosen by voters. In the face of widespread resistance, the National Assembly then required the Catholic clergy to take a loyalty oath to the new government and become just so many more employees of the state. The pope formally condemned this attempt to subjugate the church, and only half the priests of France took the oath of allegiance. The result was a deep division within both the country and the clergy on the religious question; confusion and hostility among French Catholics were pervasive. The attempt to remake the Catholic church, like the Assembly's abolition of guilds and workers combinations, sharpened the conflict between the educated classes and the common people that had been emerging in the eighteenth century. This policy toward the church was the revolutionary government's first important failure.

World War and Republican France, 1791–1799

When Louis XVI accepted the final version of the completed constitution in September 1791, a young and still obscure provincial lawyer and member of the National Assembly named Maximilien Robespierre (1758–1794) evaluated the work of two years and concluded, "The Revolution is over." Robespierre was both right and wrong. He was right in the sense that the most constructive and lasting reforms were in place. Nothing substantial in the way of liberty and useful reform would be gained in the next generation. He was wrong in the sense that a much more radical stage lay ahead. New heroes and new ideologies were to emerge in revolutionary wars and international conflict.

Foreign Reactions and the Beginning of War

The outbreak and progress of revolution in France produced great excitement and a sharp division of opinion in Europe and the United States. Liberals and radicals saw a mighty triumph of liberty over despotism. In Great Britain especially, they hoped that the French example would lead to a fundamental reordering of Parliament, which was in the hands of the aristocracy and a few wealthy merchants. After the French Revolution began, conservative leaders

FRENCH DEMOCRATS surprizing the Royal Runaways.

The Capture of Louis XVI, June 1791 This English cartoon satirizes the royal family's disastrous attempt to sneak out of France. Recognized and arrested only a few miles from safety across the Belgian border, Louis XVI appeared guilty of treason to many of the French. The radicalization of the Revolution accelerated. *(Courtesy of the Trustees of the British Museum)*

such as Edmund Burke (1729–1797) were deeply troubled by the aroused spirit of reform. In 1790 Burke published *Reflections on the Revolution in France,* one of the great intellectual defenses of European conservatism. He defended inherited privileges in general and those of the English monarchy and aristocracy. He glorified the unrepresentative Parliament and predicted that thoroughgoing reform like that occurring in France would lead only to chaos and tyranny. Burke's work sparked much debate.

One passionate rebuttal came from a young writer in London, Mary Wollstonecraft (1759–1797). Born into the middle class, Wollstonecraft was schooled in adversity by a mean-spirited father who beat his wife and squandered his inherited fortune. Determined to be independent in a society that generally expected women of her class to become homebodies and obedient wives, she struggled for years to earn her living as a governess and teacher—practically the only acceptable careers for single, educated women—before attaining success as a translator and author. Incensed by Burke's book, Wollstonecraft immediately wrote a blistering, widely read attack, *A Vindication of the Rights of Man* (1790).

Then she made a daring intellectual leap. She developed for the first time the logical implications of natural-law philosophy in her masterpiece, *A Vindication of the Rights of Woman* (1792). To fulfill the still-unrealized potential of the French Revolution and to eliminate the sexual inequality she had felt so keenly, she demanded that

the Rights of Women be respected . . . [and] JUSTICE for one-half of the human race. . . . It is time to effect a revolution in female manners, time to restore to them their lost dignity, and make them, as part of the human species, labor, by reforming themselves, to reform the world.

Setting high standards for women—"I wish to persuade women to endeavor to acquire strength, both of mind and body"—Wollstonecraft broke with those who had a low opinion of women's intellectual potential. She advocated rigorous coeducation, which would make women better wives and mothers, good citizens, and even economically independent people. Women could manage businesses and enter politics if only men would give them the chance. Men themselves would benefit from women's rights, for Wollstonecraft believed that "the two sexes mutually corrupt and improve each other."[6] Wollstonecraft's analysis testified to the power of the Revolution to excite and inspire outside of France. Paralleling ideas put forth independently in France by Olympe de Gouges (1748–1793), a self-taught writer and woman of the people (see the feature "Listening to the Past: Revolution and Women's Rights" on pages 722–723), Wollstonecraft's work marked the birth of the modern women's movement for equal rights, and it was ultimately very influential.

The kings and nobles of continental Europe, who had at first welcomed the revolution in France as weakening a competing power, began to feel no less threatened than Burke and his supporters. When Louis XVI and Marie Antoinette were arrested and returned to Paris after trying unsuccessfully to slip out of France in June 1791, the monarchs of Austria and Prussia issued the Declaration of Pillnitz. This carefully worded statement declared their willingness to intervene in France in certain circumstances and was expected to have a sobering effect on revolutionary France without causing war.

But the crowned heads of Europe misjudged the revolutionary spirit in France. When the National Assembly disbanded, it sought popular support by decreeing that none of its members would be eligible for election to the new Legislative Assembly. This meant that when the new representative body convened in October 1791, it had a different character. The great majority of the legislators were still prosperous, well-educated, middle-class men, but they were younger and less cautious than their predecessors. Many of the deputies were loosely allied and called **Jacobins,** after the name of their political club.

The new representatives to the Assembly were passionately committed to liberal revolution and distrustful of monarchy after Louis's attempted flight. They increasingly lumped "useless aristocrats" and "despotic monarchs" together, and they easily whipped themselves into a patriotic fury with bombastic oratory. If the courts of Europe were attempting to incite a war of kings against France, then "we will incite a war of people against kings. . . . Ten million Frenchmen, kindled by the fire of liberty, armed with the sword, with reason, with eloquence would be able to change the face of the world and make the tyrants tremble on their thrones."[7] Only Robespierre and a very few others argued that people would not welcome liberation at the point of a gun. Such warnings were brushed aside. France would "rise to the full height of her mission," as one deputy urged. In April 1792, France declared war on Francis II, the Habsburg monarch.

France's crusade against tyranny went poorly at first. Prussia joined Austria in the Austrian Netherlands (present-day Belgium), and French forces broke and fled at their first encounter with armies of this First Coalition. The road to Paris lay open, and it is possible that only conflict between the eastern monarchs over the division of Poland saved France from defeat.

Military reversals and patriotic fervor led the Legislative Assembly to declare the country in danger. Volunteer armies from the provinces streamed through Paris, fraternizing with the people and singing patriotic songs like the stirring "Marseillaise," later the French national anthem.

In this supercharged wartime atmosphere, rumors of treason by the king and queen spread in Paris. On August 10, 1792, a revolutionary crowd attacked the royal palace at the Tuileries, capturing it after heavy fighting with the Swiss Guards. The king and his family fled for their lives to the nearby Legislative Assembly, which suspended the king from all his functions, imprisoned him, and called for a new National Convention to be elected by universal male suffrage. Monarchy in France was on its deathbed, mortally wounded by war and popular upheaval.

The Second Revolution

The fall of the monarchy marked a rapid radicalization of the Revolution, a phase that historians often call the **second revolution.** Louis's imprisonment was followed by the September Massacres. Wild stories seized the city that imprisoned counter-revolutionary aristocrats and priests were plotting with the allied invaders. As a result, angry crowds invaded the prisons of Paris and summarily slaughtered half the men and women they found. In late September 1792, the new, popularly elected National Convention proclaimed France a republic.

The republic sought to create a new popular culture, fashioning compelling symbols that broke with the past and glorified the new order. It adopted a brand-new revolutionary calendar, which eliminated saints' days and renamed the days and the months after the seasons of the year. Citizens were expected to address each other with the friendly "thou" of the people rather than with the formal "you" of the rich and powerful. The republic energetically promoted broad, open-air, democratic festivals. These spectacles brought the entire population together and sought to redirect the people's traditional enthusiasm for Catholic religious celebrations to secular holidays instilling republican virtue and a love of nation. These spectacles were less successful in villages than in cities, where popular interest in politics was greater and Catholicism was weaker.

All of the members of the National Convention were republicans, and at the beginning almost all belonged to the Jacobin club of Paris. But control of the Convention was increasingly contested by two bitterly competitive groups—the **Girondists,** named after a department in southwestern France, and **the Mountain,** led by Robespierre and another young lawyer, Georges Jacques Danton. The Mountain was so called because its members sat on the uppermost left-hand benches of the assembly hall. A majority of the indecisive Convention members, seated in the "Plain" below, floated back and forth between the rival factions.

This division was clearly apparent after the National Convention overwhelmingly convicted Louis XVI of treason. By a narrow majority, the Convention then sentenced him to death in January 1793. Louis died with tranquil dignity on the newly invented guillotine. One of his last statements was "I am innocent and shall die without fear. I would that my death might bring happiness to the French, and ward off the dangers which I foresee."[8]

Both the Girondists and the Mountain were determined to continue the "war against tyranny." The Prussians had been stopped at the Battle of Valmy on September 20, 1792, one day before the republic was proclaimed. French armies then invaded Savoy and captured Nice, moved into the German Rhineland, and by November 1792 were occupying the entire Austrian Netherlands. Everywhere they went, French armies of occupation chased the princes, "abolished feudalism," and found support among some peasants and middle-class people.

But the French armies also lived off the land, requisitioning food and supplies and plundering local treasures. The liberators looked increasingly like foreign invaders. International tensions mounted. In February 1793, the National Convention, at war with Austria and Prussia, declared war on Britain, Holland, and Spain as well. Republican France was now at war with almost all of Europe, a great war that would last almost without interruption until 1815.

As the forces of the First Coalition drove the French from the Austrian Netherlands, peasants in western France revolted against being drafted into the army. They were supported and encouraged in their resistance by devout Catholics, royalists, and foreign agents.

In Paris the quarrelsome National Convention found itself locked in a life-and-death political struggle between the Girondists and the Mountain. Both groups were sincere republicans, hating privilege and wanting to temper economic liberalism with social concern. Yet personal hatreds ran deep. The Girondists feared a bloody dictatorship by the Mountain, and the Mountain was no less convinced that the more moderate Girondists would turn to conservatives and even royalists in order to retain power. With the middle-class delegates so bitterly divided, the laboring poor of Paris emerged as the decisive political factor.

The laboring men and women of Paris always constituted—along with the peasantry in the summer of 1789—the elemental force that drove the Revolution forward. It was the artisans, day laborers, market women, and garment workers who had stormed the Bastille, marched on Versailles, driven the king from the Tuileries, and carried out the September Massacres. The laboring poor and the petty traders were often known as the **sans-culottes,** "without breeches," because sans-culottes men wore trousers instead of the knee breeches of the aristocracy and the solid middle class. The immediate interests of the sans-culottes were mainly economic, and in the

Contrasting Visions of the Sans-Culottes The woman on the left, with her playful cat and calm simplicity, suggests how the French sans-culottes saw themselves as democrats and virtuous citizens. The ferocious sans-culotte harpy on the right, a creation of wartime England's vivid counter-revolutionary imagination, screams for more blood, more death: "I am the Goddess of Liberty! Long live the guillotine!" *(Bibliothèque Nationale, Paris)*

spring of 1793 rapid inflation, unemployment, and food shortages were again weighing heavily on poor families.

Moreover, by the spring of 1793, the sans-culottes had become keenly interested in politics. Encouraged by the so-called angry men, such as the passionate young ex-priest and journalist Jacques Roux, sans-culottes men and women were demanding radical political action to guarantee them their daily bread. At first the Mountain joined the Girondists in rejecting these demands. But in the face of military defeat, peasant revolt, and hatred of the Girondists, the Mountain and especially Robespierre became more sympathetic. The Mountain joined with sans-culottes activists in the city government to engineer a popular uprising, which forced the Convention to arrest thirty-one Girondist deputies for treason on June 2. All power passed to the Mountain.

Robespierre and others from the Mountain joined the recently formed Committee of Public Safety, to which the Convention had given dictatorial power to deal with the national emergency. These developments in Paris triggered revolt in leading provincial cities, such as Lyons and Marseilles, where moderates denounced Paris and demanded a decentralized government. The peasant revolt spread, and the republic's armies were driven back on all fronts. By July 1793, only the areas around Paris and on the eastern frontier were firmly held by the central government. Defeat seemed imminent.

Total War and the Terror

A year later, in July 1794, the Austrian Netherlands and the Rhineland were once again in the hands of conquering French armies, and the First Coalition was falling apart. This remarkable change of fortune was due to the revolutionary government's success in harnessing, for perhaps the first time in history, the explosive forces of a planned economy, revolutionary terror, and modern nationalism in a total war effort.

Robespierre and the Committee of Public Safety advanced with implacable resolution on several fronts in 1793 and 1794. First, they collaborated with the fiercely patriotic and democratic sans-culottes, who retained the common people's traditional faith in fair prices and a moral economic order and who distrusted most wealthy capitalists and all aristocrats. Thus Robespierre and his coworkers established, as best they could, a **planned economy** with egalitarian social overtones. Rather than let supply and demand determine prices, the government set maximum allowable prices for key products. Though the state was too weak to enforce all its price regulations, it did fix the price of bread in Paris at levels the poor could afford. Rationing was introduced, and bakers were permitted to make only the "bread of equality"—a brown bread made of a mixture of all available flours. White bread and pastries were outlawed as luxuries. The poor of Paris may not have eaten well, but at least they ate.

They also worked, mainly to produce arms and munitions for the war effort. The government told craftsmen what to produce, nationalized many small workshops, and requisitioned raw materials and grain from the peasants. Sometimes planning and control did not go beyond orders to meet the latest emergency: "Ten thousand soldiers lack shoes. You will take the shoes of all the aristocrats in Strasbourg and deliver them ready for transport to headquarters at 10 A.M. tomorrow." But failures to control and coordinate were failures of means and not of desire. The second revolution and the ascendancy of the sans-culottes had produced an embryonic emergency socialism, which thoroughly frightened Europe's propertied classes and had great influence on the subsequent development of socialist ideology.

Second, while radical economic measures supplied the poor with bread and the armies with weapons, the **Reign of Terror** (1793–1794) used revolutionary terror to solidify the home front. Special revolutionary courts responsible only to Robespierre's Committee of Public Safety tried rebels and "enemies of the nation" for political crimes. Drawing on popular, sans-culottes support centered in the local Jacobin clubs, these local courts ignored normal legal procedures and judged severely. Some 40,000 French men and women were executed or died in prison. Another 300,000 suspects crowded the prisons and often brushed close to death in a revolutionary court.

Robespierre's Reign of Terror was one of the most controversial phases of the French Revolution. Most historians now believe that the Reign of Terror was not directed against any single class. Rather, it was a political weapon directed impartially against all who might oppose the revolutionary government. For many Europeans of the time, however, the Reign of Terror represented a frightening perversion of the generous ideals of 1789. It strengthened the belief that France had foolishly replaced a weak king with a bloody dictatorship.

The third and perhaps most decisive element in the French republic's victory over the First Coalition was its ability to draw on the explosive power of patriotic dedication to a national state and a national mission. An essential part of modern **nationalism**, this commitment was something new in history. With a common language and a common tradition newly reinforced by the ideas of popular sovereignty and democracy, large numbers of French people were stirred by a common loyalty. They developed

The French Revolution

May 5, 1789	Estates General convene at Versailles.
June 17, 1789	Third estate declares itself the National Assembly.
June 20, 1789	Oath of the Tennis Court is sworn.
July 14, 1789	Storming of the Bastille occurs.
July–August 1789	Great Fear ravages the countryside.
August 4, 1789	National Assembly abolishes feudal privileges.
August 27, 1789	National Assembly issues Declaration of the Rights of Man.
October 5, 1789	Women march on Versailles and force royal family to return to Paris.
November 1789	National Assembly confiscates church lands.
July 1790	Civil Constitution of the Clergy establishes a national church. Louis XVI reluctantly agrees to accept a constitutional monarchy.
June 1791	Royal family is arrested while attempting to flee France.
August 1791	Austria and Prussia issue the Declaration of Pillnitz.
April 1792	France declares war on Austria.
August 1792	Parisian mob attacks the palace and takes Louis XVI prisoner.
September 1792	September Massacres occur. National Convention declares France a republic and abolishes monarchy.
January 1793	Louis XVI is executed.
February 1793	France declares war on Britain, Holland, and Spain. Revolts take place in some provincial cities.
March 1793	Bitter struggle occurs in the National Convention between Girondists and the Mountain.
April–June 1793	Robespierre and the Mountain organize the Committee of Public Safety and arrest Girondist leaders.
September 1793	Price controls are instituted to aid the sans-culottes and mobilize the war effort.
1793–1794	Reign of Terror darkens Paris and the provinces.
Spring 1794	French armies are victorious on all fronts.
July 1794	Robespierre is executed. Thermidorian reaction begins.
1795–1799	Directory rules.
1795	Economic controls are abolished, and suppression of the sans-culottes begins.
1797	Napoleon defeats Austrian armies in Italy and returns triumphant to Paris.
1798	Austria, Great Britain, and Russia form the Second Coalition against France.
1799	Napoleon overthrows the Directory and seizes power.

The Last Roll Call Prisoners sentenced to death by revolutionary courts listen to an official solemnly reading the names of those selected for immediate execution. After being bound, the prisoners will ride standing up in a small cart through the streets of Paris to the nearby guillotine. As this painting highlights, both women and men were executed for political crimes under the Terror. *(Mansell/TimePix)*

an intense emotional commitment to the defense of the nation, and they imagined the nation as a great loving family that included all right-thinking patriots.

In such circumstances, war was no longer the gentlemanly game of the eighteenth century, but rather total war, a life-and-death struggle between good and evil. Everyone had to participate in the national effort. According to a famous decree of August 23, 1793:

> *The young men shall go to battle and the married men shall forge arms. The women shall make tents and clothes, and shall serve in the hospitals; children shall tear rags into lint. The old men will be guided to the public places of the cities to kindle the courage of the young warriors and to preach the unity of the Republic and the hatred of kings.*

Like the wars of religion, war in 1793 was a crusade. This war, however, was fought for a secular, rather than a religious, ideology.

The all-out mobilization of French resources under the Terror combined with the fervor of modern nationalism to create an awesome fighting machine. After August 1793, all unmarried young men were subject to the draft, and by January 1794 the French had about 800,000 soldiers on active duty in fourteen armies. A force of this size was unprecedented in the history of European warfare, and recent research concludes that the French armed forces outnumbered their enemies almost four to one.[9] Well trained, well equipped, and constantly indoctrinated, the enormous armies of the republic were led by young, impetuous generals. These generals often had risen from the ranks, and they personified the opportunities the Revolution seemed to offer gifted sons of the people. Following orders from Paris to attack relentlessly, French generals used mass assaults at bayonet point to overwhelm the enemy. "No maneuvering, nothing elaborate," declared the fearless

General Hoche. "Just cold steel, passion and patriotism."[10] By the spring of 1794, French armies were victorious on all fronts. The republic was saved.

The Thermidorian Reaction and the Directory, 1794–1799

The success of the French armies led Robespierre and the Committee of Public Safety to relax the emergency economic controls, but they extended the political Reign of Terror. Their lofty goal was increasingly an ideal democratic republic where justice would reign and there would be neither rich nor poor. Their lowly means were unrestrained despotism and the guillotine, which struck down any who might seriously question the new order. In March 1794, to the horror of many sans-culottes, Robespierre's Terror wiped out many of the angry men who had been criticizing Robespierre for being soft on the wealthy and who were led by the radical social democrat Jacques Hébert. Two weeks later, several of Robespierre's long-standing collaborators, led by the famous orator Danton, marched up the steps to the guillotine. A strange assortment of radicals and moderates in the Convention, knowing that they might be next, organized a conspiracy. They howled down Robespierre when he tried to speak to the National Convention on 9 Thermidor (July 27, 1794). On the following day, it was Robespierre's turn to be shaved by the revolutionary razor.

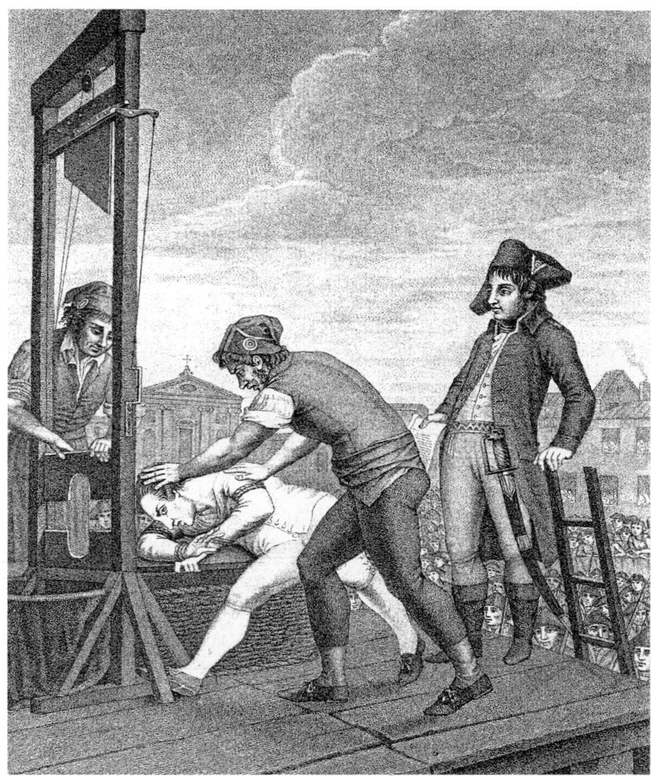

The Execution of Robespierre The guillotine was painted red and completely wooden except for the heavy iron blade. Large crowds witnessed the executions in a majestic public square in central Paris, then known as the Place de la Revolution and now called the Place de la Concorde (Harmony Square). *(Musée Carnavalet/Edimedia)*

As Robespierre's closest supporters followed their leader, France unexpectedly experienced a thorough reaction to the despotism of the Reign of Terror. In a general way, this **Thermidorian reaction** recalled the early days of the Revolution. The respectable middle-class lawyers and professionals who had led the liberal revolution of 1789 reasserted their authority, drawing support from their own class, the provincial cities, and the better-off peasants. The National Convention abolished many economic controls, let prices rise sharply, and severely restricted the local political organizations where the sans-culottes had their strength. And all the while, wealthy bankers and newly rich speculators celebrated the sudden end of the Terror with an orgy of self-indulgence and ostentatious luxury, an orgy symbolized by the shockingly low-cut gowns that quickly became the rage among their wives and mistresses.

The collapse of economic controls, coupled with runaway inflation, hit the working poor very hard. The gaudy extravagance of the rich wounded their pride. The sans-culottes accepted private property, but they believed passionately in small business, decent wages, and economic justice. Increasingly disorganized after Robespierre purged radical leaders, the common people of Paris finally revolted against the emerging new order in early 1795. The Convention quickly used the army to suppress these insurrections and made no concessions to the poor. In the face of all these reversals, the revolutionary fervor of the laboring poor in Paris finally subsided. Excluded and disillusioned, the urban poor would have little interest in and influence on politics until 1830.

In villages and small towns there arose a great cry for peace and a turning toward religion, especially from women, who had seldom experienced the political radicalization of sans-culottes women in the big cities. Instead, these women had tenaciously defended their culture and religious beliefs against the often heavy-handed attacks of antireligious revolutionary officials after 1789. As the government began to retreat on the religious question from 1796 to 1801, the women of rural France brought back the Catholic church and the open worship of God. In the words of a leading historian, these women worked for a return to a normal and structured lifestyle:

Peacefully but purposefully, they sought to re-establish a pattern of life punctuated by a pealing bell and one in which the rites of passage—birth, marriage, and death—were respected and hallowed. The state had intruded too far and women entered the public arena to push it back and won. It was one of the most resounding political statements made by the populace in the entire history of the Revolution.[11]

As for the middle-class members of the National Convention, in 1795 they wrote yet another constitution, which they believed would guarantee their economic position and political supremacy. As in previous elections, the mass of the population voted only for electors, whose number was cut back to men of substantial means. Electors then elected the members of a reorganized legislative assembly, as well as key officials throughout France. The new assembly also chose a five-man executive—the Directory.

The Directory continued to support French military expansion abroad. War was no longer so much a crusade as a means to meet ever-present, ever-unsolved economic problems. Large, victorious French armies reduced unemployment at home and were able to live off the territories they conquered and plundered.

The unprincipled action of the Directory reinforced widespread disgust with war and starvation. This general dissatisfaction revealed itself clearly in the national elections of 1797, which returned a large number of conservative and even monarchist deputies who favored peace at almost any price. The members of the Directory, fearing for their skins, used the army to nullify the elections and began to govern dictatorially. Two years later, Napoleon Bonaparte ended the Directory in a *coup d'état* and substituted a strong dictatorship for a weak one. The effort to establish stable representative government had failed.

The Napoleonic Era, 1799–1815

For almost fifteen years, from 1799 to 1814, France was in the hands of a keen-minded military dictator of exceptional ability. One of history's most fascinating leaders, Napoleon Bonaparte (1769–1821) realized the need to put an end to civil strife in France, in order to create unity and consolidate his rule. And he did. But Napoleon saw himself as a man of destiny, and the glory of war and the dream of universal empire proved irresistible. For years he spiraled from victory to victory, but in the end he was destroyed by a mighty coalition united in fear of his restless ambition.

Napoleon's Rule of France

In 1799 when he seized power, young General Napoleon Bonaparte was a national hero. Born in Corsica into an impoverished noble family in 1769, Napoleon left home and became a lieutenant in the French artillery in 1785. After a brief and unsuccessful adventure fighting for Corsican independence in 1789, he returned to France as a French patriot and a dedicated revolutionary. Rising rapidly in the new army, Napoleon was placed in command of French forces in Italy and won brilliant victories there in 1796 and 1797. His next campaign, in Egypt, was a failure, but Napoleon returned to France before the fiasco was generally known. His reputation remained intact.

Napoleon soon learned that some prominent members of the legislature were plotting against the Directory. The dissatisfaction of these plotters stemmed not so much from the fact that the Directory was a dictatorship as from the fact that it was a weak dictatorship. Ten years of upheaval and uncertainty had made firm rule much more appealing than liberty and popular politics to these disillusioned revolutionaries. The abbé Sieyès personified this evolution in thinking. In 1789 he had written that the nobility was grossly overprivileged and that the entire people should rule the French nation. Now Sieyès's motto was "Confidence from below, authority from above."

Like the other members of his group, Sieyès wanted a strong military ruler. The flamboyant thirty-year-old Napoleon was ideal. Thus the conspirators and Napoleon organized a takeover. On November 9, 1799, they ousted the Directors, and the following day soldiers disbanded the legislature at bayonet point. Napoleon was named first consul of the republic, and a new constitution consolidating his position was overwhelmingly approved in a plebiscite in December 1799. Republican appearances were maintained, but Napoleon was already the real ruler of France.

The essence of Napoleon's domestic policy was to use his great and highly personal powers to maintain order and end civil strife. He did so by working out unwritten agreements with powerful groups in France whereby these groups received favors in return for loyal service. Napoleon's bargain with the solid middle class was codified in the famous Civil Code of 1804, which reasserted two of the fundamental principles of the liberal and essentially moderate revolution of 1789: equality of all male citizens before the law and absolute security of

The Napoleonic Era

November 1799	Napoleon overthrows the Directory.
December 1799	French voters overwhelmingly approve Napoleon's new constitution.
1800	Napoleon founds the Bank of France.
1801	France defeats Austria and acquires Italian and German territories in the Treaty of Lunéville. Napoleon signs the Concordat with the pope.
1802	France signs the Treaty of Amiens with Britain.
December 1804	Napoleon crowns himself emperor.
October 1805	Britain defeats the French and Spanish fleet at the Battle of Trafalgar.
December 1805	Napoleon defeats Austria and Russia at the Battle of Austerlitz.
1807	Napoleon redraws the map of Europe in the treaties of Tilsit.
1810	The Grand Empire is at its height.
June 1812	Napoleon invades Russia with 600,000 men.
Fall–Winter 1812	Napoleon makes a disastrous retreat from Russia.
March 1814	Russia, Prussia, Austria, and Britain form the Quadruple Alliance to defeat France.
April 1814	Napoleon abdicates and is exiled to Elba.
February–June 1815	Napoleon escapes from Elba and rules France until he is defeated at the Battle of Waterloo.

wealth and private property. Napoleon and the leading bankers of Paris established the privately owned Bank of France, which loyally served the interests of both the state and the financial oligarchy. Napoleon's defense of the new economic order also appealed successfully to the peasants, who had gained both land and status from the revolutionary changes. Thus Napoleon reconfirmed the gains of the peasantry and reassured the solid middle class, which had lost a large number of its revolutionary illusions in the face of social upheaval.

At the same time, Napoleon accepted and strengthened the position of the French bureaucracy. Building on the solid foundations that revolutionary governments had inherited from the Old Regime, he perfected a thoroughly centralized state. A network of prefects, subprefects, and centrally appointed mayors depended on Napoleon and served him well. Nor were members of the old nobility slighted. In 1800 and again in 1802, Napoleon granted amnesty to 100,000 émigrés on the condition that they return to France and take a loyalty oath. Members of this returning elite soon ably occupied many high posts in the expanding centralized state. Only one thousand die-hard monarchists were exempted and remained abroad. Napoleon also created a new imperial nobility in order to reward his most talented generals and officials.

Napoleon's skill in gaining support from important and potentially hostile groups is illustrated by his treatment of the Catholic church in France. In 1800 the French clergy was still divided into two groups: those who had taken an oath of allegiance to the revolutionary government and those in exile or hiding who had refused to do so. Personally uninterested in religion, Napoleon wanted to heal the religious division so that a united Catholic church in France could serve as a bulwark of order and social peace. After arduous negotiations, Napoleon and Pope Pius VII (1800–1823) signed the Concordat of 1801. The pope gained for French Catholics the precious right to practice their religion freely, but Napoleon gained political power: his government now nominated bishops, paid the clergy, and exerted great influence over the church in France.

The domestic reforms of Napoleon's early years were his greatest achievement. Much of his legal and administrative reorganization has survived in France to this day. More generally, Napoleon's domestic initiatives gave the great majority of French people a welcome sense of stability and national unity.

Order and unity had their price: Napoleon's authoritarian rule. Women, who had often participated in revolutionary politics without having legal equality, lost many of the gains they had made in the 1790s. Under the law of the new Napoleonic Code, women were dependents of either their fathers or their husbands, and they could not make contracts or even have bank accounts in their own names. Indeed, Napoleon and his advisers aimed at reestablishing a **family monarchy,** where the power of the husband and father was as absolute over the wife and the children as that of Napoleon was over his subjects.

Free speech and freedom of the press were continually violated. By 1811 only four newspapers were left, and they were little more than organs of government propaganda. The occasional elections were a farce. Later laws prescribed harsh penalties for political offenses.

These changes in the law were part of the creation of a police state in France. Since Napoleon was usually busy making war, this task was largely left to Joseph Fouché, an unscrupulous opportunist who had earned a reputation for brutality during the Reign of Terror. As minister of police, Fouché organized a ruthlessly efficient spy system, which kept thousands of citizens under continual police surveillance. People suspected of subversive activities were arbitrarily detained, placed under house arrest, or consigned to insane asylums. After 1810 political suspects were held in state prisons, as they had been during the Terror. There were about twenty-five hundred such political prisoners in 1814.

Napoleon's Wars and Foreign Policy

Napoleon was above all a military man, and a great one. After coming to power in 1799, he sent peace feelers to Austria and Great Britain, the two remaining members of the Second Coalition, which had been formed against France in 1798. When these overtures were rejected, French armies led by Napoleon decisively defeated the Austrians. In the Treaty of Lunéville (1801), Austria accepted the loss of almost all its Italian possessions, and German territory on the west bank of the Rhine was incorporated into France. Once more, as in 1797, the British were alone, and war-weary, like the French.

Still seeking to consolidate his regime domestically, Napoleon concluded the Treaty of Amiens with Great Britain in 1802. France remained in control of Holland, the Austrian Netherlands, the west bank of the Rhine, and most of the Italian peninsula. Napoleon was free to reshape the German states as he wished. The Treaty of Amiens was clearly a diplomatic triumph for Napoleon, and peace with honor and profit increased his popularity at home.

In 1802 Napoleon was secure but unsatisfied. Ever a romantic gambler as well as a brilliant administrator, he could not contain his power drive. Aggressively redrawing the map of Germany so as to weaken Austria and attract the secondary states of southwestern Germany toward France, Napoleon tried to restrict British trade with all of Europe. Deciding to renew war with Britain in May 1803, Napoleon concentrated his armies in the French ports on the Channel in the fall of 1803 and began making preparations to invade England. Yet Great Britain remained dominant on the seas. When Napoleon tried to bring his Mediterranean fleet around Gibraltar to northern France, a combined French and Spanish fleet was, after a series of mishaps, virtually annihilated by Lord Nelson at the Battle of Trafalgar on October 21, 1805. Invasion of England was henceforth impossible. Renewed fighting had its advantages, however, for the first consul used the wartime atmosphere to have himself proclaimed emperor in late 1804.

Austria, Russia, and Sweden joined with Britain to form the Third Coalition against France shortly before the Battle of Trafalgar. Actions such as Napoleon's assumption of the Italian crown had convinced both Alexander I of Russia and Francis II of Austria that Napoleon was a threat to their interests and to the European balance of power. Yet the Austrians and the Russians were no match for Napoleon, who scored a brilliant victory over them at the Battle of Austerlitz in December 1805. Alexander I decided to pull back, and Austria accepted large territorial losses in return for peace as the Third Coalition collapsed.

Victorious at Austerlitz, Napoleon proceeded to reorganize the German states to his liking. In 1806 he abolished many of the tiny German states as well as the ancient Holy Roman Empire. Napoleon established by decree the German Confederation of the Rhine, a union of fifteen German states minus Austria, Prussia, and Saxony.

The Coronation of Napoleon, 1804 (detail) In this grandiose painting by Jacques-Louis David, Napoleon prepares to crown his beautiful wife, Josephine, in an elaborate ceremony in Notre Dame Cathedral. Napoleon, the ultimate upstart, also crowned himself. Pope Pius VII, seated glumly behind the emperor, is reduced to being a spectator. *(Louvre/Réunion des Musées Nationaux/Art Resource, NY)*

Naming himself "protector" of the confederation, Napoleon firmly controlled western Germany.

Napoleon's intervention in German affairs alarmed the Prussians, who mobilized their armies after more than a decade of peace with France. Napoleon attacked and won two more brilliant victories in October 1806 at Jena and Auerstädt, where the Prussians were outnumbered two to one. The war with Prussia, now joined by Russia, continued into the following spring, and after Napoleon's larger armies won another victory, Alexander I of Russia wanted peace.

For several days in June 1807, the young tsar and the French emperor negotiated face to face on a raft anchored in the middle of the Niemen River. All the while, the helpless Frederick William III of Prussia rode back and forth on the shore anxiously awaiting the results. As the German poet Heinrich Heine said later, Napoleon had but to whistle and Prussia would have ceased to exist. In the subsequent treaties of Tilsit, Prussia lost half of its population, while Russia accepted Napoleon's reorganization of western and central Europe and promised to enforce Napoleon's economic blockade against British goods.

Increasingly Napoleon saw himself as the emperor of Europe and not just of France. The so-called Grand Empire he built had three parts. The core, or first part, was an ever-expanding France, which by 1810 included Belgium, Holland, parts of northern Italy, and much German territory on the east bank of the Rhine. Beyond French borders Napoleon established the second part: a number of dependent satellite kingdoms, on the thrones

MAP 21.1 Napoleonic Europe in 1810 Only Great Britain remained at war with Napoleon at the height of the Grand Empire. Many British goods were smuggled through Helgoland, a tiny but strategic British possession off the German coast.

of which he placed (and replaced) the members of his large family. The third part comprised the independent but allied states of Austria, Prussia, and Russia. Both satellites and allies were expected after 1806 to support Napoleon's continental system and cease trade with Britain.

The impact of the Grand Empire on the peoples of Europe was considerable. In the areas incorporated into France and in the satellites (see Map 21.1), Napoleon introduced many French laws, abolishing feudal dues and serfdom where French revolutionary armies had not already done so. Some of the peasants and middle class benefited from these reforms. Yet Napoleon had to put the prosperity and special interests of France first in order to safeguard his power base. Levying heavy taxes in money and men for his armies, Napoleon came to be regarded more as a conquering tyrant than as an enlightened liberator. Thus French rule sparked patriotic upheavals and encouraged the growth of reactive nationalisms, for individuals in different lands learned to identify emotionally with their own embattled national families, as the French had done earlier.

The first great revolt occurred in Spain. In 1808 a coalition of Catholics, monarchists, and patriots rebelled against Napoleon's attempts to make Spain a French satellite with a Bonaparte as its king. French armies occupied Madrid, but the foes of Napoleon fled to the hills and waged uncompromising guerrilla warfare. Spain was a clear warning: resistance to French imperialism was growing.

Yet Napoleon pushed on, determined to hold his complex and far-flung empire together. In 1810, when the Grand Empire was at its height, Britain still remained at war with France, helping the guerrillas in Spain and Portugal. The continental system, organized to exclude British goods from the continent and force that "nation of shopkeepers" to its knees, was a failure. Instead, it was France that suffered from Britain's counter-blockade,

The War in Spain This unforgettable etching by the Spanish painter Francisco Goya (1746–1828) comes from his famous collection "The Disasters of the War." A French firing squad executes captured Spanish rebels almost as soon as they are captured, an everyday event in a war of atrocities on both sides. Do you think these rebels are "terrorists," or "freedom fighters"? *(Foto Marburg/Art Resource, NY)*

which created hard times for French artisans and the middle class. Perhaps looking for a scapegoat, Napoleon turned on Alexander I of Russia, who in 1811 openly repudiated Napoleon's war of prohibitions against British goods.

Napoleon's invasion of Russia began in June 1812 with a force that eventually numbered 600,000, probably the largest force yet assembled in a single army. Only one-third of this Great Army was French, however; nationals of all the satellites and allies were drafted into the operation. (See the feature "Individuals in Society: Jakob Walter, German Draftee with Napoleon.") Originally planning to winter in the Russian city of Smolensk if Alexander did not sue for peace, Napoleon reached Smolensk and recklessly pressed on toward Moscow. The great Battle of Borodino that followed was a draw, and the Russians retreated in good order. Alexander ordered the evacuation of Moscow, which then burned in part, and he refused to negotiate. Finally, after five weeks in the abandoned city, Napoleon ordered a retreat. That retreat was one of the great military disasters in history. The Russian army, the Russian winter, and starvation cut Napoleon's army to pieces. When the frozen remnants staggered into Poland and Prussia in December, 370,000 men had died and another 200,000 had been taken prisoner.[12]

Leaving his troops to their fate, Napoleon raced to Paris to raise yet another army. Possibly he might still have saved his throne if he had been willing to accept a France reduced to its historical size—the proposal offered by Austria's foreign minister, Prince Klemens von Metternich. But Napoleon refused. Austria and Prussia deserted Napoleon and joined Russia and Great Britain in the Fourth Coalition. All across Europe, patriots called for a "war of liberation" against Napoleon's oppression, and the well-disciplined regular armies of Napoleon's enemies closed in for the kill. This time the coalition held together, cemented by the Treaty of Chaumont, which created a Quadruple Alliance intended to last for twenty years. Less than a month later, on April 4, 1814, a defeated Napoleon abdicated his throne. After this unconditional abdication, the victorious allies granted Napoleon the island of Elba off the coast of Italy as his own tiny state. Napoleon was even allowed to keep his imperial title, and France was required to pay him a yearly income of 2 million francs.

The allies also agreed to the restoration of the Bourbon dynasty, in part because demonstrations led by a few dedicated French monarchists indicated some support among the French people for that course of action. The new monarch, Louis XVIII (r. 1814–1824), tried to consolidate that support by issuing the Constitutional Charter, which accepted many of France's revolutionary changes and guaranteed civil liberties. Indeed, the charter gave France a constitutional monarchy roughly similar to that established in 1791, although far fewer people had the right to vote for representatives to the resurrected Chamber of Deputies. Moreover, in an attempt to strengthen popular support for Louis XVIII's new government, France was treated leniently by the allies, which agreed to meet in Vienna to work out a general peace settlement.

Yet Louis XVIII—old, ugly, and crippled by gout—totally lacked the glory and magic of Napoleon. Hearing of political unrest in France and diplomatic tensions in Vienna, Napoleon staged a daring escape from Elba in February 1815. Landing in France, he issued appeals for support and marched on Paris with a small band of followers. French officers and soldiers who had fought so long for their emperor responded to the call. Louis XVIII fled, and once more Napoleon took command. But Napoleon's gamble was a desperate long shot, for the allies were united against him. At the end of a frantic period known as the Hundred Days, they crushed his forces at Waterloo on June 18, 1815, and imprisoned him on the rocky island of St. Helena, far off the western coast of Africa. Old Louis XVIII returned again—this time "in the baggage of the allies," as his detractors scornfully put it—and recommenced his reign. The allies now dealt more harshly with the apparently incorrigible French. As for Napoleon, he took revenge by writing his memoirs, skillfully nurturing the myth that he had been Europe's revolutionary liberator, a romantic hero whose lofty work had been undone by oppressive reactionaries. An era had ended.

Summary

The French Revolution left a compelling and many-sided political legacy. This legacy included, most notably, liberalism, assertive nationalism, radical democratic republicanism, embryonic socialism, and self-conscious conservatism. It also left a rich and turbulent history of electoral competition, legislative assemblies, and even mass politics. Thus the French Revolution and conflicting interpretations of its significance presented a whole range of political options and alternative visions of the future. For this reason, it was truly the revolution in modern European politics.

The revolution that began in America and spread to France was a liberal revolution. Revolutionaries on both sides of the Atlantic wanted to establish civil liberties and equality before the law within the framework of representative government, and they succeeded. In France liberal nobles and an increasingly class-conscious middle

Individuals in Society

Jakob Walter, German Draftee with Napoleon

In January 1812, a young German named Jakob Walter (1788–1864) was recalled to active duty in the army of Württemberg, a Napoleonic satellite in the Confederation of the Rhine. Stonemason and common draftee, Walter later wrote a rare enlisted man's account of the Russian campaign, a personal history that testified to the terrible price paid by the common people for a generation of war.

Napoleon's invasion of Russia was a desperate gamble from the beginning. French armies were accustomed to living off well-developed local economies, but this strategy did not work well in poor, sparsely populated eastern Europe. Scrounging for food dominated Walter's recollection of earlier fighting in Poland, and now, in 1812, the food situation was much worse. Crossing into Russia, Walter and his buddies found the nearby villages half-burned and stripped of food. Running down an occasional hog, they greedily tore it to pieces and ate it raw. Strangled by dust and thirst and then pelted for days by cold rain, the Great Army raced to catch the retreating Russians and force them into battle. When the famished troops stopped, the desperate search for food began.

In mid-August Walter's company helped storm the city of Smolensk in heavy fighting. From there onward, the road was littered with men, horses, and wagons, and all the towns and villages had been burned by the Russians to deprive the enemy of supplies. Surrounded by all these horrors, Walter almost lost his nerve, but he drew on his Catholic faith and found the courage "to go on trustingly to meet my fate."* Fighting at the great Battle of Borodino, "where the death cries and the shattering gunfire seemed a hell," he and the allied troops entered a deserted and fire-damaged Moscow in mid-September. But food, liquor, and fancy silks were there for the taking, and the weather was warm.

On October 18, the reprieve was over, and the retreating allied infantrymen re-entered Hell. Yet Walter, "still alert and spirited," was asked by an officer to be his attendant and received for his services a horse to ride. The horse proved a lifesaver. It allowed Walter to forage for food farther off the highway, to flee from approaching Cossacks, and to conserve his strength as vicious freezing winter weather set in. Yet food found at great peril could be quickly lost. Once Walter fought off some French soldiers with the help of some nearby Germans, who then robbed him of his bread. But what, he reflected later, could one expect? The starving men had simply lost their humanity. "I myself could look cold-bloodedly into the lamenting faces of the wounded, the freezing, and the burned," he wrote. When his horse was stolen as he slept, he silently stole someone else's. Struggling on in this brutal every-man-for-himself environment, Walter reached Poland in late December and hobbled home, a rare survivor. He went on to recover, marry, and have ten children.

The retreat from Moscow; detail of an engraving by G. Küstler. Soldiers strip the sick of their blankets and boots, leaving them to die in the cold.
(New York Public Library, Slavonic Division)

Why did Jakob Walter survive? Pure chance surely played a large part. So did his robust constitution and street smarts. His faith in God also provided strength to meet each day's challenges. The beautiful vision of returning home and seeing his family offered equal encouragement. Finally, he lacked hatred and animosity, whether toward the Russians, the French, or whomever. He accepted the things he could not change and concentrated on those he could.

Questions for Analysis

1. Why was obtaining food such a problem for Jakob Walter and his fellow soldiers?
2. What impresses you most about Walter's account of the Russian campaign?

*Jakob Walter, *The Diary of a Napoleonic Foot Soldier,* ed. with an introduction by M. Raeff (New York: Penguin Books, 1993), p. 53. Also pp. 54, 66.

class overwhelmed declining monarchical absolutism and feudal privilege, thanks to the intervention of the common people—the sans-culottes and the peasants. Featuring electoral competition and civil equality, the government established by the Declaration of the Rights of Man and the French constitution of 1791 was remarkably similar to that created in America by the federal Constitution and the Bill of Rights. France's new political system reflected a social structure based increasingly on wealth and achievement rather than on tradition and legal privileges.

After the establishment of the republic, the radical phase of the Revolution during the Terror, and the fall of Robespierre, the educated elites and the solid middle class reasserted themselves under the Directory. And though Napoleon sharply curtailed representative institutions and individual rights, he effectively promoted the reconciliation of old and new, of centralized bureaucracy and careers open to talent, of noble and bourgeois in a restructured property-owning elite. Louis XVIII had to accept the commanding position of this restructured elite, and in granting representative government and civil liberties to facilitate his restoration to the throne in 1814, he submitted to the rest of the liberal triumph of 1789 to 1791. The liberal core of the French Revolution had successfully survived a generation of war and dictatorship.

Revolution in France, as opposed to in the United States, also left a multiplicity of legacies that extended well beyond the triumphant liberalism of 1789. Indeed, the lived experience of the French Revolution and the wars that went with it exercised a pervasive influence on politics and the political imagination in the nineteenth century, not only in France but throughout Europe and even the rest of the world. First, there was the radical legacy of the embattled republic of 1793 and 1794, with its sans-culottes democratic republicanism and its egalitarian ideology and embryonic socialism. This legacy would inspire republicans, democrats, and early socialists. Second, there was the legacy of a powerful and continuing reaction to the French Revolution and to aggressive French nationalism. Monarchists and traditionalists now believed that 1789 had been a tragic mistake. They concluded that democratic republicanism and sans-culottes activism led only to war, class conflict, and savage dictatorship. And even though revolutionary upheaval encouraged generations of radicals to believe that political revolution might remake society and even create a new humanity, conservatives and many comfortable moderates were profoundly disillusioned by the revolutionary era. They looked with nostalgia toward the supposedly ordered world of benevolent monarchy, firm government, and respectful common people.

Key Terms

liberty and equality
sovereignty
bourgeoisie
representative government
checks and balances
classical liberalism
estates
manorial rights
Great Fear
constitutional monarchy
Jacobins
second revolution
Girondists
the Mountain
sans-culottes
planned economy
Reign of Terror
nationalism
Thermidorian reaction
family monarchy

Notes

1. Quoted in R. R. Palmer, *The Age of the Democratic Revolution,* vol. 1 (Princeton, N.J.: Princeton University Press, 1959), p. 239.
2. G. Lefebvre, *The Coming of the French Revolution* (New York: Vintage Books, 1947), p. 81.
3. P. H. Beik, ed., *The French Revolution* (New York: Walker, 1970), p. 89.
4. G. Pernoud and S. Flaisser, eds., *The French Revolution* (Greenwich, Conn.: Fawcett, 1960), p. 61.
5. O. Hufton, *Women and the Limits of Citizenship in the French Revolution* (Toronto: University of Toronto Press, 1992), pp. 3–22.
6. Quotations from Wollstonecraft are drawn from E. W. Sunstein, *A Different Face: The Life of Mary Wollstonecraft* (New York: Harper & Row, 1975), pp. 208, 211; and H. R. James, *Mary Wollstonecraft: A Sketch* (London: Oxford University Press, 1932), pp. 60, 62, 69.
7. Quoted in L. Gershoy, *The Era of the French Revolution, 1789–1799* (New York: Van Nostrand, 1957), p. 150.
8. Pernoud and Flaisser, *The French Revolution,* pp. 193–194.
9. T. Blanning, *The French Revolutionary Wars, 1787–1802* (London: Arnold, 1996), pp. 116–128.
10. Quoted ibid., p. 123.
11. Hufton, *Women and the Limits of Citizenship,* p. 130.
12. D. Sutherland, *France, 1789–1815: Revolution and Counterrevolution* (New York: Oxford University Press, 1986), p. 420.

Suggested Reading

For fascinating eyewitness reports on the French Revolution, see the edited works by Beik and by Pernoud and Flaisser mentioned in the Notes. In addition, A. Young, *Travels in France During the Years 1787, 1788 and 1789* (1969), offers an engrossing contemporary description of France and Paris on the eve of revolution. E. Burke, *Reflections on the Revolution in France,* first published in 1790, is the classic conservative indictment. The intense passions the French Revolution has generated may be seen in nineteenth-century French historians, notably the enthusiastic J. Michelet, *History of the French Revolution;* the hostile H. Taine; and the judicious A. de Tocqueville, whose masterpiece, *The Old Regime and the French Revolution,* was first published in 1856. Important general studies on the entire period include the work by

Palmer, cited in the Notes, which paints a comparative international picture; E. J. Hobsbawm, *The Age of Revolution, 1789–1848* (1962); and O. Connelly, *French Revolution—Napoleonic Era* (1979). P. Schroeder, *The Transformation of European Politics, 1763–1848* (1994), is a masterful synthesis and reinterpretation, which may be compared with L. Dehio, *The Precarious Balance: Four Centuries of the European Power Struggle* (1962).

Revisionist scholarship has created a wealth of new scholarship and interpretation. A. Cobban, *The Social Interpretation of the French Revolution* (1964), and F. Furet, *Interpreting the French Revolution* (1981), are major reassessments of long-dominant ideas, which are admirably presented in N. Hampson, *A Social History of the French Revolution* (1963), and in the volume by Lefebvre listed in the Notes. F. Furet, *Revolutionary France, 1770–1880* (1995), is an extended development of the author's revisionist interpretations. E. Kennedy, *A Cultural History of the French Revolution* (1989), beautifully written and handsomely illustrated, and W. Doyle, *Origins of the French Revolution,* 3d ed. (1988), are excellent on long-term developments. Among valuable studies, which generally are often quite critical of revolutionary developments, several are noteworthy: J. Bosher, *The French Revolution* (1988); S. Schama, *Citizens: A Chronicle of the French Revolution* (1989); W. Doyle, *The Oxford History of the French Revolution* (1989); and D. Sutherland, *France, 1789–1815: Revolution and Counterrevolution* (1986).

Two excellent anthologies concisely presenting a range of interpretations are F. Kafker and J. Laux, eds., *The French Revolutions: Conflicting Interpretations,* 4th ed. (1989), and G. Best, ed., *The Permanent Revolution: The French Revolution and Its Legacy, 1789–1989* (1988). G. Rudé makes the men and women of the great days of upheaval come alive in *The Crowd in the French Revolution* (1959), whereas R. R. Palmer studies sympathetically the leaders of the Terror in *Twelve Who Ruled* (1941). Four other particularly interesting, detailed works are B. Shapiro, *Revolutionary Justice in Paris, 1789–1790* (1993); D. Jordan, *The Revolutionary Career of Maximilien Robespierre* (1985); J. P. Bertaud, *The Army of the French Revolution: From Citizen-Soldier to Instrument of Power* (1988); and C. L. R. James, *The Black Jacobins* (1938, 1980), on black slave revolt in Haiti. Other significant studies on aspects of revolutionary France include P. Jones's pathbreaking *The Peasantry in the French Revolution* (1988); W. Sewell, Jr.'s imaginative *Work and Revolution in France: The Language of Labor from the Old Regime to 1848* (1980); and L. Hunt's innovative *The Family Romance of the French Revolution* (1992). M. Ozouf, *Festivals and the French Revolution* (1988), is a pioneering cultural study focusing on revolutionary symbols. Two major studies on the era's continuous wars are Blanning, cited in the Notes, and O. Connelly, *Blundering to Glory: Napoleon's Military Campaigns* (1987).

Studies on women in the French Revolution present conflicting interpretations. This may be seen by comparing two particularly important works: J. Landes, *Women and the Public Sphere in the Age of the French Revolution* (1988), and Hufton, listed in the Notes. D. Outram, *The Body and the French Revolution: Sex, Class and Political Culture* (1989), and L. Hunt, *The Family Romance of the French Revolution* (1992), provide innovative analyses of the gender-related aspects of revolutionary politics and are highly recommended. H. Applewhite and D. Levy, eds., *Women and Politics in the Age of Democratic Revolution* (1990), compares developments in leading countries. Mary Wollstonecraft's dramatic life is the subject of several good biographies, including those by Sunstein and James, cited in the Notes.

Two important works placing political developments in a comparative perspective are P. Higonnet, *Sister Republics: The Origins of French and American Republicanism* (1988), and E. Morgan, *Inventing the People: The Rise of Popular Sovereignty in England and America* (1988). B. Bailyn, *The Ideological Origins of the American Revolution* (1967), is also noteworthy.

The best synthesis on Napoleonic France is L. Bergeron, *France Under Napoleon* (1981). E. Arnold, Jr., ed., *A Documentary Survey of Napoleonic France* (1994), includes political and cultural selections. K. Kafker and J. Laux, eds., *Napoleon and His Times: Selected Interpretations* (1989), is an interesting collection of articles, which may be compared with R. Jones, *Napoleon: Man and Myth* (1977). Good biographies are J. Thompson, *Napoleon Bonaparte: His Rise and Fall* (1952); F. Markham, *Napoleon* (1964); and V. Cronin, *Napoleon Bonaparte* (1972). Wonderful novels inspired by the period include Raphael Sabatini's *Scaramouche,* a swashbuckler of revolutionary intrigue with accurate historical details; Charles Dickens's fanciful *A Tale of Two Cities;* and Leo Tolstoy's monumental saga of Napoleon's invasion of Russia (and much more), *War and Peace*.

Listening to the Past

Revolution and Women's Rights

The 1789 Declaration of the Rights of Man was a revolutionary call for legal equality, representative government, and individual freedom. But the new rights were strictly limited to men; Napoleon tightened further the subordination of French women.

Among those who saw the contradiction in granting supposedly universal rights to only half the population was Marie Gouze (1748–1793), known to history as Olympe de Gouges. The daughter of a provincial butcher and peddler, she pursued a literary career in Paris after the death of her husband. Between 1790 and 1793, she wrote more than two dozen political pamphlets under her new name. De Gouges's great work was her "Declaration of the Rights of Woman" (1791). Excerpted here, de Gouges's manifesto went beyond the 1789 Rights of Man. It called on males to end their oppression of women and give women equal rights. A radical on women's issues, de Gouges sympathized with the monarchy and criticized Robespierre in print. Convicted of sedition, she was guillotined in November 1793.

. . . Man, are you capable of being just? . . . Tell me, what gives you sovereign empire to oppress my sex? Your strength? Your talents? Observe the Creator in his wisdom . . . and give me, if you dare, an example of this tyrannical empire. Go back to animals, consult the elements, study plants . . . and distinguish, if you can, the sexes in the administration of nature. Everywhere you will find them mingled; everywhere they cooperate in harmonious togetherness in this immortal masterpiece.

Man alone has raised his exceptional circumstances to a principle. . . . [H]e wants to command as a despot a sex which is in full possession of its intellectual faculties; he pretends to enjoy the Revolution and to claim his rights to equality in order to say nothing more about it.

DECLARATION OF THE RIGHTS OF WOMAN AND THE FEMALE CITIZEN

For the National Assembly to decree in its last sessions, or in those of the next legislature:

Preamble

Mothers, daughters, sisters and representatives of the nation demand to be constituted into a national assembly. Believing that ignorance, omission, or scorn for the rights of woman are the only causes of public misfortunes and of the corruption of governments, [the women] have resolved to set forth in a solemn declaration the natural, inalienable, and sacred rights of woman. . . .

. . . the sex that is as superior in beauty as it is in courage during the sufferings of maternity recognizes and declares in the presence and under the auspices of the Supreme Being, the following Rights of Woman and of Female Citizens:

I. Woman is born free and lives equal to man in her rights. Social distinctions can be based only on the common utility.

II. The purpose of any political association is the conservation of the natural and imprescriptible rights of woman and man; these rights are liberty, property, security, and especially resistance to oppression.

III. The principle of all sovereignty rests essentially with the nation, which is nothing but the union of woman and man. . . .

IV. Liberty and justice consist of restoring all that belongs to others; thus, the only limits on the exercise of the natural rights of woman are perpetual male tyranny; these limits are to be reformed by the laws of nature and reason.

V. Laws of nature and reason proscribe all acts harmful to society. . . .

VI. The law must be the expression of the general will; all female and male citizens must contribute either personally or through their representatives to its formation; it must be the same for all: male and female citizens, being equal in the eyes of the law, must be equally admitted to all honors, positions, and public employment according to their capacity and without other distinctions besides those of their virtues and talents.

VII. No woman is an exception; she is accused, arrested, and detained in cases determined by law. Women, like men, obey this rigorous law.

VIII. The law must establish only those penalties that are strictly and obviously necessary. . . .

IX. Once any woman is declared guilty, complete rigor is [to be] exercised by the law.

X. No one is to be disquieted for his very basic opinions; woman has the right to mount the scaffold; she must equally have the right to mount the rostrum, provided that her demonstrations do not disturb the legally established public order.

XI. The free communication of thoughts and opinions is one of the most precious rights of woman, since that liberty assures the recognition of children by their fathers. Any female citizen thus may say freely, I am the mother of a child which belongs to you, without being forced by a barbarous prejudice to hide the truth. . . .

XIII. For the support of the public force and the expenses of administration, the contributions of woman and man are equal; she shares all the duties . . . and all the painful tasks; therefore, she must have the same share in the distribution of positions, employment, offices, honors, and jobs. . . .

XIV. Female and male citizens have the right to verify, either by themselves or through their representatives, the necessity of the public contribution. This can only apply to women if they are granted an equal share, not only of wealth, but also of public administration. . . .

XV. The collectivity of women, joined for tax purposes to the aggregate of men, has the right to demand an accounting of his administration from any public agent.

XVI. No society has a constitution without the guarantee of rights and the separation of powers; the constitution is null if the majority of individuals comprising the nation have not cooperated in drafting it.

XVII. Property belongs to both sexes whether united or separate; for each it is an inviolable and sacred right. . . .

The late-eighteenth-century French painting *La Liberté*. *(Bibliothèque Nationale, Paris/Art Resource, NY)*

Postscript

Women, wake up. . . . Discover your rights. . . . Oh, women, women! When will you cease to be blind? What advantage have you received from the Revolution? A more pronounced scorn, a more marked disdain. . . . [If men persist in contradicting their revolutionary principles,] courageously oppose the force of reason to the empty pretensions of superiority . . . and you will soon see these haughty men, not groveling at your feet as servile adorers, but proud to share with you the treasure of the Supreme Being. Regardless of what barriers confront you; it is in your power to free yourselves; you have only to want to. . . .

Questions for Analysis

1. On what basis did de Gouges argue for gender equality? Did she believe in natural law?
2. What consequences did "scorn for the rights of woman" have for France, according to de Gouges?
3. Did de Gouges stress political rights at the expense of social and economic rights? If so, why?

Source: Olympe de Gouges, "Declaration of the Rights of Woman," in Darline G. Levy, Harriet B. Applewhite, and Mary D. Johnson, eds., *Women in Revolutionary Paris, 1789–1795* (Urbana: University of Illinois Press, 1979), pp. 87–96.

Index

Timeline A History of Western Society: A Brief Overview

	Government	Society and Economy
3200 B.C.	Dominance of Sumerian cities in Mesopotamia, ca 3200–2340 Unification of Egypt; Archaic Period, ca 3100–2660 Old Kingdom of Egypt, ca 2660–2180 Dominance of Akkadian empire in Mesopotamia, ca 2331–2200 Middle Kingdom in Egypt, ca 2080–1640	Neolithic peoples rely on settled agriculture, while others pursue nomadic life, ca 7000–ca 3000 Development of wheeled transport in Mesopotamia, by ca 3200 Expansion of Mesopotamian trade and culture into modern Turkey, the Middle East, and Iran, ca 2600
2000 B.C.	Babylonian empire, ca 2000–1595 Hyksos invade Egypt, ca 1640–1570 Hittite Empire, ca 1600–1200 New Kingdom in Egypt, ca 1570–1075	First wave of Indo-European migrants, by 2000 Extended commerce in Egypt, by ca 2000 Horses introduced into western Asia, by ca 2000
1500 B.C.	Third Intermediate Period in Egypt, ca 1100–700 Unified Hebrew Kingdom under Saul, David, and Solomon, ca 1025–925	Use of iron increases in western Asia, by ca 1300–1100 Second wave of Indo-European migrants, by ca 1200
1000 B.C.	Hebrew Kingdom divided into Israel and Judah, 925 Assyrian Empire, ca 900–612 Phoenicians found Carthage, 813 Kingdom of Kush conquers and reunifies Egypt, 8th c. Medes conquers Persia, 710 Babylon wins independence from Assyria, 626 Dracon issues law code at Athens, 621 Cyrus the Great conquers Medes, founds Persian Empire, 550 Solon's reforms at Athens, ca 549 Persians complete conquest of ancient Near East, 521–464 Reforms of Cleisthenes in Athens, 508	Concentration of landed wealth in Greece, ca 750–600 Greek overseas expansion, ca 750–550 Beginning of coinage in western Asia, ca 640
500 B.C.	Battle of Marathon, 490 Xerxes' invasion of Greece, 480–479 Delian Confederacy, 478/7 Twelve Tables in Rome, 451/0 Valerio-Horatian laws in Rome, 449 Peloponnesian War, 431–404 Rome captures Veii, 396 Gauls sack Rome, 390 Roman expansion in Italy, 390–290 Conquests of Alexander the Great, 334–323 Punic Wars, 264–146 Reforms of the Gracchi, 133–121	Building of the Via Appia begins, 312 Growth of Hellenistic trade and cities, ca 300–100 Beginning of Roman silver coinage, 269 Growth of slavery, decline of small farmers in Rome, ca 250–100 Agrarian reforms of the Gracchi, 133–121

Religion and Philosophy	Science and Technology	Arts and Letters
Growth of anthropomorphic religion in Mesopotamia, ca 3000–2000 Emergence of Egyptian polytheism and belief in personal immortality, ca 2660 Spread of Mesopotamian and Egyptian religious ideas as far north as modern Anatolia and as far south as central Africa, ca 2600	Development of wheeled transport in Mesopotamia, by ca 3200 Use of widespread irrigation in Mesopotamia and Egypt, ca 3000 Construction of the first pyramid in Egypt, ca 2600	Sumerian cuneiform writing, ca 3200 Egyptian hieroglyphic writing, ca 3100
Emergence of Hebrew monotheism, ca 1700 Mixture of Hittite and Near Eastern religious beliefs, ca 1595	Construction of the first ziggurats in Mesopotamia, ca 2000 Widespread use of bronze in the ancient Near East, ca 1900 Babylonian mathematical advances, ca 1800	*Epic of Gilgamesh,* ca 1900 Code of Hammurabi, ca 1790
Exodus of the Hebrews from Egypt into Palestine, 13th c. Religious beliefs of Akhenaten, ca 1367	Hittites introduce iron technology, ca 1400	Phoenicians develop alphabet, ca 1400 Naturalistic art in Egypt under Akhenaten, ca 1367 Egyptian Book of the Dead, ca 1300
Era of the prophets in Israel, ca 1100–500 Intermixture of Etruscan and Roman religious cults, ca 753–509 Growing popularity of local Greek religious cults, ca 700 B.C.–A.D. 337 Babylonian Captivity of the Hebrews, 586–539	Babylonian astronomical advances, ca 750–400	Beginning of the Hebrew Bible, ca 9th c. First Olympic Games, 776 Babylonian astronomical advances, ca 750–400 Homer, traditional author of the *Iliad* and *Odyssey,* ca 700 Hesiod, author of the *Theogony* and *Works and Days,* ca 700 Archilochos, lyric poet, 648 Aeschylus, first significant Athenian tragedian, 525/4–456
Pre-Socratic philosophers, 5th c. Socrates, 469–399 Plato, 429–347 Diogenes, leading proponent of cynicism, ca 412–323 Aristotle, 384–322 Epicurus, 340–270 Zeno, founder of Stoic philosophy, 335–262 Emergence of Mithraism, ca 300 Spread of Hellenistic mystery religions, 2nd c. Greek cults brought to Rome, ca 200	Hippocrates, formal founder of medicine ca 430 Theophrastus, founder of botany, ca 372–288 Aristarchos of Samos, advances in astronomy, ca 310–230 Euclid codifies geometry, ca 300 Herophilus, discoveries in medicine, ca 300–250 Archimedes, works on physics and hydrologics, ca 287–212	Sophocles, tragedian who used his plays to explore moral and political problems, ca 496–406 Euripides, the most personal of the Athenian tragedians, ca 480–406 Thucydides, historian of the Peloponnesian War, ca 460–400 Aristophanes, the greatest writer of Old Comedy, ca 457–ca 385 Herodotus, the father of history, ca 450

	Government	Society and Economy
100 B.C.	Dictatorship of Sulla, 88–79 Civil war in Rome, 78–27 Dictatorship of Caesar, 45–44 Principate of Augustus, 31 B.C.–A.D. 14	Reform of the Roman calendar, 46
A.D. 300	Constantine removes capital of Roman Empire to Constantinople, ca 315 Visigoths defeat Roman army at Adrianople (378), signaling massive German invasions into the empire Bishop Ambrose asserts church's independence from the state, 380 Death of emperor Romulus Augustus marks end of Roman Empire in the West, 476 Clovis issues Salic law of the Franks, ca 490	Growth of serfdom in Roman Empire, ca 200–500 Economic contraction in Roman Empire, 3rd c.
500	Law Code of Justinian, 529 Dooms of Ethelbert, king of Kent, ca 604 Spread of Islam across Arabia, the Mediterranean region, Spain, North Africa, and Asia as far as India, ca 630–733	Gallo-Roman aristocracy intermarries with Germanic chieftains Decline of towns and trade, ca 500–700 Agrarian economy predominates in the West, ca 500–1500
700	Charles Martel defeats Muslims at Tours, 732 Pippin III anointed king of the Franks, 754 Charlemagne secures Frankish crown, r. 768–814	Height of Muslim commercial activity, ca 700–1300
800	Imperial coronation of Charlemagne, Christmas 800 Treaty of Verdun, 843 Viking, Magyar, and Muslim invasions, ca 845–900	Byzantine commerce and industry, ca 800–1000 Invasions and unstable conditions lead to increase of serfdom
1000	Seljuk Turks conquer Muslim Baghdad, 1055 Norman conquest of England, 1066 Penance of Henry IV at Canossa, 1077	Agrarian economy predominates in the West, 1000–1500 Decline of Byzantine free peasantry, ca 1025–1100 Growth of towns and trade in the West, ca 1050–1300 Domesday Book, 1086
1100	Henry I of England, r. 1100–1135 Louis VI of France, r. 1108–1137 Frederick I of Germany, r. 1152–1190 Henry II of England, r. 1154–1189 Thomas Becket murdered, 1170 Philip Augustus of France, r. 1180–1223	Henry I of England establishes the Exchequer, 1130 Beginnings of the Hanseatic League, 1159

Religion and Philosophy	Science and Technology	Arts and Letters
Mithraism spreads to Rome, 27 B.C.–A.D. 270 Dedication of the Ara Pacis Augustae, 9 Traditional birth of Jesus, ca 3	Pliny the Elder, student of natural history, 23 B.C.–A.D. 79 Frontinus, engineering advances in Rome, 30 B.C.–A.D. 104	Virgil, 70–19 B.C. Livy, ca 59 B.C.–A.D. 17 Ovid, 43 B.C.–A.D. 17
Constantine legalizes Christianity, 312 Theodosius declares Christianity the official state religion, 380 Donatist heretical movement at its height, ca 400 St. Augustine, *The City of God,* ca 425 Clovis adopts Roman Christianity, 496		St. Jerome publishes the Latin *Vulgate,* late 4th c. St. Augustine, *Confessions,* ca 390 Byzantines preserve Greco-Roman culture, ca 400–1000
Rule of St. Benedict, 529 Monasteries established in Anglo-Saxon England, 7th c. Muhammad preaches reform, ca 610 Publication of the Qu'ran, 651 Synod of Whitby, 664	Using watermills, Benedictine monks exploit energy of fast-flowing rivers and streams Heavy plow and improved harness facilitate use of multiple-ox teams; harrow widely used in northern Europe	Boethius, *The Consolation of Philosophy,* ca 520 Justinian constructs church of Santa Sophia, 532–537 Pope Gregory the Great publishes *Dialogues, Pastoral Care, Moralia,* 590–604
Missionary work of St. Boniface in Germany, ca 710–750 Iconoclastic controversy in Byzantine Empire, 726–843 Pippin III donates Papal States to the papacy, 756	Byzantines successfully use "Greek fire" in naval combat against Arab fleets attacking Constantinople, 673, 717	Lindisfarne Gospel Book, ca 700 Bede, *Ecclesiastical History of the English Nation,* ca 700 *Beowulf,* ca 700 Carolingian Renaissance, ca 780–850
Foundation of abbey of Cluny, 909 Byzantine conversion of Russia, late 10th c.	Stirrup and nailed horseshoes become widespread in shock combat Paper, invented in China ca 2d c., enters Europe through Muslim Spain in 10th c.	Byzantines develop the Cyrillic script, late 10th c.
Beginning of reformed papacy, 1046 Schism between Roman and Greek Orthodox churches, 1054 Pope Gregory VII, 1073–1085 Peter Abelard, 1079–1142 St. Bernard of Clairvaux, 1090–1153 First Crusade, 1095–1099	Arab conquests bring new irrigation methods, cotton cultivation, and manufacture to Spain, Sicily, southern Italy Avicenna, Arab scientist, d. 1037	Romanesque style in architecture and art, ca 1000–1200 *Song of Roland,* ca 1095 Muslim musicians introduce lute, rebec—stringed instruments and ancestors of violin
Universities begin, ca 1100–1300 Concordat of Worms ends investiture controversy, 1122 Height of Cistercian monasticism, 1125–1175 Aristotle's works translated into Latin, ca 1140–1260 Third Crusade, 1189–1192 Pope Innocent III, 1198–1216	In castle construction Europeans, copying Muslim and Byzantine models, erect rounded towers and crenelated walls Windmill invented, ca 1180 Some monasteries, such as Clairvaux and Canterbury Cathedral Priory, supplied by underground pipes with running water and indoor latrines, elsewhere very rare until 19th c.	*Rubaiyat of Umar Khayyam,* ca 1120 Dedication of abbey church of Saint-Denis launches Gothic style, 1144 Hildegard of Bingen, 1098–1179 Court of troubador poetry, especially that of Chrétien de Troyes, circulates widely

	Government	Society and Economy
1200	Spanish victory over Muslims at Las Navas de Tolosa, 1212 Frederick II of Germany and Sicily, r. 1212–1250 Magna Carta, 1215 Louis IX of France, r. 1226–1270 Mongols end Abbasid caliphate, 1258 Edward I of England, r. 1272–1307 Philip IV (the Fair) of France, r. 1285–1314 England and France at war, 1296	Economic revival, growth of towns, clearing of wasteland contribute to great growth of personal freedom, 13th c. Crusaders capture Constantinople (Fourth Crusade) and spur Venetian economy, 1204 Agricultural expansion leads to population growth, ca 1225–1300
1300	Philip IV orders arrest of Pope Boniface at Anagni, 1303 Hundred Years' War, 1337–1453 Political chaos in Germany, ca 1350–1450 Merchant oligarchies or despots rule Italian city-states	European economic depression, ca 1300–1450 Black Death appears ca 1347; returns intermittently until 18th c. Height of the Hanseatic League, 1350–1450 Peasant and working-class revolts: France, 1358; Florence, 1378; England, 1381
1400	Joan of Arc rallies French monarchy, 1429–1431 Medici domination of Florence begins, 1434 Princes in Germany consolidate power, ca 1450–1500 Ottoman Turks under Mahomet II capture Constantinople, May 1453 Wars of the Roses in England, 1453–1471 Ferdinand and Isabella complete reconquista in Spain, 1492 French invasion of Italy, 1494	Population decline, peasants' revolts, high labor costs contribute to decline of serfdom in western Europe Christopher Columbus reaches the Americas, October 1492 Portuguese gain control of East Indian spice trade, 1498–1511 Flow of Balkan slaves into eastern Mediterranean; of African slaves into Iberia and Italy, ca 1400–1500
1500	Charles V, Holy Roman emperor, 1519–1556 Imperial sack of Rome, 1527 Philip II of Spain, r. 1556–1598 Revolt of the Netherlands, 1566–1609 St. Bartholomew's Day massacre, August 24, 1572 Defeat of the Spanish Armada, 1588 Henry IV of France issues Edict of Nantes, 1598	Balboa discovers the Pacific, 1513 Magellan's crew circumnavigates the earth, 1519–1522 Spain and Portugal gain control of regions of Central and South America, ca 1520–1550 Peasants' Revolt in Germany, 1524–1525 "Time of Troubles" in Russia, 1598–1613
1600	Thirty Years' War, 1618–1648 Richelieu dominates French government, 1624–1643 Frederick William, Elector of Brandenburg, r. 1640–1688 English Civil War, 1642–1649	Chartering of British East India Company, 1600 Famine and taxation lead to widespread revolts, decline of serfdom in western Europe, ca 1600–1650 English Poor Law, 1601

Religion and Philosophy	Science and Technology	Arts and Letters
Maimonides, d. 1204 Founding of Franciscan order, 1210 Fourth Lateran Council, 1215 Founding of Dominican order, 1216 Thomas Aquinas (1225–1274) marks height of Scholasticism Pope Boniface VIII, 1294–1303	*Notebooks* of Villard de Honnecourt, a master mason (architect), a major source for Gothic engineering, ca 1250 Development of double-entry bookkeeping in Florence and Genoa, ca 1250–1340 Venetians purchase secrets of glass manufacture from Syria, 1277 Mechanical clock invented, ca 1290	*Parzifal, Roman de la Rose, King Arthur and the Round Table* celebrate virtues of knighthood Height of Gothic style, ca 1225–1300
Babylonian Captivity of the papacy, 1307–1377 John Wyclif, ca 1330–1384 Great Schism in the papacy, 1377–1418	Edward III of England uses cannon in siege of Calais, 1346	Petrarch, 1304–1374 Paintings of Giotto, ca 1305–1337 Dante, *Divine Comedy,* ca 1310 Boccaccio, *The Decameron,* ca 1350 Jan van Eyck, 1366–1441 Brunelleschi, 1377–1446 Chaucer, *Canterbury Tales,* ca 1385–1400
Council of Constance, 1414–1418 Pragmatic Sanction of Bourges, 1438 Expulsion of Jews from Spain, 1492	Water-powered blast furnaces operative in Sweden, Austria, the Rhine Valley, Liège, ca 1400 Leonardo Fibonacci's *Liber Abaci* (1202) popularizes use of Hindu-Arabic numerals, "a major factor in the rise of science in the Western world" Paris and largest Italian cities pave streets, making street cleaning possible Printing and movable type, ca 1450	Masaccio, 1401–1428 Botticelli, 1444–1510 Leonardo da Vinci, 1452–1519 Albrecht Dürer, 1471–1528 Michelangelo, 1475–1564 Raphael, 1483–1520 Rabelais, ca 1490–1553
Lateran Council attempts reforms of church abuses, 1512–1517 Machiavelli, *The Prince,* 1513 Concordat of Bologna, 1516 More, *Utopia,* 1516 Luther, *Ninety-five Theses,* 1517 Henry VIII of England breaks with Rome, 1532–1534 Loyola establishes Society of Jesus, 1540 Calvin establishes theocracy in Geneva, 1541 Merici establishes Ursuline order for education of women, 1544 Council of Trent, 1545–1563 Peace of Augsburg, 1555 Hobbes, 1588–1679 Descartes, 1596–1650	Copernicus, *On the Revolutions of the Heavenly Bodies,* 1543 Galileo, 1564–1642 Kepler, 1571–1630 Harvey, 1578–1657	Erasmus, *The Praise of Folly,* 1509 Castiglione, *The Courtier,* 1528 Cervantes, 1547–1616 Baroque movement in the arts, ca 1550–1725 Shakespeare, 1564–1616 Rubens, 1577–1640 Montaigne, *Essays,* 1598 Velazquez, 1599–1660
Huguenot revolt in France, 1625	Bacon, *The Advancement of Learning,* 1605 Boyle, 1627–1691 Leeuwenhoek, 1632–1723	Rembrandt van Rijn, 1606–1669 Golden Age of Dutch culture, 1625–1675 Vermeer, 1632–1675 Racine, 1639–1699

	Government	Society and Economy
1600 (cont.)	Louis XIV, r. 1643–1715 Peace of Westphalia, 1648 The Fronde in France, 1648–1660	Chartering of Dutch East India Company, 1602 Height of Dutch commercial activity, ca 1630–1665
1650	Protectorate in England, 1653–1658 Leopold I, Habsburg emperor, r. 1658–1705 Treaty of the Pyrenees, 1659 English monarchy restored, 1660 Siege of Vienna, 1683 Glorious Revolution in England, 1688–1689 Peter the Great of Russia, r. 1689–1725	Height of mercantilism in Europe, ca 1650–1750 Principle of peasants' "hereditary subjugation" to their lords affirmed in Prussia, 1653 Colbert's economic reforms in France, ca 1663–1683 Cossack revolt in Russia, 1670–1671
1700	War of the Spanish Succession, 1701–1713 Peace of Utrecht, 1713 Frederick William I of Prussia, r. 1713–1740 Louis XV of France, r. 1715–1774 Maria Theresa of Austria, r. 1740–1780 Frederick the Great of Prussia, r. 1740–1786	Foundation of St. Petersburg, 1701 Last appearance of bubonic plague in western Europe, ca 1720 Enclosure movement in England, ca 1730–1830 Jeremy Bentham, 1748–1823
1750	Seven Years' War, 1756–1763 Catherine the Great of Russia, r. 1762–1796 Partition of Poland, 1772–1795 Louis XVI of France, r. 1774–1792 American Revolution, 1776–1783 Beginning of the French Revolution, 1789	Start of general European population increase, ca 1750 Growth of illegitimate births, ca 1750–1850 Adam Smith, *The Wealth of Nations,* 1776 Thomas Malthus, *Essay of the Principle of Population,* 1798
1800	Napoleonic era, 1799–1815 Congress of Vienna, 1814–1815 "Battle of Peterloo," Great Britain, 1819	European economic imperialism, ca 1816–1880
1825	Greece wins independence, 1830 Revolution in France, 1830 Great Britain: Reform Bill of 1832; Poor Law reform, 1834; Chartists, repeal of Corn Laws, 1838–1848 British complete occupation of India, 1848 Revolutions in Europe, 1848	Height of French utopian socialism, 1830s–1840s German Zollverein founded, 1834 European capitalists begin large-scale foreign investment, 1840s Great Famine in Ireland, 1845–1851 Marx, *Communist Manifesto,* 1848
1850	Second Empire in France, 1852–1870 Crimean War, 1853–1856 Unification of Italy, 1859–1870 Civil War, United States, 1861–1865 Bismarck leads Germany, 1862–1890 Unification of Germany, 1864–1871 Britain's Second Reform Bill, 1867 Third Republic in France, 1870–1940	Crédit Mobilier founded in France, 1852 Japan opened to European influence, 1853 Mill, *On Liberty,* 1859 Russian serfs emancipated, 1861 First Socialist International, 1864–1871 Marx, *Das Capital,* 1867

Religion and Philosophy	Science and Technology	Arts and Letters
Patriarch Nikon's reforms split Russian Orthodox church, 1652 Test Act in England excludes Roman Catholics from public office, 1673 Revocation of Edict of Nantes, 1685 James II tries to restore Catholicism as state religion, 1685–1688 Montesquieu, 1689–1755 Locke, *Second Treatise on Civil Government,* 1690 Pierre Bayle, *Historical and Critical Dictionary,* 1697	Tull (1674–1741) encourages innovation in English agriculture Newton, *Principia Mathematica,* 1687 Newcomen develops steam engine, 1705	Construction of baroque palaces and remodeling of capital cities throughout central and eastern Europe, ca 1650–1725 J. S. Bach, 1685–1750 Fontenelle, *Conversations on the Plurality of Worlds,* 1686 The Enlightenment, ca 1690–1790 Voltaire, 1694–1778
Wesley, 1703–1791 Hume, 1711–1776 Diderot, 1713–1784 Condorcet, 1743–1794	Charles Townsend introduces four-year crop rotation, 1730	Montesquieu, *The Spirit of Laws,* 1748
Ricardo, 1772–1823 Fourier, 1772–1837 Papacy dissolves the Jesuits, 1773 Church reforms of Joseph II in Austria, 1780s Reorganization of the church in France, 1790s	Hargreaves's spinning jenny, ca 1765 Arkwright's water frame, ca 1765 Watt's steam engine promotes industrial breakthroughs, 1780s War widens the gap in technology between Britain and the continent, 1792–1815 Jenner's smallpox vaccine, 1796	*Encyclopedia,* edited by Diderot and d'Alembert, published, 1751–1765 Mozart, 1756–1791 Rousseau, *The Social Contract,* 1762 Beethoven, 1770–1827 Wordsworth, 1770–1850 Romanticism, ca 1790–1850 Wollstonecraft, *A Vindication of the Rights of Women,* 1792
Napoleon signs Concordat with Pope Pius VII regulating Catholic church in France, 1801 Spencer, 1820–1903		Staël, *On Germany,* 1810 Liszt, 1811–1886
Comte, *System of Positive Philosophy,* 1830–1842 List, *National System of Political Economy,* 1841 Nietzsche, 1844–1900 Sorel, 1847–1922	First railroad, Great Britain, 1825 Faraday studies electromagnetism, 1830–1840s	Balzac, *The Human Comedy,* 1829–1841 Delacroix, *Liberty Leading the People,* 1830 Hugo, *Hunchback of Notre Dame,* 1831
Decline in church attendance among working classes, ca 1850–1914 Pope Pius IX, *Syllabus of Errors,* denounces modern thoughts, 1864 Doctrine of papal infallibility, 1870	Modernization of Paris, ca 1850–1870 Great Exhibition, London, 1851 Darwin, *Origin of Species,* 1859 Pasteur develops germ theory of disease, 1860s Suez Canal opened, 1869 Mendeleev develops the periodic table, 1869	Realism, ca 1850–1870 Freud, 1856–1939 Flaubert, *Madame Bovary,* 1857 Tolstoy, *War and Peace,* 1869 Impressionism in art, ca 1870–1900 Eliot (Mary Ann Evans), *Middlemarch,* 1872

	Government	Society and Economy
1875	Congress of Berlin, 1878 European "scramble for Africa," 1880–1900 Britain's Third Reform Bill, 1884 Berlin conference on Africa, 1884 Dreyfus affair in France, 1894–1899 Spanish-American War, 1898 Boer War, 1899–1902	Full property rights for women, Great Britain, 1882 Social welfare legislation, Germany, 1883–1889 Second Socialist International, 1889–1914 Witte directs modernization of Russian economy, 1892–1899
1900	Russo-Japanese War, 1904–1905 Revolution in Russia, 1905 Balkan wars, 1912–1913	Women's suffrage movement, England, ca 1900–1914 Social welfare legislation, France, 1904, 1910; England, 1906–1914 Agrarian reforms in Russia, 1907–1912
1914	World War I, 1914–1918 Easter Rebellion, 1916 U.S. declares war on Germany, 1917 Bolshevik Revolution, 1917–1918 Treaty of Versailles, 1919	Planned economics in Europe, 1914 Auxiliary Service Law in Germany, 1916 Bread riots in Russia, March 1917
1920	Mussolini seizes power, 1922 Stalin uses forced collectivization, police terror, ca 1929–1939 Hitler gains power, 1933 Rome-Berlin Axis, 1936 Nazi-Soviet Non-Aggression Pact, 1939 World War II, 1939–1945	New Economic Policy in the Soviet Union, 1921 Dawes Plan for reparations and recovery, 1924 The Great Depression, 1929–1939 Rapid industrialization in Soviet Union, 1930s Roosevelt's "New Deal," 1933
1940	United Nations, 1945 Cold war begins, 1947 Fall of colonial empires, 1947–1962 Communist government in China, 1949 Korean War, 1950–1953 "De-Stalinization," 1955–1962	The Holocaust, 1941–1945 Marshall Plan, 1947 European economic progress, ca 1950–1969 European Coal and Steel Community, 1952 European Economic Community, 1957
1960	The Berlin Wall goes up, 1961 United States in Vietnam, ca 1961–1973 Student rebellion in France, 1968 Soviet tanks end Prague Spring, 1968 Détente, 1970s Soviets in Afghanistan, 1979	Civil rights movement in United States, 1960s Collapse of postwar monetary system, 1971 OPEC oil price increases, 1973 and 1979 Stagflation, 1970s Women's movement, 1970s
1980	U.S. military buildup, 1980s Solidarity in Poland, 1980 Gorbachev takes power, 1985 Unification of Germany, 1989 Revolutions in eastern Europe, 1989–1990 End of Soviet Union, 1991 War in former Yugoslavia, 1991–1995	Growth of debt, 1980s Economic crisis in Poland, 1988 Maastricht Treaty proposes monetary union, 1990 Conservative economic policies in western Europe, 1990s European Community becomes European Union, 1993 Migration to western Europe grows, 1990s
2000	Terrorist attack on United States, Sept. 11, 2001 War in Afghanistan, 2001	Euro note enters circulation, 2002

Religion and Philosophy	Science and Technology	Arts and Letters
Growth of public education in France, ca 1880–1900 Growth of mission schools in Africa, 1890–1914	Emergence of modern immunology, ca 1875–1900 Trans-Siberian Railroad, 1890s Marie Curie, discovery of radium, 1898 Electrical industry: lighting and streetcars, 1880–1900	Zola, *Germinal,* 1885 Kipling, "The White Man's Burden," 1899
Separation of church and state, France, 1901–1905 Jean-Paul Sartre, 1905–1980	Planck develops quantum theory, ca 1900 First airplane flight, 1903 Einstein develops relativity theory, 1905–1910	"Modernism," ca 1900–1929 Conrad, *Heart of Darkness,* 1902 Cubism in art, ca 1905–1930 Proust, *Remembrance of Things Past,* 1913–1927
Schweitzer, *Quest of the Historical Jesus,* 1906	Submarine warfare, 1915 Ernest Rutherford splits the atom, 1919	Spengler, *The Decline of the West,* 1918
Emergence of modern existentialism, 1920s Wittgenstein, *Essay on Logical Philosophy,* 1922 Revival of Christianity, 1920s and 1930s	"Heroic age of physics," 1920s First major public radio broadcasts in Great Britain and the United States, 1920 Heisenberg, "principle of uncertainty," 1927 Talking movies, 1930 Radar system in England, 1939	Gropius, the Bauhaus, 1920s Dadaism and surrealism, 1920s Woolf, *Jacob's Room,* 1922 Joyce, *Ulysses,* 1922 Eliot, *The Waste Land,* 1922 Remarque, *All Quiet on the Western Front,* 1929 Picasso, *Guernica,* 1937
De Beauvoir, *The Second Sex,* 1949 Communists fail to break Catholic church in Poland, 1950s	Oppenheimer, 1904–1967 "Big Science" in United States, ca 1940–1970 U.S. drops atomic bombs on Japan, 1945 Watson and Crick discover structure of DNA molecule, 1953 Russian satellite in orbit, 1957	Cultural purge in Soviet Union, 1946–1952 Van der Rohe, Lake Shore Apartments, 1948–1951 Orwell, *1984,* 1949 Pasternak, *Doctor Zhivago,* 1956 The "beat" movement in the U.S., late 1950s
Catholic church opposes the legalization of divorce and abortion, 1970 to present Pope John Paul II electrifies Poland, 1979	European Council for Nuclear Research (CERN), 1960 Space race, 1960s Russian cosmonaut first to orbit globe, 1961 American astronaut first person on the moon, 1969	The Beatles, 1960s Solzhenitsyn, *One Day in the Life of Ivan Denisovitch,* 1962 Friedan, *The Feminine Mystique,* 1963 Servan-Schreiber, *The American Challenge,* 1967
Revival of religion in Soviet Union, 1985 to present Fukuyama proclaims "end of history," 1991 Growth of Islam in Europe, 1990s	Reduced spending on Big Science, 1980s Computer revolution continues, 1980s and 1990s "Dolly," first genetically cloned sheep, 1996 U.S. Genome Project begins, 1990	Solzhenitsyn returns to Russia, 1994 Author Salman Rushdie is exiled from Iran, 1989